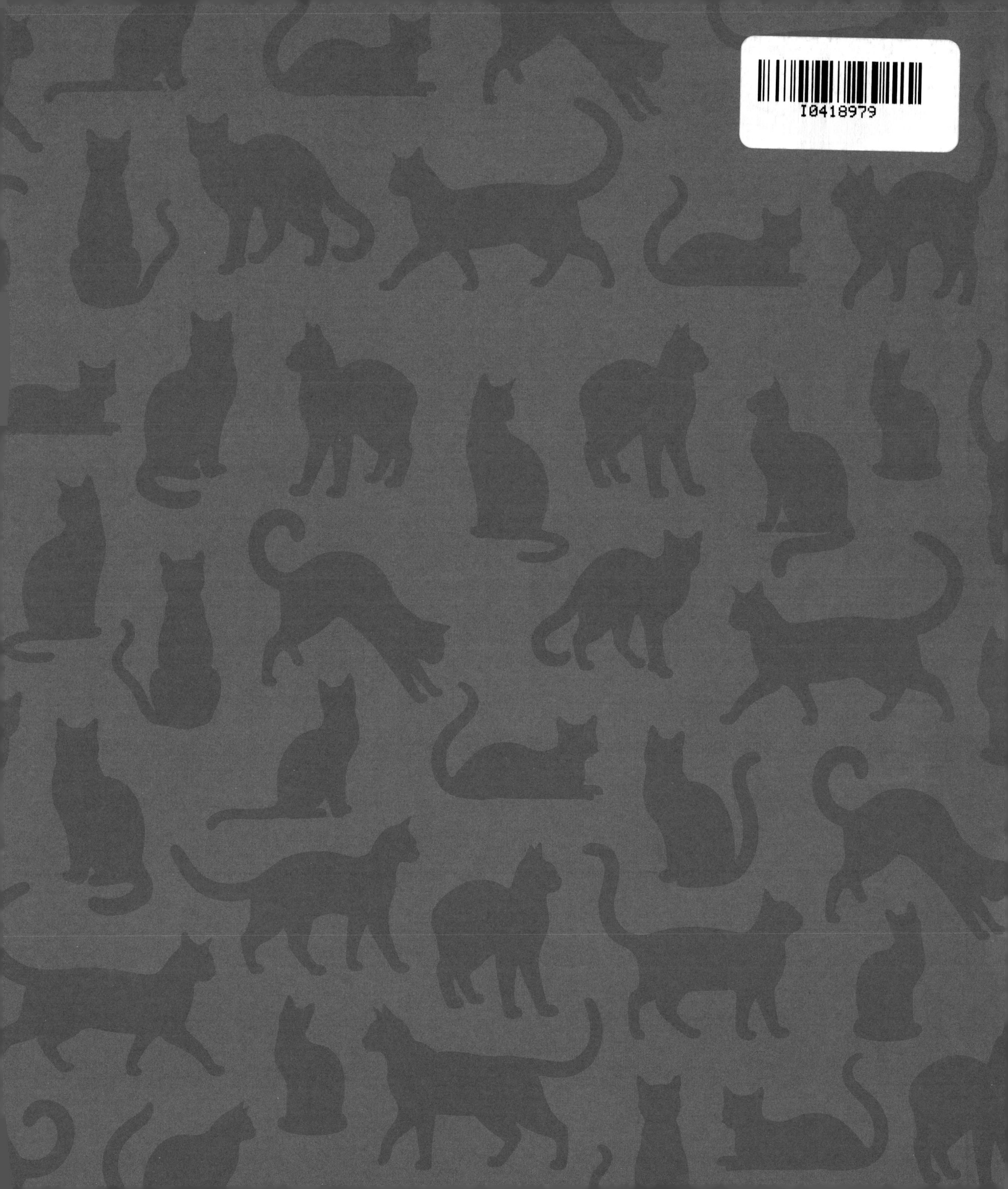

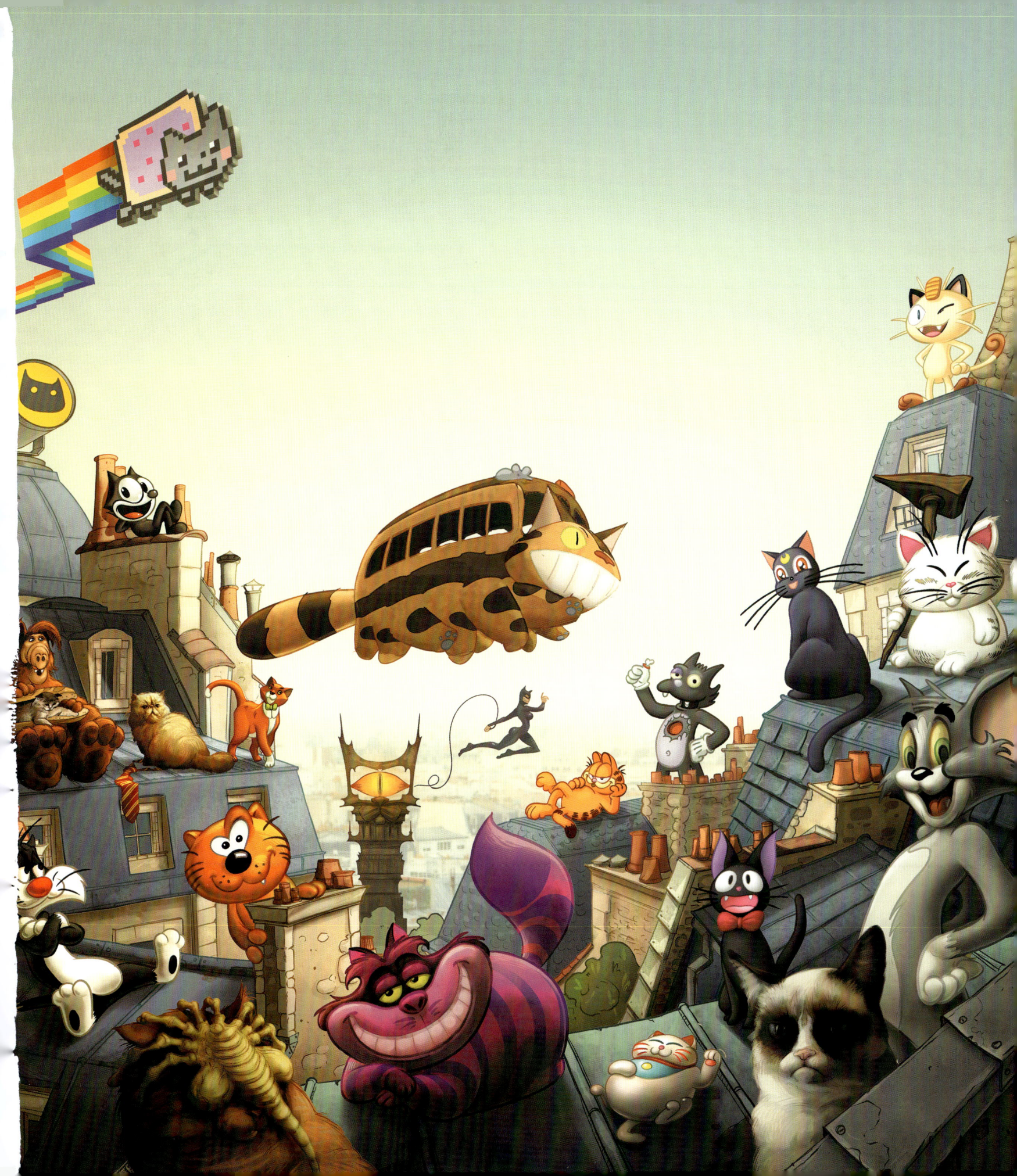

Stéphanie Chaptal · Claire-France Thévenon

CATS
IN POP CULTURE

Translated by Beth Smith

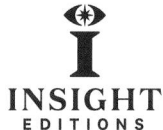

INSIGHT
EDITIONS

SAN RAFAEL · LOS ANGELES · LONDON

Contents

Women and Cats

Cats and Science (Fiction)

Super Cute and Funny Cats

Cats As Artists' Muses

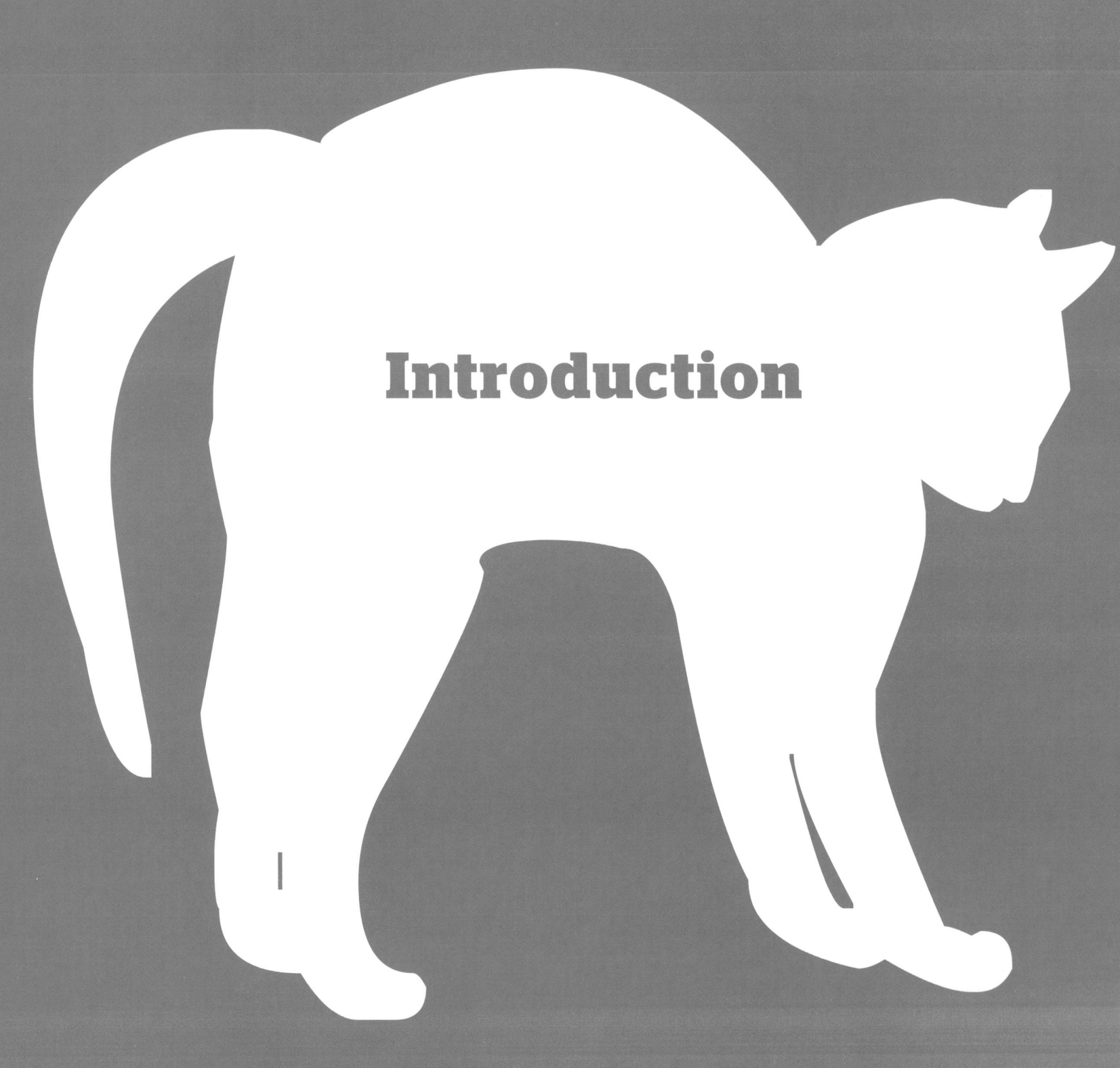

Introduction

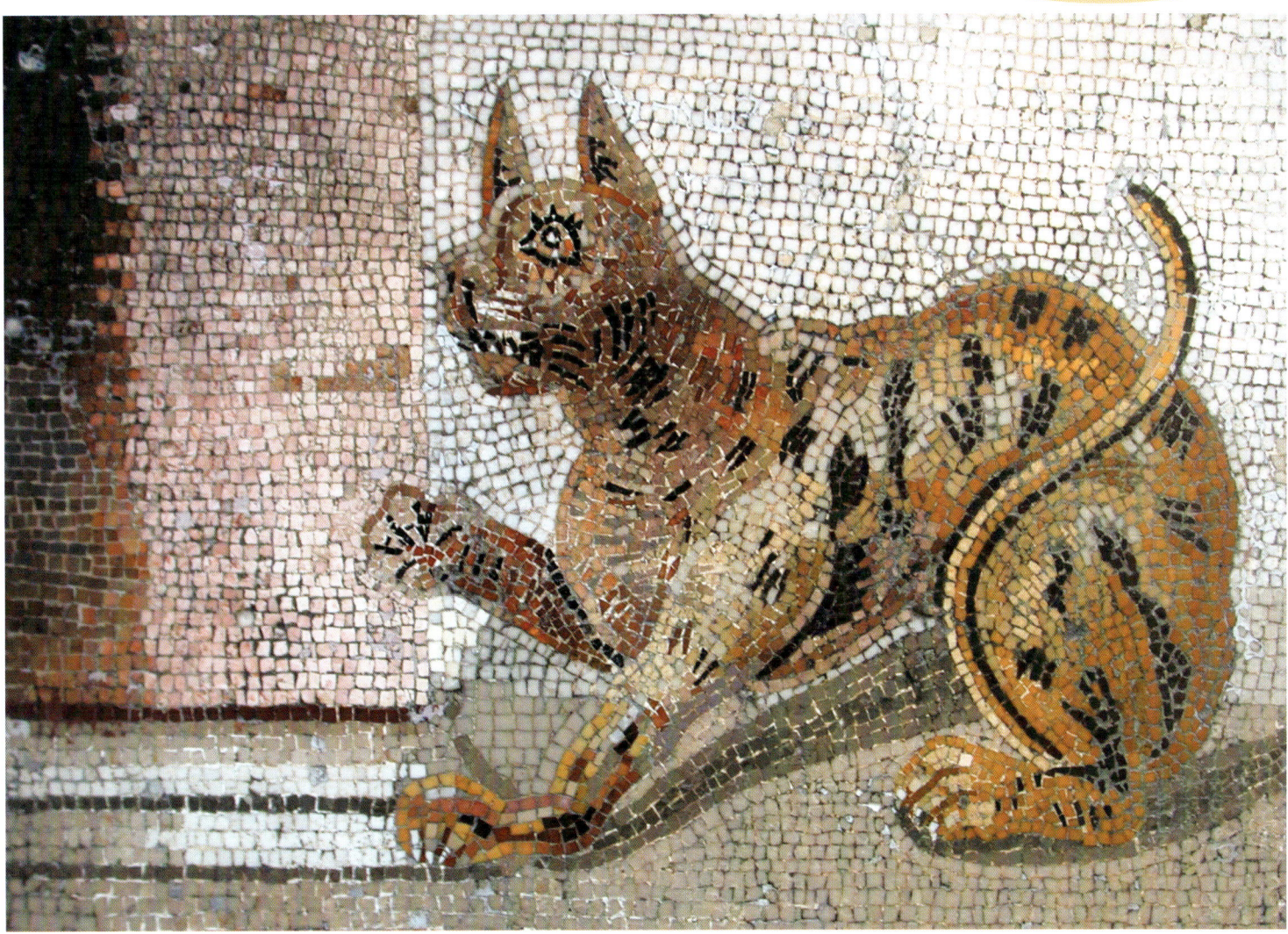

Cat mosaic in Pompeii, National Museum of Archaeology, Naples. Photo by Massimo Finizio.

"A carnivorous mammal (Felis catus) long domesticated as a pet and for catching rats and mice." With this definition from Merriam-Webster, we're well on the way to defining what a cat is and its role in relation to human beings.

Biologically speaking, cats belong to the *Felidae* family. These carnivorous placental mammals are characterized by their round heads, shortened skulls, jaws with around thirty teeth, and, with a few exceptions, retractable claws. The "small felines," including our domestic cats, are distinguished from their big cat cousins not only by their size, but also by their inability to roar, even though they are perfectly capable of making themselves heard from afar when their adopted humans have forgotten about their mealtimes. However, they can purr instead. And of the thirty or so species of "small felines" currently identified, they are the only ones to have come close to humans long enough for dictionaries to define them as pets. And what extraordinary animals they are!

If we take France as an example, according to the latest figures published by FACCO (the French federation of manufacturers of cat, dog, bird, and other pet food) in November 2020, France had 14.2 million cats.[1] That's around one cat for every five inhabitants in the country! With the exception of fish in aquariums and ponds, cats are France's favorite pets, ahead of birds and dogs. Since people and cats first began to cohabit in the Neolithic period, guided by converging interests arising from agriculture,[2] the history of cats and humans has been a complicated one, with many ups and downs. At certain times, cats were adored, venerated, and pampered, while at others, they were hunted down, martyred, and vilified. Sometimes, hunger and greed meant that they were merely animals to be hunted or raised for their meat and the quality of their fur. And to complicate matters, at any given time, the cat's status in human society varied enormously from one country to another and from one people to another.

This long, eventful history spawned a profusion of myths, symbols, and works of art in which the cat plays a central role. Their foray into popular culture, past and present, will be the focus of this book. It's not about boring you with biological, historical, economic, religious, or other considerations about the cat's place in our society. Instead, this book shows you how our relationship with this special animal has woven the fabric of a varied and abundant body of work. Throughout the pages, you'll come across works in which the cat plays the starring role as adviser, protector, or, quite simply, heroic figure in his own right. And others in which the cat is used as the ideal antagonist, either as Satan's minion or as a creature that is simply evil by nature. Sometimes, the cat is there just to make us laugh with his antics and the human qualities and faults we attribute to him. At other times, he terrifies us by being ferociously free and independent, never really tamed, and always uncompromising in his affection or indifference. In these cases, our fear is twofold, either because of his violence and predatory instincts,

linked to malice or a desire for vengeance on the part of the animal, or because of the fear his fate inspires in us and, on the contrary, our desire to protect him and save him from suffering. All of which are unreal, because in fiction, unlike in science, the cats concerned are rarely hurt, being no more than actors, mere splashes of color on paper or computer-generated pixels.

This book is about more than just cats. It explores the various facets the animals take on in our popular culture and teaches us about our own humanity and our relationship with these companions who have lived alongside us since the dawn of time. 🐾

[1] This figure includes animals in homes or shelters but doesn't include stray cats in towns or the countryside, for whom, by definition, no one buys bags or cans of cat food.
[2] Agriculture means seeds, which means food for mice. And mice mean cats that will hunt and eat them and human farmers who encourage this predatory behavior and protect their reserves.

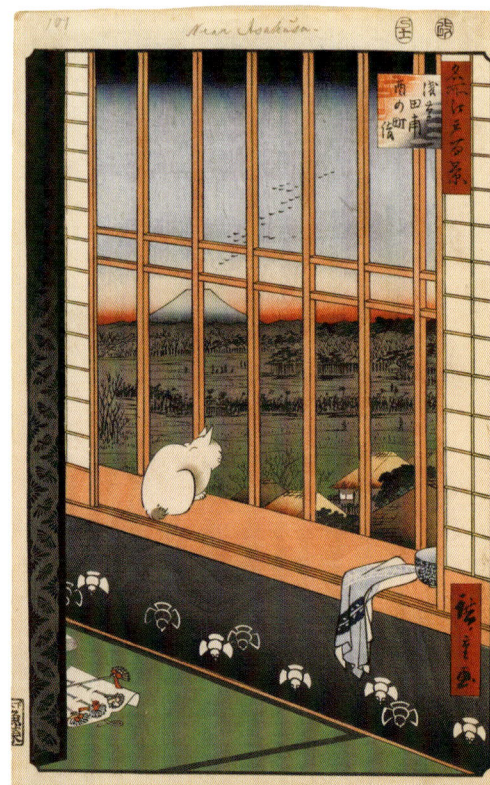

From *One Hundred Famous Views of Edo*, Utagawa Hiroshige, between 1857 and 1858, Brooklyn Museum.

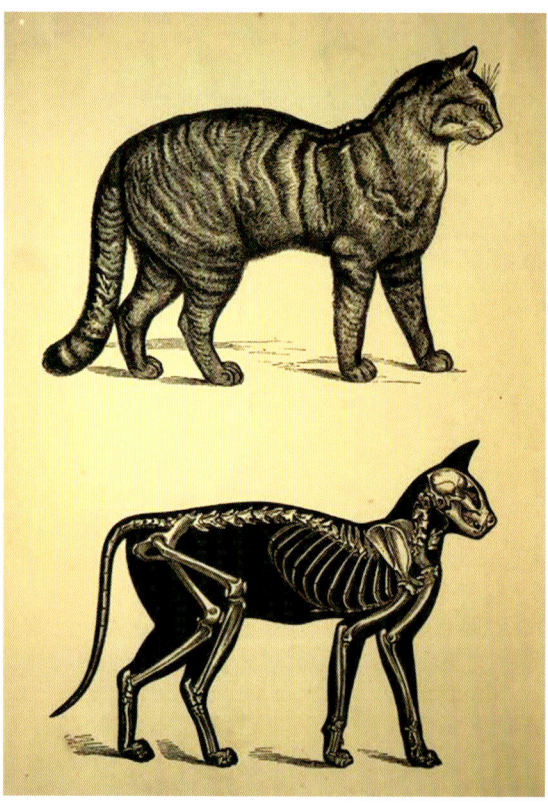

Cat Skeleton, drawing, St. George Mivart, 1881.

Cats vs. Other Animals: Let the Fun Begin!

Introduction: Cats Against the World

To be the hero of his own story, a cat doesn't need a human foil. However, whether they're protagonists or not, cats are regularly portrayed in conflict with other animals for comedic purposes, even if they are not traditionally seen as enemies.

Let's not kid ourselves: Humor, and in particular the situational comedy in which cats are often used, is based on conflict between two opposing forces. Their mutual misunderstandings and clashes, staged in a slapstick manner, generate plenty of laughs. That's why felines are regularly pitted against other animals. At the top of the list is the one animal considered their hereditary enemy, as it competes with them for the position of favorite household pet: the dog.

Cats and Dogs

Many stories about cats also feature canines. So why are dogs almost always pitted against them? The first factor is the contrasting personalities of the two animals. Cats are idle by nature. Their active times don't necessarily match those of the *Homo sapiens* with whom they live. Cats like to sleep, whereas dogs like to run or play in the house at times when humans are active. Dogs are accustomed to living in packs and are sociable. Felines also enjoy social contact but remain solitary animals. Moreover, their need for interaction varies greatly from one individual to another. And their games are often solitary. It's not unusual to see a cat chasing a string or a reflection against a wall.

The mostly successful domestication of the two animals is often at the heart of the gags in their relationship. The cat is seen as an indoor animal, while its antagonist is often identified with the outdoors and the backyard. With the advent of sedentary lifestyles and urbanization, dogs are moving into our homes more and more, but their sleeping space is often designated by a basket or a dedicated area, whereas felines sleep wherever they please, be it a bed, a closet, or a chair. In older stories, the dog has their doghouse and is destined to stay outside. This element figures prominently in Warner cartoons with Claude Cat. He regularly taunts Marc Anthony, the bulldog who has been kicked out of the house. This explains why, in the antagonistic duo, the feline always plays the bad guy against the ever-benevolent dog. It also stems from the vision of the temperamental cat versus the compassionate guard dog. The role of guardian is also opposed to the independence of an animal that is almost impossible to train.

The two species also contrast in size. The canine is often much larger than the feline, and if this isn't the case, it

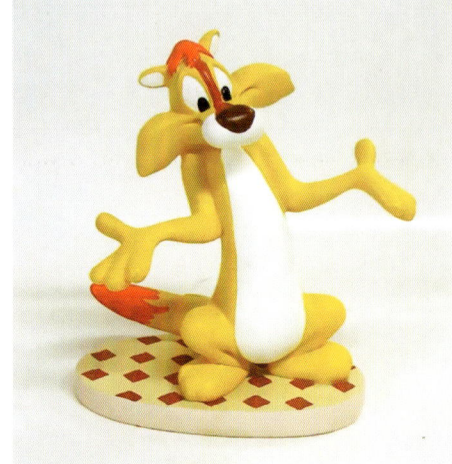

Claude Cat figurine.

becomes an interesting comic element in the narrative. While dogs don't eat cats, they tend to hunt and kill them when they haven't learned to cohabit with them. However, this aspect of predation and gratuitous violence is never used to the dog's disadvantage in fiction. On the contrary, the cat is seen as a relatively cunning animal, and its victimization rarely moves the

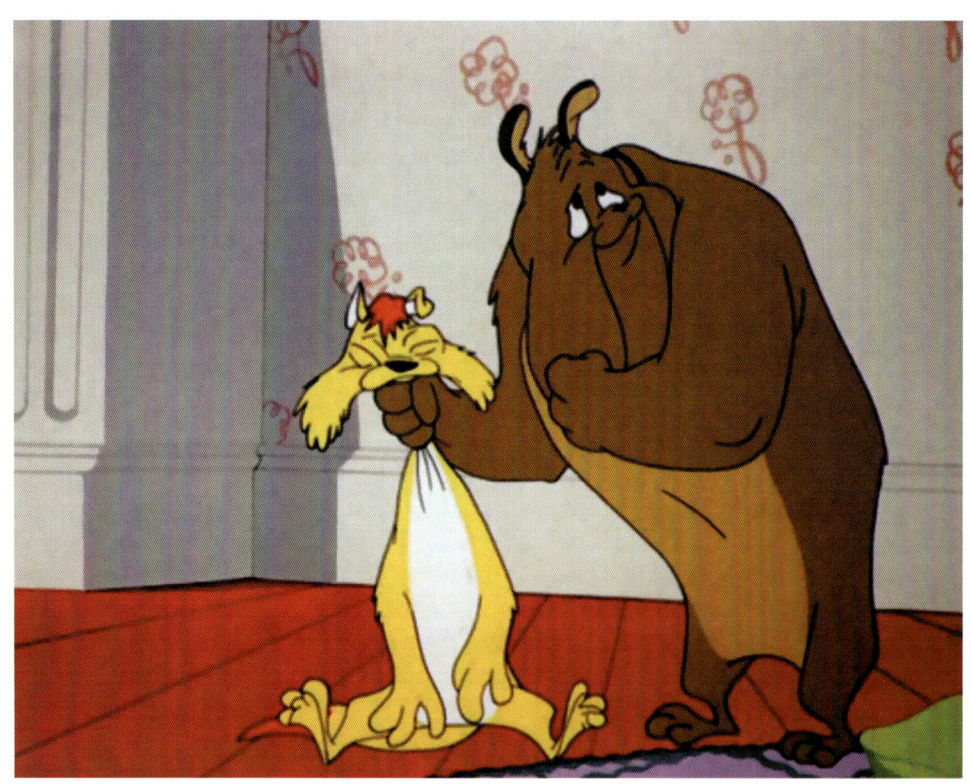

audience. In *ALF*, for example, the alien who wants to eat his host family's cat is a recurring gag that entertains the audience. This undoubtedly stems from society's view of the canine as a well-meaning guardian of human safety. And yet, both species are domesticated and condemned to live together, despite their opposite natures. Both are furry animals deemed cute by humans. These common traits explain why they are not systematically opposed to each other. They can even be friends, as in *Oliver and Company*. Animals living together despite their differences is a theme that's regularly used to create a clear narrative opposition or to create funny scenes.

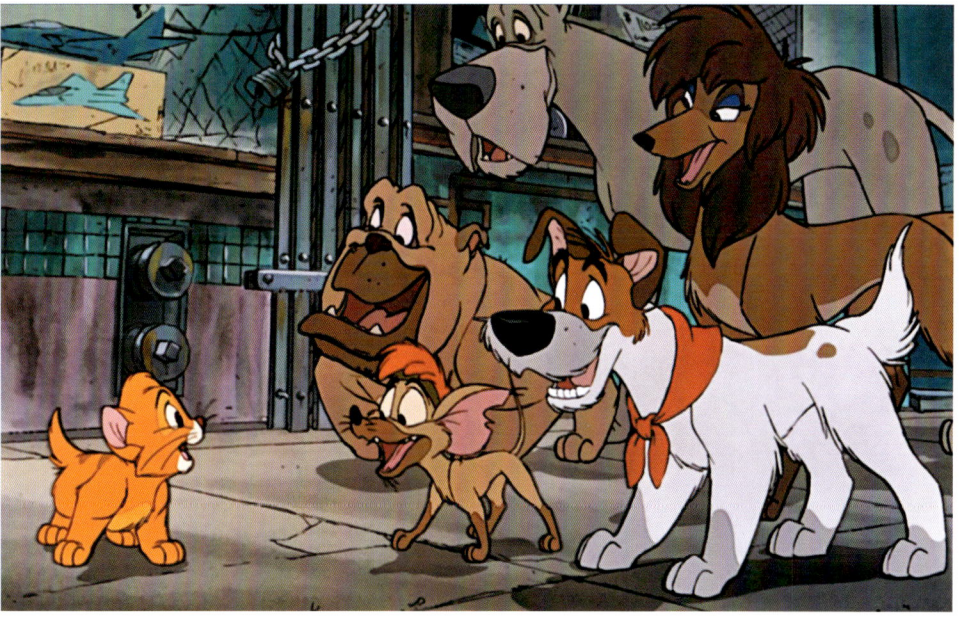
Oliver and Company.

The Cats of Animation

While the predatory aspect is never used in stories featuring cat-dog relationships, it's regularly brought to the fore when the feline is the predator, usually of mice or birds. The domestic cat then rediscovers its hunting instinct and wants to attack the other animal

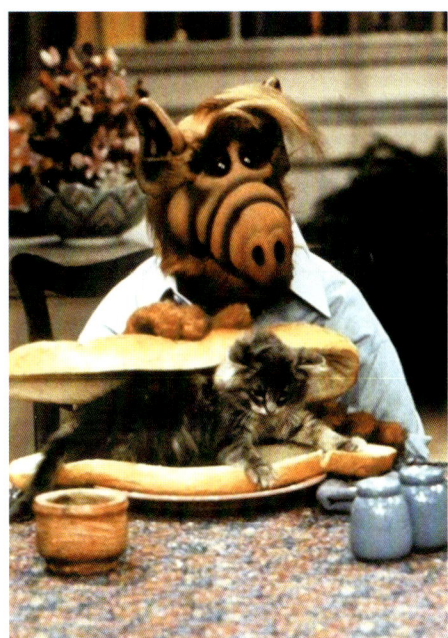
ALF.

in the household, whether out of greed or just out of sadism and for fun. The motive for clashing with another animal can also be linked to the possessive nature of the feline, which considers that people, the home, and, above all, the food in the house belong to him. This is the case with Claude Cat, a hypocritical and sadistic animal that tries to attack a cute little kitten in several episodes. The feline hates everyone, even his own species. His comfortable home isn't threatened, but he refuses to share it with anyone else.

The Looney Tunes cat Sylvester is most often pitted against the canary Tweety, but also against the mouse Speedy Gonzales. His attitude is Manichean, and he's calculating, even though his plans always fail. With Tom and Jerry, there's less of a moral dimension between the supposedly good guy and the bad guy. In some cases, Tom is just trying to keep the sometimes-sadistic rodent from stealing. The feline may defend the house from a cheese-stealing or mischievous mouse in many stories but is rarely presented as such. More often,

he's considered the aggressor and the one the viewers want to see fail.

A cat can also be the prey's ally, whether for personal gain or out of attachment. This is the case in the film *Stuart Little*, in which Snowbell gets used to the house mouse. Occasionally, the cat and its enemy become friends, as happens with Tom and Jerry, who

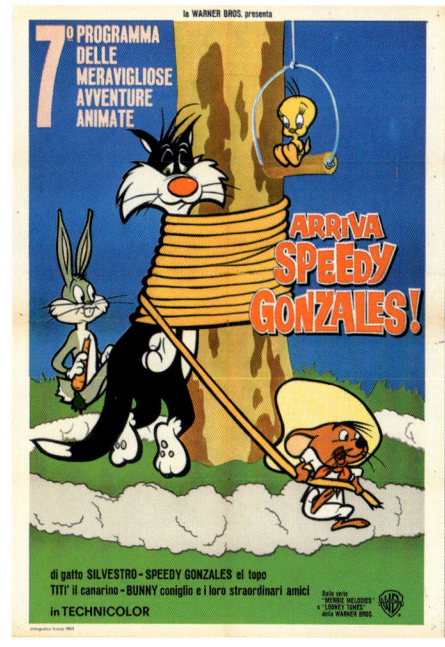
Sylvester taking on Speedy Gonzales.

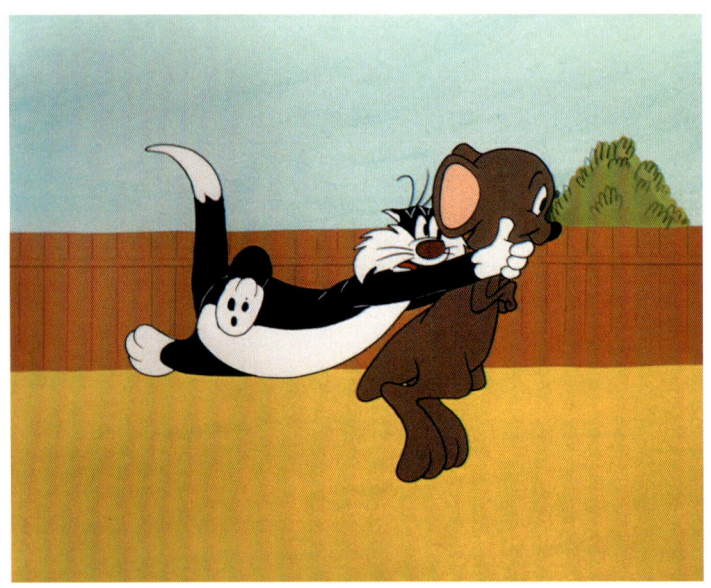
Sylvester with Hippety Hopper, the kangaroo he mistakes for a mouse.

One of the rare examples of this willing domestication of cats with other animals can be found in *The Secret Life of Pets* (2016). The obese cat Chloe belongs to the same group as the guinea pig Norman and the bird Sweet Pea and doesn't try to devour them. This emphasizes the feline's total domestication. In the 2019 sequel, she teaches the dog Gidget how to become a cat. She caricatures the cat's perspective as follows: A cat never fetches a ball, it always lands on its feet, it uses a litter box, and it eats other animals. Chloe says, "Cats eat birds; that's nature."

In *The Diary of a Killer Cat*, Anne Fine chronicles the adventures of Tuffy, a bird killer who is falsely accused of murdering the neighbors' rabbit. In this cat autobiography, the animal is likened to a human, and thus to a psychopathic killer, since he can't help but kill the animals that cross his path. The feline's humanized point of view is the funniest thing about the book. Tuffy is obviously not scary; he's like a child who doesn't take responsibility for his misdeeds and always

have a complex, dynamic relationship. In *The Sylvester & Tweety Mysteries*, the two Looney Tunes characters fight, but also have periods of truce for the sake of their mission.

Cats As an Allegory for Human Violence

There's much more physical violence between cats and other animals than with dogs. When cats are in a position of power, they are regularly perceived as dangerous and cruel in their abuse of power. Plus, cats like to play with their food. The house cat's ability to remain a hunter and a predator is a recurring theme in portraying cats as antagonists. Sylvester's failures and inability to kill the "giant mouse" in front of his son are a disgrace to the son. Killing is a way for domestic cats to prove to themselves that they are still wild animals. The cat's desire to assert that it can hunt and kill, and that it is still a wild beast, is an anthropomorphic transposition of the virile man. Showing that it's not a domesticated cat—a cat that has lost its instincts—is akin to a modern man's struggle to be seen as an alpha male. This stigmatization of domestication is a recurring comic element in the conflict between the feline and the animals it pursues. It wouldn't be nearly as funny to see modern cats happily cohabiting with other animals, even though this is the case in many homes.

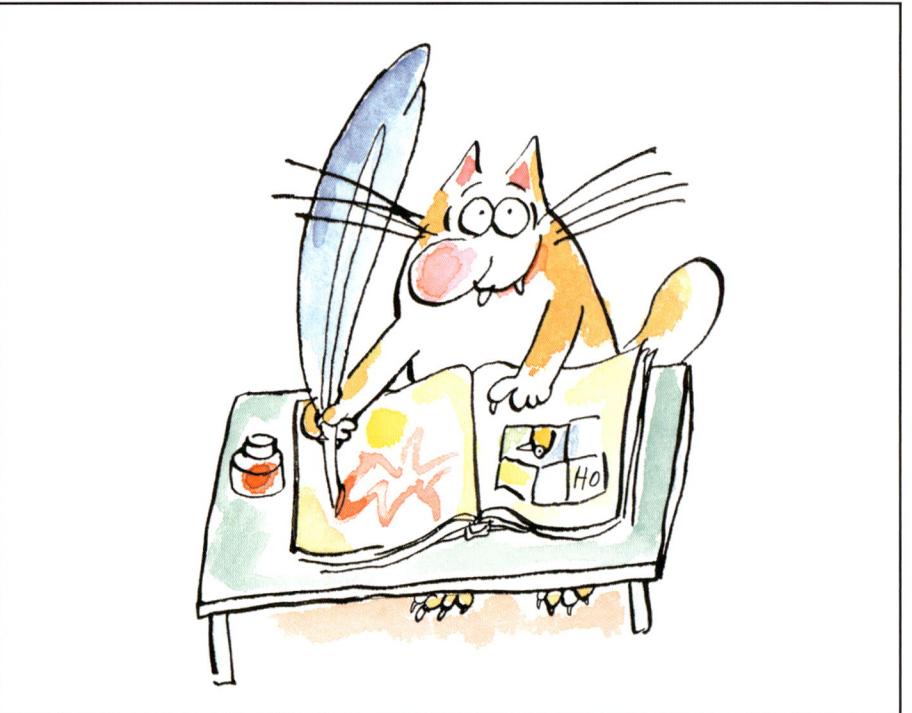
Cover artwork from the French edition of Anne Fine's *The Diary of a Killer Cat.*

has an excellent excuse for his mistakes. When he kills a bird, it's obviously the bird's fault. The feline's glaring bad faith is easy for kids to identify with, making this book a favorite in children's literature. Cats' domesticated savagery is once again a humorous element. 🐾

CATS:
ANTAGONISTS OR PROTAGONISTS?

Etymologically, a protagonist is the main character in a story. Felines are often protagonists, like in Disney's *The Aristocats* and *Oliver and Company*. However, the cats in these works have no real adversaries. In stories based on strong rivalries between characters, the cat is so closely associated with its opponent that it is sometimes difficult to define who is the protagonist and who is the antagonist. In *Tom and Jerry*, the gray cat isn't a hero, as he is motivated by a desire to harm the mouse. However, the director usually adopts Tom's point of view. The protagonist is the character with whom viewers empathize and whose goals and inner conflicts they understand. Based on this definition, Jerry is the story's antagonist. By the same token, whether he's battling Tweety, Speedy Gonzales, or the kangaroo, Sylvester is the protagonist of the Looney Tunes shorts in which he appears.

   This archetypal feline protagonist is paradoxical, because he's doomed to fail. The audience laughs at him, not with him, despite the empathy he's supposed to evoke. This process is at the heart of Buster Keaton's comic success, as he noted that his audience loved to see him suffer physically. The viewer's cruelty in seeing the cat miss his targets or endure physical abuse is one of the reasons for his success. A cat's love of violence and delight in torture is taken to extremes as the basis for *Itchy and Scratchy* in *The Simpsons*. If he's an antagonist, he'll be equally abused by his rival(s). The damage done to Mr. Tinkles's ego in *Cats & Dogs* is hilarious. The psychology of the cat in fiction is very black and white, but no matter how important his role, as long as he's involved in an adversarial relationship with another animal, he can't be the hero. Whether he's central to the narrative or a minor character, his contribution will always be negative and doomed to failure.

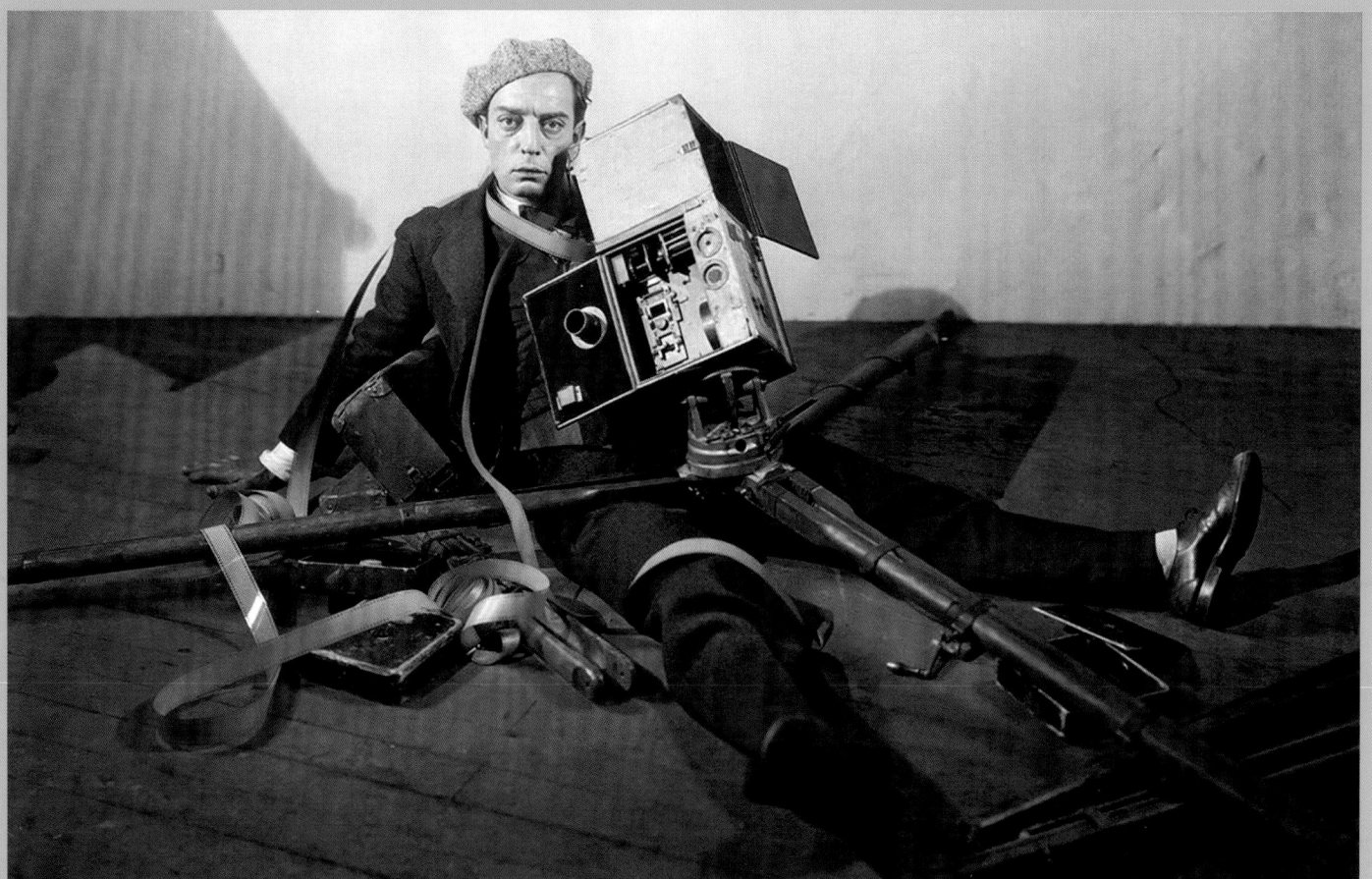

Buster Keaton.

Viewpoint

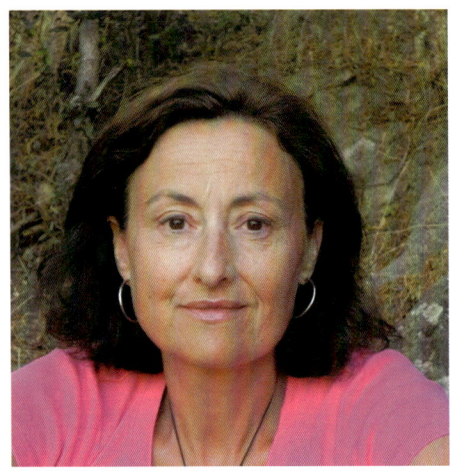

Emmanuelle Titieux, Veterinary Behaviorist

Emmanuelle Titieux is an animal behavior specialist at the National Veterinary School of Alfort in France. She explains why cats amuse humans and how the behaviors of the two species are connected.

It seems to me that cats were not domesticated in the same way as other animals.

There are several definitions of domestication. There was one that said it was the fact that a species could be fed, housed, and have its reproduction controlled by humans. Cats don't fall into this category. For millennia, they've eaten near farms and reproduced as they pleased. Another definition that we use a lot at the veterinary school is Price's from 1999, which states that genetic modifications made from generation to generation allow an individual of a species to live in conditions that are, let's say, defined and controlled by humans. In other words, in a captive environment, and this is underway in cats, but it hasn't quite been perfected, either.

So, why do people want to live with them?

Felines are very attractive to humans. That athletic gait, their way of pouncing and being flexible, we have to admire, I think. Baudelaire wrote poems about them. Then there are the eyes. That wild aspect that we can't domesticate attracts humans. Domestication isn't that simple. People who are incompetent with animals get rejected by the cat. They pay dearly. Those who succeed don't even know why. They have a sense of observation, a gift for it. That's why, when you manage to get along with a cat, you say to yourself, "Wow, I've done it, but it wasn't that easy!" But what about being good with a dog? Dogs erase human mistakes. They're more tolerant of mistreatment; it's atrocious. With the average cat, you can't go wrong even once or twice. Do you know why cat videos are so popular? People watch them because they're procrastinating. So, they watch cat videos, which do them a world of good and soothe the guilt they feel for procrastinating.

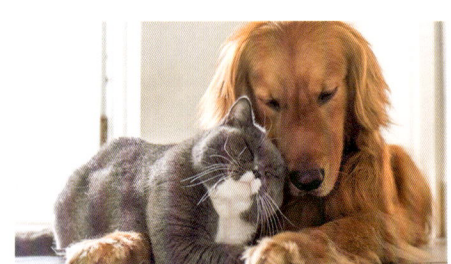

Cats are often associated with a variety of character traits in our culture. There's the lazy cat, the thieving cat, and so on. Have these traits been present in cats since they were domesticated, or are they innate? For example, cats sleep a lot, like most felines.

So do wild canines. But when you're an herbivore, because you must eat a huge amount of foliage and grass to get your daily calorie intake, you spend sixty percent of your time walking and eating, so there's less time for sleeping.

When a cat is associated with a particular fault, is this justified by the animal's characteristics, or is it the human being bringing their own feelings to it?

I think it's human projection. Like cats living in captivity: Some will engage in the repetitive activity of eating. They're going to become obese, and they're going to move around a lot less. To have individuals that can live in the enclosed environment of an apartment, it's better to select individuals that are not very active.

What about lust in cats? Is it because some females are rather noisy when they're in heat?

That's beyond me. I don't have an answer, because I don't see lust in cats. One thing's for sure: A cat in heat is noisy. She has to make herself heard for there to be males. The males may fight, and the female cat may mate with several toms when she's in heat to increase her chances of being pregnant. There's no such thing as one big tomcat winning everything and the others being losers. In any case, it's always like that with humans; they always want to reproduce a vision. It's terrible, and I say this as a woman because male researchers don't always understand, but there's an extremely macho vision of all reproduction, whatever the animal. With the exception of a few species like ducks, dolphins, and humans, it's always the female who gives the green light. Always! And the male waits and says okay. This dominant-subordinate hierarchy that researchers have tried to show in all species is completely false. Looking at animals through a human lens and seeing things that we would appreciate in humans or justify as natural in humans just isn't right.

How can we tell if a cat is happy or not?

Some domestic cats definitely have problems, but with others, who's to say they don't? Who's to say your cat is happy in an apartment? That's not for me to say. It's up to the cat. We started to develop a cat well-being indicator to measure the well-being of cats who were mutilating their necks.[1] It's an environmental disease, and if you change the cat's environment, it can be cured for good. But as soon as you put it back in its original environment, where there are too many constraints, the disease reappears. I think a cat can adapt to life in an apartment, but it has to have vacations, just like we do. I beg cat owners to give them a vacation, to rent something in the countryside where there are no roads, of course. My aim is not to have the cats run over, but that from time to time, they have access to freedom. I'm always reminded of something I heard at an animal welfare conference, where one of the specialists asked, "In a zoo, do you think the animals with the most behavioral problems are those born in a zoo or those born in the wild?" And obviously, everyone thought it was the free-born ones who had a much harder time adapting to life in a zoo. Well, not at all. The ones with the most stereotypes and repetitive behaviors were those born in a zoo. Developing in an environment where all behaviors can develop in a normal way results in a more balanced individual than in an environment where they can't develop all those behaviors that will enable them to adapt later on. These repetitive behaviors will appear.

Most of the cats you see in consultation have behavioral problems. How does a consultation with you work?

I don't have to go to people's homes. I ask the humans questions and observe the cat during the consultation, cross-checking what they tell me with what I see. Afterward, I examine the cat, if necessary, if I have any doubts about the presence

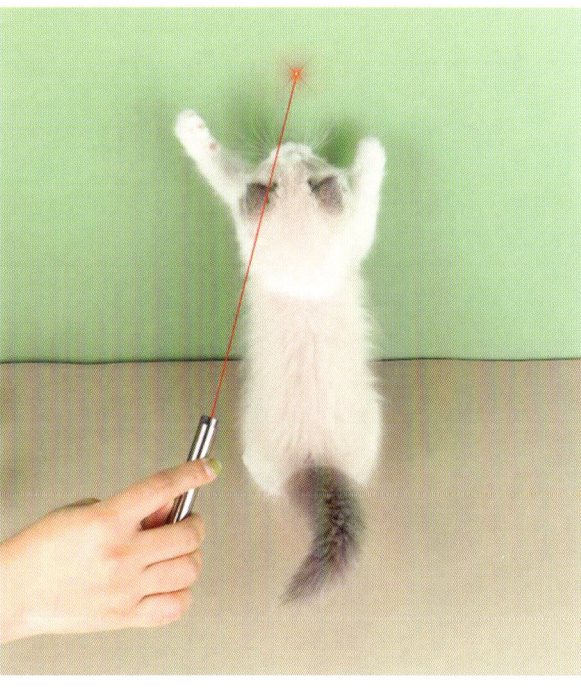

of a disease, or if it's purely due to the environment. I include humans in the environment.

Besides obesity, why else do they come?

They don't come at all for obesity. Never. The problem with obese cats is that they develop diabetes. Vets haven't become tyrants about weight, but with cats, we know they're going to pay dearly for it. And so will the owner, because between blood tests, insulin injections, and so on, it's quite expensive. The problems I encounter are aggressiveness, uncleanliness, inter- and intraspecies aggressiveness (cats that attack humans or cats that don't get along with other cats), compulsive licking, compulsive scratching, and excessive meowing.

So, these are things that bother the owners more than anything else?

Some people come because it's bothering them, and some people come because they think their cat isn't doing well. Some people come in, and I ask them, "What are you hoping for?" They say, "I'd like to know why my cat is meowing." I ask, "Don't you want me to solve the problem?" They say, "Oh, yes . . ." But first, they want to know what they're doing wrong.

Usually, to solve a cat's problem, do you have to change behavior and the environment in which it lives? Change the owner's attitude?

Yes. 🐾

---

[1] https://pubmed.ncbi.nlm.nih.gov/29713639/

Tom and Jerry

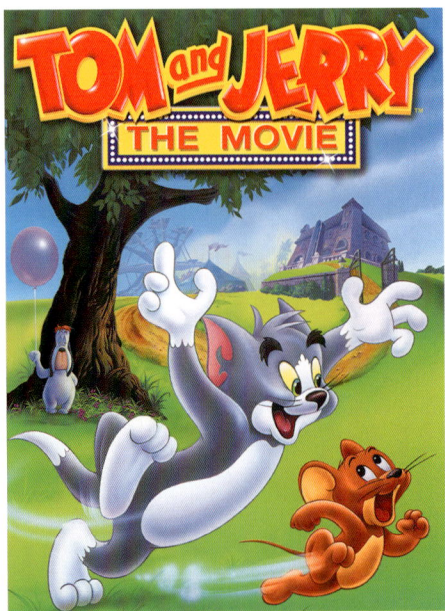

During the golden age of Hollywood studios, Warner Bros. dominated animation with its Looney Tunes shorts that were shown before feature films, but MGM also had an animated production arm, which brought Tom and Jerry *to the public.*

The series began with Hanna-Barbera's short film "Puss Gets the Boot" in 1940. The film about Jasper the cat and Jinx the mouse was a hit with audiences and critics alike. Except for their names, the concept was already there, with an emphasis on physical humor: the cat and mouse hit each other, chased each other, and laughed at each other's pain. In 1941, in the middle of World War II, they became Tom and Jerry in "The Midnight Snack." The name Tom is said to be a reference to "Tommies," the English nickname for English soldiers, and Jerry to "Jerries," which was slang for German soldiers.

The entire Hollywood industry was called upon to do its part during the war, so the duo also participated in more partisan films, such as 1943's "Yankee Doodle Mouse." The film went on to win an Oscar the following year. It featured a long chase between Tom and Jerry that was staged like a war film. A cheese grater with USA insignia becomes a jeep, eggs become grenades, and light bulbs turn into bombs.

The First Frenemies of the Animal Kingdom

While cat-and-mouse antagonism is a common comedic device, the special feature of the series is that Tom pursues Jerry, whether it be to eat him, make him suffer, or simply to keep him from stealing something, but the mouse is not to be outdone. Jerry is often violent and sadistic when it comes to Tom. From his very first appearance in "The Midnight Snack," he understands that the feline will be in trouble if he breaks anything in the house. So, he decides to threaten to break some dishes.

The two characters' sadism toward each other is one of the hallmarks of the series. Like many cartoons of the period, the series was inspired by silent burlesque movies. The characters' violence can be traced back to slapstick comedy; derived from theatrical chase scenes, it literally means "stick used for slapping." Fatty Arbuckle and Buster Keaton were the stars of the genre, first together and then separately. In the cartoon, there is no single victim or aggressor, as Tom and Jerry take turns in each role.

The two characters have a complicated relationship. Although most often antagonistic, they sometimes join forces or worry about each other, as the game is ultimately more important than killing the other. In 1956's "Blue Cat Blues," they are close friends, and Jerry tells the story of the blue-gray cat's unhappy love affair. The episode's ending is controversial, as both protagonists seem to be on the verge of committing suicide under a train.

In the original cartoons, Tom is usually an indoor cat cared for by an overweight maid, with only her legs revealed in the cartoon.

The maid is abrupt and not at all gentle with the feline. However, some films break with this pattern and offer parodies. One example is *The Two Mouseketeers*, which won the Oscar for best animated short in 1952. Three other films were produced to build on the Mouseketeers' success. The comic duo's popularity grew in the 1950s, and

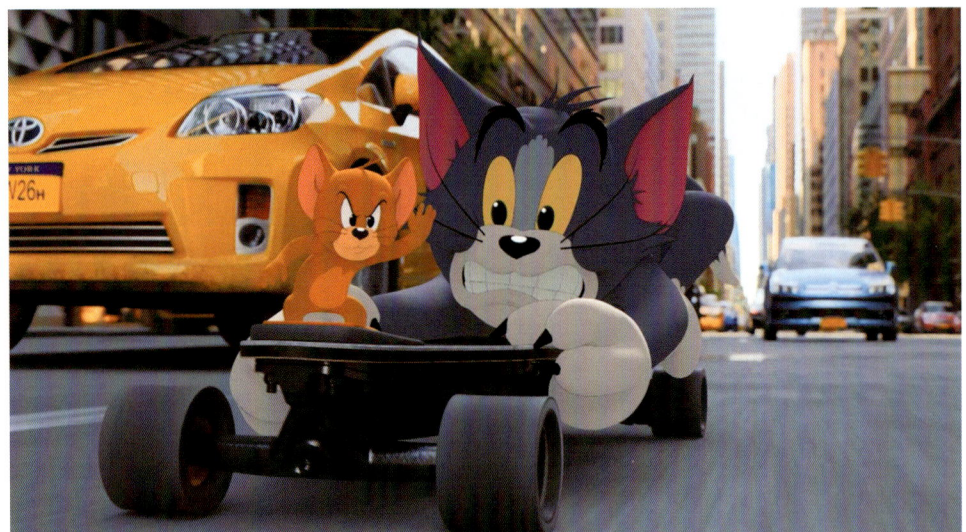

Tom and Jerry, 2021.

they remained mainly silent, although the characters regularly cried out in pain or spoke briefly. The success of the series inspired various productions to revive the franchise in each decade.

From Television to Movie Theater

In 1992, the cat and mouse moved to the big screen with *Tom and Jerry: The Movie*. The challenge of transposing a film that lasts less than ten minutes into a full-length feature forced the producers to make some tough choices. The duo talks, probably too much. But it was perhaps the heartfelt sentiments that were too far removed from the cartoon's original violence that led to the film's failure. The film was not a hit, earning a paltry $3 million out of an $8 million investment.

In 2021, Warner Bros., which has owned the rights since 2006, also adapted the adventures of the cat and mouse for the big screen. For the first time, they appeared in a live-action film, like the classic *Who Framed Roger Rabbit?* (1988) or the Looney Tunes film *Space Jam* (1996). Taking a lesson from 1992, the studio made the two protagonists mute again, apart from a serenade that Tom plays on the piano. He never speaks, but he sings. The other animals, on the other hand, from pigeons to cats and even elephants, speak in this *Tom and Jerry*.

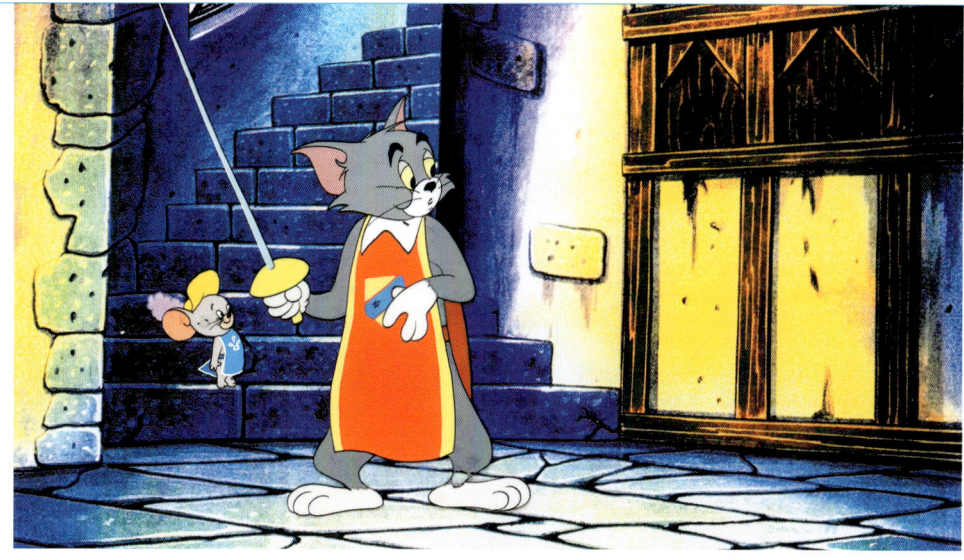
The Two Mouseketeers.

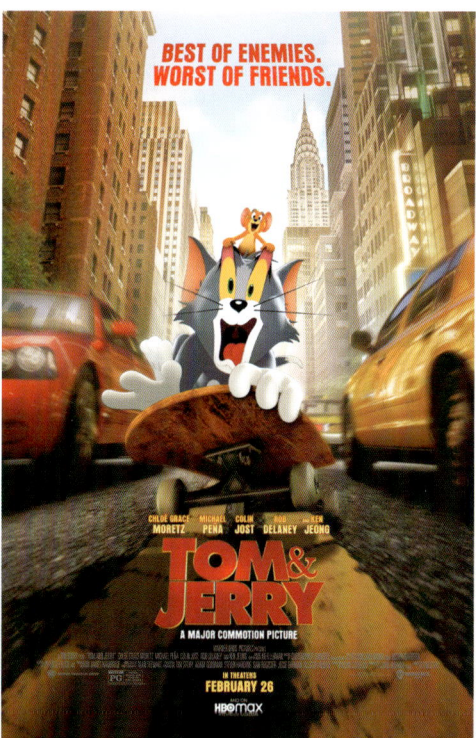

From a technical standpoint, the characters' animation is highly meticulous. Made with cel-shading computer graphics, the characters fit in much better with real-life shots than they would in a classic cartoon. The realistic aspect of the film is not at all shocking. In terms of storytelling, an hour-and-a-half-long film can't limit itself to chases and physical gags. Tom is hired to chase Jerry out of a luxury hotel. The two become friends and try to help a woman, Kayla, keep her job at the hotel. Although it's not captivating, the human storyline is enough to entertain. 🐾

SPEC SHEET

WORK: *Tom and Jerry*.
CREATORS: William Hanna and Joseph Barbera.
DATE CREATED: 1941.
DISTRIBUTOR: Warner Bros.
CAT'S NAME AND ROLE IN THE WORK: Tom, a blue alley cat; one of the members of the duo.

Sylvester

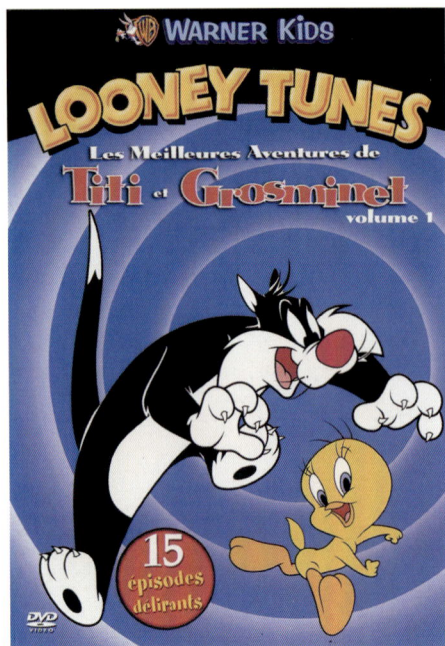

Sylvester is undoubtedly the star cat of Looney Tunes. Created by Friz Freleng, he's as well known as his various opponents, including the most famous, the yellow canary Tweety.

Sylvester is a black-and-white tuxedo cat (meaning that he has white on his front that makes it look like he's wearing a tuxedo). He's short-tempered and has trouble pronouncing Fs, which gives the impression that the character is constantly babbling. Like in most Looney Tunes and Merry Melodies cartoons, the character is driven by a simple goal—to devour the bird Tweety—but he differs from Wile E. Coyote, who also dreams of feasting on a bird. An episode's structure may resemble that of a Coyote and Road Runner cartoon, with its use of convoluted plans and absurd ACME gadgets, but it usually incorporates interactions with other characters, such as Hector the Bulldog and Granny.

Some episodes are parodies, such as 1955's "Red Riding Hoodwinked," a funny, modern adaptation of "Little Red Riding Hood," and 1960's "Hyde and Go Tweet," in which Tweety falls into a "Hyde potion" that turns him into a giant monster, an obvious reference to *Dr. Jekyll and Mr. Hyde*. The 1953 cartoon "Tom Tom Tomcat" reflected the Native American films of the time, as well as American history. In it, Sylvester and his band of native cats attack the peaceful Granny and Tweety. Since it conveys historical untruths and, above all, racist prejudices, it hasn't been broadcast since the 1990s.

Although when he first appeared in 1945, Sylester was more of an alley cat who wanted to devour a bluebird, he was later clearly a house cat belonging to Granny. The old woman also owns Tweety and Hector. She regularly uses her rolling pin to calm the cat down when he tries to attack her bird. It wasn't until 1947 that the duo appeared in Freleng's cartoon "Tweety Pie." The dynamic between Sylvester and Tweety is based on the cat's malicious intentions, the canary's supposed innocence (although the bird is often innocently sadistic with the cat), and recurring punchlines. Tweety systematically says, "I thought I saw a puddy tat," "It *was* a puddy tat," and "Bad puddy tat," while Sylvester sticks with "Sufferin' succotash!"

The cat doesn't necessarily have nine lives, but he often ends up leaving his body behind in the hunt for the little bird. He dies in more than a dozen episodes. He then appears with wings and a halo to go to heaven or elsewhere. This is the case in 1954's "Satan's Waitin'," in which Sylvester uses up his nine lives and then descends into hell.

He stars in around one hundred episodes and is consistently the villain the audience loves to see fail. He also appears in episodes with Speedy Gonzales, where he becomes Grosso Mineto, supposedly the stupidest cat in Mexico.

A recurring character outside his adventures with the canary is his son, Sylvester Junior. A miniature version of Sylvester, he spends his episodes complaining that his father makes him feel ashamed because he systematically fails, whether it's at fishing or, more often than not, at catching a "giant mouse" that's actually a kangaroo.

One of the most famous Warner Bros. characters, Sylvester appeared

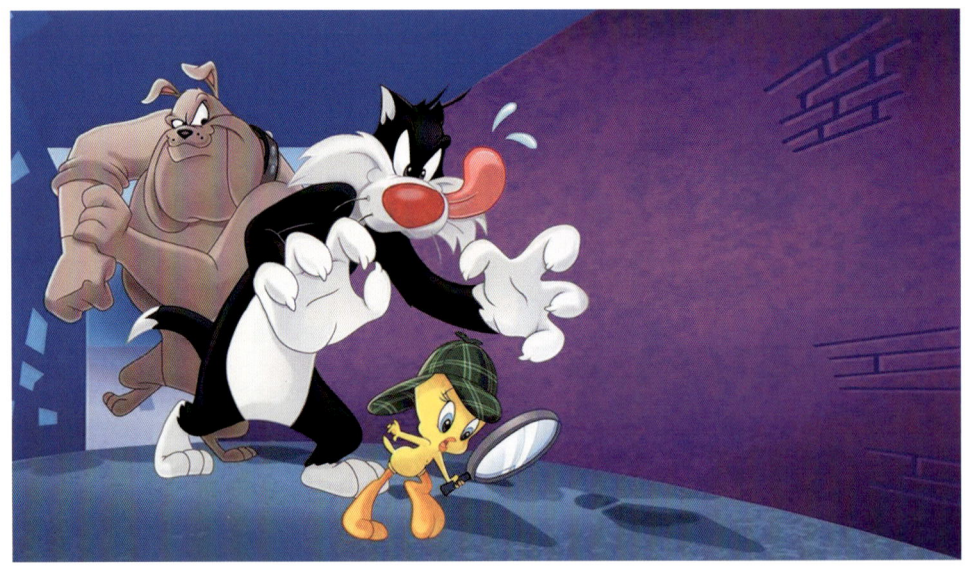

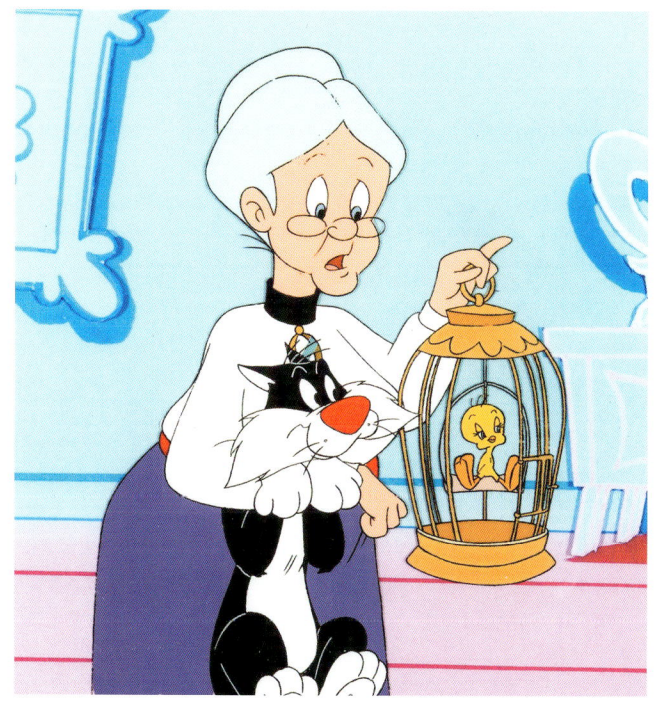

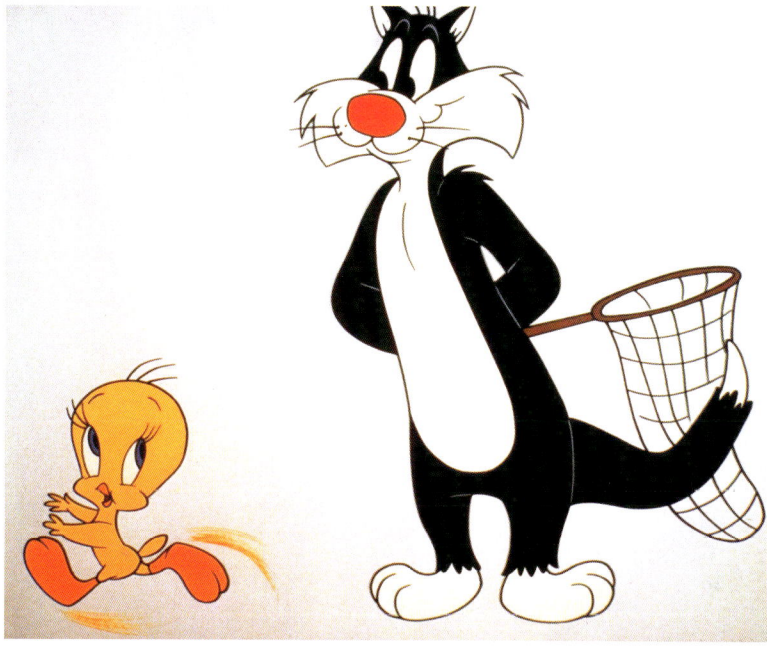

Sylvester the Cat's main preoccupation is chasing Tweety, a yellow canary bird.

alongside Michael Jordan in the 1996 film *Space Jam*, in 2003's *Looney Tunes: Back in Action*, and in *2021's Space Jam* 2 with LeBron James. These films combine live action and cartoons, as in the landmark film *Who Framed Roger Rabbit?* (1988), in which the cat made a cameo. Unlike *Roger Rabbit*, however, the plots of these films struggle to go beyond a series of gags, and the features don't keep the same pace as the studio's classic cartoons.

In the 1990s, Steven Spielberg began producing Tiny Toons using Warner's character license. Capturing the adventures of young toons in thirty-minute episodes, the cartoon introduced Furball as one of the main characters, as well as his mentor, Sylvester. Above all, this series marked Looney Tunes's transition to modern cartoon formats.

In 1995, Warner Bros. began production on fifty twenty-two-minute episodes of *The Sylvester and Tweety Mysteries*. For five seasons, the duo helped Granny, who had become a detective for the show, to solve cases.

In 2001, the cat appeared again in *Baby Looney Tunes*, aimed at a younger audience. The characters wore diapers and lacked any real malice.

SPEC SHEET

CAT'S NAME: Sylvester.
WORK: *Tweety and Sylvester*.
CREATOR: Friz Freleng.
DATE CREATED: 1945.
DISTRIBUTOR/AVAILABILITY: Warner Bros. Multiple DVDs and streaming services, and on cartoon TV channels.
CAT'S CHARACTERISTICS: Black and white, red nose, speech impediment on the letter F.

Hercules

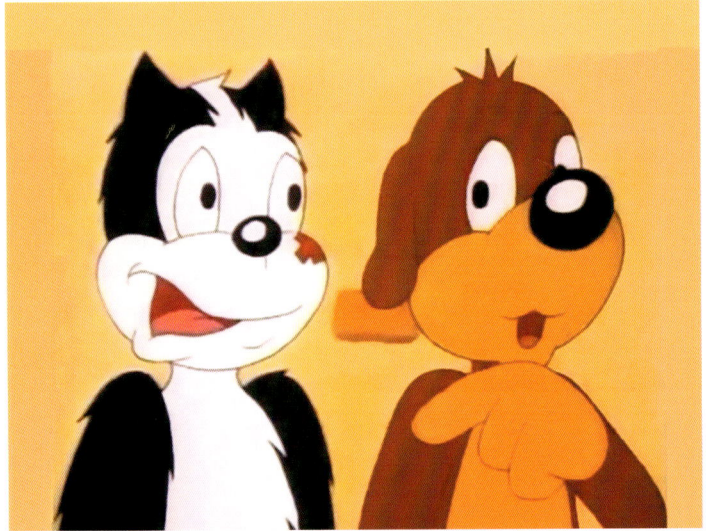

Spiff's companion and adversary, this black-and-white alley cat with an ever-present red bandage on his face, has valiantly passed the age of seventy. And he's been part of every version of the French magazine Pif Gadget *since its creation.*

Two years after Spiff, a beagle, first appeared in the pages of the French Communist daily *L'Humanité*, he was joined by a tuxedo cat reminiscent of Felix the Cat. The duo of Spiff and Hercules was born. And from the very first four-frame gag published on August 28, 1950, at the bottom of an inside page of *L'Humanité*, these two were inseparable. From publication to publication (*Vaillant* and *Pif Gadget* and its various revivals in France, as well as in the UK in the *Daily Worker* and *The Morning Star*), they were adapted into an animated series and even a film.

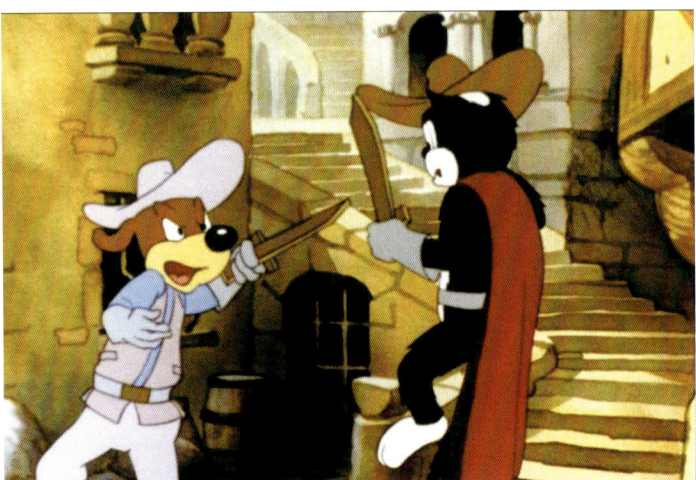

At first, Hercules plays the classic role of Spiff's adversary, starting by stealing a sausage. But over the course of their adventures and gags, the two grow closer. They join forces and protect each other from the wrath of Spiff's owner, Tonton, before becoming the best of friends, even though they continue to squabble on a regular basis. And little by little, the human characters and the animals' dependence on them fade from the pages. Nevertheless, Hercules retains his typical alley cat personality: quarrelsome, teasing, full of himself, and totally unscrupulous when it comes to making mischief. Over time, however, his character softens, even in the adventures he has without Spiff guiding him. But in his first solo adventures, accompanied by two young children, he plays a string of dirty tricks on the poor keeper of a municipal square who's just trying to enforce the ban on walking on the grass.

Like Spiff, he even had his own magazine, *Super Hercules*, for a time. Just like in *Spiff and Hercules*, in which the cat is the distorting mirror image of the dog but with a little more malice, *Super Hercules* was the sarcastic counterpart to *Pif Gadget* magazine. From 1986 to 1992, its seventy-one monthly issues and specials were packed with gags and original comics, but the editorial line was resolutely focused on humor and less on information or educating young people (which was the case in *Vaillant* and then in *Pif Gadget*). Even the magazine's gadgets were more like jokes and novelties than those usually found in

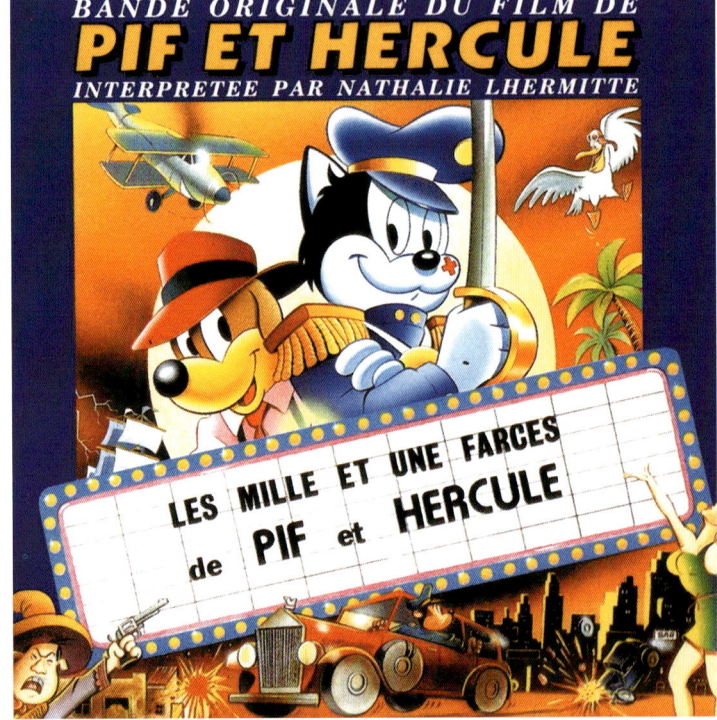

Pif Gadget. Despite his solo adventures and the publication of four comic strip books dedicated to him, Hercules was never far from Spiff and took part in the various attempts to relaunch the magazine. 🐾

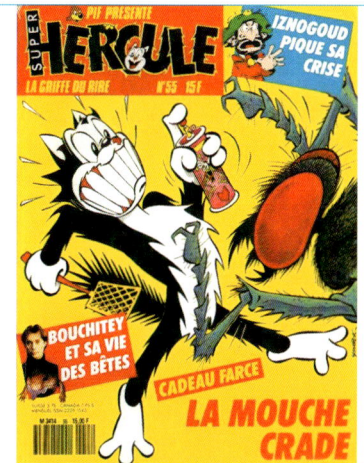

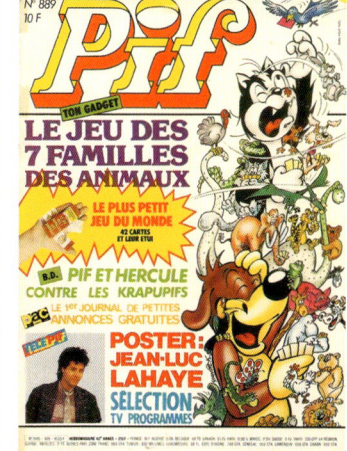

A NEW YOUTH IN ANIMATION

While the first fans of *Spiff and Hercules* discovered them in their parents' newspaper or in children's magazines, kids in the 1980s discovered the feisty cat Hercules on television. On October 30, 1989, a cartoon series brought the two friends front and center. *Spiff and Hercules* was broadcast on the French channel TF1 and ran for 130 ten-minute episodes. It was followed in 1993 by a feature-length animated film, *The 1001 Gags of Spiff & Hercules*, in which Hercules, dreaming of being a star in his own right and no longer a dog's stooge, retreats to an island to tell his own story and make a film of his adventures. Over the course of eighty minutes, he recalls his best exploits with Spiff, making himself look his best, even if that was sometimes far from what really happened.

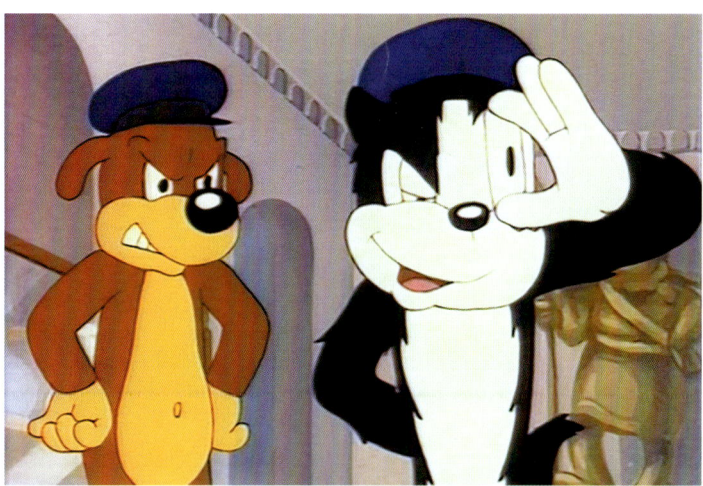

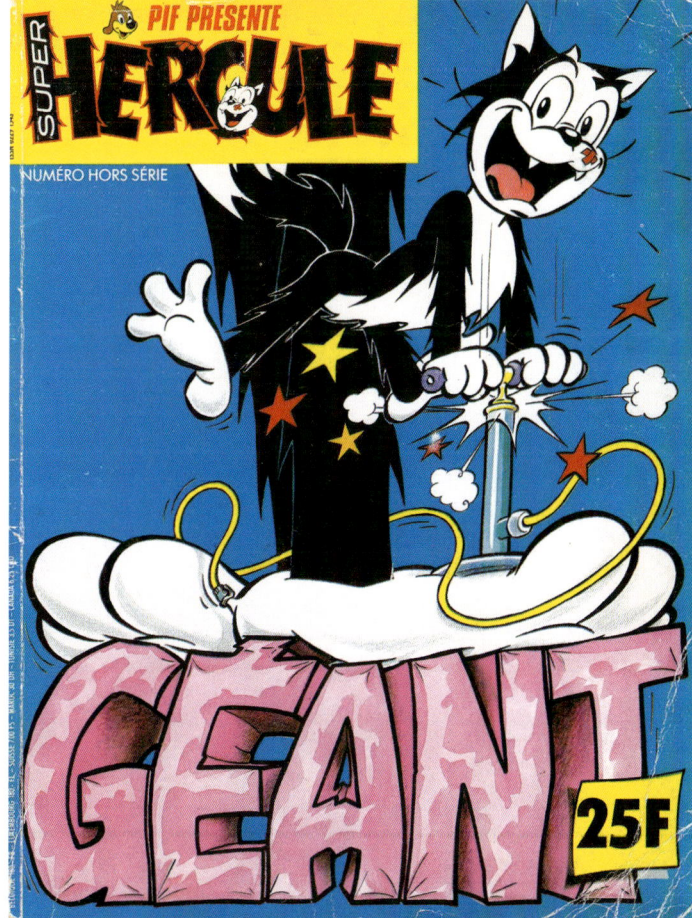

SPEC SHEET

CAT'S NAME: Hercules.
WORK: *Spiff and Hecules.*
CREATOR: José Cabrero Arnal.
DATE CREATED: August 28, 1950, in the pages of the daily L'Humanité.
PUBLISHER/AVAILABILITY: Éditions Vaillant and Bamboo for the comics; four books by Yannick Hodbert.
CAT'S CHARACTERISTICS: Anthropomorphic black-and-white tuxedo cat, with a red bandage on the left side of his mouth.

Itchy and Scratchy

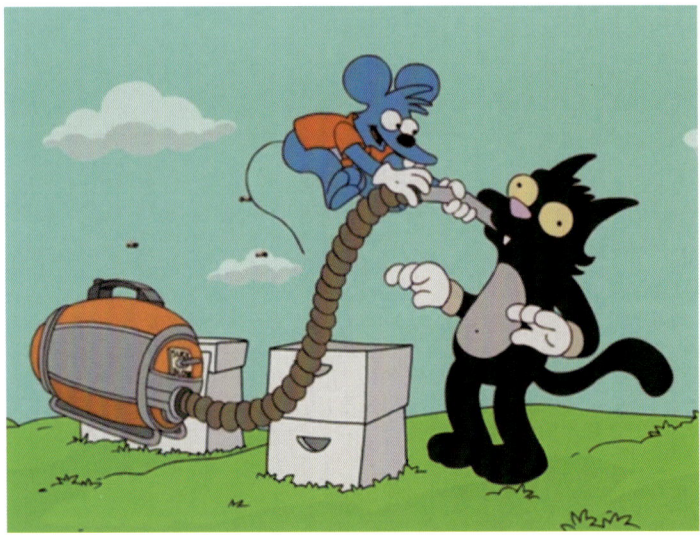

Since 1989, the whole world has been watching The Simpsons, the animated comedy series about the adventures of an average American family. Still on-screen more than twenty-two years after it was launched on Fox, it deals with all kinds of topics, including cats.

Living in suburban Springfield, Homer and Marge Simpson are raising three children, Bart, Lisa and baby Maggie, in increasingly offbeat situations. They also have a cat and a dog. While the dog, Santa's Little Helper, is a recurring character in many episodes, the cat, Snowball II, makes more limited appearances. A black cat, unlike his white predecessor, Snowball I, he is heroic in the episode "Old Yeller-Belly," where he saves his master's life, unlike the cowardly dog. Only the episode "I, (Annoyed Grunt)-Bot" in Season 15 deals more with the subject of cats and the Simpsons. It features Lisa's curse with her cats. Snowball II dies, as do Snowball III and Coltrane. The episode ends with the adoption of Snowball V, who is renamed Snowball II, officially for practical reasons, such as the name on the bowl, but obviously more simply for undisguised storytelling reasons. The Simpsons series is based on an episode concept, not on continuity. The choice of the name Snowball II is not insignificant. It's funny because the cat is black and not at all snow-colored, but above all, it implies that the animals are interchangeable. The dog is unique, but the cat is just a number. The dog is beloved, and the cat is a secondary animal.

However, the most famous cat in the series isn't Snowball II, but Scratchy. The Simpson children, raised on TV, swear by *The Krusty the Clown Show*. In 1990, a cartoon appeared on the show: *The Itchy and Scratchy Show*. In 1988, the cartoon within the cartoon featuring the comic duo had already appeared in the episode "The Bart Simpson Show" while the yellow family was still just a segment on *The Tracey Ullman Show*. In general, the cartoon follows the adventures of a cat and a mouse. They're a clear reference to Tom and Jerry, except that they take violence to another level, making it completely explicit. There's blood and exploding eyeballs, and the mouse tortures the cat with incredible sadism.

Scratchy is a black cat, a bit naive and foolish. Most of the time, he's a rather peaceful cat who is attacked gratuitously by Itchy. Itchy is a sadistic gray mouse. He attacks the cat for no reason at all and cuts him to pieces with great inventiveness. The comic duo plays a big part in the lives of the Simpson children. The adaptation of their adventures for the big screen in the Season 4 episode "Itchy and Scratchy: The Movie" is the subject of an educational battle between Bart and Homer. Broadcast in 1992, this episode raised the possibility of creating a film for an animated series, but it didn't happen for *The Simpsons* until 2007.

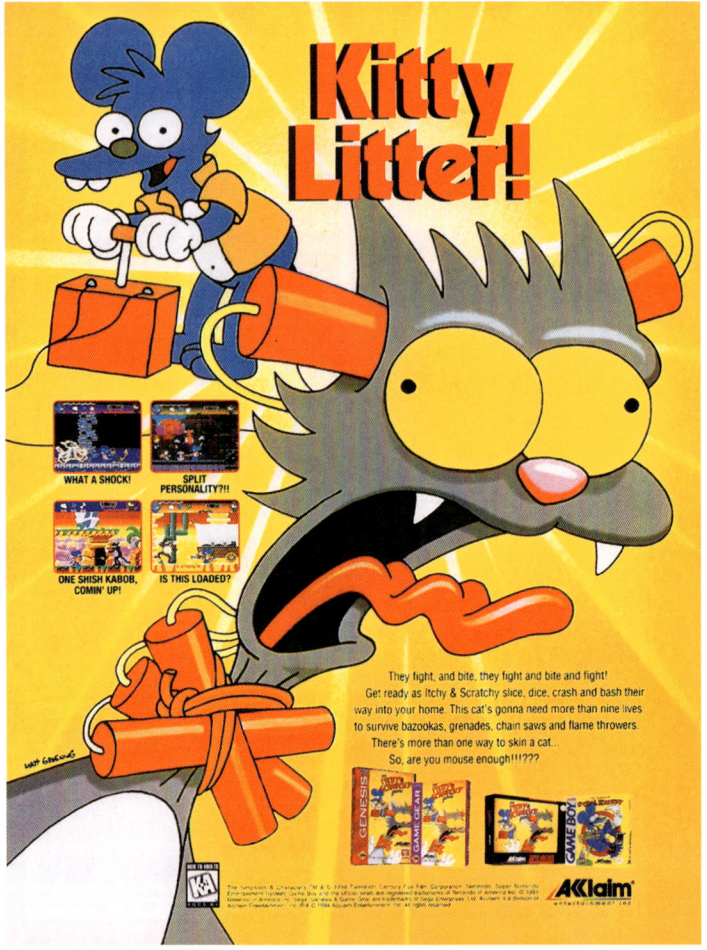

One of the *Itchy and Scratchy* video games.

The film adaptation of the cat-and-mouse duo isn't the only one in the series: In *The Simpsons Movie*, the opening scene features the *Itchy and Scratchy* film, which the family is watching. Homer stands up and shouts, "Boring!" This new *mise en abyme* is a way of making fun of any future criticisms the Springfield family's film may receive. In the end, the critics were fairly lenient, and the production pocketed more than $500 million for $75 million invested.

Like the series that frames it, *Itchy and Scratchy* takes provocation to a new level. Ever acerbic and defiant in its criticism, Itchy uses the American flag to pierce the cat's heart after he has just planted it on the moon, asserting that they have both come in peace. During the Iraq War in the Bush years,

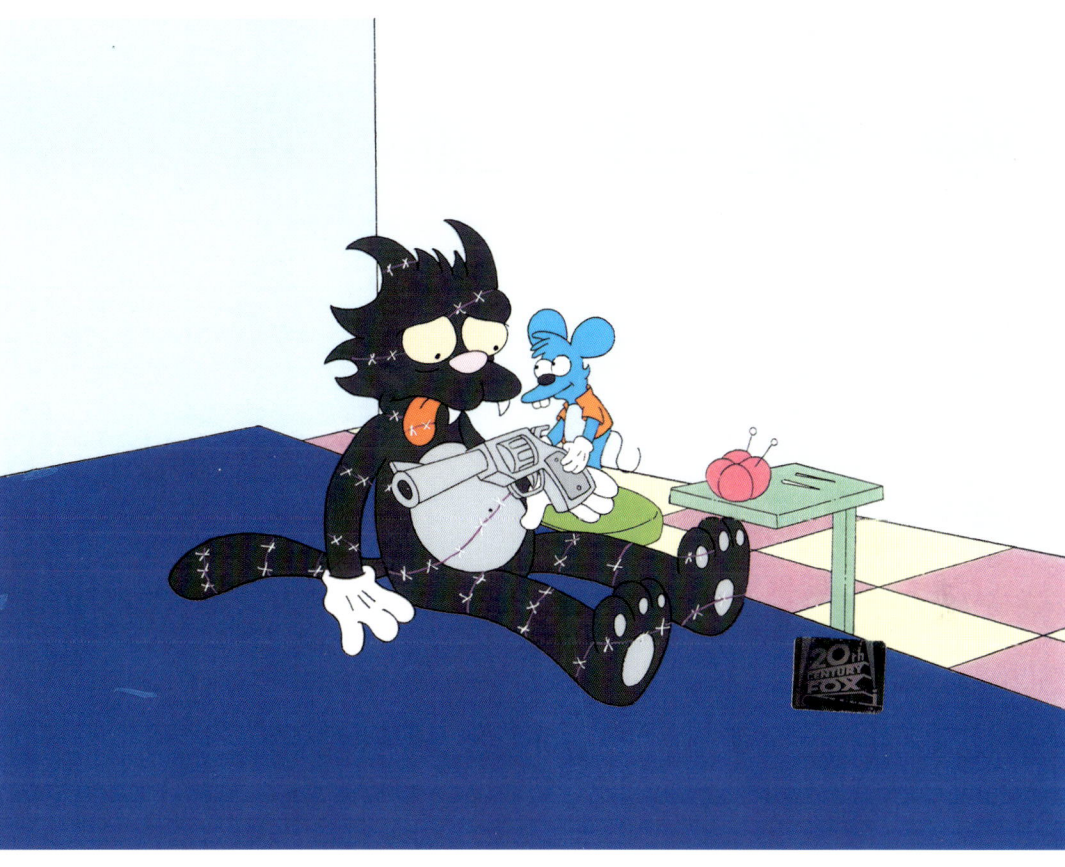

it was no coincidence that the same mouse found himself elected to the White House in the sequel to the film within the film. The series created the character of a dog in Season 8 in "The Itchy & Scratchy & Poochie Show." Poochie is a marketing idea in the fictional *Simpsons* universe to revive the flagging franchise. The supposedly cool dog voiced by Homer is sanctimonious and hated by the public. He is finally killed at the end of the episode. The episode isn't a great success, but it's

really about the longevity of *The Simpsons* and the difficulty of maintaining audiences. Over the years, the *Itchy and Scratchy* cartoons have become classic, eagerly anticipated moments in the series, much like the "Treehouse of Horror" Halloween specials. In reality, the cartoon within the cartoon is regularly used to lengthen episodes that are several minutes short.

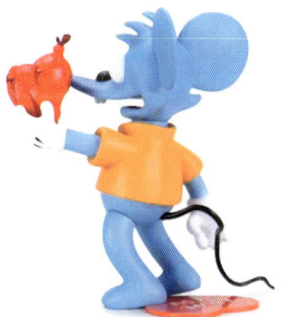

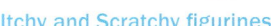

Itchy and Scratchy figurines.

SPEC SHEET

WORK: *The Simpsons*.
CREATOR: Matt Groening.
FIRST BROADCAST: December 17, 1989.
DISTRIBUTOR/AVAILABILITY: 20th Century Studios. Available on DVD, streaming, and regularly broadcast on TV.
CAT'S NAME AND ROLE IN THE WORK: Scratchy, the black cat from the *Itchy and Scratchy* cartoon that Bart and Lisa Simpson watch.

Lucky and Zorba

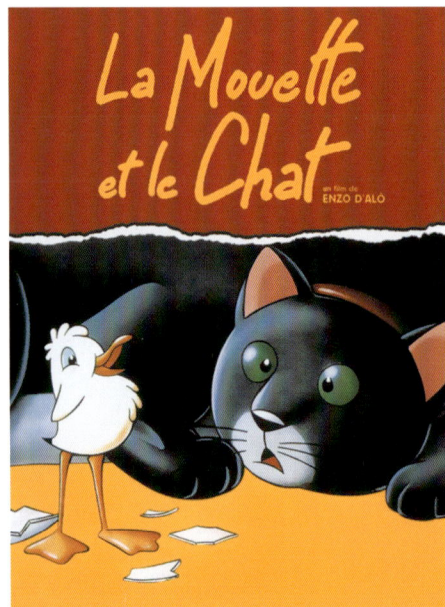

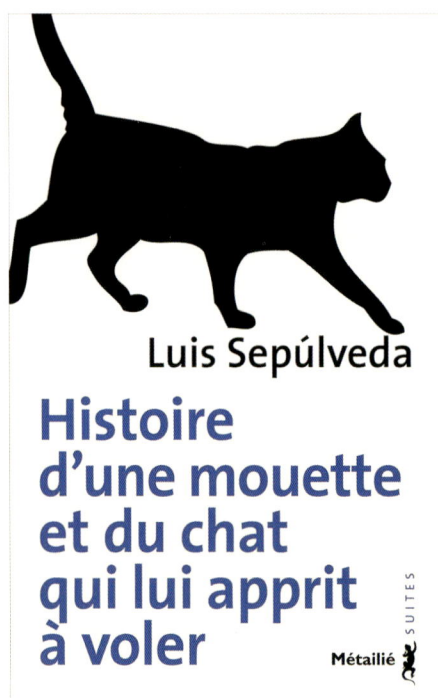

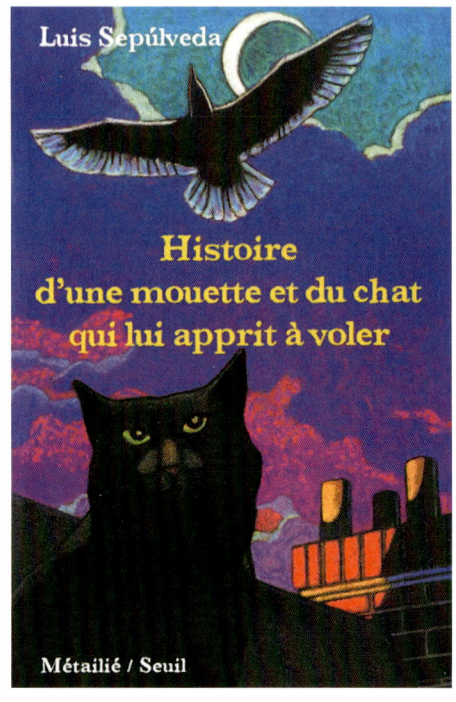

A delightful, animated tale for children aged four or five and up, but also enjoyable for adults, **Lucky and Zorba** *shows felines in a positive light, working together and with other animals to help a newborn seagull take flight.*

In fictional portrayals of cats in relation to other animals, whether felines are the protagonists of the story or the antagonists, they are often predators (or sometimes prey of dogs) and always with a comic edge. But there are exceptions, such as *Lucky and Zorba*, a gentle, funny story released in 1998. This Italian animated film goes against the grain by making the port's tomcats the protectors of a little seagull.

It all begins for the small crew when a young seagull, which had fallen into an oil slick, lands in Zorba the cat's garden to lay its egg and die. She elicits three promises from him: to not eat the egg, to incubate it, and to raise the chick and teach it to fly. The process is complicated by the war being waged at the same time by the city's cats and rats, led by Big Rat.

With their deeply feline behavior, even though the cats and other animals talk to and understand each other normally to make it easier for us to understand them, the port cats escape the worst of the feline clichés, particularly their hunters' cruelty toward the birds and rodents that are their usual prey. Only the kitten, Pallino, shows a hint of malice in a scene in which he tells the young seagull, Lucky, that she's not a cat like him, and that the reason they're raising her is to fatten her up, because cats eat birds. This action is not due to animal instinct, but to jealousy, as he is no longer the smallest of the group and no longer the center of attention.

While cats and birds find common ground in the film, the cats still have a natural enemy: rats. And the battle

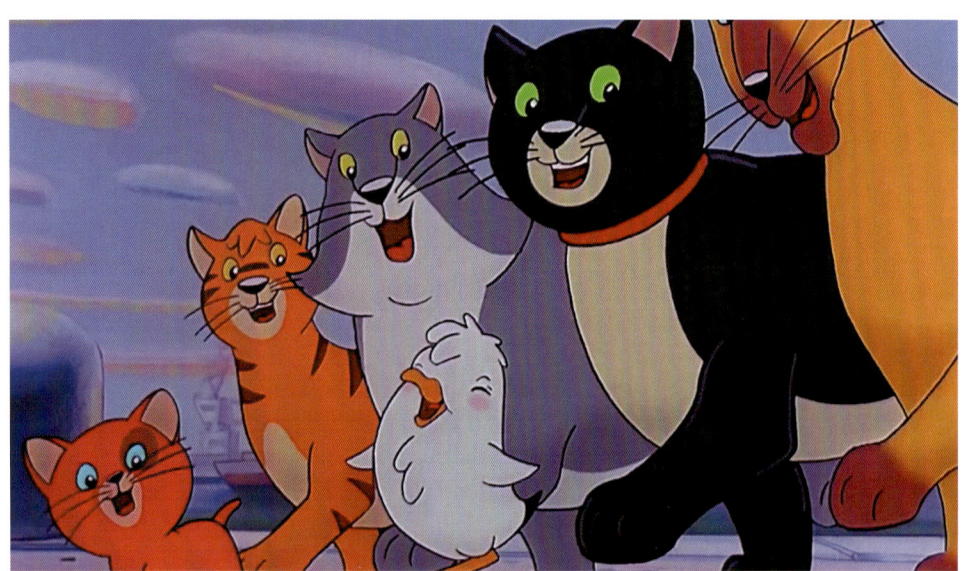

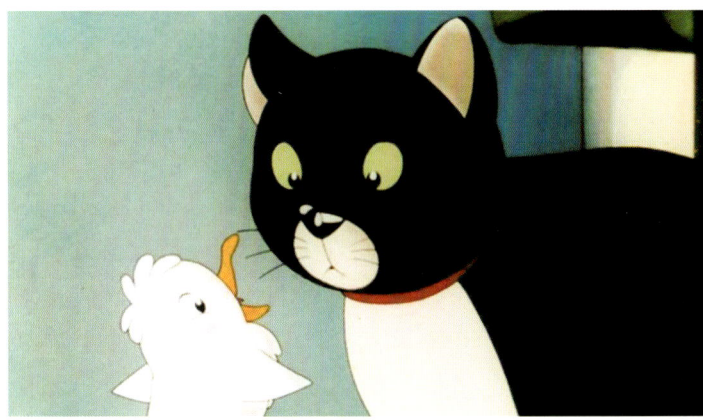

against the rodents that proliferate and thrive on humanity's trash is far more evenly matched than usually presented. The rats are dangerous adversaries for the cats, who have to resort to ruses to defeat them (like a Trojan cheese to get back Lucky and Pallino, who have fallen into the rats' paws). And what about humans? Most of them are just extras in the story, totally unaware of what their pets are up to. Only the poet's daughter, who is still a child with the ability to dream and a wide-open imagination, suspects something and gives the final nudge to help Lucky take flight.

While some of the themes in Luis Sepúlveda's novel take a back seat (such as the part about pollution, which is dealt with more lightly), the emphasis is on collaboration between animals and the fact that love makes it possible to overcome one's instincts. Even though, at the very end, Lucky follows her own instincts and, after her first successful flight, sets off on the great migration.

THE BOOK THAT INSPIRED THE FILM

Lucky and Zorba is a very loose adaptation of the children's story by Chilean writer Luis Sepúlveda, *The Story of a Seagull and the Cat Who Taught Her to Fly.* The action isn't set in a southern European port, but in Hamburg. While the causes of the mother seagull's death are the same, and the promises she wrings from the cat Zorba are similar, the plot is very different. Rats are only one of the story's complications, and far less frightening than in the film. On the other hand, there's also an inconvenient monkey and a lighthouse with its keeper.

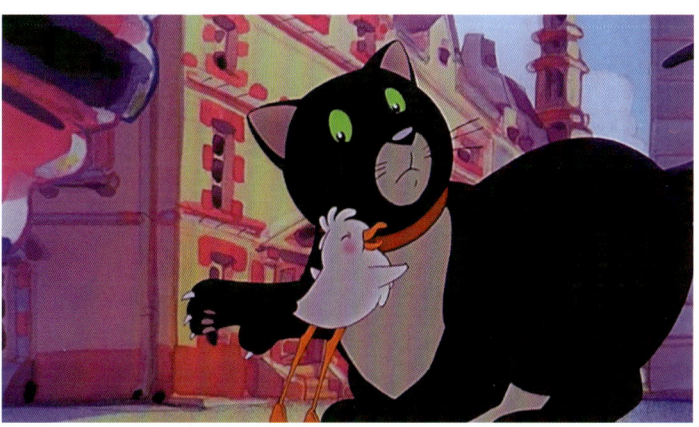

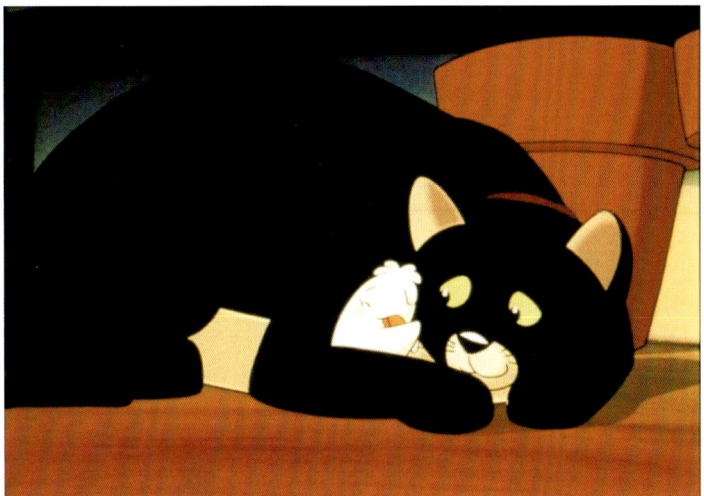

SPEC SHEET

WORK: *Lucky and Zorba*.
CREATORS: Enzo D'Alò (director); Enzo D'Alò and Umberto Marino (screenwriters).
RELEASE DATE: December 23, 1998.
DISTRIBUTOR/AVAILABILITY: Cecchi Gori Group Tiger Cinematografica and Lanterna Magica. Available on DVD and various streaming services.
CAT'S NAME AND ROLE IN THE WORK: Zorba, a black-and-white cat with green eyes. The dying seagull lands in his garden, and he raises the chick with help from the port's other cats.

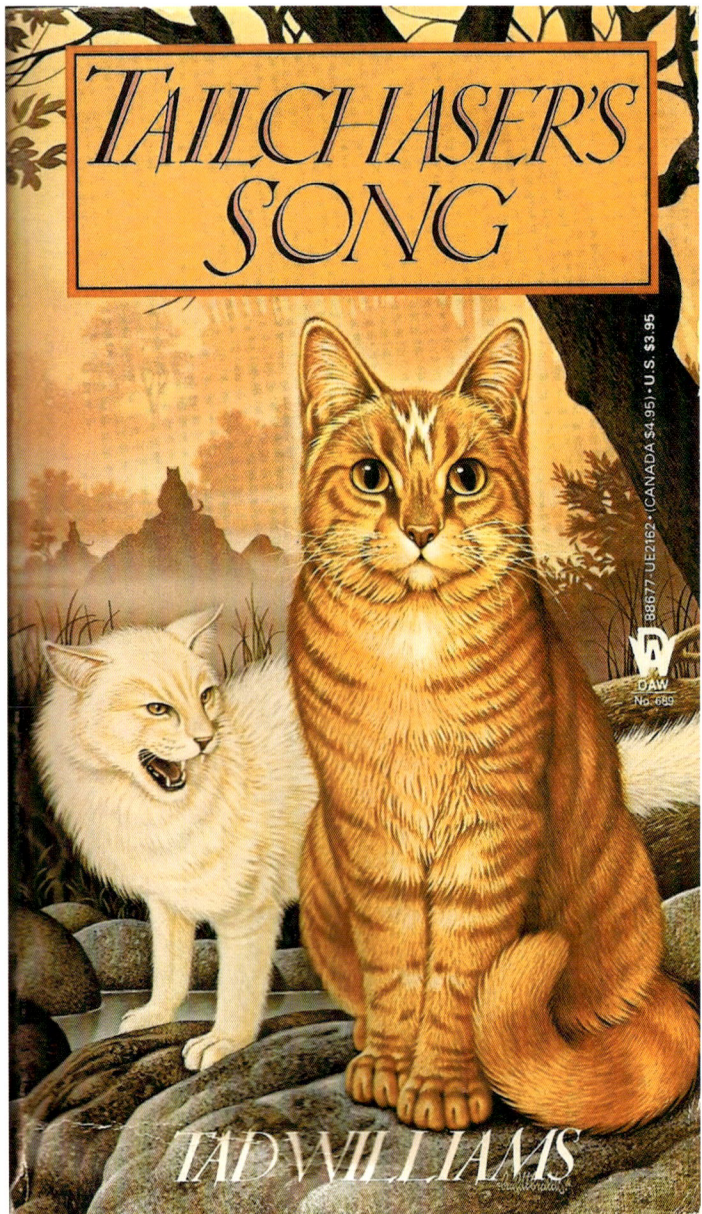

Long before the Warriors saga, animal fantasy had its own version of The Lord of the Rings, with Fritti Tailchaser as the feline version of Frodo Baggins.

Writer Tad Williams's first novel, *Tailchaser's Song*, is the only one of its kind in his body of work, which touches on every variation of the imaginary. If the plot reminds you of *Warriors*, it's probably because both stories are about feral cats, i.e., domestic cats who have returned to the wild, either through abandonment or of their own free will. But *Tailchaser's Song* was published in 1985, while the *Warriors* saga began in 2003.

Tailchaser is a young orange tabby cat with a white star on his forehead. Living half with a family of humans and half as a feral cat, he embarks on a quest to find out where several of his friends have disappeared to, including Hushpad, a young cat to whom he was to become engaged. Along the way, he meets several allies, including the kitten Pouncequick, who has followed him from the start. He also faces a terrible threat from a feline mythological figure and encounters all sorts of fantastic creatures.

It has the plot of a classic epic fantasy novel. But the whole story is seen at whisker level, and the cats never deviate from feline behavior, even when magic is involved; they don't suddenly stand on two legs or use tools.

However, contrary to what one might think on first reading this text, Tad Williams isn't necessarily a fan of domestic cats. In the early 1980s, when he wrote what was to become his very first novel, he even described himself as more of a "dog person," and it was while walking his dog that he got the idea for the plot. His wife was a cat lover and had brought her two feline companions with her when they moved in together. Observing these strange creatures daily, he tried to understand them

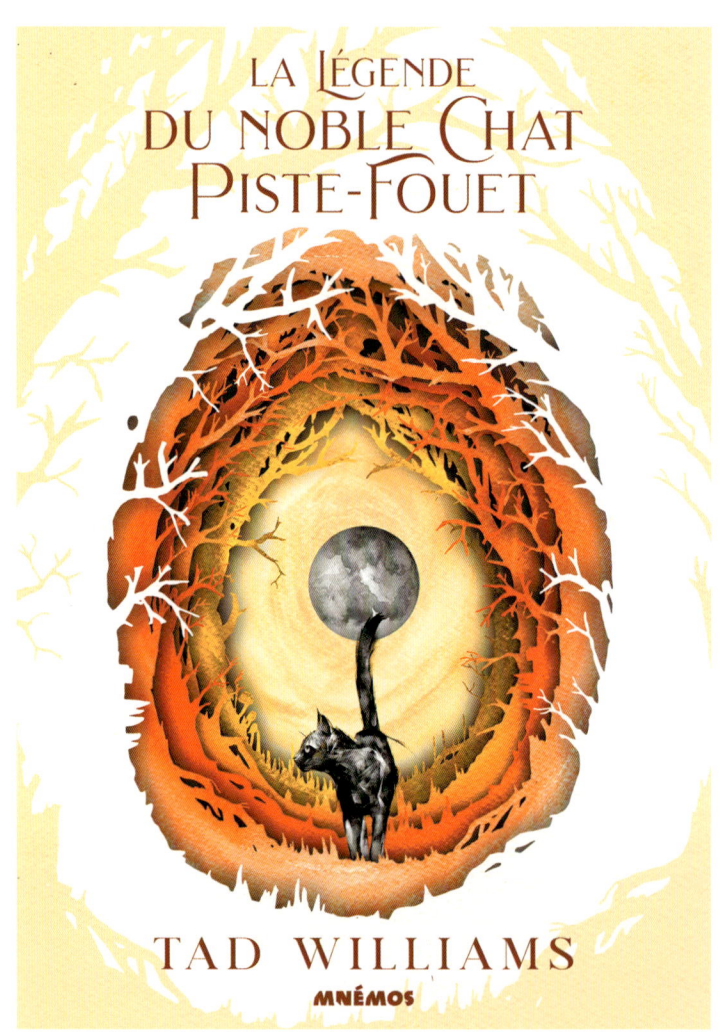

and put himself in their shoes, and the basic idea for *Tailchaser's Song* was born. And perhaps, he sees himself in the particularly demeaning position of M'an, the hairless bipedal giant, forever subservient to his more perfect cousins, the People (i.e., cats).

On the other hand, while the novel is clearly inspired by the well-known works of J. R. R. Tolkien, even copying or parodying certain passages in animal form, it's much shorter, at 364 pages. Its mythology is just as rich, with its first-borns, its explanations of the creation of the sun and moon and humans, and the importance of the cat's three names: the heart name given by the mother to her kittens; the face name, known to all, which is given by the members of the clan; and the tail name, which the cat must discover and which sums up its life. Tad Williams even goes so far as to invent terms and indicate their pronunciation. Without going so far as to create new languages, like J. R. R. Tolkien did with Elvish, he defines two languages: Common Singing used by all animals, with the exception of M'an, who have become a bit silly since their transformation from cat to biped, and the Higher Singing, which is practiced almost exclusively by cats. Interspersed with poetry and "songs" by the various animals, *Tailchaser's Song* is classified as a children's book, as is Richard George Adams's *Watership Down* (1972). Yet whether it's Tad Williams's cats or Richard Adams's rabbits, the themes explored in these books are fairly stark, not at all watered down in the Disney way, and the action can be particularly intense and brutal at times. 🐾

SPEC SHEET

WORK: *Tailchaser's Song*.
CREATOR: Tad Williams.
DATE CREATED: 1985.
PUBLISHER: Daw Books, Hodder Paperbacks.
CAT'S NAME AND ROLE IN THE WORK: Fritti Tailchaser, a curious, stubborn young cat on a quest to find his fiancée.

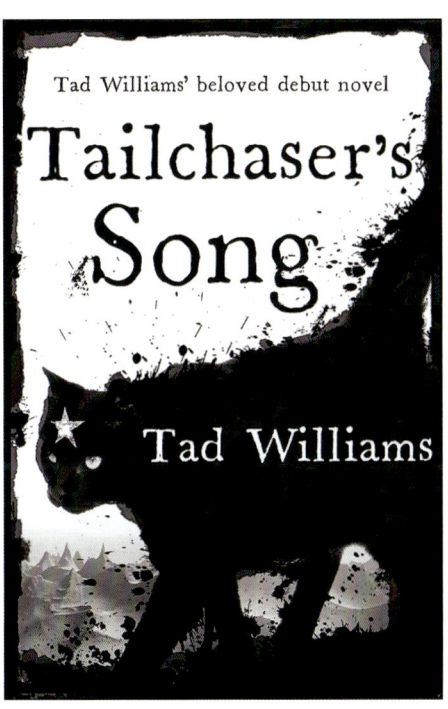

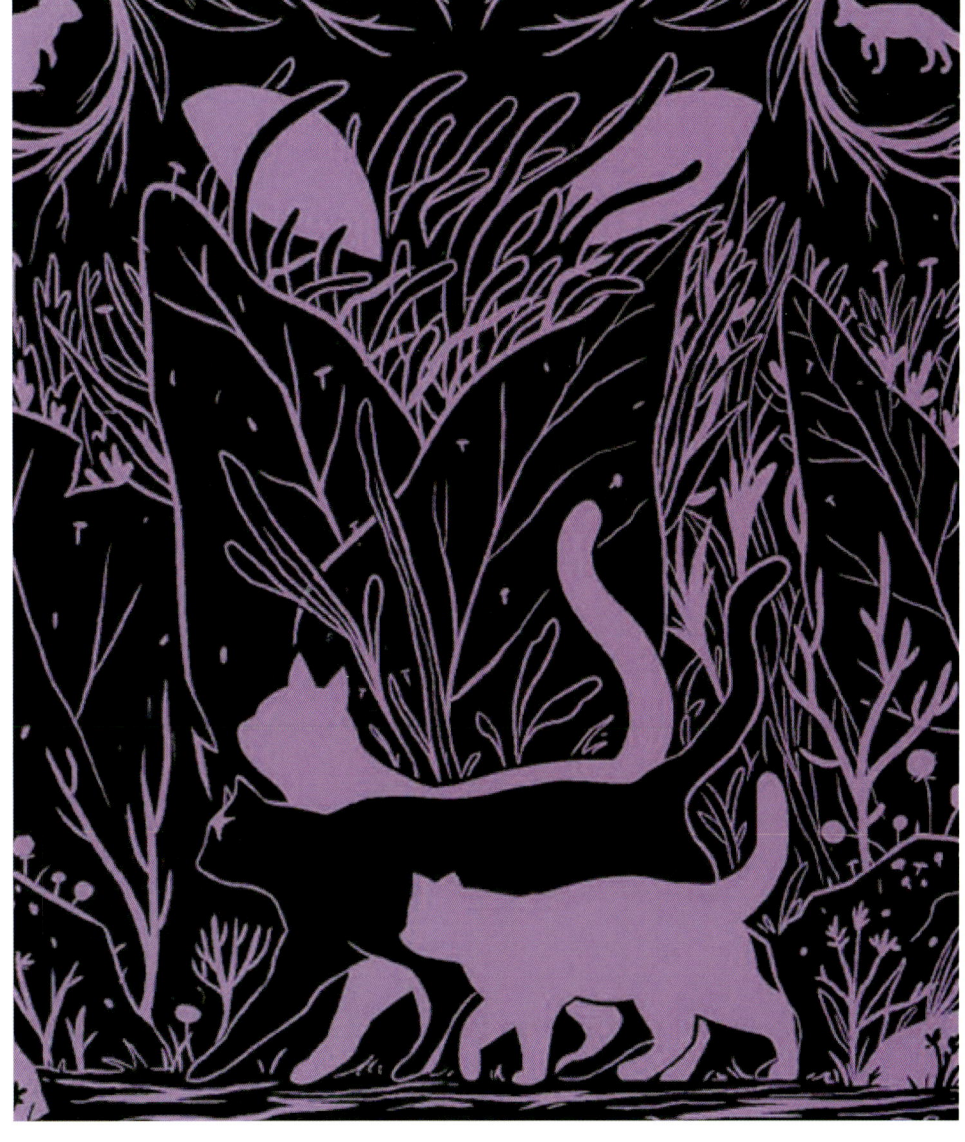

Warriors

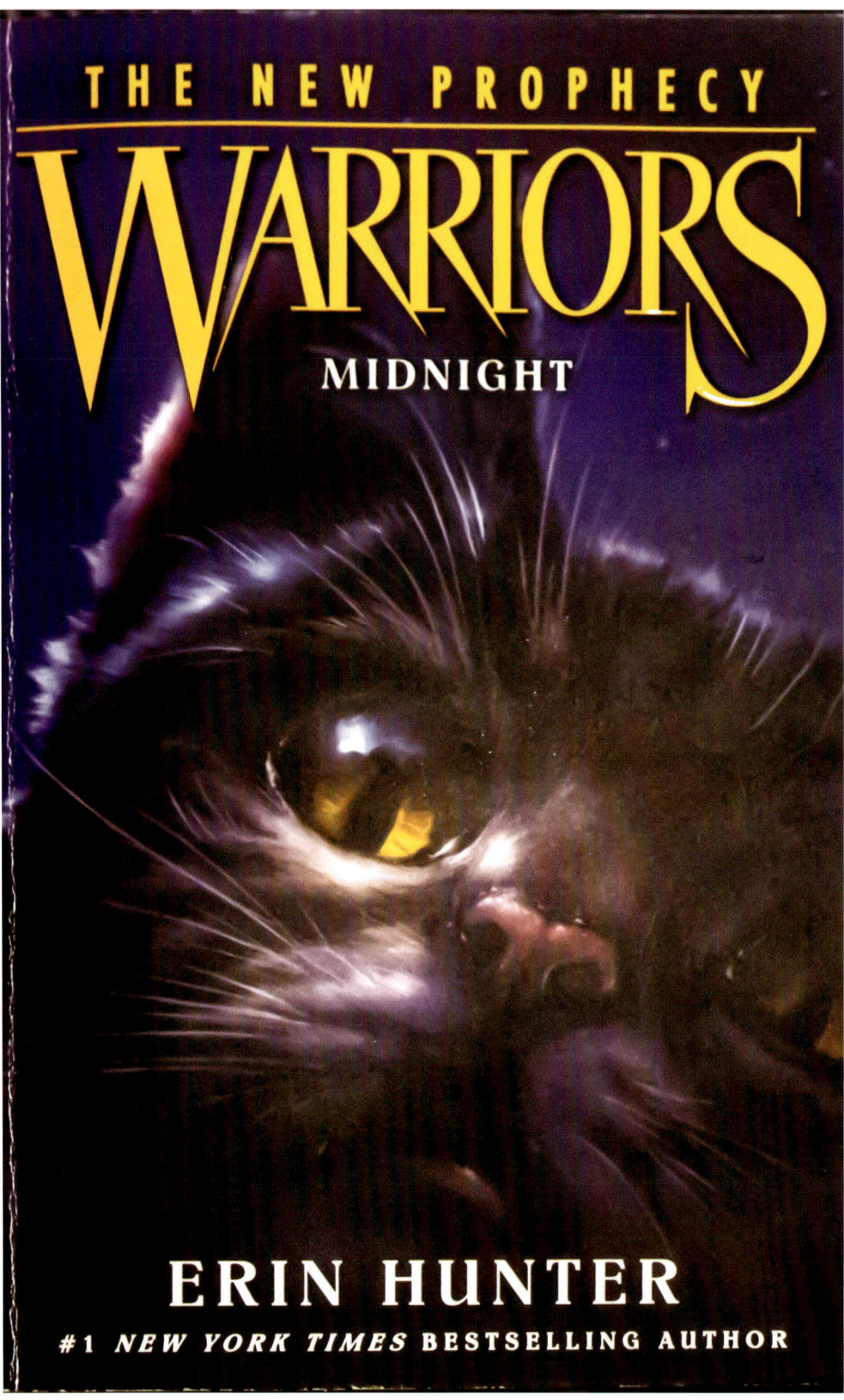

THE NEW PROPHECY

WARRIORS

MIDNIGHT

ERIN HUNTER

#1 *NEW YORK TIMES* BESTSELLING AUTHOR

More of a publishing success than a literary masterpiece, Warriors *is one of the world's most widely read and sold fantasy sagas for young people. Its heroes are cats that have gone feral.*

Who says that a literary work must be the product of one author? American comic books and, to a lesser extent, some of the great successes of Franco-Belgian comics have proved that sagas can live and flourish with a succession of authors. In conventional publishing, the phenomenon is rarer. But with the right idea, it's entirely possible. *Warriors* is a case in point. Although this fantasy series for young people has the immense advantage of having cats as its main characters, this alone doesn't explain how, since the release of the first volume, *Into the Wild*, this series has generated a multitude of books (to date, seven cycles of six books, short novels, novellas, and manga) and related products. Most likely because Victoria Holmes, the editor who has overseen the project since it was launched in the early 2000s, decided to combine what makes good sagas successful (wars, politics, revenge, impossible love affairs, religious conflicts) with an animal beloved by her young readers, and to make him independent, both to simplify the narrative without involving humans and to satisfy the dreams of independence of the teenagers and preteens for whom this series is intended.

The first cycle, *Warriors: The Prophecies Begin*, tells how a young orange cat (rather like Tad Williams's Fritti Tailchaser, see p. 26) leaves home to venture into the forest behind his humans' home and join a group of feral cats, ThunderClan. He climbs the ranks

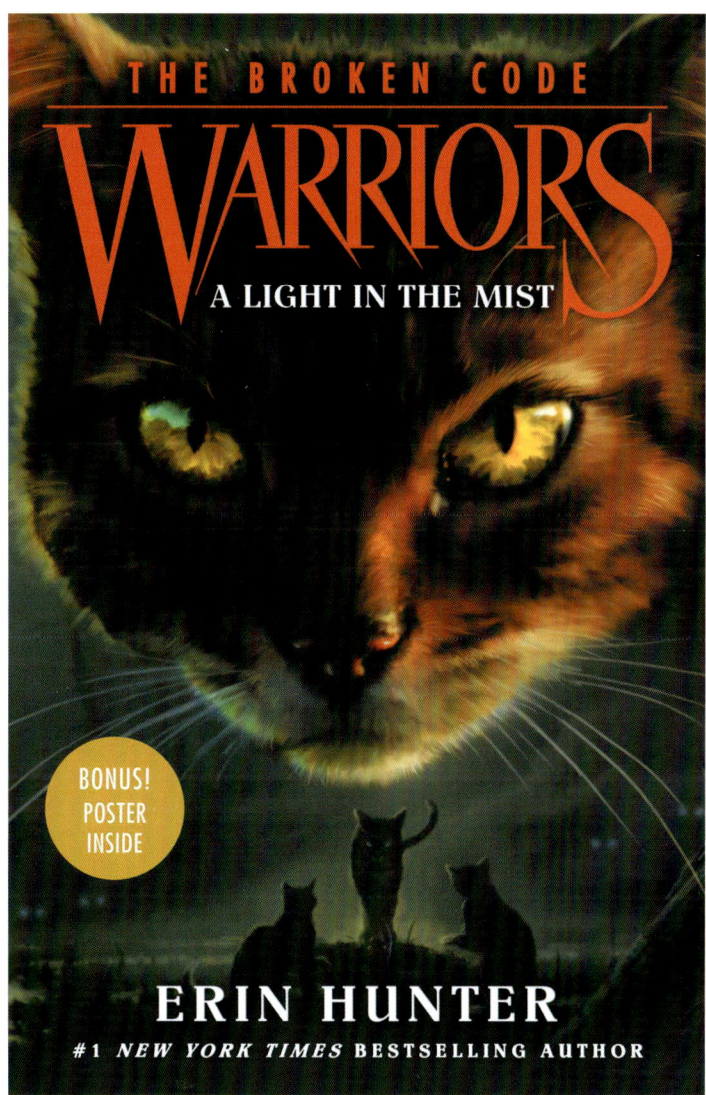

THE BROKEN CODE

WARRIORS
A LIGHT IN THE MIST

BONUS!
POSTER
INSIDE

ERIN HUNTER
#1 *NEW YORK TIMES* BESTSELLING AUTHOR

AN EXPANDING WORLD

In addition to the original books (fifty-six volumes to date), the *Warriors* series is also available in comic books (fifteen volumes to date), plays (*After Sunset: We Need to Talk* and *Brightspirit's Mercy*, whose scripts are available on the series' official website,[1] along with plenty of merchandising and related products), a video game (in-browser from the website), a mobile app for iOS and Android, and trading cards with 3D effects for the Chinese market. In 2016, Chinese producer Alibaba Pictures expressed its intention to make a film based on the series, with a script to be written by Jonathan Aibel and Glenn Berger, but there has been no further information on the matter since 2019.

[1] https://warriorcats.com/

and eliminates the traitors in his midst. The other cycles all feature other cats as main characters and take place either in the past or in the future, in relation to the first cycle, although there are slight elements that link them together. Like all epic fantasy stories, *Warriors* is based on a consistent mythology. In addition to the four original clans (ThunderClan, WindClan, RiverClan, and ShadowClan), there are other tribes made up of living cats (Tribe of Rushing Water for the mountain cats, BloodClan for city street cats, SkyClan) and dead cats (StarClan, made up of dead ancestors inhabiting a heavenly forest and the Dark Forest, a kind of feline hell). There are also three mythical clans linked to the big cats (lions, tigers, panthers), which inspired the present-day cat clans. And all felines are expected to follow the seventeen teachings of the warrior code (inspired by the Bushido of the Japanese samurai). Each clan also has its own rules and special talents and forges alliances or wages wars with opposing clans for a variety of reasons, not to mention external forces such as other forest animals that are enemies of the cats (like foxes and badgers) and human urbanization, which drives them out of the woods to take refuge near a lake.

SPEC SHEET

WORK: *Warriors*.
CREATOR: Under the single pseudonym of Erin Hunter, we find Kate Cary, Cherith Baldry, and Victoria Holmes, then Tui Sutherland, Gillian Philip, and Inbali Iserles.
DATE CREATED: January 21, 2003.

PUBLISHER/AVAILABILITY: HarperCollins in the US and UK. Seven series of six novels, plus fourteen stand-alones, are available in English and are gradually being translated into other languages.
CATS' NAMES AND ROLE IN THE WORK: Almost all the characters are cats. The first character we follow is Rusty, a house cat who decides to go feral.

Stuart Little

Stuart Little *follows the adventures of a mouse who has to adapt his size to his life as a human. Inspired by E. B. White's classic children's book, the 1999 film includes a hostile but not necessarily evil cat character: Snowbell. Who is he?*

In the book, Snowbell is a menacing white cat who shows the mouse his teeth as soon as he appears. Even though it's just a matter of comparing their teeth, the first meeting between the two characters creates suspense. Will Snowbell want to eat him? In the end, he won't, but the cat will provoke Stuart into antics until he hurts himself. Rather than helping him, the feline steals his hat and puts it in front of a mouse hole to cover his tracks and play a trick on him. The cat is cunning, but he won't threaten the youngest member of the family directly. On the other hand, he is out to eat Margalo, a bird stranded at the Littles' home, which the mouse will defend with his bow, shooting Snowbell in the ear with an arrow.

The writing style is very direct and is reminiscent of a fairy tale. It doesn't

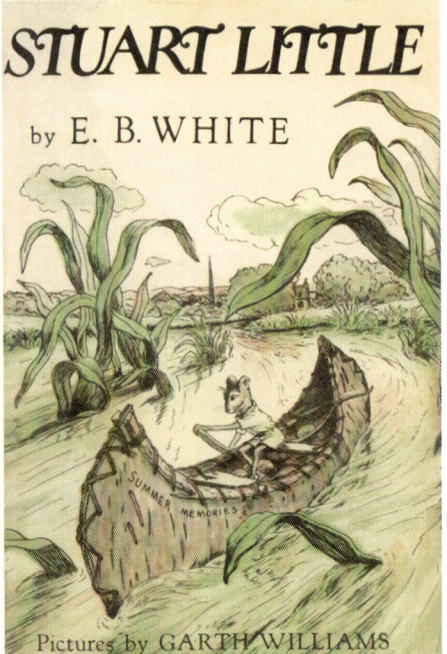

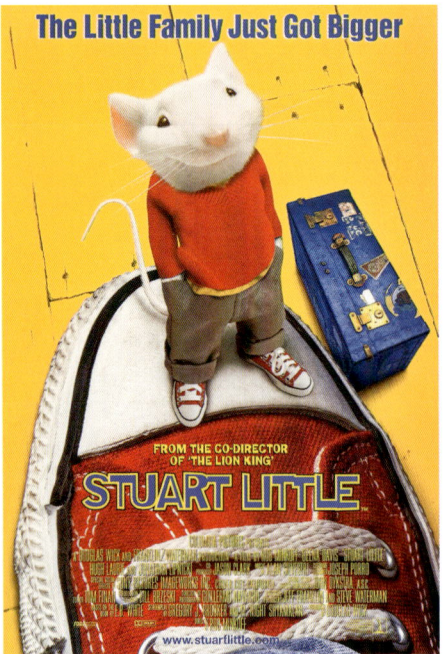

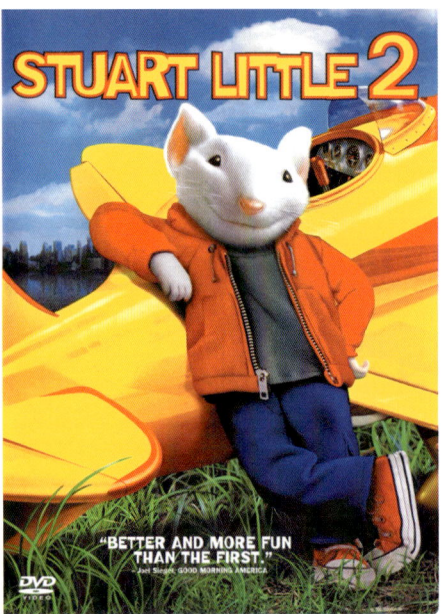

leave room for many descriptions of the cat's feelings. It's made clear that the animal doesn't appreciate the presence of the young boy who looks like and is the size of a mouse. He negotiates with a neighboring Angora cat to get rid of Stuart and Margalo, explaining that this unusual cohabitation with prey doesn't sit well with him.

The first Gath William drawings in the book illustrating Snowbell are much more realistic and frightening than how the character is developed in the movies.

In the live-action version, the cat tries to eat the Littles' youngest son as soon as they meet. He's also hostile to him, plotting to get rid of him. But over the course of the film, he grows accustomed to his presence. Insulting and malevolent, he ends up showing a typical feline affection for Stuart, going so far as to carry him on his back like a horse.

Snowbell, the Story's Comic Highlight

Although the book and the film are very different, particularly in terms of Stuart's birth, they are each very successful in their own way. The originality of the novel, in which a family sees a mouse-like boy born as their youngest son, becomes the adoption of a mouse as a child by a gently eccentric family. The adaptation features a top-notch cast, including Geena Davis as Mrs. Little, Hugh Laurie (with the acerbic Dr. House as a bespectacled family man), and Michael J. Fox as the impetuous mouse. Rob Minkoff's (*The Lion King*, 1995) direction adds to the overall quality of this children's film.

In both versions, Snowbell's presence is fundamentally comic. Stuart is a member of the Little family, so technically, the cat is the mouse's pet. The movie places great emphasis on this paradox.

The screenplay incorporates a storyline revolving around the relationship between Stuart and his brother George, as well as one focusing on Snowbell's acceptance of the mouse. M. Night Shyamalan, master of the fantastic thriller with such films as *The Sixth Sense*, took the lead on the script.

In the novel, the cat is cunning, but in the film, he's more stupid and cowardly. He grumbles and is an indoor cat, mocked by the alley cats. A precious hypochondriac, in later films, he becomes a sidekick to Stuart, who is simple and resourceful. The Angora cat is foolishly possessive of his home but lacks the scope and megalomania of a power-hungry villain. Snowbell's domestication is a recurring comic element throughout the series. He's also often involved in physical gags, which gives him a rather

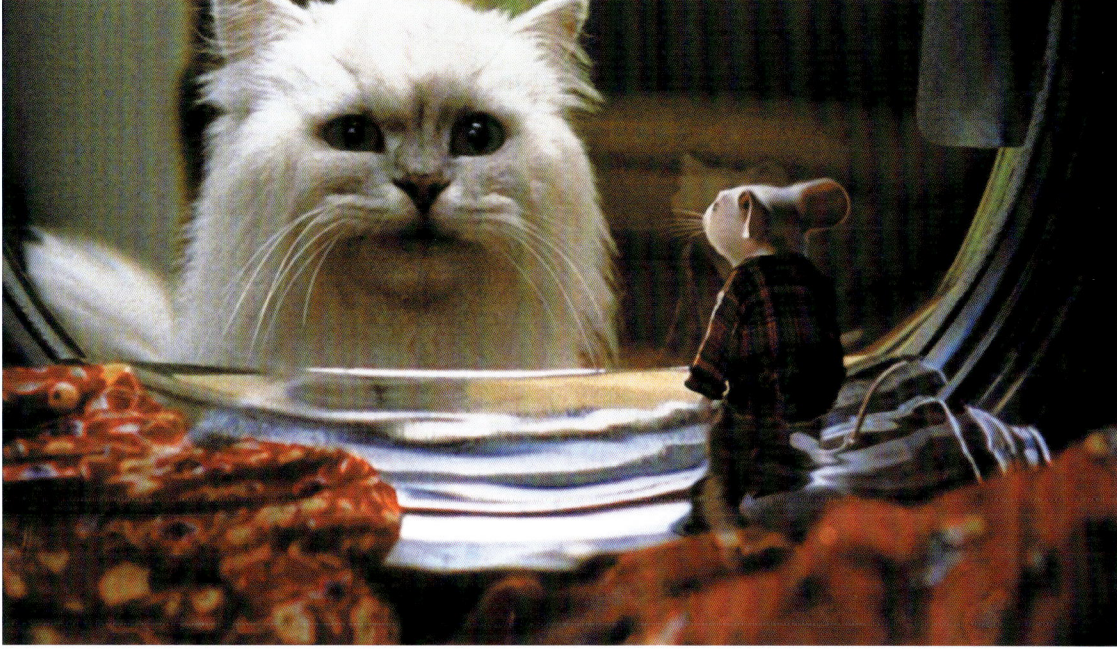

slapstick role. The ridiculousness of the character's dialogue is amplified by the grandiloquent voice acting of Nathan Lane, who was also the voice of Timon in *The Lion King*.

Snowbell's movements are animated with a real cat, and only his face incorporates CGI during dialogue. The quality of the animation is worthy of the production and has stood the test of time. The first film was a huge success, grossing $300 million against a $133 million budget. The second film, released in 2002, was a more modest success, grossing $169 million for a budget of $133 million. However, the soundtrack's song "I'm Alive," performed by Céline Dion, was a 2002 hit. In

2005, a third installment titled *Stuart Little 3: Call of the Wild* was released directly to video. Although it features the original cast, this is not a live-action film, but rather cel-shaded animation. This 3D animation method gives the shots a cartoonish effect. 🐾

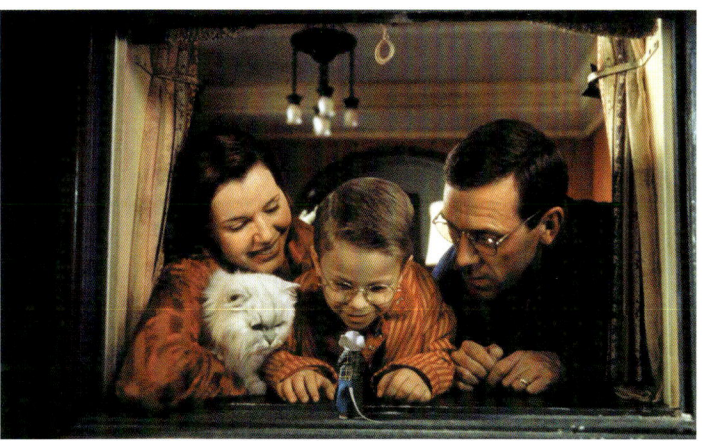

SPEC SHEET

WORK: *Stuart Little*.
CREATORS: Book written by E. B. White; film directed by Rob Minkoff from a screenplay by M. Night Shyamalan.
RELEASE DATE: 1945 (book); December 5, 1999 (film).
PUBLISHER/DISTRIBUTOR: HarperCollins for the book; Sony Pictures for the film.
CAT'S NAME AND ROLE IN THE WORK: Snowbell, the pet of Stuart Little's family.

Calvin and Hobbes

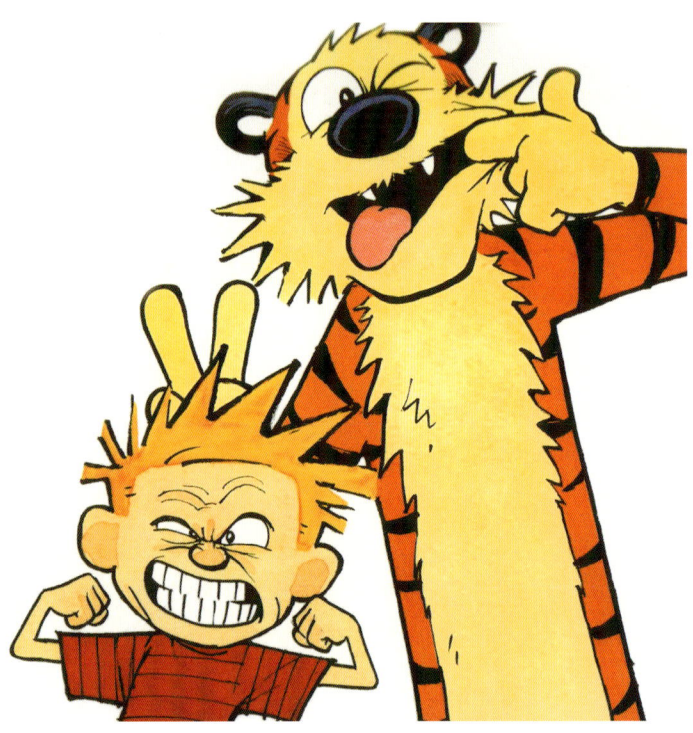

SPEC SHEET

CAT'S NAME: Hobbes.
WORK: "Calvin and Hobbes."
CREATOR: Bill Watterson.
RELEASE DATE: November 18, 1985.
PUBLISHER/AVAILABILITY: Andrews
McMeel Publishing.
CAT'S NAME AND ROLE IN THE WORK:
Plush orange-and-black tiger with
a white belly. He comes to life and
becomes more detailed when Calvin is
alone with him.

This half-animal, half-toy tiger from the Calvin and Hobbes duo has all the characteristics of a domestic tomcat and is the more or less effective conscience of a six-year-old boy. He's also the nostalgic and rather ironic personification of the comic's readers.

Technically, Hobbes isn't a cat or even a pet. He's a stuffed tiger who belongs to a little boy, Calvin, who has an overactive imagination. So why did we include him in this book? Quite simply because when Hobbes comes to life to take part in Calvin's games, he behaves much more like a house cat than a big cat. For the grown-ups around Calvin, Hobbes is nothing more than a cuddly toy that he's owned since he was very young (although in one comic strip, he describes how he lured him with a tuna fish sandwich). But for the little boy, he's a genuine anthropomorphic, talking animal who accompanies him in all his antics and mischief. The tiger's behavior is a cross between that of a domestic cat (his love of tuna, the way he curls up on the sofa) and that of a little boy. Slightly more considered than Calvin, he tries to reason with his master before letting himself be drawn into new adventures.

Like the philosopher Thomas Hobbes, from whom he takes his name, the beast is quite disillusioned with human nature. Hobbes is also lazier and less ambitious than Calvin; his most cherished wish is a large field where he can fall asleep in the sun, while the little boy dreams of conquests and adventures.

Bill Watterson's "Calvin and Hobbes," which ran for more than ten years in daily newspapers, is both a funny, tender comic strip about childhood and nostalgia for a certain carefree spirit and a critique of human failings, society, and art. Although originally published in news publications, the series itself makes little reference to current events, avoiding naming personalities or specifying events. At the height of its success, it was published in 2,400 different newspapers around the world and in a series of books. It also won several awards.

In the absence of a Cold War between the major powers, let's turn to the animal world's most famous Cold War with this family-friendly spy film that pits canines and felines against each other in a merciless battle.

It's well known that cats are megalomaniacs with a thirst for world domination. *Cats & Dogs* portrays a secret organization of cats plotting to prevent a scientist from finding the formula for a vaccine against allergies to dogs. Unbeknownst to humans, pets talk and have access to cutting-edge technology. Inspired by spy films such as the James Bond series, the film's storyline essentially pits kind, loyal dogs against completely evil, duplicitous cats. At the heart of the evil organization is Mr. Tinkles, a white Persian whose physique mirrors that of the cat belonging to 007's famous adversary, Blofeld.

In this case, the villain is grotesque. The film uses every possible pretext to put him in ridiculous situations: in a bathtub with wet fur, as a dictatorial orator, as a crane operator, and even in various costumes, such as a clown and a cheerleader. The cat's dubbing and very serious dialogue also contribute to the character's humorous quality. The cute name of Mr. Tinkles also contrasts with his dark intentions.

In this 2001 film, the use of puppets, CGI, and real animals has aged rather well. The dogs—undoubtedly easier to train—are real animals whose mouths have been animated for their dialogue. As for the cats, Mr. Tinkles's monologues are computer animated. His action scenes were mostly done using puppets, with CGI to animate his face.

Animating the Siamese cats was more demanding: As feline agents, they act like ninjas and require more movement. These characters are animated in CGI for a fight sequence, as is the puppy, Lou.

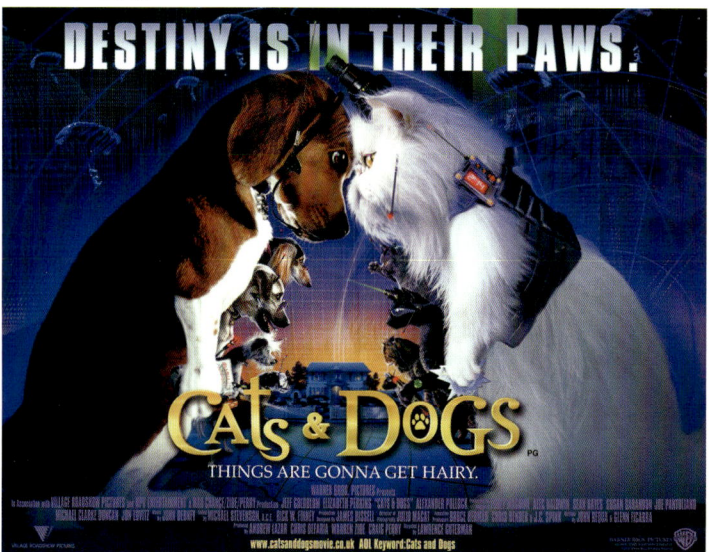

This children's film was a hit, earning its producers more than $200 million against a budget of just $60 million. In 2010, a second film was released under the title *Cats & Dogs: The Revenge of Kitty Galore*. The film earned $115 million at the box office for an investment of $85 million. The last film of the series, *Cats & Dogs 3: Paws Unite!*, was released in 2020. It was a flop, with an investment of $17 million and worldwide box-office receipts of $3 million. 🐾

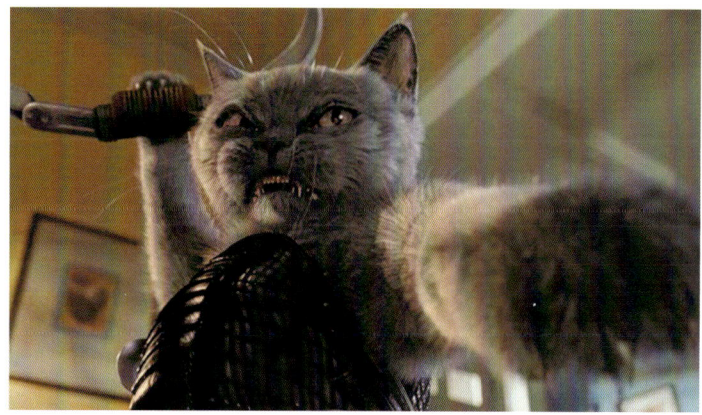

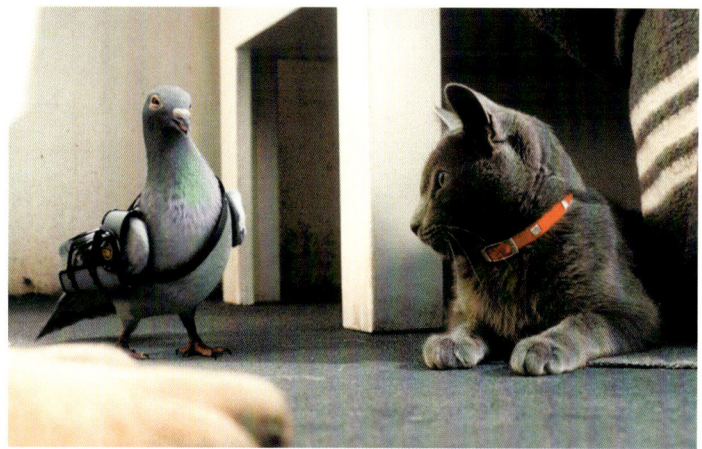

SPEC SHEET

WORK: *Cats & Dogs*.
CREATORS: Lawrence Guterman (director); John Requa and Glenn Ficarra (screenwriters).
RELEASE DATE: August 15, 2001.
DISTRIBUTOR: Warner Bros. Available on DVD, Blu-ray, and streaming services.
CAT'S NAME AND ROLE IN THE WORK: Mr. Tinkles, the story's villain.

CatDog

Sometimes, the opposition between cats and other animals is more organic. The duality between cat and dog behavior is at the heart of the CatDog character, providing most of the gags in this animated series.

For some, a creature made up of two half-animals as different as a dog and a cat would be an inexhaustible source of nightmares. For Peter Hannan, creator of the *CatDog* cartoon, it's an inexhaustible source of jokes for children. Commissioned by Nickelodeon, *CatDog* chronicles the adventures of Siamese twins who are joined at the abdomen. What makes them special? One half is a cat, the other half a dog. And while they may face common enemies, the two get along . . . like a cat and a dog. Their temperaments are polar opposites. Dog is impulsive, always ready to have fun, loves rock 'n' roll, and

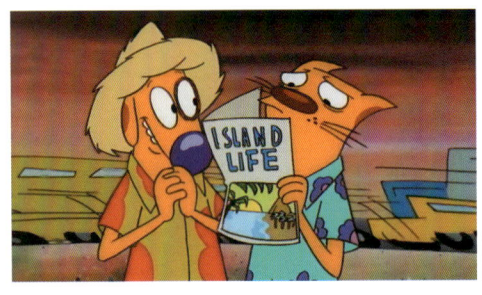

is a bit silly. Cat is more of a homebody, more thoughtful, and it's often his intelligence that gets them out of trouble. But he's also quick-tempered, gaining incredible strength and terrifying those around him, including his brother.

Their main antagonists also match their characters. While Dog gets on quite well with Winslow Oddfellow, who lives in their house, this is not at all the case with Cat, who's the target of the mustelid's

critical reflections and traps (and whom he has tried to eat in the past, we learn in one of the last episodes). Outdoors—the

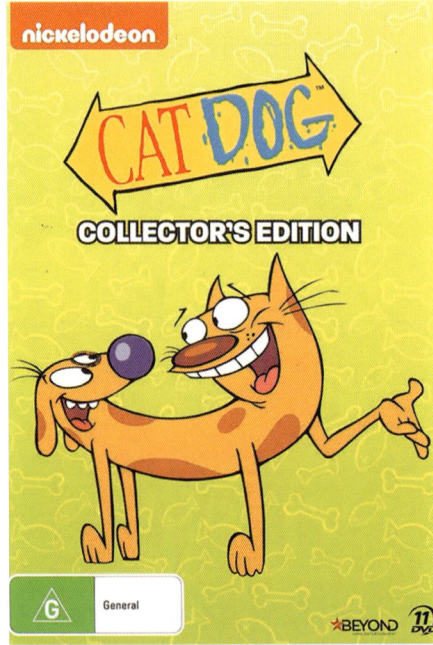

traditional domain of canines in the cartoon imagination— it's mainly Rancid Rabbit and the gang of street dogs led by Lube who attack Dog, as the dogs view him as competition, and the rabbit views him as a natural predator.

Other animals that are featured in the show include Eddie the squirrel and Randolph the dandy cat, who is willing to try anything at least once in his life. 🐾

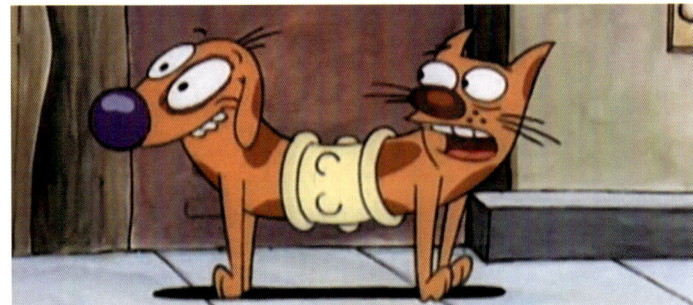

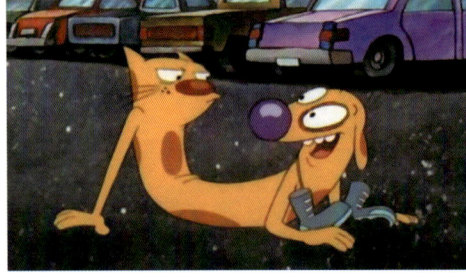

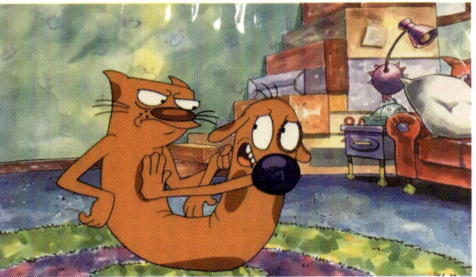

SPEC SHEET

WORK: *CatDog*.
CREATOR: Peter Hannan.
DATE CREATED: April 4, 1998.

DISTRIBUTOR/AVAILABILITY: Nickelodeon. Available on DVD and on certain streaming services such as AppleTV, as well as being rebroadcast quite frequently on TV.
CAT'S NAME AND ROLE IN THE WORK: Cat, the more thoughtful, intelligent feline half of the Siamese twin brothers.

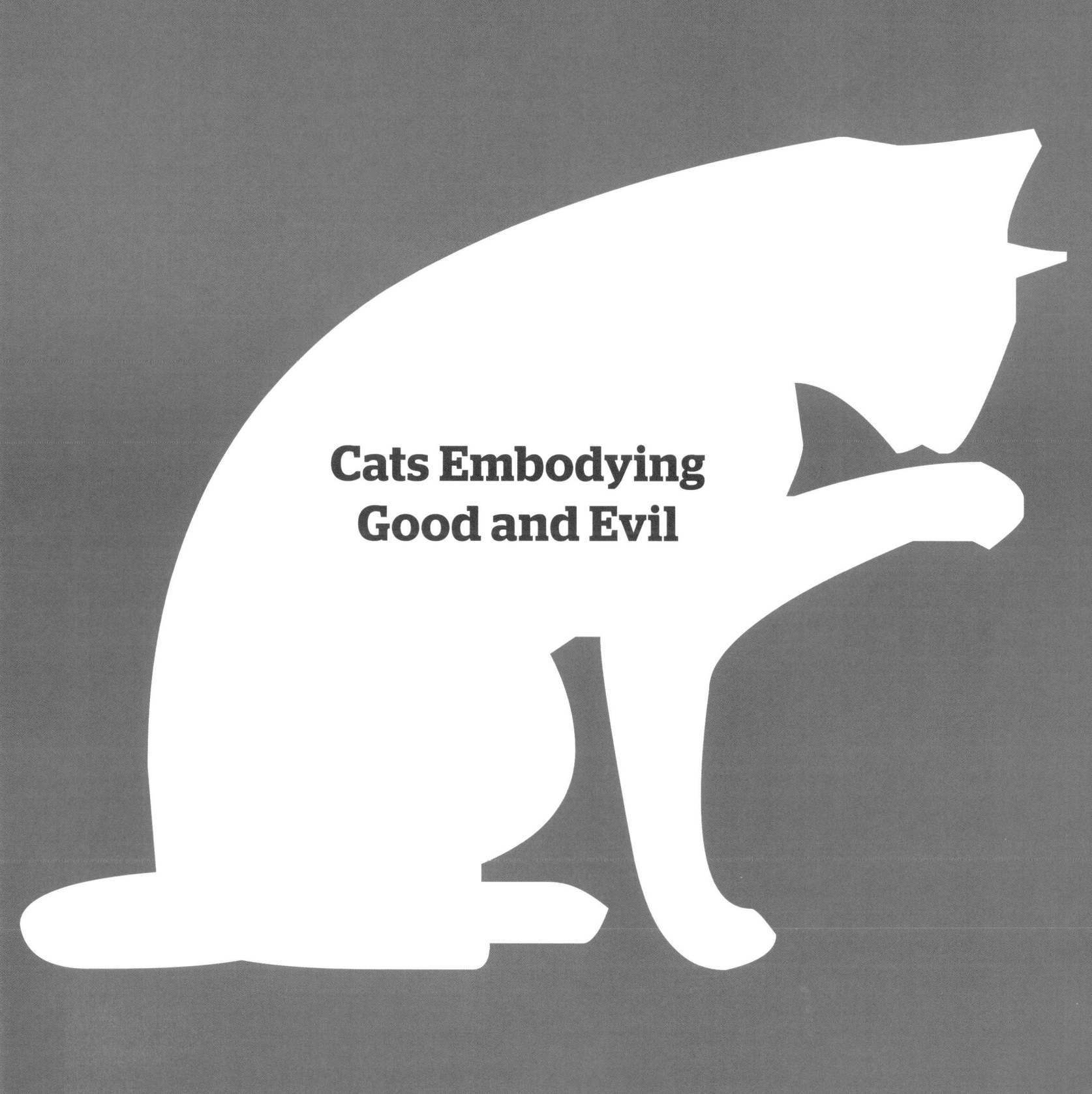

Cats Embodying
Good and Evil

Are These Animals Good or Evil?

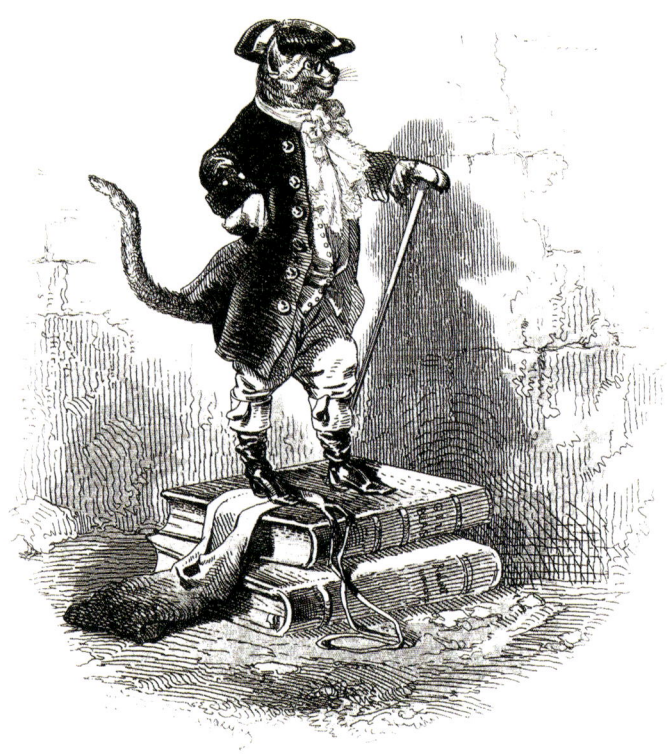

Cover of *Tales of Passed Times*, 1843.

Cats are animals that almost systematically trigger passions. This is true in real life, as well as in legends, beliefs, and fiction. Felines appear regularly in animation and in works aimed at young audiences and are often portrayed in a very Manichean light, the legacy of a long, shared history.

Cats: Evil or Divine

While divine and mystical cats have their own chapter, it's interesting to note that cats are rarely negative animals in modern fiction. They are often deified or mystified, like Korin, the Tower Master in *Dragon Ball*. The rest of the time, they're known for their flaws or their cunning, in both senses of the word. Historically, in fairy tales and in the common imagination, cats are often ambivalent. The difficulties in domesticating them

and their natural independence have undoubtedly contributed to this image. In ancient times, in Egypt as in other cultures, they were deified. The image changed in the Middle Ages, when cats were demonized by the Catholic Church. During this period, the growing power of the clergy over the world led to a negative vision of the feline. They were considered demonic and persecuted during the Inquisition.

While felines have been subjected to various types of abuse, the most common was probably burning at the stake. In the Middle Ages, the Midsummer fire became a pretext for burning cats.[1] In Paris, for the occasion, barrels and sacks filled with black cats were suspended over a blaze in the Place de Grève. The popular spectacle lasted for several centuries, until it was banned by Louis XV. Black cats in particular were associated with witchcraft, which was forbidden by the Church and Christianity in general. In the United States, which was predominantly Protestant and far removed from the papacy, black cats also became bad-luck charms and were massively persecuted during the witch hunts of the late seventeenth century. They were suspected of being transformed witches. The association between cats and witchcraft is a recurring theme in fiction, from *Sabrina the Teenage Witch* to *Kiki's Delivery Service*.

In the fourteenth century, cats were accused of transmitting the bubonic plague, or black death, which was ravaging Europe. With the disease causing the death of a third of the population,[2] the four-legged companions were massacred. However, the disease originated from fleas, which were mainly spread by rodents. In retrospect, exterminating cats at the time may well have contributed to the spread of the virus, as there would have been more rats in the absence of predators. Cats weren't exonerated by the Church until the early seventeenth century.[3] All these elements of Western culture go some way to explaining why they are so often perceived as malevolent, and this is reflected in fiction.

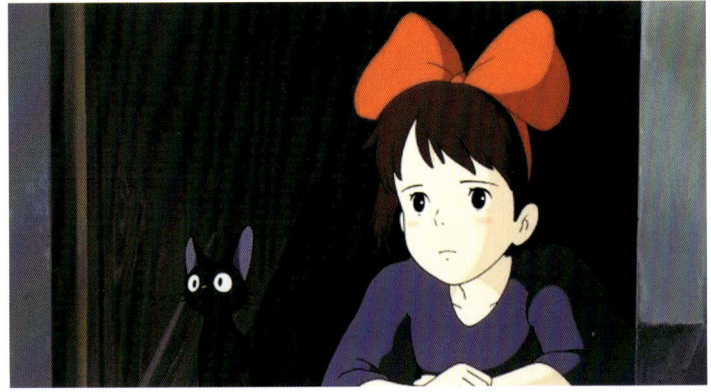

Jiji and Kiki.

[1] https://oatao.univ-toulouse.fr/1817/1/celdran_1817.pdf
[2] https://www.nationalgeographic.fr/sciences/les-rats-ne-seraient-pas-responsables-de-la-peste-noire
[3] https://www.franceinter.fr/societe/les-chats-nous-protegent-peste

Silver Cats

French folklore says that an evil cat can bring wealth to its master. Called a silver cat in Brittany, it's known as a *matagot* in Provence and a *madragot* in Gascony. Whatever it's called, it's traditionally black. These legends of the silver cat are less common in fictional worlds, although *Puss in Boots* has many of its attributes, except for the color.

The legend of Dick Whittington and his cat is another example of a *matagot*. Well known in British folklore, it tells how the poor child made his fortune thanks to his cat and eventually became mayor of London in the fourteenth century. However, the stories linked to his cat didn't appear until the early seventeenth century. Adapted into ballads, plays, and tales, he is said to have launched his financial empire by selling his cat to a merchant ship. With no other goods to sell, he gave away his pet in exchange for what it would bring back from other lands. There, in a kingdom plagued by mice, his cat drove away the vermin. The king thanked the travelers by buying their goods back at ten times their value. While legend has no basis in fact for the cat's role, Dick Whittington's existence has been proved. He is known for his investment in charity work in the fifteenth century, bequeathing his fortune to the Charity of Sir Richard Whittington Foundation, which is still active today.

Images of Dick Whittington always show him with a cat. In the tradition of the silver cat, there is often talk of summoning the devil to the crossroads of five paths or baiting him at the crossroads of four paths with a dead chicken. It's strange that a cat that brings money should be closely linked to the devil and negative values. This is partly explained by the way money was viewed in Christian society. In the Gospel according to Matthew, it is said that: "No one can serve two masters at the same time, for either you will hate the one and love the other, or you will be devoted to one and despise the other. You cannot serve God and Money at the same time." Having money is therefore wrong. The silver cat is linked to the evil one and requires a soul to be invoked. The legend of the *matagot* cat has led to numerous swindles over the centuries. A cat that was supposed to bring in money for its master was sold at a high price to the greediest person and, of course, turned out to be just a cat.

Little Ones Are Always Nice

Although cats are more often portrayed as bad than good, little ones are a systematic exception. Kittens are always nice. Such cute little things can't be negative. This is striking in Warner

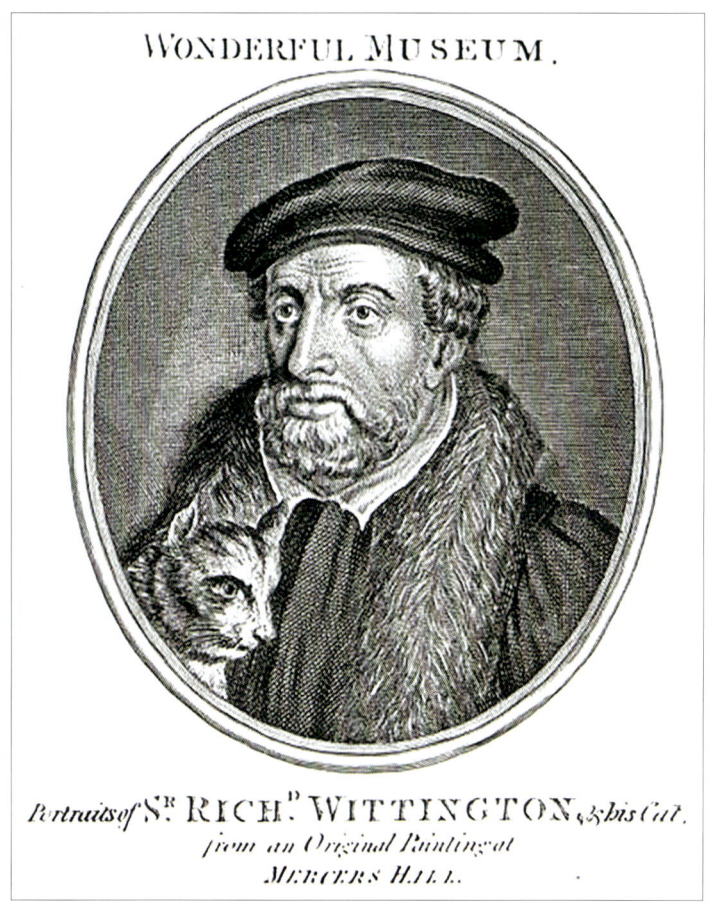

Richard Wittington and His Cat, engraving by Guillaume Philippe Benoist, 19th century, Mercers Hall.

Bros. cartoons, in which the adult cat Claude is an embittered old grump, while the little one is so cute and delicate that he even attracts the dog's sympathy. In *The Aristocats* and *Oliver and Company*, cuteness is never associated with negativity. Kittens aren't like adult cats in fiction, who are cruelly handsome. However, the image of the cat in Disney animated films isn't always flattering. They are often evil, like Lucifer in *Cinderella*.

It's legitimate to wonder why felines rarely appear in a more measured role, like in *The Rescuers*. Cats' ambivalent nature is obviously one possible answer to this negative view of the animal. However, the narrative structure of these films also explains the beasts' dual nature. The movies are aimed at a young Western audience accustomed to clear conventions of good and evil. While the tales are full of violence and morally ambiguous behavior, their adaptation by the American studio has always respected Walt Disney's conservative Christian values.

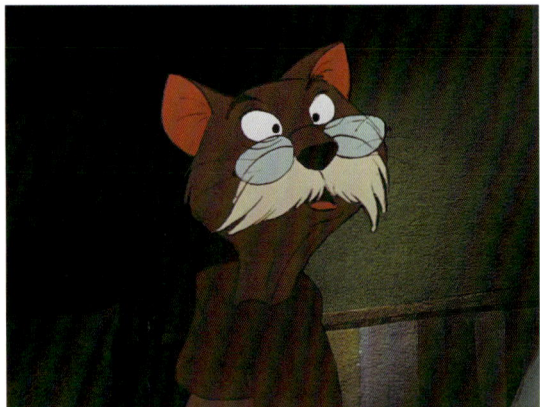
Rufus in *The Rescuers*.

These Animals Are Too Much Like Humans

Cats' ambivalent nature is regularly highlighted in legends and stories. Puss in Boots serves his master's interests, while using cunning to kill the ogre and achieve his aims. In the end, the cat is quite human. Fiction pushes anthropomorphism to the point of making cats talk, like in *The Aristocats*, or stand on their hind legs, like in *Heathcliff and the Catillac Cats* and *Hello Kitty*. Humans project their own behaviors onto cats because they're so similar. We are mammals, carnivores, and capable of both gentleness and violence. This projection is very clear in films like *The Voices*, in which the cat is the human being's guilty conscience. When there's a dog, the cat is always the evil one.

When not pitted against other animals, cats often embody a dual nature, both good and evil. This is the case with Garfield,

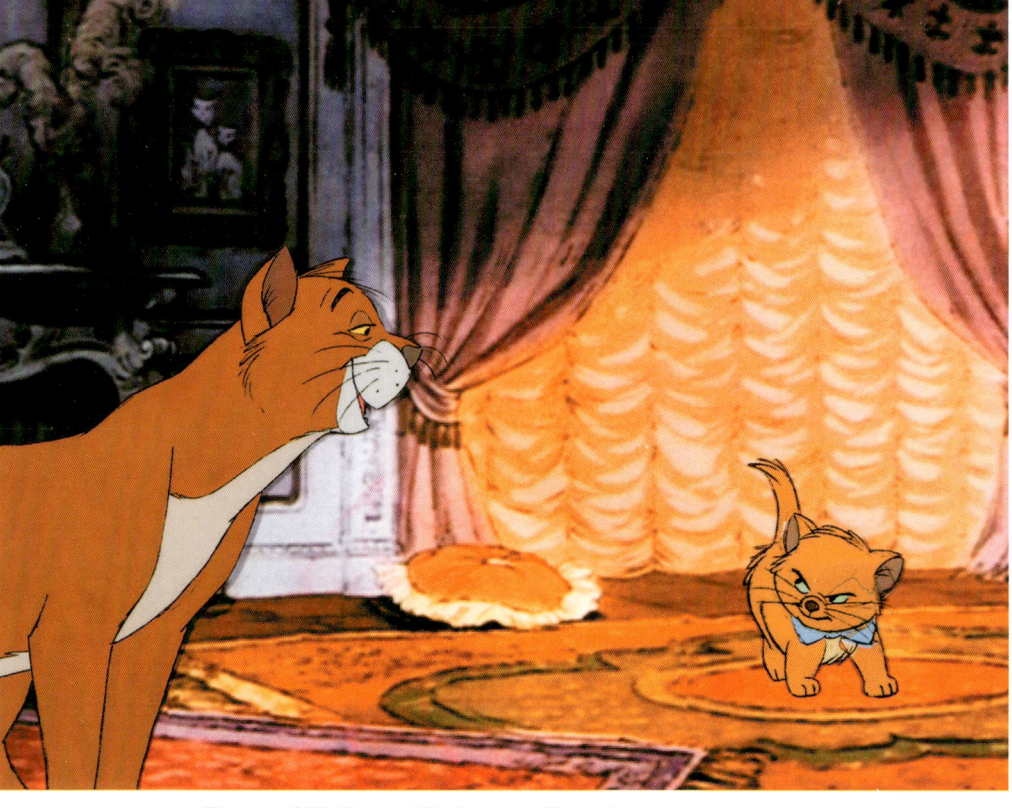
Thomas O'Malley and Toulouse in *The Aristocats*.

who is both obnoxious and endearing, and Snowbell in the *Stuart Little* films, who is hostile to the mouse but ultimately kind. Cats are often beautiful, belying their evil character. This is why white Persians have come to be regarded as evil cats in the collective unconscious. Recognizable by their rare beauty and fur, they have become the symbol of evil thanks to their appearance in James Bond films.

Cats' Eyes

In Greek mythology, much-coveted beauty could also be a curse, as in the case of Helen of Troy, whose beauty led to the Trojan War. Beauty is also a double-edged sword for felines, the counterpart of a dark heart. Cats' piercing gaze also explains why they are seen as evil animals. With retracted pupils, deep-colored eyes that reflect light in the dark, and the ability to see in the dark, they leave no one indifferent. In fiction, a cat's eyes are sometimes seen before his face, revealing his cunning (or at least unsettling) nature. One example is the appearance of Puss in Boots in *Shrek 2*.

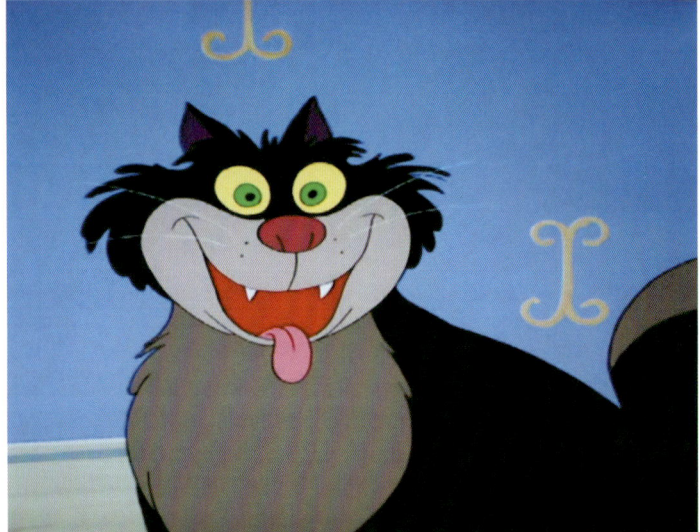
Lucifer in *Cinderella*.

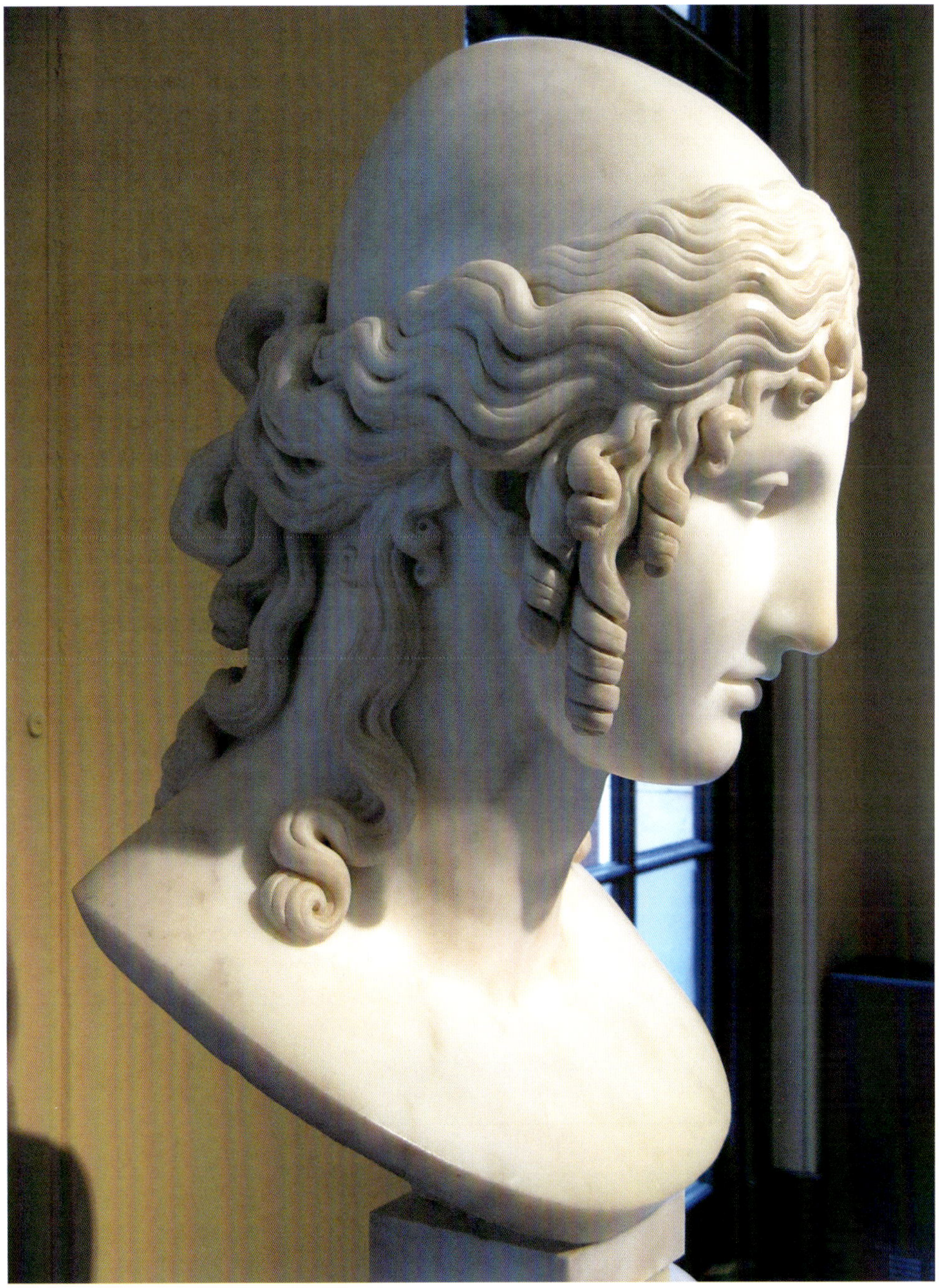

Helen of Troy, Antonio Canova (1757–1822), Victoria and Albert Museum. Photo by Yair Haklai.

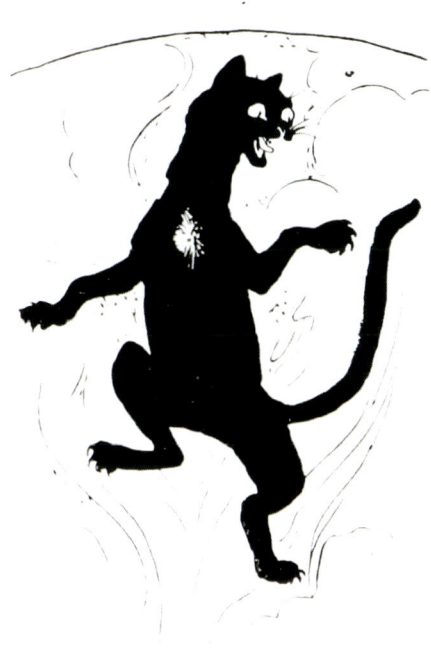

The legendary Cat Sìth (Scottish folklore), John D. Batten, 1894.

Black Cat/White Cat: Good or Bad?

The way colors are perceived is intimately linked to each country's culture. For example, red, the color of passion in the West, is the color of success and fortune in China. However, black is almost universally recognized as the color of mourning or death. It's therefore regularly associated with the negative. The black cat may be considered the devil's beast, but British folklore, particularly in Scotland, makes it a lucky charm. In fiction, black cats aren't necessarily evil. They are regularly associated with witchcraft, but this isn't always the case. They are also used in more neutral worlds, such as that of Felix the Cat. Paradoxically, white cats aren't always symbols of purity. In *The Voices*, the orange cat is the diabolical part of the character. In Asia, the *maneki-neko* is always a good-luck charm, whatever its color. White ones signify purity, while black ones ward off evil spirits, and red ones protect health. 🐾

Viewpoint

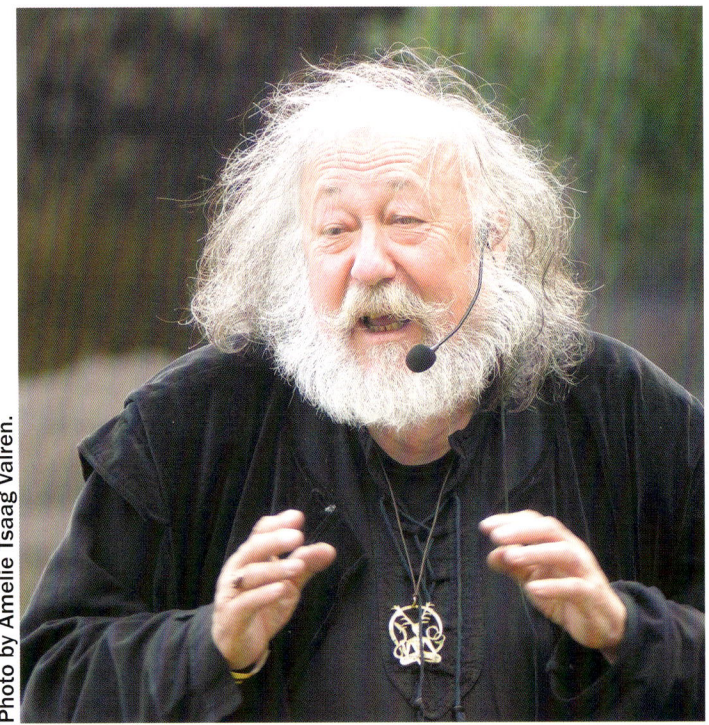

Photo by Amélie Tsaag Valren.

Pierre Dubois, "Elficologist" and Storyteller

"Cats remain two-sided: both good and evil."

A specialist in myths and legends, and a connoisseur of fairy-tale people whose secrets he reveals in his many books, Pierre Dubois has always lived with cats. He reveals why these mysterious animals have enchanted us since the dawn of time.

Are cats an integral part of tales and legends around the world? Where does this fascination come from?

Cats are omnipresent, truly in every tale: in England, in France, in China, everywhere. Cats are always there, and they're always ambivalent. They're on both the side of good and that of evil. Why are they on both sides? Because, as we know, every time God created either a plant or an animal, the devil imitated him or went on to make another. Except that, since it was the devil, obviously it would be bad. For example, God made a horse, which was superb, and the devil tried to imitate him and made a donkey. It was always the same: One made boxwood, the other holly, one a beautiful oak, the other hawthorn, which curiously enough is the devil's tree, but which would also become the fairies' tree. There's always ambivalence. But then one day, God created a particularly pretty animal: agile, flexible,

cuddly, with soft fur. He was making the cat. The devil thought, "I have to get my hands on this animal. It's too beautiful." He said to God, "You can make the cat if you like, but its head will be mine." That's why cats have all the positive qualities—they're beautiful, flexible, etc.—but they're also cruel. There's a bit of the devil in them. You can see it right away in their eyes, which are very open and sparkling in the night. They are God's animals, but with cruelty and gratuitous crime somehow involved; they do harm in their games. They go out at night. They have a mysterious life that belongs to the devil. That's why there's this kind of ambiguity in cats. So, a hero like Puss in Boots helps his brave marquis, but they can also be evil. To the point where cats were even killed in some countries. For example, in Belgium, in Ypres, where there's a very, very high belfry, cats were killed every year. Litters of cats were thrown off because they were witches' pets, their familiars. This went on for a very long time. Today, it's no longer possible to throw cats like that; it's too cruel. But people still throw stuffed cats from the belfry.

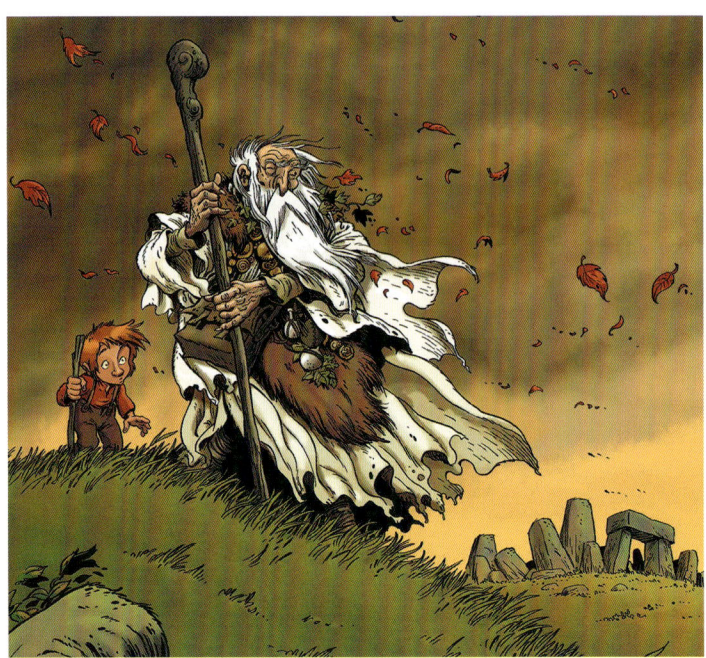

Detail from a book cover by Pierre Dubois.

So, has the way we perceive cats changed?

Nowadays, cats are really tame. Cats are in the house; we see them in commercials; we give them foie gras in commercials; we cuddle them. Whereas when I was a child, we gave cats leftovers. We also gave them milk, milk soup with bread, a little butter, sometimes margarine in it, but they had to fend for themselves. So, these cats would prowl around the neighbors' homes, especially in the country. They went to see what was going on, which made them seem much more diabolical. People told each other stories, secrets that shouldn't be told, family secrets, and the neighbor, or rather the woman next door who was a bit of a witch and didn't leave her house, but who had cats, would send them to listen in at the neighbor's door. Even if, in reality, cats were mostly hungry and tried to steal food, they would tell the neighbor all your secrets just by being there. When I was looking for stories in the countryside, I was told the same thing more than once. There was at least one like it in every village. A cat was always there when people were telling secrets. In one case, someone took a poker from the stove and burned it. In others, they threw the fryer at it or broke one of its paws. Strangely enough, within the next day or two, people noticed that the neighbor woman had stopped going out, and in fact, she had broken her leg or her arm or suffered a serious burn.

Have cats long been associated with the devil in legends?

They've always had a slightly diabolical side. The cat was the witch's pet who went to the sabbath with her. For example, not far from where I live, near Elsene in the Belgian Ardennes, there's the Cat Sauvage [Wild Cat] mill, and it was a sabbath site. The *matagot* cats, in other words, the sorcerer cats, went to find the devil in the form of a much larger cat . . . There were short cats; it was the Great Marcaou; it was the Beelzebub of cats; and they always met between the night of Shrove Tuesday and Ash Wednesday, at the intersection of four roads in Brittany. It was a true sabbath. If you had a cat's paw in your pocket, you could hear what he was saying. In other words, you could hear that he was speaking the language of men. He was blaspheming. But when you didn't have that paw, all you heard was meowing, terrible screeching and screaming, and they danced together until they fought, too. Like at any carnival, there was always blood.

In all our traditional festivals, there was always a moment when blood had to be shed: There was a brawl, a fight, a sort of obligatory sacrifice. And so, just like that, there was always a cat there. If you went out on the moors at night, it was better to avoid these areas; otherwise, you'd run the risk of walking into their sabbath and being mauled

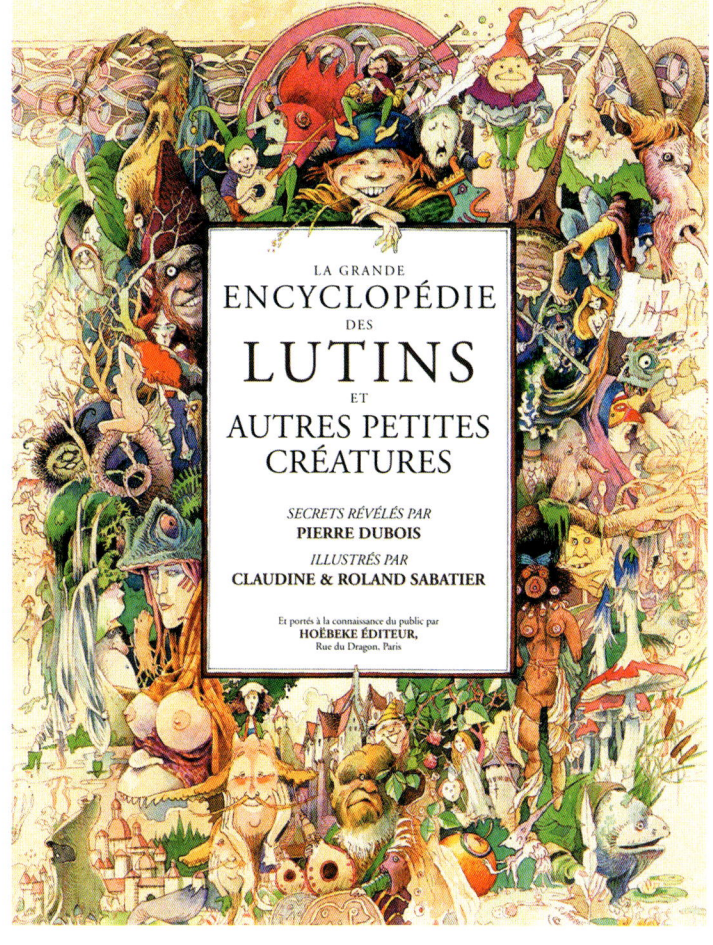

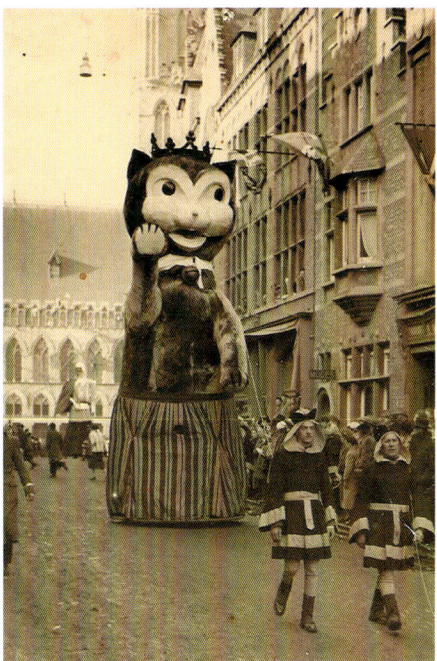

Cat parade, Ypres, 1950s. Photo by Delorme.

or killed. Even if sometimes things didn't go too badly, a cat intervened because it recognized its master and didn't want him to be touched. It became its master's advocate, and the cats didn't touch him. Or else, the man recognized the cat. To prevent your cat from going to the sabbath, all you had to do was trim its ear a little, trim its whiskers or a bit of its tail. Or burn it a little. All it took for the cat to be banned from the sabbath circle was for it to be missing something. It had to have an absolutely pristine coat, and it had to be beautiful, otherwise it wouldn't fit in.

In some stories, cats are likened to werewolves, but cat skins can be found in tree trunks. It's said that when pollarded willows were pruned in Isère, a skin could be found in the hollows of certain

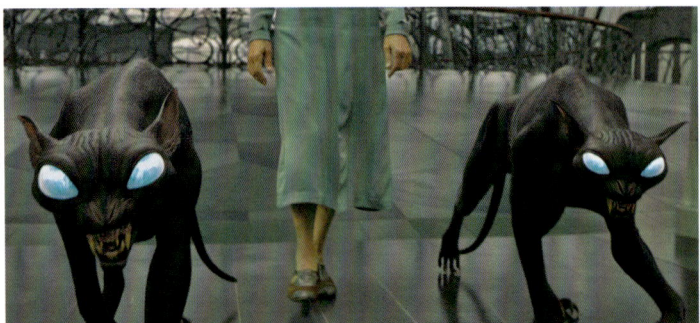

Matagots in *Fantastic Beasts: The Crimes of Grindelwald.*

trees. A wolf's skin, and if you burned it, someone from the village would suddenly turn up roasting on the spot. He'd arrive to retrieve his werewolf skin, which he'd hide in a hollow tree. When he wanted to be a werewolf during the full moon, he'd go and get his skin and put it on. No one knew who he was, but burning his skin betrayed who the werewolf was. Once the skin was burned, he was free. The same applied to cats. Sometimes, an old woman would come along, and she was a witch whose pet's skin was being burned, a *matagot* cat or a *matagon* cat or a *foireau*. That's how she gave herself away.

There are *matagot* cats, but are there also good cats in the fairy world?

Of course. But there are very few fairy cats. There is the fairy Margotine, the cat Margotine, who is one of the only cat-women who is benevolent. Even in this case, the cat remains both good and evil. The cat is nature. In other words, it has every opportunity to be cruel and evil, just as nature is. It isn't, though; it simply is. There are storms, there are tempests, but at the same time, nature is beneficial, just as cats are part God and part devil. They're a kind of Jekyll and Hyde: They can help the Marquis de Carabas. But if the other party betrays them just once, if they break the pact, they immediately become witches. They'll be angry, and their anger is terrible. Cats are felines. They can grow huge and devour someone who betrays them.

Like Bastet and Sekhmet in Egyptian mythology?

Yes, exactly like that. Fairy tales are derived from mythological stories. Even today. Today, we're invaded by manga and things like that, but they're just drawing from the great cauldron of tales and mythology, which they adapt, repurpose, and even lie about. They tell untruths. Nevertheless, they always start from this innate philosophy, this wisdom and madness that is described by mythologies, whether Egyptian, Scandinavian, or Celtic. It's always the same, as if something came to us from elsewhere, a kind of warning that hangs over us like this.

And from ancient times to today, cats have haunted our imaginations, haven't they?

Strangely enough, cats have adapted. They've never left us, as if they were one of our images. They reflect who we are. Often, when alone with a cat, old people who have no other companions say, "He understands what I'm saying. Ah, what if I didn't have him! When I'm sad, he's sad, and he consoles me. He sees things I don't." They tell themselves that cats sense ghosts, see ghosts. There are lots of stories about cats leaving the house when they sense a threat. They don't want to go into a room where there's been a ghost. When we wanted to know if a house was haunted, we'd send a cat in to check whether or not it smelled anything. Suddenly, it would spit.

Speaking of spitting, people used to say that when the neighbor's cat spat in the soup, it brought disease. On the other hand, when it spits in the face of danger, it's because it senses something. It doesn't want to stay in the house because it senses things; cats are mediums. The world is changing, becoming more covered in concrete and asphalt, but cats are adapting. They've become city dwellers. They're with us; they're still here. They're always attracted to children, with whom they feel at home. Even a cat that's not always very nice won't do anything to a child, whereas in the past, people used

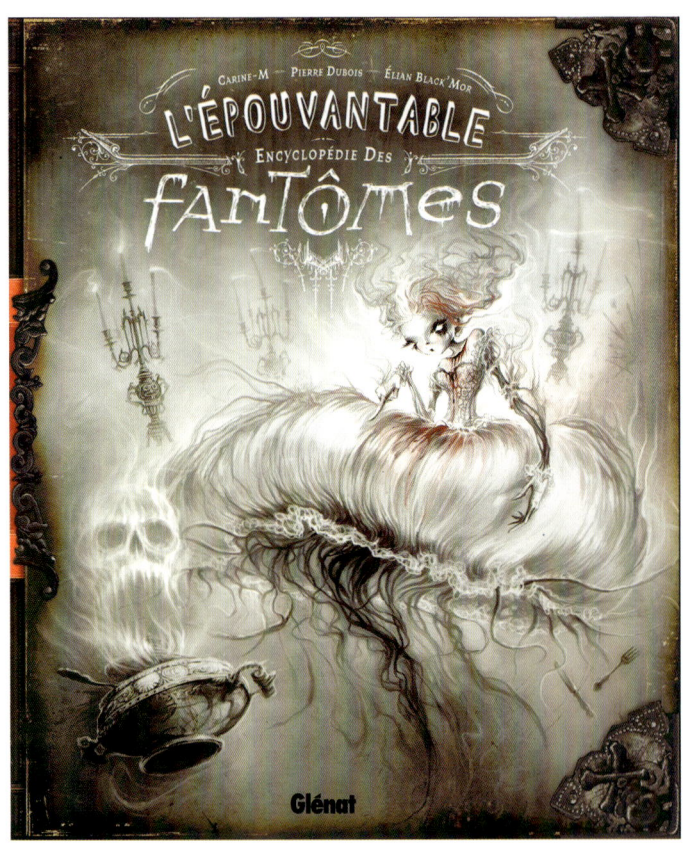

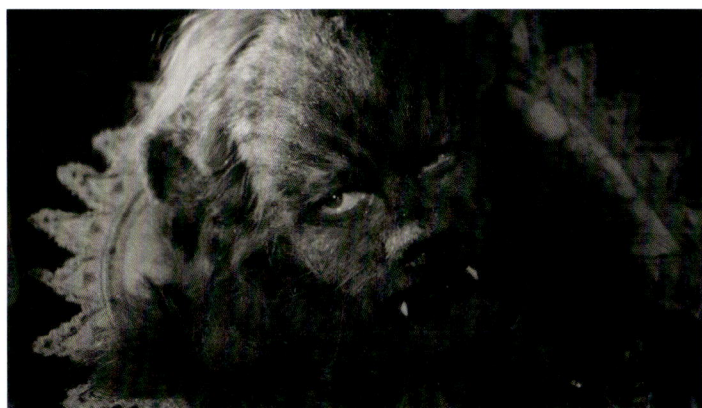

Beauty and the Beast.

to say, "Yes, yes, cats suffocate children." They'll get into the cradle, and that's the devilish side that we wanted to attribute to cats. Despite what some people say, cats are loyal. Some are abandoned and come back, traveling miles, sometimes wearing out their paw pads, to find their home, their master. And that, too, is what gives the animals their fantastic side. Dogs are nice, but there aren't too many legends about them.

Are cats our doubles?

Cats are the animals that are closest to humankind, but at the same time, they're also the ones that scare us. It's funny, because with people who don't like cats and are afraid of them, the cat often comes right into their lap, as if to say, "You see? I'm nice. Don't worry; it's going to be all right. I'm giving you a chance. Do you want to find your animality with me or not?"

Cats give their fur, too. If a hero has to go somewhere and needs certain objects, sometimes the cat gives him some of its fur. It gives him back his femininity, his wild side, so that he understands and can return to this form of animality in which he can understand something or fight the dragon. The cat will side with him to help him regain his magic and animality. It wasn't for nothing that Cocteau, a poet who was very close to all these mysteries, gave the Beast the face of a cat, a feline (see poster, right). When we read *Beauty and the Beast,* some people have given him a boar's head, others a dragon's or a lizard's head. Cocteau's *Beauty and the Beast* is truly the finest tribute ever paid to cats, fairies, and fairy tales. 🐾

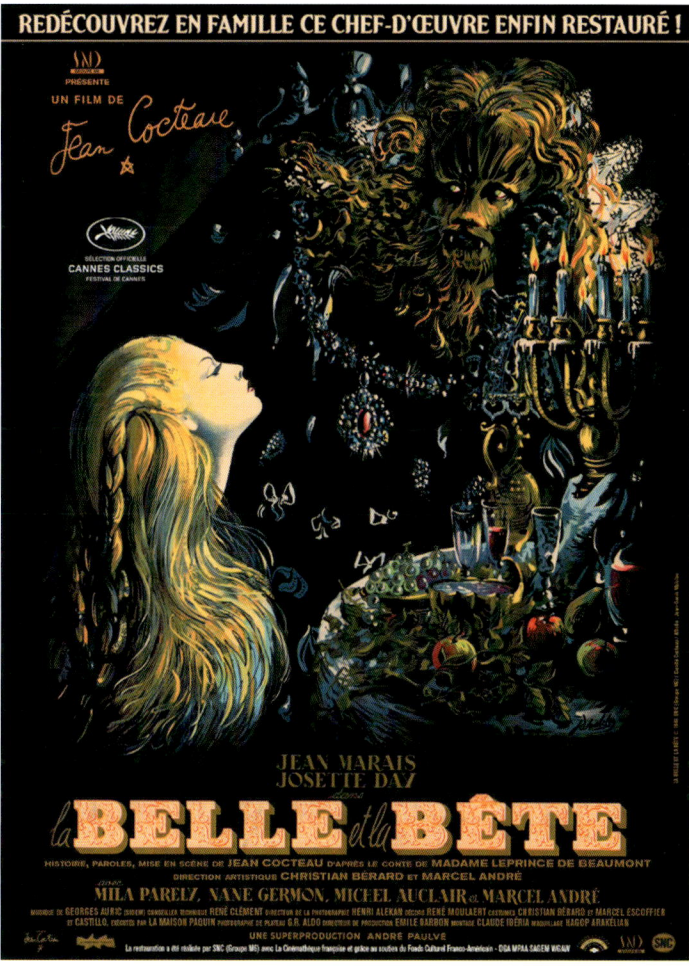

Blofeld's Persian

While Ian Fleming's James Bond series of spy books is best known for its charismatic Agent 007, its most iconic villain is undoubtedly Ernst Stavro Blofeld. In the film adaptations, he is known for his white Persian cat.

First appearing in the second film of the series, *From Russia with Love*, in 1963, Blofeld is never seen directly in front of the camera. Director Terence Young hid him off-screen, showed him from behind, or simply framed his shots on the arms of Bond's enemy. This technique would be used in the character's numerous appearances, until his face was revealed at the end of *You Only Live Twice* (1967). Blofeld, also known as Number 1 in his terrorist organization, SPECTRE, appeared in nine films, including the latest one, *No Time to Die*, in which the role was taken over by Christoph Waltz.

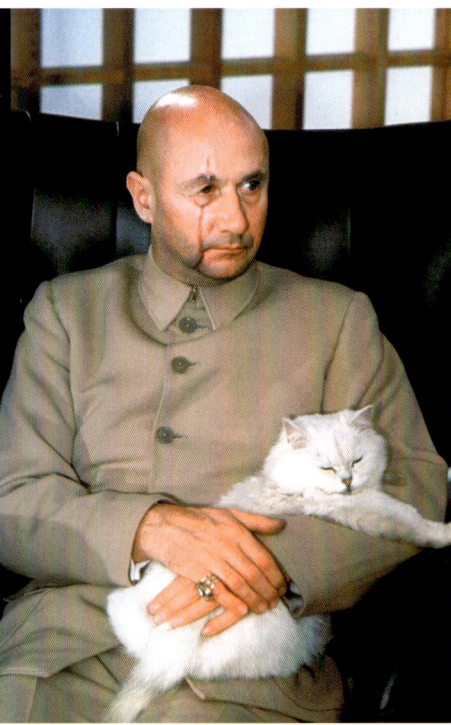

You Only Live Twice.

Number 1's physique evolves throughout the series, although he is often depicted as bald and wearing a Mao suit. His white Persian is the thread that runs through the films. Never seeing his face in the early films, viewers identify the villain with his cat, which sits calmly on the terrorist's lap, letting himself be petted and observing the situation.

In *From Russia with Love*, Blofeld shows his most manipulative side by commenting on a fight between two fish while his cat looks on, impassive and observant. "He lets the other two fight while he waits. Waits until the survivor is so exhausted that he cannot defend himself. And then, like SPECTRE, he strikes."

Blofeld's Persian, often filmed to justify his facelessness, is ascribed his master's evil intentions. The villain is identifiable by his cat. The Persian archetype would later be assimilated to a negative character in the collective unconscious. It was so pervasive that it led to tributes and parodies ranging from *Cats & Dogs* to *Inspector Gadget*.

The choice of a Persian cat is not insignificant. Its distinguished character matches Blofeld's fascinating side quite well. Its calm, precious nature contributes to the character's haughty demeanor. Moreover, cats are virtually impossible to train and very tricky to direct in films. The Persian is a relatively docile breed of cat and easier to manage on film. The Chinchilla version—a cat with predominantly light fur, but with a dark tip to create a kind of halo around the animal and surround its eyes with a line of natural kohl—is even more sought-after by breeders and luxury enthusiasts. This fits perfectly with Ernst Stavro Blofeld's refinement and need for order. Once Number 1's face is revealed, the cat continues to appear, though less systematically. In *On Her Majesty's Secret Service* (1967), Blofeld hides his true identity from Bond. He has no cat then, a clue that makes the plot too obvious to the viewer. 🐾

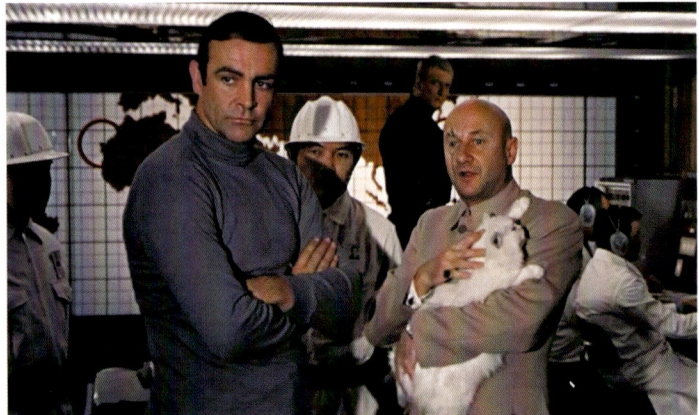

You Only Live Twice.

SPEC SHEET

WORK: *From Russia with Love* and seven other James Bond films.
CREATORS: Directed by Terence Young; screenplay by Richard Maibaum; based on the novel by Ian Fleming.
DATE CREATED: 1963.
PUBLISHER/DISTRIBUTOR: MGM/United Artists.
CAT'S NAME AND ROLE IN THE WORK: Anonymous Chinchilla Persian.

Parodies of Blofeld's Cat

Following the success of the James Bond series, the visuals and role of Blofeld's cat have been reused many times in film and on television, either as an homage or a parody, in brief appearances or in starring roles.

While the James Bond films brought the elegant suit and pistol into everyday imagery, they also established the image of the bald, scarred villain accompanied by a white cat. This cat appears in many films and series that caricature spy movie clichés, even if it's just for a single scene.

Mr. Tinkles in *Cats & Dogs* (see p. 33) directly embodies the villain of a spy story. In fact, the entire film refers to this genre. And it's not the only one! *Austin Powers* openly pays tribute to Blofeld and his cat. The most famous reference is no doubt found in *Inspector Gadget*, a cartoon also inspired by the American comedy series *Get Smart* and Inspector Clouseau from *The Pink Panther*. Created in 1983, this Franco-American-Japanese oddity follows the adventures of Gadget, a clumsy secret agent with a multitude of spy gadgets. With the help of his niece Sophie and his dog Brain, Gadget regularly foils the plans of the villainous Dr. Claw. All the audience sees of the villain is his iron glove and his snide cat, M.A.D. Cat. Visually, he's more inspired by cats in Disney films, such as *Cinderella* or *Alice in Wonderland*, than by Blofeld's cat. However, his role is identical, and the animation often shows him laughing at his master's diabolical plans. When his master's plans fail, on the other hand, he is often the victim of his anger.

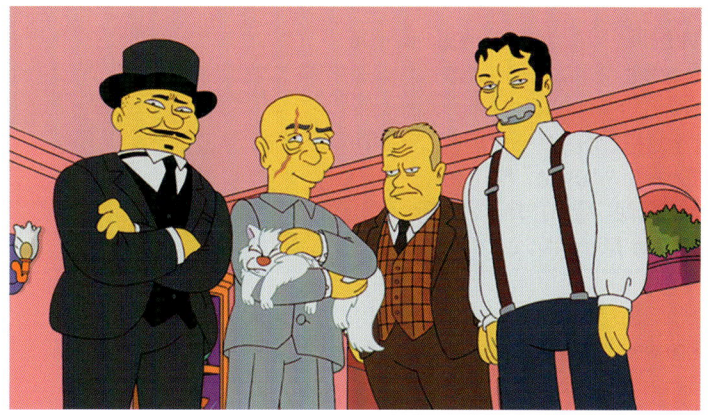

The Simpsons.

Buoyed by its international success, Hollywood had the bad idea of adapting *Inspector Gadget* into a live-action film in 1999. In this version, the big cat became a white cat that looked more like Blofeld's cat than the original. In 2015, a new 3D animated series was created, in which M.A.D. Cat was a female (in the James Bond series, the gender isn't specified).

The character of Blofeld's cat is so enduring that today, the reference feeds on itself. Younger generations may not have seen the James Bond films but are familiar with the parodies that recur regularly in cartoons. In more recent allusions, Giovanni, the leader of Team Rocket, enemies of Ash Ketchum and his gang in *Pokémon*, is shown sitting in an armchair accompanied by a Pokémon cat, Persian, which is an evolution of Meowth. 🐾

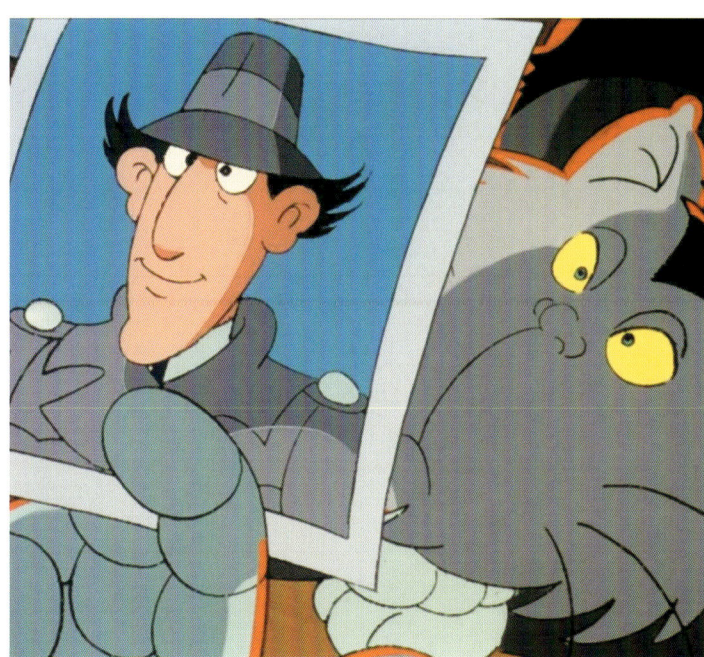

M.A.D Cat in *Inspector Gadget.*

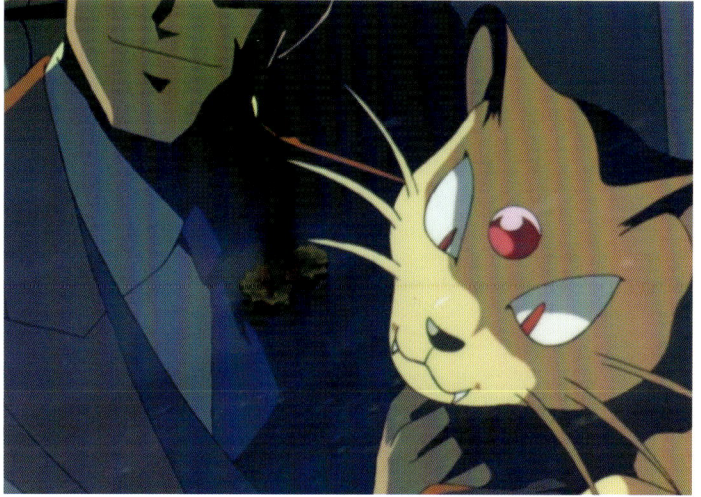

Pokémon.

Mr. Bigglesworth

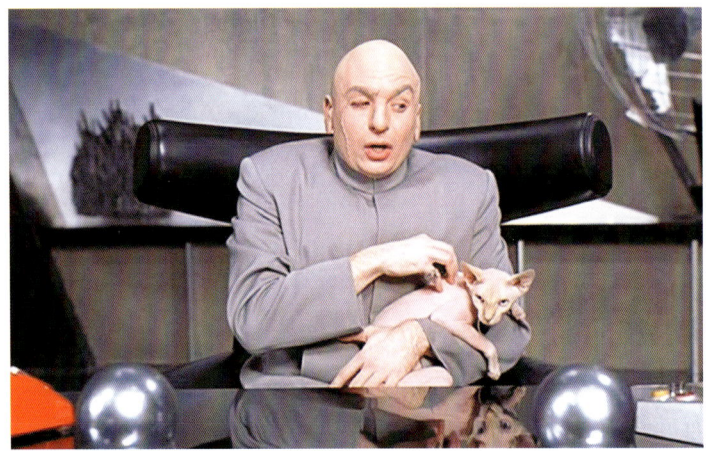

In 1997, Mike Myers invented the spy character Austin Powers, the polar opposite of James Bond. With huge glasses, crooked teeth, and a ruffled shirt, he fights the plans of the Machiavellian Dr. Evil, who is accompanied by his feline sidekick, Mr. Bigglesworth.

After the colossal success of the *Wayne's World* film in 1992 and the failure of its sequel the following year, comedian Mike Myers went through a period of limbo. A well-known comedian on *Saturday Night Live*, he began a parody of spy films with the gritty jokes so appreciated by his fans, which relaunched his career. He enjoyed playing a variety of characters, taking on both the lead role and that of his adversary, Dr. Evil. The bald, megalomaniacal mad scientist has the same features as Blofeld in the James Bond franchise. A scar on the right side of his face, a suit reminiscent of a military uniform, and a pinkie ring define the character. However, the living accessory essential to the viewer's direct perception of the caricature is a white Persian cat.

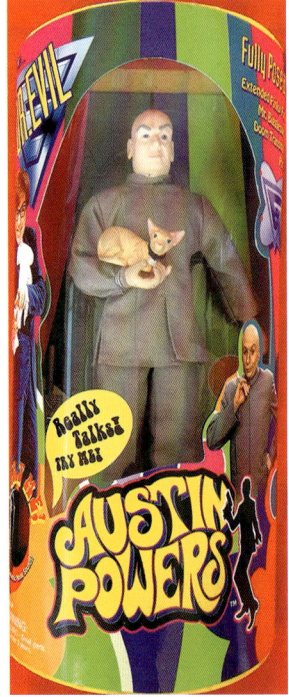

The docile cat lets the psychopath stroke him. Mr. Bigglesworth's fur is one of the film's running gags. At the beginning of the film, Dr. Evil is cryogenically frozen and sent thirty years back in time to escape Austin Powers. When he returns, at a meeting of his terrorist organization, he announces that a technical problem has occurred with his cat. The Persian lost all its hair due to cryonics. From then on, he's naked and played by a sphynx cat. Mustafa, who is responsible for this error, is thrown into the fire through a trapdoor in one of the running jokes that Myers is so fond of.

The sphynx regularly reappears in his master's arms, further underlining the ridiculousness of the character. In the 1999 sequel, *Austin Powers: The Spy Who Shagged Me*, Mr. Bigglesworth is replaced as sidekick by Dr. Evil's clone, Mini-Me.

He returned in the third installment, *Austin Powers in Goldmember*, released in 2002. The opening sequence is a *mise en abyme* in which Steven Spielberg is making a film about Austin's life, with a cast that includes Tom Cruise. In this version, Mr. Bigglesworth appears in the arms of a Dr. Evil portrayed by Kevin Spacey. 🐾

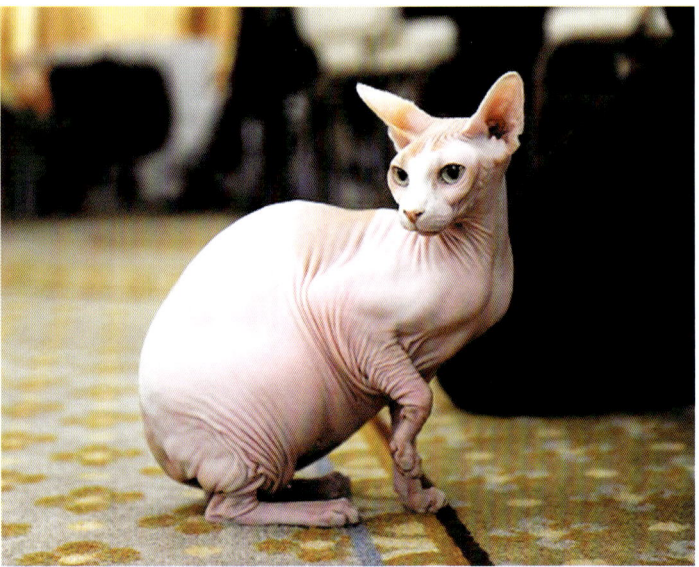

SPEC SHEET

CAT'S NAME: Mr. Bigglesworth.
WORK: *Austin Powers* and *Austin Powers in Goldmember*.
CREATORS: Mike Myers (screenwriter) and Jay Roach (director).
DATE CREATED: May 2, 1997.
DISTRIBUTOR/AVAILABILITY: New Line, available on DVD and Blu-ray and on various streaming services.
CAT'S CHARACTERISTICS: White Persian that becomes a sphynx cat after an accident.

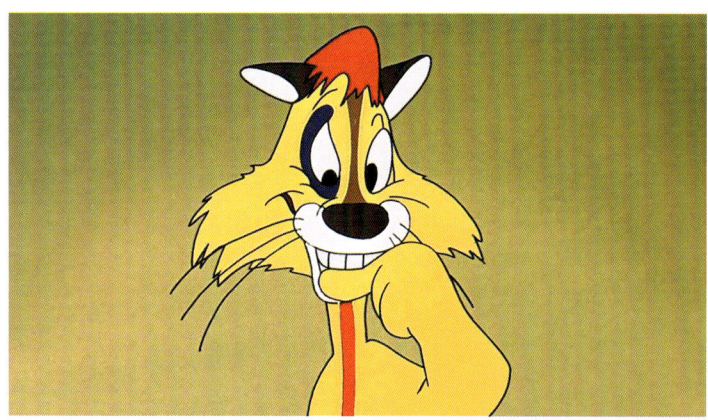

Less well known than Sylvester, the Looney Tunes character Claude first appeared around the same time. Created by cartoon genius Chuck Jones, he is endowed with the worst possible cat personality: he is possessive, jealous, and idle, and every intention seems more evil than the last.

A yellow cat with a white belly, Claude has red fur on the top of his head and at the tip of his tail. The short film "The Aristo-Cat," considered Claude's first appearance, presented a very different image of the character, who was then black and white and from a privileged background. The cartoon wasn't particularly successful, presenting a cat whose only common traits with the character he would later become were an appreciation of luxury and a fickle temperament. The character's visual identity didn't appear until 1949, with the Oscar-nominated "Mouse Wreckers." In this short, however, he is only a secondary character, victimized by the two mice, Hubie and Bertie. He is more upper-class, living in a comfortable house.

In 1950's "The Hypo-Chondri-Cat," Claude is a complete hypochondriac. In "Two's a Crowd," the character finally breaks

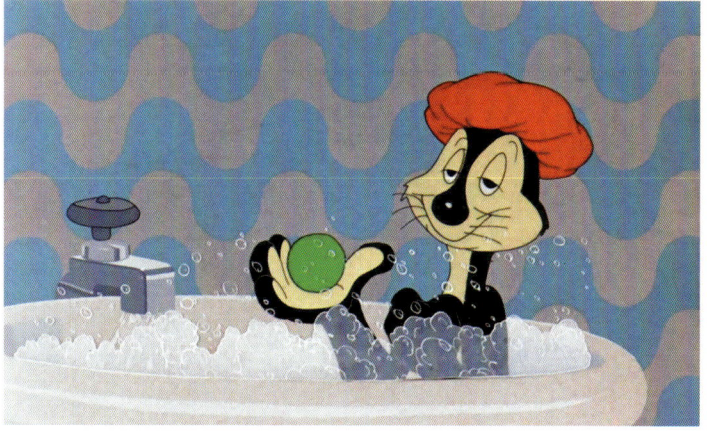

A well-born cat, first appearance of the character.

free from the two rodents. This time, the arrival of a dog threatens his established place in the household, and he tries to get rid of it. This storyline was reused in 1954 in "Feline Frame-Up," in which the family adopts a cute little kitten. Marc Anthony the bulldog tries to keep Claude from harming the kitten.

Over time, Claude becomes mute, which is offset by his cunning expressions. He shows himself to be a hypocrite, pretending to love animals in front of his masters, but then tries to kick them out. Despite his evolution, he remains extremely skittish. Every surprise makes him literally jump to the ceiling, only to fall and stop a few inches from the ground to turn around, landing on his paws in true feline fashion.

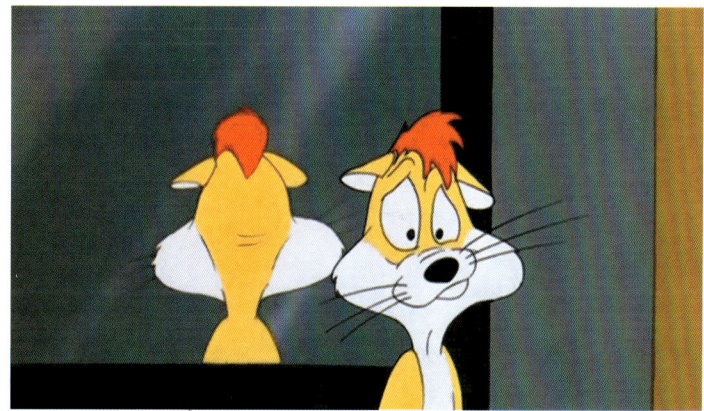

With a dozen appearances in animated shorts, the four episodes based on Claude's cruelty to kittens and puppies most clearly define the character. Cunning and cruel, he uses trickery to achieve his ends, but never succeeds. This form of narrative construction is very reminiscent of Wile E. Coyote and the Road Runner, which were developed at the same time and by the same creator. 🐾

SPEC SHEET

CAT'S NAME: Claude.
WORK: *Claude Cat.*
CREATOR: Chuck Jones.
DATE CREATED: 1943.
DISTRIBUTOR: Warner Bros.
CAT'S CHARACTERISTICS: Yellow-and-white cat with a bit of red on his head. An unlikable main character.

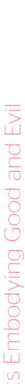

The Voices

Jerry is a lonely guy trying to fit in at his new job. He can count on help from his dog, Bosco, and his cat, Mr. Whiskers, who can give him advice on social situations when he stops taking his medication and starts killing.

A schizophrenic who hears voices isn't a new storyline in the movies. The originality of *The Voices* lies in two elements. The first is that most of the film follows the story from the patient's point of view. The viewer is plunged into Jerry's delirium, played with sincerity by Ryan Reynolds. The costumes, sets, and even the colors are reminiscent of classic Hollywood. The world is bright and sanitized, in contrast with the violence of the sick man's murders.

The second interesting aspect of the film is the voices Jerry hears when he stops treatment. These voices, which give the film its name, correspond to those of the protagonist's good and bad conscience and are embodied by his pets. The dog, representing the good, is understanding with his master. He has a big, reassuring voice and advises his master wisely. Of course, the bad side of his mind, which drives him to kill, is portrayed by the cat. Mr. Whiskers, an animal regularly seen as cunning and cruel, completely reflects this archetype. While the main character gradually hears other voices, those of his two pets stay with him throughout the film.

Jerry is presented as a weak victim when faced with the voices that drive him to kill, such as Mr. Whiskers. However, the cat clearly tells him, "You know there's no such thing as a talking cat. So, whatever I say, you're the one who's thinking it." The orange cat, whose mouth is computer animated, draws him into predatory instincts that he shares. "The only time I've felt truly alive is when I'm killing," he tells him. Scenes in which Jerry takes his pills or when another character comes to his house show the sordid reality and, ultimately, the innocence of the cat to whom the serial killer lends his voice and dark thoughts.

Marjane Satrapi, the Franco-Iranian author of the graphic novel and 2007 film *Persepolis*, won numerous awards and

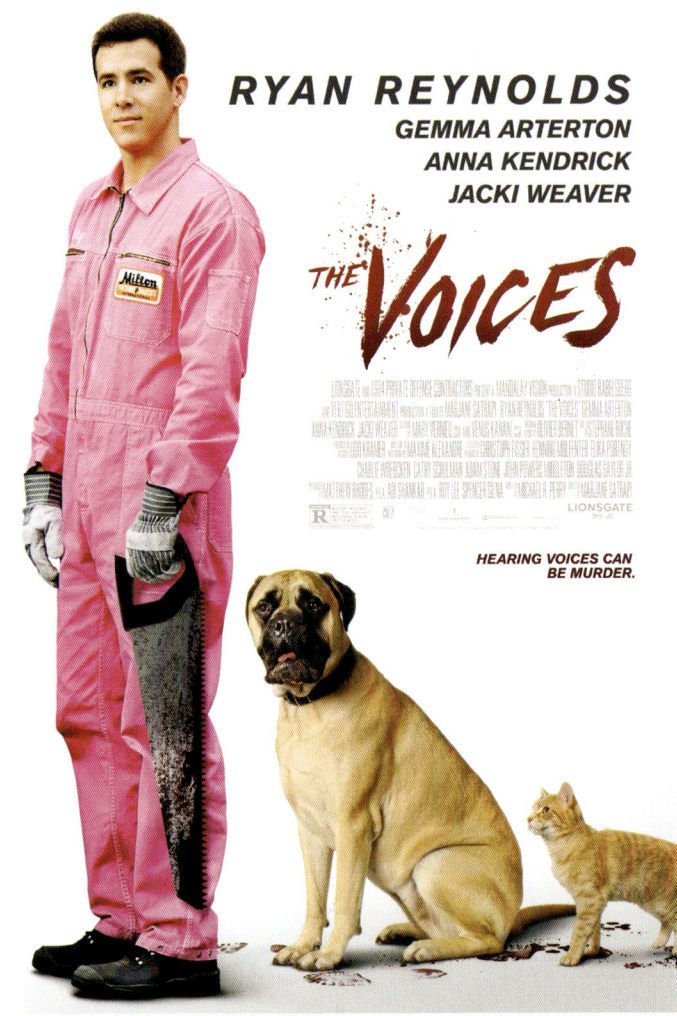

nominations for *The Voices,* including at the Fantastic'Arts festival in Gérardmer and the Sundance Film Festival. However, this critical acclaim didn't have much impact on the film's box-office success, which remained relatively modest. 🐾

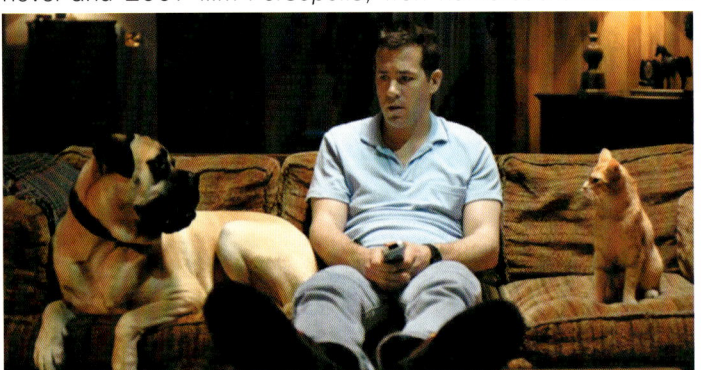

Les Nuls l'Émission

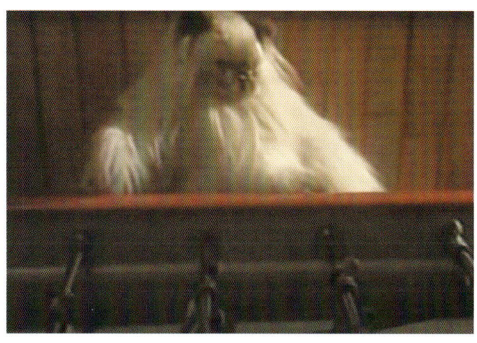 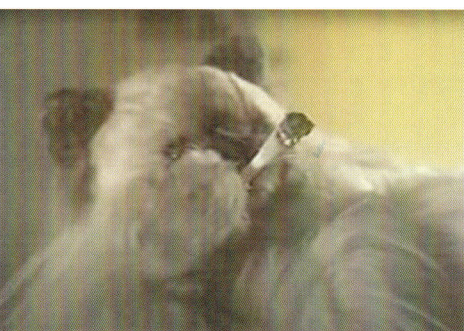

In 1990, the French comedy group Les Nuls, then made up of Alain Chabat, Chantal Lauby, and Dominique Farrugia, created a French-style Saturday Night Live. Their fake commercials—some of them featuring cats—became cult favorites, like the one for Kwiskas.

Over the course of two years, the show in the form of an American talk show with parodies performed alongside a prestigious guest (such as Jean Reno or Vanessa Paradis), the comedians of Canal+'s golden age produced several commercials featuring cats. Not out of love for felines, but with the intention of making fun of them, their supposed cunning and laziness, as well as the consumerist wastefulness of their human owners, the ideal target of the consumer society. For example, one of the show's best-known fake commercials was for cat food. Kwiskas was a fake advertisement for canned cat food, using real Whiskas advertising images. Alain Chabat's voice-over deliberately repeated a naive, redundant line about how "cats would buy Kwiskas." He also stressed the unappetizing aspect of the food. The music heavily emphasized the cuteness of the images, as in the original ad. However, in the middle of the spot, shots filmed for the occasion show a stuffed cat smoking marijuana, playing foosball, and being thrown at the ceiling with a comical meow.

Then the narrator's tone changed. "Instead of that, cats spend their money on foosball; they spend their time smoking joints and climbing the ceiling. Cats are just a bunch of slackers." He finally announced to the viewer: "That was an announcement from the CCC, the Committee Against Cats (*Comité contre les chats*)."

A stuffed cat being tormented, with an off-screen sound of a cat struggling, is also the comic device behind the fake Le Chat Machine commercial. Imitating the Le Chat laundry detergent campaign launched in the 1990s with a white-haired announcer, this time, Alain Chabat pulls a cat out of a package of detergent. The stuffed cat struggles. "Le Chat Machine is all natural," he says, before tossing the animal into the washing machine. There would be two fake ads, both reminding us "Don't forget to boil your cat" before clarifying that it was actually a CCC statement.

Another ad reused images from the Fido commercial, showing fussy cats who didn't want to eat just anything. Dominique Farrugia provided the voice-over. Where the viewer expected to be offered Fido cat food, the narrator suggested "a kick in the ass." A stuffed cat was kicked, flying away with an exaggerated meow. Another example of cat-related comic violence in *Les Nuls* was a fake commercial for a Moulinex vacuum cleaner. The "Founinex Dirt-Eater" suggested that a vacuum cleaner could be used to suck up kittens. Since then, the CCC has spawned several Facebook groups, T-shirts,[1] and internet memes, and even thirty years later still advocates fighting the tyranny of domestic felines in the guise of humor. 🐾

[1] https://t-s.fr/contents/t-shirt-comite-contre-les-chats_92_1_0.html

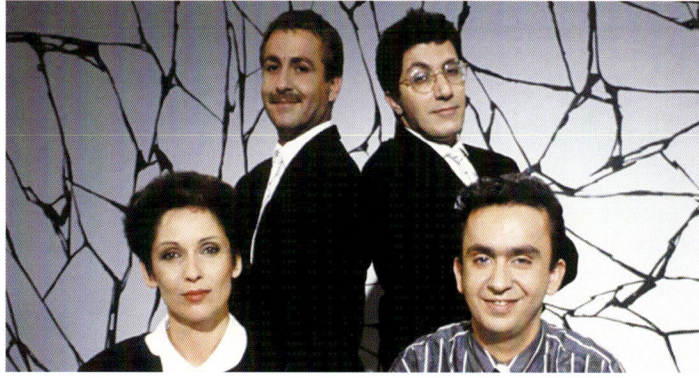

From left to right: Chantal Lauby, Bruno Carette, Alain Chabat, Dominique Farrugia.

SPEC SHEET

WORK: *Les Nuls, l'Émission*.
CREATORS: Alain Chabat, Chantal Lauby, Dominique Farrugia, Alexandre Pesle, Christian Borde, Jean-Marie Gourio, Marion Ciblat, and Jean-Michel Thiriet.
DATE CREATED: 1990.
DISTRIBUTOR: Studio Canal.
CATS' NAMES AND ROLES IN THE WORK: No cats are named or (hopefully) mistreated. They star in several of the show's fake commercials.

Cats: The Other Disney Stars

Although it was a mouse that brought Walt Disney success, cats were not to be outdone. His studio has regularly produced outstanding animated films featuring animals, especially felines.

Before taking an interest in cats, Walt Disney focused on wild animals, such as the tiger and panther in *The Jungle Book* and the various lions that appear in his movies.

Cats' Cousins

Starting with the production of *Snow White and the Seven Dwarfs*, the first animated feature released in 1937, Disney Studios has developed new methods to make drawings more realistic. To better render animals' movements and appearance, animators observed them directly. This approach is now standardized, whether for classic animation or CGI. While it's easy to observe cats, producing *The Lion King* (1994) required more resources. Before that, the company had already created lions with Prince John and King Richard in its animated version of *Robin Hood* (1973), but the film's anthropomorphism required less realism.

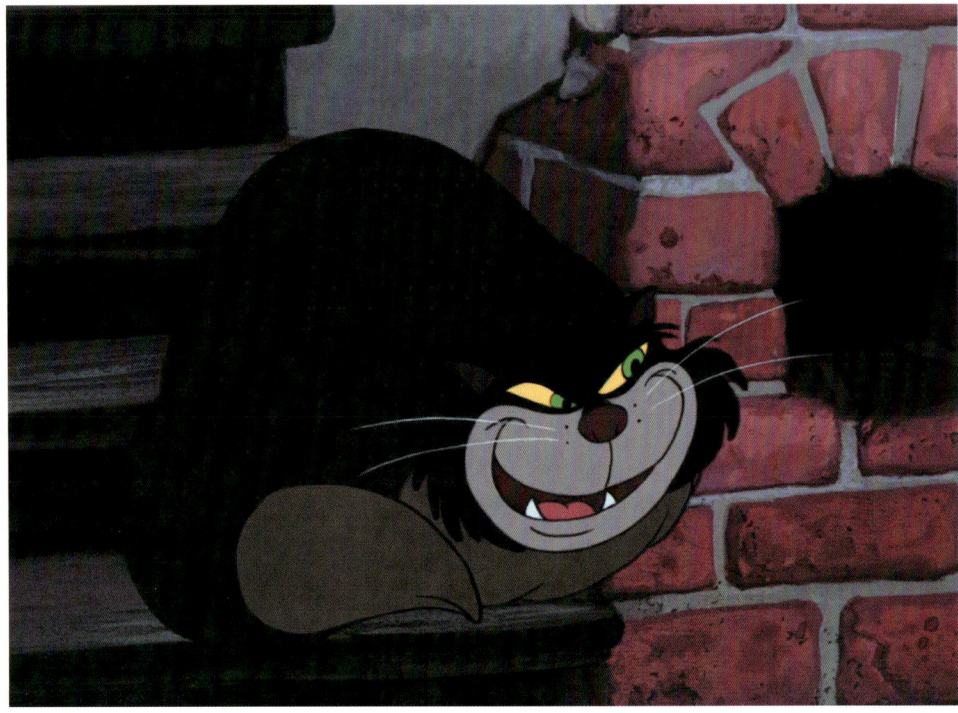

Lucifer in *Cinderella*.

Cats in Disney Films

Like many Hollywood movies, Disney films are rather simplistic. Whether transposing fairy tales or creating new stories with animals, it's common to see cats whose character is sometimes evil, sometimes good. The perception of the cat depends mainly on the context in which it appears. If the story features friendly mice, the cat will more often than not be an antagonist, endowed with all the usual faults. Sometimes, however, the narrative revolves around cats in leading roles, and the antagonists are humans or another species that, paradoxically, is never the dog. The animation's realism then emphasizes their cute, lovable side.

Lucifer in *Cinderella*

In Disney's 1950 film *Cinderella*, the young woman is bullied by her stepmother, who treats her like a servant. The stepmother shows affection for only one creature: Lucifer. The cat with the demonic name is a classic example of an evil cat. Loosely inspired by Perrault's fairy tale, Disney used its usual narrative tricks to brighten up a story that was originally quite dark and frightening. The studio's recipe for success included songs and comical talking animals, and *Cinderella* was built on this model. The young woman is helped by animals, such as

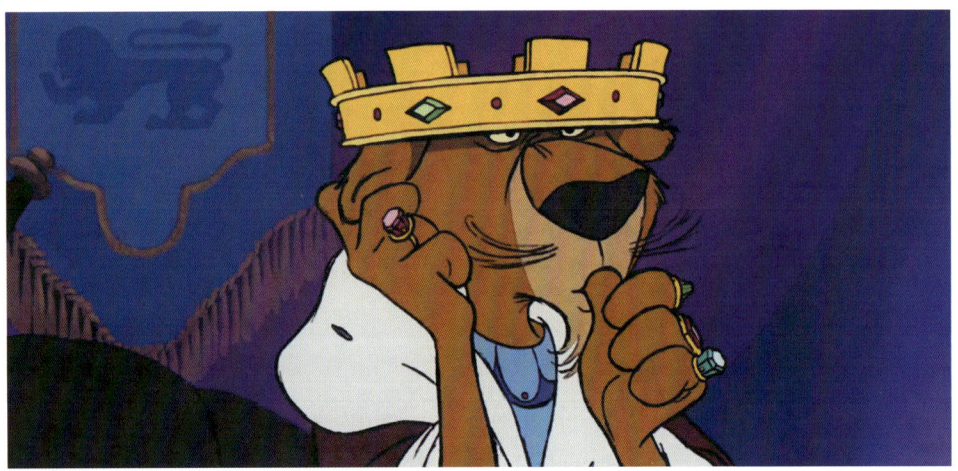

Prince John in *Robin Hood*.

her dog Bruno, birds, and even the mice, Jaq and Gus. Her cold, calculating stepmother is regularly accompanied by the cat Lucifer. He sleeps next to her, and she caresses him, making him the character closest to her. With his yellow eyes and sly smile, the feline regards the young woman as his servant, whom he ironically refers to as "Your Highness." Cinderella is deeply naive and refuses to accept that the animal can only be deceitful. "There must be something good about him," she says. And yet, the cat intentionally puts dust everywhere she has cleaned. Unusually for a Disney villain's sidekick, the cat is pushed out a window and can be assumed dead by the viewer. Lucifer's design and cunning smile would be used for that of the Cheshire Cat in the animated version of *Alice in Wonderland*, released the following year (see p. 90).

Lady and the Tramp

Lady and the Tramp was released in 1955, depicting the adventures of a dog who has taken a back seat in her family following the birth of a baby. She meets a stray dog, Tramp, and their romance leads to the classic scene of eating and kissing over a plate of spaghetti. Left in the care of an aunt with the newborn, Lady escapes in her owners' absence after being forced to wear a muzzle. The catalyst for this episode is the arrival of the aunt's Siamese cats, which are deceitful, evil, and manipulative. They try to eat the goldfish, ransack the house, threaten to take the baby's food, and blame Lady for the damage they've caused.

Like *The Aristocats*, the cats are now perceived as conveying racist clichés. They are indistinguishable and almond-eyed, have a strong accent, and appear to a deliberately Asian-sounding soundtrack.

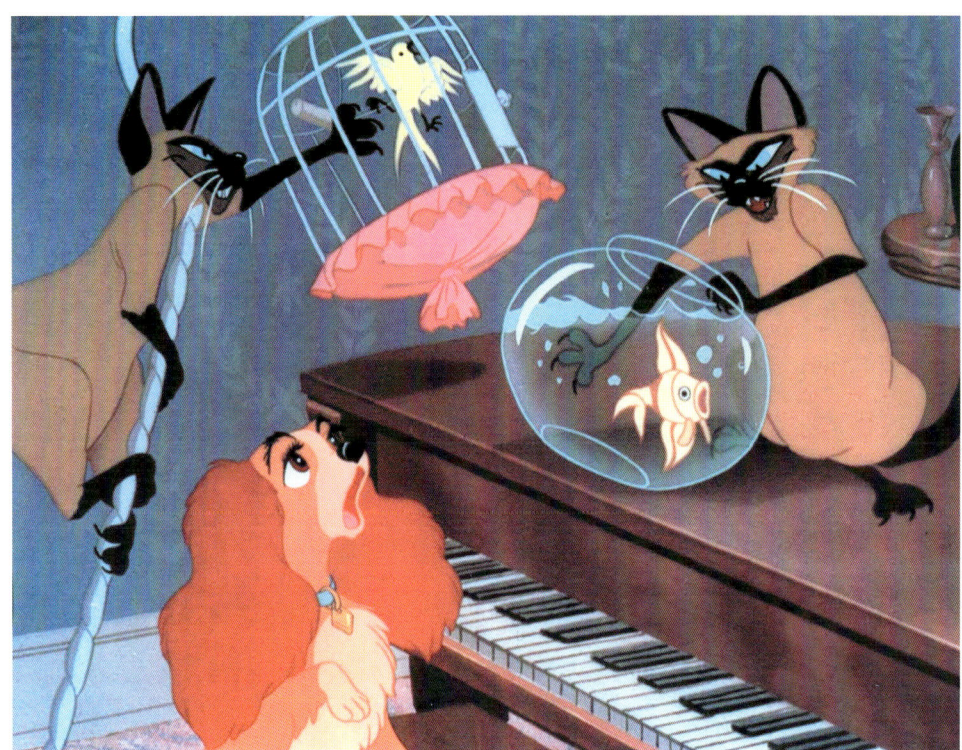

Lady and the Siamese bothers in *Lady and the Tramp*.

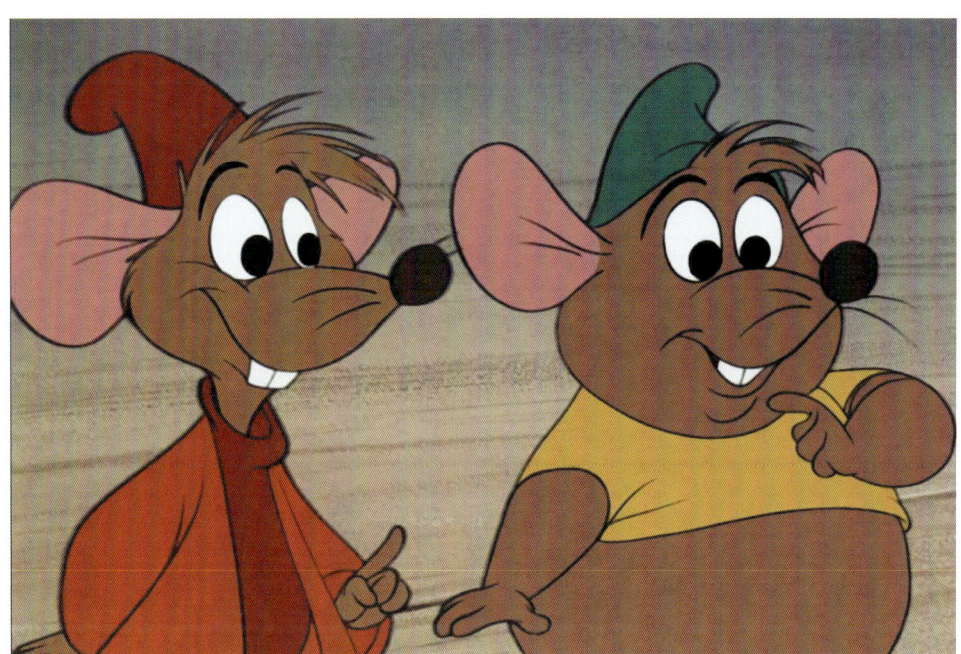

Jaq and Gus in *Cinderella*.

In 2019, Disney produced a live-action version that's fairly faithful to the original but changed the cats' song to suit the moral values of our time. Their role in the narrative and their cunning remain the same, but they are no longer Siamese cats. Their bodies are still slender and trim, but they're gray tabbies. Their accents are no longer Asian, but bourgeois. And finally, their song no longer incorporates gongs, and the instrumentation is jazzier.

The Rescuers

Released in 1977, *The Rescuers* tells the story of a young orphan's rescue by two mice from the Rescue Aid Society, an international mouse organization. Along the way, Bernard and Bianca meet Rufus, a cat with a rare role in fiction: that of a guardian. He's an elderly cat who works in the orphanage where little Penny lived before she was kidnapped. The brown feline wears a scarf and glasses and has a white moustache, accentuating his old age. The two mice come across the feline during their investigation. The two protagonists are afraid until Rufus reassures them: "I'm too old to be chasing mice." He's kind-hearted, and a flashback shows the cat's tenderness as he rubs against Penny's face and comforts her when she's rejected by potential adoptive parents. 🐾

PETE, A SPECIAL CASE

The quintessential antagonist of Donald Duck and Mickey Mouse in both cartoons and comics, Pete (also known as Black Pete, Pistol Pete, or Peg Leg Pete) has two particularities. The first is that since he is highly anthropomorphized like Goofy, few viewers or readers of modern comics realize that the crook is actually a big black cat with three legs, as the fourth one is artificial (and in the early days, was a simple wooden stump). The second is that he's the oldest character in the Disney stable, even preceding the famous Mickey Mouse. Pete made his first appearance in the 1925 short "Alice Solves the Puzzle." Initially a bear, he became a big cat in 1928 when Mickey Mouse became the studio's star. His role in American films was simple: to be the hero's antagonist (more or less sympathetic, depending on the era). This all changed with the development of Disney comics produced in Italy (and mostly reused in the group's newspapers in France), in which the scriptwriters gave him a girlfriend and then a nephew, often turning him into a sympathetic anti-hero, like the Beagle Boys.

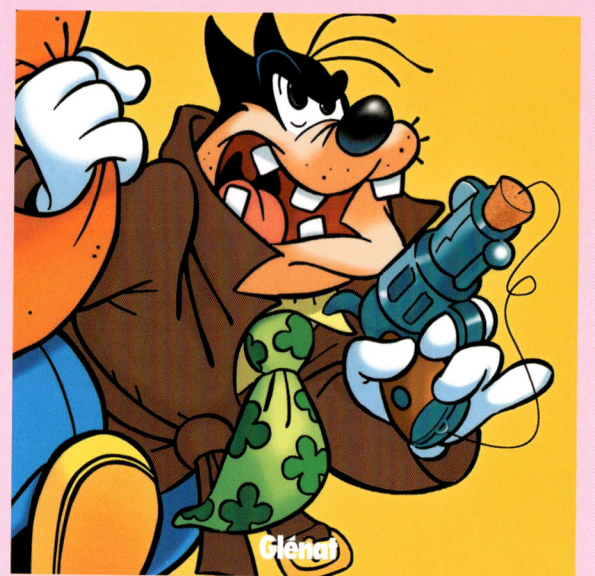

In the early twentieth century, a wealthy Parisian woman decides to leave her fortune to her cat, Duchess, and her kittens. Eager to inherit in their place, the butler abandons the cats in the countryside, where they meet the alley cat Thomas O'Malley.

Besides the typical Disney cuteness of the animals, thanks to the detailed animation and the finesse of the traits observed in feline behavior, *The Aristocats* is a light-hearted film, but it's actually quite profound and referential. The film is naive, and the main characters are innocent and mostly well-meaning. The cat family interacts with many animals, including mice, geese, dogs, and cats. The only hostile being in the film is Edgar, a human. And yet . . .

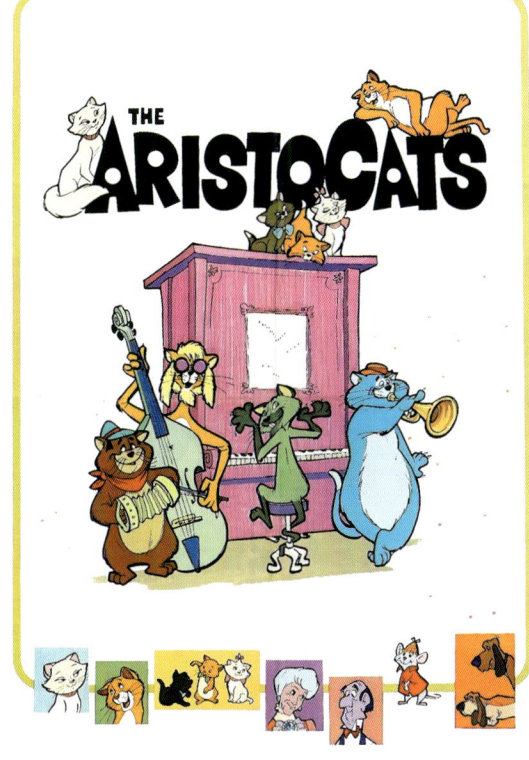

O'Malley, social background is mainly a comic element.

French Clichés

Set in France at the turn of the last century, the film features many American clichés about the country. Maurice Chevalier, a 1930s music hall star, was hired to sing the title song—"Ev'rybody Wants to Be a Cat"—in both the English and French versions. In English, he sings the *Aristocats* theme song with a thick accent over an accordion background. The scenes of the city, the Eiffel Tower, the accordion notes in the romantic sequences, and even the watercolor backdrops reinforce the film's clichéd imagery.

Duchess's education of her kittens, with its emphasis on politeness, is also a stereotype of the French-style education still prevalent in American society. She teaches them the arts, whether painting or music, and the kittens' names are themselves references to the arts.

Berlioz, the gray musician kitten, obviously refers to Hector Berlioz, the French classical composer. The name of the orange kitten, Toulouse, on the other hand, refers not to the city, but to the painter Henri de Toulouse-Lautrec. One scene shows the kitten painting at his mother's request. It's amusing to note such a reference in a Disney film to a painter known for his promiscuous lifestyle. The girl kitten's name, Marie, could be a reference to the singer Maria Callas, as she sings in the sequence about raising kittens.

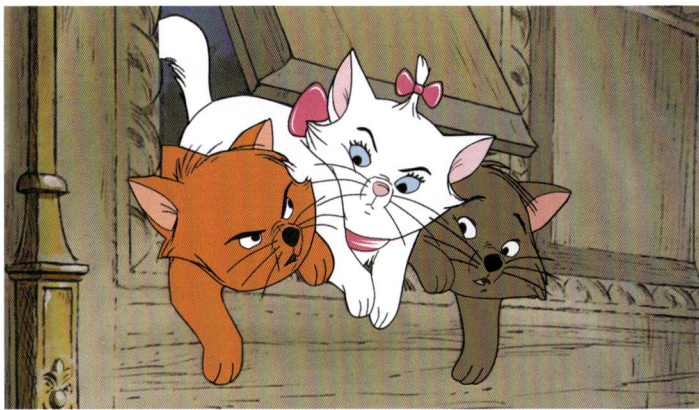

Toulouse, Marie, and Berlioz.

No Class Struggle for Cats

The last film approved for production by Walt Disney himself, it was released in 1970 and is based on the theme of class differences. Duchess and her kittens, Marie, Berlioz, and Toulouse, live in a big house with a butler, while Thomas O'Malley, an orange cat, lives in the country. As the family's protector, he teaches them how to survive in the wild and in the city. This contrast is also reflected in the music, with its mix of opera and jazz. The class difference isn't a real struggle, however, as Disney isn't known for its communist values. Used as a dramatic device in the romance between Duchess and

Anachronistic Jazz

Many Disney films have left their mark on our childhood with catchy soundtracks. *The Aristocats* is no exception, with music composed by the Sherman brothers, who had already penned many hits, including for *Mary Poppins* (1964) and *The Jungle Book* (1967). The jazz sounds already present in the latter are found again here, but this time with a group of jazz-mad cats, including Scat Cat, a trumpet-playing cat inspired by Louis Armstrong. However, the film is set in Paris in 1910, so the presence of this musical style is an anachronism. The musical genre appeared around this time in New Orleans, but didn't really achieve international success until the 1920s. However, in an animated film about cats who talk, sing, and play music, it's perfectly possible to overlook a slight inaccuracy.

The Film's Controversy

Other aspects of the film are more difficult to overcome. Although Disney films have a reputation for being timeless, passing down from generation to generation, this trend seems to have been challenged in recent years. A controversy over content in some of the company's works gained momentum with the launch of the Disney+ video-on-demand platform, where some Disney classics were accompanied by a warning: "This program includes negative depictions and/or mistreatment of people or cultures. These stereotypes were wrong then and are wrong now. Rather than remove this content, we want to acknowledge its harmful impact, learn from it, and spark conversation to create a more inclusive future together."

More recently, the films in question were removed from the company's children's catalog and then returned with a warning. *The Aristocats* is on the list of films with racist clichés. This controversy is centered on the appearance of a Siamese cat during the key musical scene, "Ev'rybody Wants to Be a Cat." He has slanted eyes, big teeth, plays the piano with chopsticks, and speaks with a strong Asian accent. Although he only appears in the film for a few seconds, objectively, this cat has all the hallmarks of a racist caricature. This raises the question of the evolution of a work of art and society's perception of it. 🐾

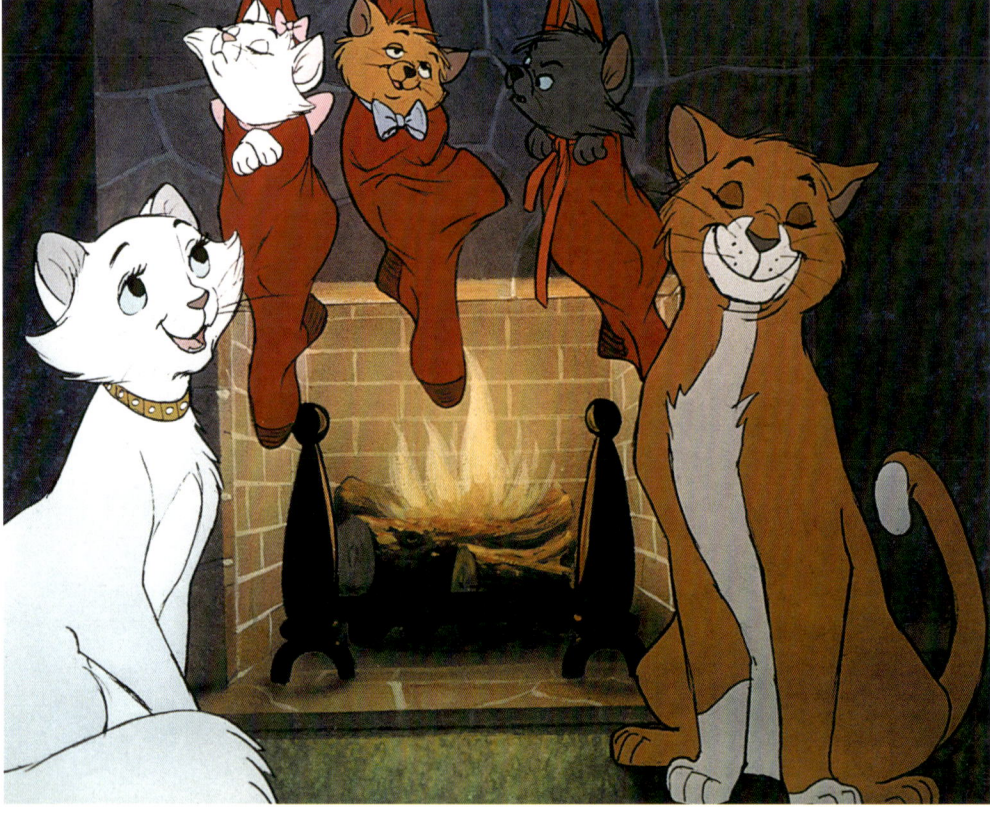
Duchess and Thomas O'Malley.

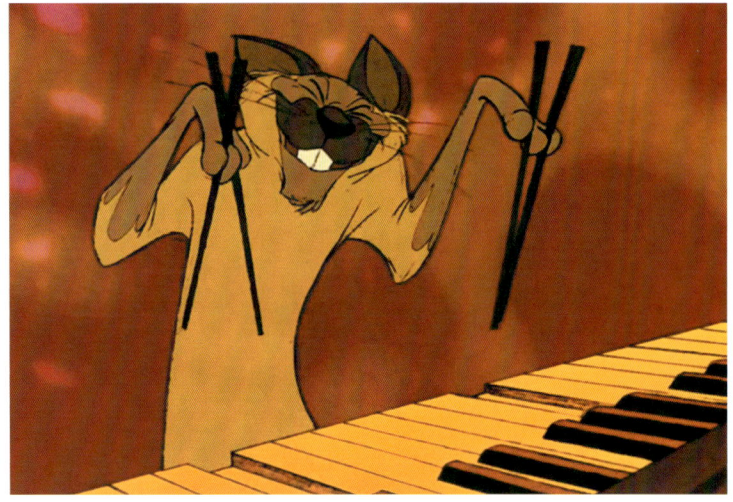
Shun Gon.

SPEC SHEET

WORK: *The Aristocats*.
CREATORS: Wolfgang Reitherman (director); Larry Clemmons, Vance Gerry, Ken Anderson, Frank Thomas, Eric Cleworth, Julius Svendsen, and Ralph Wright (screenwriters).
DATE CREATED: December 11, 1970.
DISTRIBUTOR/AVAILABILITY: Walt Disney Company. Available on Blu-ray and DVD and on the company's streaming platform.
CATS' NAMES AND ROLES IN THE WORK: Thomas O'Malley, Duchess, Marie, Toulouse, and Berlioz; they play the leading roles.

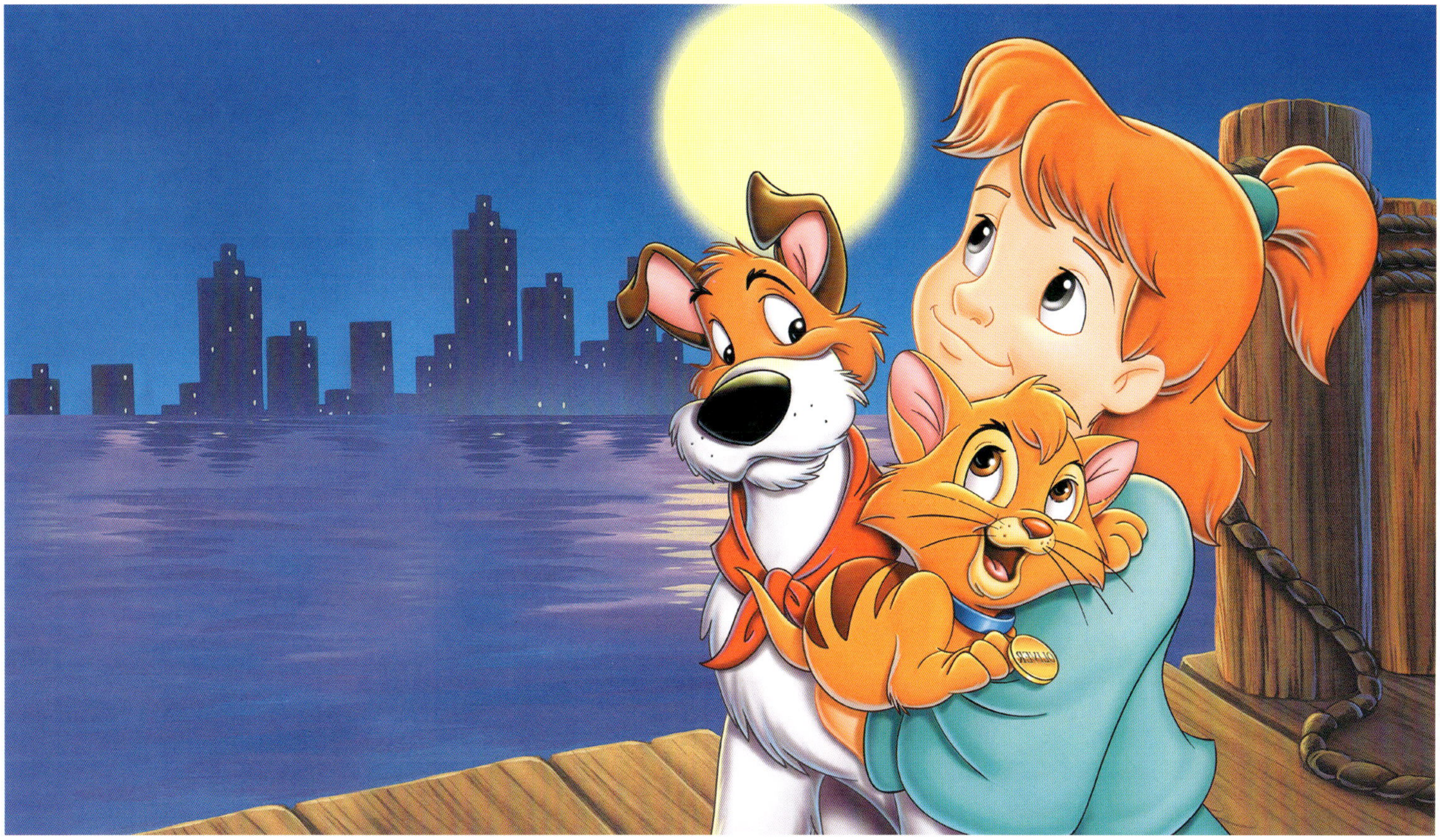

When Disney Studios tackled a Charles Dickens work, the result was Oliver & Company, *an adventure film with a kitten and a pack of dogs lost in New York, punctuated by songs such "Why Should I Worry?" which was nominated for a Golden Globe in 1989.*

It all began at Disney with a pitch (a very short summary that determines whether a film will be developed) in the office of the company's decision-makers. Jeffrey Katzenberg, who was then president of Disney animation and the future founder of Pixar, was interested in artist Pete Young's project to produce an animated version of the English literary classic *Oliver Twist*. The original work, which was published as a serial between 1837 and 1839, tells the adventures of a child left in a home after his mother's death. After much mistreatment, he eventually joins the Artful Dodger and his gang to commit petty theft. The novel is dark, set in a squalid London. On the surface, it has little in common with Disney's usually light-hearted world.

The company used its favorite method to make the classic story accessible to a younger audience: adding songs and animals. Oliver becomes an orange kitten abandoned in a cardboard box, while Dodger is a member of a New York dog gang. Filthy Victorian London is easily transposed to 1980s New York, where the social divide is omnipresent. The poor, like Fagin and his dogs, live in the city alongside the rich, like Jenny's family; the little girl eventually adopts Oliver. The sadness of the original world is toned down in the film, since the kitten is only abandoned and alone at the beginning. He soon makes friends, and Dodger's song sets a lighter tone.

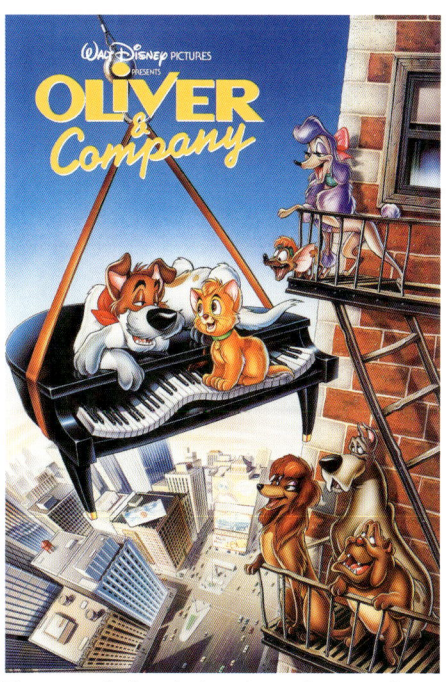

The result is obviously a far cry from the original novel, which was more a source of inspiration, rather than a real adaptation.

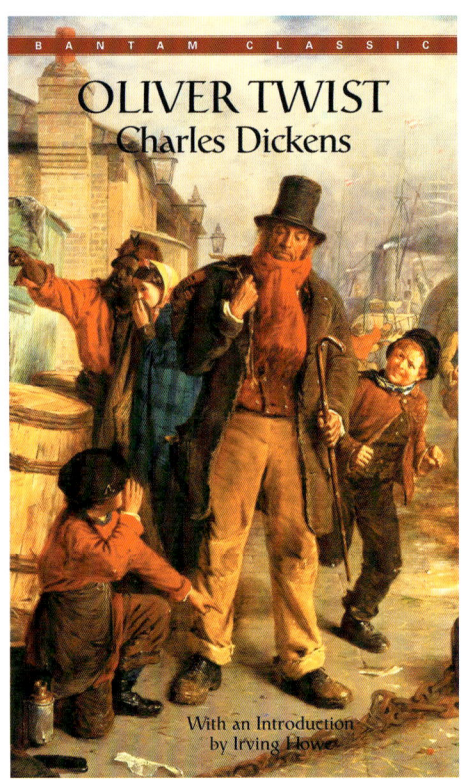

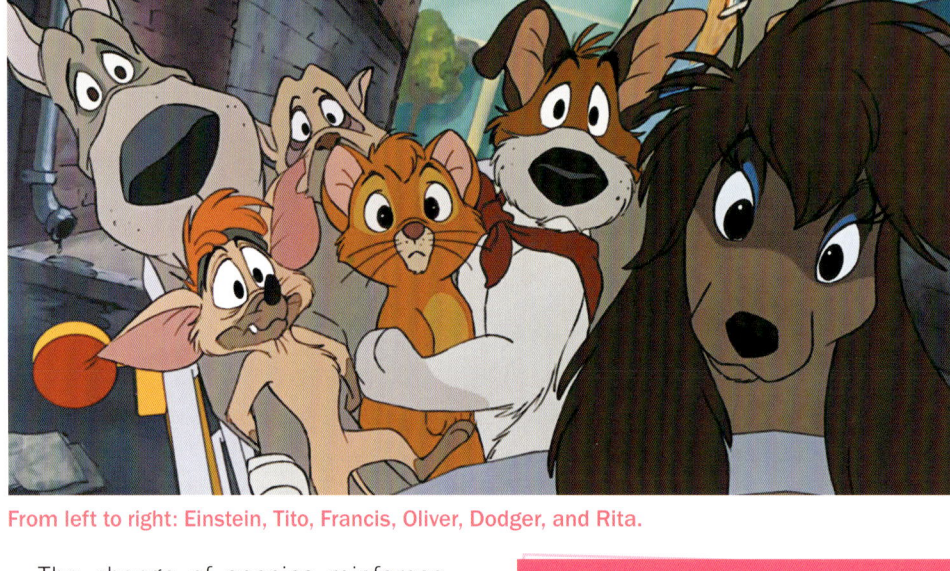

From left to right: Einstein, Tito, Francis, Oliver, Dodger, and Rita.

While Oliver joins a pack of dogs, the decision to make him a cat is undoubtedly an attempt to marginalize him. "Why would a cat follow a dog?" one of the dogs asks, realizing the irrationality of what later becomes a team. The kitten's role here is to be naive and cute, unlike in most fiction, where he's just the dog's antagonist.

The change of species reinforces the contrast more than if he had been just another puppy in the gang. And Disney's gamble paid off. The film was a success, grossing $74 million for a budget of $31 million, even though the critical reception was far more mixed. Considered a part of Disney's second golden age, the choice of watercolor-like sets for an oversized, inhuman New York now gives the impression of a drop in animation quality compared to most of the studio's films that preceded it, as well as those that followed. 🐾

SPEC SHEET

WORK: *Oliver & Company.*
CREATORS: George Scribner (director); Jim Cox, Tim Disney, and James Mangold (screenwriters). Based on the novel *Oliver Twist* by Charles Dickens.
DATE CREATED: November 13, 1988.
DISTRIBUTOR/AVAILABILITY: Walt Disney. Available on DVD and Blu-ray and on the company's streaming service, Disney+.
CAT'S CHARACTERISTICS: Small and orange.

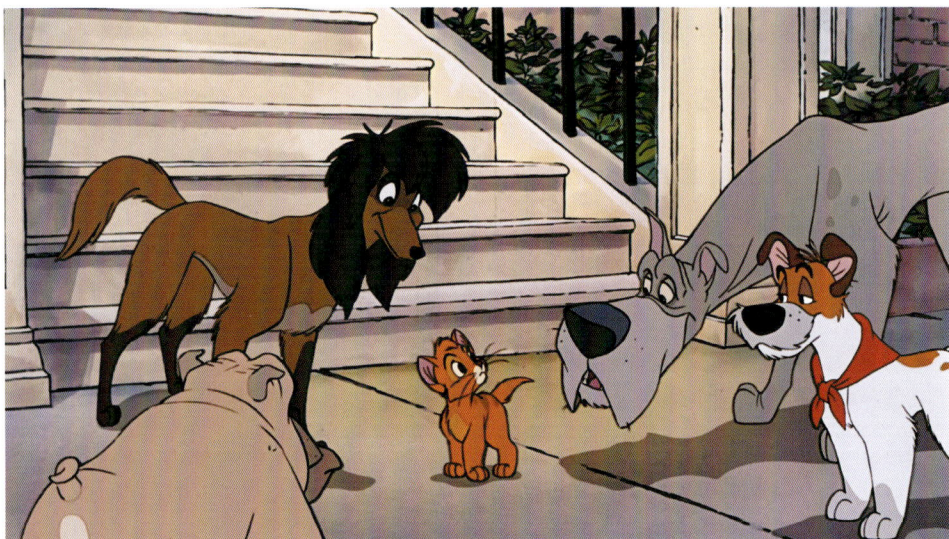

The Cat in the Hat

In Dr. Seuss's classic book of the same name, the Cat in the Hat invites himself into the home of two bored children on a rainy day. Sporting a big red-and-white hat, he encourages the children to get into mischief while their mother is out.

A mischievous, surrealistic cat, the Cat in the Hat knows how to play tricks and has a box, a sort of Santa's sack, containing Thing One and Thing Two, creatures designed to play, but above all to create bedlam in the house. He stands on two legs, wears a hat and a red bow tie, carries an umbrella, and wants to play without ever thinking about the consequences. He's the children's guilty conscience. Mr. Krinklebein, the goldfish, is his antagonist, playing the children's good conscience. He's the cat's target throughout the book, his natural enemy.

A colossal success in children's literature, its moral remains more ambiguous than in most of Dr. Seuss's works. After helping to turn the house upside down, the cat is sent away but returns to help the children clean up, so they manage to cover up their silliness. The story has an open ending, as the author asks the reader what they would say to their mother if they were in the children's shoes.

The cat isn't evil. He likes to play and have fun without thinking about the consequences. It's a trait that doesn't appear in Bo Welch's 2003 live-action adaptation. Starring Mike Myers as the Cat in the Hat, the film was a critical failure and met with lukewarm commercial success. Under the guise of creating a "cartoonish" character in both color and slapstick gags, the cat refuses to leave the house and is ultimately quite malevolent. This led to eight nominations at the 2004 Razzie Awards, including Worst Film.

Not all adaptations featuring the cat have been so unfortunate. In 1971, a medium-length film directed by Hawley Pratt offered a fairly faithful version made with the collaboration of Dr. Seuss. In 2012, Netflix created an animated series, *The Cat in the Hat Knows a Lot About That!* comprising some forty episodes made with modern animation methods; the choice of colors and the aesthetics of the characters are modeled on the original design. The cat is less childish and more kind-hearted than in the original version, and is more of a guide to a wonderful, wacky world than a troublemaker. 🐾

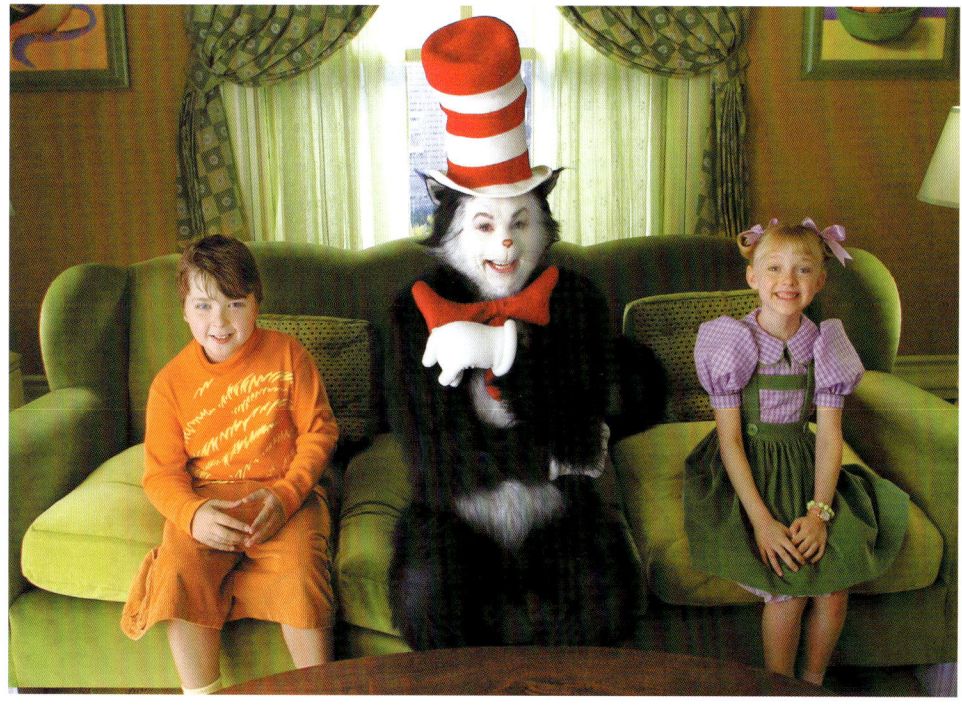

SPEC SHEET

WORK: *The Cat in the Hat*.
CREATORS: Theodor Seuss Geisel, known as Dr. Seuss.
DATE CREATED: 1957.
PUBLISHER: Random House.
CAT'S NAME AND ROLE IN THE WORK: The Cat in the Hat. An anthropomorphic black-and-white cat with a red-and-white top hat and a big red bow tie; he is one of the main characters.

Master Korin

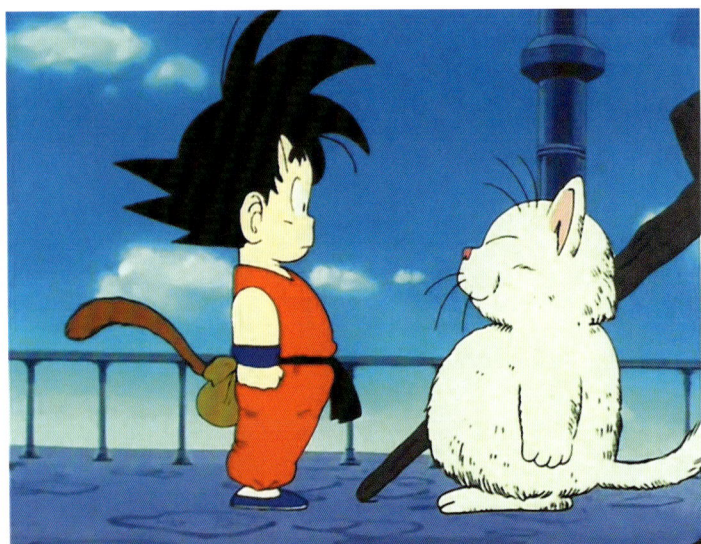

A manga classic, Dragon Ball *chronicles the adventures of young Goku, the monkey-tailed warrior. His adventures take place over several years and soon lead him to Master Korin, also known as Cat Hermit.*

Whether in Goku's quest for the crystal balls or in other works by mangaka Akira Toriyama, it's not uncommon to see animals talking without it shocking any of the characters. In Volume 6, the young hero climbs Korin Tower after being left for dead by Tao Pai Pai, a fearsome hitman recruited by the Red Ribbon Army. Goku hopes to reach the top to drink a legendary elixir that will make him strong enough to defeat the assassin. At the top of the tower, he meets Korin, a white cat he doesn't yet know is the master of the premises. He's small, slightly round, white, and looks gentle, with his eyes always closed and a shepherd's crook in his hand.

Master Korin trains Goku for three days, but the hermit reappears regularly in both the manga and the anime. His role in the storytelling is essential for two elements that will recur in the rest of the comics. In Volume 11, Goku returns to the top of the tower, hoping for the cat's help with further training, but the wise one has nothing more to teach him. He does, however, reveal the existence of the Castle of God above Korin Tower, which can be reached with the Power Pole. Training in this palace leads to Goku's transformation from child to adult, making the manga darker thereafter.

In addition to his wisdom, which regularly characterizes the episodes in the follow-up to *Dragon Ball* and the *Dragon Ball Z* anime, Korin brings an essential resource to the Z Fighters[1]: Senzu Beans. Initially, the cat emphasizes a bean's ability to satiate a person for two weeks. However, when he returns in Volume 11, the hermit uses the Senzu Beans to restore Goku's strength when he's on the verge of death. From then on, the characters no longer go into battle without Senzu Beans. At several points in the manga, they are used as a narrative dilemma when, for example, only one bean remains for two characters. More than eight hundred years old, his original name of Karinto is a play on words meaning both "Korin Tower" and the name of a Japanese doughnut. Carrying a name associated with food like many of Toriyama's characters (like Gohan and Vegeta), Korin's physique is said to have been inspired by his cat.[2]

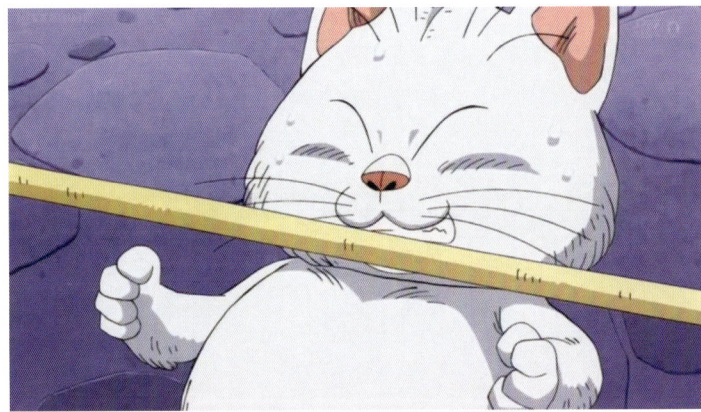

SPEC SHEET

CAT'S NAME: Master Korin.
WORK: *Dragon Ball*.
CREATOR: Akira Toriyama.
DATE CREATED: 1984.
PUBLISHER: Viz Media.
CAT'S CHARACTERISTICS: White-coated sage, martial arts expert, always carries a shepherd's crook.

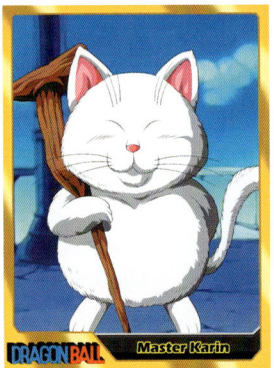

Trading card.

---

[1] Nickname given to the team of heroes in the series.
[2] http://www.dragonball-ultimate.com/encyclopedia/characters/karin.

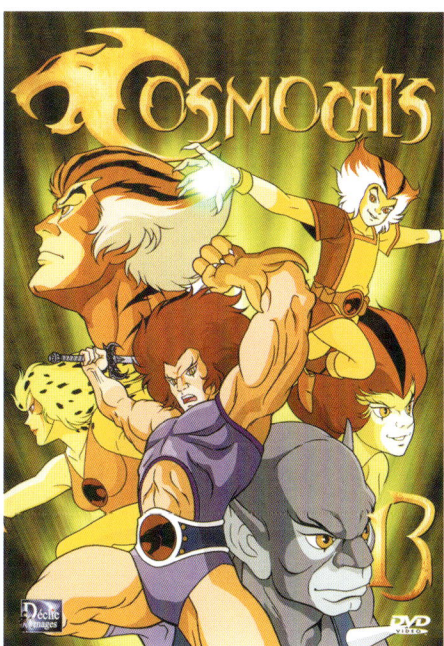

The original 1984 series.

The animated series ThunderCats tells the story of cat-like humanoid aliens facing off against a band of mutants inspired by various animal species for control of a mystical sword.

A pure product of American-style children's cartoons of the 1980s, the *ThunderCats* series is based on the hero myth and a confrontation between the forces of good and evil. Here, the forces of good are represented by the ThunderCats, a band of refugees who have fled the destruction of Thundera and are protecting the crown prince, Lion-O, who will become the hero. These aliens borrow their appearance from the Earth's beasts: the lion, king of animals for the Crown Prince; the black panther for Panthro; the cheetah for Cheetara; the tiger for Tigra; and domestic cats for Snarf and the twins, Wilykat and Wilykit, who are as carefree as kittens. Although they supposedly belong to the same species, each character has their own set of talents: Cheetara has

psychic abilities and can run very fast, Tigra can make himself invisible, Snarf understands all animal languages, and so on. They face off against a troop of mutants in the service of Mumm-Ra, a thousand-year-old mummy inhabited by "ancient evil spirits." These are represented by a set of humanoid animals whose potential to be likable and elegant is far inferior to that of felines in a children's world: a reptile, a monkey, a jackal, a rat, and a vulture. Their goal is to seize the Sword of Omens from Lion-O, which is the source of the group's power and a symbol of its authority. But to what end? The series ended after 130 episodes (four seasons) without a clear answer. And the second series, developed in 2011, and the third, from 2020, still failed to answer the question: Why take the sword? The 2011 version, co-developed with Japanese

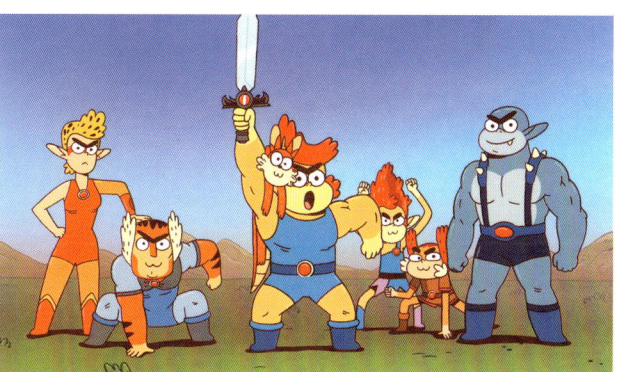

ThunderCats Roar.

STUDIO4°C, was much darker and more violent than the original cartoon, while the 2020 version, *ThunderCats Roar*, went in the opposite direction and was much funnier. Both attempts were unsuccessful. Nevertheless, in 2021, Warner Bros. announced the relaunch of a live-action film based on the series, which is to be directed by Adam Wingard, whose credits include the live-action versions of *Death Note* and *Godzilla vs. Kong*. 🐾

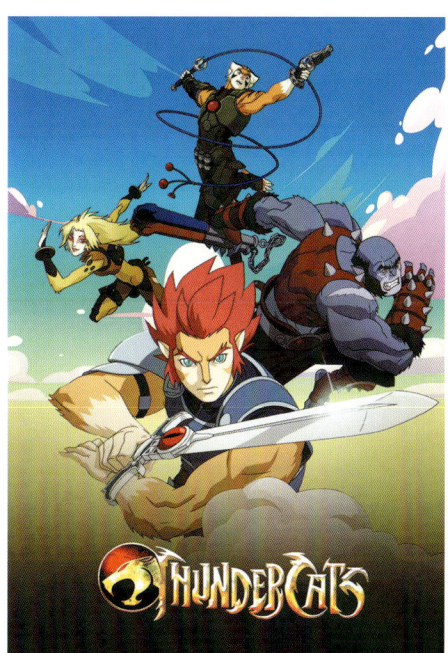

The 2011 series.

SPEC SHEET

WORK: *ThunderCats*.
CREATOR: Ted Wolf.
DATE CREATED: January 23, 1985.
DISTRIBUTOR/AVAILABILITY: Warner Bros. Available on DVD and streaming services.
CATS' NAMES AND ROLES IN THE WORK: Lion-O, Tigra, Cheetara, Panthro, Wilykat and Wilykit, Jaga, Snarf, and the others, who are the last representatives of a race of humanoid felines stranded on Third Earth.

Pet Sematary

Inspired by the death of a real cat, Pet Sematary is, according to Stephen King, his book that scares him the most.[1] Twice adapted for the big screen, in addition to its various morals, the story shows the cat in the terrifying role of psychopomp for the rest of the family.

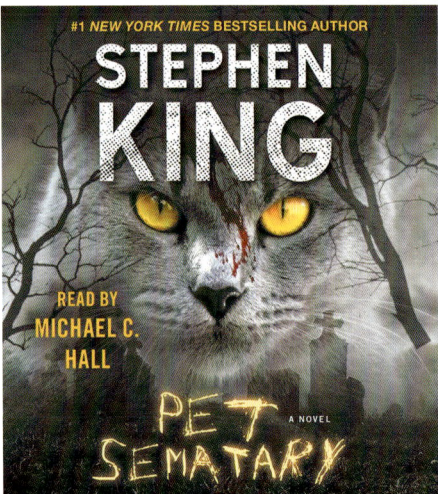

Then writer-in-residence at the University of Maine, Stephen King was inspired by the death of his daughter Naomi's cat, which was run over by a truck, to write the novel *Pet Sematary*. In it, a cat named Church is the main catalyst and one of two antagonists. When protagonist Louis Creed buries the cat in an ancient Indian burial ground with astonishing properties in an attempt to spare his daughter, Ellie, the grief of having lost a beloved pet, he sets in motion a vicious spiral that will ultimately destroy his family. A true Stephen King classic, written during the most prolific and terrifying period of his career, fans of the master of horror often cite *Pet Sematary* as one of their favorite books (along with *It* and *The*

Dark Tower series). Why? Because it's one of the books that best combines the supernatural, horror, and the tragedy of everyday life. Under the guise of terrifying us, he talks about finding the balance between protecting your loved ones and letting them live and grow, as well as the difficulty of mourning and coming to terms with the reality of death. As one of the characters explains, when talking about death, "[I]t's not such a bad idea to be on nodding acquaintance with it. These days . . . I don't know

. . . no one wants to talk about it or think about it [. . .], it just seems like people want to forget it."

To this end, Church plays the role of both catalyst and psychopomp. He's a catalyst because the various family members confront death by evoking his neutering to prevent him from being

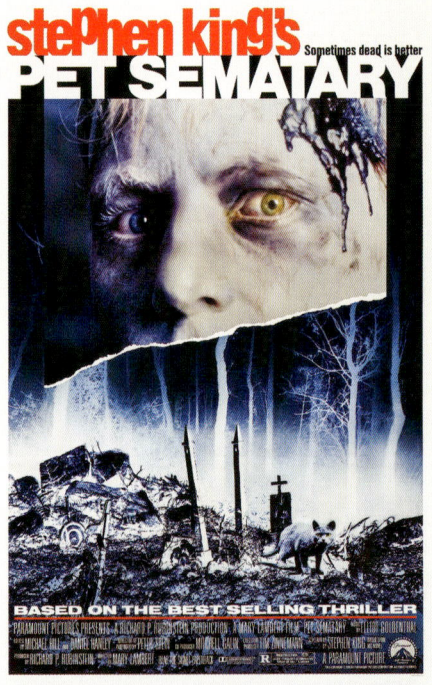

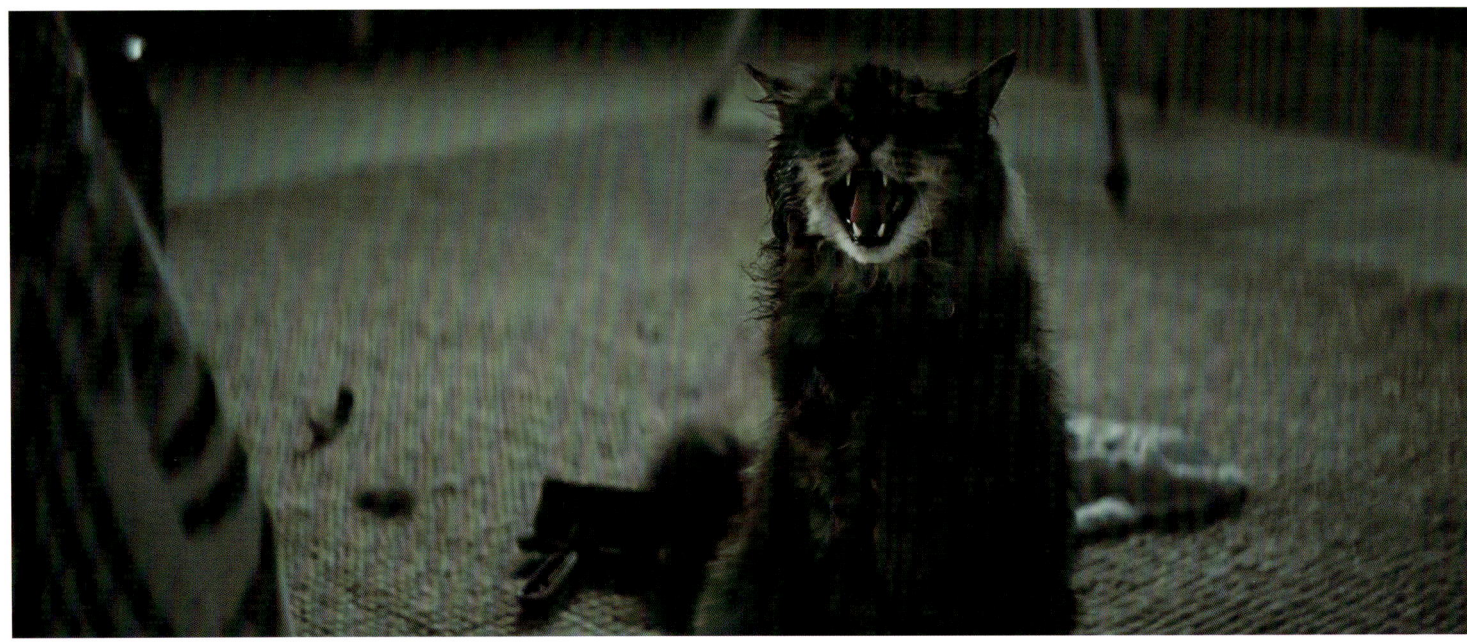

[1] In *Haunted Heart: The Life and Times of Stephen King* by Lisa Rogak.

TWO FILM ADAPTATIONS AND A SEQUEL

Stephen King is one of the modern writers who most inspires Hollywood. Among the various adaptations of his films, 1989's *Pet Sematary*, directed by Mary Lambert (also known for directing music videos and TV series episodes), is one of the few in which the author himself wrote the screenplay; he also plays a small role as a priest. This explains its faithfulness to the original novel, despite a few omissions. Although the special effects have aged rather badly, the atmosphere remains unsettling from one end of the film to the other, and certain scenes (such as the appearance of the ghost jogger or the flashbacks to Rachel Creed's sister) remain truly striking. Its closing theme song, *Pet Sematary*, was one of the most successful commercial hits by the punk band the Ramones. This prompted Paramount to commission a sequel, *Pet Sematary 2*, from the same director a few years later. Gorier and featuring a dog instead of a cat, the sequel was disavowed by Stephen King and remains largely forgettable. In 2019, Kevin Kölsch and Dennis Widmyer directed a remake whose main distinction was switching which child died. While in both the novel and the 1989 film, the younger Gage dies and comes back zombified like the cat, in this version, it's the elder child, Ellie, who ends up buried in the Native American cemetery. Despite having more technical resources, the result is not as frightening as the 1989 version. Nevertheless, the film also has a sequel, or rather a prequel, exploring the childhood mythology of the town of Ludlow and the creation of the pet cemetery. It's available for streaming.

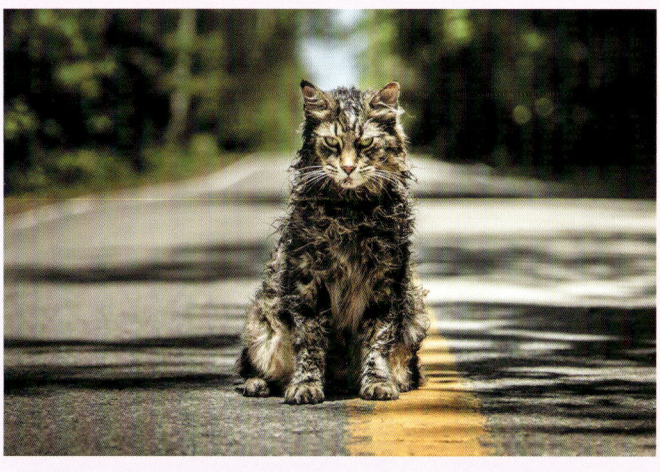

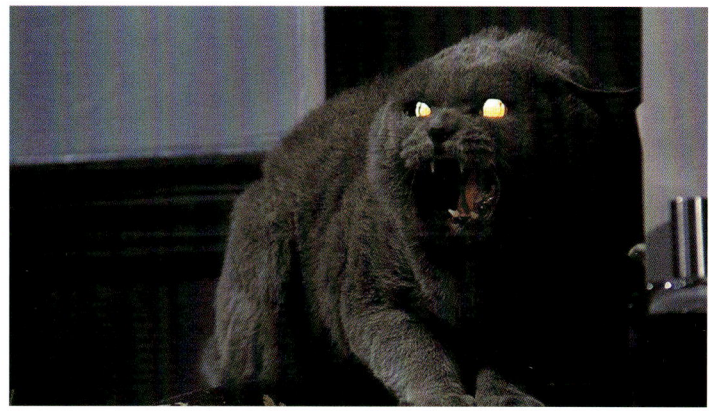

crushed to death on the busy road beside the house, with more or less rational and clear-cut reactions depending on age and experience. He's a psychopomp, or passer of souls from one world to another (usually from life to death), as his return from the Native American cemetery and his radically altered behavior foreshadow what will later happen to one of the children, and the final tragedy that will ensue. The cat made the journey himself once, and, as Ellie's father wanted to spare her the pain of mourning, Church had to return to "help" his humans make the long journey. By necessity, he's an evil psychopomp, much like the cat-sith, the black demon cat with a white spot from Scottish and Irish folklore. On the other hand, while *Pet Sematary* warns us of the danger of not accepting that all life has an end and that some lives are by nature shorter than others, Stephen King doesn't venture—at least not in this book—to explain how to accept this reality and overcome the pain it brings. 🐾

SPEC SHEET

WORK: *Pet Sematary*.
CREATOR: Stephen King.
DATE CREATED: November 14, 1983.
PUBLISHER: Doubleday.
CAT'S NAME AND ROLE IN THE WORK: Winston Churchill, aka Church, Ellie Creed's male cat. In the book, he is not described physically, except to say that he has agate-green eyes. In the 1989 film, he is portrayed by various British Shorthair cats, and in the 2019 film by long-haired tabby cats.

Meowing in Terror

Since Jacques Tourneur and the early days of genre cinema, cats have been key players in horror films. The addition of a feline, whether a member of the protagonist's family, the antagonist's pet, or the monster itself, is often enough to make a horror film even more terrifying.

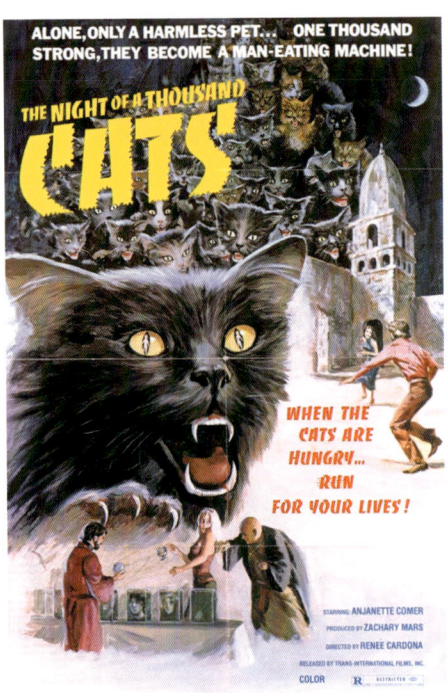

The many incarnations of *Cat People*, *Alien*, *Pet Sematary* and its remake, *House* (*Hausu* in Japanese), all the big-screen adaptations of Poe's story "The Black Cat," *Blood Feast*, and the horror-comedy *The Corpse Grinders* series prove it: Cats have a special place in horror films. Whether they're used as evil creatures, the monster's sidekicks, antagonists, mere extras intended to divert attention, the heroes of the story (as in *Sleepwalkers* or *Cat's Eye*, both inspired by Stephen King, in which the cats come to the protagonists' rescue), or a family member the viewer will worry about, horror films rely on the various preconceived ideas associated with cats to heighten the on-screen tension.

When the cat is a victim, its everyday companionship and cuddliness are exploited. In Sam Raimi's *Drag Me to Hell*, the protagonist must sacrifice her kitten to get rid of the Lamia pursuing her, with no other result than to show the desperation of her situation on-screen.

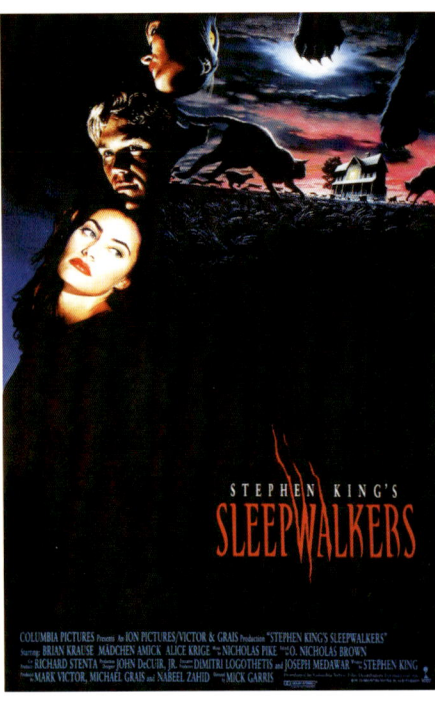

Similarly, in *Willard*, the protagonist, who has a monstrous affinity with rats,

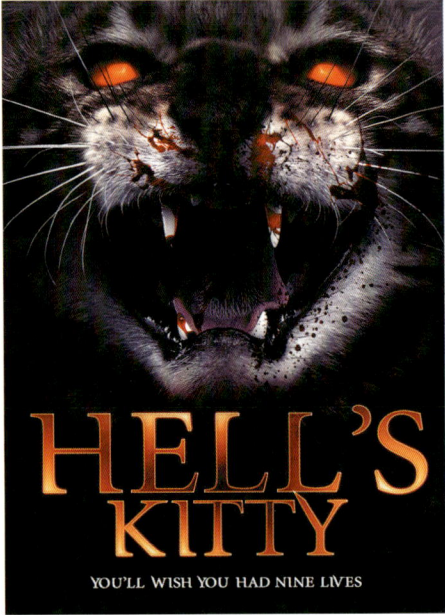

is given a cat by his co-workers. In the 1971 original, the orange tomcat gets away, but in the 2003 remake, he's mauled by his natural enemies. And then there's Rufus, the roommate's cat who serves as Herbert West's first resurrection guinea pig in *Re-Animator*.

Sometimes, the cat's role as psychopomp and supernatural detector comes to the fore. In *Let the Right One In* and *Coraline*, for example, cats warn the protagonists of danger and even

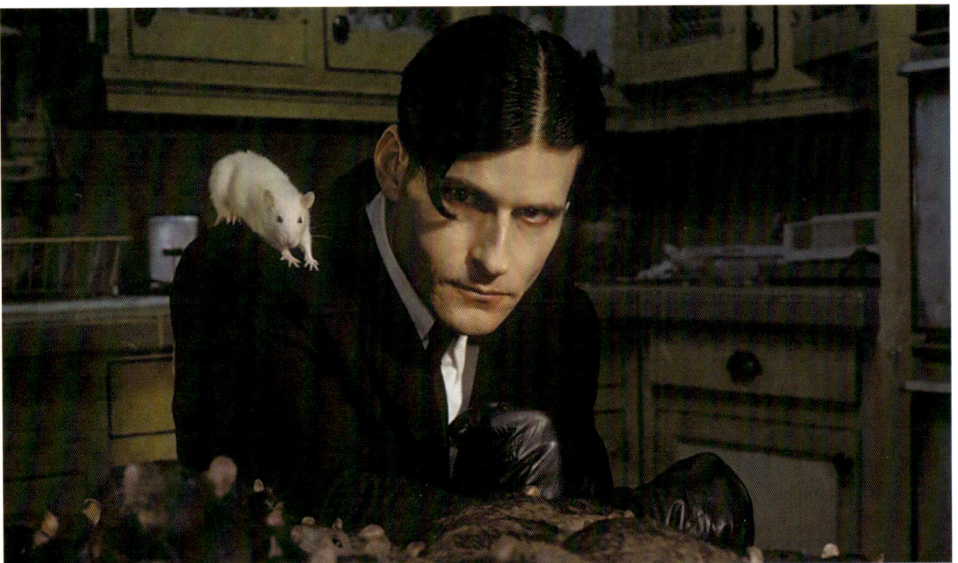

Willard, 2003.

lend a helping paw to get rid of enemies. This association with the supernatural is also reversed to make them the monster's sidekicks. In addition to the many witches' cats found in various films, in *A Girl Walks Home Alone at Night*, the vampire is accompanied by a cat who could be the reincarnation of her mother.

While *Strays* and *Uninvited* are rare examples of killer cats without supernatural intervention in the horror bestiary, monstrous felines often serve as mouthpieces for evil. This may be literal, like in *The Voices* (see p. 48), or through more classic possession, as in *House of the Damned* or the horror comedy *Hell's Kitty* (2018).

Finally, more inoffensive for the actors, and much less so for viewers with a heart condition, the cat is used to divert attention via "cat scares," which were invented in *Cat People* and have been reused regularly in horror films ever since. Such is the case of Chester, the black cat in *When a Stranger Calls*, Mar in *The Grudge* (whether in the original Japanese film or its American remake), and, more recently, the Persian belonging to the heroine of *Hush* (2016). With all these different variations, horror fans have learned to be wary of cats while watching out for them: Friend, enemy, or mere decoy, their presence in their favorite genre films is never as innocuous as it seems. 🐾

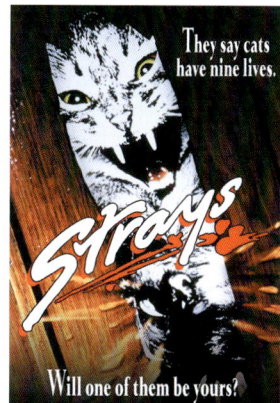
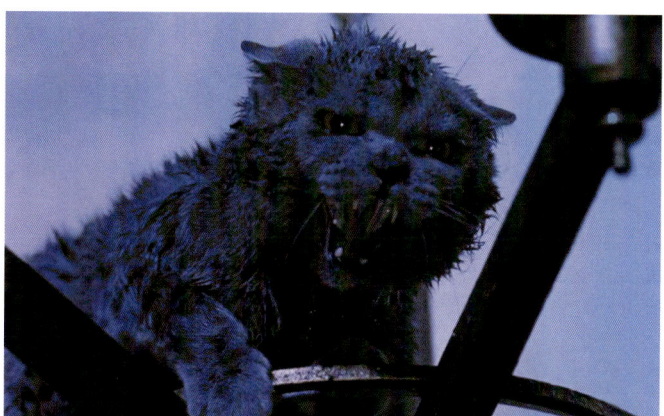
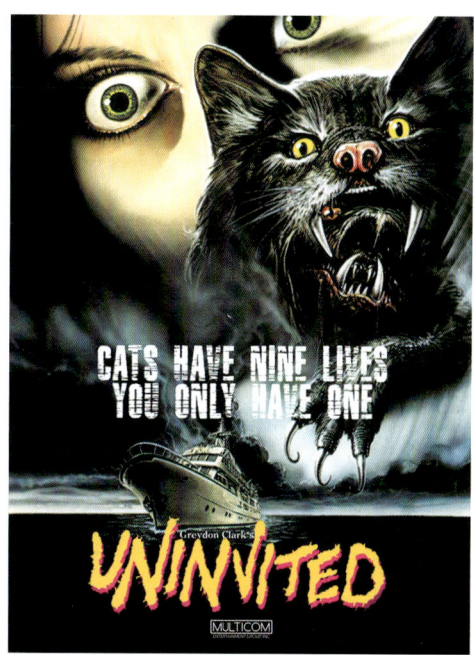
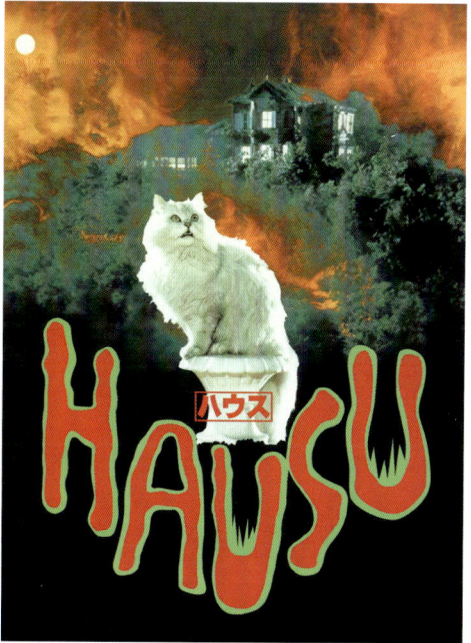
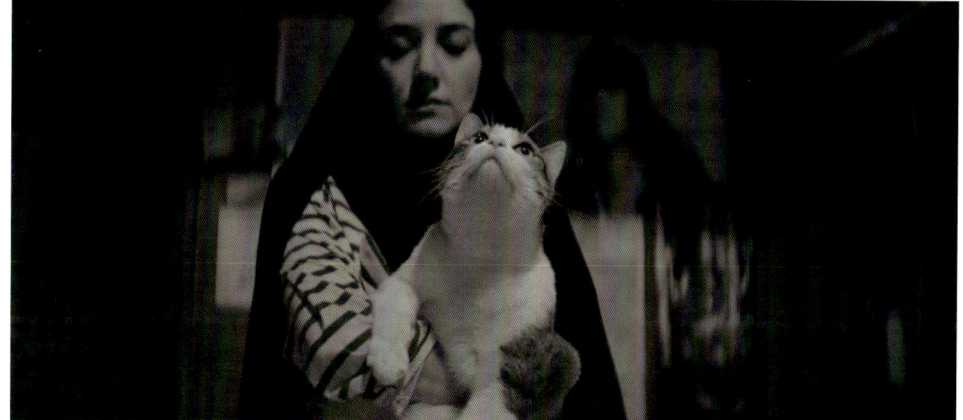

A Girl Walks Home Alone at Night.

Cats in the World of Harry Potter

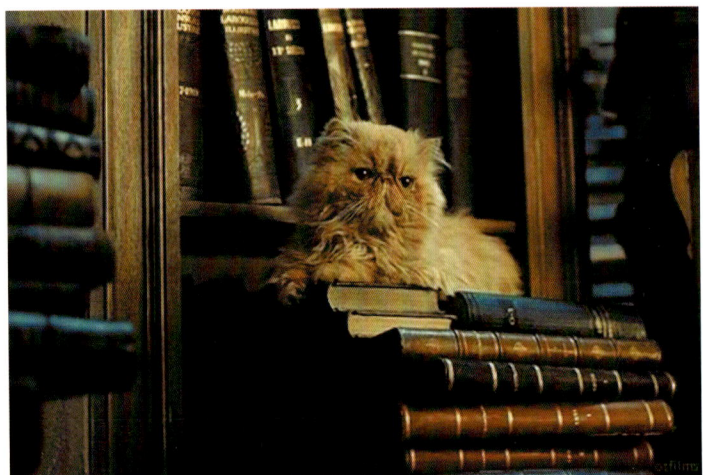

Hermione Granger's Persian cat Crookshanks.

Cats are abundant in the wizarding world created by J. K. Rowling. Wizards and Muggles alike enjoy having these animals as companions, although some of them have more intense magical sensibilities.

In her Harry Potter novels, J. K. Rowling has created a world that combines many legends of European magical folklore with the hushed atmosphere of English boarding schools. So, it was only natural that the author should take an interest in cats and their place in the wizarding world. As a general rule, among wizards and Muggles alike, the attraction or repulsion to cats varies from person to person. For example, Rubeus Hagrid, the Hogwarts gamekeeper and sometime professor of Care of Magical Creatures, declares in the very first book that he doesn't like cats because they make him sneeze. However, cats are among the pets (along with toads and owls, and in Ron Weasley's unfortunate case, a rat) that students can bring along to keep them company during their studies.

Contrary to the myths she was inspired by, J. K. Rowling's books don't take a clear position on the animal's role as good or evil. One of the series' two main cats is an ally of the Golden Trio of protagonists, while the other is a secondary antagonist. The first, Hermione Granger's Persian cat Crookshanks, has the added distinction of not being a simple domestic feline, but a cross between an ordinary (albeit pedigreed) cat and a Kneazle. This cat-like species can be identified physically by its lion-like tufted tail and long ears. Kneazles are sensitive to a character's aura and can spot unfriendly people. This helped Crookshanks understand the true nature of Ron's rat, Scabbers.

In addition to pets, cats are one of the favorite forms taken by Animagi, meaning wizards who can transform themselves into animals. One notable example is Minerva McGonagall, the Transfiguration teacher who is the Deputy Headmistress of the school and Head of Gryffindor House at the beginning of the series. In her animal form, she's a tabby cat with eyeglass-shaped markings around her eyes. Her Patronus—a kind of spirit/totem that can be used as a protector or messenger—is also a cat, as is that of one of the series' most detestable adversaries, Dolores Umbridge. Once again, the feline balance between good and evil is strictly respected. 🐾

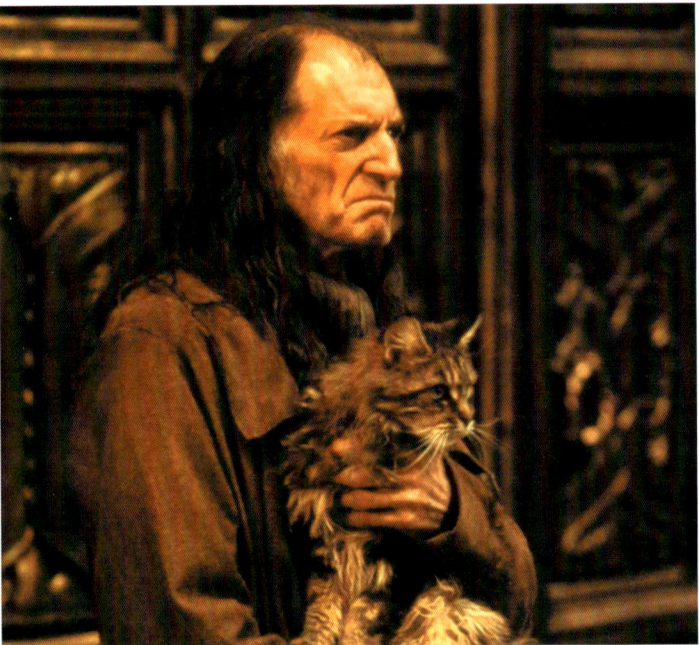

Mrs. Norris, the pet cat of Hogwarts caretaker Argus Filch.

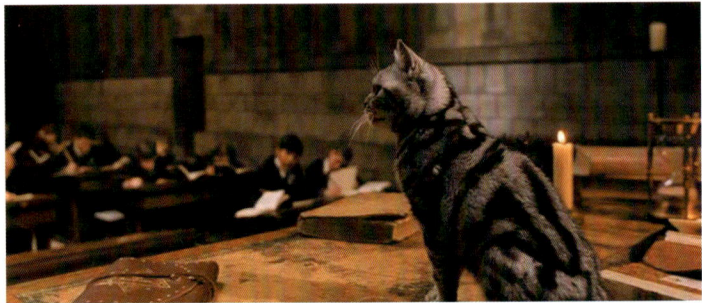

Minerva McGonagall in Animagus form.

Mystical
Cats

The Source of Many Legends

The animal has fascinated us ever since the first cat approached the first human dwelling to chase a mouse or curl up by the fire. It's central to many myths, both religious and otherwise. These myths themselves have been recycled in our favorite works of fiction.

Having lived alongside mankind since the dawn of agriculture but never fully tamed, cats are an endless source of myths and legends. All kinds of powers are attributed to cats, including the power to ward off evil spirits, just as they chase away rodents that plunder the crops and food supplies of the humans they live alongside, as well as the power to spread plague and disease or, on the contrary, to offer protection from them. Cats are strict carnivores and can sometimes be scavengers, but they often have a delicate palate and will turn away from meat that has been aged—unless they have no other choice. This habit allows them to easily detect corpses, as well as sick animals and people. In some cases, they'll reassure them and ease their death, like the cat in Stephen King's sequel to *The Shining, Doctor Sleep*. In others, the cats will run away from them. And based on observations, cats have earned a reputation as psychopomps and messengers between the afterlife and the real world.

In many civilizations, cats are honored as gods. The fertility of the species, their territorial tendency to always return to their nest (or the home of the humans with whom they live), their hunting habits (often at dawn or dusk), their ability to see in the dark, their meticulous cleanliness, and the phosphorescence of their eyes have all contributed to making cats mysterious creatures.

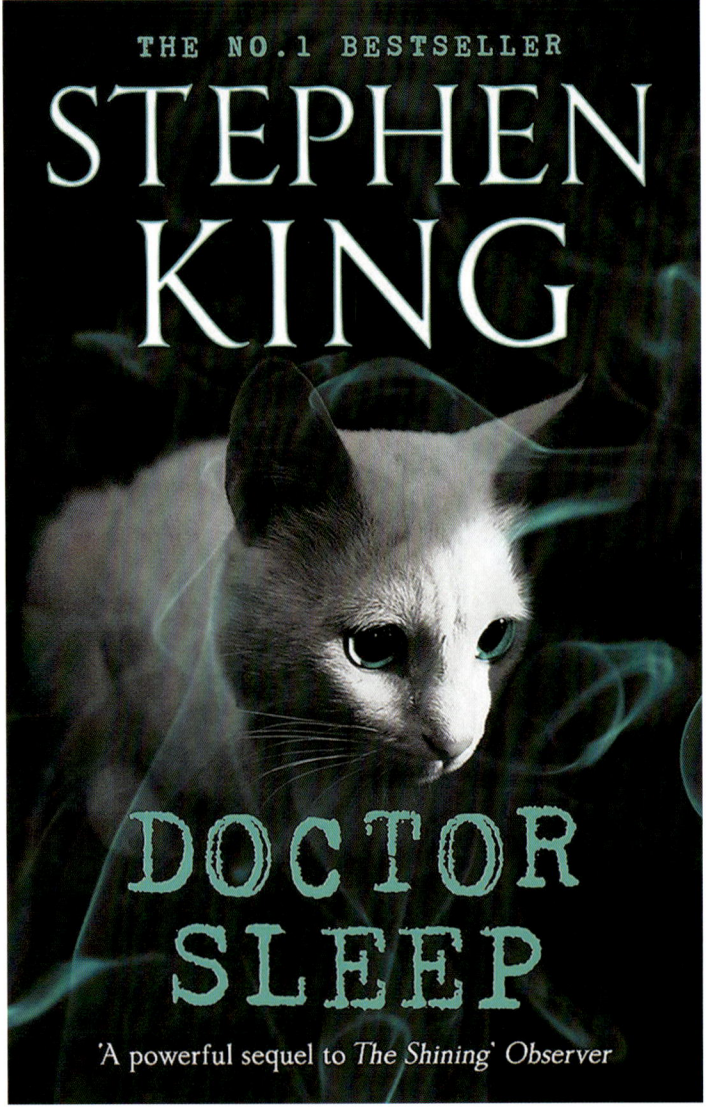

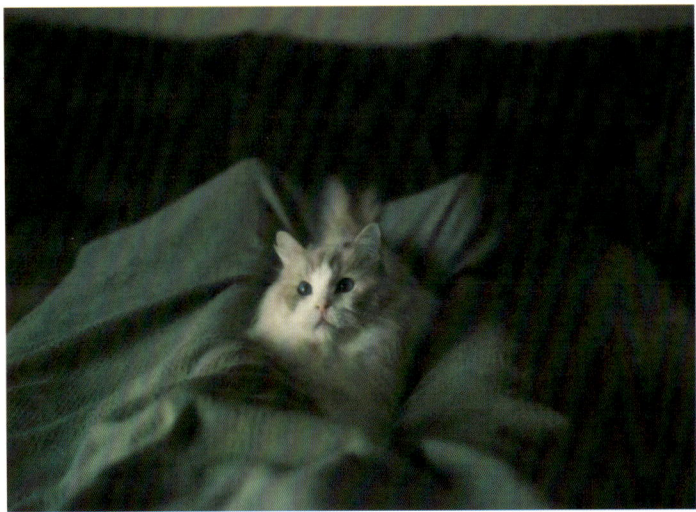

Azrael, the cat in *Doctor Sleep*, settles on the beds of hospice patients just before they're about to die.

When considered a god, or rather a goddess, a cat's role is twofold. Most often associated with fertility and protection, the divine cat is likely to be angry and destructive. This is true of the most famous of cat goddesses, the Egyptian Bastet. Not only was her worship the cause of a veritable carnage of cats and kittens that were mummified as votive offerings, but she herself was a warrior by night, too dangerous in her form as the lioness Sekhmet, as well as being a protector of young children by day and a music lover at all times. Mishipeshu, the panther that lives under the waters of the First Nations in the Great Lakes region, can also be destructive, causing storms, whirlpools, and drownings, but can protect travelers and guarantee abundant fishing for those who are hungry.

When downgraded from gods to mere spirit familiars, cats retain their great versatility. Sometimes, they're the pets of

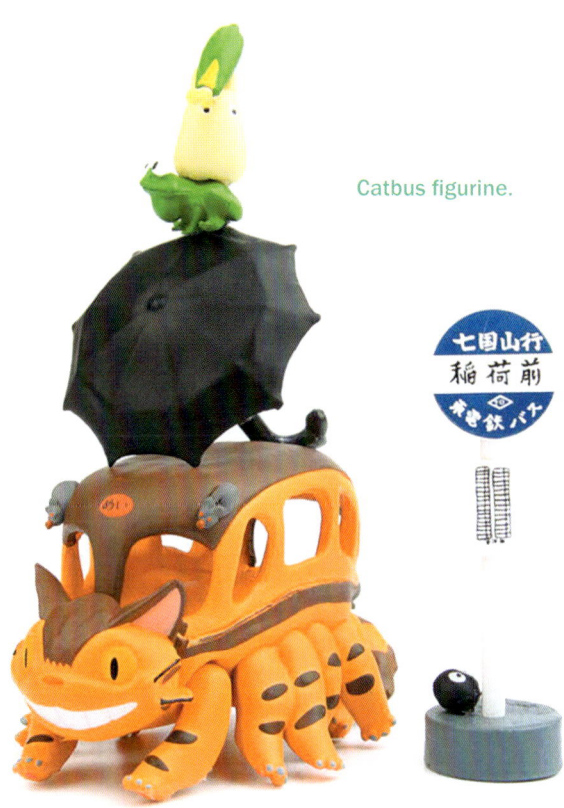

Catbus figurine.

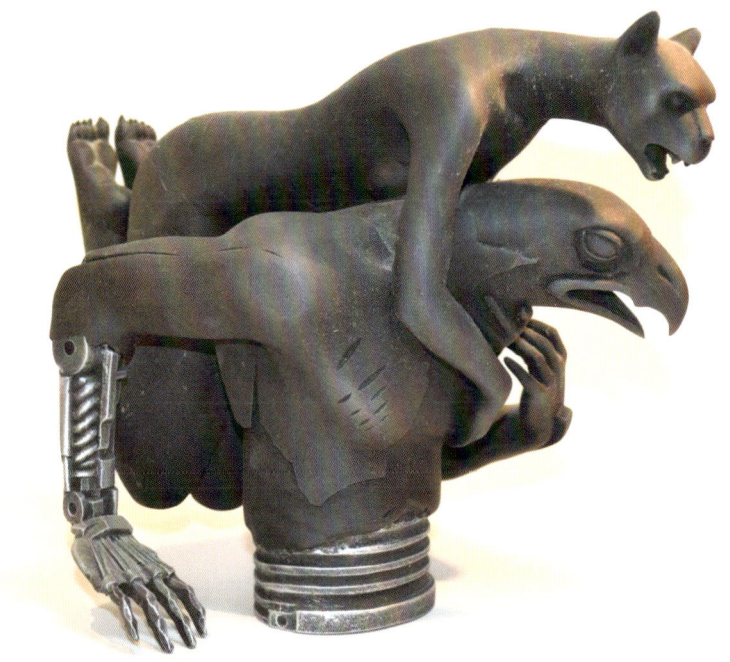

Bastet and Horus, based on Enki Bilal's *The Nikopol Trilogy*.

magicians and witches, like the fictional Salem, Sabrina's cat in the comics and TV series, or Jiji, who accompanies the young witch Kiki in Hayao Miyazaki's film. Sometimes, they serve as more or less reliable guides. The Cheshire Cat offers good advice, but can you really take advice from a drug addict who claims to be crazy? And Luna and Artemis have a hard time guiding the various Sailors when they're not bickering amongst themselves. At times, cats denounce and reveal something that's been hidden. This is notably the case of the unfortunate tomcat in Edgar Allan Poe's "The Black Cat," or more recently, the role of Lying Cat in the *Saga* series by Brian K. Vaughan and Fiona Staples. Sometimes, those around them don't get the message at all, as in Emir Kusturica's *Black Cat, White Cat*, in which only attentive viewers are able to decipher the warnings of the two animals. While cats' mystical side is sometimes combined with other attributes, such as their supposed affiliation with the devil since at least the Middle Ages in Europe, or the various feline monsters of Asian folklore, some of their roles are unique. This can be explained by the mixture of familiarity and strangeness we feel for these independent creatures that have shared the fate of the human race for over ten thousand years, without ever having been completely tamed. 🐾

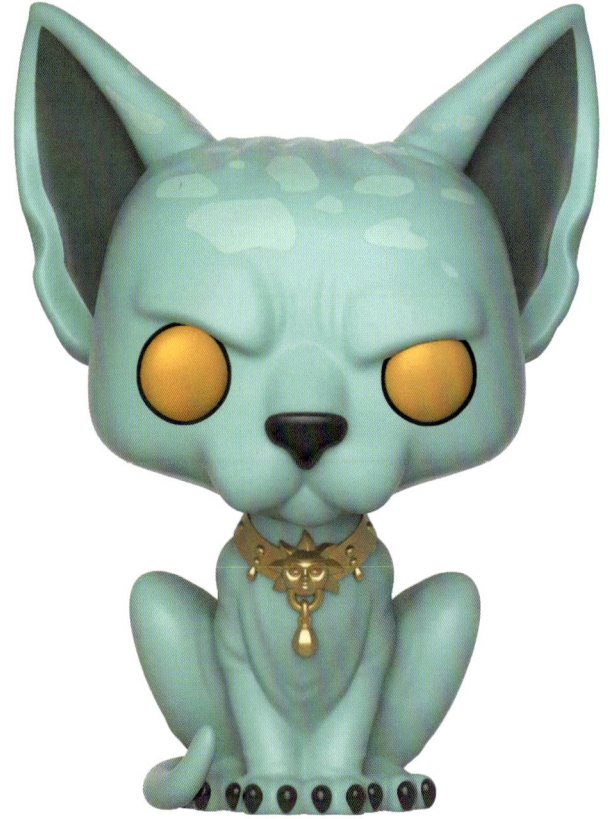

Lying Cat figurine.

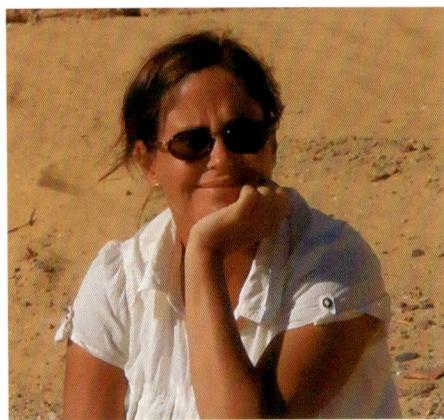

**Cécile Callou,
Archaeozoologist at
the French National
Museum of Natural
History**

**"With cats, we haven't
achieved complete
domestication."**

*Cécile Callou, a specialist in the
shared history of human beings
and domesticated animals, traces
the history of our encounters
with small cats and how this
companionship has evolved and
changed both species.*

How did cats become domesticated?

There's some debate, depending on
who you ask. What is a domesticated
animal? You'll get a slightly different
answer, but you can be sure that it
reflects a process with stages. And
this is especially true with cats. I used
to have great discussions with my
colleague, Jean-Denis Vigne. [1] He was
the one who discovered the oldest cat
buried on the island of Cyprus, and he
doesn't have a cat. I think that's the
difference, too. It's whether you have a
cat or you don't. He was talking about
the domestication of cats. As I also
have cats, I said to him, "But you know,
cats domesticate us, too. I mean, we're
tamed by the cat, because the cat can
do just about anything it wants with us."
If a cat wants to leave and find another
master, he'll do it without any problem.
He can do it, whereas with a dog, it's a
lot more complicated.

When did the relationship between cats and humans begin?

How did they meet? A lion is a big
cat. When we use the term "cat,"
we're talking about felines, and there
were wild felines in many places, on
many continents. Domestication is a
complex, multistage process. First,
there has to be contact. With cats, this
happened when people began farming
and building granaries. Felines came
to eat around these granaries because
they attracted mice. This happened
in the Neolithic period, although the
date of the Neolithic era varies from
continent to continent. And, as with all
domestication, all it took was a litter
of kittens nearby. Humans must have
taken kittens and raised them or kept
them close by as mouse hunters. One
constant in cats is that they have always
been, and still are, mouse hunters. The
shift toward becoming a pet was
actually quite recent. Whatever we want
from cats, even magnificent breeds that
are incapable of hunting anything, we
think of them as hunters.

Was only one species of feline involved in this process?

For a long time, when we said "cats,"
we weren't sure which cats we were
talking about. It took a lot of time for cat
genetics to be properly analyzed. First,
something happened in the Near East;
there was a wildcat there, *Felis silvestris
lybica*, but there was also one in Europe
(*Felis silvestris silvestris*), plus *Felis
silvestris ornata* in Central Asia and
other species in China, for example.
There were several moves to get closer
to each other in all these areas. This
all became clearer in 2009, so it's very
recent. Today, we have proof that all our
domestic cats are descended from the
lybica line.

Is it possible to cross a domestic cat with a European wildcat, for example?

Yes, no problem at all. But wildcats are
anthrophobic and won't get close to
humans. Their heads aren't quite the
same: They're much bigger, and their

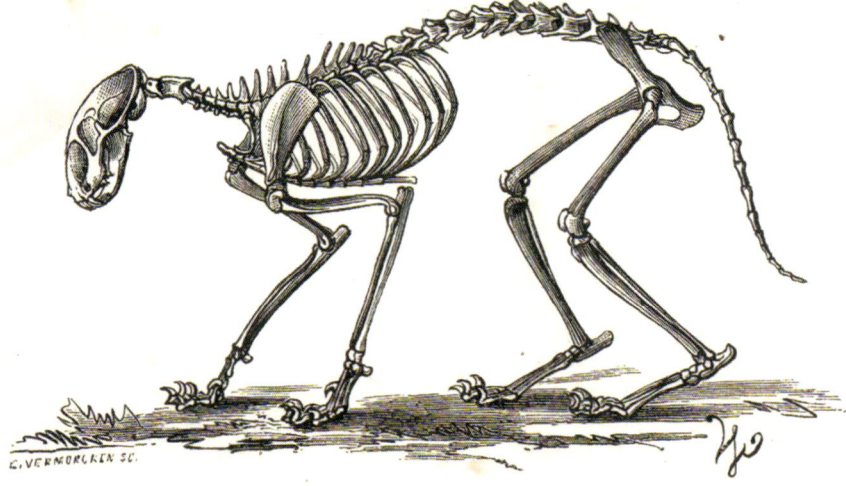

FIG. 2. — Squelette de Chat.

Felis silvestris catus, 1890.

[1] See "D'où viennent nos chats?" by Jean-Denis Vigne, *Espèces* No. 33, September 2019.

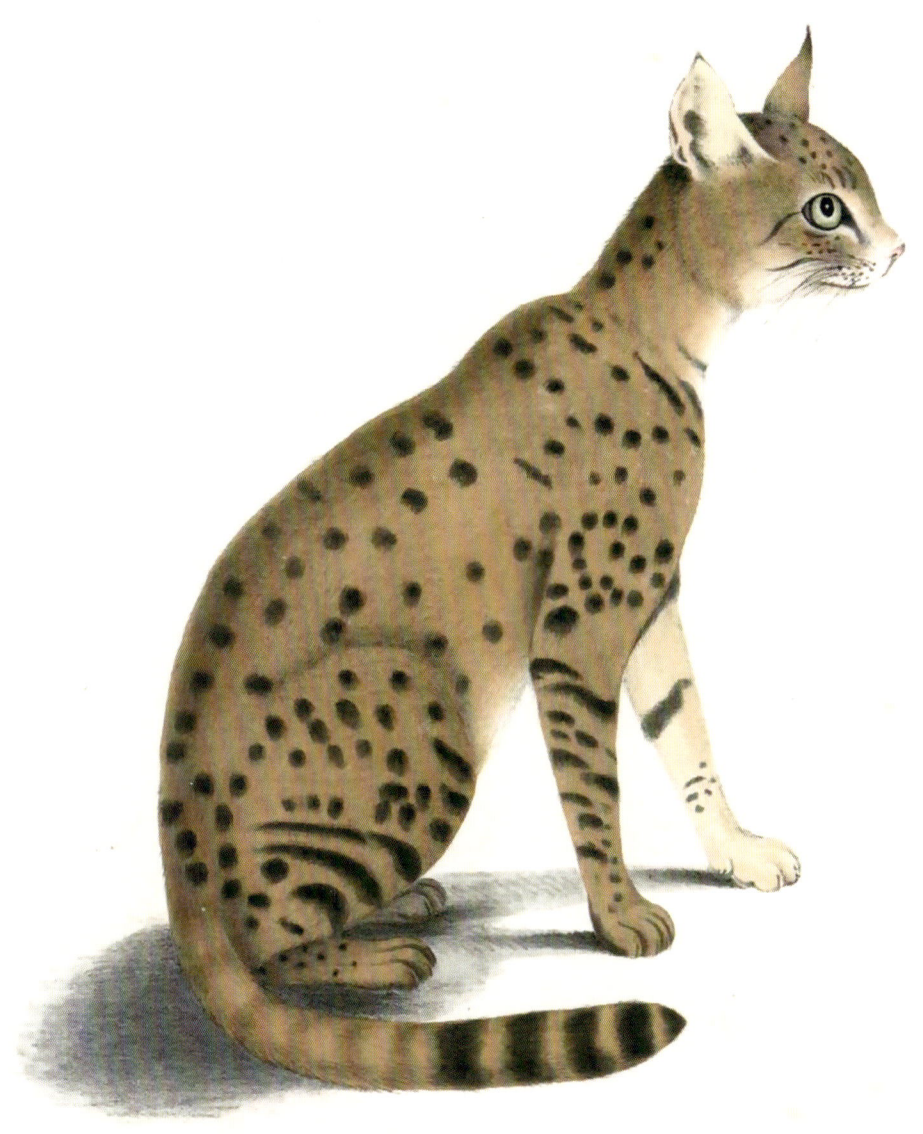

Felis silvestris ornata, Thomas Hardwicke.

and dog owners aren't the same, and cat owners are very happy with their independence. Cat owners like to have their own territory, whereas dog owners are much more interested in controlling their pets. So, I don't think it's quite the same thing. The other point, which is why I think the number of cats in households is exploding compared to the number of dogs, is that you can go away for two or three days over the weekend and leave your cat with no worries. But you can't do that with a dog.

Has the company of cats changed us?

I think it has changed us, but only very recently: when they came into our houses, and we started spoiling them during the industrial age. Before that, and even today in the countryside, cats can be in the house; they can be outside; they're very noticeable. In urban areas, cat owners like their cats to stay home for the cuddly aspect, and I think this is a very recent development. For many people, having a cat means having a nice companion who doesn't grumble, who may sometimes pout a bit, but who is sometimes much more pleasant than a human companion.

How were cats originally perceived?

Cats have been found in graves and the like, so were they buried with humans? In Egypt, don't get me wrong, they've often been found alongside humans, but in fact, that's not how they were seen in Egypt. There was a cult of animals in general. There were several series of cults in different eras. There was a period when single animals were worshipped. And then there was a shift toward a cult for what we call "plural" animals, and that's where we find cats, dogs, ibises. And then we move on to the industrial scale of mummification. There's a place of worship with a temple

ears are shorter. They avoid humans at all costs.

Unlike dogs, cats haven't evolved much from a physical point of view since Neolithic times, have they?

Well, no! Cats are still mouse hunters. They're still strict carnivores, even with dry food. They're still hunters, and their flexibility hasn't changed at all. If you look at their skeletons, today's cats, even those of highly developed breeds, aren't very different from wildcats or

cats domesticated five hundred years ago. In time, we'll start to see things, but they will remain minute differences compared to the dog, where you have a bull terrier and a Chihuahua. It's no longer the same animal.

Could it be because you don't need to change a cat's character to get what you want: a mouse hunter or a companion?

Why do we get cats? It's for their independent side, too. Cat owners dedicated to a god or goddess, cat or dog. For cats, there were several gods, including the very famous Bastet. Animal mummies were put in these places of worship in the hope of obtaining all manner of good things from the god or goddess. Cats were carriers of fertility, as they produced many kittens. And cats were bred: to kill them, to make mummies of them, to offer them as gifts. There was the temple, and around it, the breeding facilities. People could bring their favorite cats and have them buried. Or they could buy ready-made mummies on the spot, to make *ex-voto* offerings. What changed things a little was the discovery of several tombs on the island of Cyprus dating back six to eight thousand years. And there's another one in China, where a cat grave

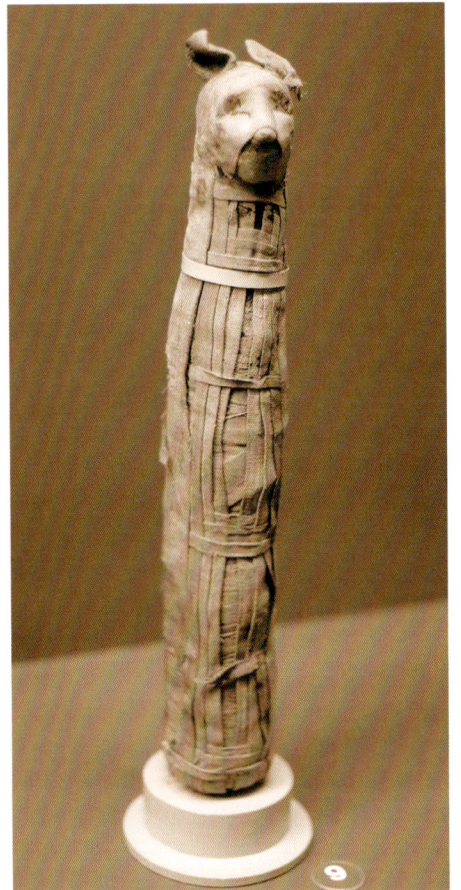

Cat mummy, Rosicrucian Egyptian Museum, San Jose. Photo by E. Michael Smith.

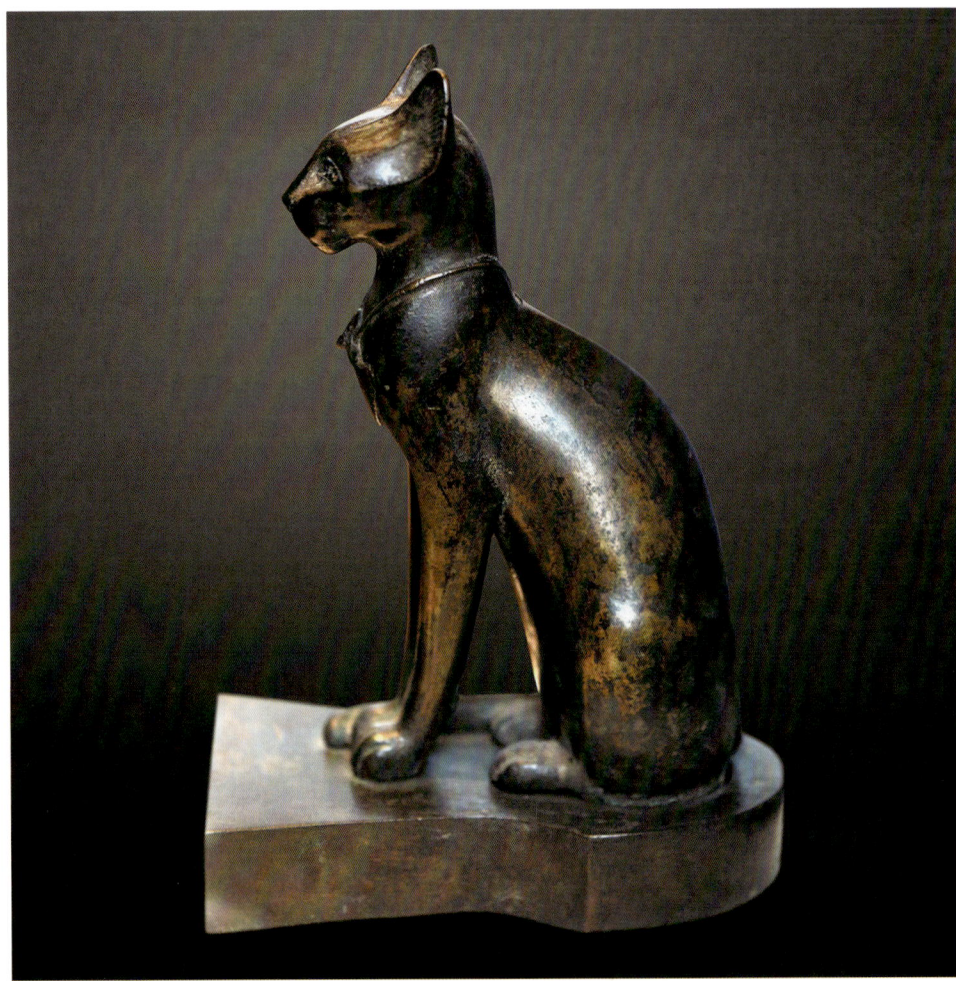

Statue of Bastet, Department of Antiquities, the Louvre. Photo by Rama.

was discovered next to a human grave. The thing about Cyprus is that, first of all, it was much older than what had been discovered in Egypt. Above all, there were no cats on the island. This one must have been brought there, because cats don't swim very well. When you start taking animals with you, moving them around, it's because there's this closeness and, moreover, you take special care of them.

How do you differentiate between taming and domestication?

Domestication is really the culmination of a long process that involves commensalism, meaning that the animal is nearby. Then we tame it, give it water, feed it. He comes closer; he leaves

again. Until we get through the whole process. Then there's the anthropophilic stage, where we take great interest in it. And then there's domestication, where we actually have control over the animal. And this control means controlling its descendants. We control its reproduction; we make a selection. The animal is in our sphere, which is a pretty

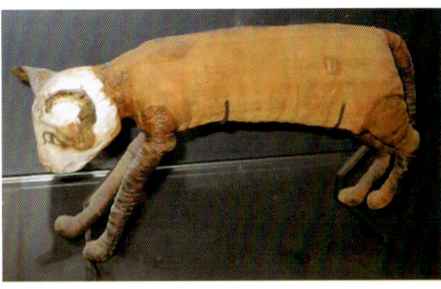

Mummy, Department of Antiquities, the Louvre. Photo by Rama.

small sphere in terms of distance. That's why I make a distinction. Can we say that the animal in Cyprus was domesticated? Was it on its own? There was no control, really, so for me, it was tame, but I find it hard to talk about domestication for the cat in Cyprus.

On the other hand, even for the cats we now have, I'm not sure we can speak of domestication. If you read Pastoureau, a science historian who works a lot on animals, you'll see that a domesticated animal is one that's in or around the house. But cockroaches are around the house, so in that sense, they're domesticated. I like the definition suggested by Jean-Denis Vigne, because it's more complex than that. And this notion of domestication, of control over cats ... I also like the fundamental idea that they need us, but that we need them, too. It's not strict domestication, but that's my perception. That's why I have a cat and not a guinea pig. Compared to dogs, to come back to them, with cats, we haven't achieved complete domestication. For me, it's still a work in progress, and that's great. 🐾

LES ANIMAUX CÉLÈBRES.

Michel Pastoureau

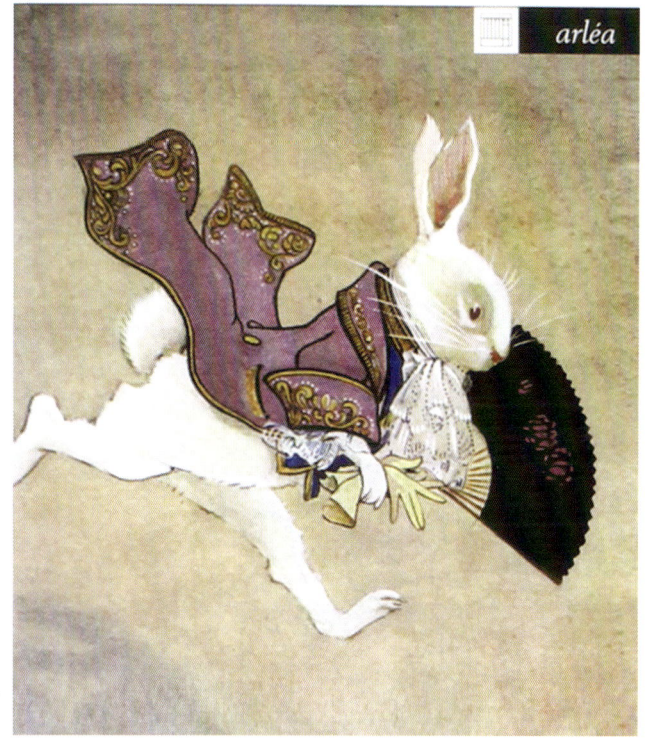

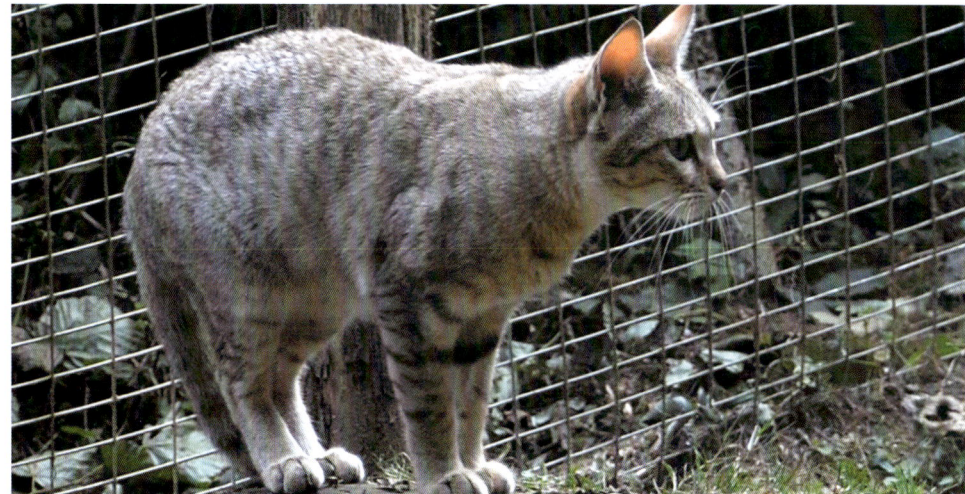

Felis silvestris lybica (gordoni), Parc des Félins [Cat Park]. Photo by Vassil.

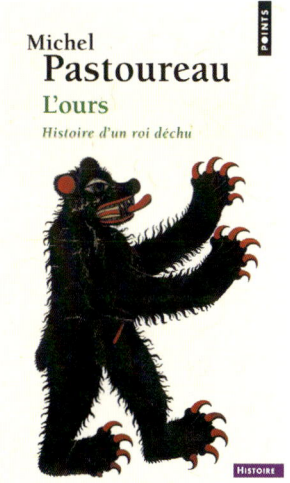

Divine Avatars of the Cat

Throughout our shared history, cats have been seen as either divine or diabolical creatures. From intensive breeding to honor Bastet in ancient Egypt to Freya's cats in Scandinavia, not to mention South America and China, many gods are associated with felines.

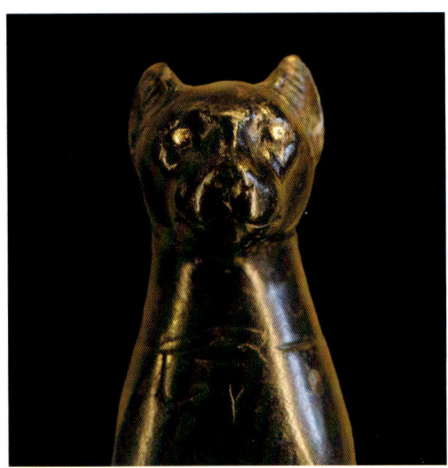

Bastet, 664–332 BCE, Department of Antiquities, the Louvre.

"In ancient times, cats were worshipped as gods; they haven't forgotten that." Regularly attributed to the English satirical author and cat lover Terry Pratchett, this quote doesn't appear in any of his works. But it's not unrealistic, given that cats and divinities have been associated since the earliest antiquity. This has been the case throughout the world, as cats sought out human companionship.

In Ancient Egypt

For a long time, Egypt was seen as the cradle of cat domestication throughout the world, and in fact, it was where the deification of the animal was most impressive, with temples dedicated to it, or more precisely to one of the many cat goddesses in the local pantheon. The best known of these was Bast or Bastet. She was mainly honored in the

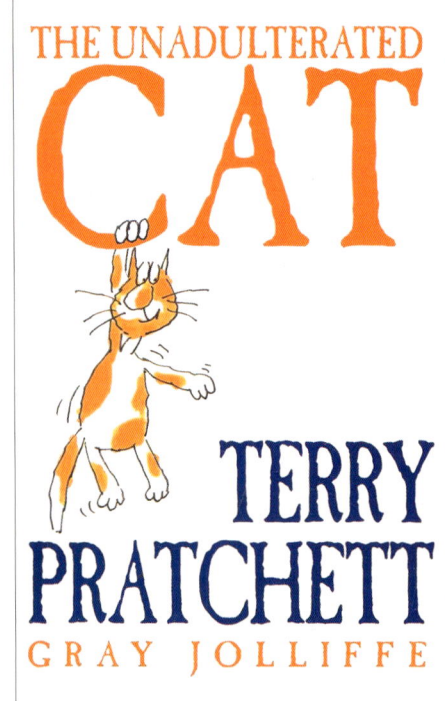

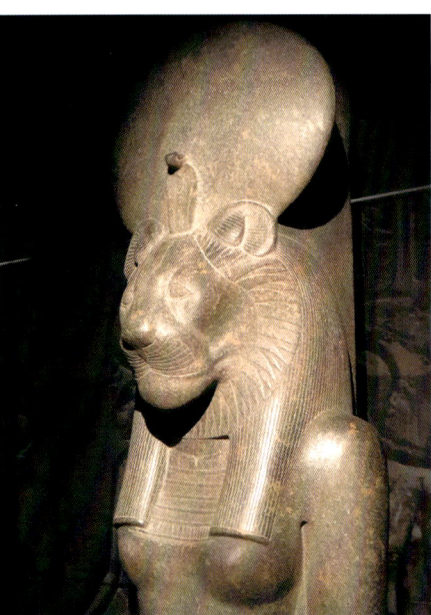

Sekhmet, 664–332 BCE, Musée de Montréal. Photo by Maksim Sokolov.

city bearing her name, Bubastis, in the eastern delta. Who was she? In myth, she was the daughter of Ra, the sun, and the wife of Ptah, the creator god and patron of craftsmen and architects. She was a double goddess. In her lioness form, Sekhmet was Ra's destructive

weapon and leader of his armies. In her cat form, she was one of the goddesses protecting the home, children, and pregnant women, as well as femininity and "creative" energy, a euphemism for sexual desire. She also represented the warmth of the sun. Her dual nature as both wild beast and domestic animal is

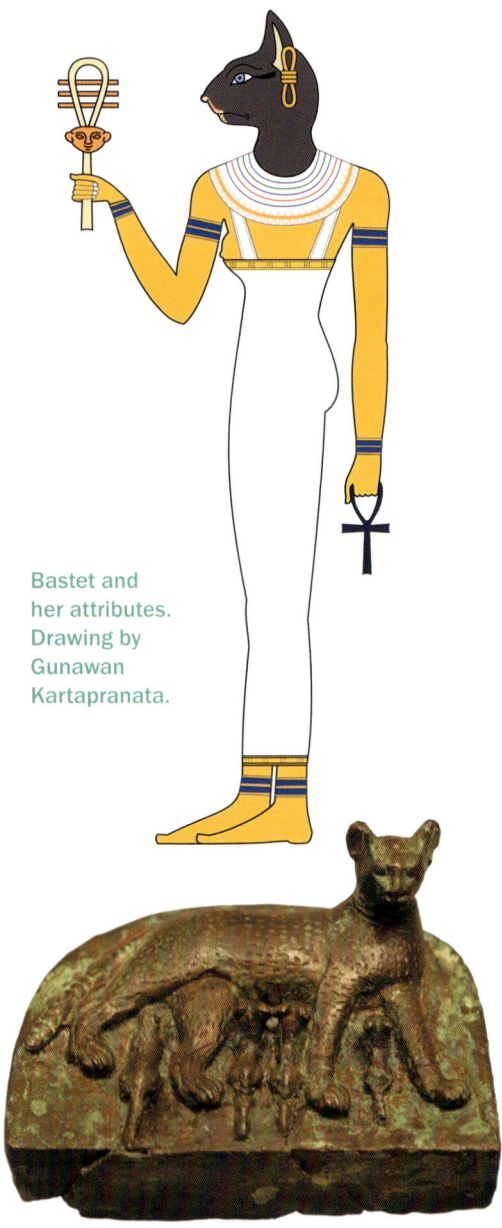

Bastet and her attributes. Drawing by Gunawan Kartapranata.

Statue, Egyptian and Near Eastern Collection, Kunsthistorisches Museum. Photo by Captmondo.

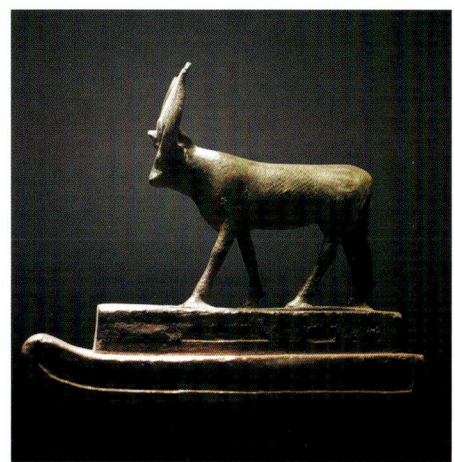

Hathor, 664–332 BCE, Department of Egyptian Antiquities, the Louvre. Both the cow goddess and the cat goddess, Bastet, are incarnations of love and refer to the lion-goddess Sekhmet.

illustrated by several myths. Every night, she was said to stand on Ra's back, protecting the god on his journey to the world below from Apophis, the chaotic serpent who tried to swallow him before his rebirth at dawn. In addition, when her warrior avatar Sekhmet went mad with rage after too many battles and couldn't help destroying men, Isis, the goddess of magic (and in some versions, mother of Bastet), advised Ra to prepare a large quantity of beer mixed with pomegranate juice. Mistaking it for blood, Sekhmet drank so much that she fell asleep drunk. When she awoke, she had calmed down and, according to some versions, went away under her feline guise, Bastet. In other versions of the legend, the goddess of love, Hathor (often depicted with a cow's head), was the one who walked away. Femininity and love were so important to the Egyptians that two goddesses were needed to embody these concepts.

Bastet was represented either as a cat, usually black, that was sitting and sometimes nursing her kittens or a Pharaoh, or as a cat-headed woman holding a sistrum in one hand (which is fitting, as she was a goddess of music)

and an ankh cross, the symbol of life, in the other.

Bast was not the only cat goddess. Before her, the Egyptians worshipped Mafdet, the runner, the goddess who protected against snakebites and scorpion stings (as Sekhmet would later), and the executor of divine justice who brought the heart of the criminal to her master's feet, like a cat brings back its prey. Gradually, her role and attributes were transferred to Bastet/Sekhmet, and Mafdet faded from memory.

In Europe

Unlike in Egypt, the goddesses of the various European pantheons rarely took on feline attributes. However, they did like to surround themselves with cats and use them as messengers. In Greece, Bastet was honored and merged with the cult of the goddess of hunting and young children, Artemis (Diana to the Romans). But it was above all Hecate, the goddess of magic, the new moon, and crossroads (and sometimes also assimilated to Artemis, or to the Egyptian Isis), who was associated with cats. After the war between the Titans and the gods, she took the form of a cat to escape the fury of the monster Typhon, instrument of Gaia's vengeance. This might explain why, according to Pausanias, the Greek city of Colophon sacrificed black cats to her in memory of the event, instead of the dogs that were usually dedicated to her.

Farther north, Ceridwen, a Welsh magician and goddess of death and fertility, used white cats as messengers. Freyja, the Nordic goddess of love and fertility, and one of the most important figures in the pantheon, is the protector of cats. Her chariot is drawn by two giant blue cats, named either Thófnir

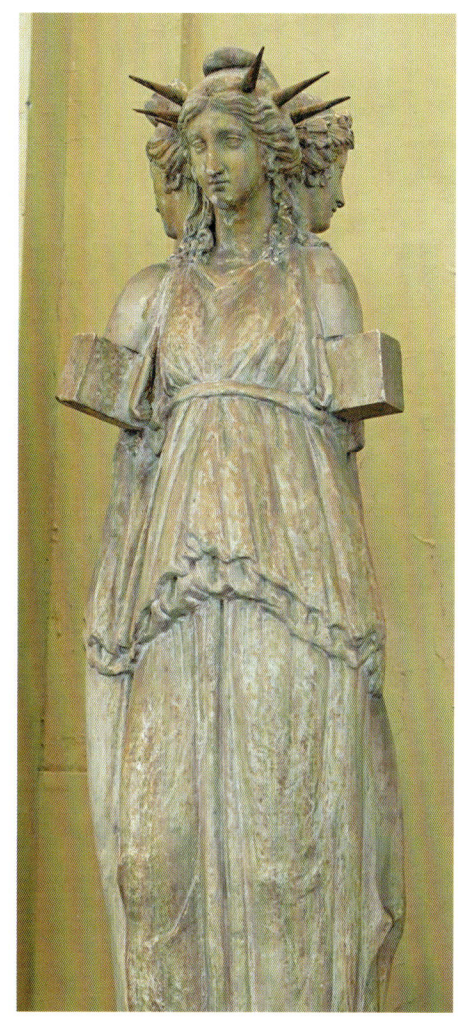

Hecate, date and artist unknown, Chiaramonti Museum. Photo by Jastrow.

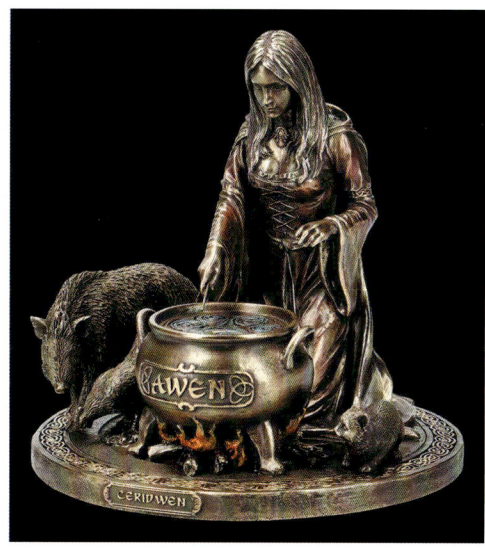

Ceridwen figurine.

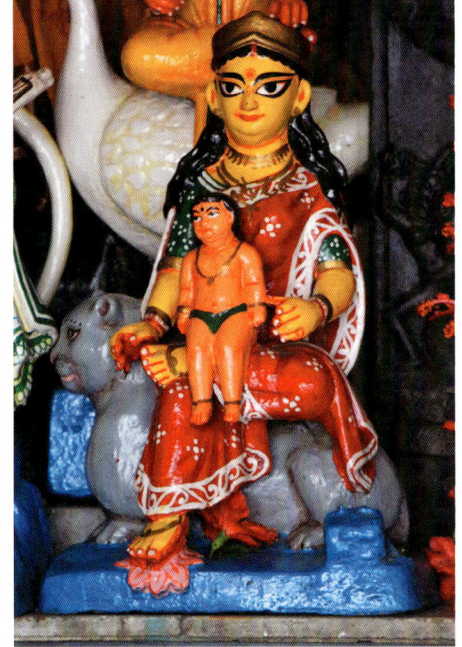

Freya, Johannes Gehrts, 1901.

and Högni, or Brundr and Kælinn. The cats were a gift from Thor, who met their father during one of his adventures. Since then, Freyja has looked kindly on anyone who leaves a bowl of milk for her cats in their field and guarantees their prosperity.

In the East, halfway between a god and a familiar spirit, is Slavic mythology's Ovinnik. He's most often depicted as a more or less anthropomorphic black cat, with glow-in-the-dark eyes and a dog-like bark. Most often associated with barns and granaries, he protects farm animals and grain, as long as locals remember to feed him with offerings of blinis or roosters. If not, he plays all sorts of tricks on them before setting fire to the barn!

In Asia

On a continent where felines are plentiful, it's easy to imagine that the local gods and goddesses were somehow linked with these animals. And yet, domestic cats weren't favored by the great gods and goddesses, who preferred wild beasts, like the Hindu goddess Parvati and the tigers she used as a means of transport. In India, it's Shashthi who uses the cat as a means of transportation and as a seat. Once again, the fertility and protective behavior of female cats with their young are the reasons for this connection. Shashthi is a goddess who protects children. In addition to the cat that carries her, she is often depicted

The Goddess Shashthi, temple near Bagbazar, India. Photo by Arnab Dutta.

with one or more children, whom she nurses and holds in her many pairs of arms. Her animal transport is seen as a hunter of evil spirits.

In China, it's cats' mouse-hunting ability that comes to the fore. The goddess in question is Li Shou, mentioned in the *Book of Rites*. Appointed by the other gods to oversee the smooth running of the world, she was efficient in her task until she fell asleep for a nap. After three

Ovinnik, Anton Shipitsa.

awakenings and three reprimands, she declared herself unfit to watch over the world and suggested entrusting the Earth to humans. She and her followers, which are ordinary cats, took charge of protecting crops and food from rodents and other animals that might want them. Particularly honored by farmers, she is also, in some legends, associated with the passage of time and the phases of the moon, due to the way the pupils in cats' eyes vary according to the lighting and their daily rhythm, alternating long periods of rest and short phases of very intense activity.

In Japan, cats are not officially deified but rather seen as more or less evil *yokai* (see p. 80). This didn't stop painter Toru Kaya from creating the Nyan Nyan Ji Cat Temple in Kyoto in 2016. This monastery, named after his cat Koyuki (a white stray with eyes of two different colors), is unique in that it only has cat monks, dressed as such. Part cat café, part tourist attraction, part animal sanctuary, the place has become quite a success, taking the veneration of an animal by its master to a rare extreme. 🐾

IN THE AMERICAS

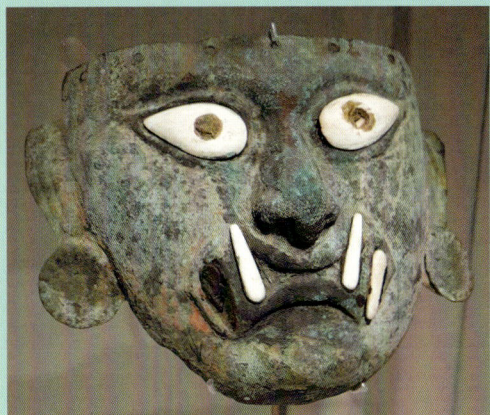

Ai Apaec, Rowan Windwhistler.

Originally from Africa and having grown closer to man during the Neolithic period, domestic cats didn't reach the American continents with the first waves of migration (those of Paleolithic hunter-gatherers), but much later. The various cat gods found there were more inspired by local animals (lynx, puma, jaguar). In Peru, for example, the punishing god of the Moche, Ai Apaec, was a big fan of human sacrifice, mostly decapitated prisoners. He was often described as an old man with the fangs and whiskers of a cat or jaguar, or as a spider with a feline face and long fangs. Since then, in popular culture, he has become a familiar spirit with the look of a brawling tomcat, and at Marvel, a Spider-Man antagonist recruited by Norman Osborn in *Dark Avengers* #175.

In North America, in the Great Lakes region straddling the United States and Canada, the Ojibwe nations knew Mishipeshu, the underwater lynx or panther. Appearing as a large, horned feline with copper scales on its back and tail, Mishipeshu was a water god. Associated with swift waters, it was believed to be responsible for drowning caused by whirlpools, rapids, or people venturing onto thin ice in the winter. But it was also considered a protector of travelers and fishermen who knew how to charm it.

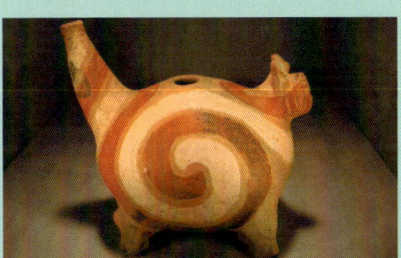

Mishipeshu, 1400–1600, National Museum of the American Indian, New York.

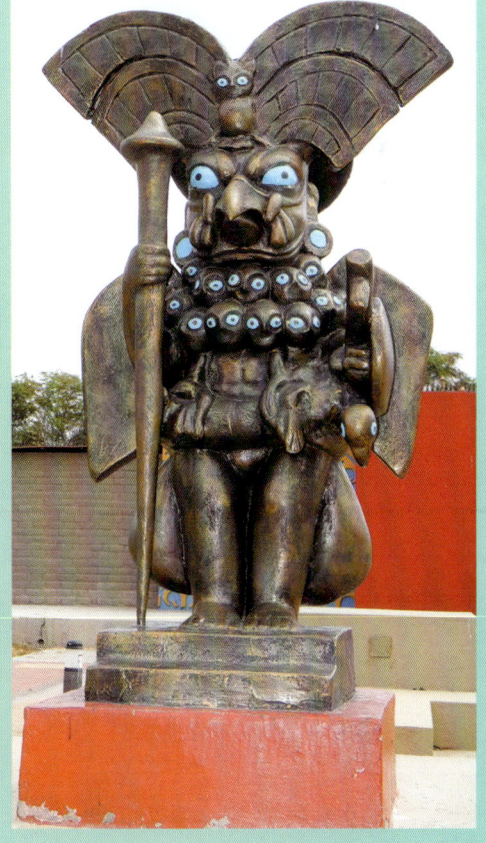

Ai Apaec, Huaca Rajada Museum, Sipan, Peru. Photo by BluesyPete.

Black Cat, White Cat

In Emir Kusturica's comedy about the Romani world, the two title cats appear as visual punctuation. Yet without saying a word and just living their feline lives, they comment on what's happening on-screen.

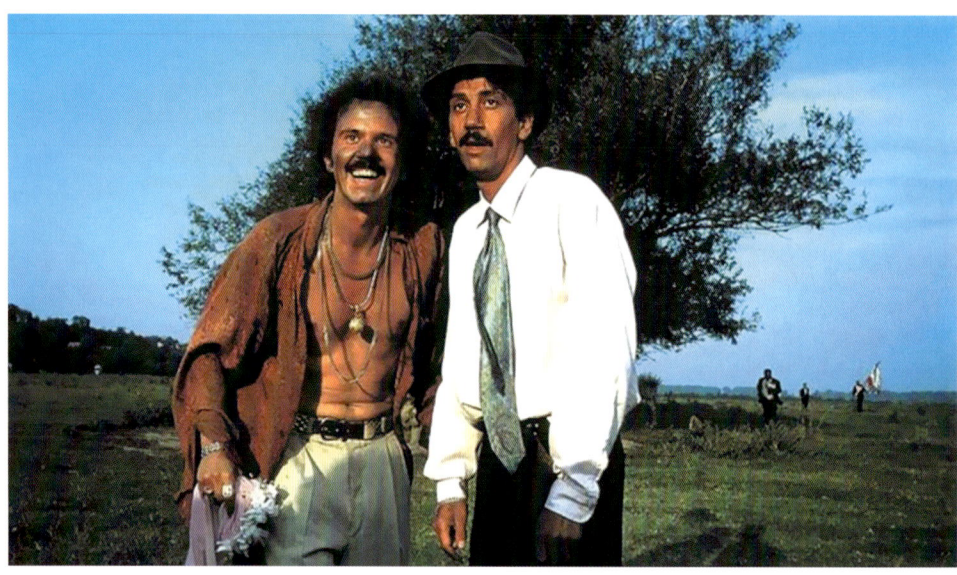

Summarizing the plot of *Black Cat, White Cat*—the film that relaunched Emir Kusturica's career in 1998 and won him a Silver Lion at that year's Venice Film Festival—is a challenge. On the banks of the Danube, a Romani man named Matko makes a living out of petty crime. When one of his schemes goes wrong, he is forced to marry off his son to the dwarf sister of his childhood friend and cocaine-addicted gangster, Dadan. But Matko is in love with someone else, and the boy's grandfather and the local godfather don't see things that way. All's well that ends well after two hours and thirteen minutes of music, misunderstandings, slapstick action, and colorful dialogue.

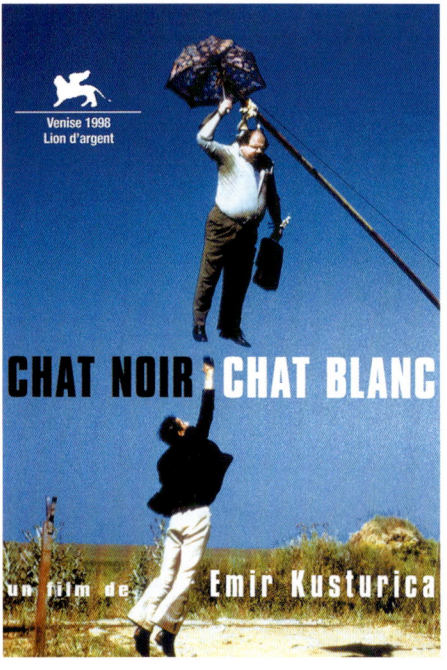

And what about the cats? From the very start of the film, a pair of cats, a white male and a black female (contrary to the original Serbian title), roam the screen. More often than not, they serve as transitions between scenes, or as clues to underline an important point. So, when the giant Grga explains to his grandfather that he'll only marry after love at first sight, he spots the cats and chases them away before we can hear the answer. They gain importance at the end of the film, waking up the grandfather who had been left for dead and then serving as impromptu witnesses to the grandson's real wedding. And their relationship and the contrast between their coats can also be seen as a symbol of the friendship between the local godfather and the grandfather when both have taken diametrically opposite paths in life and their children clash. It's the next generation who, like the cats, decide to live their lives without worrying about obligations and receive the strong support of the two old-timers. Even after death. 🐾

SPEC SHEET

WORK: *Black Cat, White Cat*.
CREATORS: Emir Kusturica (director) and Gordan Mihic (screenwriter).
DATE CREATED: June 1, 1998.
DISTRIBUTOR/AVAILABILITY: October Films. Available for streaming on Klassiki.
CATS' NAMES AND ROLE IN THE WORK: A pair of anonymous cats, one black, the other white. They wander around the screen, highlighting the action, even triggering it, by living their lives without bothering about humans.

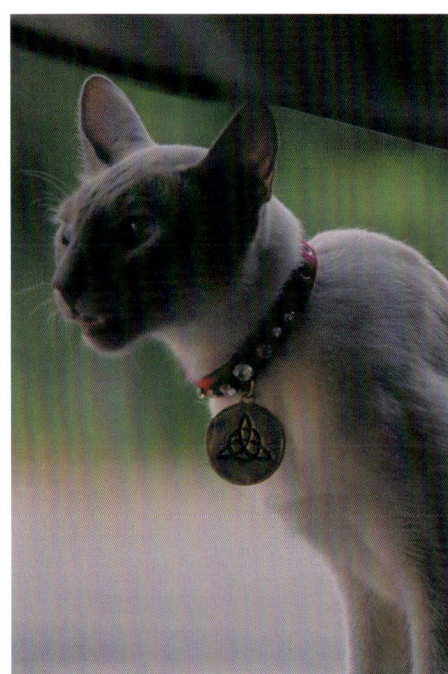

In 1998, Aaron Spelling produced what would become his last great success: Charmed. *A master of series production since the 1970s with* Charlie's Angels *and* The Love Boat, *he rode the wave of the supernatural by telling the story of three witches.*

Three sisters, Prue, Piper, and Phoebe, discover that they are descended from a long line of witches, and that they have powers of their own. Together, they hold the "power of three" that allows them to fight the forces of evil. With the fantasy teen drama craze launched by *Buffy the Vampire Slayer* in 1997, The WB invested in this witch story, supported by a popular cast featuring Shannon Doherty and Alyssa Milano, teen idols of the 1980s and 1990s.

Loosely revolving around the myths and legends of witchcraft, the three protagonists adopt a cat in the first episode, unless it's the other way around. Kit belongs to a witch, Serena Fredrick, who is murdered at the beginning of the series. This Siamese cat becomes the sisters' pet, regularly warning them of danger.

The cat wears a necklace and pendant with a triquetra symbol, representing the power of three possessed by the sisters. Although she's not black, she's a typical witch's companion. She often has a very secondary role, with powers that are often underutilized, but she is part of witchcraft folklore. In Season 4, conflicts on the set led to Shannon Doherty's departure from the show and, thus, her character Prue. Rose McGowan, who has since become known as one of the first Harvey Weinstein victims to speak out, replaced her at short notice in the role of Paige, the family's long-lost sister. Kit follows Paige until she joins the trio of witches. The cat is rewarded for her work with them by being transformed into a human. Her mistresses think that she has run away. She returns in her human form, Katrina, in Season 5, in the episode "Cat House." The death of the cat who played Kit in the first three seasons doesn't really explain her disappearance, since she appears again in this episode, played by another cat. The cat's role had undoubtedly reached its limits, story-wise. 🐾

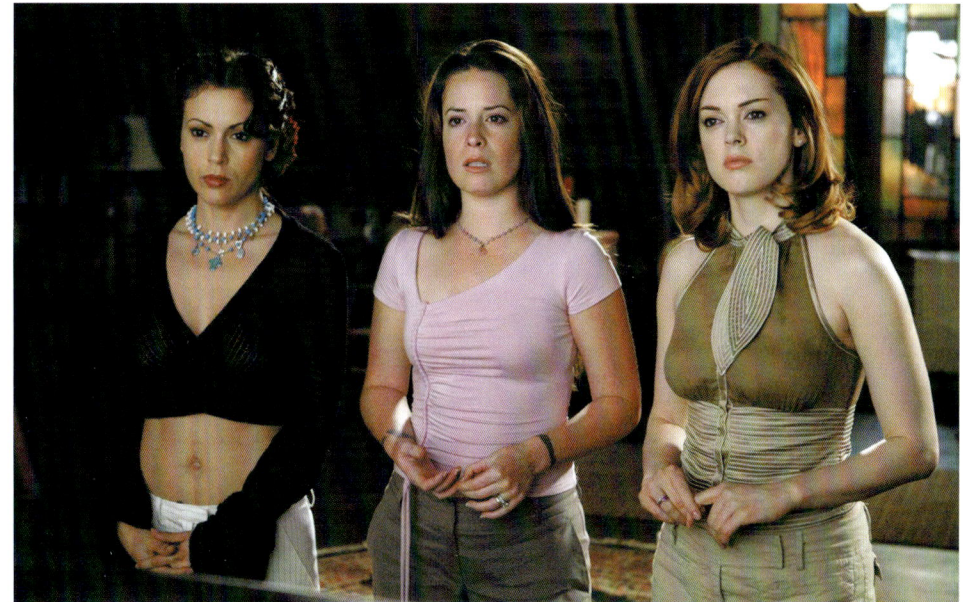

Phoebe, Piper, and Paige.

SPEC SHEET

CAT'S NAME: Kit.
WORK: *Charmed*.
CREATOR: Constance M. Burge.
DATE CREATED: 1998.
DISTRIBUTOR/AVAILABILITY: Available on DVD (Paramount Pictures), through various streaming services, and on TNT (US television channel).
CAT'S CHARACTERISTICS: Siamese blue point with triquetra pendant.

The Rabbi's Cat

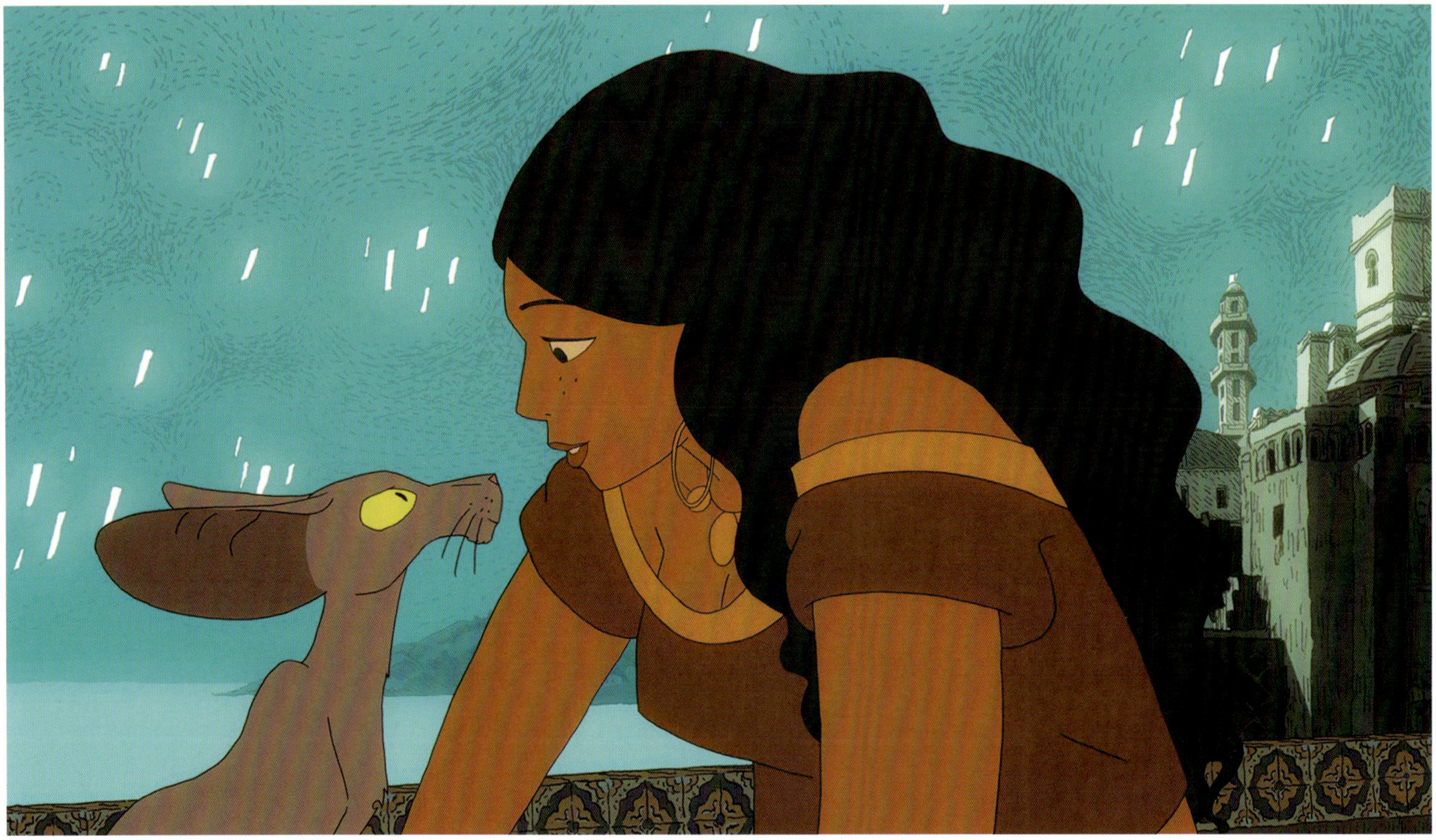

Cat lover Joann Sfar also likes to talk about religion and human idiosyncrasies. Through a gangly cat that is gifted with speech if not wisdom, he nostalgically evokes the Algeria of the 1920s and 1930s, and a certain idea of tolerance.

When a kitten, "the ugliest and strangest cat,"[1] slipped into his coat pocket, Joann Sfar had no idea that this feline would inspire him to create one of his most famous series two years later: *The Rabbi's Cat*. "I really got the idea for these books from watching him. He looked at everyone with such intensity with his big eyes that you had the impression he wanted to talk. Plus, he meowed all the time," he said in an interview with *Le Parisien*. Like his flesh-and-blood model, Imhotep, the rabbi's (anonymous) cat spies on the humans around him and tries to understand them. Giving himself the gift of speech by eating a parrot in the first book, he serves as narrator and guide for

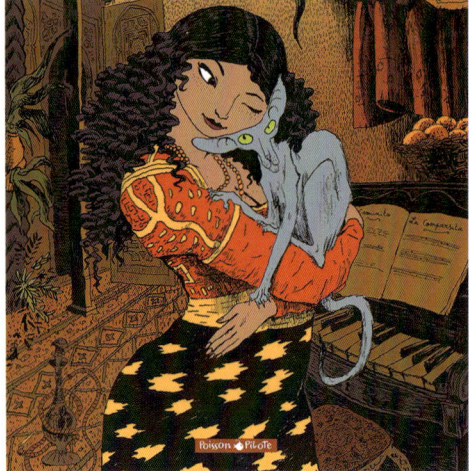

twenty-first-century readers, discovering Jewish culture and twentieth-century Algeria before the War of Independence. He is in love with his mistress, Zlabya, and enjoys debating with the rabbi, pointing out his contradictions. From the height of a four-legged companion, he shows a nostalgic Algiers that his author never knew (that of the 1920s and 1930s). The religions in the book are cousins, like the rabbi and the Sufi musician, who are both descendants of the same Sfar and celebrate him in song and dance every year.

After becoming gifted with words intelligible to felines, humans, and other animals, the cat struggles between his animal instincts and his philosophical aspirations. In the opening line of the first book, the cat explains, "Jews have been bitten, chased, and barked at for so long that in the end, they prefer cats." For Joann Sfar, it's an opportunity to talk about subjects that are important to him, such as religious tolerance (between different faiths, but also with regard to the behavior of others, whether believers or

---

[1] https://www.leparisien.fr/culture-loisirs/livres/bande-dessinee-le-vrai-chat-du-rabbin-de-joann-sfar-est-mort-24-02-2018-7577304.php

THE ANIMATED FILM

Comic book author Joann Sfar is also a film director, so it was a natural step for him to take on the task of adapting his cult comic for the big screen in 2011 with Antoine Delesvaux. The story blends the plot of Volumes 1 (The Bar Mitzvah), 2 (The Malka of the Lions), and 5 (African Jerusalem) into one complete story, leaving out the rabbi's son-in-law and any time spent outside Africa. Faithful to the graphics of the comics, with a little more action and a little less philosophy, this cartoon running an hour and forty minutes will appeal to the whole family. Children will be fascinated first by the cat's antics and then by the adventures of the rabbi, the painter, and the Sufi in search of the Jerusalem of the Queen of Sheba, crossing the continent from Algiers to Ethiopia. Older viewers will appreciate the dialogue and the sometimes-wicked humor in situations that aren't all that funny, such as the Russian pogroms or the encounter with the fundamentalist nomads (more developed than in the comics, but also much milder in its treatment). The voices, led by François Morel in the role of the cat, and the soundtrack complement the artwork admirably. So much so, in fact, that when you return to the books after viewing them, you'll hear the actors' voices as you read the characters.

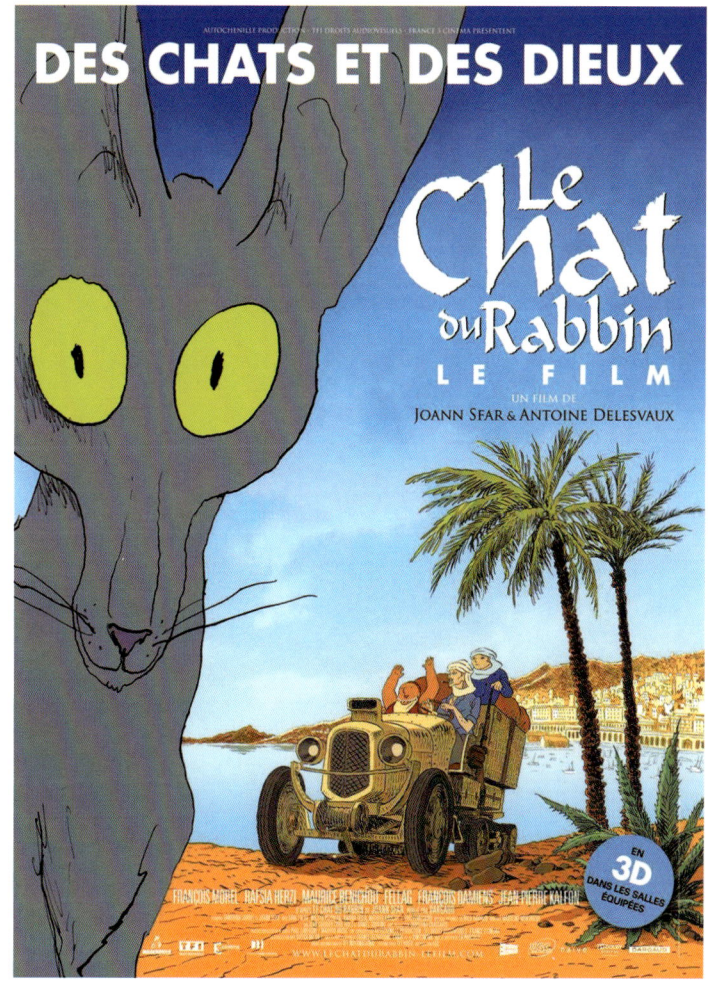

not), Judaism as its own identity, racism, and anti-Semitism, as well as food, music, and art in general. All of this is done with a great deal of humor and finesse, so that most of the books can be read with as much pleasure by children as by adults, even though adults will find references that are difficult for younger children to understand. Please note, however, that these books aren't particularly aimed at young people, so some of the panels may not be suitable for very young children. It's best to introduce them to this world through the animated film first, which is one of several adaptations of the comic strip, along with two plays (one by Camille Nahum and the other by Sarah and Xénia Marcuse), a radio series by Katell Guillou and Cédric Aussir for France Culture, and a live-action film project with no release date. 🐾

SPEC SHEET

WORK: *The Rabbi's Cat*.
CREATORS: Joann Sfar (script and drawings); Brigitte Findakly (colors).
DATE CREATED: 2002.
PUBLISHER: Pantheon.
CAT'S NAME AND ROLE IN THE WORK: An anonymous, skinny street cat with the ability to speak and reason, much to the rabbi's dismay.

Yokai Cats: Are They Dangerous Monsters?

Cats have long featured in Japanese illustrations and literature, but in Japan as in the West, they haven't always had a good reputation in legends. It took the arrival of certain anime and manga characters to reverse the trend.

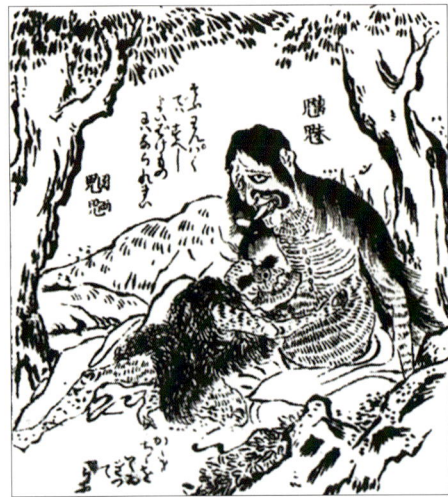

Chimimōryō, Mountain and River Spirit, Sekien Toriyama, 1802.

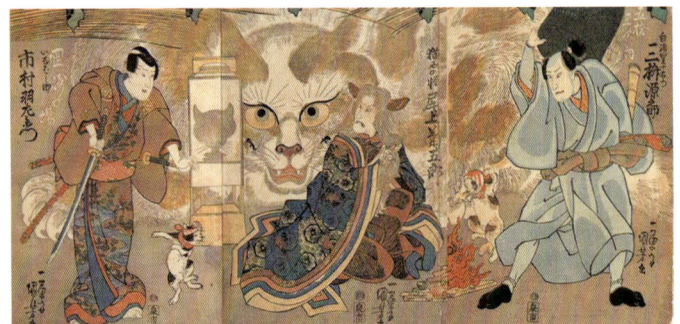

Bakeneko (center), *Kabuki Scene*, Utagawa Kuniyoshi, 1835.

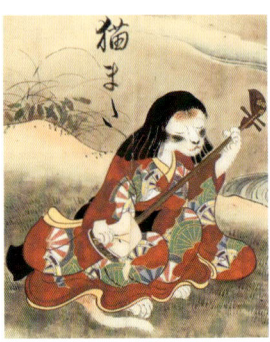

Nekomata, Sawaki Suushi, 1737.

Looking at the various prints and sculptures from Japanese history or strolling through the nation's towns and looking at the *maneki-neko* at store entrances, one could easily believe that Japan is a paradise for cats. Admittedly, these fish- and mouse-loving animals, which protect rice fields and crops from pests, have always been appreciated by some of the population.

With Age Comes the *Bakeneko*

If it's too fat or too old, according to local beliefs, a cat will turn into a terrible monster, the *bakeneko*. This evil cat, which is half succubus, half vampire, will prey on newcomers to its host family or neighbors. By day, it's the same old cat, but by night, it will approach its sleeping victims to brutalize them or rob them of their very breath. Traditionally,

any cat over ten years of age or over a certain weight was considered capable of becoming a *bakeneko* and often preventively put to death. Shigeru Mizuki even points out that it was often advisable to give the cat away when a death occurred in the family. This may have something to do with the Tsushima Island legend of a demon descending from the sky to steal the body at a funeral. It was said that the demon was the deceased's transformed cat. Since then, it has been a local custom to lock up old cats.

This type of theft is not unlike the behavior of the *kasha*, literally "cat on fire" or "burning chariot."

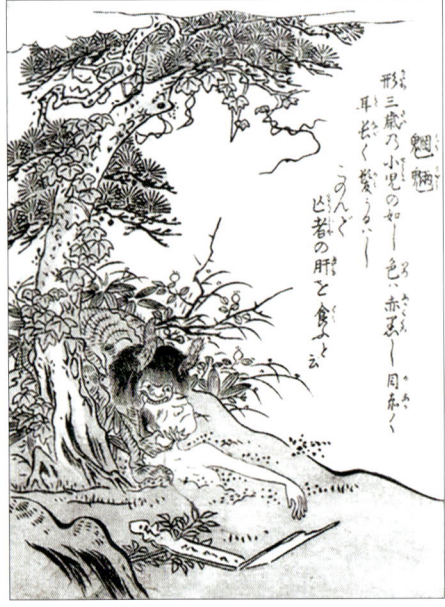

Mōryō, Cat of Mountains and Rivers, Trees and Rocks, Sekien Toriyama, 1779.

Usually arriving at night or during thunderstorms, these funereal cats seize the remains of the deceased who have led a bad life before they are cremated. It's not a question of feeding on the body of the deceased, which is the task of the *mōryō*, another *yokai* associated with funerals, but of using it as a garment to come and go in the world of the living. Or, in a less selfish interpretation, to act as a conductor to the underworld for the less-deserving dead. They are also sometimes messengers between the two worlds. The existence of *kasha* and *mōryō* explains why there are sometimes two funeral ceremonies: one with a false coffin filled with stones, the other with the real thing. The attendees also bang cymbals to frighten the supernatural animal away.

Cat-Vampires Drawing Out the Vital Essence

Although the *bakeneko*, the best-known feline *yokai*, is sometimes compared to a vampire, it's not the cat-vampire par excellence of Japanese folklore. That role is shared equally between two closely related monsters: the *gotokuneko* (or "tripod cat") and the *nekomata no hi* (or "will-o'-the-wisp split-tailed cat"). So much so that the former is often considered a variant of the latter. According to Shigeru Mizuki, the *gotokuneko* was created by Nakazawa, who lived with five cats and used to carry one of them in his pocket when paying his respects when someone died in the neighborhood. The cat would then go out and suck out the vital essence of the dead person, until one of them acquired the ability to speak. Nakazawa, who was married, often abandoned his wife to go to the theater. One day, she complained to the cat, who made her laugh by performing a play. Sometime later, while her husband was away, a samurai showed up and seduced the wife, who was grieving the loss of that same cat. When asked, "Who are you?" he simply replied, "I'm the cat." But when the affair was discovered, both cat and samurai had disappeared, and the woman was found dead, with a feline bite mark on her neck.

Traditionally, the *gotokuneko* is depicted as a cat with a trivet on its head, stoking the heat of a cooking fire with a bamboo pipe. The *nekomata* is distinguished from the classic *bakeneko* by its double tail, known as a "split tail" or "forked tail," depending on the story. It's also a much more powerful *yokai*, with necromantic talents capable of raising the dead and controlling them. Transforming himself at will into a will-o'-the-wisp or an old lady, he enters certain homes to feed on the lives of the inhabitants. To get rid of him, you must kill him during the day and check that he has two tails.

Some Rather Friendly *Yokai* in Fiction

Not all feline *yokai* are so horrible, however. The *sunekosuri* is merely unpleasant. On rainy or snowy days, or in the dead of night, this phantom crawls between the legs of passersby, rubbing against their shins to frighten or disorient them. Sometimes, the

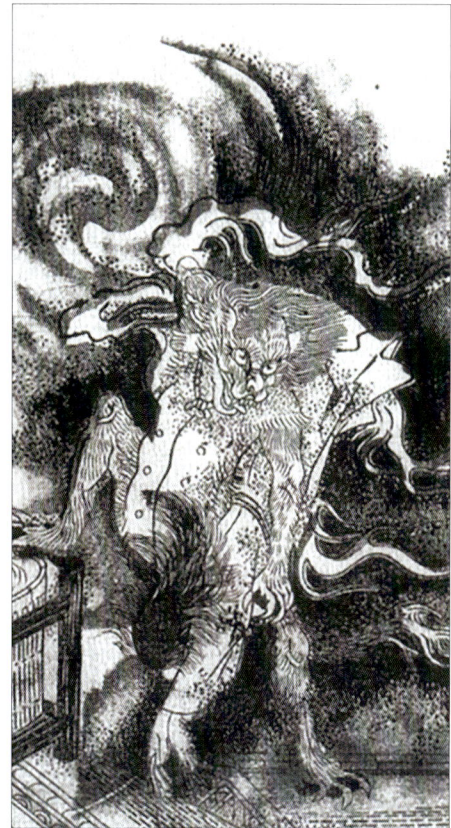

Kasha, Sekien Toriyama, 1781.

consequences can be catastrophic when the person gets lost, but more often than not, they just get a good scare. And then in the twentieth century, along came Hayao Miyazaki. A connoisseur of Japanese myths, the animator/director often incorporates them into his works, transforming them in the process. In 1988's *My Neighbor Totoro* (*Tonari no Totoro*), for example, he featured several spirits, including a *bakeneko*. This is the famous Catbus, which, unlike the legendary monsters, is totally benevolent. At Totoro's request, he takes the two little girls in the story across fields and forests to the hospital where their sick mother is. In the short film sequel, *Mei and the Kittenbus*,[1] the family expands to include an extremely old grandmother and a whole series of fantastic cat-vehicles (trains, an airship, etc.). The *Yo-kai Watch* video

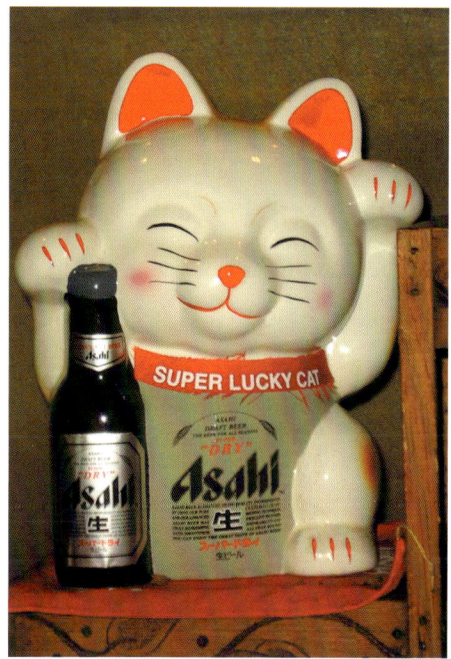

Maneki-neko, New York. Photo by Berto.

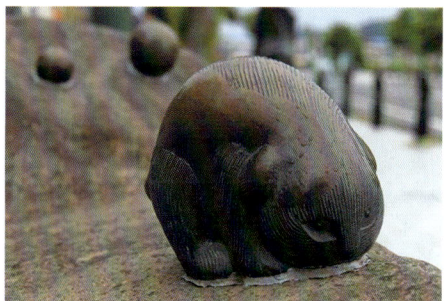

Statue of Sunekosuri, Mizuki Shigeru Road, Sakaiminato, Japan.

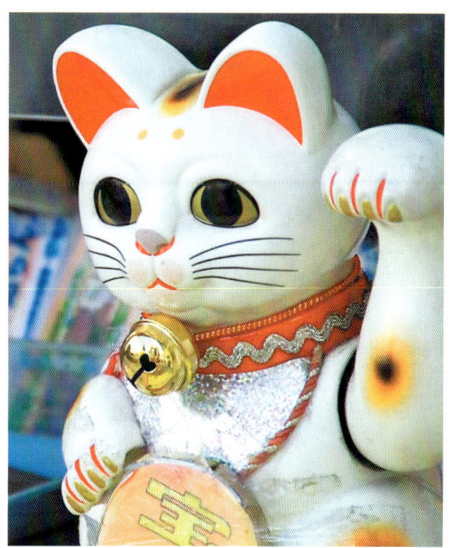

Maneki-neko, Tokyo.

---

[1] It can only be seen at the Ghibli Museum.

game franchise, which is also available in manga and anime, has featured a whole host of likable *bakeneko* and *nekomata* since its inception, starting with Jibanyan, the franchise mascot. Many Pokémon are also inspired by feline *yokai*: Meowth and Persian, as well as Espeon, with his double tail and psychic powers. 🐾

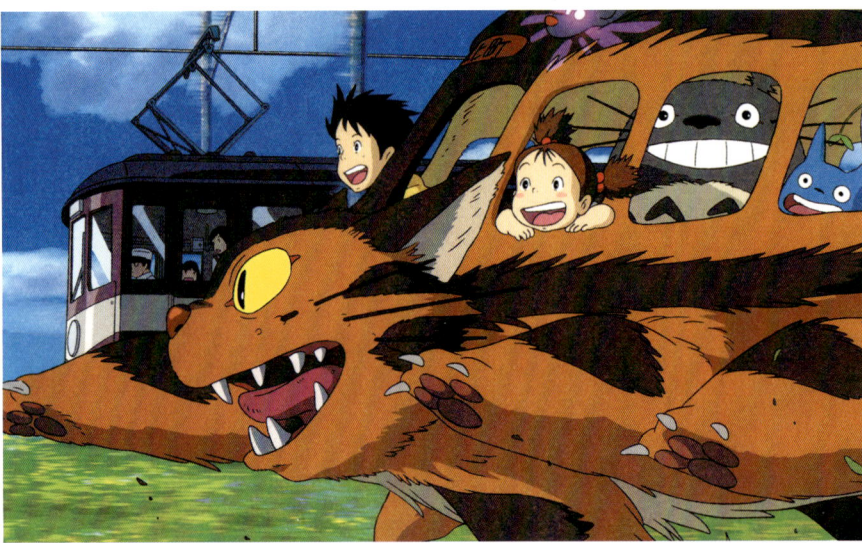

Catbus, a nice variation on the bakeneko in *My Neighbor Totoro*.

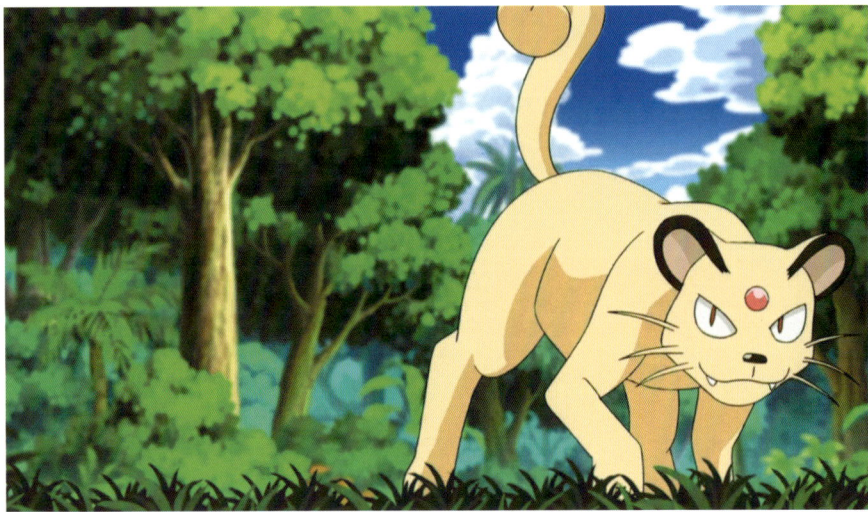

Persian in *Pokémon.*

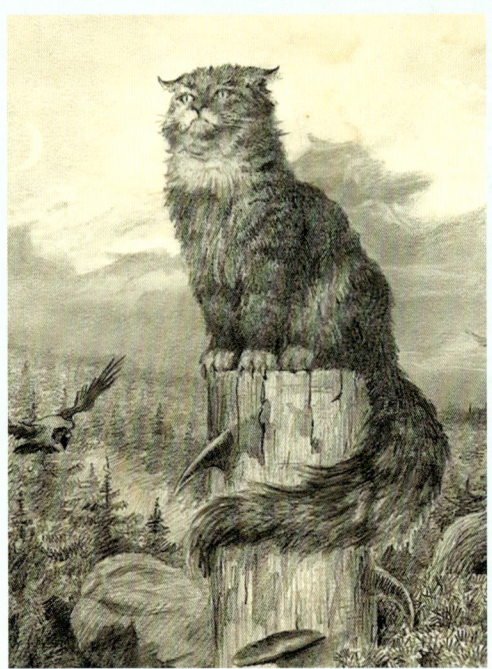

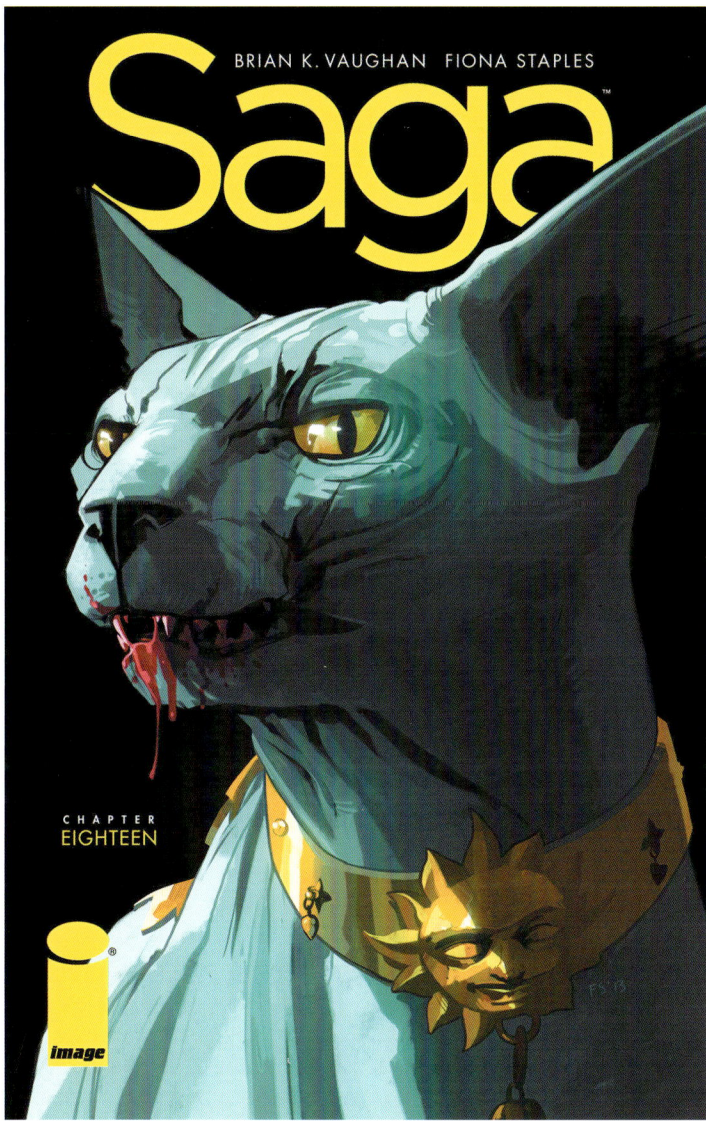

One of the Saga series antagonists, Lying Cat has become one of the comic's most iconic characters, thanks to her psychic abilities and ethical integrity.

A comic book series created by Fiona Staples and Brian K. Vaughan in 2012, *Saga* is a story that combines magic and space opera, love, betrayal, politics, and false pretenses. Of all the characters and their many secrets, only one maintains a steady ethical line from one end of the comic's twelve volumes to the other: Lying Cat, the companion of The Will, who is the mercenary pursuing the hero couple and their daughter, Hazel.

Physically, although Lying Cat was the weakest of her litter, she looks like a giant sphynx cat with blue-green skin and a few yellow markings. The creature isn't very talkative, but she is able to detect lies in the words or behavior of those around her and asserts this loudly with a resounding "Lying." In fact, this is the only word the cat says. She is also subject to certain rules, like all of her kind, which force her to accept ethical as well as factual truths. This allows her, for example, to reassure Sophie that what she has suffered in a planetary brothel doesn't make her dirty or impure.

Playing the role of living conscience for The Will, Lying Cat is nonetheless a feline like any other. She hates to be ignored, loves to be cuddled, and is often playful and attentive to the actions and feelings of the humans around her, especially The Will. And like all *Saga* characters, she's not entirely on the side of good. In addition to being one of the antagonists, she proves particularly vicious in her method of combat, much like a house cat acts when hunting, playing with its prey at length, only to abandon it once dead without even taking a bite. Lying Cat has won herself a fan club outside her original comics, making an appearance in the *Supernatural* TV series, as well as in two different Marvel comics (*Daredevil* and *Siege*). She is also available in tie-in products and plush toys. 🐾

SPEC SHEET

CAT'S NAME: Lying Cat.
WORK: The *Saga* comic book series. She appears in the very first chapter.
CREATORS: Fiona Staples (drawing) and Brian K. Vaughan (script).
DATE CREATED: March 2012.
PUBLISHER/AVAILABILITY: Image Comics. The comics are published monthly, and there are currently twelve collected editions.
CAT'S CHARACTERISTICS: Giant feline that looks like a sphynx cat with blue-green skin and yellow stripes on her back. Wears jewels.

Salem

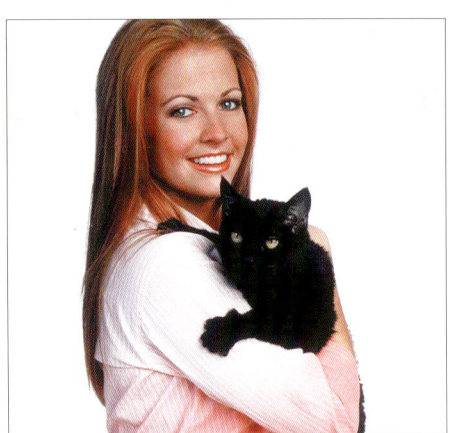

The 1990s series.

Salem is the black cat belonging to teenager Sabrina Spellman, a mixed-blood novice witch. First appearing in comic books in the 1960s, the young witch's companion is best known for his humorous role in the 1990s sitcom, which led to a resurgence in his popularity in comics.

After a 1996 *Sabrina the Teenage Witch* TV movie starring Melissa Joan Hart, ABC decided to produce a series with the same cast. The sitcom ran for four seasons on the network and then was produced by Warner Bros. until 2003. This light-hearted series shows the trials and tribulations of the social life and adventures of a teenager living with a secret. Her cat, Salem, comments on the Spellman family's every move with the show's best punchlines.

Costumes are also used regularly to enhance Salem's comedy. Mafioso, angel, king, fireman, or even a ghost: any excuse to make the audience laugh, years before the emergence of lolcats. His gluttony and desire for domination are also recurrent comic themes.

Animated using a mechanical puppet that allows him to articulate words, his movements are achieved with a black cat. Salem's lack of realism is no more shocking than the show's sitcom setting or the lack of special effects (mostly mechanical or pyrotechnic). Humor predominates, primarily thanks to the secondary characters, whether it be Salem or the two aunts, Hilda and Zelda.

A simple cat in the original comics, the series creators invented a past for him. Trapped in the body of a cat, Salem Saberhagen is a warlock condemned to remain in this body for 100 years. Apart from the fact that he can speak, he no longer has any powers. The cat/warlock has been punished for seeking to conquer the world. This is totally in keeping with Salem's character; he's ridiculously megalomaniacal and always amused by others' misfortunes.

Two animated series of sixty-five and twenty-six episodes were produced in 1999 and 2003, as well as an animated film in 2002 (*Sabrina the Teenage Witch: Friends Forever*), using the sitcom's clichés. In 2009, Archie published *Young Salem*, a comic book about the adventures of young Salem, before he was turned into a cat. In 2018, Netflix produced a four-part, thirty-two-episode miniseries, *Chilling Adventures of Sabrina,* based on the comic book *Chilling Adventures of Sabrina*. The atmosphere is completely different: darker, more violent, and adventure-oriented. Salem's role is considerably reduced. Speaking only in meows, he acts as an occasional guide to help the young witch. 🐾

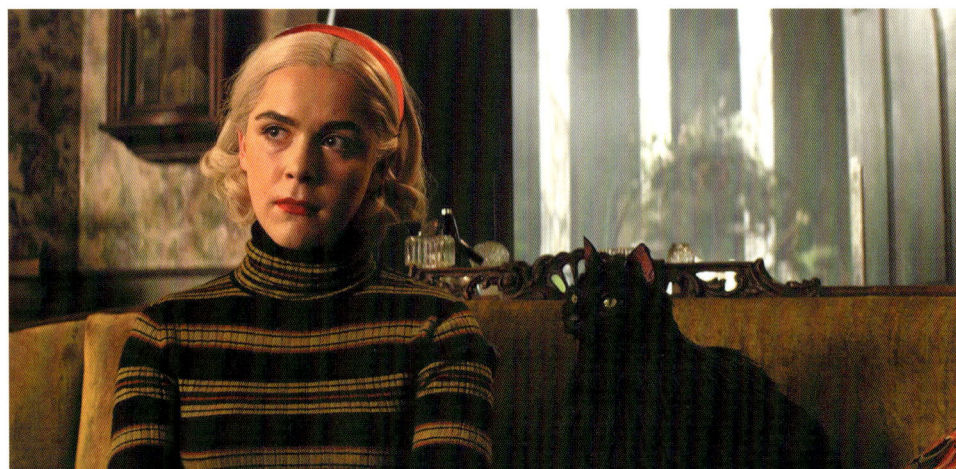

The new series.

SPEC SHEET

CAT'S NAME: Salem Saberhagen.
WORK: *Sabrina the Teenage Witch* (comics, TV series, animation).
CREATORS: George Gladir and Dan DeCarlo.
DATE CREATED: October 1962 (in comics).
PUBLISHER/DISTRIBUTOR: Archie Comics/Paramount.
CAT'S CHARACTERISTICS: Black American Shorthair cat (or black and white in the comics). A former wizard, he's sarcastic and serves as the witch's guide.

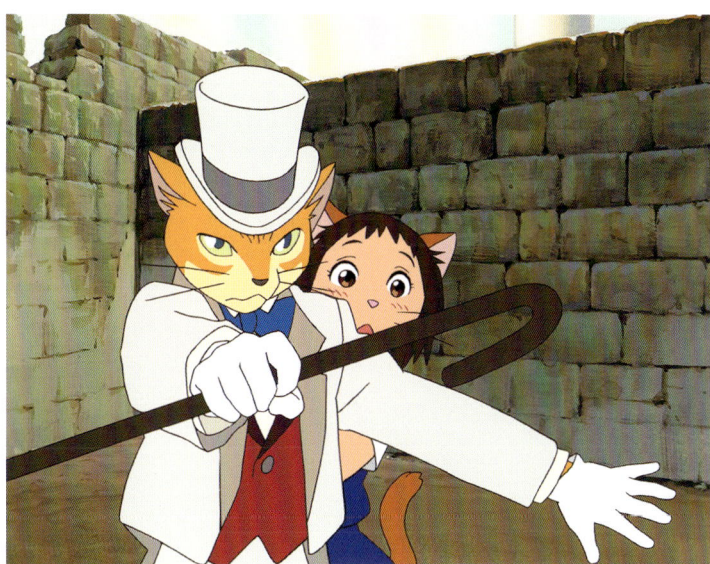

*Entertaining for the whole family, **The Cat Returns** is one of Studio Ghibli's shortest films. Inspired by the cats (both real and statues) in **Whisper of the Heart**, which was released a few years earlier, this movie is a dreamlike journey into a feline world.*

Originally commissioned for an amusement park that was never completed due to lack of funds, *The Cat Returns* ended up being one of Studio Ghibli's shortest films, and one of the most endearing and accessible to young children. Hayao Miyazaki conceptualized the film, even though he later moved on to other projects. He took the two cats in *Whisper of the Heart* (Moon, now Muta, and the Baron statuette), for which he had written the screenplay, and built the story around them. He asked mangaka Aoi Hiiragi, one of whose stories had already inspired the previous film, to write a manga around them to serve as the basis for what was to be a short film. She got a bit carried away, and the story turned out to be much longer than expected, so the film was eventually extended from twenty minutes to seventy-five.

As with *Whisper of the Heart* and many of the films directed by Hayao Miyazaki, the heroine of *The Cat Returns* is a teenager in a transitional time. Here, seventeen-year-old Haru is a dreamy, insecure high school student. After saving the life of a cat who turns out to be the prince of the Cat Kingdom, she finds herself having to get out of a marriage that is arranged against her will, and by the end of her adventure, she gains self-confidence and maturity. In any case, with its anthropomorphic animals and animated objects, *The Cat Returns* offers accessible family entertainment for ages three and up. The story is full of twists and turns, and the cats' antics will appeal to younger children, whereas *Whisper of the Heart*, in which the cats are only secondary characters, will appeal more to teenagers and adults. *The Cat Returns* draws inspiration from classic fairy tales but reverses the ending: The heroine doesn't marry the handsome prince she was promised; she returns home and goes back to her studies. This plot twist will appeal to adults, too, offering some interesting food for thought. 🐾

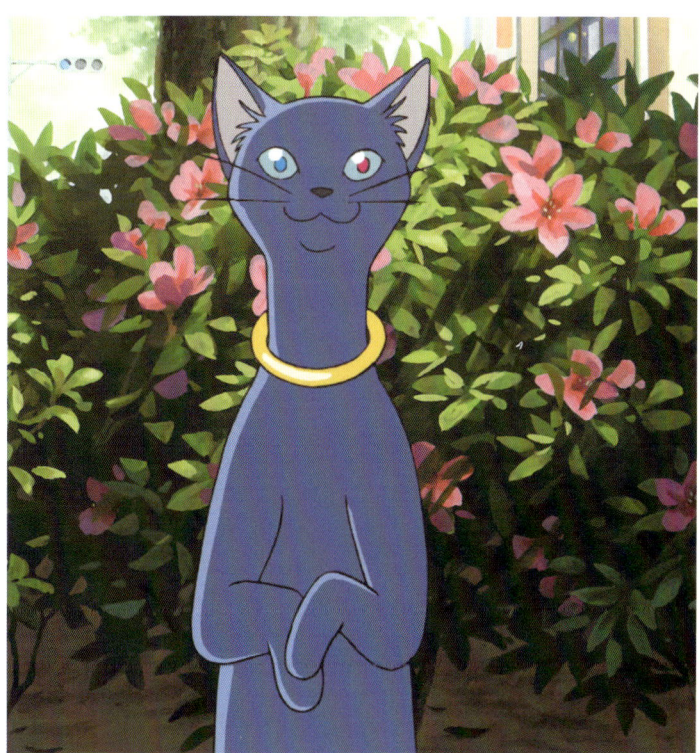

SPEC SHEET

WORK: *The Cat Returns* (*Neko no Ongaeshi*, 猫の恩返し).
CREATORS: Hiroyuki Morita (director); Reiko Yoshida (scriptwriter). Based on a manga by Aoi Hiiragi.
DATE CREATED: July 20, 2002.
PRODUCTION/AVAILABILITY: Studio Ghibli. Available on DVD, Blu-ray, and some streaming services.
CATS' NAMES AND ROLES IN THE WORK: Baron Humbert von Gikkingen and Muta, who already appeared in *Whisper of the Heart*, are the Cat Kingdom's official representatives in the human world, while Prince Lune and Yuki have been rescued by the human heroine and will help her.

Sailor Moon

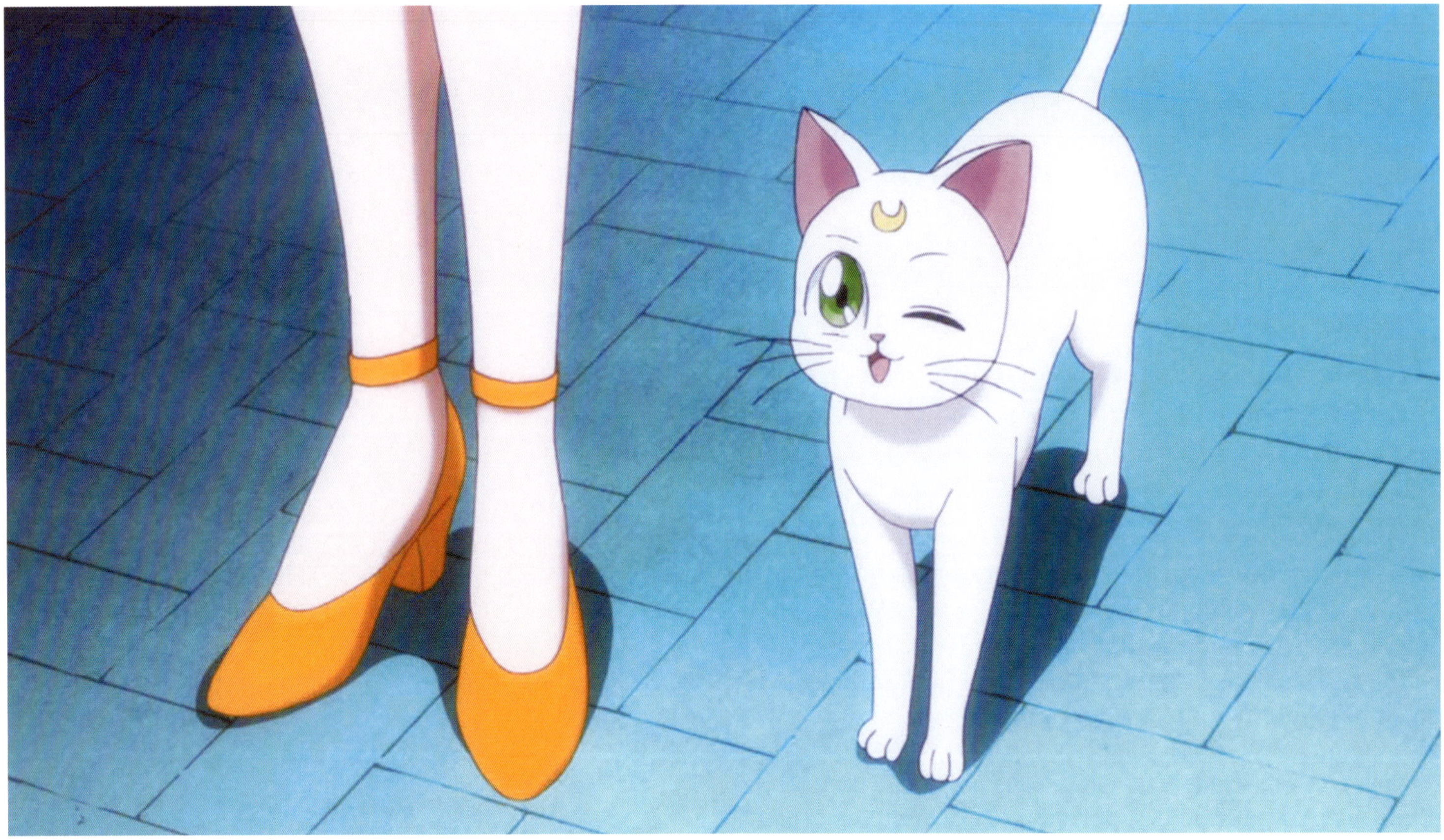

The iconic anime Sailor Moon **tells the story of the reincarnation of Serenity, Princess of the Moon, as a Japanese teenager. Guided by the cat Luna, Usagi seeks victory for love and justice.**

In both the manga and the original anime, Sailor Moon's powers on Earth are bestowed upon her by Luna, a midnight-blue cat. Luna has a moon on her forehead and reveals that Sailor Moon is the reincarnation of the Princess of the Moon. Luna and her companion, Artemis, are the guardian cats of the Moon's powers, originally from the planet Mau. Together, they have a kitten named Diana.

The reincarnation of a Princess of the Moon is a clear reference to the Japanese legend of Princess Kaguya. Dark and sometimes violent, Sailor Moon has the decidedly *kawaii* aesthetic typical of "magical girls" series. Adapted from Naoko Takeuchi's manga, the series marked the revival of the genre of stories about young girls possessing magical powers in the world of *shōjo* (manga for girls). The first animated version ran for two hundred episodes.

The cat characters contribute to the work's cute aesthetic, whether on paper

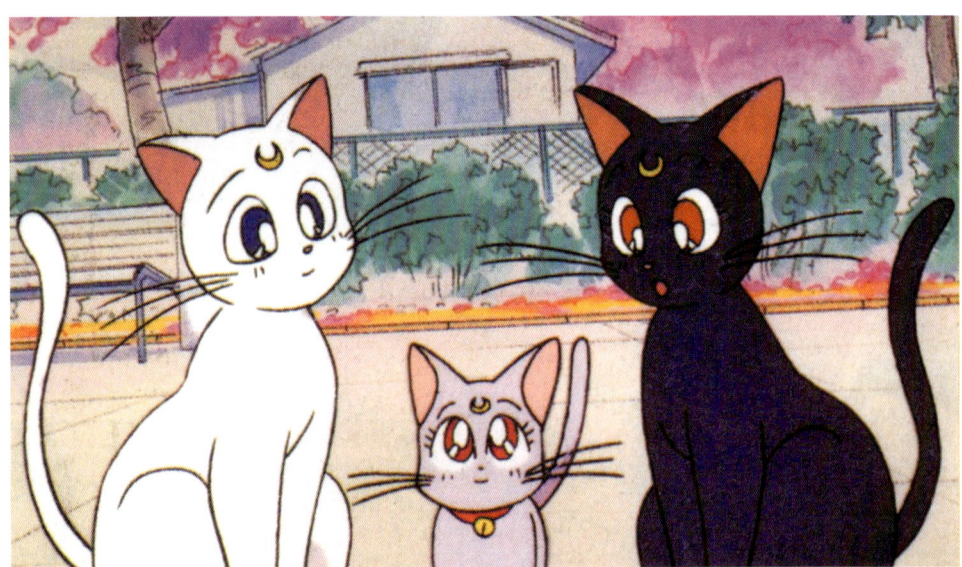

From left to right: Artemis, Diana, and Luna.

or in animation. Many merchandising products feature the felines, especially Luna. Luna is a wise cat. She guides the characters and plays a key role in the narrative. An adviser to the Queen of the Moon, Luna has been sent down to protect the Earth in case of danger.

Although wise, Luna is used as a comic character in two different pairings. The first duo is the one she forms with Usagi. The girl is, apart from her alter ego Sailor Moon, naturally eccentric and outgoing. She spends her time talking about or proposing ridiculous ideas, to which Luna responds with either scathing comments or an expression of despair. The other comic duo is the one she forms with Artemis, another feline guardian. Often on the same wavelength when it comes to saving the world, the pair regularly share domestic scenes. The discovery of Diana, a cat from the future, is particularly funny, as she introduces herself to her father in front of her mother. The gag involves Luna's emotional outburst when she is convinced that Artemis has cheated on her and has an illegitimate child.

The choice of a cat as spiritual guide is in keeping with the manga's *kawaii* style and also helps to lighten its darker side. A story is often less dramatic when told by a cat! The success of the 1990s has faded worldwide, but it continues in Japan, where films such as *Pretty Guardian Sailor Moon Eternal* are regularly released in theaters. 🐾

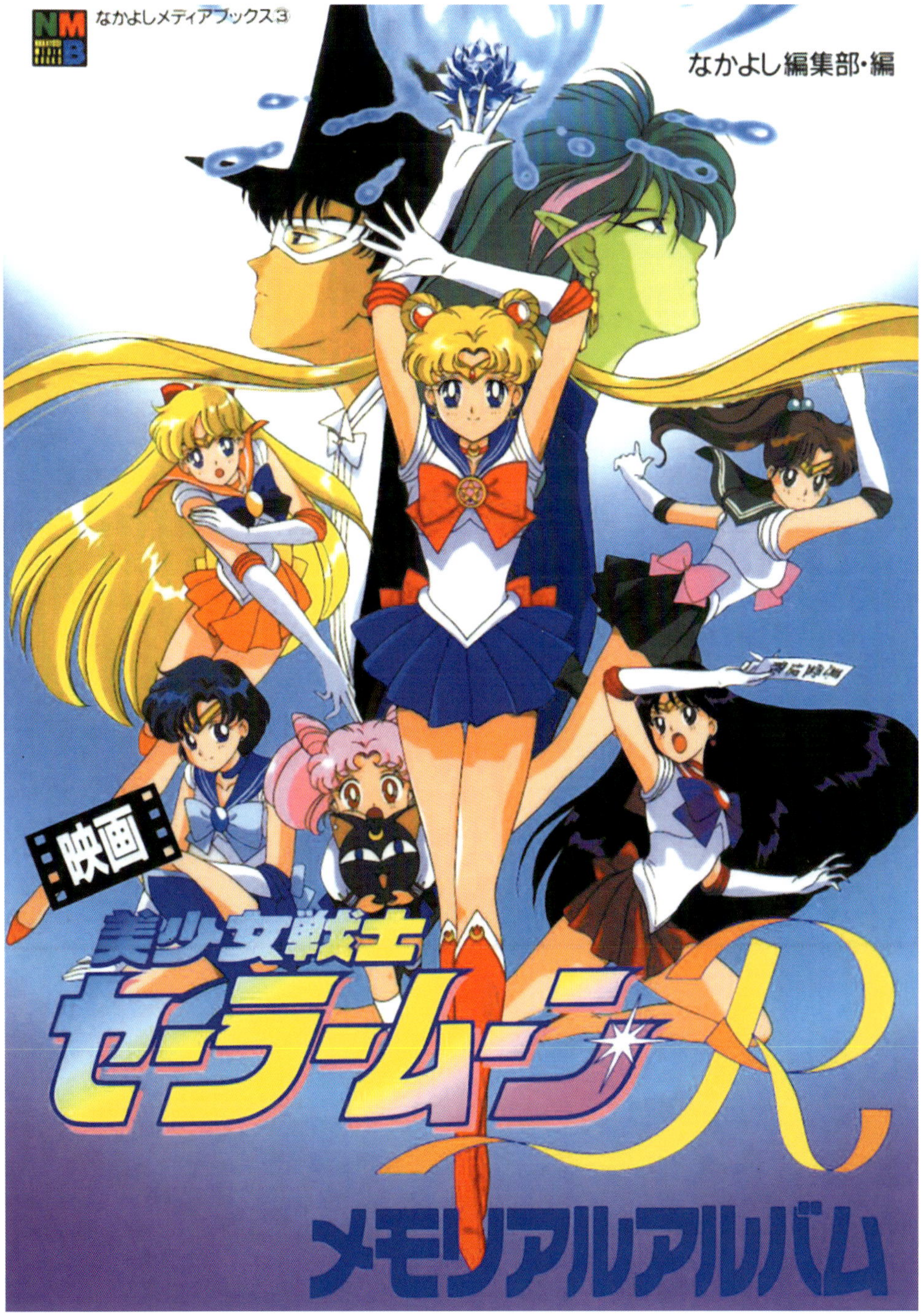

なかよしメディアブックス③

なかよし編集部・編

映画

美少女戦士
セーラームーンR

メモリアルアルバム

SPEC SHEET

WORK: *Sailor Moon*.
CREATOR: Naoko Takeuchi.
DATE CREATED: 1991 for the manga.
PUBLISHER/DISTRIBUTOR/ AVAILABILITY: Kodansha for the manga, Toei Animation for the anime. Available on DVD and Netflix.
CATS' NAMES AND ROLE IN THE WORK: Luna, Artemis, and Diana, the heroines' spiritual guides.

Mr. Mittens

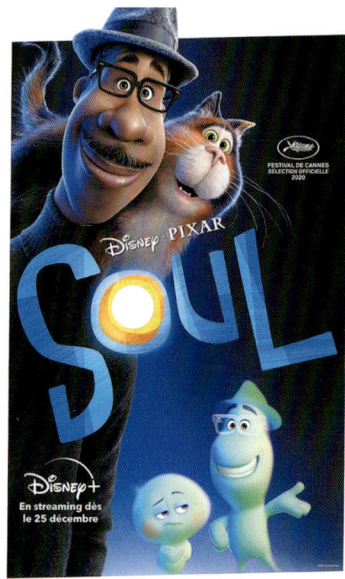

One of the many adventures awaiting musician Joe Gardner as he passes from life to death occurs when he takes over the body of a New York tomcat and guides an indecisive little soul.

When musician Joe Gardner nearly dies suddenly at the beginning of *Soul*, he doesn't expect to become the mentor for 22, a soul who isn't quite ready to take on a body. After a series of twists and turns, he returns to Earth, but in the body of a big, long-haired tomcat, and has to guide 22, who has taken refuge in his own body. Aside from the comic potential of seeing a cat, even a therapy cat, act and talk like a human being, this transposition is a way for Joe to rediscover his hometown from another point of view. And he sees himself with fresh eyes, watching the people he knows interact with his body, unaware that it harbors a soul other than his own. As he guides 22's steps on Earth, his cat side (greedy with the pizza slice, dependent on a human for certain actions) will count just as much as the schoolteacher and jazz musician that he is. As for the soul of the cat whose place he has taken, it makes the long journey to the afterlife without discussion at the time of transfer, and without the shadow of a regret. (Don't worry; he comes back in the end. Cats have nine lives, you know!)

He is also left with the task of acting as a shamanic guide for soul 22, inspiring her to take human form and live. Similarly, as a therapy animal in a hospital, the cat's soul helped patients endure pain and sometimes cross over to the other side. Could Pete Docter be alluding to Azrael, aka Azzie, the nursing home cat in Stephen King's novel *Doctor Sleep* who always settles on the beds of residents who are about to die? On a lighter note, because this is a cartoon for the whole family, Joe Gardner will accomplish his mission, as a cat and as a man, and be rewarded for it. 🐾

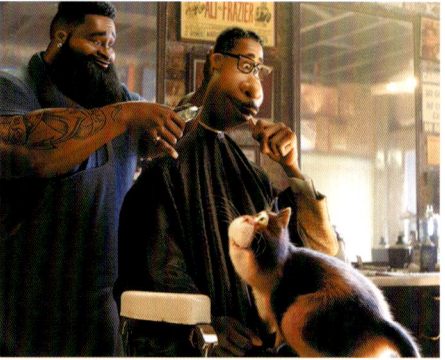

SPEC SHEET

CAT'S NAME: Mr. Mittens.
WORK: *Soul*.
CREATORS: Pete Docter and Kemp Powers (directors); Pete Docter, Kemp Powers, and Mike Jones (screenwriters).
RELEASE DATE: December 25, 2020.
DISTRIBUTOR/AVAILABILITY: Pixar Animations Studios, Walt Disney Pictures. Available on DVD, Blu-ray, and Disney+.
CAT'S CHARACTERISTICS: Chunky calico therapy cat with green eyes.

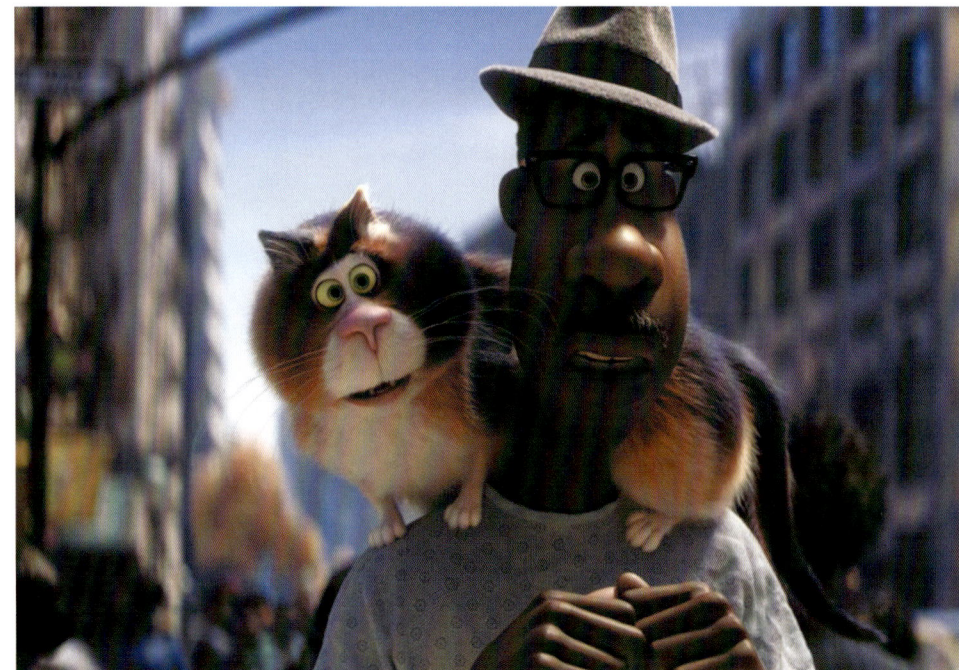

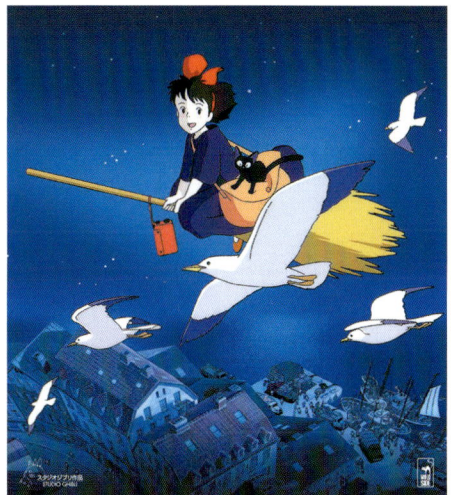

Kiki's companion in both Hayao Miyazaki's animated film and Eiko Kadono's book series, Jiji seems to embody all the stereotypes of the magical familiar. In practice, he's more of a guide in the teenager's learning process.

Whether you discovered *Kiki's Delivery Service* through Hayao Miyazaki's film or Eiko Kadono's books, it's impossible to forget her companion, Jiji. A witch's cat, his coat is as black as his human's apprentice dress, conforming in this respect to the stereotypes of the magical pet. In this world, he was raised with the young witch since birth. He has been her companion since she was ten, helping her when she has to leave her family at age thirteen to set up on her own as a witch in a new town. He's the only link she has left with her childhood, and the only touch of home.

The cat is more than just a companion. Through his conversations and antics, he is also one of the main sources of comedy in both the film and the book and serves as a sounding board for Kiki to test her ideas (even if it means being mauled by a young customer who thinks he's a stuffed toy) and encourage or warn her when she makes risky decisions. A young adult cat at the beginning of the story, he grows up with his protégée. And in the film, he loses his voice when she loses her magic. Except that when Kiki, who gains more confidence in herself, regains her powers, Jiji remains mute. The witch has grown up, completed her apprenticeship, and become totally independent. Meanwhile, Jiji has fallen in love and started a family with the neighbor's white cat. While he remains close to the witch, he no longer needs to be anything more than an ordinary cat to her. Many years later, another chatty black cat finds himself helping another magical child in a Studio Ghibli film: Thomas, the familiar of a "wicked" witch in *Earwig and the Witch*, the 2021 film directed by Goro Miyazaki. 🐾

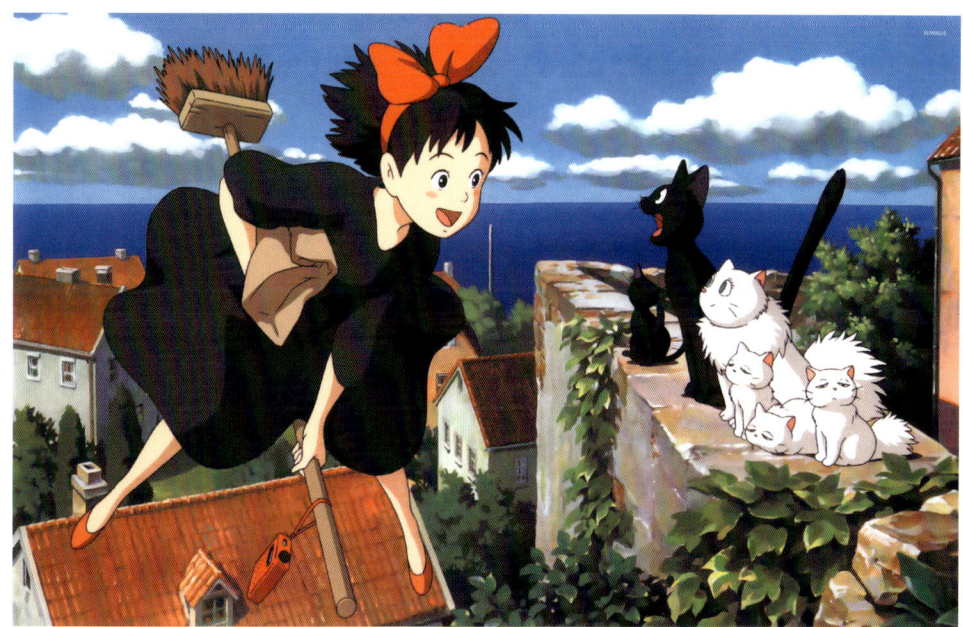

SPEC SHEET

CAT'S NAME: Jiji.
WORK: *Kiki's Delivery Service*.
CREATORS: Eiko Kadono (for the book) and Hayao Miyazaki (the film's director and screenwriter).
DATE CREATED: January 25, 1985 (publication date of the first book).
PUBLISHER/DISTRIBUTOR/AVAILABILITY: Annick Press published the first English edition. Walt Disney Pictures was the original US distributor. Available on DVD, Blu-ray, and some streaming services.
CAT'S CHARACTERISTICS: Black witch's cat who is talkative and teasing.

The Cheshire Cat

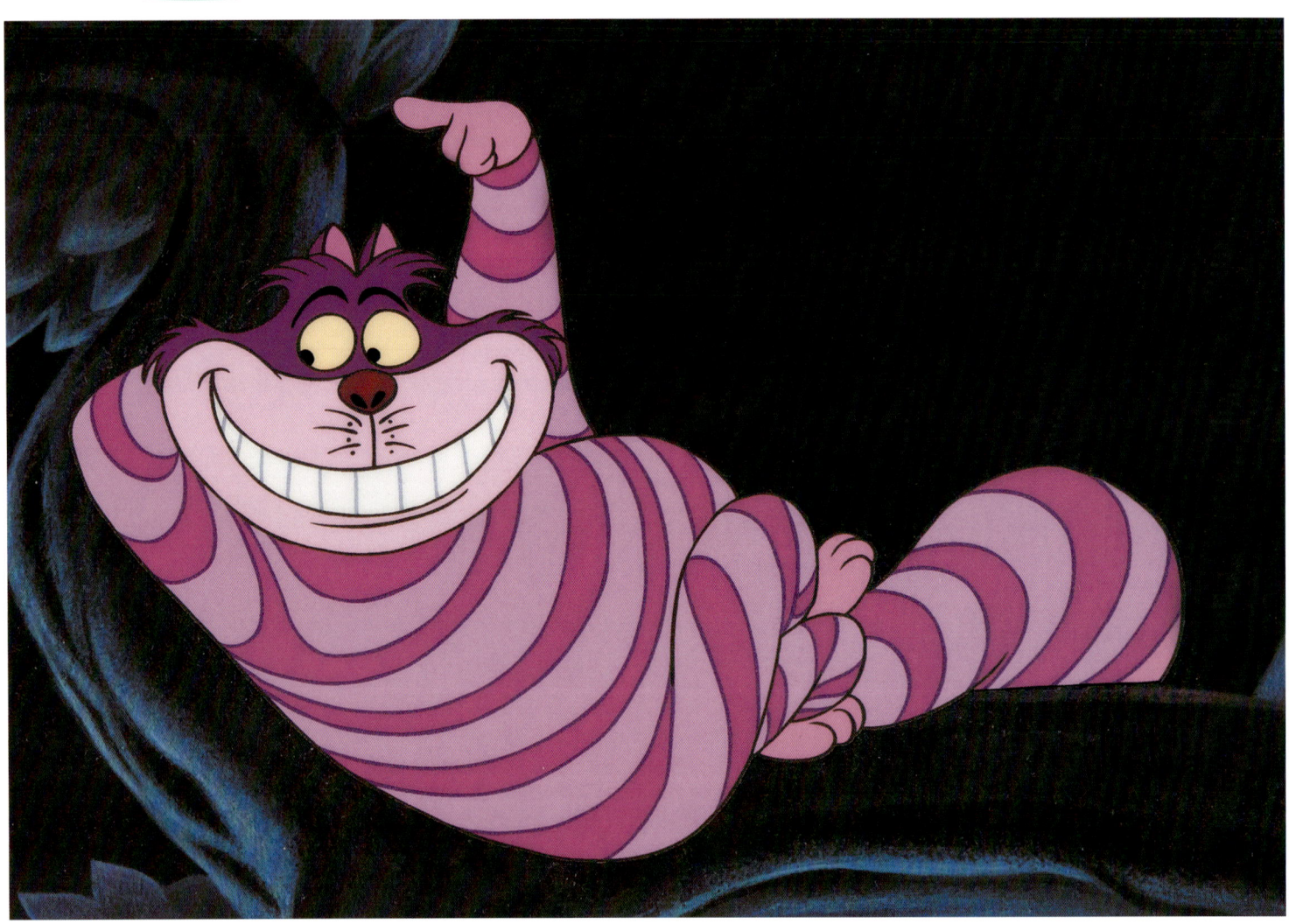

In Alice's Adventures in Wonderland, *Lewis Carroll describes a fantastical, surreal world where a young girl encounters a cast of characters, each one more unlikely than the last. Along the way, she meets the strange Cheshire Cat.*

In every adaptation of the novel, the cat's smile is his main characteristic. In fact, it's the first thing that catches the eye of the novel's heroine. The author's description says, "it had very long claws and a great many teeth," which makes him a little unsettling, in line with most of the other characters.

When he meets Alice, the Cheshire Cat explains that he is, in essence, crazy. To illustrate his point, he compares the behavior of a cat and a dog. The canine barks when he's upset and wags his tail when he's happy. "Now I growl when I'm pleased and wag my tail when I'm angry. Therefore, I'm mad," he adds to justify his reasoning.

The question of madness and normality is at the heart of this work, which combines all the characteristics of a children's story with adult issues. The novel has become a reference point in pop culture, as in the *Matrix* film, and is regularly associated with a trip on psychotropic drugs.

But the cat isn't as crazy as he claims. His role is that of a guide in the broadest sense of the word. The animal also has the power to disappear and reappear wherever it pleases. Not only does he point the way to the Mad Hatter, but he also shares a philosophical reflection with the protagonist, telling her that she's sure to get somewhere "if only you walk long enough."

Alice's Adventures in Wonderland has been a major inspiration for film, television, and literature. The novel has also had several adaptations, all featuring the Cheshire Cat. Disney Studios tackled the story in 1951. The cat initially appears off-camera, singing a nonsensical song. The viewer first sees his smile in the dark before being able to make out his psychedelic pink-and-purple striped coat. In this adaptation, the cat is clearly mad. He leaves paw prints when he's invisible, sings incoherently, and loses his memory in the middle of conversations. His exuberance isn't enough to mitigate the film's unsettling strangeness. Directed by Clyde Geronimi, Wilfred Jackson, and Hamilton Luske, *Alice in Wonderland* remains a unique film in Disney's filmography, both in terms of narrative and tone, and is a mash-up of the original book and its sequel, *Through the Looking Glass*, which was published in 1871.

While this is undoubtedly the most famous adaptation of the novel, it wasn't the studio's first. Walt Disney himself initiated the *Alice Comedies* series of short films. This project, whose pilot film was called *Alice's Wonderland*, was produced in 1923. It combined live action and animation. It depicted the adventures of Alice, a young girl who sees characters from an animation studio come to life around her. The seed of what would become the Disney theme parks was already there. Yet, as innovative as the project was, the production costs led to the downfall of Laugh-O-Gram, the first production company founded by Mickey's then twenty-one-year-old creator. With his pilot in hand, the young producer headed to California to sell his project, with which he would create the Disney Brothers Studio.

In 2010, master animator and gothic filmmaker Tim Burton took on the classic. The eccentric director shot a live-action film starring his muse, Johnny Depp, as the Mad Hatter. The

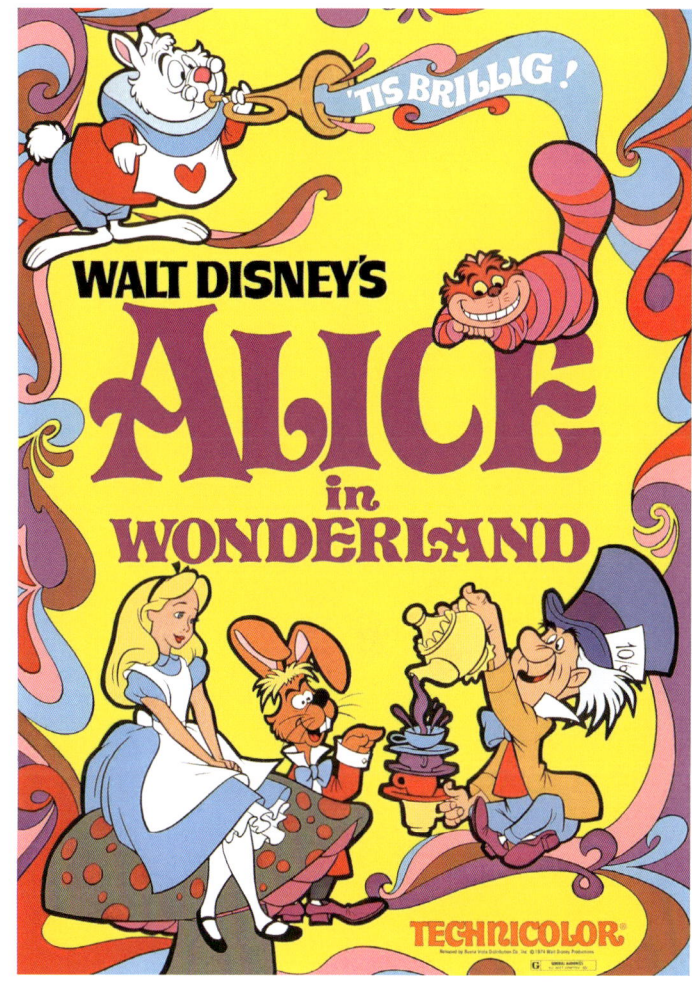

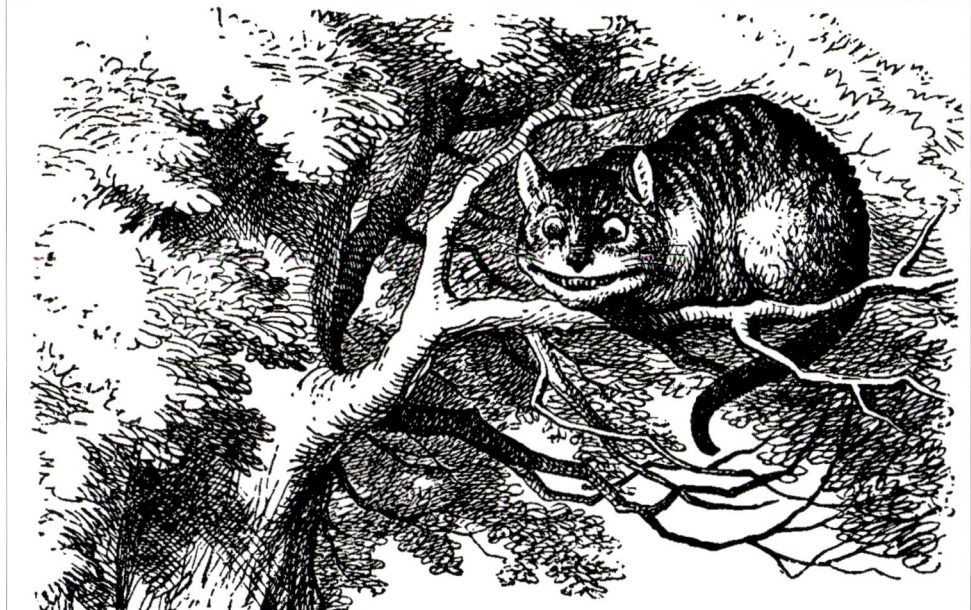

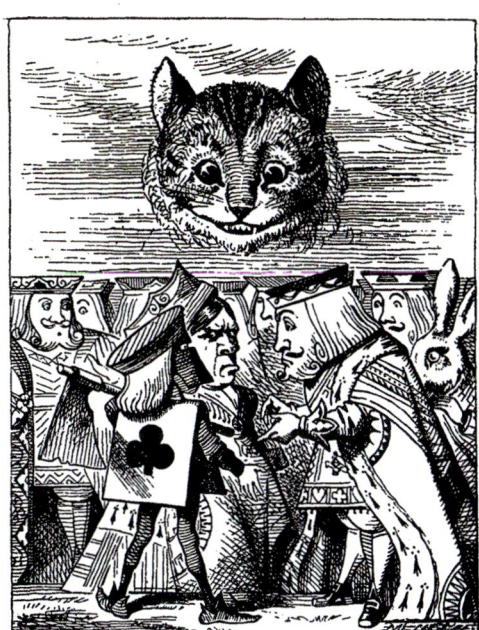

The Cheshire Cat, illustrations for the novel, John Tenniel, 1869.

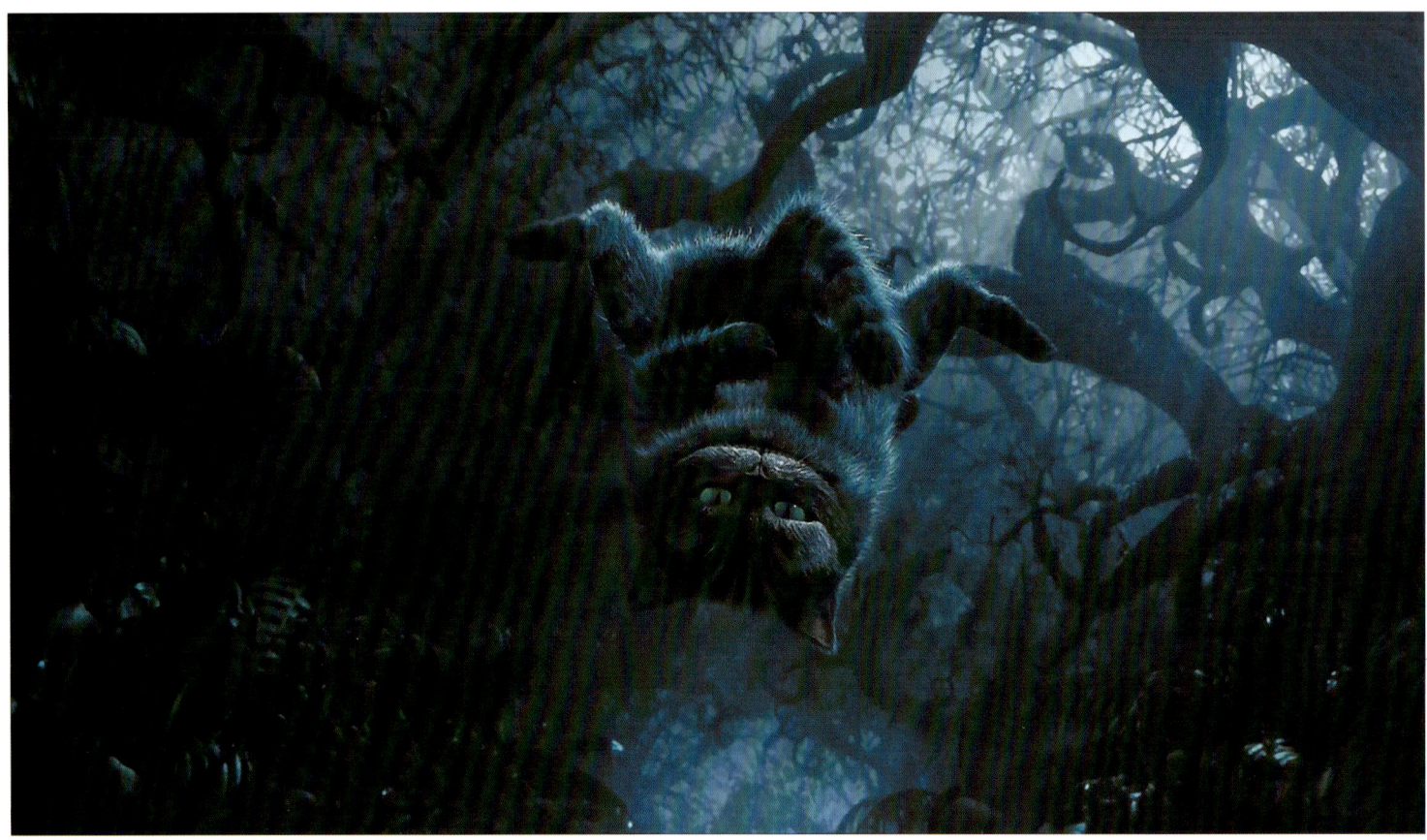

In the Tim Burton film.

movie's world is generally dark. The dull blue colors that filter through the images contribute to the impression of a frightening tale. A former Disney animator, Burton clearly drew inspiration from the original animated film for the cat's movements and disappearances. The feline flies and, like in the animated version, manages to separate his head from his body. He's still striped, but this time he's gray and green (an unearthly bright green). He's no longer exuberant, but glides with light detachment. His voice is so soft that, combined with his broad smile, it becomes somewhat disturbing. The character fits well with the director's imagination, in which the bizarre becomes normal and vice versa. This is the case in many of his films, such as *Edward Scissorhands* and *Beetlejuice*. The film cost Disney Studios $200 million to produce but grossed a billion dollars during its run. In 2016, the team was reunited for *Alice Through the Looking Glass*. It was a more mixed success, with a box office of $299 million against a budget of $170 million.

SPEC SHEET

CAT'S NAME: The Cheshire Cat.
WORK: *Alice's Adventures in Wonderland*.
CREATOR: Lewis Carroll.
DATE CREATED: 1865.
PUBLISHER: First published by Macmillan.
CAT'S CHARACTERISTICS: A big, toothy smile. He talks and calls himself mad.

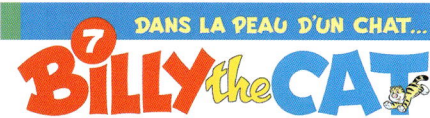

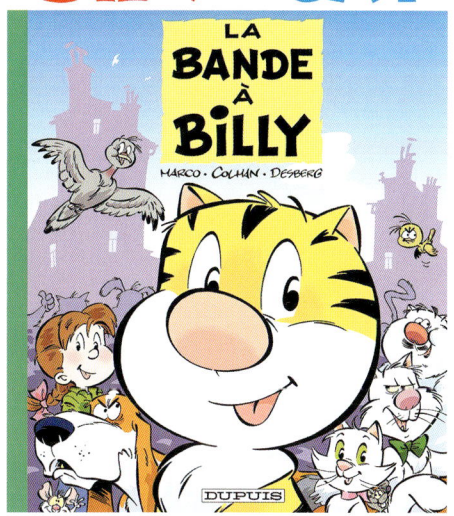

Billy, a young boy who is cruel to animals, is turned into a kitten and must learn to atone for his behavior if he is ever to become human again. In his new life as a cat, he will change and make friends with other animals.

In 1982, *Le Journal de Spirou*, the iconic Franco-Belgian comics magazine, published the adventures of Billy, a boy who was transformed into a cat after a car accident. Having made mistakes all his life, Billy can't go to heaven and is, ironically, forced to turn into an animal. In 1989, Dupuis published a complete volume of the comic titled *Dans la peau d'un chat* [*In the Body of a Cat*]. Billy makes friends like the cat Monsieur Hubert, who gives him a place to sleep and introduces him to feline life and the joys of freedom. In the first few volumes, Saucisse, Billy's basset hound when he was human, takes revenge for his past behavior and mean tricks. But as the story progresses, the one-eyed cat Sanctifer becomes the comic strip's main antagonist.

At the end of the sixth volume, series creator and illustrator Stéphane Colman handed *Billy the Cat* over to fellow writer Stephen Desberg. Desberg himself abandoned the series in Volume 9, and after that, the series, headed by Jean-Louis Janssens and Peral, didn't fully convince readers and was discontinued after two more volumes.

In 1996, an animated version, *Billy the Cat, dans la peau d'un chat*, was produced by Les Films du Triangle. The narrative was changed for television. It's less subtle and, above all, not as sad. In this version, Billy doesn't die. He is transformed into a kitten by a sorcerer after mistreating his cat. Any violent or overly emotional character

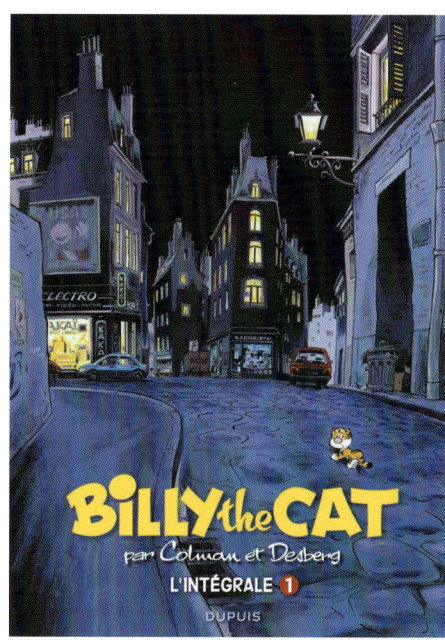

is erased in favor of action and adventure. Nevertheless, the fifty-two episodes produced over two seasons are well-made. In the paper version, the characters often had dark pasts, such as Monsieur Hubert's tragic romance, or the explanation of Billy's behavior. The young boy's mischief is attributed to the

pain of having a father who is too often absent. A cast of strong characters who evolve over the course of each volume, combined with meticulous graphic design, make *Billy the Cat* an essential in modern Franco-Belgian comics.

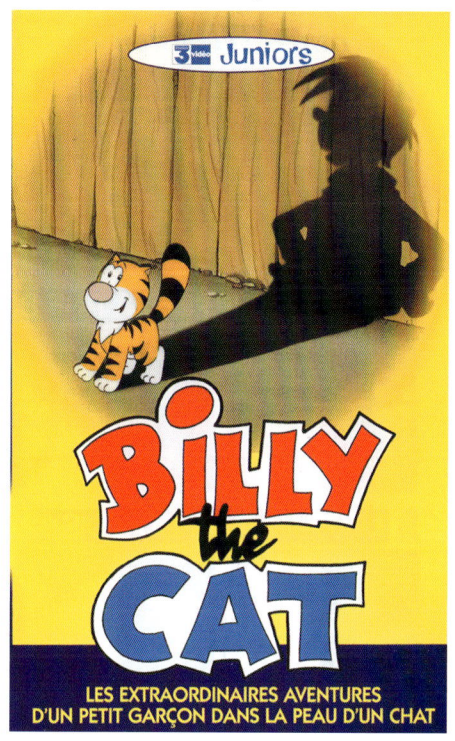

SPEC SHEET

CAT'S NAME: Billy.
WORK: *Billy the Cat*.
CREATORS: Stéphane Colman and Stephen Desberg.
DATE CREATED: 1981.
PUBLISHER/AVAILABILITY: Dupuis. Eleven books and two collections. (In French.)
CAT'S CHARACTERISTICS: Orange kitten with black stripes, a pink nose, and a white chest.

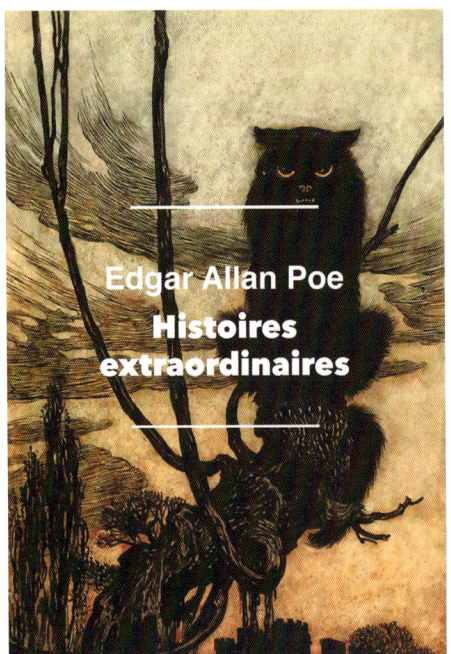

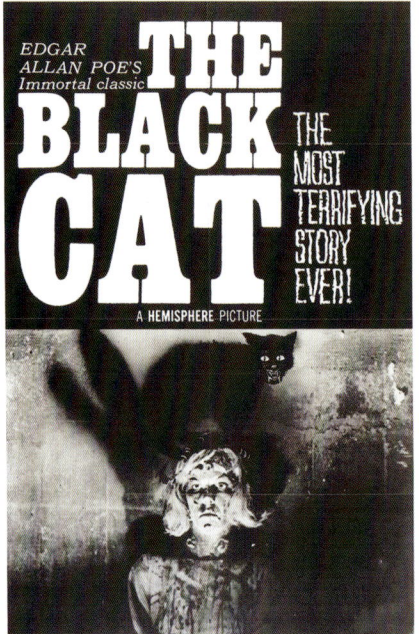

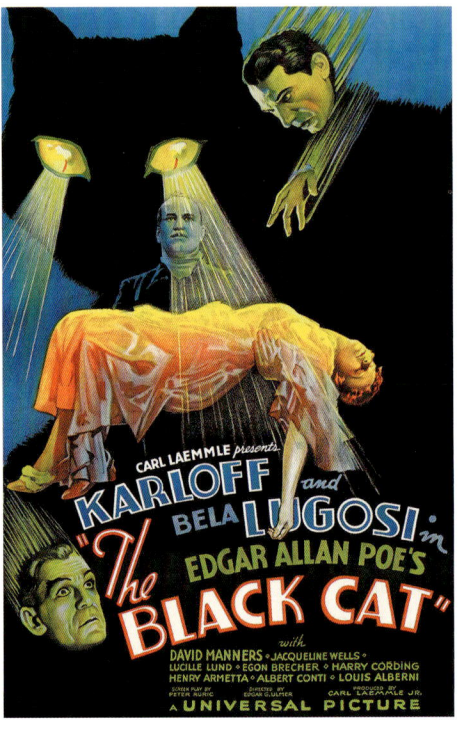

A short story bordering on the fantastic, Edgar Allan Poe's tale has been the subject of many adaptations and variations, further anchoring the black cat in the horror imagination and making it an animal personification of vengeance.

Edgar Allan Poe's "The Black Cat" is one of the author's most memorable tales. Told in the first person from the point of view of the cat's "victim," this tale treads the borderline between the supernatural and the delusions of an alcoholic. Although he claims to love animals, the narrator, who is driven to violence by his excessive drinking, mutilates and then kills the black cat he claims to love so much. Haunted by the cat, or by the personification of his guilt, he ends up driven to murderous madness and directly to the gallows. The cat also plays a psychopomp role, not announcing the narrator's death, but revealing the fate of one of his victims to the authorities.

In addition to the ambiguity of the text itself and its strange coincidences, "The Black Cat" leaves its mark through the way the feline's position evolves in the narrator's eyes. So much so, in fact, that this short story became one of the author's best-known and most studied texts and was widely adapted in all kinds of media: comic books, video games, horror and fantasy anthology episodes, radio serials, and, of course, film adaptations featuring some of the biggest names in horror (Bela Lugosi, Boris Karloff, Dario Argento, Lucio Fulci, and many others). Some of these works clearly display their kinship in the title, while others play around with the theme, like Roger Corman's *The Tomb of Ligeia* (1965), which merges the plot of this short story and another by Edgard Allan Poe, "Ligeia," in which a nobleman's first wife comes back to haunt the second, ultimately driving the narrator to madness. In the film, the black cat is one of the incarnations of the deceased wife, but once again, the cat acts as a bad conscience and psychopomp, playing on the guilt of both the new bride and the husband. 🐾

SPEC SHEET

WORK: "The Black Cat."
CREATOR: Edgar Allan Poe.
DATE OF FIRST PUBLICATION: August 19, 1843.
PUBLISHER/AVAILABILITY: It was first published in the *Saturday Evening Post*. It's available from many publishers.
CAT'S NAME AND ROLE IN THE WORK: Pluto, the narrator's cat, originally with all-black fur.

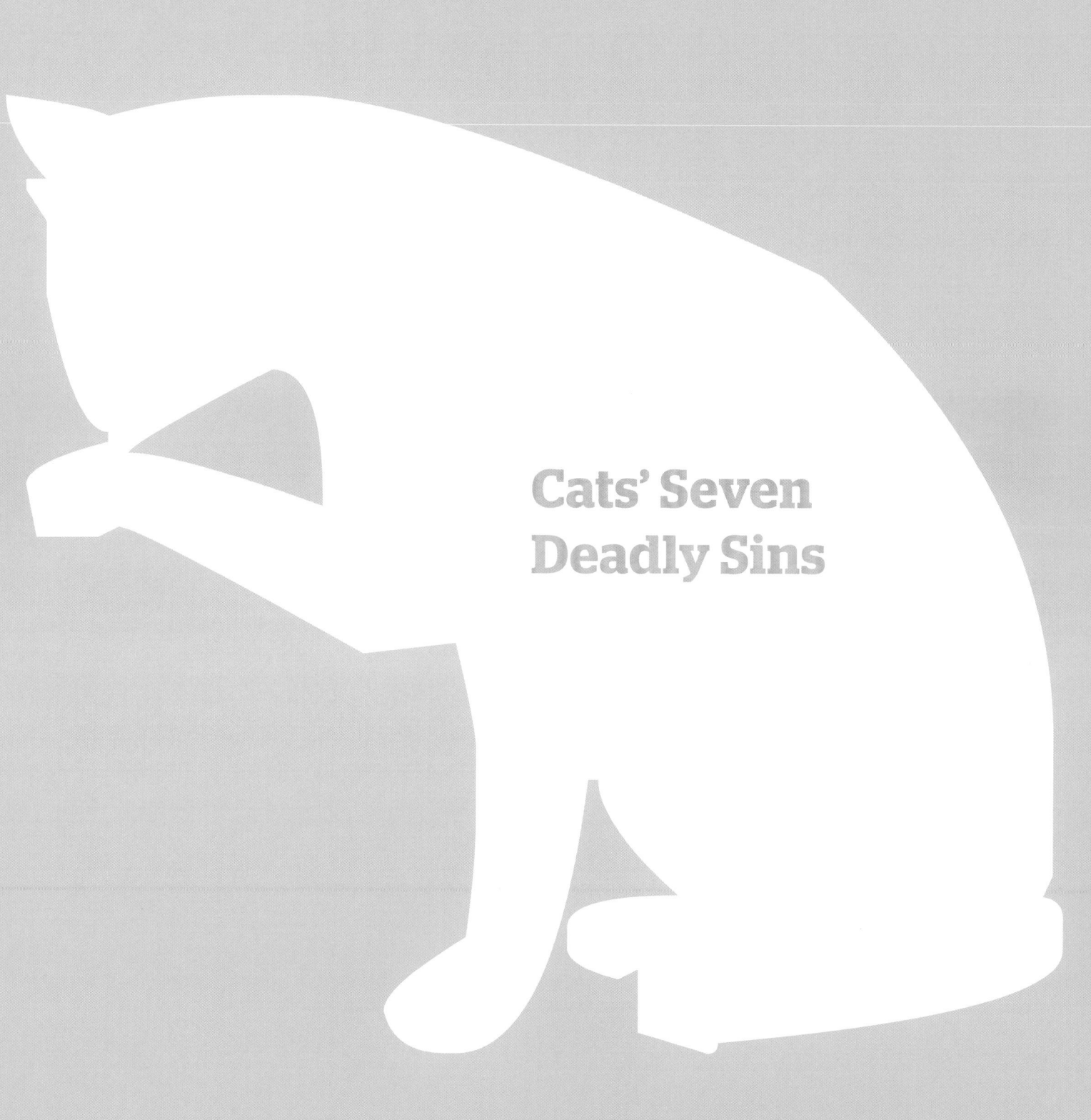

Cats' Seven
Deadly Sins

Cats' Seven Deadly Sins

While cats' elegant, clever, and cute sides are regularly featured in fiction and pop culture in general, feline vices are also widely portrayed. The animals are loved as much for their sinful instincts as for their virtues.

Gluttony

The seven deadly sins are pride, envy, sloth, greed, wrath, lust, and, of course, gluttony. Cats are rightly or wrongly associated with all these vices in works of fiction. Gluttony is undoubtedly the one that comes up the most. This can be made clear to the viewer by emphasizing the cat's overindulgence. This is the case with Garfield, whose love of food goes beyond mere hunger. The cat is fed by his owner, and his love of food goes beyond simply enjoying a meal. Dogs are also voracious animals, but cats' decidedly thieving nature highlights this trait in the feline more than in the canine (although poorly trained dogs can be just as thieving, if not more so, than some cats).

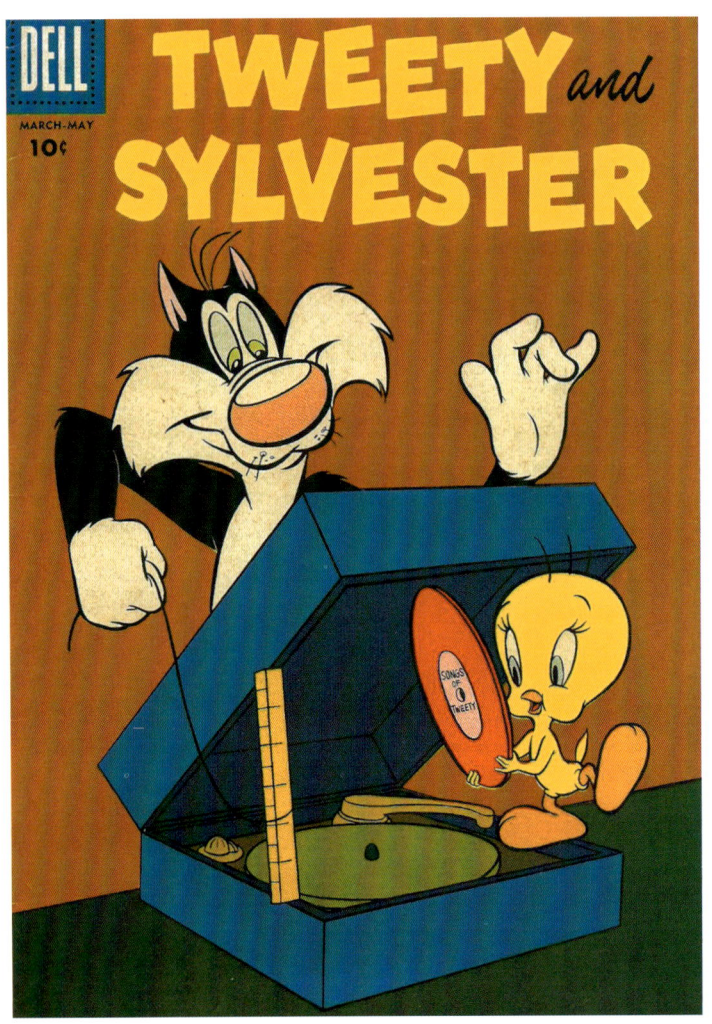

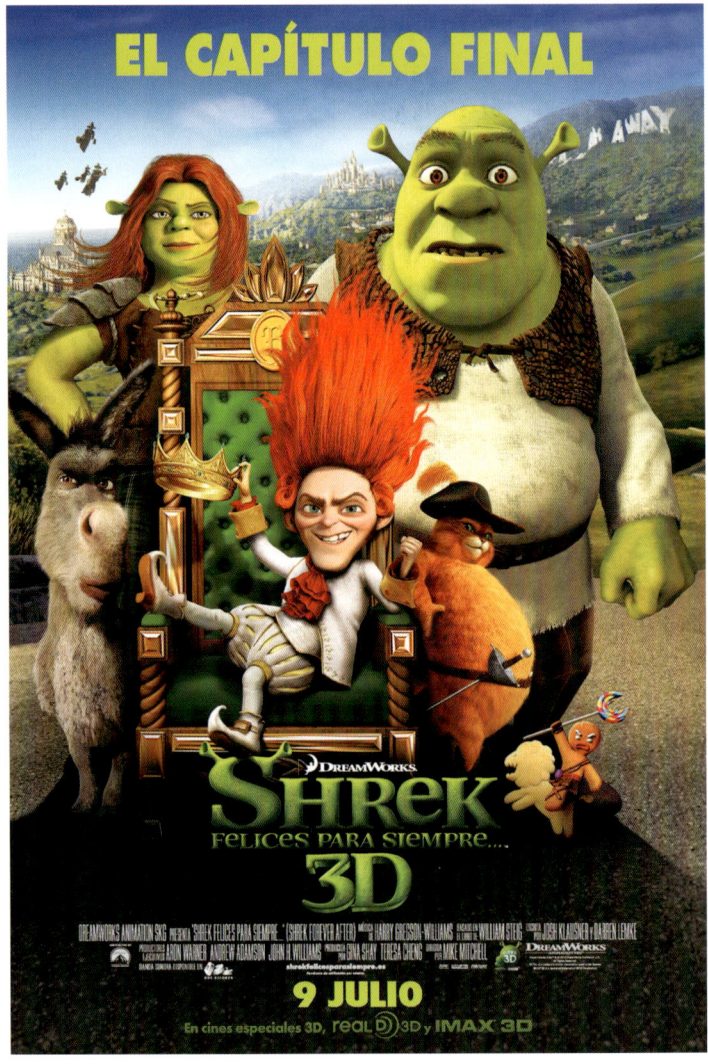

Gluttonous cats are often large and sedentary. They have been domesticated by humans, and they hunt for the simple pleasure of playing and killing. Eating is often a secondary objective in the pursuit of their prey. Although Sylvester hunts his prey with the aim of eating it, Tom doesn't usually go after Jerry for food. In anthropomorphic representations of cats, gluttonous cats are an image of sedentary modern humans. The idleness associated with obesity even prevents them from hunting. This is the case in *Shrek 4*, where the obese Puss in Boots lets a mouse drink milk from his plate because he's too lazy to catch it. While gluttony is a trait that appears regularly in cats, it's the result—obesity—that represents domestication and the loss of their wild nature.

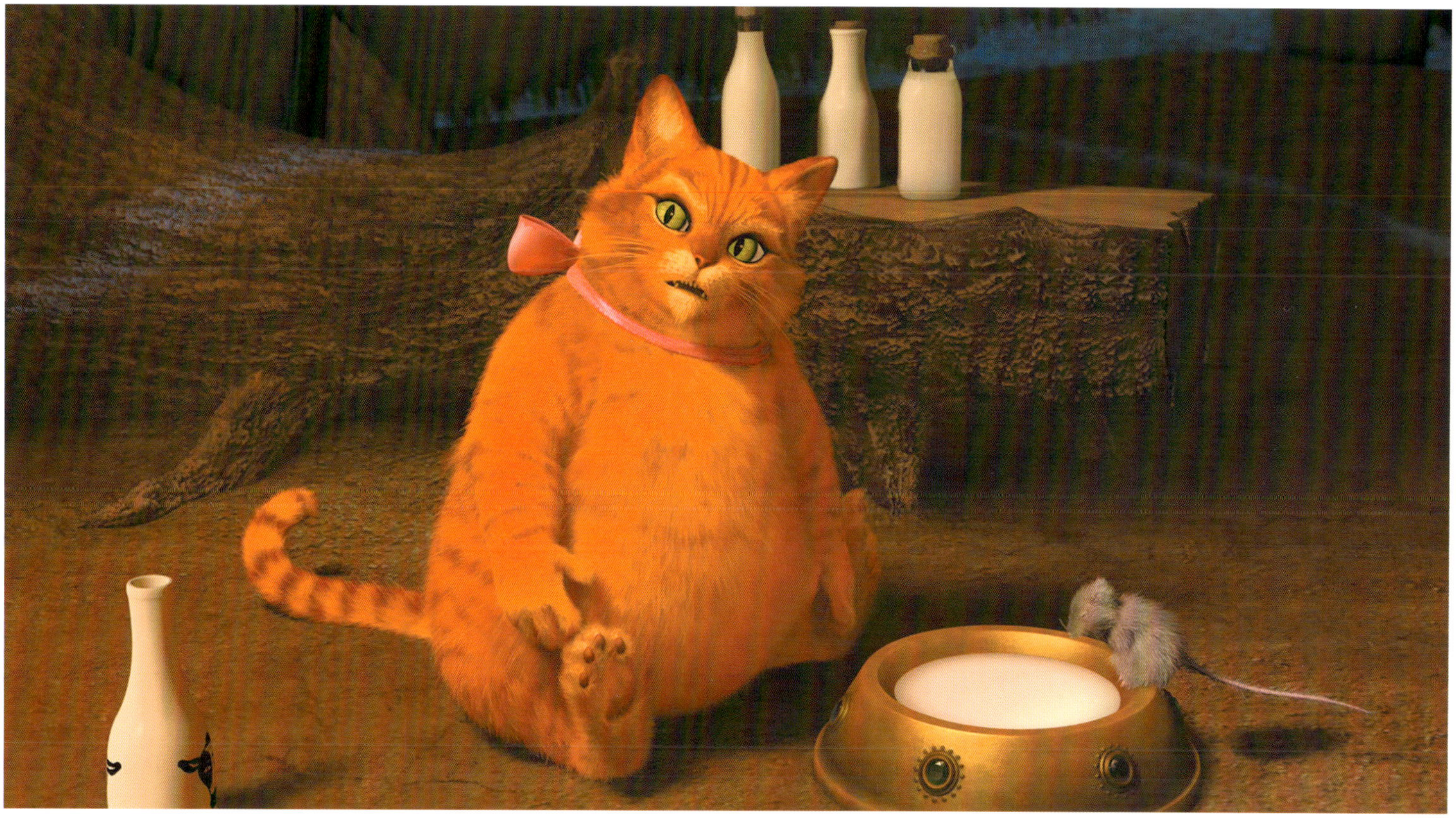

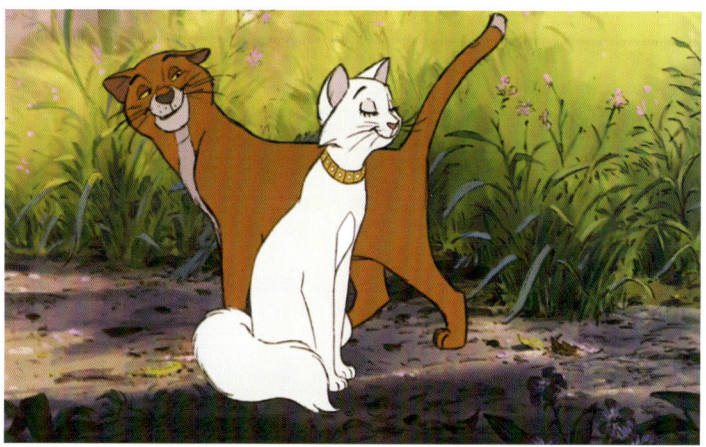

Pride

Unlike good-natured dogs, cats are known for their strong, sometimes cantankerous character. Their egos are big and regularly put to the test when they fail to capture prey. Pride is, by definition, having a high opinion of oneself. Felines' haughty way of walking contributes to this impression of being proud animals; sometimes they're considered aristocratic, like in *The Aristocats*, and other times, they're seen as full of themselves, such as in *Cats & Dogs*. This flaw is regularly used in comedy, as viewers enjoy watching a cat drape himself in pride despite failure or disappointment.

In the cartoon classics, the chase may start out as defending the home from a thieving mouse, or just as a simple hunt. Later, the cat's objective often turns into an obsession with stalking. It's not uncommon for Looney Tunes's Sylvester to have blueprints or develop machines from the Acme company to achieve his goals. Pride pushes the animal to go beyond the reasonable point of giving up.

In *Stuart Little*, the cat's frustration is based on the fact that one of his masters is a mouse. In *Shrek 2*, spared by the green ogre, Puss in Boots puts his honor at the service of the hero. This time, pride is associated with a positive value rather than a sin.

Envy

While envy can refer to general desire, in religious terms, this sin is more synonymous with covetousness. It can also generate very negative feelings, such as resentment and, above all, jealousy. Someone else has a material or immaterial possession, and the feline wants the same. Cats are perceived as deeply selfish animals who will always put their own needs before those of their masters. In fiction, if they're envious,

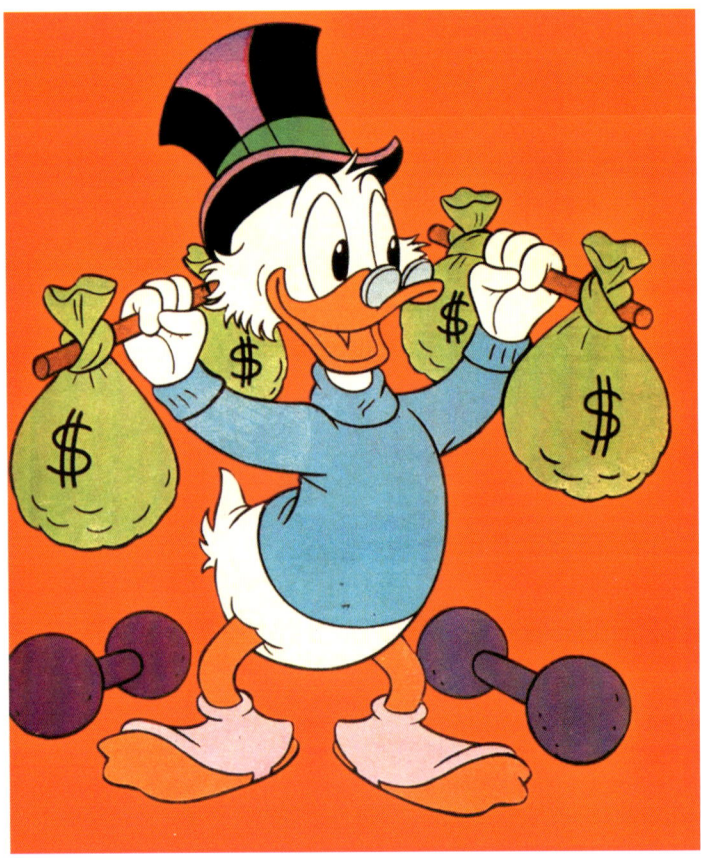

Greed

Greedy fictional cats love to hoard money and possessions. Unlike Uncle Scrooge, the millionaire duck, most cats don't use money. Aesop's ant isn't a lender, and neither are felines. Cats want more attention, more food, more possessions, and they're not prepared to share the benefits of their domestication. Such is the case with Looney Tunes's Claude, who isn't ready to open his home to another pet, whatever it may be. This fault is less often associated with laziness and gluttony. Stingy cats are cantankerous and malicious. "Plague take all misers and all miserly ways!" Molière said in *The Miser*. Cats' greed is more of a possessive nature than a true desire to accumulate. However, cats in fiction like gold and love to steal. Puss in Boots shows his venality when he agrees to kill Shrek for a bag of gold. In general, cats in fiction steal for pleasure and rarely out of need.

Wrath

Wrath is probably the least common flaw in fictional cats, who are often portrayed as cold and calculating. Cats typically lose self-control less often than dogs, which are considered more impulsive. Explosive anger is seen in Mr. Tinkles, the power-hungry cat from *Cats & Dogs*. He screams and lashes out repeatedly in the film, displaying excessive, over-the-top emotion. Salem, the four-legged companion in *Sabrina the Teenage Witch*, shares these feelings, which lead to him being cursed and turned into a cat. Meowth, Team Rocket's Pokémon, is another example of angry feline behavior.

they won't stay that way for long; they will act to capture the object of their desire, even if it means stealing. They covet not only objects, but also the attention their human might give to someone else. This trait of cats is often associated with pride and greed, symbolizing the archetypal thieving cat. In the *Shrek* film series, Puss in Boots is envious of the donkey's role as best friend. Similarly, Mr. Tinkles wants to prevent the creation of a vaccine against dog allergies, so that humans don't prefer them to his own species.

Sloth

On average, cats sleep between twelve and sixteen hours a day. Since the average human sleeps only eight hours, it's not surprising that we have the impression that felines spend their lives sleeping, and they're associated with laziness, a fault that is often linked to gluttony. In Western societies, obesity is seen as a sign of laziness, and the same applies to our four-legged companions.

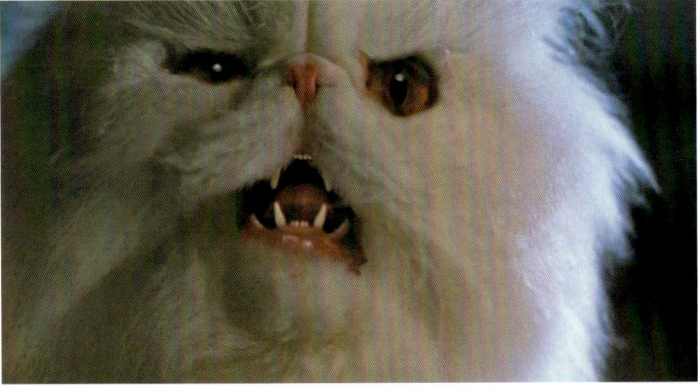

Mr. Tinkles.

BELOVED CATS: HUMANIZATION AND ANTHROPOMORPHISM

Cats are sinners, and that doesn't necessarily make them the villains of the works in which they appear. Sometimes secondary characters, sometimes main characters, or even full-fledged antagonists, their flaws are far from making them unpopular. On the contrary, cats are deeply humanized by their character traits.

Cats are often caricatures of human behavior. The sum of all these sins sometimes makes them complex beings, and even psychiatric cases. In the film *The Voices*, the pet cat is the guilty conscience of a madman. Cats are amplified versions of all our faults. Our anthropomorphic projection makes them funny. Cats render the amorality of these feelings acceptable. It's unimaginable that audiences would watch an adult human being try to kill a baby because it's going to disrupt their daily life. Yet this is how the adventures of the cartoon cat Claude (see p. 47) would be transposed.

It would also be difficult to make a comedy about an obese man who just likes to sleep and eat without it being a little tragic or very dubiously humorous. Garfield's cat condition makes his comics funny. As humans, we project our desire to be carefree onto our furry companions. A sinfully naughty cat has a cathartic function. In a way, felines are the psychopaths we all dream of being.

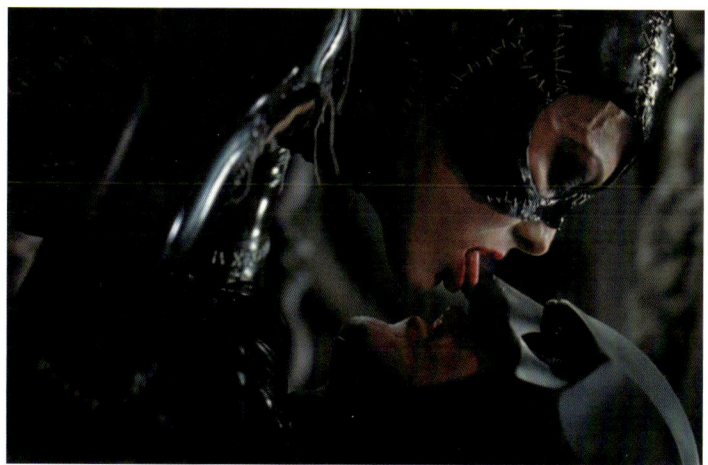

Batman Returns, Catwoman and Batman.

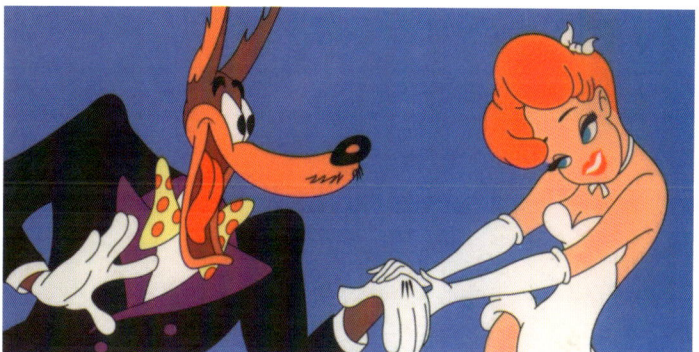

Tex Avery's wolf.

Lust

Lust is the pursuit of sexual pleasure. The sexualization of cats in pop culture is fundamentally feminine. The animals' curves and swaying gait are used both sensually and sexually in characters such as Catwoman and the many cat women in American and Japanese comics. Fictional cats may be interested in sex, but this is rarely their main failing. Wolves are more commonly used for this type of analogy, like in Tex Avery cartoons. Puss in Boots, with his supposedly sexy Latino accent, makes use of the register of seduction with women or female cats, but it's often more a means of getting his way than a real search for sexual satisfaction. 🐾

ALF

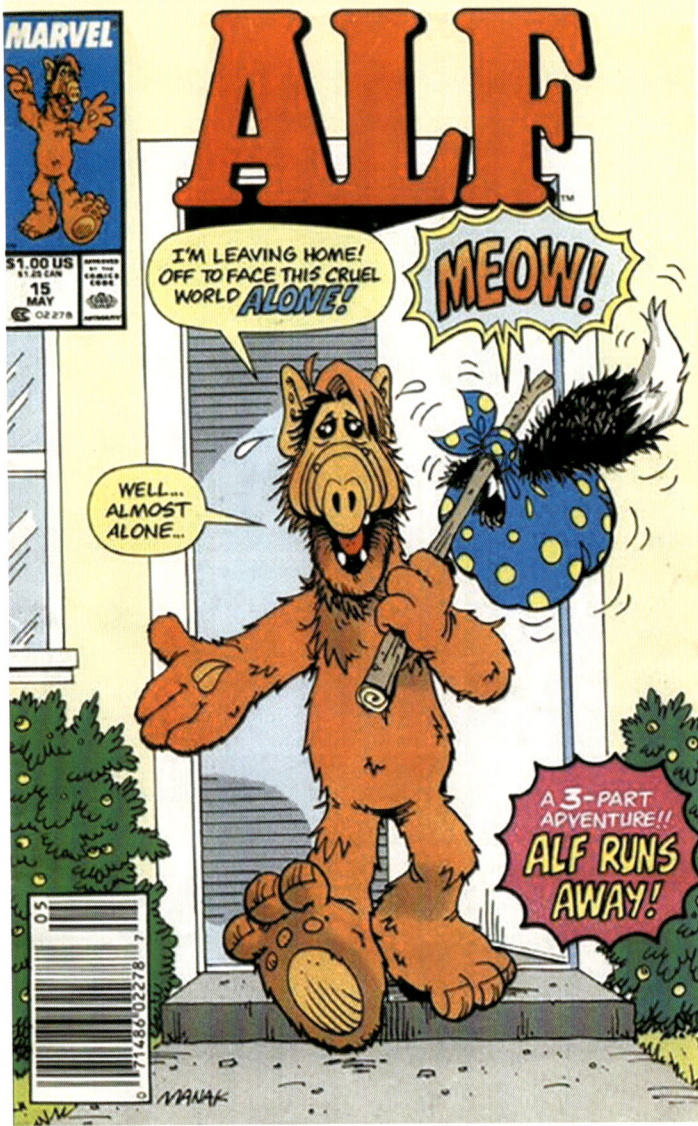

In 1986, NBC launched ALF, a sitcom about an alien adopted by a California family. Cultural differences are at the heart of the show's humor, as is the alien's fondness for eating cats.

ALF is a mainstream comedy in the tradition of the good-natured, politically correct TV shows of the time, such as *Diff'rent Strokes* and its spin-off, *The Facts of Life*. After the planet Melmac is destroyed, ALF (an acronym for Alien Life Form) discovers Earth and family life. He spends the series hiding from the authorities and nosy neighbors.

The show's humor is based on ALF's unfamiliarity with human life and social interaction. This comic device is regularly used in a caricatured way, like in the film *Little Indian, Big City* (1994). The primary incompatibility between the alien and his

hosts is his taste for cat meat. The character is a bit of a rock 'n' roller in the early episodes. In fact, the title of each episode is a song title. At NBC's request, jokes about the hairy alien's alcohol consumption were dropped, but not those about cats.

In every episode, the alien tries to eat the family cat or raises the possibility of doing so. The animal would have been one of the tastiest delicacies on Melmac. Perhaps the strangest thing is the reaction of the Tanner family: They aren't particularly bothered by this permanent threat to their pet. They stop him from carrying out his plan, but beyond that, they don't worry about ALF's obsession.

The feline in the ALF series represents envy and gluttony, but here, these aren't the cat's faults. His only sin is tasting good. The cat is a bit of a whipping boy with jokes made at his expense. A Chinese man wanting to cook the family dog, or a Frenchman wanting to cook their rabbit would be shocking for the audience, but viewers find the cat/alien mix an acceptable joke.

The cat's name is Lucky, which is ironic, since he's under constant threat of death. However, the first cat dies in his sleep in Episode 9 of Season 4, titled "Live and Let Die." Willy Tanner suggests that his son get a dog, but the boy replies emphatically, "I don't want a dog." To which ALF replies, "Me neither, it's much too stringy." The jokes about eating felines

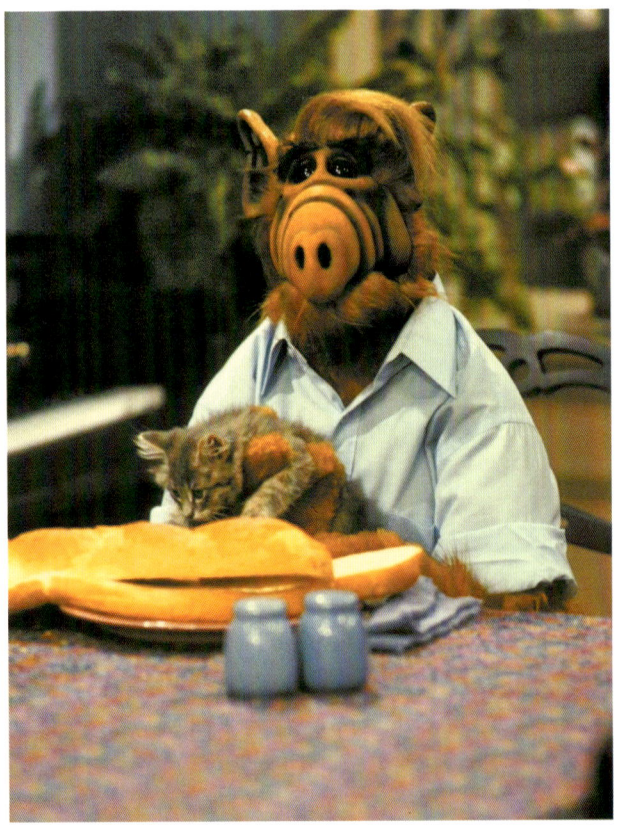

continue throughout the episode, as the alien orders himself a box of kittens.

In a hilarious scene, he wants to eat them in a sandwich. He gives up eating the first cat, claiming it's too cute. He figures he'll manage to eat an uglier one but is interrupted by the arrival of the Tanners. In the end, he's the one who arranges to adopt the kitten, which they unimaginatively name Lucky II.

In the last episode of the series, ALF is finally captured by the army in a cliffhanger preceding the end of the show. The creators hoped to convince NBC to extend the show for a fifth season, but the network refused. It wasn't until 1996 that the series came to a conclusion in the much-maligned *Project: ALF*. With the Tanner family out of the picture and the format completely different from that of a sitcom, the TV movie's dynamics were completely at odds with the series, and fans were not happy.

In 1987, there was an animated version of his adventures in the form of a prequel chronicling his life before he was stranded on Earth.

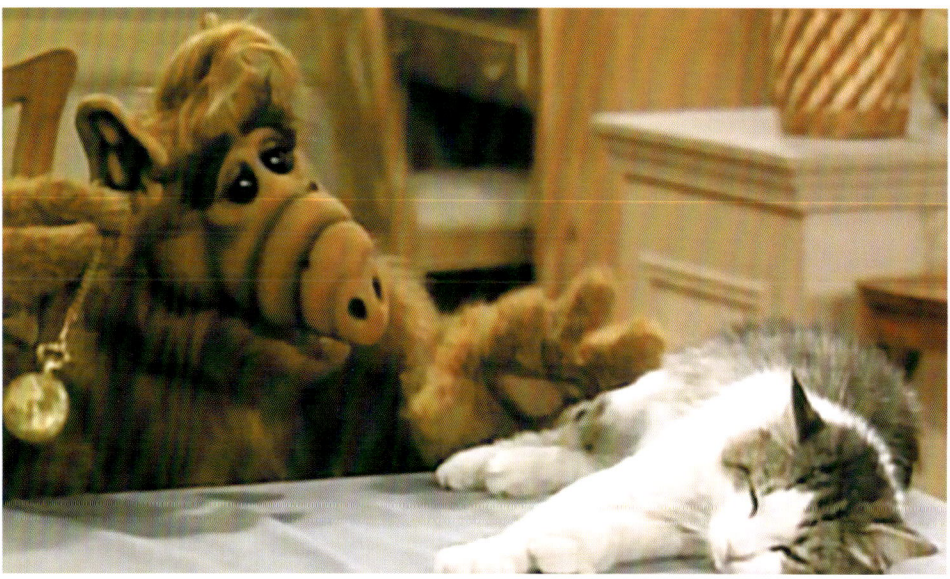

A second animated series, *ALF Tales*, ran between 1989 and 1990. This featured fairy tales portrayed by ALF and his friends. In 2018, following in the footsteps of sequels to series such as *Dallas* and *Full House*, rumors of a reboot of the ALF sitcom with Warner Bros. circulated. However, the project has yet to see the light of day, so cats can still sleep soundly. 🐾

SPEC SHEET

WORK: *ALF*.
CREATORS: Paul Fusco and Tom Patchett.
DATE CREATED: September 22, 1986.
DISTRIBUTOR/AVAILABILITY: Warner Bros. Available on DVD and on several steaming services.
CATS' NAMES AND ROLE IN THE WORK: Lucky, then Lucky II. Cats in the Tanner household. Hors d'oeuvres that always escape ALF and are a source of jokes.

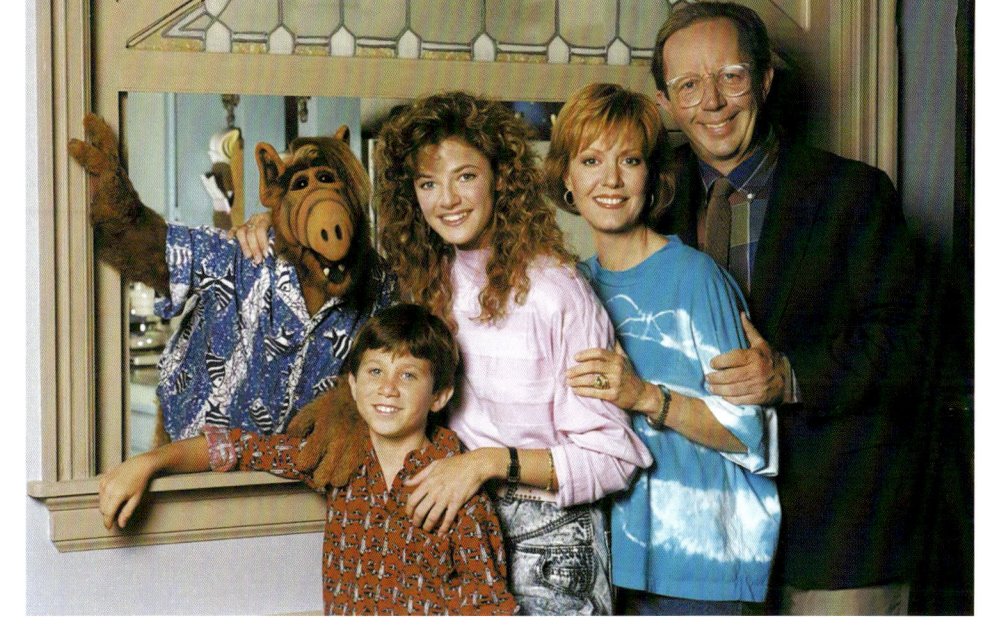

Garfield

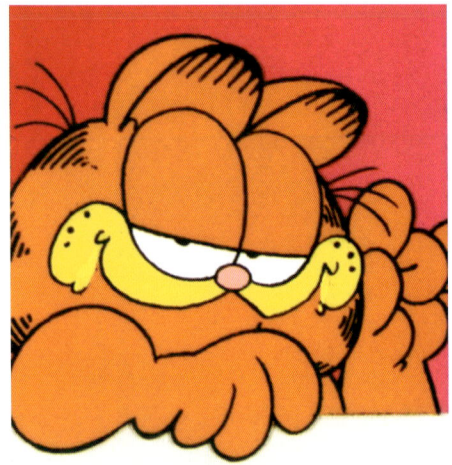

Garfield is arguably the best-known cat in the world of comics. He's greedy, overweight, and especially egocentric, and fans have enjoyed watching him get into trouble and annoy those around him since 1978.

A Comic Strip Success Story

The comic strip is a comics format that has been used in US newspapers since the nineteenth century. It then became popular throughout the world. The generally funny genre took off in the twentieth century. Cartoonist Jim Davis had already published this type of comic strip but didn't hit his stride with *Gnorm Gnat*, which was about insects. The humor and tone were already there, but he didn't find success until *Garfield*. Distributed by the United Feature Syndicate, which supplies many of the country's newspapers with strips, *Garfield* was published by some forty dailies from the outset. Today distributed in more than one hundred countries, the adventures of the mischievous cat have now appeared in more than seventy books since their first publication in hardcover in 1981. Its creator is the head of a financial empire thanks to his company, Paws, Inc., which holds the rights to the character.

The cat's appearance has evolved over time, particularly in terms of face and color. His slightly sunken face became smiling and rounder. His eyes became larger and half-closed, reinforcing his lazy side. The color of his fur has also gotten lighter over the years.

Garfield and Gluttony

Garfield has an obsession with food other than cat food. He's particularly partial to lasagna, probably because he was born in Mama Leone's Italian restaurant. He hates it when his owner, Jon, puts him on a diet. As with many fictional cats, gluttony is linked to laziness. In Garfield's case, it's extreme.

He used to stand on all fours, but over time, the comic strip became increasingly anthropomorphic. His laziness is that of a human, and he hates Mondays and mornings, although in real life, cats don't work and don't have the same notion of time as we do.

Domesticated, but Not Too Domesticated

Garfield is a modern cat. He uses technology, like the phone that reminds him to harass Odie the dog, and even a computer. Endless chases with dogs and mice aren't his thing. He lives with a canine that he never forgets to annoy, and he's happy to let his master think he's hunting mice for food. In reality, he's friends with Squeak the mouse. The protagonist is totally sedentary and domesticated in the sense that he stays in the house, yet he's not an obedient cat. He's not affectionate, and he's uncommonly selfish. While he's not really mean, he's only interested in others when he wants to deliver scathing punchlines or play tricks on them. Over the years, a gallery of

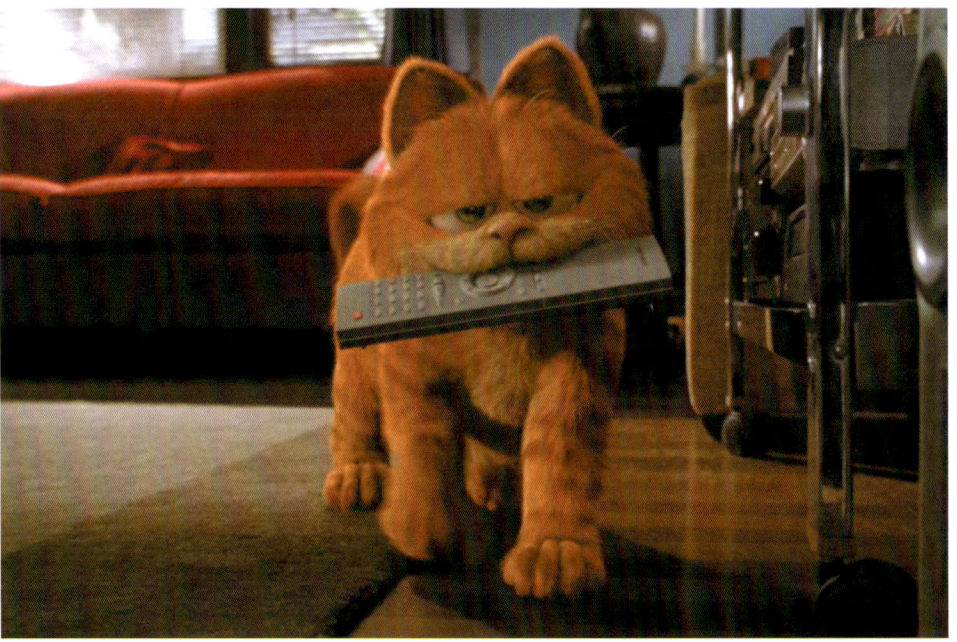

The 2004 *Garfield* film.

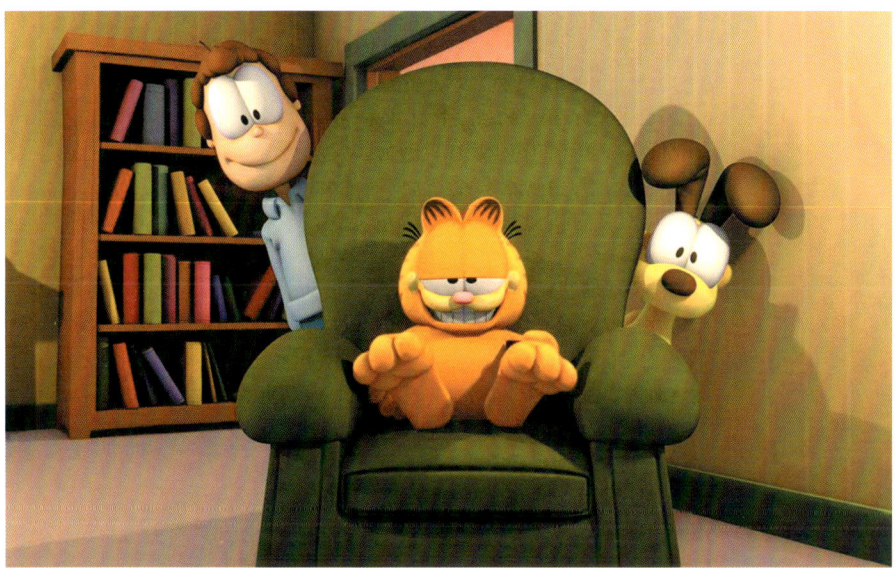

The Garfield Show.

by Bill Murray, the ever-jaded star of *Ghostbusters*. Three other fully 3D films were also produced but were only released on DVD. 🐾

SPEC SHEET

CAT'S NAME: Garfield.
WORK: *Garfield.*
CREATOR: Jim Davis.
DATE CREATED: June 19, 1978.
PUBLISHER/AVAILABILITY: Random House. The seventy-sixth book was published in 2024.
CAT'S CHARACTERISTICS: Big orange cat with black stripes.

recurring characters has been added, creating amusing interactions with the orange cat.

TV Adaptations

Over the years, publishers and producers have seen *Garfield* as a financial windfall, and there have been many adaptations of the comic strip. In addition to the fifteen or so video games based on the franchise, the adventures of the orange cat have been brought to the small screen in three animated series. The first, *Garfield and Friends*, was first produced in 1988. This 124-episode production offered a version that was fairly faithful to the original work, succeeding in adapting the comic strip to a twenty-five-minute format. It ended in 1994 after seven well-made seasons.

In 2008, *The Garfield Show* moved into 3D, following in the footsteps of the film. However, this production has aged very poorly, and the plots struggle to keep viewers on the edge of their seats. Nevertheless, this Franco-American co-production lasted for five seasons and 214 episodes.

In 2019, the cat returned to classic animation for another highly successful adaptation, *Garfield Originals*. This series of just twenty-four episodes is also a French co-production and, like its predecessor, co-created by Philippe Vidal. There is no dialogue, and the beautiful, modern graphics are a pleasure to look at.

Film Adaptations

When there's a hit or a franchise, when there's money to be made, Hollywood is never far away. In 2004, Peter Hewitt directed a live-action film about the lazy cat. The production is decent, and Garfield is his usual egotistical, gag-loving self. However, the film lacks unity, which earned it some very bad reviews. Nevertheless, its popularity with children helped the production rake in $200 million in profits for a $50 million investment. Building on this success, a second film was produced two years later, grossing $140 million. For the occasion, the mischievous cat found himself playing king at the court of London. The films' greatest achievement was surely the voice-over

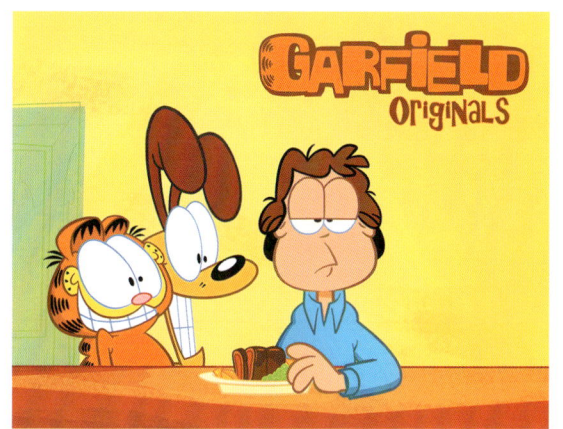

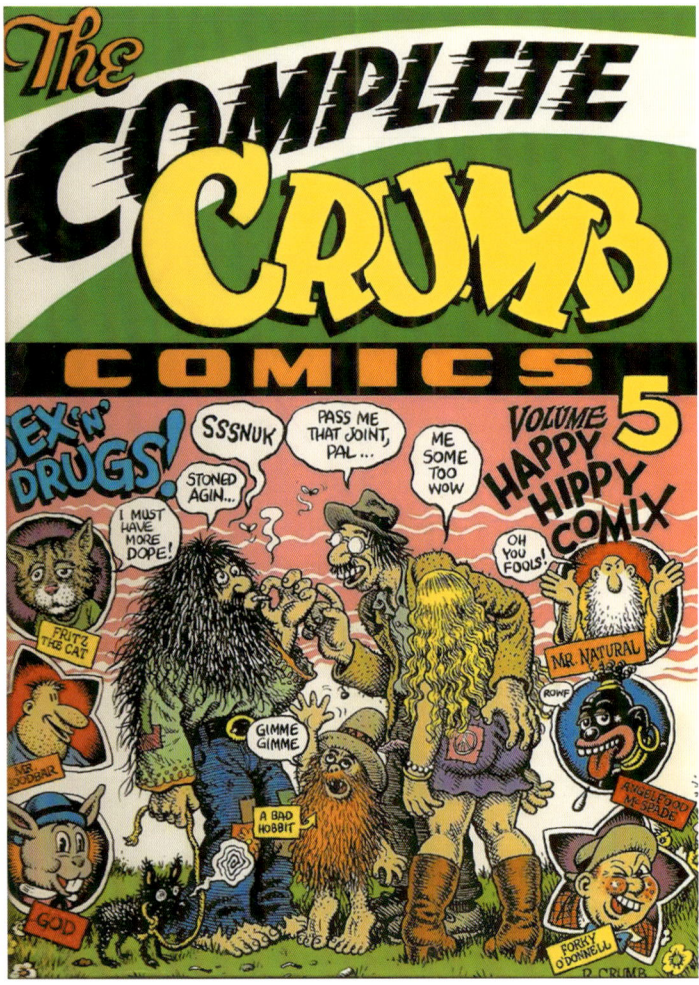

Robert Crumb's best-known creation, Fritz the Cat, is often seen as an icon of the American counterculture of the 1960s and 1970s, even though it's a biting caricature and an acerbic critique of society at the time.

In fifteen fairly short stories, from "Fritz Comes on Strong" (January 1965) to "Fritz the Cat: 'Superstar'" (September 1972), some intended for publication and others originally not, such as "R. Crumb's Comics and Stories" and "Fritz the Cat, Ace Salesman," Robert Crumb's bipedal anthropomorphic cat quickly acquired the status of counterculture icon. And yet . . .

Although inspired by the tomcat, Fred, that his family had when he was a teenager, Fritz has all the human faults: He's by turns cowardly, weak, lazy (to the point of burning his lessons instead of studying, even if it means setting fire to the whole building), an alcoholic, a drug addict, a thief, and more. He's not exactly a choirboy, and his only limits are his survival instinct and his desires. When he's not indulging in an incestuous interlude with his sister in "R. Crumb's Comics and Stories," he eats his latest conquest after putting her through the wringer in "Fred, the Teen-Age Girl Pigeon." Inspired by hippie culture and the various social upheavals in the United States at the time, Fritz the Cat served as a magnifying glass to show the failings of a more or less well-to-do intellectual fringe of society. As tensions between white and Black people grew in a United States seeking to free itself from segregation, Robert Crumb's "Fritz Bugs Out" depicted his character venturing into the ghetto populated by crows and accumulating racist clichés, even though he knows, "It ain't no picnic, man! I know, I've studied the racial problem!" As if books could somehow equal everyday experience.

Although he was the first character created by Robert Crumb, when he wrote "Cat Stories" with his older brother Charles for the amusement of the family (Robert drew Fred the Cat, the hero, while Charles drew the other animal antagonists), the artist never felt any particular attachment to his character. He said, "I couldn't stop drawing him. I liked drawing Fritz; he was fun to draw."[1] It kept him busy while the artist was a teenager,

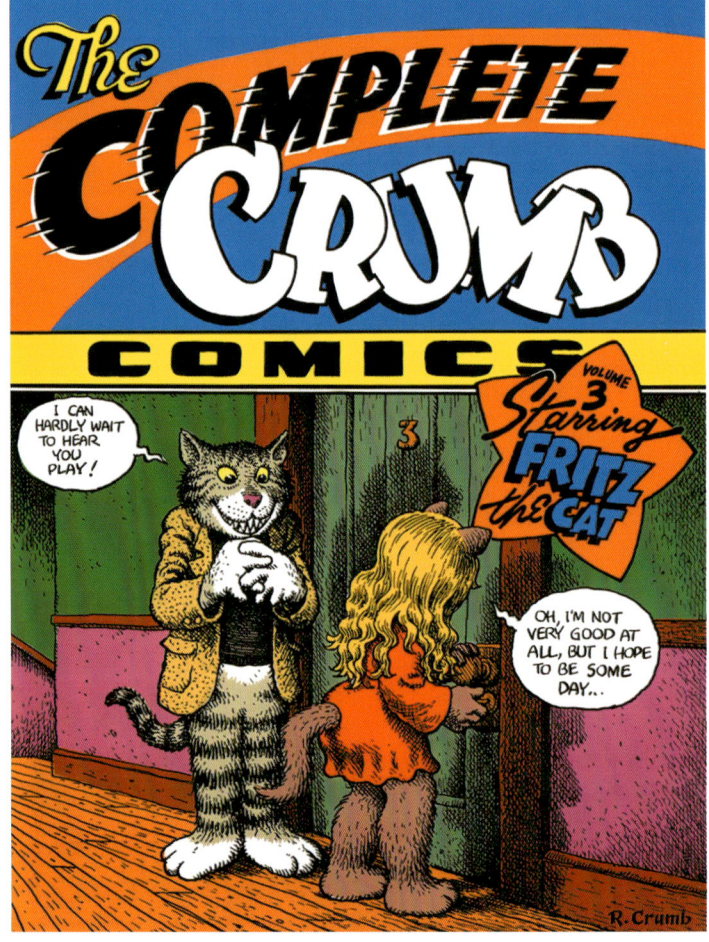

---

[1] In *Funnyworld*, No. 14, "The Filming of Fritz the Cat: Crumb, His Cat and the Dotted Line," by Michael Barrier, http://www.michaelbarrier.com/Funnyworld/ FritzPartOne/ FritzThree.htm

TWO FILMS FOR ONE COMIC

Although Fritz the Cat was created by Robert Crumb, the comic strip is now less well known than the film, *Fritz the Cat*, which was the first American cartoon to be rated X for pornography and drug use, in 1972. Directed and scripted by Ralph Bakshi, for whom it was the first feature film, *Fritz the Cat* was shocking for its content, which was deemed pornographic, anti-Semitic (with the Jewish pig policeman who doesn't appear in the comics), and racist. It displeased Robert Crumb to the point that he asked to have his name removed from the poster, arguing that the contract had been signed by his first wife, Dana, in his absence. Nevertheless, the film was a success, paving the way for more mature, irreverent animation such as *The Simpsons*, *Beavis and Butt-Head*, and *South Park*. In light of this success, the producer hired Robert Taylor to make a second film, *The Nine Lives of Fritz the Cat*, but it failed to live up to the quality and commercial success of the first. While the first film, with an estimated budget of $700,000, earned $25 million in the United States and $90 million worldwide, that wasn't the case for the second, despite its participation in the 1974 Cannes Film Festival.

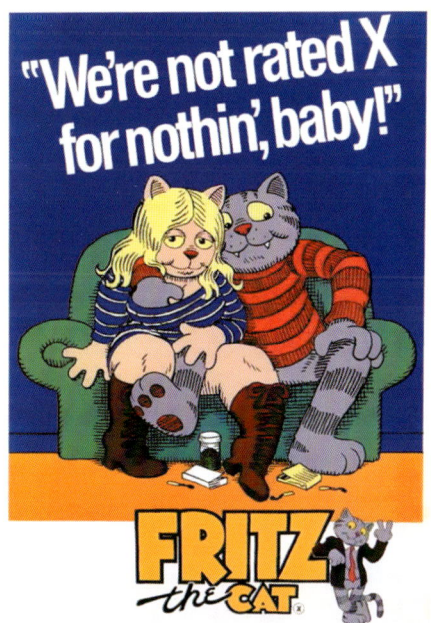

"We're not rated X for nothin', baby!"

FRITZ the CAT

He's X rated and animated!

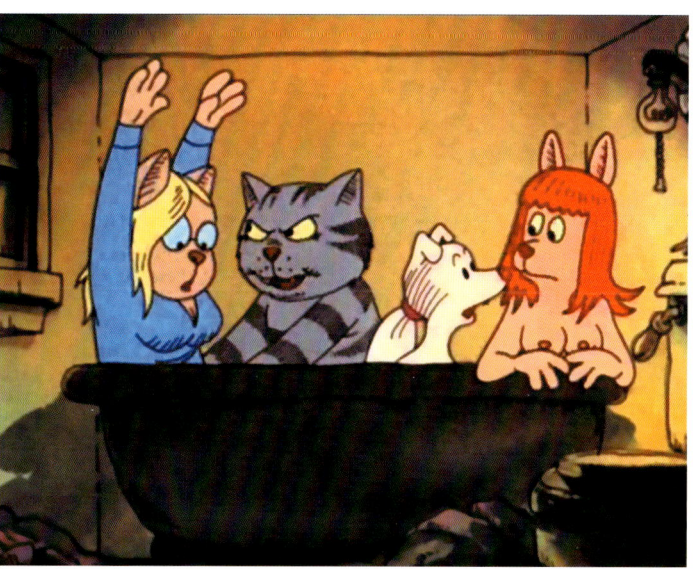

Ralph Bakshi's film.

then a lonely student with a gangly physique that, according to him, didn't help him pick up girls. Once he'd found a group of friends and a sexual outlet, he didn't have as much energy to draw his character, according to Marty Pahls, one of his childhood friends.[2] So, when he saw his creation leave the world of underground comics to take his first steps on the silver screen, and in an incarnation that didn't suit his vision, he killed off the character in "Fritz the Cat: 'Superstar,'" after portraying him as a disillusioned movie star. He used an ice pick to end the career of the feline who had launched his own.

---

[2] Quoted in *The Art of the Comic Book: An Aesthetic History* by Robert C. Harvey (1996).

Felix the Cat

One of the first icons of animated film, Felix appeared in the silent era and survived well into the twenty-first century. The tuxedo cat makes people of all ages smile and dream, with or without his bag of tricks.

When *Feline Follies* hit theaters on November 9, 1919, Master Tom was still just an ordinary black cat who played the seducer and forgot to chase mice, eventually committing suicide to escape fatherhood. He soon returned, taking the name Felix in his third installment, *The Adventures of Felix*. As the stories continued, his figure became rounder, his personality more mischievous, curious, and open, and a silent movie icon was gradually born. Initially in black and white, Felix the Cat's stories were aimed at an adult audience, touching on the theory of evolution and alcoholism in his jokes, or advocating a certain form of redistribution of wealth akin to socialism in *The Goose That Laid the Golden Egg* (1936), a talking color adaptation of Jean de La Fontaine's fable, "The Hen with the Golden Eggs." Although the first shorts weren't free of the shortcomings of their time, including a rather caricatured depiction of Black children, the character maintained his popularity throughout his life, gradually erasing his flaws. Moving from studio to studio (Paramount in the early days, then Winkler Pictures, Educational Pictures, and RKO, among others), Felix the Cat soon became an advertising tool (for Mazda light bulbs around 1925), a mascot (starting in 1926), a comic strip (from 1923), and even the subject of several animated series (two American ones and one, *Baby Felix and Friends*, that was originally broadcast on NHK in Japan in 2000).

Who is Felix? At first, Felix was simply a street tomcat who ran amuck in the first silent shorts, but his personality grew as he moved from one medium to another. He retained

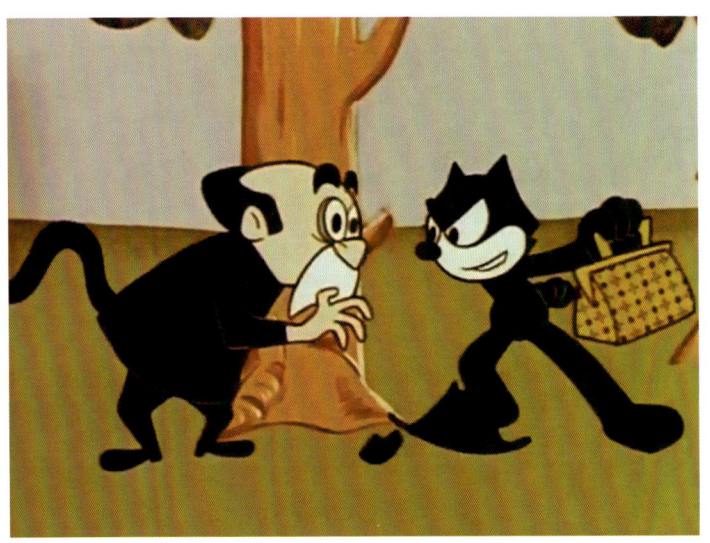

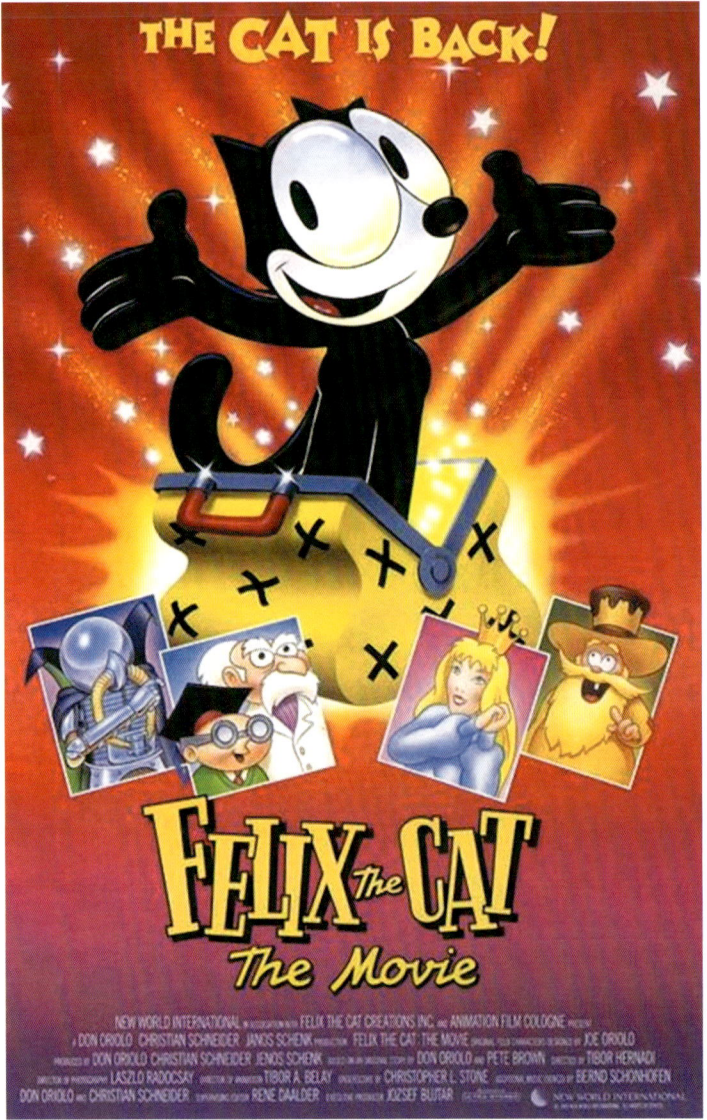

positive qualities associated with cats, such as cunning and a particularly well-developed curiosity, without having any of their flaws. He's a fundamentally nice character, attached to his friends (as evidenced by his relationship with the golden goose in one of his first talking cartoons), who doesn't have the faults usually attributed to felines, such as cruelty, laziness, gluttony, or thievery. Even before Joe Oriolo added his "magic bag of tricks" to the 1953 cartoon (when he moved to the small screen), Felix the Cat was already the embodiment of a certain sense of surrealism and childlike wonder in the most concrete of everyday situations (such as when he tries to help a hobo friend kick his drinking problem). This bag, which looks like a yellow doctor's bag with black decorations when it's not in use, can take any shape (regardless of size or volume) to satisfy its owner's needs, but on two conditions: that he doesn't use it to do anything wrong and that he doesn't reveal its secret

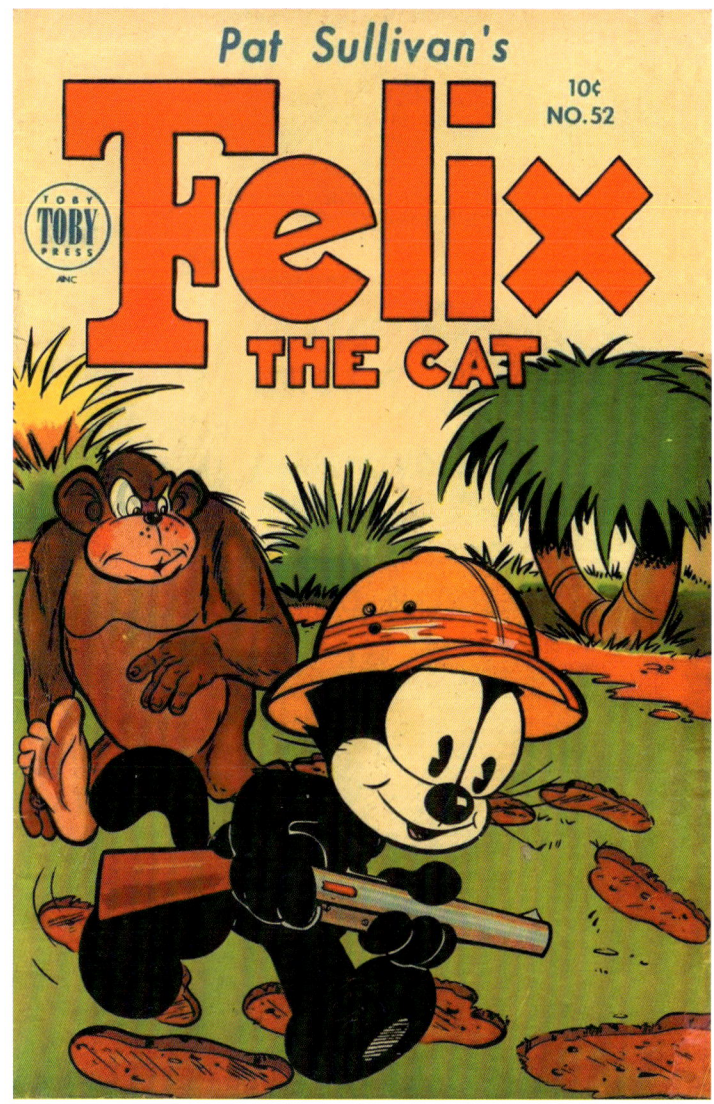

NOT TO BE CONFUSED WITH FELIX CAT FOOD

While Felix was originally a common name for any type of cat, since the character's popularity, it has come to be associated with black-and-white cats (much like Socks, for those with white paw tips, named after Chelsea Clinton's, which occupied the White House from 1993 to 2001 under President Bill Clinton). And this popularity was used beginning in 1989 by the English pet food manufacturer Felix when it relaunched in the European market. Created at the end of World War II, the brand was losing ground to the other market giant, Whiskas, and its tabby cat. The brand, therefore, created a mascot in 1989, in the form of a smiling black-and-white cat with large, arched eyes. The design is more detailed, with the appearance of whiskers, but the relationship to the original Felix the Cat is clear. This Felix behaves more like a real, four-legged cat, but his antics and gluttony shine through in the commercials and poster campaigns. Since 1997, the brand has been part of the Nestlé Purina group, and it is marketed as an entry-level product intended to be a cat treat or reward, rather than a primary food.

SPEC SHEET

CAT'S NAME: Felix the Cat.
WORKS: Initially silent films, then comic strips, video games, films, and various objects.
CREATORS: Pat Sullivan, Otto Messmer, and Joe Oriolo.
DATE CREATED: 1919 (*Feline Follies*).
DISTRIBUTOR: Since 2014, DreamWorks Animation.
CAT'S CHARACTERISTICS: Anthropomorphic tuxedo cat (black with a white chest), a big smile, white eyes, and, in more recent versions, long legs and a magic bag that can transform into anything. Felix also demonstrates shapeshifting abilities in his earliest appearances.

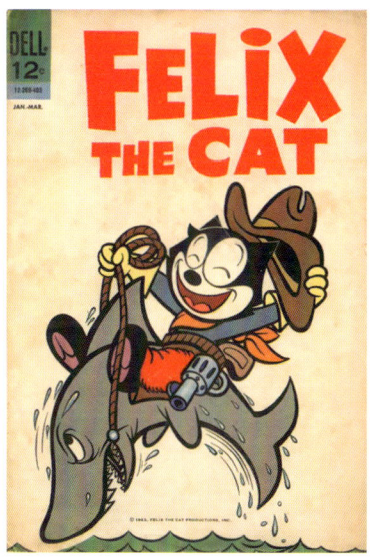

to anyone. These rules, and the transmission of a prototype of the bag from adult Felix to Baby Felix, will be one of the driving forces behind the plot of *Baby Felix and Friends*. Even without the bag, the cat's ability to transform is put to good use, but in the end, it's the way he thinks, taking long strides with his hands behind his back, that remains his best-known characteristic. 🐾

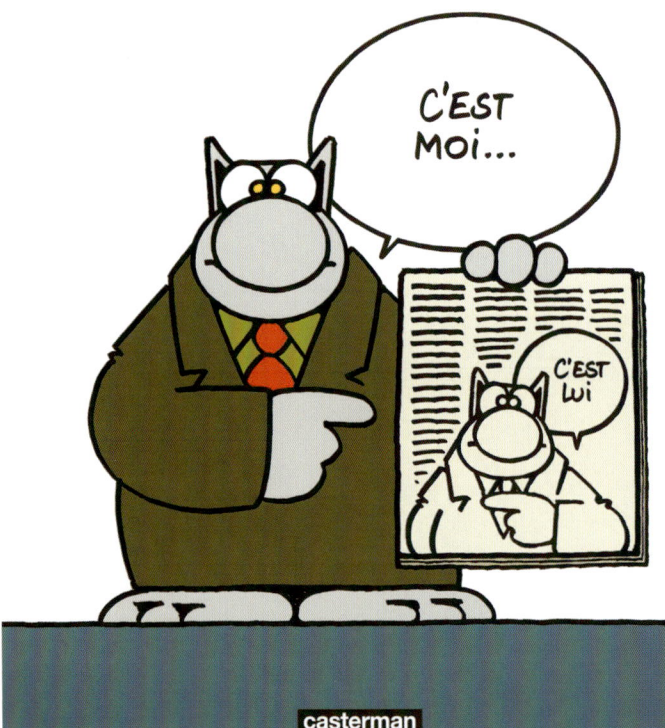

PHILIPPE GELUCK
LE CHAT

casterman

Commenting on current affairs in the Belgian newspaper Le Soir for thirty years, Le Cat has also made his mark on TV and the arts and has been seen almost everywhere. Never at a loss for words, he says the most horrifying things despite his benign appearance.

On March 22, 1983, a sketched cat in a suit made his first official appearance in the pages of the Belgian newspaper *Le Soir*. Still relatively svelte and in black and white at the time, this was the first official appearance of Le Cat, the creature that made Philippe Geluck famous far beyond his native Belgium. Geluck confided in 2016[1] that the character had already had a private existence before (like Robert Crumb's Fritz), notably to decorate announcements. Le Cat was inspired by a real cat he had known as a child, ironically nicknamed Passe-Partout [Go Anywhere] because he was too fat to fit in anywhere.

For thirty years, every day, he commented on current affairs in the daily newspaper, making him, in the words of his creator, "the modern-day Confucius." And it has to be said that, with his good-natured air, Le Cat never misses a beat: A veritable itching powder, he annoys the self-righteous and the sectarians of every stripe by highlighting their shortcomings or using the absurd to divert them.

Artistically, Le Cat is a striking example of false simplicity. The animal is fat, gray, usually dressed (to avoid having to draw its muscles), but shoeless and facing the front. He doesn't open his mouth, and his gestures are kept to a minimum. When humans appear, like Roger the bartender, they're mostly outside the panel, with only a speech bubble. And yet, on occasion, Le Cat's panels will reproduce and modify famous works with a wealth of detail, even if it means that the cat himself isn't present. Over the years, Le Cat's world has expanded. In addition to the aforementioned Roger and the feline's favorite snacks and punching bags, mice, we meet Mrs. Cat, who may or may not participate in the conversation, a plethora of kittens (some nephews who drive their uncle crazy, and some children, including a son who would have his own comic book series), a certain Mr. G.—a cartoonist with round glasses who bears a

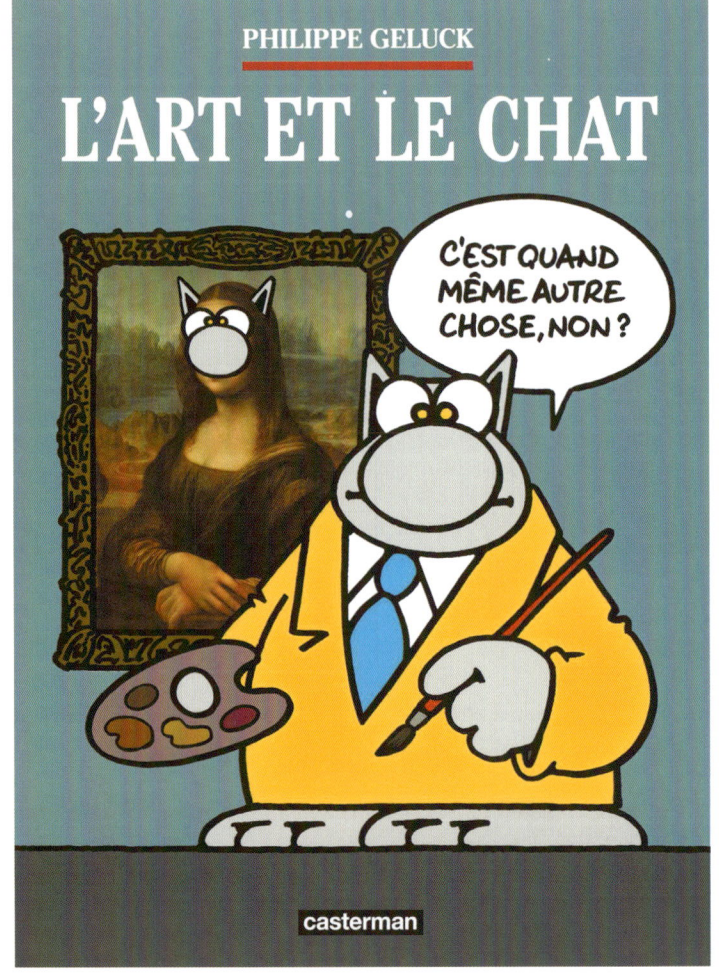

PHILIPPE GELUCK
L'ART ET LE CHAT

casterman

[1] *Paris-Match*, September 29, 2016.

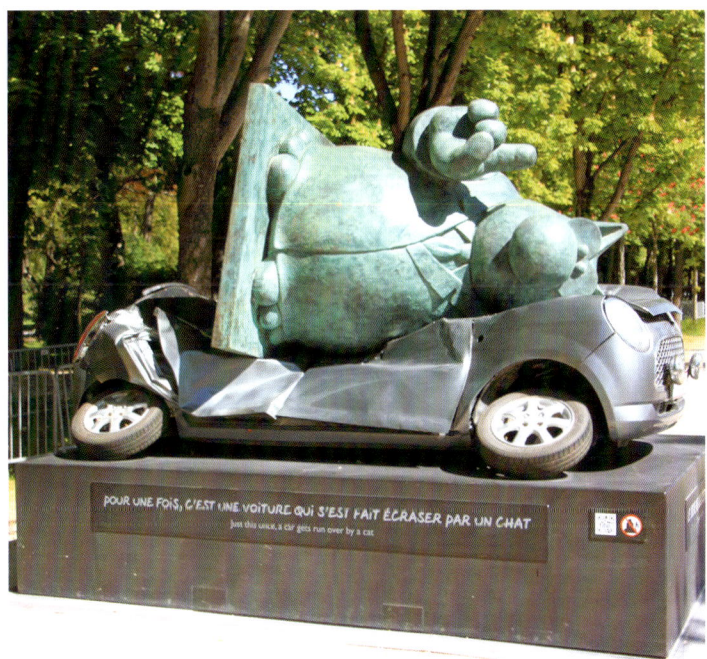

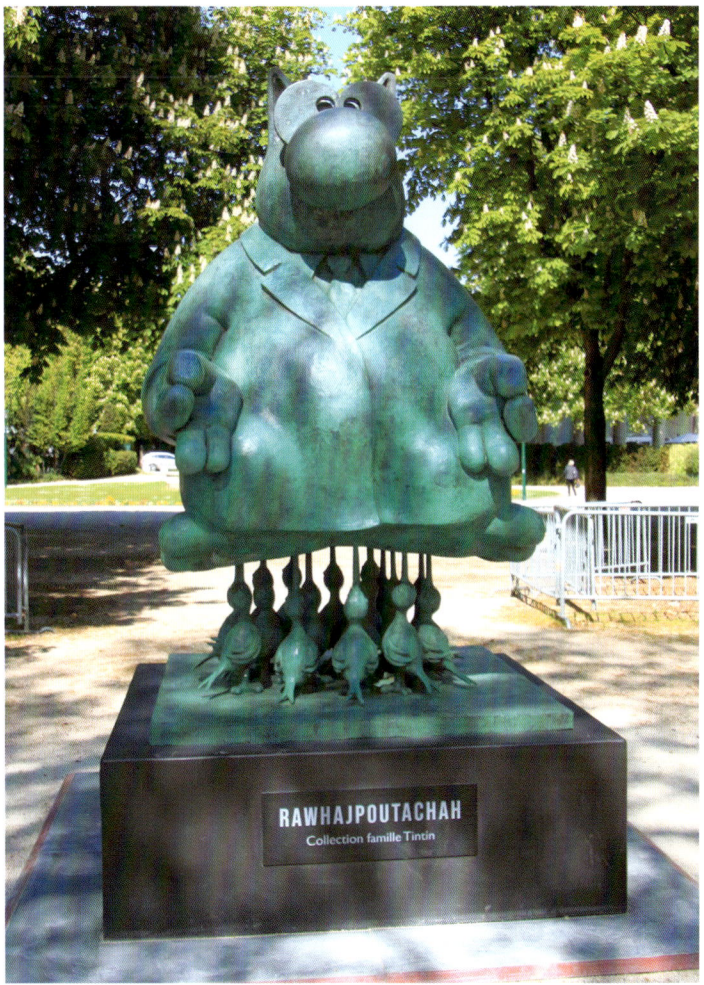

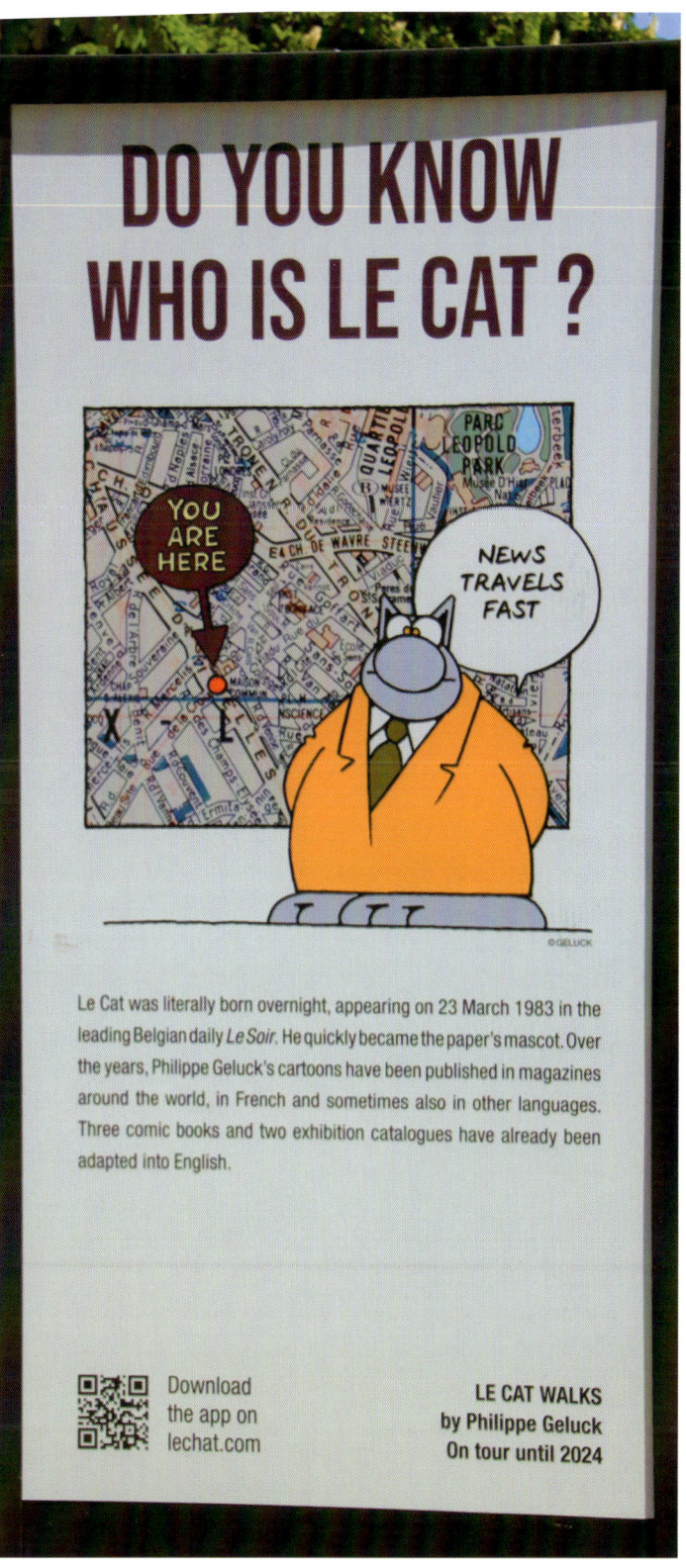

Le Cat exhibition, Champs-Élysées, Paris, 2021.
Photos by Ludovic Dugué.

strong resemblance to Philippe Geluck himself—and Le Cat's shrink, whom the animal often drives to the brink of madness. Le Cat's horizons have also expanded. From the pages of *Le Soir*, he has infiltrated those of other newspapers and magazines (such as *Sud-Ouest* and *Midi Libre* in France) and taken part in TV shows (notably *On a tout essayé* with Laurent Ruquier and *Vivement Dimanche!* with Michel Drucker). He's even been animated, using the voice of comedian Jean-Yves Lafesse for short vignettes combining 3D, 2D, and stop-motion for the Belgian media service RTBF. And since 1986, he's been available in albums from Casterman, who first reprinted the French-language comic strips that had already appeared in the press and then launched original productions. Casterman has also extended the Le Cat family with special issues and comics devoted to Le Cat's son (with nine volumes to date).

When Philippe Geluck stopped working with *Le Soir* on March 22, 2013, he wasn't signing his character's death warrant. Quite the opposite, in fact. For a time, Le Cat had his own app on Android and iOS, where the cartoonist regularly sent jokes to users. Le Cat has also become an icon on display. In 2008, Hotton, Belgium, inaugurated a Place du Chat with a statue of the feline at its center. From October 2020 to September 2021,[2] Le Cat was exhibited at the Musée Soulages in Rodez, France, where it paid tribute to the Aveyron painter and engraver Pierre Soulages with paintings, drawings, and sculptures. In March 2021, under the name "Le Chat déambule" [Le Cat Wanders], some twenty sculptures of Le Cat were installed on the Avenue des Champs-Élysées, including three fountains. Some were created for the occasion; others came from private collections. When the Paris exhibition ended in June 2021, Le Cat's sculptures embarked on a tour of France. At one point, there was even talk of inaugurating a Museum of Le Cat and Humorous Drawing in Brussels, but the controversy surrounding the cost of the building to house it reached such proportions that in May 2021, Philippe Geluck said he was ready to abandon the project.[3]

---

[2] https://musee-soulages-rodez.fr/oeuvres/le-chat-visite-le-musee-soulages/

[3] https://www.lecho.be/culture/general/philippe-geluck-pret-a-faire-une-croix-sur-le-musee-du-chat/10302721.html

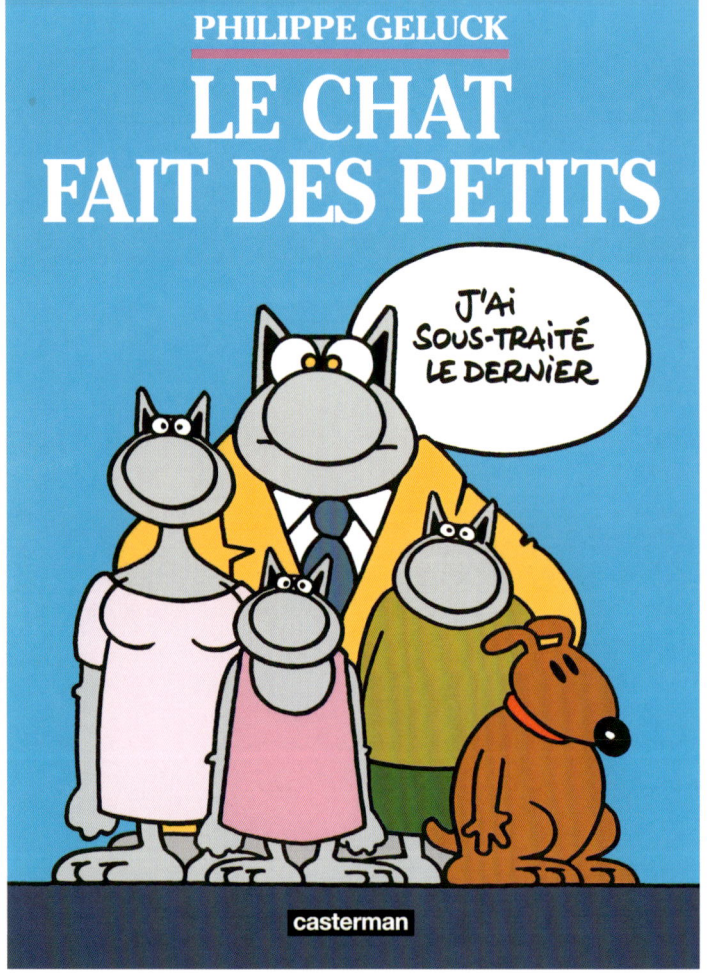

SPEC SHEET

CAT'S NAME: Le Cat.
WORKS: Humorous newspaper illustrations, comics, sculptures.
CREATOR: Philippe Geluck.
DATE CREATED: March 22, 1983, in the pages of the Belgian daily *Le Soir*.
PUBLISHER/AVAILABILITY: Casterman in French, with sixty-four albums available, plus six collections and three special issues. Rue Elise Editions in English, with a few available titles.
CAT'S CHARACTERISTICS: Big, gray, Chartreux-type cat, usually wearing a suit and tie.

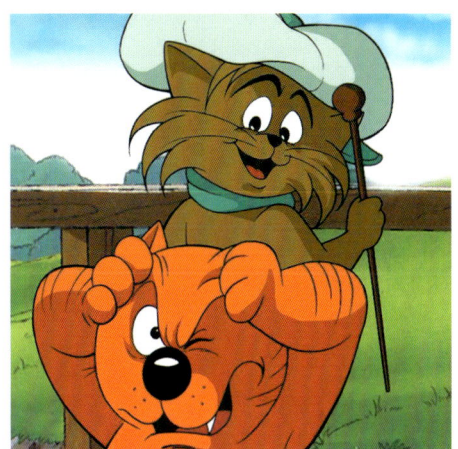

Riff-Raff (top) and Heathcliff (bottom).

A Franco-American series from the 1980s, Heathcliff and the Catillac Cats *follows the adventures of Heathcliff, a middle-class cat, and Riff-Raff and his gang, who are strays living in a junkyard. Each episode is divided in two, with each part featuring one of the two protagonists.*

Adapted from the *Heathcliff* comics created by George Gately in 1973, this children's series features light-hearted plots based on the characters' desire to find food or have fun. A cartoon about a gluttonous, lazy orange cat is bound to evoke Garfield, for whom he must have been an inspiration.

In the cartoon, gluttony is the primary sin of Heathcliff and the Catillac Cats. In the case of the obese house cat, it's not just a question of getting something to eat, but actual gluttony.

As the bigshot in his residential neighborhood, he can steal or get into mischief for his own amusement, such as by harassing the dog Spike. Riff-Raff and his gang were an original invention for the animated series. These alley cats live in a Cadillac in a junkyard. While Heathcliff crosses paths with the gang in some episodes, the two protagonists never see each other. Riff-Raff is small, smart, and angry.

The style of Riff-Raff's crew is strongly influenced by the 1980s. Their leader wears a cap and scarf evoking a bourgeois look. The Catillac Cats have no masters, but are elegant or cool, in keeping with the standards of the time (like Saturn, who wears a Walkman and roller skates). Riff-Raff's girlfriend Cleo's look is equally distinctive. She has big hair and wears pink leggings, accessories that became extremely popular after the 1983 film *Flashdance*.

Like many cartoons of the time, each episode ends with a little moral lesson from Heathcliff. Given Heathcliff's disrespectful attitude and the gang aspect of the Catillac Cats, this conclusion could be at odds with the show's premise, but it's done with a great deal of humor. This is the case, for example, when Heathcliff explains that you have to watch your pets' weight, joking about his own excess weight. The series consists of eighty-six independent episodes. A 1986 TV movie featuring Heathcliff was animated by the same team. 🐾

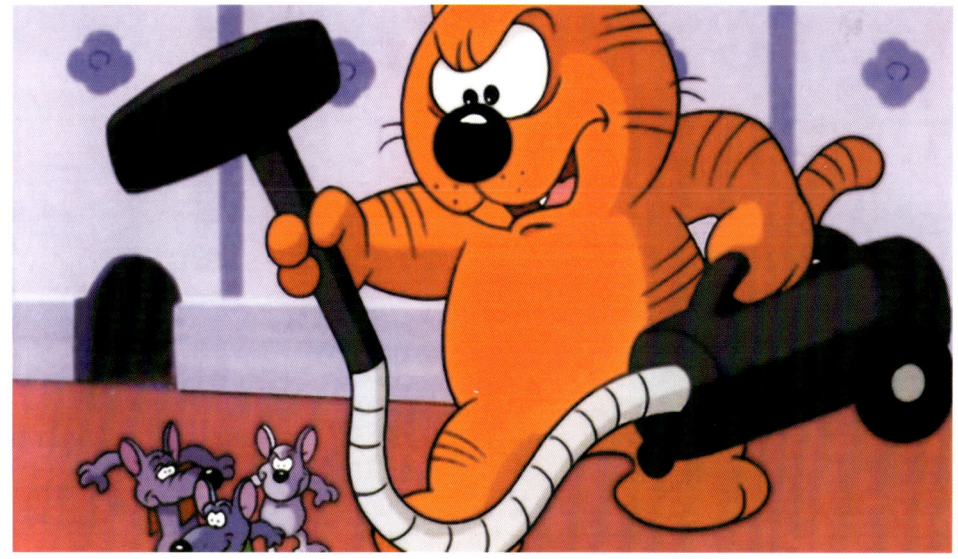

SPEC SHEET

WORK: *Heathcliff and the Catillac Cats.*

CREATORS: George Gately, Jean Chalopin, and Bruno Bianchi.

ORIGINAL BROADCAST DATES: October 15, 1984–November 30, 1987, on FR3 in France. Released in first-run syndication in the United States on September 15, 1984.

DISTRIBUTOR/AVAILABILITY: WildBrain. Available on DVD and through several streaming services.

CATS' NAMES AND ROLE IN THE WORK: Heathcliff, Riff-Raff, Cleo, Sonja, Hector, Mungo, Wordsworth W. Wordsworth. House cats or alley cats, they're the stars of the series.

Puss in Boots

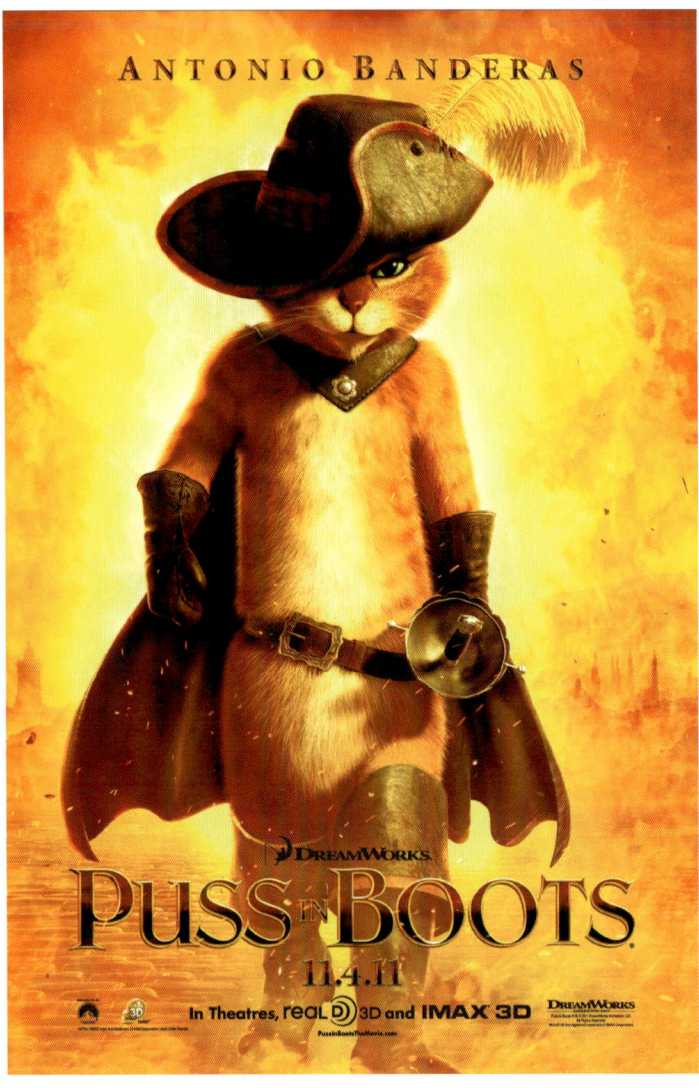

In 2001, DreamWorks released Shrek, its eponymous adaptation of William Steig's 1990 novel. Given its success, the animation studio decided to produce an equally successful sequel in 2004. This installment introduced one of the series's iconic characters: Puss in Boots.

A Puss in Boots Caricature

Whether in the original book or in its adaptations, *Shrek* caricatures fairy tales. In the second movie, Princess Fiona's father, the king of Far Far Away, hires a killer to deal with the ogre. That killer is Puss in Boots, a beautiful orange cat who knows how to swordfight. While the boots are a reference to Charles Perrault's *Puss in Boots*, the rest of the character is a far cry from the Marquis de Carabas's cat. The reference

to this tale is clever from a narrative point of view, since in the fairy tale, Puss in Boots kills an ogre transformed into a mouse. Unable to defeat Shrek, Puss becomes his friend and a recurring character in the series, to the point of having his own spin-offs.

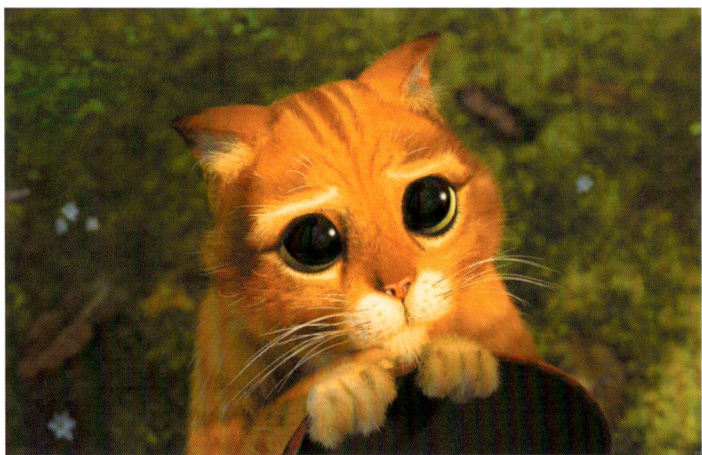

A Hispanic Cat

The reference to the *Puss in Boots* story isn't used much later on, as the character is deliberately compared to Zorro. When he enters a scene, he swings his sword in the shape of a P for "Puss in Boots." The iconology of this sequence echoes the Latino character played by Antonio Banderas in *The Mask of Zorro*. This Latin Robin Hood stole for good, so the choice of the actor to voice Puss in Boots was no coincidence. The cat may be a thief, but he loves just causes, and this aspect was developed in the 2011 film, *Puss in Boots*.

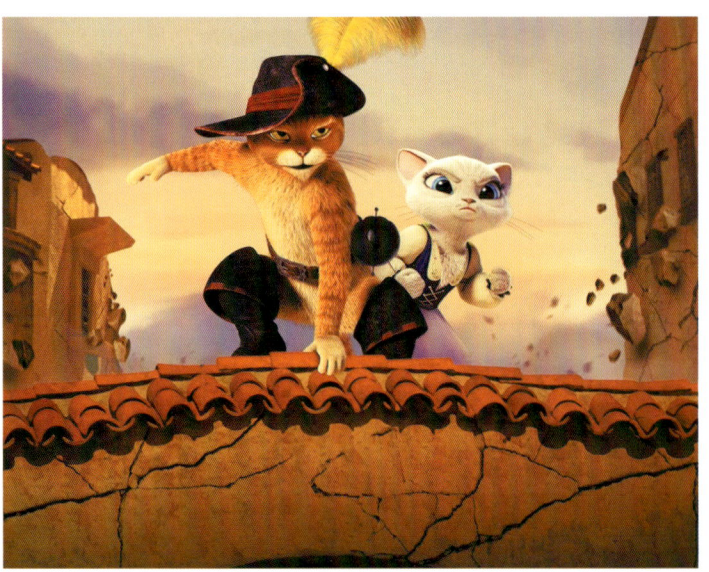

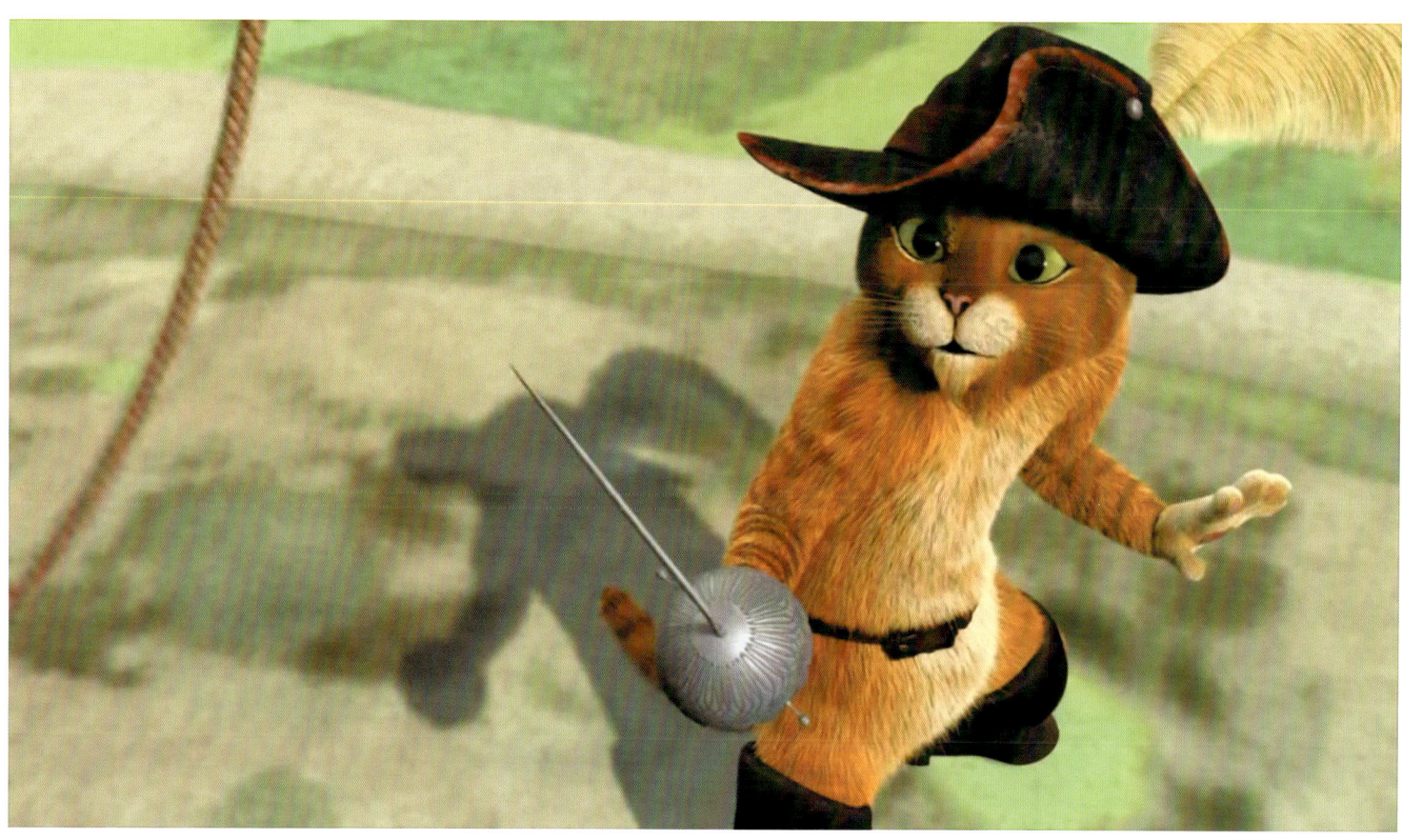

The Look That Kills

Puss in Boots is a thief, a virtue often attributed to cats. He's cunning like the cat in the fairy tale, but he's also cute. One of the film's most memorable gags, which is repeated in every episode of the franchise, is the moment when he gives a soulful look. He opens his eyes wide and dilates his pupils, making all those who would oppose him give in, as if by hypnosis. This running gag is also used in the short film *Puss in Boots: The Three Diablos*, in a staring duel with kittens.

The Puss in Boots License

From his very first appearance, the cat made a big impression on audiences, and DreamWorks saw it as a financial windfall. The cat appeared in all the *Shrek* shorts, in his spin-off, and on Netflix with a seventy-eight-episode series, *The Adventures of Puss in Boots* (2015). After years of speculation about possible sequels in the Shrek universe, Universal released the sequel to *Puss in Boots—Puss in Boots: The Last Wish—*in 2022. 🐾

SPEC SHEET

CAT'S NAME: Puss in Boots.
WORKS: *Shrek 2, 3*, and *4*, *Puss in Boots*, *Puss in Boots: The Last Wish*, and several animated series.
CREATORS: Andrew Adamson, Joe Stillman, J. David Stem, and David N. Weiss.
DATE CREATED: June 23, 2004.
DISTRIBUTOR/AVAILABILITY: DreamWorks. Available on Blu-ray, DVD, and streaming services.
CAT'S CHARACTERISTICS: Orange cat, big hat, boots, sword. A thief and a smooth talker.

Samurai Pizza Cats

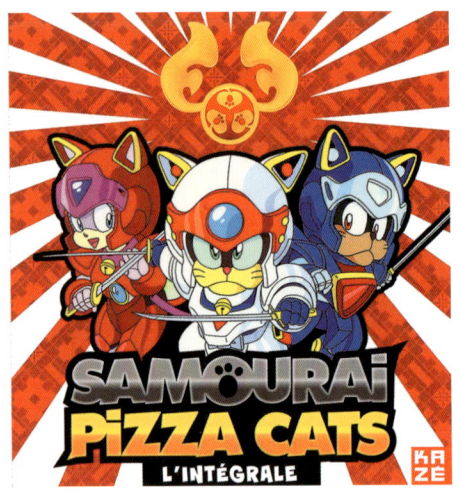

The series is a hallucinatory mix of mecha and pizza-delivering samurai cats.

In the 1990s, many Japanese cartoons were criticized for their violence. This was because they were not actually intended for children, as in the case of *Fist of the North Star*, whose brutality caused a scandal, but which wasn't geared to young people. *Samurai Pizza Cats*, on the other hand, is a *kodomo*, i.e., a work created for children. But this didn't stop the series from being censored. Only fifty-two of the fifty-four episodes were broadcast, due to sequences that were deemed too violent. Similarly, all references to alcohol or the location of the action were censored by cuts. The desire to transpose the Japanese story to France led to the deletion of shots with ideograms. And yet, the world of *Samurai Pizza Cats* is steeped in Japanese culture, with samurai, temples, constant references to Japanese food, and mecha. It's hard to understand the purpose of the Frenchification, except that it was done systematically in the 1990s. Kenji Kawai's soundtrack is a reflection of the series, mixing traditional sounds with synthesizer arrangements typical of the era in which it was produced.

Speedy, Guido, and Polly are delivery cats for the famous Pizza Cats Restaurant. They are also ninjas who save the world from the evil plans of Seymour "The Big" Cheese and other recurring enemies. Seymour often uses robots to attack the city's inhabitants. Meanwhile, the delivery team is all about having fun and eating, in the tradition of greedy cats. In this parallel universe where it's normal for samurai cats with mechanical armor to deliver pizzas and fight evil, the two cats Speedy and Guido vie for Lucille's favor. The young female sheep is often at the heart of both the banter between the cats and the narration. The three cats are funny, with a succession of jokes and fights. The humor is rather immature. The voice-over regularly comments on the action, adding to the comedy of the scenes by putting situations in context. Sound effects also punctuate the funny scenes in the cartoon tradition, confirming that it's aimed at a young audience. 🐾

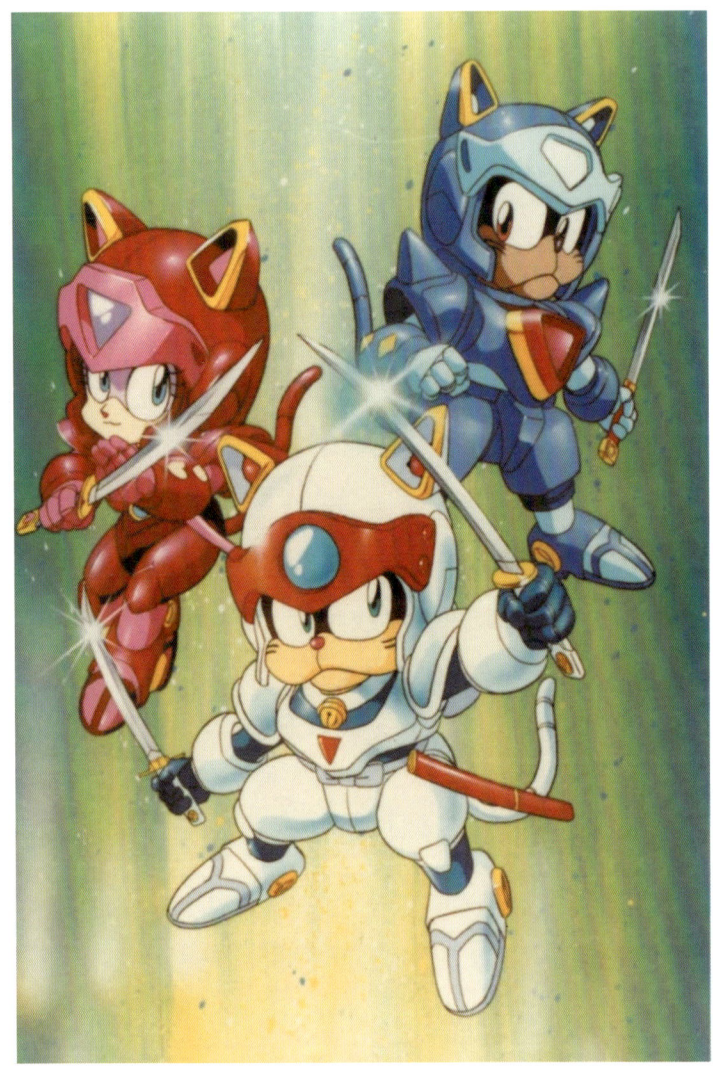

SPEC SHEET

WORK: *Samurai Pizza Cats*.
CREATORS: Kunitoshi Okajima and Mayori Sekijima.
DATE CREATED: February 1, 1990.
DISTRIBUTOR/AVAILABILITY: Discotek Media. Available on several streaming services.
CATS' NAMES AND ROLES IN THE WORK: Speedy, Guido, and Polly are the main characters' names in English.

While the golden years of the iconic **Club Dorothée** *TV show in France were based on adaptations of manga for boys (shōnen), shōjo—or manga for girls—also had their moment of glory, with* Love Me, My Knight.

Broadcast in 1988 on *Youpi! L'école est finie* on the now-defunct La Cinq, a French channel owned by Silvio Berlusconi, the romantic cartoon was widely rebroadcast on TF1 beginning in 1991. It tells the story of Yaeko, a young Tokyo student working in her father's restaurant, caught in a love triangle between Go and Satomi. The two young men are friends and play in the same rock band, Bee Hive. The melodrama lasts forty-two episodes, at the end of which the young woman chooses Go.

He's raising his little brother, Hashizo, and also taking care of his talking cat, Juliano. The big orange cat with purple stripes is known throughout the series for his gluttony. He's all about food and only cooperates when offered a pancake from Yaeko's family restaurant. Of course, the joy of the French adaptation is that in the original version, it's not a crêperie but a restaurant serving *okonomiyaki*, a typical Japanese savory pancake.

The systematic translation of names in accordance with the practices of the time and the choice to transpose the story

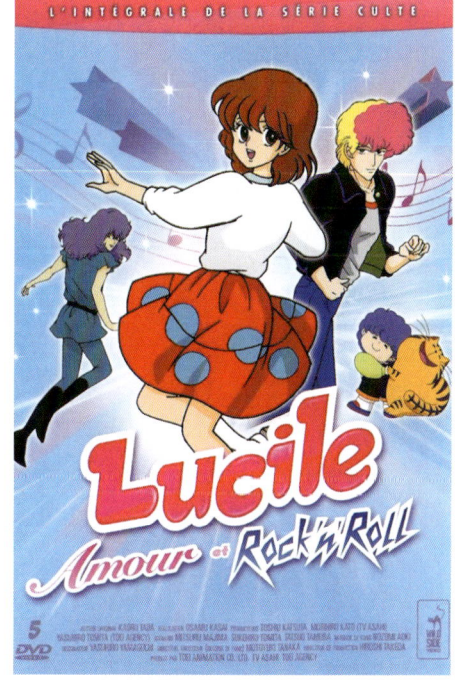

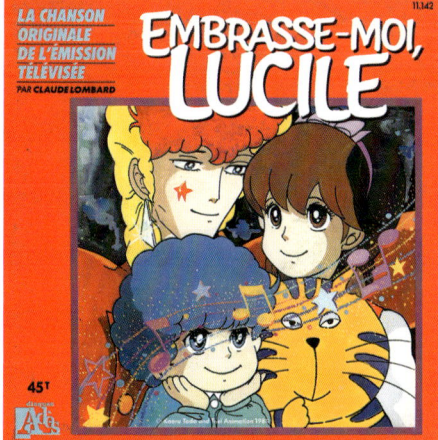

to France create inconsistencies, most famously in the series finale when one of the characters actually returns from France. The choice was then made to resituate the whole original story in Japan, making the entire translation of the series completely incoherent.

Like in *Maison Ikkoku*, Japanese culture is very much in evidence, whether in the role of women, romantic conventions, or the social pressure faced by young people in the 1980s. Nevertheless, the anime won over Western audiences. It was such a success in Italy that a live-action adaptation, *Licia Dolce Licia*, was created, combining a French sitcom with a cosplay competition. In this version, Juliano (in this case Giuliano) is extremely talkative. Played by a cat in the non-moving close-ups, he's a stuffed animal in all the more complicated group sequences.

The most obvious peculiarity of the cartoon is that Juliano speaks. He just quietly comments on what the humans are saying, often complaining or asking for something to eat. If the people don't seem to hear the feline speak, they often understand his intentions. The cat is also treated like a human being, eating at the table in the restaurant and sharing Hashizo's meals without anyone seeming surprised. The cat's role is often secondary to the plot but lends the series a touch of comedy. 🐾

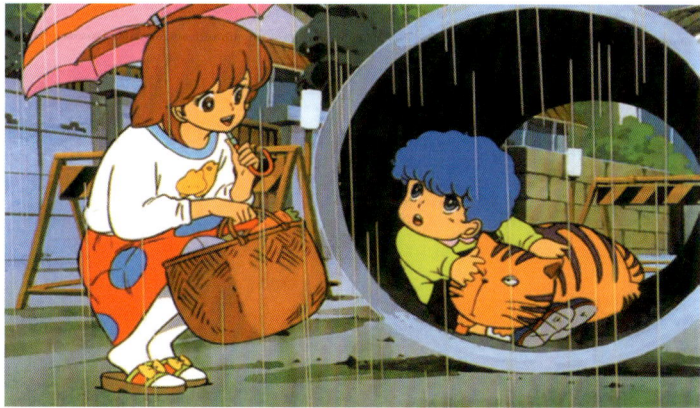

SPEC SHEET

CAT'S NAME: Juliano.
WORK: *Love Me, My Knight*.
CREATOR: Osamu Kasai (based on a manga by Kaoru Tada).
FIRST BROADCAST: 1983.
DISTRIBUTOR/AVAILABILITY: Not available in English.
CAT'S CHARACTERISTICS: Big orange tabby with purple stripes. Lover of okonomiyaki and a misogynist.

Koketsu

Before Love Me, My Knight*'s Juliano, before Studio Ghibli, there were the cats in Isao Takahata's* Chie the Brat. *Although Kotetsu and his adversaries don't take center stage in this animated film, they do provide much of the comic relief.*

Chie the Brat tells the story of a modern-day Cinderella. In a poor neighborhood of Osaka, eight-year-old Chie lives alone with her father, Tetsu, who is a lazy, hard-drinking gambler and brawler. In addition to going to school, since her mother left, she must also run the family restaurant and make up for her father's missteps with the city's yakuza. Kotetsu, an alley cat enticed by Chie's skewered meat, becomes a kind of fairy godmother for the little girl. The tomcat subdues the neighborhood's feline terror, castrating him in the process, and even prevails over Tetsu.

While the confrontations between Kotetsu and Antonio, the local godfather's cat, are resolutely comic, borrowing from conventions of the spaghetti western, their consequences drive the story forward. For example, when Antonio loses his "golden ball" (a slang euphemism for testicle), he loses his role as leader and, through a cascade of events, Tetsu, Chie's father, is saved. By the same token, when Kotetsu follows in his human family's footsteps and refuses to strike back at Antonio Jr., who has come to avenge his father, peace is established among the felines, just as Chie's parents have reconciled.

In a departure from the 1980s standard, Kotetsu walks on his hind legs—without humans saying anything about it—and, like Antonio Sr., has all the classic flaws of the anime cat: He's a glutton (and his love of meat skewers prefigures Juliano's love of pancakes

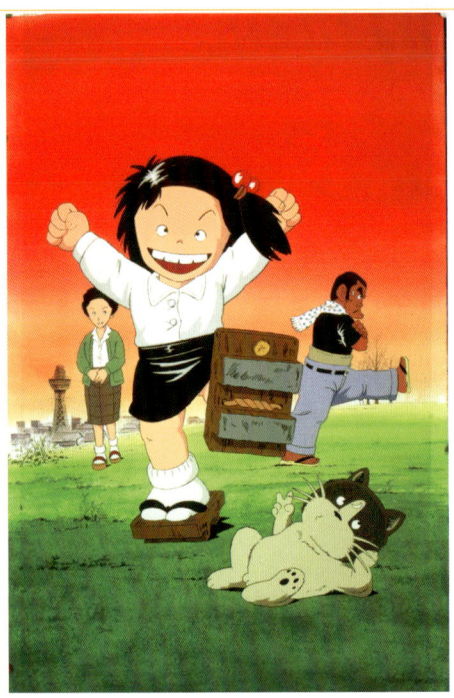

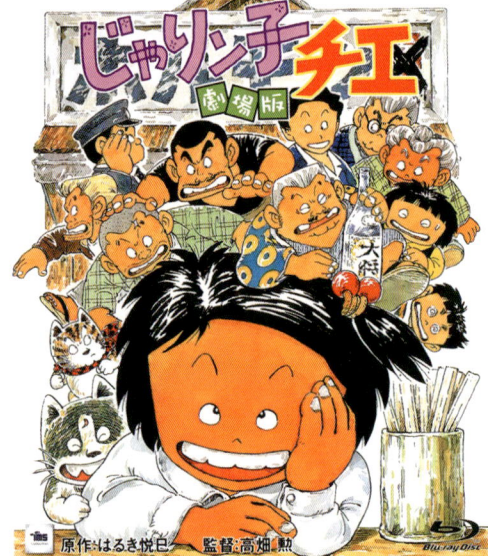

or *okonomiyaki*), short-tempered, and feisty. Antonio, on the other hand, is envious and jealous. But Kotetsu's role as protector is signaled from the outset by the crescent moon on his forehead, foreshadowing Luna, the guardian cat in the *Sailor Moon* universe (see p. 86). For those who want to understand cats in modern Japanese animation and have a good time with laughter and emotions, *Chie the Brat* is the film to see. 🐾

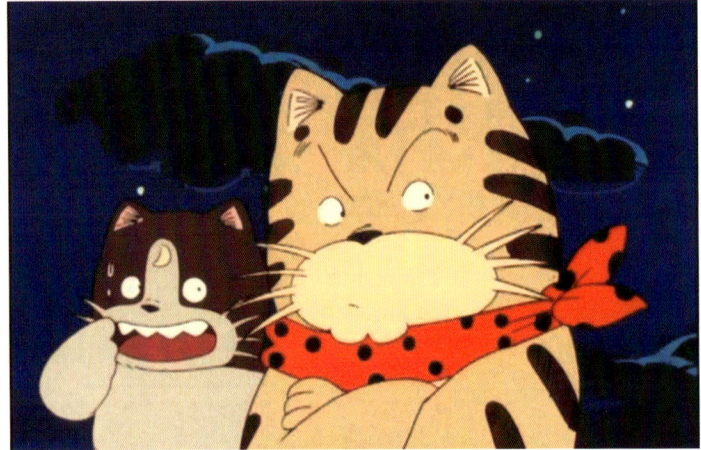

From left to right: Kotetsu and Antonio.

SPEC SHEET

CAT'S NAME: Kotetsu.
WORK: *Chie the Brat (Jarinko Chie)*.
CREATORS: Isao Takahata (director) and Noboru Shiroyama (scriptwriter), based on a work by Etsumi Haruki.
DATE CREATED: April 11, 1981.
DISTRIBUTOR/AVAILABILITY: Not available in English.
CAT'S CHARACTERISTICS: Gray-and-white male cat with a moon on his forehead. Chie's protector and neighborhood terror.

Women and Cats

Cats and Women: A Timeless Bond

If dogs are man's best friend, perhaps cats are woman's. In fiction, cats are seducers, winning over both animals and humans with their beauty and gentle ways. Sometimes cats are women's companions. Others, they are the object of comparison with women, who are said to borrow cats' virtues and faults.

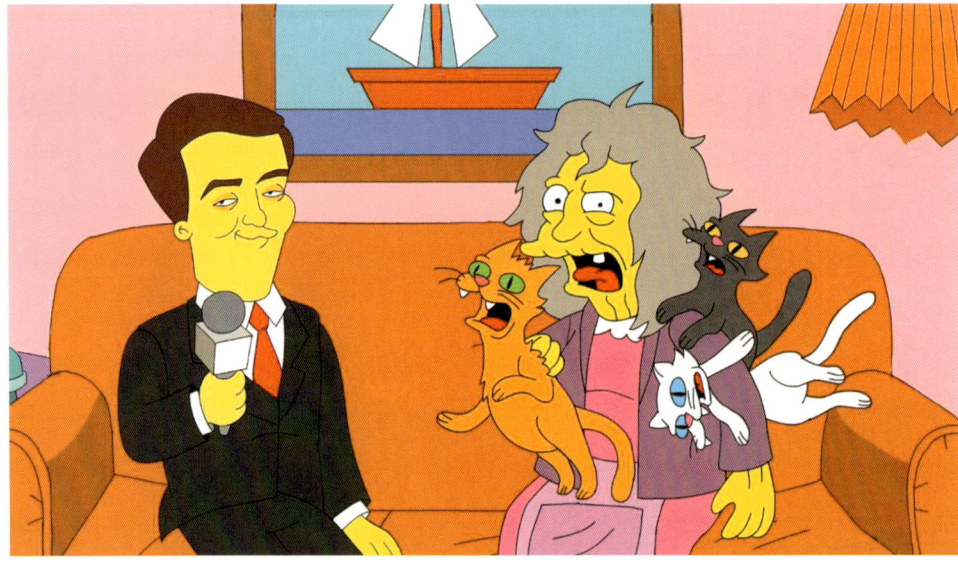

The Don Juan Cat

The archetypal Don Juan cat is Puss in Boots, the charismatic character from the Shrek franchise. His natural charm, shiny coat, and gentle, deep gaze make him irresistible. He seduces cats, especially in the spin-off devoted to him. However, he openly flirts with Princess Fiona when they first meet. This personality trait is reinforced by his "Latin lover" accent. His Don Juan attitude with humans, like his fickle nature, is highlighted to amuse viewers. The song "Le Chat" (The Cat) by the French group Pow woW also emphasizes these aspects of the animal.

The seduction of female cats becomes embarrassing in the Looney Tunes cartoon character Pepé Le Pew. Created by Chuck Jones in 1945, the French-accented skunk pursues a little cat (retroactively named Penelope Pussycat) that he mistakes for a skunk. Although hilarious since its creation, it was recently removed from the final cut of *Space Jam 2* for reasons of political correctness. A reassessment of the character argued that the cartoon's humor and narrative were based on Pepé being a sexual abuser. The unpleasant-smelling "French lover" constantly pursues a poor cat, despite her obvious refusal to give in to his advances. It should also be mentioned that the word "pussy" has more than one meaning.

Woman's Companion

The feline's natural duality of beauty and wildness aligns it with society's image of the independent woman. This also explains why cats are often seen as the companions of lonely women (especially "old maids"). Cats have therefore become the preferred companion of women in fiction. Nevertheless, there are many clichés about female cat owners. They are often unmarried, as well as frustrated, crazy, or just depressed. This cliché is a sexist myth that rarely has a male counterpart. The orange cat Garfield living with Jon, a bachelor with strange habits, is one counterexample. However, his bachelorhood came to an end in comic books in the 2000s. A common figure in pop culture, an old cat lady appears in *The Simpsons*. Afflicted with Noah syndrome, which involves adopting more animals than is reasonable, old Eleanor Abernathy is an alcoholic. She regularly throws the cats

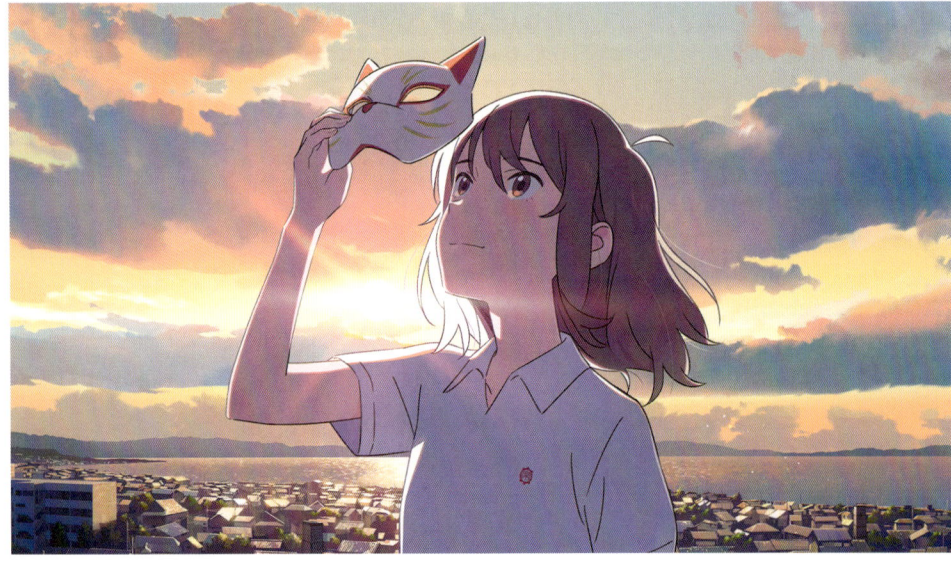

A Whisker Away.

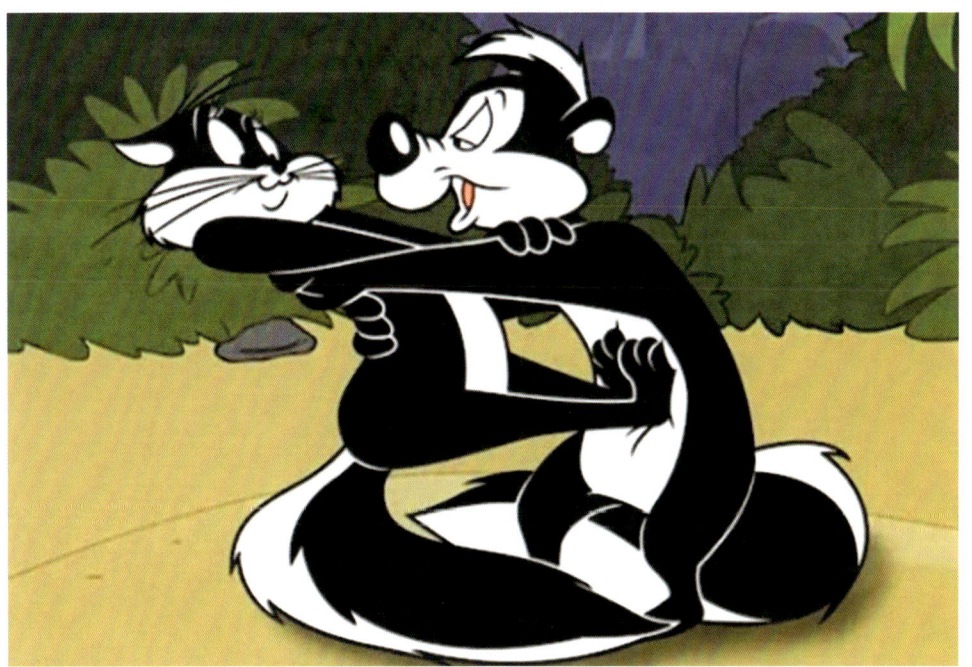

Pepé le Pew and . . . his sweetheart?

creatures in fiction. These characters are also imbued with an aura of danger. After all, the cat is a paradoxical animal, both close to and distant from man. It wants to be close to humans, while retaining the advantages of its freedom and a somewhat wild nature. Various authors have made the analogy with the figure of the woman, which explains why the two beings are so closely associated in both fiction and pop culture. Dark, mysterious feline beauty is ultimately a metaphor for the "feminine mystique." 🐾

[1] http://www.slate.fr/story/181026/stereotype-femme-chats-depression-anxiete-solitude

she takes in at the people of Springfield. The animal is seen as a companion for those suffering from depression, but no study to date has demonstrated such a link.[1]

The Cat As Woman's Alter Ego

Cats share many attributes with women, which are often highlighted in fiction. A cat wandering along gutters demonstrates its talent for flexibility and agility, as seen in the film *A Whisker Away* by Jun'ichi Satō and Tomotaka Shibayama. Freedom and the absence of a fear of heights are fantasies transposed to human life. Fictional women are empowered, freeing themselves from gravity with feline ease.

The thieves in *Cat's Eye* regularly leap into the void, as do Catwoman, the famous character from the DC Comics universe, and Marvel's Black Cat and Hellcat. The cat women's leap into the void has not only a mental significance,

but also a psychoanalytical undertone of letting go.

Cat women's freedom goes hand in hand with a wild, undomesticated, or downright aggressive side. In Catwoman's case, she's armed with a whip. Her aim isn't violence, but like a wild animal, she doesn't hesitate to use it when her life or freedom is at risk. Physical or psychological captivity (in a relationship, for example) is a recurring problem for this type of character. In *Cat's Eye*, the thieves are always trying to escape from the police, even though they have provoked them. One of them, Hitomi, runs away from her detective fiancé. This represents a metaphorical flight from commitment.

The cat's gentleness is also a feminine quality that is highlighted, among other instances, when the heroine of *A Whisker Away* is in her kitten form, striking cuddly poses with the young man she's in love with. This kind of behavior was already found in Jacques Tourneur's film *Cat People*, and in all the half-woman, half-cat

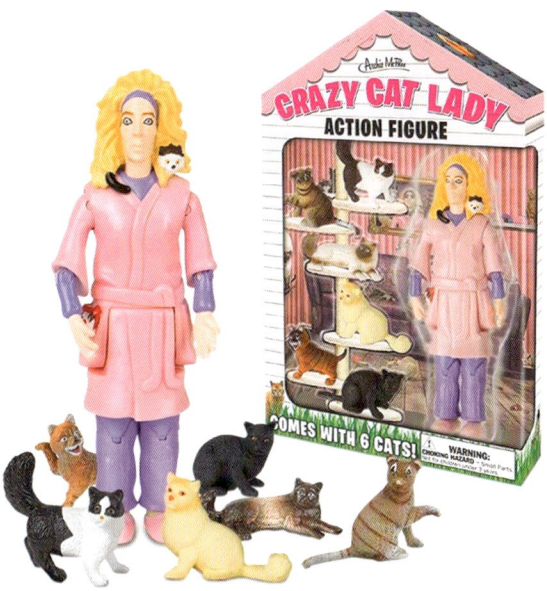

Crazy Cat Lady figurine.

Interview with . . . Maliki, Web Cartoonist

"Cats have always been part of my daily life."

When Souillon launched his blog to post the adventures of Maliki and her cats, did he have any idea that the stories about his female alter ego would be so successful? And that the cats, past or present, who appear in them would become icons of twenty-first-century pop culture?

How did Maliki come into being? And why did you start her adventures on the web before moving on to traditional publishing, then self-publishing while still on the web?

Maliki was born on the corner of a sheet of paper, during my middle school and high school years. As I drew her more and more, I decided to feature her on a blog bearing her name, starting in 2004, in the form of stories drawn from my daily life. The web was an ideal medium for introducing her, first to my family and friends, and then to the many people who became interested in her adventures. Ankama came across

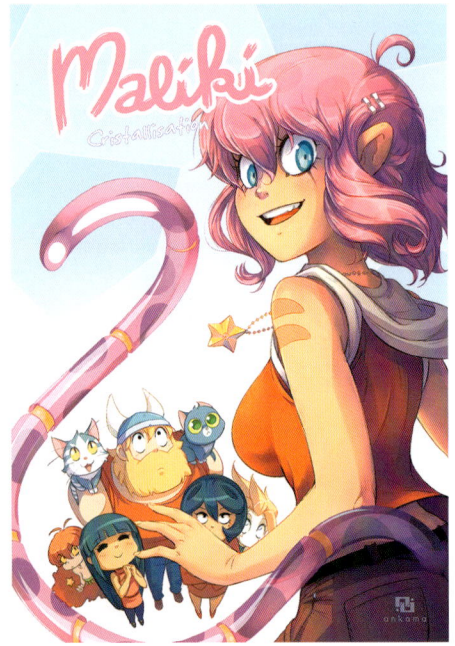

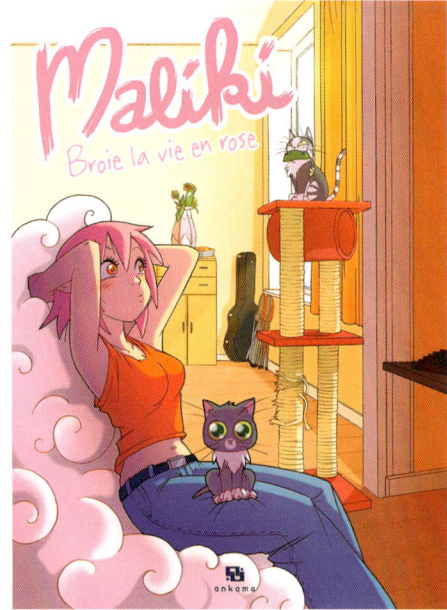

this blog and offered me a job, as well as publishing a collection of strips, which I liked. So, I left my job at GOA (a France Télécom subsidiary specializing in online gaming, which disappeared in 2010) to set up in Roubaix. Self-publishing came much later, when I decided to become totally independent with Becky. I explain all the reasons for this change in an online strip.[1] [*Editor's Note:* Since 2016 and the switch to crowdfunding, three albums have been released, in addition to the seven published by Ankama and the three novels published by Bayard.]

How have your real-life cats inspired their counterparts in blogs, comics, and novels?

Cats have always been part of my daily life, from a very early age. There are many stories to tell about them, and it's always easy to find a place for them in the Maliki universe. They evolve over time: some leaving us,[2] others finding us again. If you add a touch of the supernatural, you've got a good mix of ideas for comics and novels.

Why, when there's now a proliferation of realistic or fantastic characters and animals, are cats still the common thread?

It's true that many strips revolve around cats. But other animals have joined in, especially since I moved to Brittany: axolotls, hens, roosters, peacocks, and even alpacas. So even though people have long associated Maliki with the girl who tells stories about cats, because they're the original animals, I think that today, they're part of a whole group of beings living in harmony, or almost.

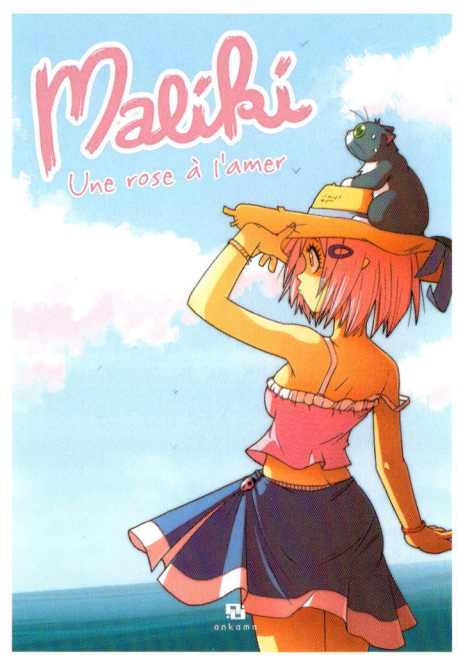

How do you plan to develop the Maliki universe?

I'd like to be able to see into the future to answer that question! We do have projects in mind, such as an anime, a video game, and one-shots, but Maliki is unpredictable, so we'll have to wait and see in the years to come. :) 🐾

---

[1] https://maliki.com/en/strips/at-a-crossroads/
[2] https://maliki.com/en/strips/minor-god/

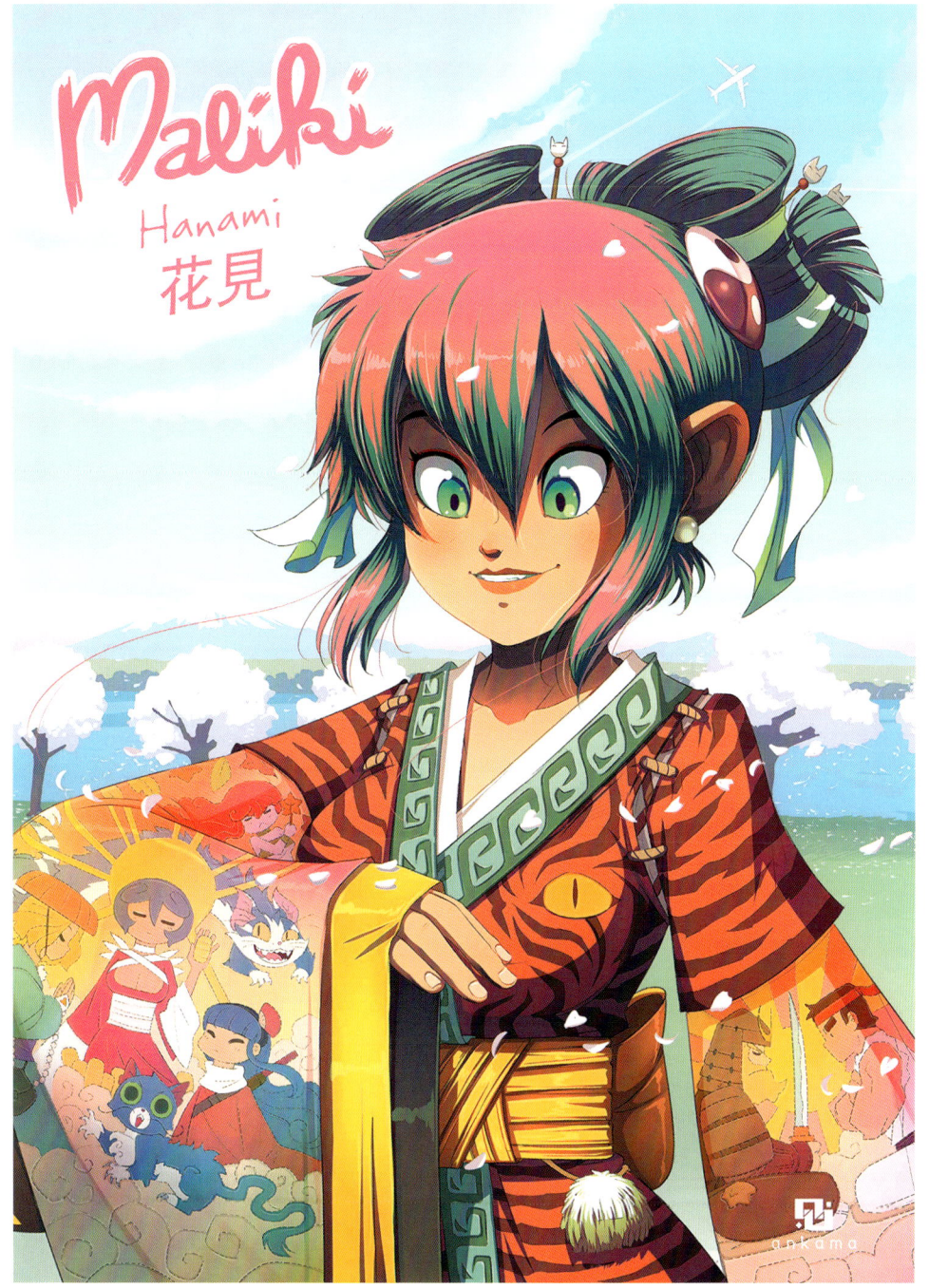

MALIKI: A CAT LADY

From her very first appearances on the web, Maliki and her pink hair have had a loyal following. This included cat lovers who wanted above all to know about the adventures of Fëanor and Fleya, the two felines who shared her life. The brother and sister have since died, but other cats have joined her household and her comics: Arya and Luma, Arcturus (also deceased), Gueulard, and Capucine. However, the two original cats are still present in the merchandising and, to a certain extent, in the comics. As for her supernatural avatar, Savage Ladybird, also known as Ladybird (Maliki's other favorite animal, along with cats) or Lady, she is also linked to felines. Not only does her look evoke the cat-women of Japanese animation, but it is also said to have been created by the fusion of the soul of a cat she had as a child and the little girl she was at the time, traumatized by the death of the animal. Usually floating a meter above the ground, Lady can solidify to interact with the outside world, and like the Hulk, her strength increases with her anger, or more precisely, the strength of the emotions felt by Maliki.

Cat People

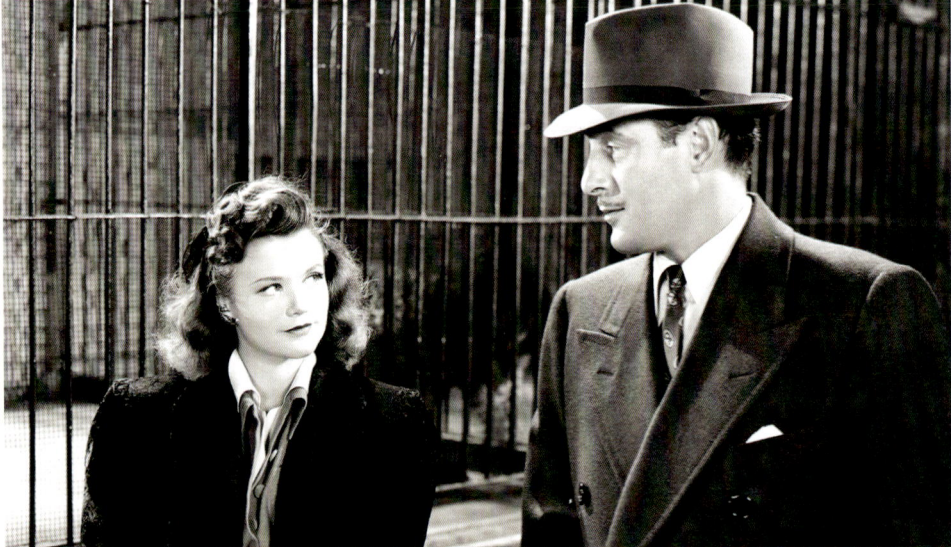

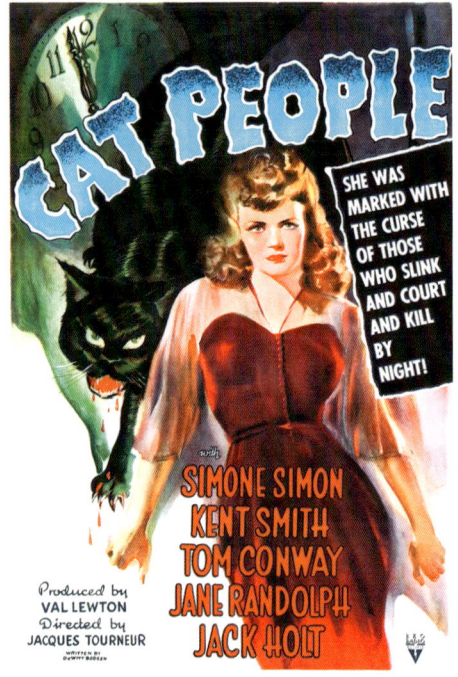

Among the very first films to feature cats in fantasy and horror, Jacques Tourneur's Cat People *stands out in more ways than one. It's both one of the oldest films in the genre and one of the first to exploit the seductive and destructive ambivalence of women and cats.*

When *Cat People* was released in 1942, it was classified as a second-rate horror film. Viewed from the 2020s, this description seems ludicrous. Second-rate? Perhaps, because the movie's budget didn't exceed $150,000, and shooting lasted just eighteen days, as RKO didn't have much faith in the film. And yet, it soon proved a success, with a direct sequel released in 1944 and another film on the same theme (*The Leopard Man*) released in 1943. A horror film? Let's face it, the budgetary constraints and film censorship of the time mean that we don't see any real horror scenes, with lacerated or devoured bodies and gallons of blood. Jacques Tourneur was a master of the art of "the less you see, the more you believe." By playing with shadows and showing a detail here (such as the

Siamese kitten seized with terror in front of Irena—Simone Simon—or Alice's lacerated bathrobe), he gradually instills an oppressive, ambiguous climate that keeps viewers on the edge of their seats throughout the film's seventy-two minutes.

And yet, the plot is simple. A New York architect falls in love with a Serbian fashion designer and marries her. Terrified by an ancient family curse in her village, she refuses to consummate the marriage for fear of killing her husband. When she finally gives in to her carnal impulses, her predatory instincts are awakened and, now a panther, she kills the man who kisses her before committing suicide. However, *Cat People* isn't a manifesto against women's emancipation; quite the contrary. The other female figure in the film is an independent woman, Alice, who ends up with the man she loves and, unlike Irena, seems to be liked by the various felines featured in the movie. On the other hand, *Cat People* contrasts the sensuality of the two actresses, Simone Simon and Jane Randolph (Alice, who would also appear in the sequel), and skillfully plays on cats' association with the figure of

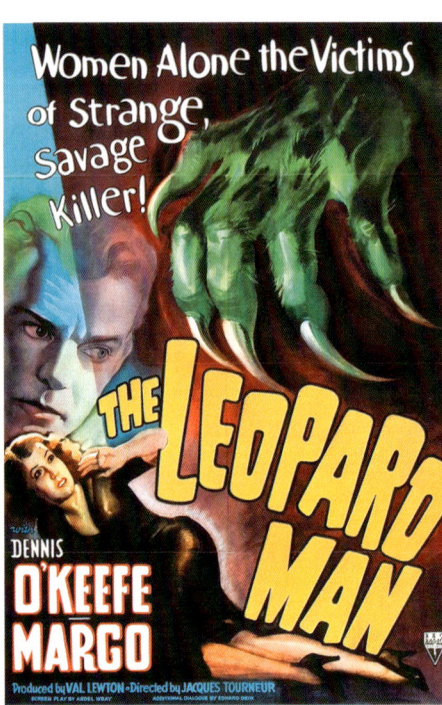

the witch. Although Irena Dubrovna is afflicted by a curse more like that of a werewolf than a true witch, she doesn't hesitate to use her charms and chastity to seduce her future husband and her psychiatrist. The legend of her native village tells of a battle against devil worshippers who worshipped him in the form of a gigantic cat. With all these elements, the director created an innovative fantasy thriller for its time, featuring the "cat scare" where, as the tension slowly mounts on-screen, the appearance of an innocuous and totally unexpected element, such as a kitten or a bus, startles the viewer. This effect and its opposite, the "jump scare" (an abrupt change of shot intended to produce a fright), later became horror film classics. 🐾

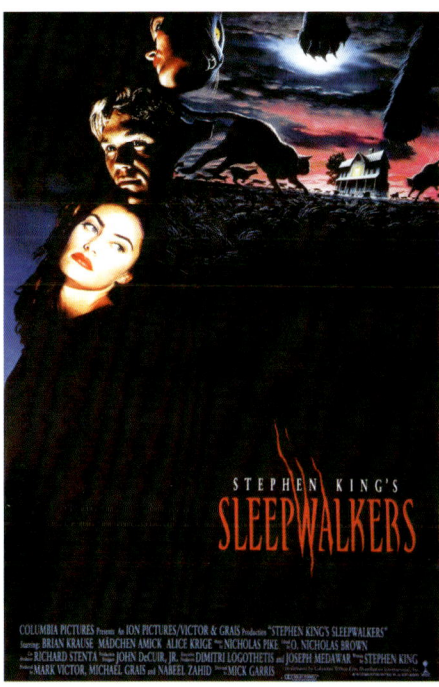

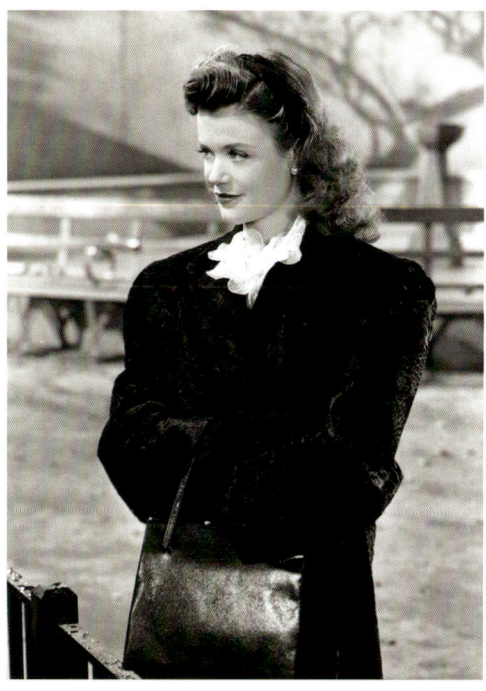

FROM SEQUELS TO REMAKES, SOME MORE OVERT THAN OTHERS

Jacques Tourneur wasn't done with cat stories after *Cat People*. He filmed *The Leopard Man*, which can be seen as the opposite of *Cat People*, with a serial killer (the first in Hollywood cinema, even though the term didn't exist) who uses an escaped leopard as a pretext to camouflage his crimes in a small New Mexico town. He moves from the big, cold city to the countryside, where white people, Latinos, and Indigenous peoples live side by side without really mixing. From fantasy disguised as a whodunit, he switches to a whodunit camouflaged behind a werewolf story. RKO commissioned Robert Wise to make a direct sequel, *Curse of the Cat People*, which featured some of the same characters as the first film but was very different in spirit, particularly as there were no cat people or cat women in the film, except as ghosts or hallucinations. In 1982, Paul Schrader remade *Cat People* with Nastassja Kinski in the title role, using the same plot as the 1942 film but transposing it to New Orleans and adding a special condition to the curse: Only incest can lift the curse. The result is an erotic-horrific film with a distinctly 1980s aesthetic, but substance too often gives way to style. Ten years later, Mick Garris's *Sleepwalkers*, based on an original screenplay by Stephen King, takes up the same idea. Here, the monsters are an incestuous vampire mother and son. Their only known predators are domestic cats, which not only see them in their true cat-headed human guise but can also use their claws to kill them. Once again, this unadmitted remake is no match for the original 1942 film.

SPEC SHEET

WORK: *Cat People*.
CREATORS: Jacques Tourneur (director) and DeWitt Bodeen (screenwriter).
DATE CREATED: 1942.
DISTRIBUTOR/AVAILABILITY: Originally, RKO Radio Pictures. Now available from the Criterion Collection on DVD and Blu-ray, and through various streaming platforms.
CAT'S NAME AND ROLE IN THE WORK: Irena Dubrovna, the film's protagonist whose cursed lineage turns her into a panther.

Catwoman

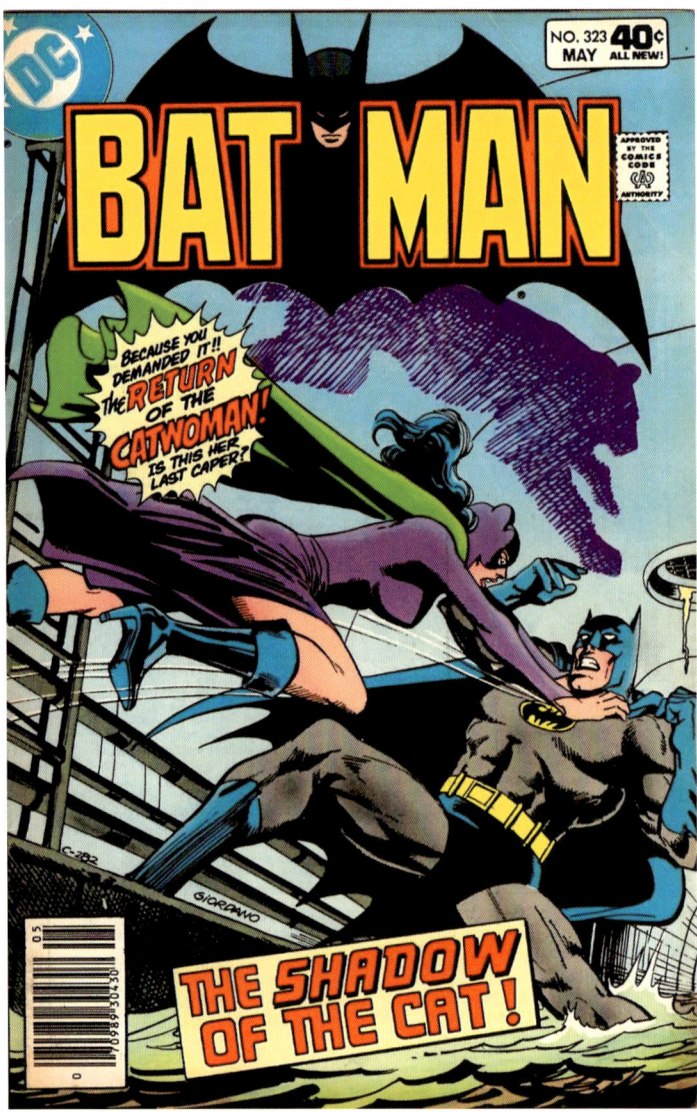

From the very first issue of Batman comics, a voluptuously curvaceous thief dressed as a cat squares off against Gotham's masked vigilante. An ambivalent, charismatic character, DC Comics began featuring her in her own comics in 1989.

Like many comic book characters, Catwoman has undergone various rewrites and reboots over the course of the DC Universe's complicated history and Batman's extended family. While the Catwoman role was temporarily embodied by the Holly Robinson character, it was mostly played by Selina Kyle. Two characteristics remain in all versions: sexualization and the character's non-Manichean aspect. The character's sexualization can be seen right from the start, with her bare legs and daring cleavage for the time. Although she wears a simple cat mask from her second appearance, she doesn't

have a specific costume at first. The character's aesthetic evolved considerably over the years. In the 1960s, her costume turned green, and she wore a cape. She then adopted a whip, which became an object of fantasy that Frank Miller used as a fetish object when he rewrote the character in 1986. In the 1990s, Tim Burton's *Batman Returns* influenced the design, turning her costume into a tight-fitting jumpsuit. She is regularly accompanied by cats who follow her or perch on her shoulder. In all cases, the choice of the cat costume is always significant. Catwoman is all about feline movement, flexibility, and beauty.

She also shares cats' first vice: theft. Her motives for stealing are deliberately ambiguous, sometimes justified, other times related only to greed or simple kleptomania. A juvenile delinquent in a crime-ridden Gotham, she sometimes defends the oppressed and becomes a jewel thief thanks to her feline

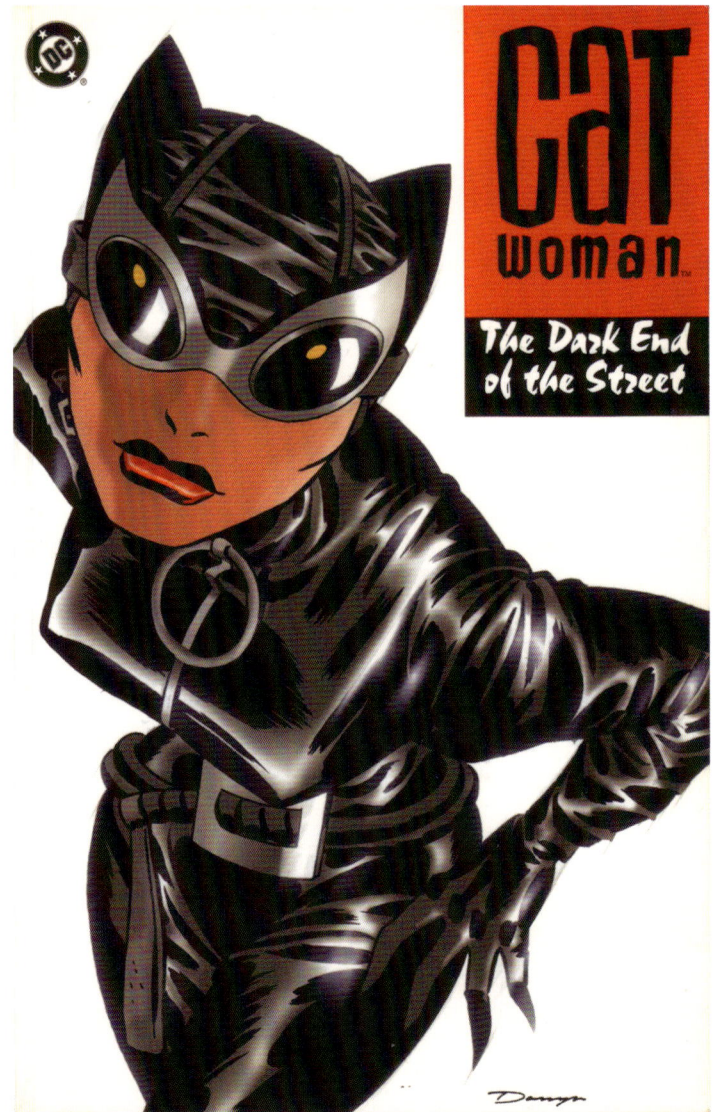

abilities. Unlike Batman's enemies, she has no inclination for violence or murder, which explains why the hero regularly lets her escape. The two characters maintain a carnal relationship in several comic book series, even going so far as to become engaged. Catwoman and Batman are then also known as Selina Kyle and Bruce Wayne.

Catwoman's confidence in her sexuality helps make her a feminist character. She's independent, not reliant on any man, and fully embraces her sexuality. In 2015, the character officially became bisexual.[1] With moral repression guiding America in the 1950s, DC was forced by the Comics Code Authority to remove Selina and her alter ego in 1954, as it deemed that the character and her sexual attitudes didn't respect the morality of the time.

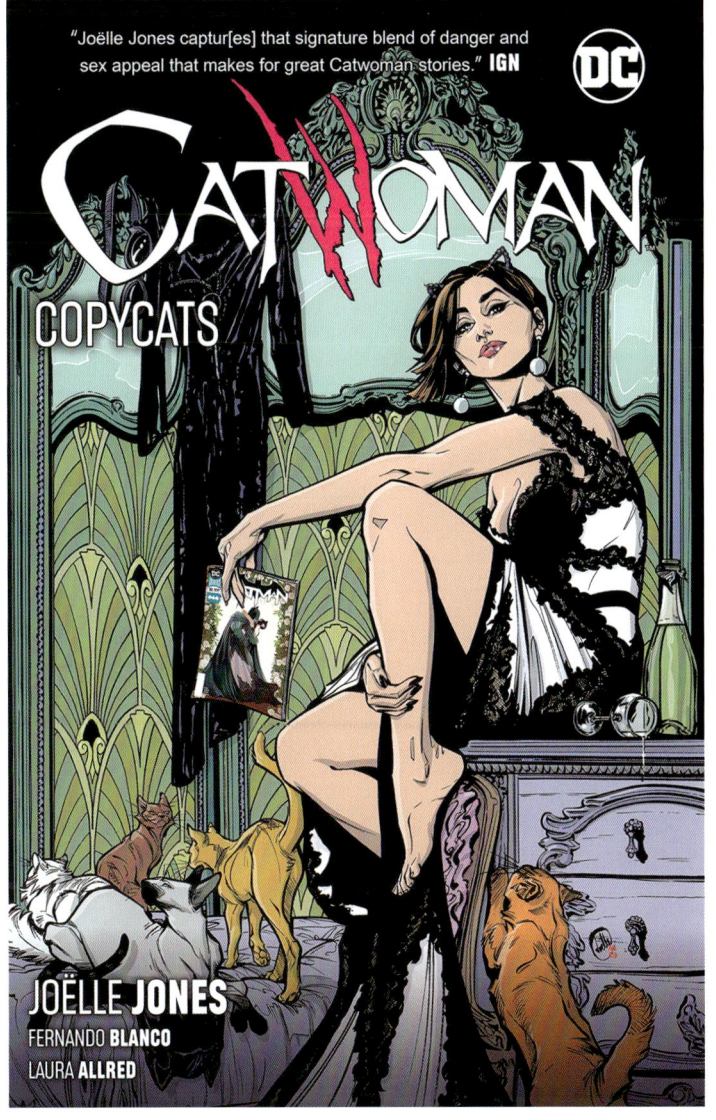

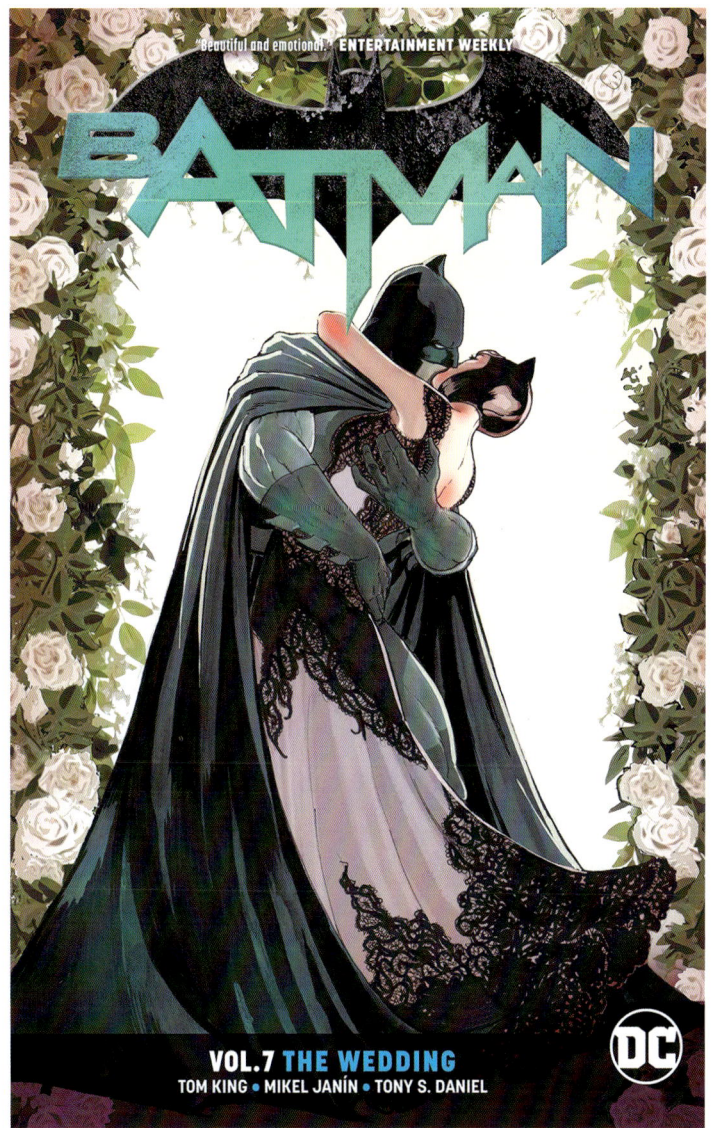

From Paper to Television Screen

The complexity of the character, who is sometimes Batman's enemy and sometimes a hero in her own right, extends beyond the comics. The characterization of the cat-woman as a feminist figure could be called into question. She could just as easily be described as a character created by misogynists because of her hypersexualization and taste for jewelry. Selina has no superhuman powers or abilities but has a gift for thievery and acrobatics that enable her to carry out her larcenies. However, several film versions feature the character's death as justification for her transformation into a cat-woman, suggesting that she has nine lives.

---

[1] https://www.dccomics.com/comics/catwoman-2011/catwoman-39

The character has been adapted many times for both film and television. The first version was played by blond Julie Newmar in the first *Batman* series of the 1960s. Sexy but decent, she's the image of the adaptation, gently grotesque. The role was taken over by brunette Lee Meriwether in the 1966 spin-off film. A new series followed, starring Eartha Kitt. The role wasn't much deeper, but it was the first time it was played by an African American actress.

A Sensual, Complementary Antagonist

In 1992, Tim Burton cast actress Michelle Pfeiffer as his Catwoman in *Batman Returns*. She has a gothic aesthetic, with seams that resemble the scars on Dr. Frankenstein's creature, as is typical of the director. Wearing skin-tight, sadomasochistic leather, this Catwoman influenced the character's appearance in the comics. In this version, she is pushed off a building by her boss and loses her life, only to be saved by Gotham's stray cats. She becomes completely psychotic and decides to dress up to steal.

In 2008, Halle Berry was chosen to play the feline heroine. French director Pitof was at the helm of what remains a monumental commercial and critical failure, and arguably the worst existing version of the character. No doubt inspired by Burton's film, the narrative begins with the death of the main character, Patience Phillipps, a reserved artist, who is resurrected by a cat. She becomes Catwoman, a confident character who takes revenge on those who killed her. The film won five Razzie awards, including Worst Actress, which Halle Berry accepted with elegance.

In 2012, Anne Hathaway played Catwoman in *The Dark Knight Rises*, the final opus in Nolan's Batman trilogy. Nolan chose to return to a more mentally stable character, focusing

on her role as a thief. Zoe Kravitz took the role opposite Robert Pattinson's Batman in 2022's film *The Batman*.

The *Gotham* TV series, centered on Inspector Gordon's role after the Wayne murders, features Selina Kyle among the characters cast. Played by Camren Bicondova for five seasons, she describes her teenage adventures with Bruce Wayne before they became the city's vigilantes.

Catwoman has also featured in various animated adaptations of *Batman*. This was especially true of Bruce Timm and Paul Dini's 1992 *Batman: The Animated Series*, whose female characters were particularly well written, and which also saw the birth of Harley Quinn. In this version, the feline criminal takes on the role of femme fatale. 🐾

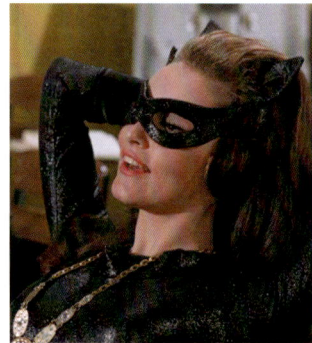

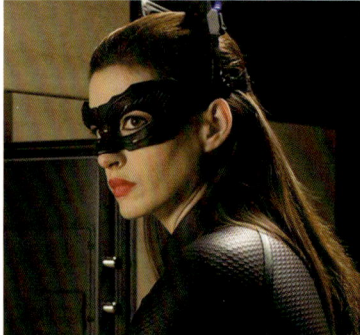

Julie Newmar.　　　　　　Anne Hathaway.

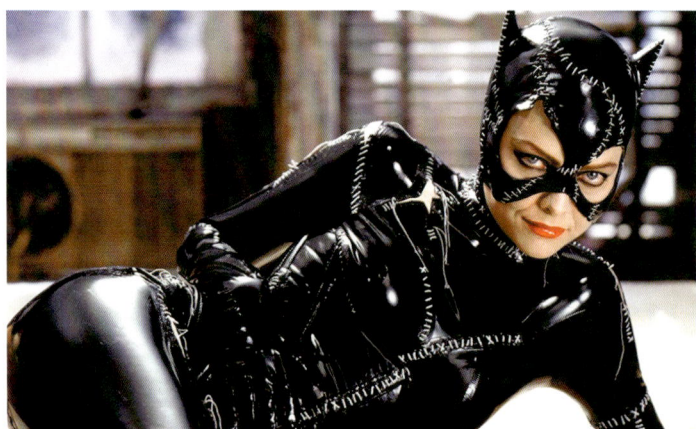

Michelle Pfeiffer.

SPEC SHEET

WORKS: The various Batman/Catwoman series set in DC's Gotham.
CREATORS: Bill Finger and Bob Kane.
DATE CREATED: Spring 1940 in the first issue of *Batman*.
PUBLISHER: DC Comics.
CAT'S NAME AND ROLE IN THE WORK: Catwoman (Selina Kyle or temporarily Holly Robinson). Recurring character in Batman stories; sometimes the hero's ally, sometimes his adversary. Acrobatic thief with no particular powers in most versions.

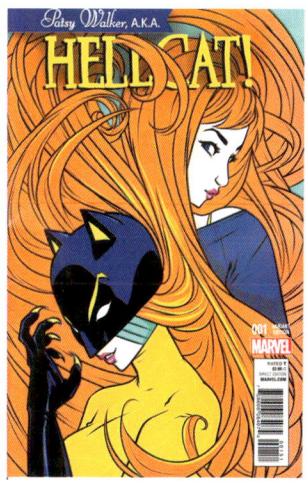
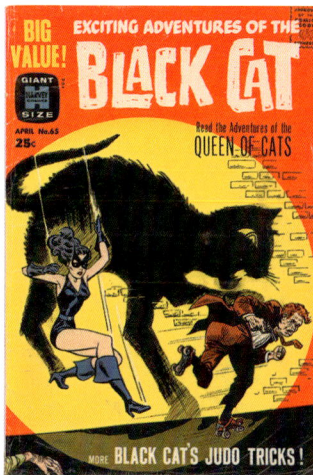
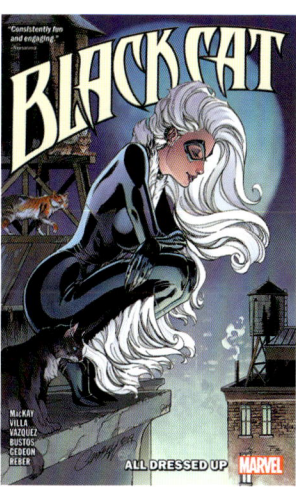

DC doesn't have a monopoly on ambiguous heroines inspired by cats. One of them was even one of the first masked superheroines, before Hellcat and Black Cat had fun blurring the lines.

DC and Marvel aren't the only publishers to issue comics featuring masked heroes. Harvey Comics, better known for publishing *Casper the Friendly Ghost*, has had its own costumed characters, including Black Cat, created by Al Gabriele in 1941. Like Catwoman, who preceded her by a year, she is the archetypal ordinary athletic woman who dons a costume (in this case, a bathing suit, motorcycle boots, vamp gloves, and a black, then blue and red, mask) to fight bad guys (in this case, Nazis). She's already on her own and doesn't serve as a foil for a male hero. To the contrary, Rick Horne is her accomplice and fiancé. Weary in 1951 after a foray into horror and westerns, she disappeared.

The next generation came from Marvel, with not one, but two heroines adopting feline costumes. The first, Patsy Walker (later Hellcat), wasn't intended to be a superhero when she was created in 1944. The redhead was a young model and celebrity, the star of the romantic-comedy comics published by Timely, the forerunner to Marvel. That all changed in the 1970s, when, because of her athletic abilities, she joined *The Avengers* after becoming friends with Hank "Beast" McCoy. Soon after, she was endowed with psychic and mystical powers (due in part to her marriage to the son of Satan, Daimon Hellstrom) and continued her career in her very discreet yellow-and-blue costume, even joining the *Jessica Jones* TV series on Netflix.

The second Marvel heroine, Felicia Hardy, known as the Black Cat, appeared in 1979 in the pages of *The Amazing Spider-Man*. Her relationship with Spider-Man is similar to Catwoman's with Batman: sometimes adversaries, sometimes allies, sometimes lovers. Like Selina Kyle, she's above all a thief by profession. However, unlike the most common incarnations of Catwoman, Black Cat doesn't rely solely on agility and seduction. She's also a mutant who, in addition to having superhuman physical abilities, can change the odds to jinx those around her, like the animal who supposedly gave her her pseudonym. She also uses a number of gadgets, including contact lenses that allow her to see far beyond the human spectrum (and thus move in the dark like a cat). 🐾

SPEC SHEET

CAT'S NAME: Patsy Walker/Hellcat.
CREATORS: Stuart Little and Ruth Atkinson.
DATE CREATED: November 1944.
PUBLISHER: Marvel.
CAT'S CHARACTERISTICS: Red-haired female acrobat with psychic and mystical powers, retractable claws in her yellow-and-blue costume, and a grappling hook.

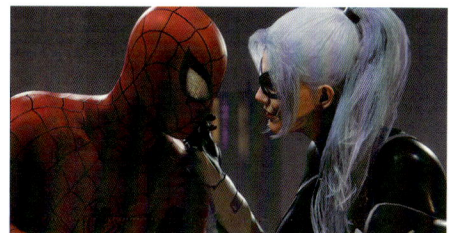

Spider-Man and Black Cat, *Marvel's Spider-Man*, PlayStation 4 video game.

SPEC SHEET

CAT'S NAME: Felicia Hardy/Black Cat.
CREATORS: Marv Wolfman and Dave Cockrum.
DATE CREATED: July 1979.
PUBLISHER: Marvel.
CAT'S CHARACTERISTICS: Burglar with platinum-blond hair and green eyes, equipped with many gadgets. A mutant who changes the odds to the detriment of others.

C'mell

A prototype of the cat-woman who would later haunt American pulp magazines and comic books, C'mell's appearance is no different from that of an ordinary human. But her temperament and behavior are fiercely feline, making her one of the most striking characters ever created by Cordwainer Smith.

In Cordwainer Smith's *Lords of Instrumentality* cycle, human beings have gradually abandoned thankless jobs, entrusting them to robots and then to animal-human hybrids, the underpeople. One of their best-known representatives is C'mell, a girly-girl working at Earthport. An underperson developed from cats, under cover of her role as an escort to travelers, she has helped Lord Jestocost in his struggle to improve conditions for the underpeople, who are considered to have no more rights than the animals from which they are derived. It's to the point that if they run out of money for food and lodging, they're taken to the Poorhouse, where they're simply euthanized with gas, like abandoned animals in an overcrowded shelter. Later, she helps Roderick McBain, the richest human being in the universe, escape his pursuers by posing as his wife when he assumes the identity of C'Roderick, a handsome but slightly dim-witted underperson.

Although the C in her name, C'mell, indicates her feline ancestry (C for cat), C'mell has a normal appearance. In the first short story in the cycle in which she appears, it says, "She was a girly-girl and they were true men, the lords of creation, but she pitted her wits against them and she won. [...] She was not even of human extraction. She was cat-derived, though human in outward shape, which explains the C in front of her name." Her physical appearance is never really described; the most we know is that she has inherited her father's athletic abilities, and that she's attractive enough to do her job. As a reward for helping Roderick McBain, she becomes the owner and chef of a restaurant, has seventy-three children, and dies at 103, a respectable age for her species.

Although Cordwainer Smith deliberately left things vague, C'mell was to become one of the prototypes of the cat-women that would later fill the comics. Unlike D'joan, the girl-dog deified by the underpeople in the

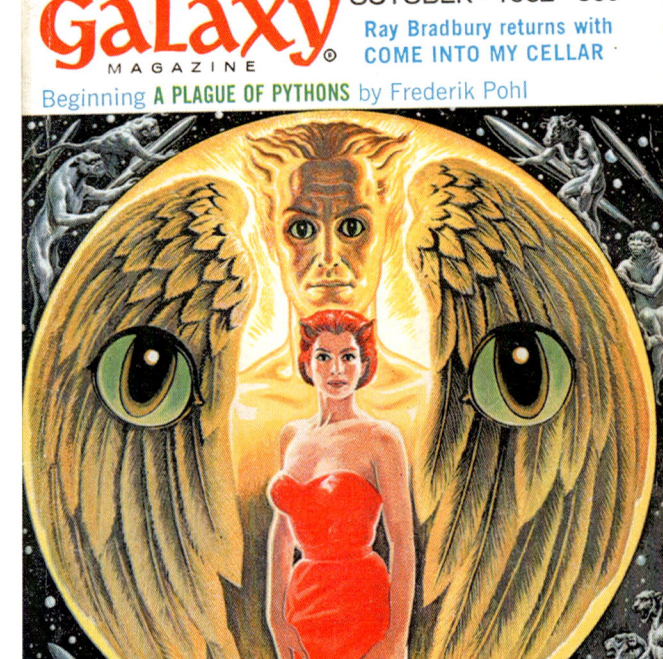

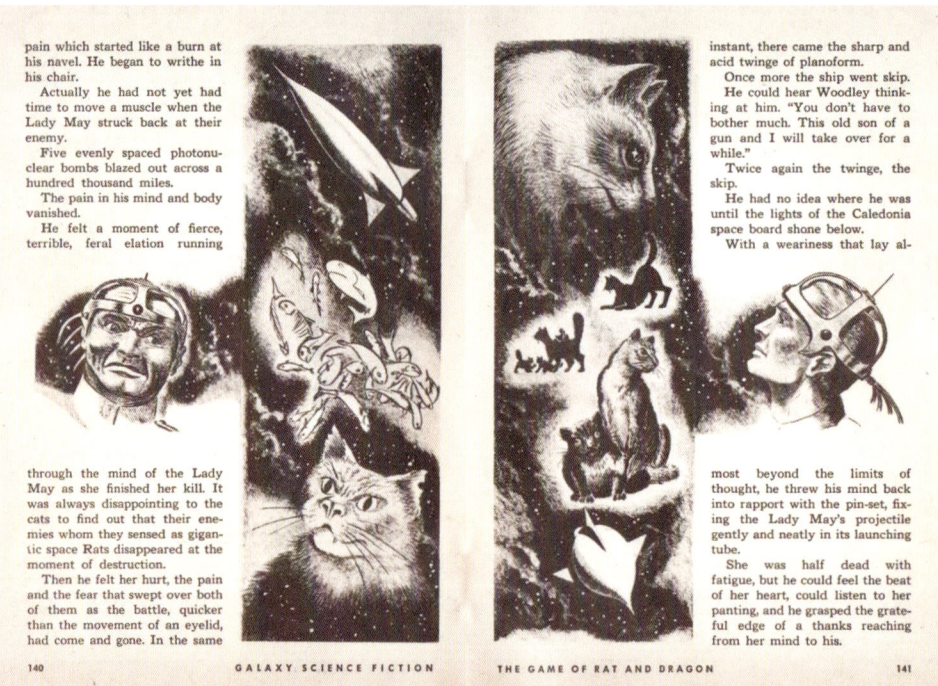

"The Game of Rat and Dragon" in *Galaxy Science Fiction* magazine, Cordwainer Smith, 1955.

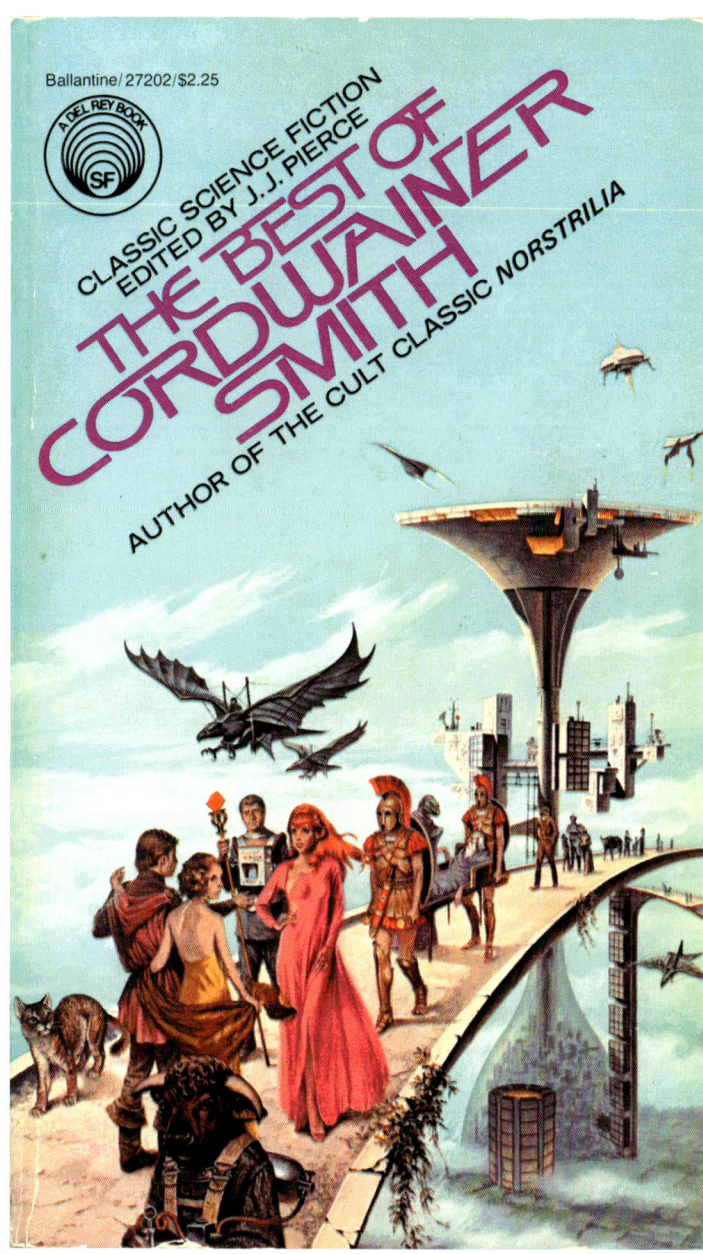

Ballantine/27202/$2.25

A DEL REY BOOK

CLASSIC SCIENCE FICTION
EDITED BY J. J. PIERCE

THE BEST OF CORDWAINER SMITH

AUTHOR OF THE CULT CLASSIC NORSTRILIA

one of his cats, Melanie,[1] a black alley cat with a particularly gentle disposition, according to the author's daughter.

C'mell and the other feline representatives of the underpeople are not the only felids in the *Lords of Instrumentality* cycle, which imagines the future of the human species from the end of World War II to twenty or thirty thousand years in the future, when various solar systems will have been conquered. These are the ones who, despite everything, have the most enviable fate. In "The Game of Rat and Dragon," ordinary cats are telepathically linked with starship pilots because of their quick reflexes and used to fight aliens attacking and driving humans mad. The casualty rate among animals is immense. On the other hand, contrary to what the title suggests, "Mother Hitton's Littul Kittons" aren't felines driven to violent, murderous madness to telepathically protect Norstralia from theft, but minks that spend most of their lives under sedation when not attacking or breeding. Would Cordwainer Smith, the cat lover, have chosen to use the predatory and territorial instincts of his favorite animals in such a cruel way? 🐾

SPEC SHEET

CAT'S NAME: C'mell.
WORKS: "The Ballad of Lost C'mell" (short story), "Alpha Ralpha Boulevard" (short story), and *The Planet Buyer* (novel) in the *Lords of Instrumentality* cycle.
CREATOR: Cordwainer Smith.
DATE CREATED: October 1962.
PUBLISHER/AVAILABILITY: His work has been published by various publishers, including Doubleday, NESFA Press, and Phoenix Pick.
CAT'S CHARACTERISTICS: Willowy young woman who appears human. Has telepathic abilities.

same cycle, C'mell is like a house cat. Fiercely independent, she never forgets her own survival, even though she is deeply loyal to the people she cares about and puts her missions first. The emphasis is on the seductive, empathetic side of her character, as well as her self-defense skills (particularly in "Alpha Ralpha Boulevard"). Like the other cat-women who follow her, C'mell knows how to break away from the mold that society wants to impose on her, using a mixture of gentleness, agility, and strength, cherishing her freedom above all else. In creating this character, Cordwainer Smith drew inspiration from

[1] http://www.cordwainer-smith.com/cmell-for-cat-lovers.htm

Catseye, Hepzibah, and Tigra: Marvel's Seductive Wildcats

By the 1970s, Marvel was no longer content with heroines dressed as cats. From then on, they would be hybrids of wild beasts and felines, usually on the side of good.

A superheroine with a feline look is all well and good, but a real heroic wildcat is even better, isn't it? Marvel's editors followed this line of reasoning, increasing the number of characters whose feminine forms blended into their feline counterparts, and vice versa, for ever more seductive appeal. While some only make short appearances for an episode or two or, like Snowbird (the embodiment of the animals of the Far North), occasionally take on a wildcat appearance, others have adopted it for good.

The first to take the plunge was Greer Grant Nelson. Created in 1972 as a crime-fighting heroine using her physical skills and numerous gadgets, she radically changed her appearance two years later, becoming Tigra. In the Marvel universe, this change is justified by the fact that, severely wounded, she is rescued and transformed into one of them by the Cat People (similar to the ancestors of the woman in the film *Cat People*, see p. 122). From a heroine symbolizing women's emancipation, she is transformed into a seductive redheaded tabby fighter dressed only in a tiny bikini, affiliated with the Avengers, the Defenders, and the New Warriors.

In October 1977, another seductive feline was created. This one, Hepzibah, is a space pirate and member of the Mephitisoid race, a kind of humanoid polecat. But, as seduction requires, she has always had the appearance of a white cat, with or without black markings, and retractable claws like cats, not ferrets. Because of her

CHEETAH, THE DC COUNTEREXAMPLE

Marvel's distinguished competitor also has its share of cat-women. But the best known of them all is Cheetah, Wonder Woman's sworn enemy since her creation in 1943. While four different people, including a man very briefly in 2001, have assumed this role, the powers and appearance of the various Cheetahs are quite similar. Physically, they can take on the appearance of a bipedal spotted wildcat, with strength, speed, and agility far superior to those of a normal human or animal. According to the creator of the first incarnation, William Moulton Marston, they symbolize femininity, giving free rein to emotions and jealousy without intellectual control. This contrasts with Wonder Woman, who, as an Amazon, embodies a Greek feminine ideal as fantasized by the American Golden Age.

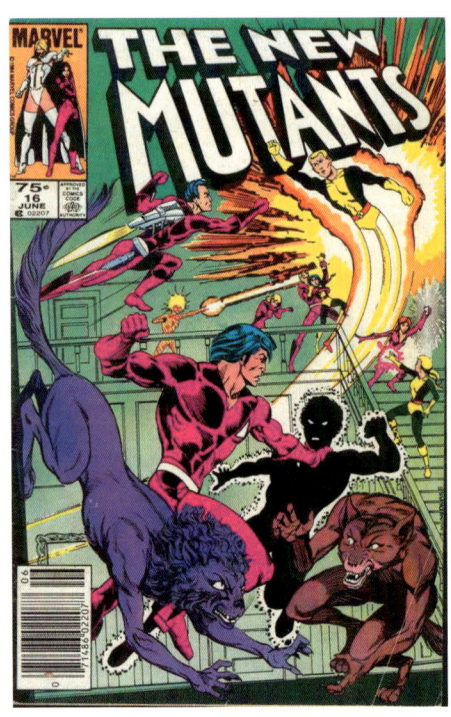

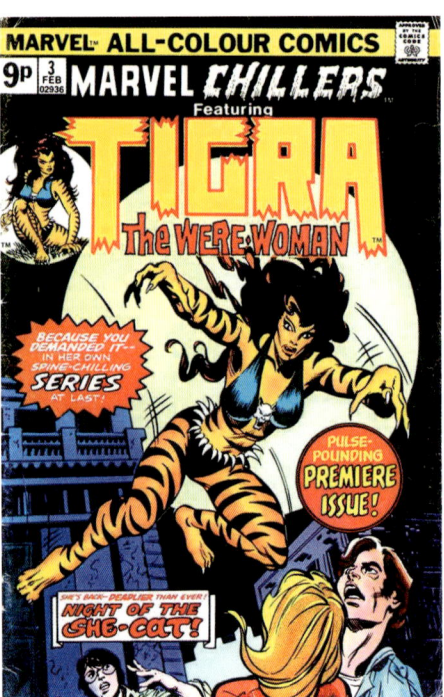

love affair with Christopher Summers (father of Cyclops and Havok of the X-Men), Hepzibah appears mainly in mutant stories, in which she plays the protective role of a mother cat for those she considers part of her family.

Finally, still in the X-Men universe, in 1984, Chris Claremont and Sal Buscema created the first official werecat. Sharon Smith, known as Catseye, is a mutant

with the ability to transform herself into a purple feline the size of a house cat, a panther, or in semi-human form. Initially part of the Hellions, the New Mutants' adversaries, she eventually bonds with them and joins the side of good, even sharing a room with Rahne Sinclair, the Scottish werewolf known as Wolfsbane. Just goes to show that cats and dogs can get along just fine when it comes to female solidarity. 🐾

Nekomimi: The Kawaii Catgirl in Japanese Pop Culture

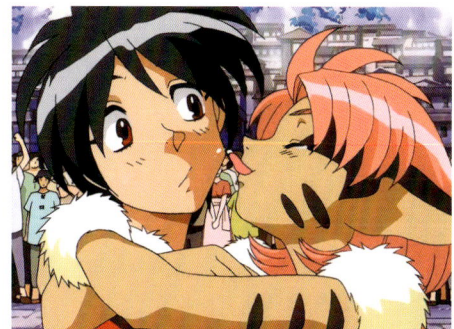

Merle in *The Vision of Escaflowne.*

The cat-woman is one of the best-known visual elements of Japanese kawaii culture. This type of character spread from manga and animation to video games, before being adopted by cosplayers all over the world.

Cats have long had a bad reputation in Japanese legends, with the notable exception of the *maneki-neko* (see p. 181). With the popularity of manga and animation, Japanese attitudes toward this animal quickly changed. So much so, in fact, that the soft, cuddly fur ball has become one of the symbols of *kawaii* culture. It has also spawned a type of character that fetishizes it: the nekomimi or catgirl. Also known as the *neko-musume* (literally "girl of the

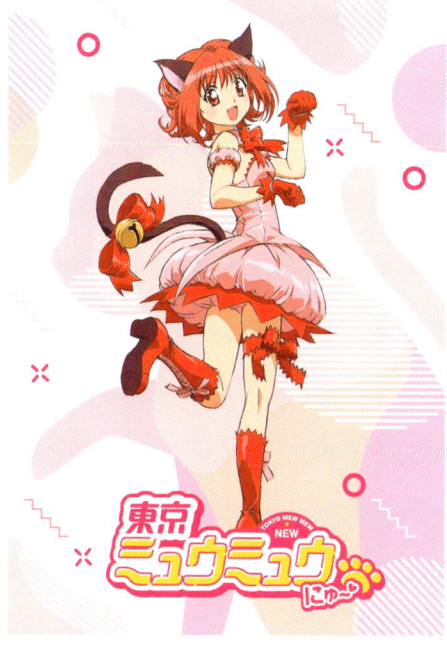

Ichigo Momomiya in *Tokyo Mew Mew.*

cat" or "cat-girl"), this character can be found in anime and manga, as well as in video games, like Felicia in the *Darkstalkers* series.

Whatever her origin, the *nekomimi* at least has cat ears with an otherwise human appearance, along with affection-seeking feline behavior (raising her paw like a *maneki-neko*, rubbing up against other people in the series where she appears) or aggression, sometimes sporting functional fangs and clawed paws. She doesn't hesitate to use them on her opponents. Unlike her Western counterparts, her way of communicating is also influenced by the animal that inspires her, ; she often punctuates her dialogue with "nya" and "meow," or the corresponding ideograms, echoing the sounds of a regular domestic cat.

Depending on the positioning of the series in which she appears, the *nekomimi* may accentuate the cute and endearing side, especially if she's very young, or the sensual and seductive side if she's a more mature character.

This second version is often taken up in fanart and cosplay, with the sale of cat-ear headbands (some of which move in response to ambient noise), tails, and paw-shaped gloves.

Among the best-known examples of catgirls in Japanese fiction are Merle, the protégé of the King of Fanelia in the anime and manga *The Vision of Escaflowne*; Hazuki/Luna in *Moon Phase*; Ichigo Momomiya, the leader of the Mew Mews in *Tokyo Mew Mew*; the Mithra race in *Final Fantasy XI* (although in this case, there are rare male representatives of the genre); Felicia in *Darkstalkers*; and the Khajiit in *The Elder Scrolls*. Even though, to the Western world, Lum from the *Urusei Yatsura* manga and anime may seem like a catgirl because of her fangs, her skimpy outfit, and her possessive and sometimes aggressive behavior, she isn't, strictly speaking, a *nekomimi*. Instead, she was one of the sources of inspiration for subsequent *nekomimi*, just like her creator, mangaka Rumiko Takahashi, who inspired a number of later works. 🐾

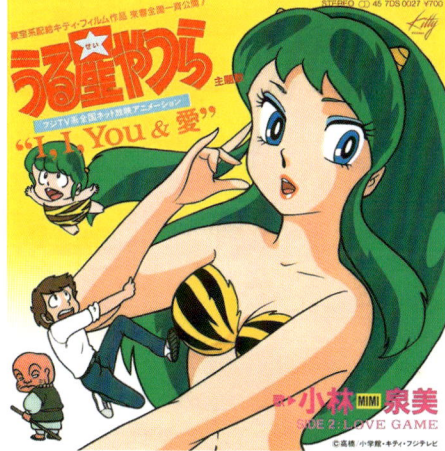

Lum in *Urusei Yatsura.*

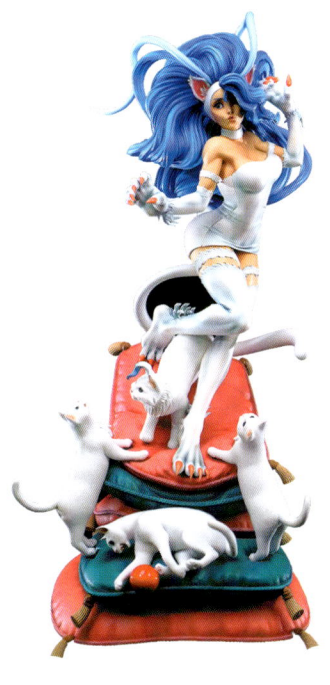

Felicia in *Darkstalkers.*

Cat's Eye

In the 1980s, manga culture spread outside of Japan. **Cat's Eye** *was also an anime series broadcast at the time, recounting the adventures of three female art thieves against a backdrop of romantic drama.*

Rui, Hitomi, and Ai Kisugi are three sisters. By day, they run the Cat's Eye café. By night, they don leotards, which were at the height of fashion at the time, and steal paintings by their late father. Going out only at night, and with the feline agility of true cat-women, they use their skills to commit museum robberies. They're provocative as cats and mock the police by sending a Cat's Eye calling card to warn them of their thefts.

Each of the female burglars has her own specialty: The eldest is the mastermind, the middle sister is the woman of action, and the youngest specializes in locks and technology. However, the narrative essentially revolves around the middle sister, Hitomi, who is engaged to Toshio, a policeman in charge of investigating the Cat's Eye gang. This adventure series is based on the dilemma of the criminal who wants to steal the paintings to find her father but is simultaneously

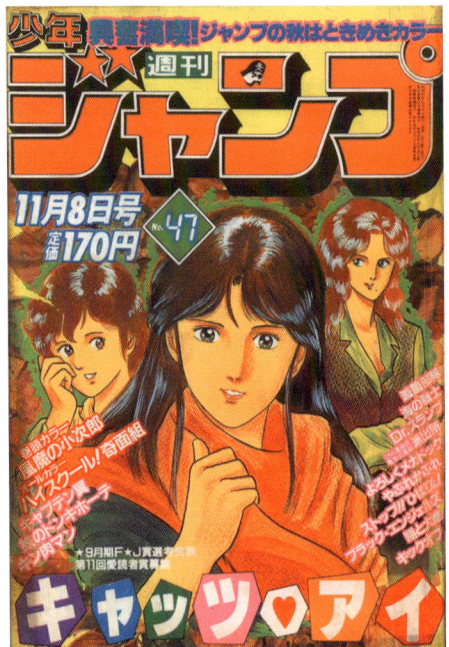

Cat's Eye featured on the cover of Weekly Shōnen Jump.

damaging the career of the man she loves.

The series is based on the manga by the famous Tsukasa Hojo. Although the manga was discontinued in 1985, the Cat's Eye café reappeared in one of his other famous works: *City Hunter*, where it's run by Miki, a retired killer. A leotard-clad thief with a Cat's Eye look also comes face-to-face with Nicky Larson in one of her adventures. *City*

Hunter: Shinjuku Private Eyes, released in 2019, features a cameo by the Kisugi sisters.

The story does contain a few narrative holes, such as Toshio's stupidity in unmasking his fiancée, and the fact that the thieves work in a café that bears their criminal name. However, Hojo's humor, rhythm, and refined drawing make *Cat's Eye* a relatively modern manga, outside of the 1980s aesthetic. The sexualization of the Cat's Eye feline women, dressed in skin-tight outfits and stealing works of art without any desire for financial gain, is reminiscent of the

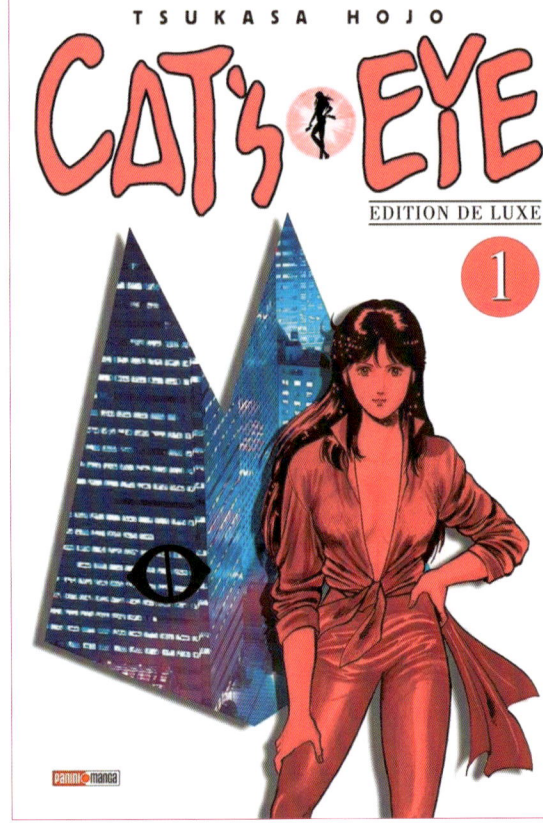

comic book character Catwoman. Like the American anti-heroine, the Kisugi sisters are independent and don't need men's gazes to exist. Moreover, each of them has a different approach to femininity, with no hierarchy between the three, allowing young viewers to identify with the model of their choice,

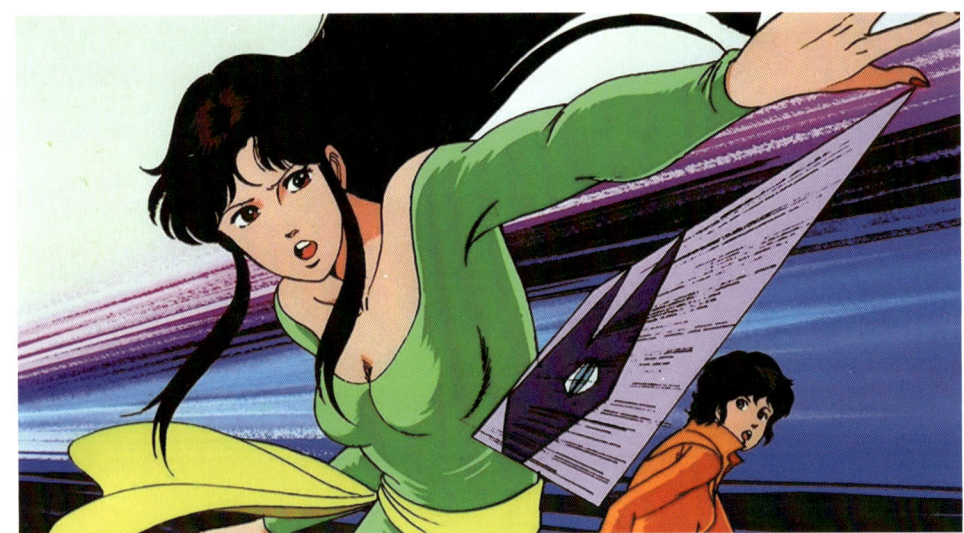

without having to fit into a mold. One can be intellectual but ultra-feminine like Rui (who is also fiercely single), interested in technology like Ai, or a mix of sweetness and action while dreaming of married life like Hitomi. 🐾

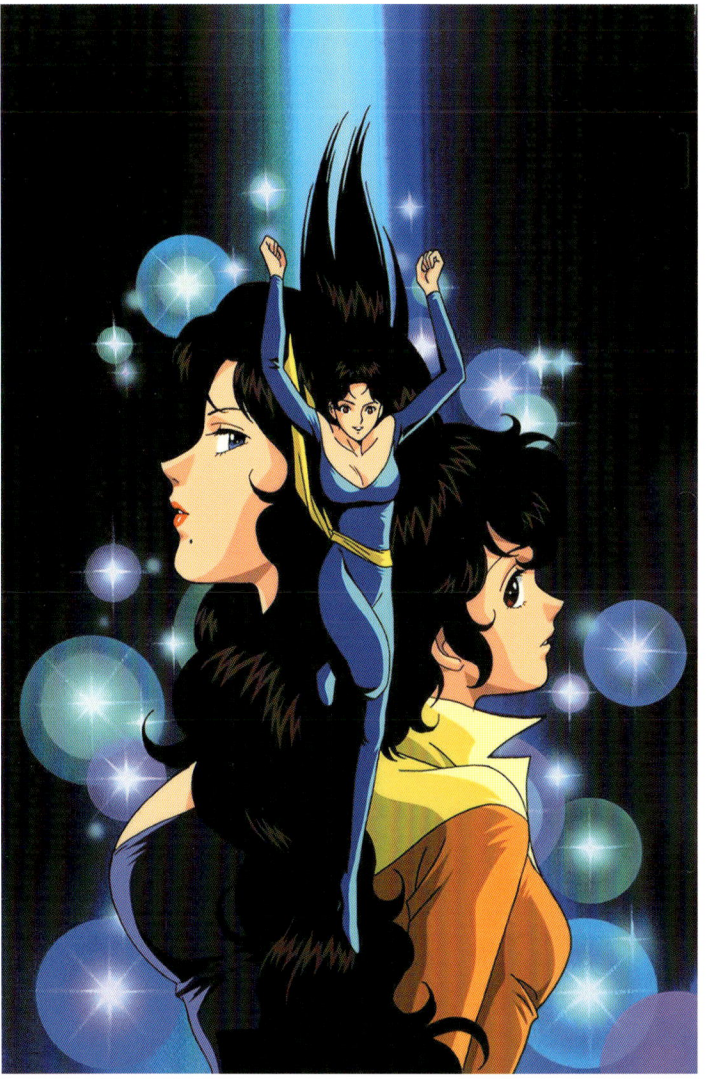

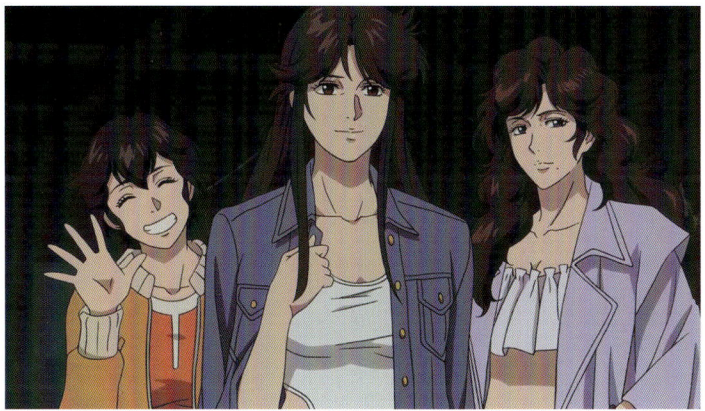

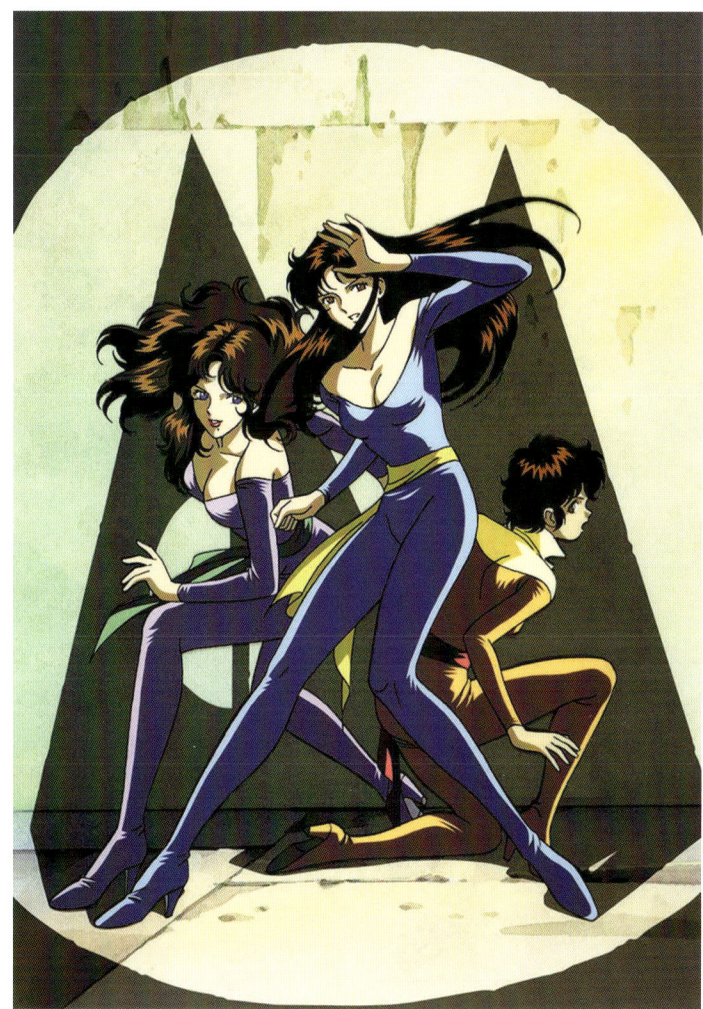

From left to right: Rui, Hitomi, and Ai.

SPEC SHEET

WORK: *Cat's Eye*.
CREATOR: Tsukasa Hojo.
DATE CREATED: 1981.
PUBLISHER: Coamix.
CATS' NAMES AND ROLE IN THE WORK: Cat's Eye is the name of the trio of female art thieves (Rui, Hitomi, and Ai Kisugi) and the bar they use as a cover.

Ugly Melanie

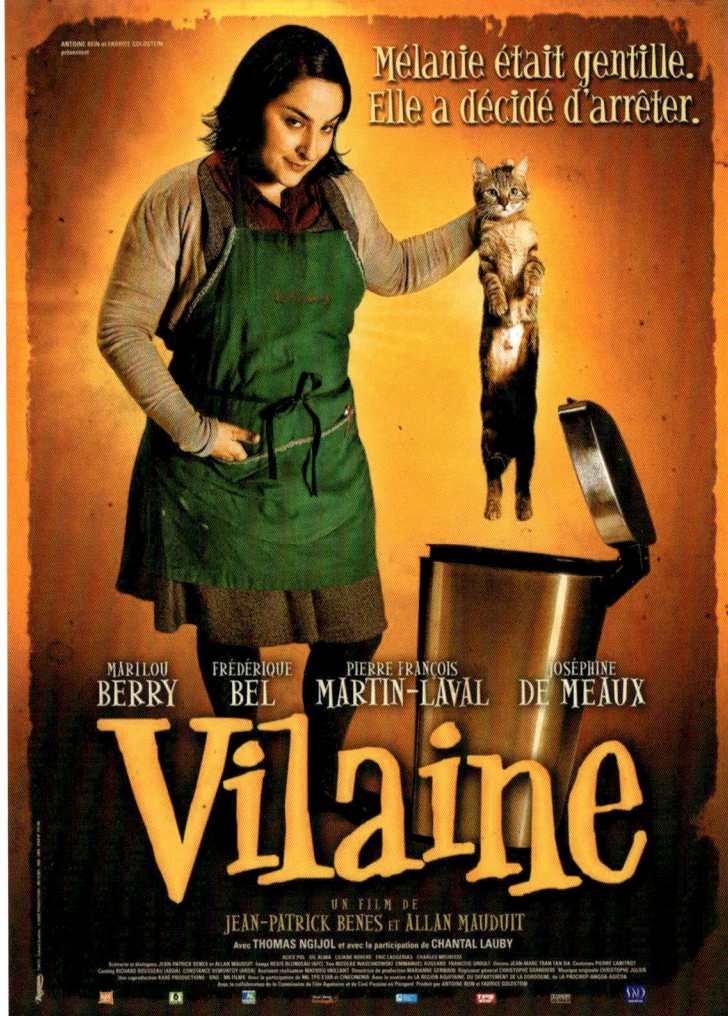

Melanie isn't pretty. Harassed for her ugliness since childhood, she makes up for her lack of beauty with extreme kindness, which is abused by those around her. One day, she decides to rebel and become mean. She tries to convince herself by mistreating a cat.

The French film *Ugly Melanie* is a sort of anti-*Amélie*; Amélie promised to make people's lives more beautiful, whereas Melanie wants to take revenge for other people's wickedness. With a story told by a narrator outside the narrative, an old-fashioned aesthetic, a yellowish image, and piano notes, *Ugly Melanie* clearly draws inspiration from Jean-Pierre Jeunet's 2001 film. The young protagonist is also a server and is worried about never having a love life, until she decides to take matters into her own hands.

When she chooses to become "evil," she puts herself through a series of tests to become mean. The second test is to go to a pet shop and not adopt a kitten. The sign in the window says, "I'm going to die. Adopt me." In the store, a Girl Scout suggests she adopt a kitten, touting how sweet it is, but she refuses. The girl offers her a second, but Melanie declines again. With the third gray tabby, the little girl adds that he has only seven days to live, accompanied by melancholy piano music. The young woman fails miserably and adopts the animal. The narrator supports this failure: "A tiny kitten was enough to shatter Melanie's hopes. She was clearly never going to be anything but a nice girl."

Once she's adopted him, she takes care of and plays with the kitten. Following another disappointment, she resumes her transformation into a mean person. This is reflected in the film's running gag, which is featured on the poster. Melanie grabs the cat and throws it into her trash can as it emits a comical meow. The kitten reappears several times, when she throws a bouquet into the garbage can and when she vomits into it, each time to the animal's lively meowing.

Regaining her natural kindness, she finally removes the kitten from the trash before the film's end. The cat, which is often used to represent the last resort of lonely women, is used here as a barometer of the protagonist's meanness. The cat's sweet nature is accentuated by its complete lack of reaction. It doesn't even struggle when it's thrown into the garbage. 🐾

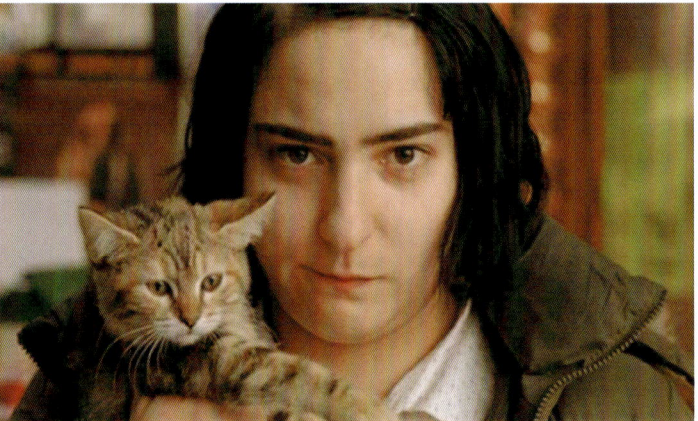

SPEC SHEET

WORK: *Ugly Melanie*.
CREATORS: Jean-Patrick Benes and Allan Mauduit.
DATE CREATED: 1981.
DISTRIBUTOR/AVAILABILITY: Currently unavailable in the United States.
CAT'S NAME AND ROLE IN THE WORK: Anonymous tabby kitten who serves as Melanie's punching bag and barometer of meanness.

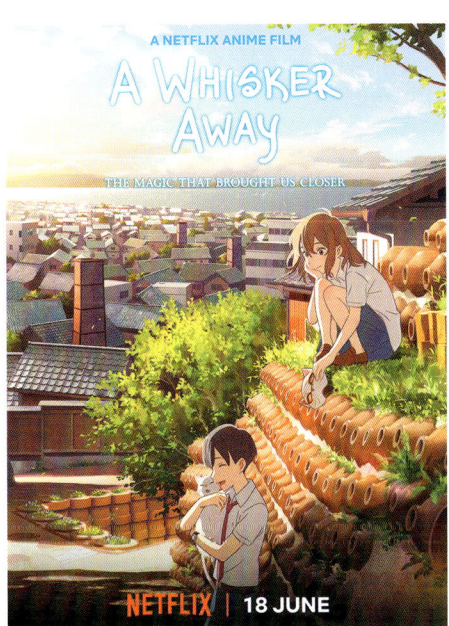

In the Japanese animated film A Whisker Away, young Miyo obtains a mask that enables her to transform into a cat. In cat form, she spends her nights with Kento, the boy she loves, and overcomes the obstacles he sets up with her in real life.

Miyo's natural goofiness and aggressive feline demeanor make it hard for her to attract Kento's attention. The young man only pays attention to her when she's Tarō, a little white fur ball with blue eyes. The reserved boy doesn't hesitate to tell his cat he loves her, to give her a hug, and to tell her about his problems. The girl is so happy with this relationship that she's willing to give up her human form for a moment. This situation is reminiscent of Andersen's fairy tale, "The Little Mermaid," where she must give up her ability to speak to become human.

Miyo is an eccentric who acts out to escape her family problems, namely her parents' separation, abandonment by her mother, and the difficulty of communicating with the stepmother she loves. As for Kento, who is under pressure to take over the family pottery workshop, he closes himself off from the world. The two misunderstood characters can't manage to get closer in life, but that's not counting the bond between the human and his cat. The refined lighting and artwork in the sequences between Kento and Tarō accentuate the intimate, poetic relationship between the two characters.

The freedom of the life of a cat who answers to no one, can roam around without going to school, and can escape from everyday problems is appealing to the girl, who ends up trapped in an existence that isn't hers. The mask seller, a large tomcat, is actually an evil genie, a sort of Tracassin dwarf who expects one important thing in return from the girl: her life expectancy. On her journey to regain her life, she visits Cat Island, where the story takes a more lyrical, fairy tale-like turn, much in the spirit of a Studio Ghibli film. Cats play a central role in the movie, as symbols of love and as non-human characters to whom people can confide all their problems without restraint. They also have unconditional love for their masters, whether it's Tarō/Miyo or her stepmother's cat, who wants to become human so he can stay with her longer. 🐾

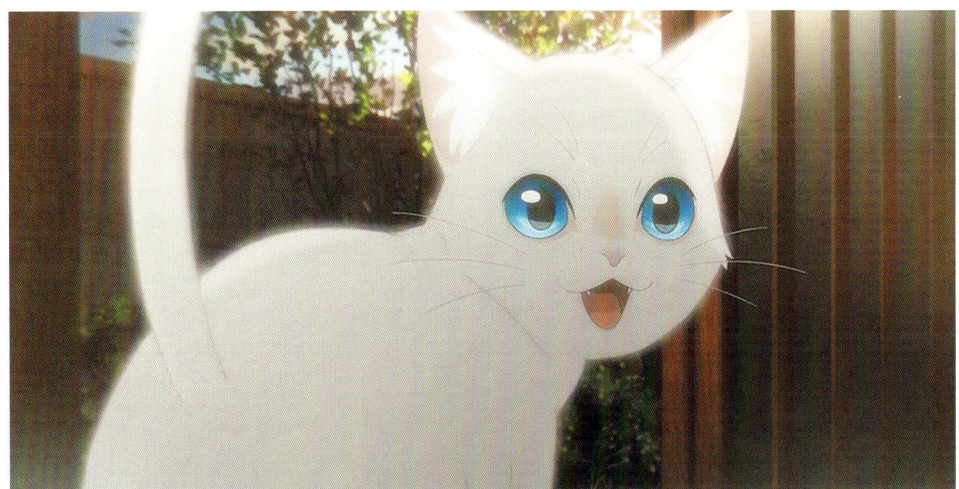

SPEC SHEET

WORK: *A Whisker Away.*
CREATORS: Jun'ichi Satō and Tomotaka Shibayama (directors); Mari Okada (screenwriter).
DATE CREATED: July 18, 2020.
DISTRIBUTOR/AVAILABILITY: Available for streaming on Netflix.
CAT'S NAME AND ROLE IN THE WORK: Tarō, a white cat with blue eyes. The main character and Miyo's alter ego.

Cats

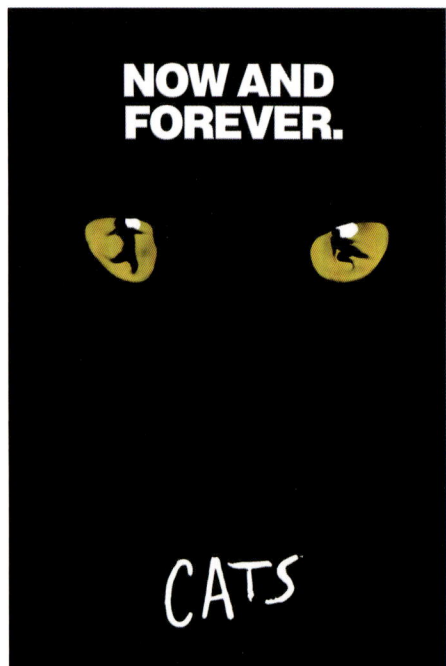

Undoubtedly composer Andrew Lloyd Webber's most incongruous work, Cats is a musical about cats singing in a junkyard. This worldwide success adapted into twenty-some languages has become a Broadway classic.

A Surreal Work

It's difficult to sum up this sung-through musical in which the Jellicle cats live among the garbage. Each cat tells its own story through musical tableaux. Every year, at a big ball, Old Deuteronomy gives one of the cats a new life. Onstage, humans are dressed as cats, with outrageous makeup, striped tights, and improbable hair extensions—everything in the aesthetic combines surrealism and the 1980s. Musically, the songs switch between rock, melodic, and disco styles.

A Surprising Success

Andrew Lloyd Webber wasn't exactly a beginner when *Cats* was released in London in 1981. He had already triumphed worldwide with *Jesus Christ Superstar* in 1971 and *Evita* in 1979. Despite the success of his previous shows, which made it all the way to Broadway, he struggled to find funding for this daring concept. He finally collaborated with young producer Cameron Mackintosh to launch his project. London critics expected the worst. Trevor Nunn, the director of the original work, would later say, "The number of people who asked me with an embarrassed smile on their face: 'You're doing a show about pussycats? Really?'"[1]

The improbable and surreal nature of the show worried the production team. Webber had to mortgage his house to finance the launch. *Cats* proved to be a huge success, with profits now estimated at more than $2 billion. It has been performed more than nine thousand times in London and 7,500 times on Broadway, and has been seen by more than eighty-one million spectators worldwide.[2]

The Musical's Origins

Andrew Lloyd Webber was born into a musical family and began composing songs at the age of five. His mother is said to have read him T. S. Eliot's poems from *Old Possum's Book of Practical Cats* when he was a child. He fell in love with these fifteen portraits of cats. In the 1980s, buoyed by both public and critical success, he undertook a short adaptation of this work for a festival. The wife of the Lost Generation poet was invited to the performance. She then gave the young composer some of her husband's unpublished poems, including "Grizabella: The Glamour Cat," which inspired the British composer. As Trevor Nunn said: "There was something that was very emotionally powerful about these characters. Especially Grizabella. I understood that the seedy neighborhood where she wandered was a place of prostitution, and that she had been ostracized from society. It was about old age and death, but also about redemption. If only one of these cats would be chosen for a better life, it would be the old cat Grizabella. That was my thread. Suddenly, I was wildly excited about this project."[3]

"Memory"

To work with audiences, a musical must contain at least one hit. For *Cats*, the defining moment is, of course, the song "Memory," in which Grizabella sings of nostalgia for the good old days. Featuring moving lyrics, interpretation, and violin accompaniment, the final version underwent a number of changes. Judi Dench, who was initially cast as Grizabella, was injured a few days before the premiere. Elaine Paige, star of the musical *Evita*, agreed to replace her at the last minute. She was the partner of Tim Rice, a former associate of Andrew Lloyd Webber, but above all, a talented lyricist. Rice tried to push through another version of the song. Trevor Nunn, the director, considered the lyrics too far removed

[1] https://www.vanityfair.fr/culture/voir-lire/articles/cats-lhistoire-de-la-comedie-musicale-de-tous-les-records/28726
[2] https://www.allocine.fr/article/fichearticle_gen_carticle=18686638.html
[3] https://www.vanityfair.fr/culture/voir-lire/articles/cats-lhistoire-de-la-comedie-musicale-de-tous-les-records/28726

from T. S. Eliot's poems. In the end, the producers decided in favor of the current version, which is closer to the original text. "Memory" experienced a second wave of international popularity the following year, with a cover by Barbra Streisand.

A Missed Opportunity in Hollywood

In 2019, Hollywood decided to adapt the musical. Major resources were invested, with a budget of $95 million.[4] It featured a prestigious cast, including singer Taylor Swift and Oscar-winning actress Judi Dench. While the American movie industry has learned to reappropriate theatrical and literary works, the gamble didn't pay off. The film was a commercial failure. It was murdered by critics and shunned by audiences. The lighting and choreography are beautiful, but the film is sanitized and unintentionally kitschy. The decision to use computer-generated images to transform humans into cats was widely contested and often criticized as ugly, if not downright disturbing. It grossed just $74 million. 🐾

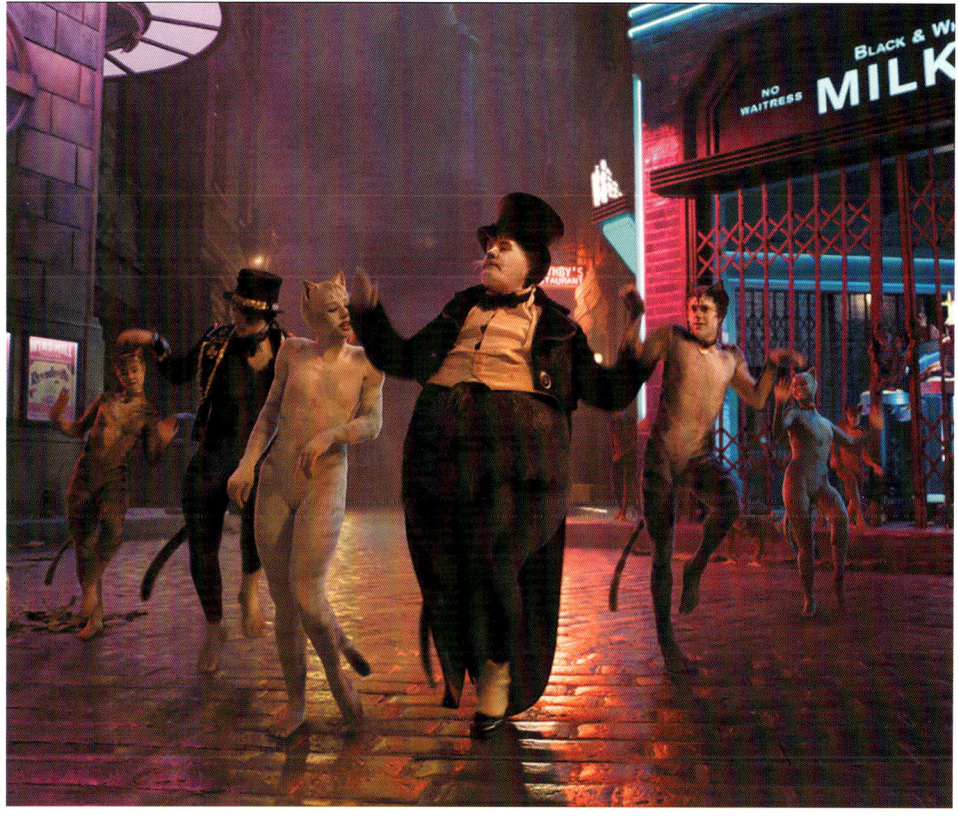

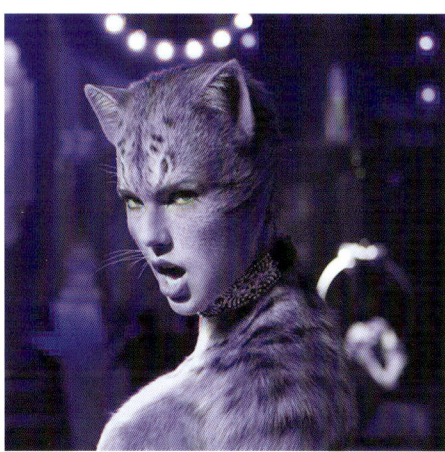

SPEC SHEET

WORK: *Cats*.
CREATORS: Composer Andrew Lloyd Webber, director Trevor Nunn, choreography by Gillian Lynne, poems by T. S. Eliot.
DATE CREATED: May 11, 1981, at the New London Theatre, London.
PUBLISHER/AVAILABILITY: Musical produced by Andrew Lloyd Webber and Cameron Mackintosh. Adapted and regularly performed around the world. A video recording was made in 1998 and is available on DVD and Blu-ray from Universal. Also available for streaming.
CATS' NAMES AND ROLES IN THE WORK: Grizabella, Bombalurina, Macavity, Old Deuteronomy, Mr. Mistoffelees, and more. All the characters are alley cats.

---

[4] https://pro.imdb.com/title/tt5697572?rf=cons_tt_atf&ref_=cons_tt_atf

Le Chat

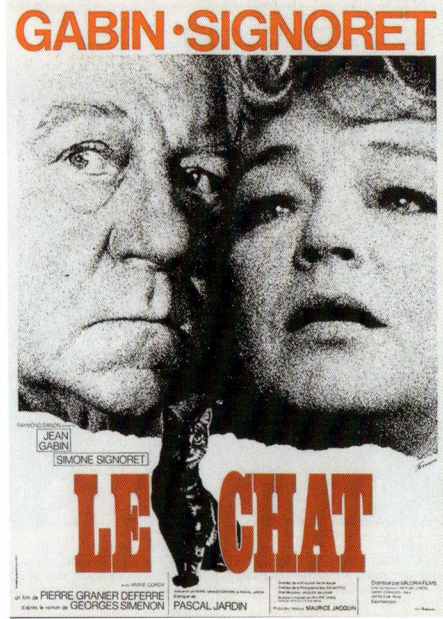

Adapted from Georges Simenon's novel of the same name, Pierre Granier-Deferre's Le Chat (The Cat) *is a masterful confrontation between Simone Signoret and Jean Gabin. A stray cat lies at the heart of their rift.*

What could be a better symbol of the theft of affection than a cat? What simpler, more fragile prey than the domestic feline for a jealous spouse? While Colette wrote a novel about this as early as 1933, imagining a young groom abandoning his wife for his pet (see p. 195), in this film, the situation is reversed. Julien (Jean Gabin) and Clémence Bouin (Simone Signoret) are retired. Married for twenty-five years and childless, the passion that made them a couple has faded, giving way to silence, arguments, irritation, and resentment. Just like the suburban neighborhood of Courbevoie where they live, which is gradually giving way to the construction sites of what will become La Défense. When Julien takes in an alley cat and showers it with affection, Clémence feels neglected, throws fits of

THE BAKER'S POMPONNETTE

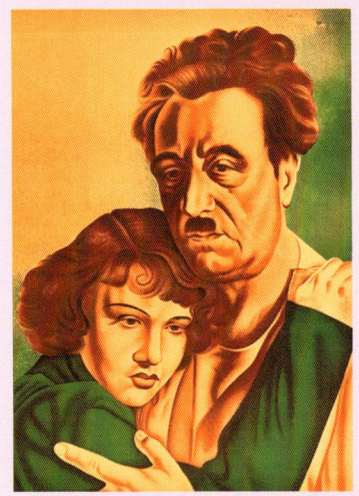

"Look at that! There she is! Do you see that? Did you see Pomponnette come back? You little bitch! Slut! Trash! Now you come back? Poor Pompon's been worried sick since yesterday. He's been looking all over for you. He's been wretched and miserable. But she'd run off with an alley cat, some good-for-nothing, a moonlit passerby. What's he got that Pompon doesn't?"

Raimu's rather frank line in Marcel Pagnol's *The Baker's Wife* (see poster, left) is addressed to the bakery's little black cat, who had spent the night outside, either hunting or in heat, the story doesn't say. It comes at the film's conclusion and is also (and above all) addressed to the baker's wife, who has had an affair. In this final scene, he explains to his younger wife, who had left their home for a shepherd of her own age, that he forgives her and agrees to resume married life, but he also expresses his sorrow at her departure and asks her to leave immediately if she's not sure she wants to stay. Here, the seasonality of feline mating and the biological fact that female cats that are left free mate with different males during their heat (even if it means having several fathers for the same litter of kittens) serves as an analogy to the behavior of the baker's wife: Married too young (and not necessarily for love) to a man older than she is, she allows herself to be seduced by the first man she meets, abandoning her husband and, above all, the entire village, which is deprived of bread due to his desperation. While it's certainly not the most influential film in the history of female emancipation, this line has become a cult classic in French cinema.

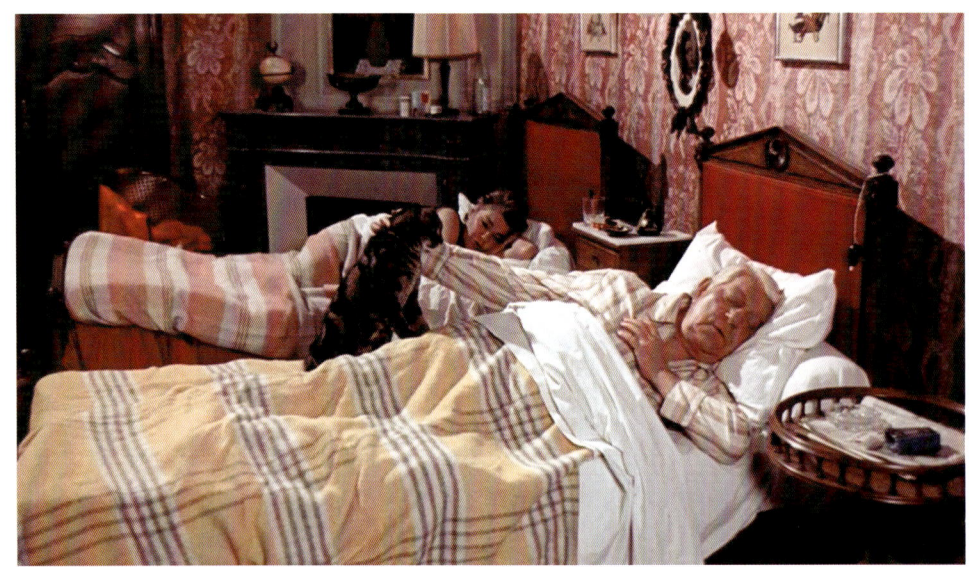

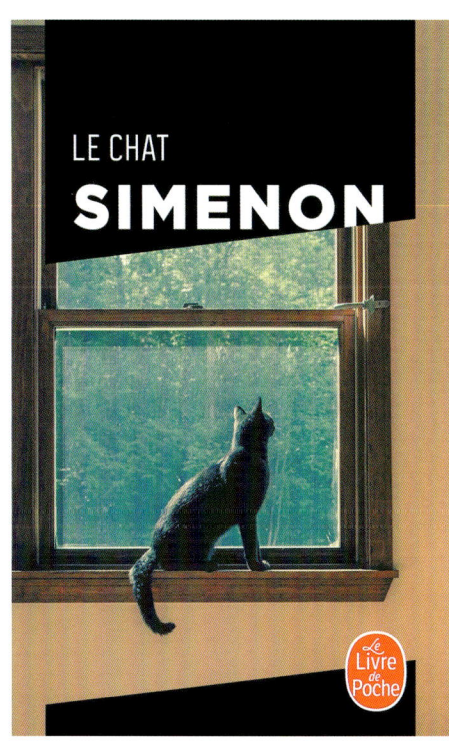

A tale of the end of a passionate love affair and the end of an era, *Le Chat* also stands out for its inversion of certain clichés. For example, the doddering pensioner with his cat isn't an embittered spinster, but a gruff old man played by an actor who was once the quintessential French male: Jean Gabin. Seeing him coddle this animal is great fun for the viewer. But it also puts him in a sympathetic position compared to Clémence, an old alcoholic whose loneliness we gradually come to understand. Compassion is reinforced by the cat's own attitude: proud, snide, and glancing disdainfully at his caretaker's wife. And once the cat's gone, there's nothing left for the couple. No one to love, no home, nothing but death. Slow, silent death.

In addition to the film, Georges Simenon's 1967 novel of the same name has been translated into English and, more recently, adapted for the stage in 2016 by Didier Long, starring Myriam Boyer and Jean Benguigui as the couple who tear each other apart. 🐾

jealousy, and ends up killing the animal. From then on, disenchantment turns to hatred and silence.

Playing on flashbacks to reveal the couple's past and shot slowly in a grayish setting (only the time he spends in the hotel run by Annie Cordy brings a touch of color to Julien's daily life), *Le Chat* is mainly driven by the acting of the three actors—Jean Gabin, Simone Signoret, and Greffier. The two humans won Silver Bears at the 1971 Berlin International Film Festival. Everything is conveyed through the looks and gestures of the various characters. Dialogue is rare, but it hits the mark. For example, Clémence confesses to the cat, "He thinks I hate you. I don't hate you. I even think you're very handsome," just before she shreds Julien's newspapers to frame the feline. And when Julien provokes her by shouting, "It'll make a great news story: acrobat kills her husband because he cheated on her with the cat!" she grabs the outstretched weapon to kill the cat.

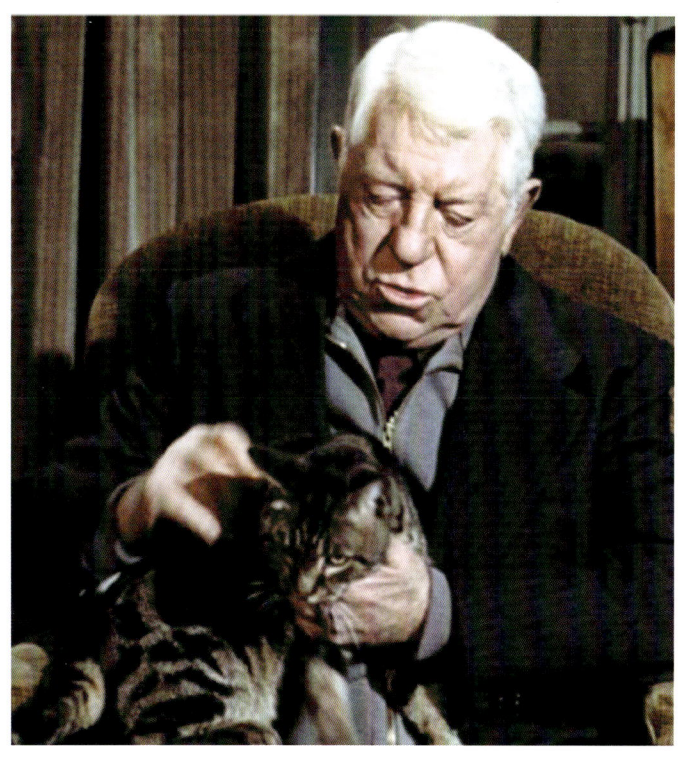

SPEC SHEET

WORK: *Le Chat*.
CREATORS: Pierre Granier-Deferre (director); Pascal Jardin (dialogue); Pierre Granier-Deferre and Pascal Jardin (screenwriters).
RELEASE DATE: April 24, 1971.
PRODUCERS: Lira Films, Cinétel, Gafer, Comacico, and Unitas Film.
CAT'S NAME: Pépère or Greffier, depending on the owner's mood. This is a perfectly ordinary, shorthaired male tabby cat with yellow-green eyes.

Jones

A companion and emotional support to the working crew of the commercial vessel Nostromo, Jones, aka Jonesy, is the only survivor, along with Ellen Ripley, of humans' first encounter with xenomorphs. They're the only ones with good survival instincts.

When Ridley Scott added a cat to the crew of the *Nostromo* in *Alien*, did he have any idea of the impact it would have on future fans? Was he trying to capitalize on the animal's cuteness to add an extra layer of emotion? Or did he want to give us a hint about how the film and franchise would unfold? In any case, this rather cuddly orange cat has won viewers' hearts, to the point that he also appeared briefly in the sequel, James Cameron's *Aliens*, at least to reassure them of his fate.

And yet, Jones, aka Jonesy, behaves like an unremarkable cat for most of the film. He first appears eating with the crew, who have just woken up from hypersleep. Then he washes while some of them explore the planet and meet the facehugger. And finally, he eats throughout the scene in which the alien brutally and noisily emerges from Kane's (John Hurt's) belly. While the book *Aliens: Colonial Marines Technical Manual* by Lee Brimmicombe-Wood states that the cats aboard Weyland-Yutani's

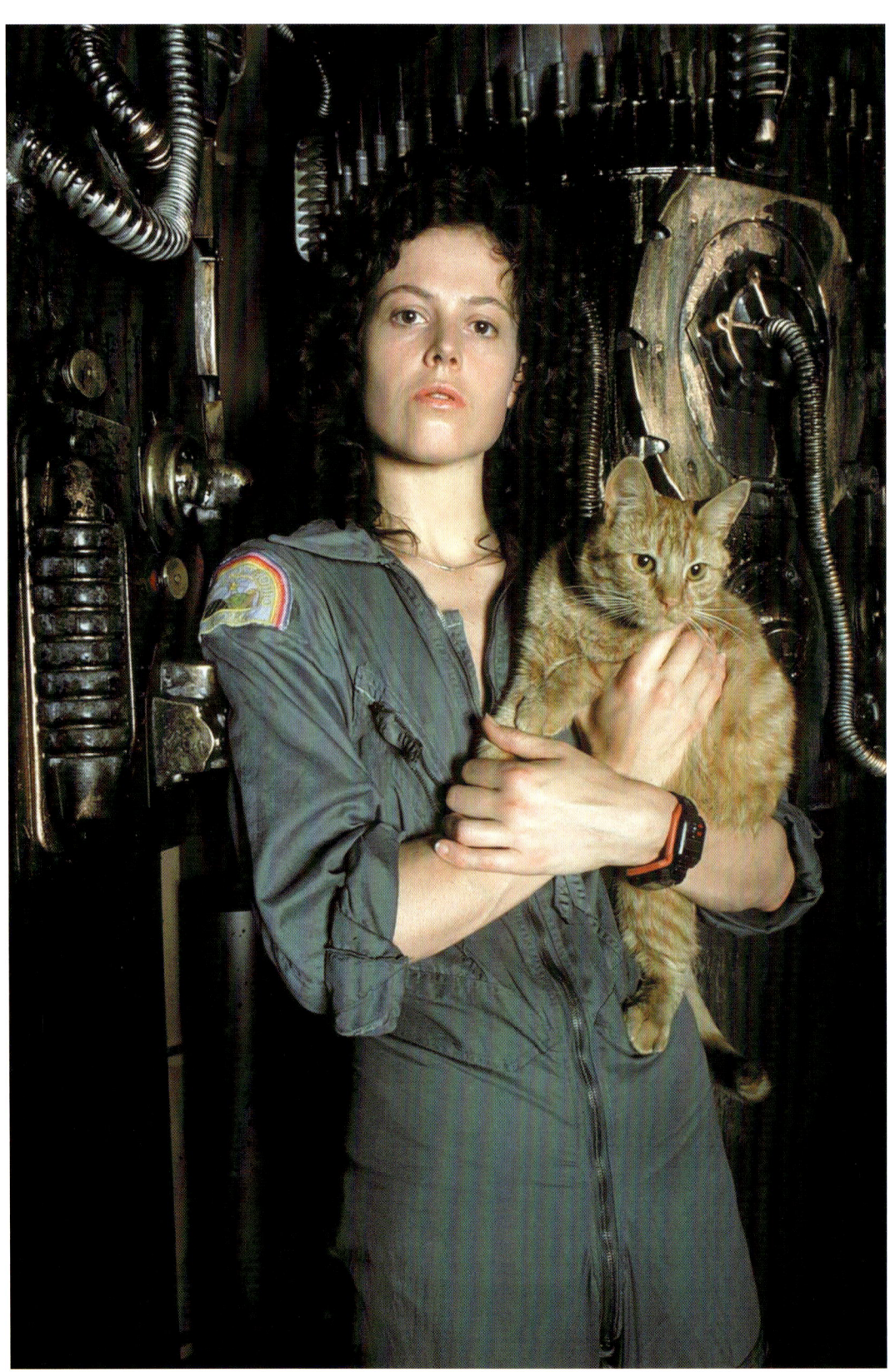

Ellen Ripley (Sigourney Weaver) and her companion.

commercial ships are there to hunt rodents, Jones is totally indifferent to the little creature as it scurries away. His hunting instinct isn't particularly well-developed. On the other hand, he proves very good at surviving, even trying to warn Brett (Harry Dean Stanton) of the alien's presence behind him, but the man doesn't understand and is killed.

Visually, this scene was created by bringing a German shepherd to the set and hiding it behind a screen. Suddenly, the screen was raised: The cat saw the dog and hissed and growled in fear. The cat also had a technical impact on the direction. Ridley Scott, like Jacques Tourneur in *Cat People* (see p. 122), used the cat as a decoy. He used it for "cat scares," those moments when the tension mounts until a totally innocuous element appears, in this case Jonesy, the crew's mascot. And in the drab world of *Alien* (the gray and black of the ships and the creature, the green and white of the crew's outfits and certain rooms), the cat's orange fur is the only touch of bright, warm color on-screen. This is in stark contrast to the blue shirt worn by Ash, the science officer who turns out to be an android on Weyland-Yutani's payroll who is willing to sacrifice the crew to get his hands on the xenomorph. In fact, he's the only crew member who has no interaction with Jones, as a machine that is totally indifferent to the concept of a pet.

In *Aliens*, Jones is only present in the first part of the film: in the hospital, then in his apartment with Ellen Ripley. She leaves him behind to once again confront the xenomorphs. And yet, once again, he serves as a warning. The way he is uncomfortable with Burke (Paul Reiser) is an indication of the turbulent role the latter will play in the rest of the story.

Beyond his mere presence, the cat also helps us to understand the behavior of the franchise's characters. After the first film, theories abounded. One explained that, in reality, he was simply an android like Ash, who used him as a scout to track and monitor the creature, which would also explain why, in the next film, it was another Weyland-Yutani agent who returned him to Ripley. Based on the xenomorph's lack of interest in him, many others drew a parallel between the small Earth predator and the large alien, perhaps even a form of understanding.

Practically speaking, the animal is too small to serve as an incubator for the xenomorph or as a real meal. He's also rather fast and slips quite well into nooks and crannies that are difficult for the creature to access. On the other hand, the way it gradually eliminates the crew in a playful manner (such as wrapping its tail around Lambert's leg) could be likened to the way cats play with their prey before killing it. Or perhaps we should look at the feline side of Ellen Ripley, Jones's caretaker. She likes routine and insists on enforcing the rules to the letter, like a cat demanding its food at a fixed time. And she doesn't hesitate to stand up to her superiors to do so, rejecting all forms of direct authority. Like a mother cat, she doesn't hesitate to put herself in danger for those in her care: She returns for Jones when it's time to evacuate the *Nostromo* and goes to great lengths to protect little Newt in *Aliens*. Finally, like a cat, she prefers avoidance or flight to combat, but when cornered, she uses every tool at her disposal to defeat the enemy, like a feline baring its claws even in the face of a larger predator. 🐾

SPEC SHEET

CAT'S NAME: Jones, aka Jonesy.
WORKS: *Alien* (1979) and *Aliens* (1986).
CREATORS: Dan O'Bannon (*Alien*'s screenwriter) and Ridley Scott (*Alien*'s director).
DATE CREATED: May 25, 1979.
DISTRIBUTOR/AVAILABILITY: 20th Century Fox. Available on DVD, Blu-ray, and various streaming services.
CAT'S CHARACTERISTICS: Jones is an orange tabby cat with green eyes. He's affectionate and cautious, with no apparent hunting instinct.

The Shadow of the Cat

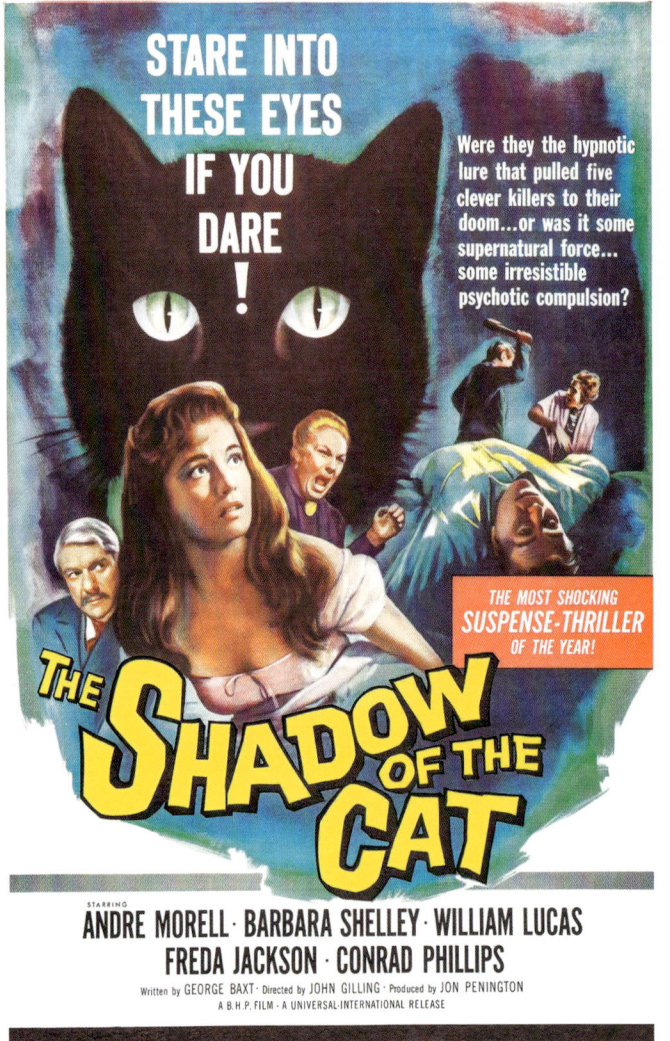

STARE INTO THESE EYES IF YOU DARE !

Were they the hypnotic lure that pulled five clever killers to their doom...or was it some supernatural force... some irresistible psychotic compulsion?

THE MOST SHOCKING SUSPENSE-THRILLER OF THE YEAR!

THE **SHADOW** OF THE **CAT**

STARRING
ANDRE MORELL · BARBARA SHELLEY · WILLIAM LUCAS
FREDA JACKSON · CONRAD PHILLIPS
Written by GEORGE BAXT · Directed by JOHN GILLING · Produced by JON PENINGTON
A B.H.P. FILM · A UNIVERSAL-INTERNATIONAL RELEASE

Although best known for its horror movies, the British Hammer Films also produced a number of more classic pictures, without a hint of the supernatural. This crime drama, for example, sees a simple house cat take revenge on those who killed her mistress.

When a cat is involved in a couple's story in a film, it often serves as a metaphor for the sensual, wayward behavior of one of the partners, or it's the object of jealousy, which is often fatal to the cat. In *The Shadow of the Cat*, there's no question of love at all, and the animal is transformed from victim to an avenging murderer. The plot begins with an old woman reading Edgar Allan Poe's "The Raven" aloud to her cat, Tabitha. Suddenly, her servant attacks her and buries the body in the woods as the cat watches. It's a heinous crime devised by her husband to

get his hands on the inheritance from his wife, Ella Venable, at the expense of her favorite niece.

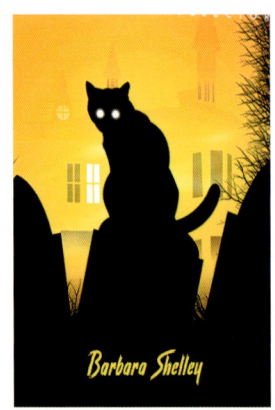

Barbara Shelley

Having seen everything, the cat does everything in her power to avenge the death of her mistress by eliminating all the culprits one by one in a series of accidents. And she forces the young niece, a journalist, and the police inspector to take a closer look at the suspicious disappearance.

Little-known among Hammer's abundant output, *The Shadow of the Cat* stands out for its total absence of supernatural elements, except perhaps for the animal's intelligence and attachment to its deceased mistress. It's also notable for certain directorial choices, such as filming some scenes in fisheye, as if they are viewed by Tabitha herself. For the rest, it's a dark crime story with British charm, reminiscent of Agatha Christie's famous *And Then There Were None*. 🐾

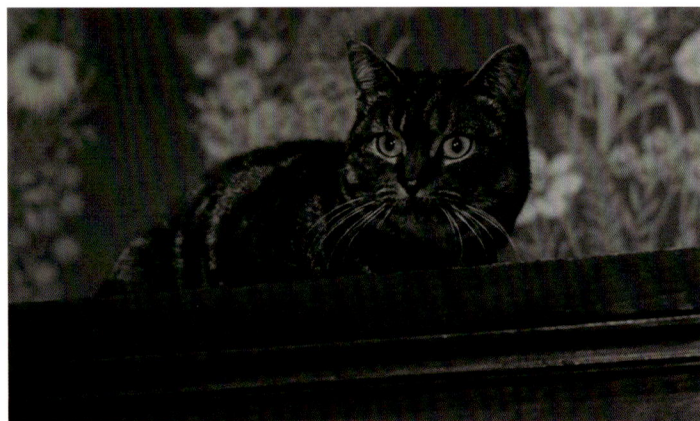

SPEC SHEET

WORK: *The Shadow of the Cat*.
CREATORS: John Gilling (director) and George Baxt (screenwriter).
RELEASE DATE: May 1, 1961.
PRODUCER: Hammer Film Productions.
CAT'S NAME: Tabitha, a shorthaired tabby cat belonging to the victim, Ella Venable.

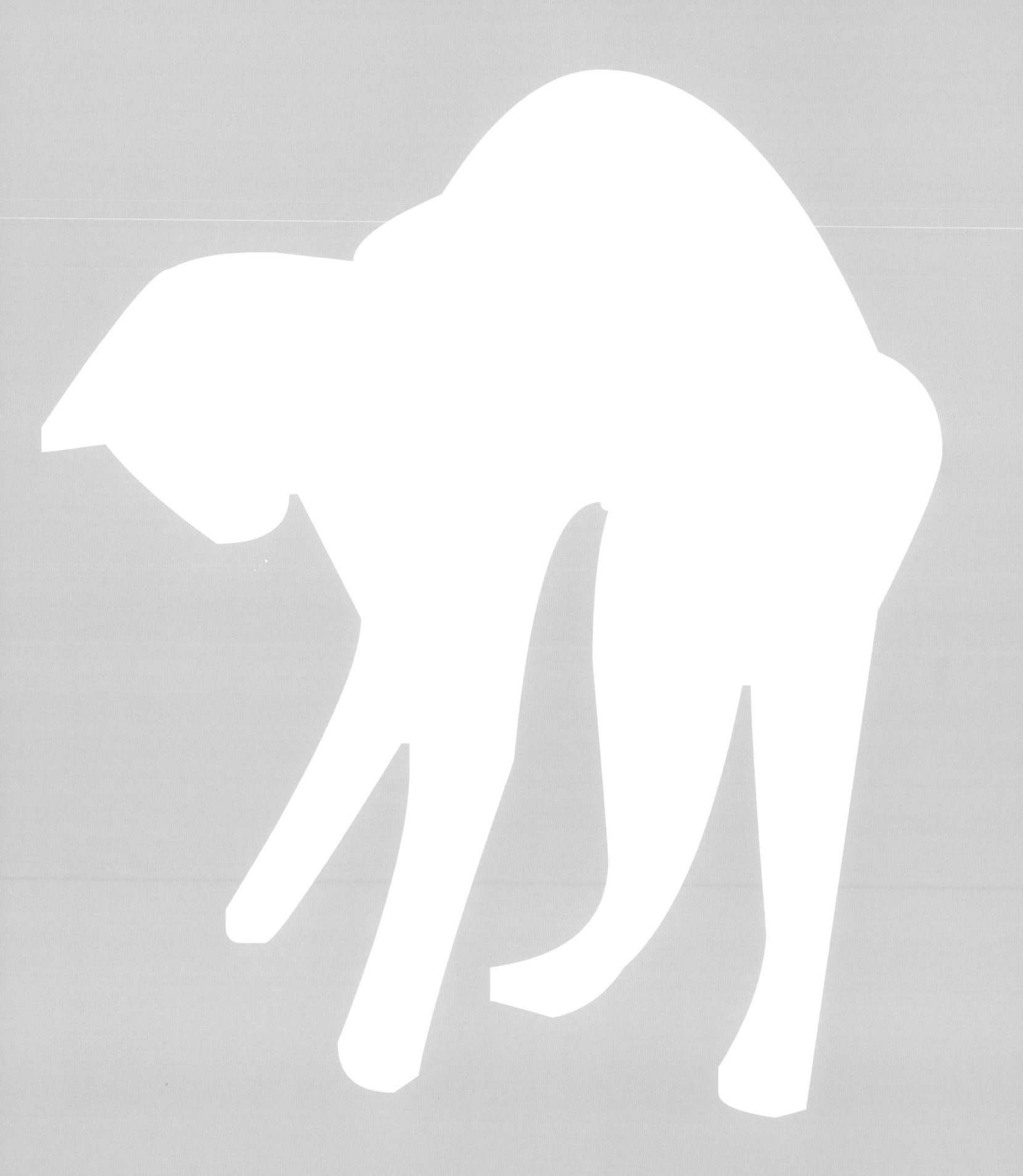

Cats in Science and Science Fiction

Cats haven't just served as ornamental pets or hunters. The feline species has also advanced science, often to its own detriment. And they've inspired some of science fiction's finest writing.

Cats haven't just inspired legends and artists. Scientists have also been fascinated by these animals and their abilities. And so have science-fiction writers; that branch of literature asks the question "What if?" based on a scientific hypothesis and imagines its consequences.

Here, the mysterious or near-supernatural aspect with which the human imagination has so frequently adorned its feline companions isn't what attracts attention. Instead, their physical abilities and actual behavior are the common denominators.

In some cases, it's simply the animal's weight and docile nature that come into play. That's what matters in thought experiments like Schrödinger's cat, where the cat was chosen because of its small size (and its love of boxes). It was also the sad case of Félicette,

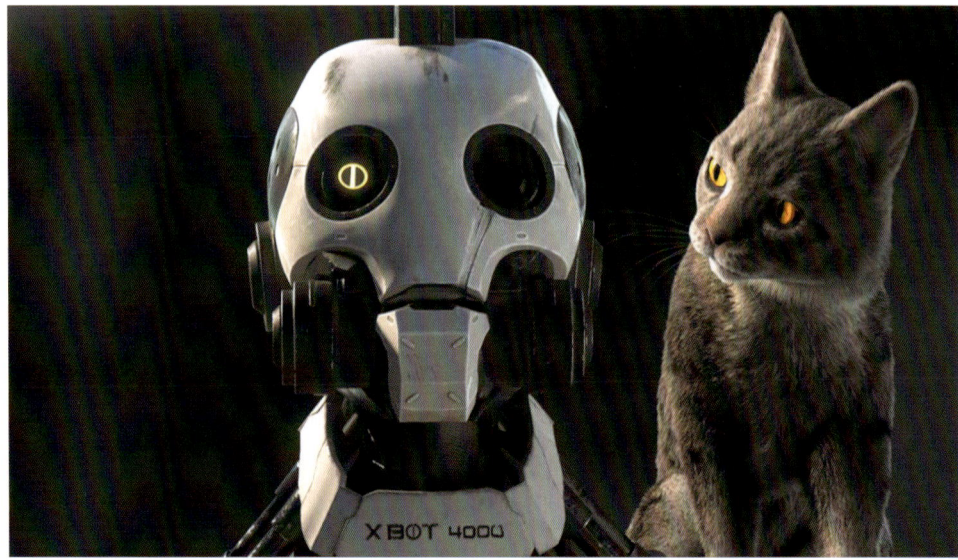

Love, Death and Robots.

the very first French astronaut in 1963, who died two months after returning to Earth so that scientists could study the effects of space flight on her physiology. In other instances, cats' proximity to humans and their susceptibility to similar illnesses are the determining factors. For example, cats have been successfully genetically modified to help fight AIDS.

Sometimes the cat's own curiosity is involved, prompting it to embark on major scientific expeditions. In the real world, cats have traveled as far as the North and South Poles and even into space, while the many feline travelers in fictional works include news anchor Groucha in *Téléchat*, Petronius the time traveler who loves his master in *The Door into Summer*, and Nimitz, Honor Harrington's treecat companion and the space representative of a long line of naval cats in David Weber's books.

On the other hand, human attachment to their feline companions is sometimes the driving force behind science, both in real life and in fiction. The desire to postpone the death of dear friends whose lives are so short has led

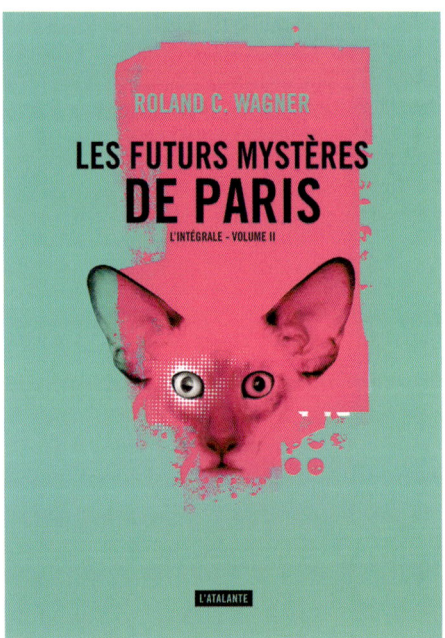

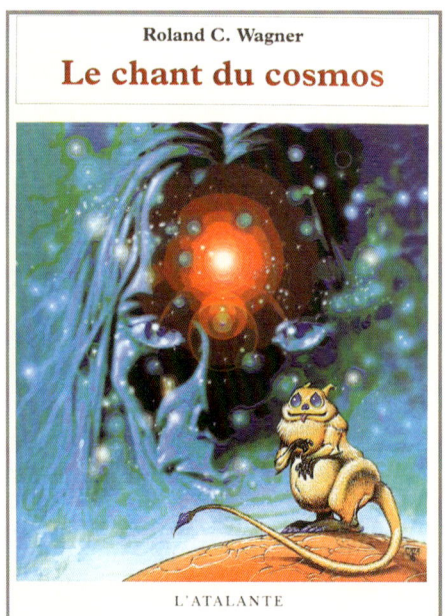

to a real business in animal cloning. Beyond the ethical problems this poses when so many cats (and other pets) are abandoned and mistreated, advances in this field have made it possible to develop cloning of other animals for breeding purposes, as well as enabling endangered species to survive. Or why not be resurrected using a close cousin as a receptacle? Humans' love of cats is evident throughout Cordwainer

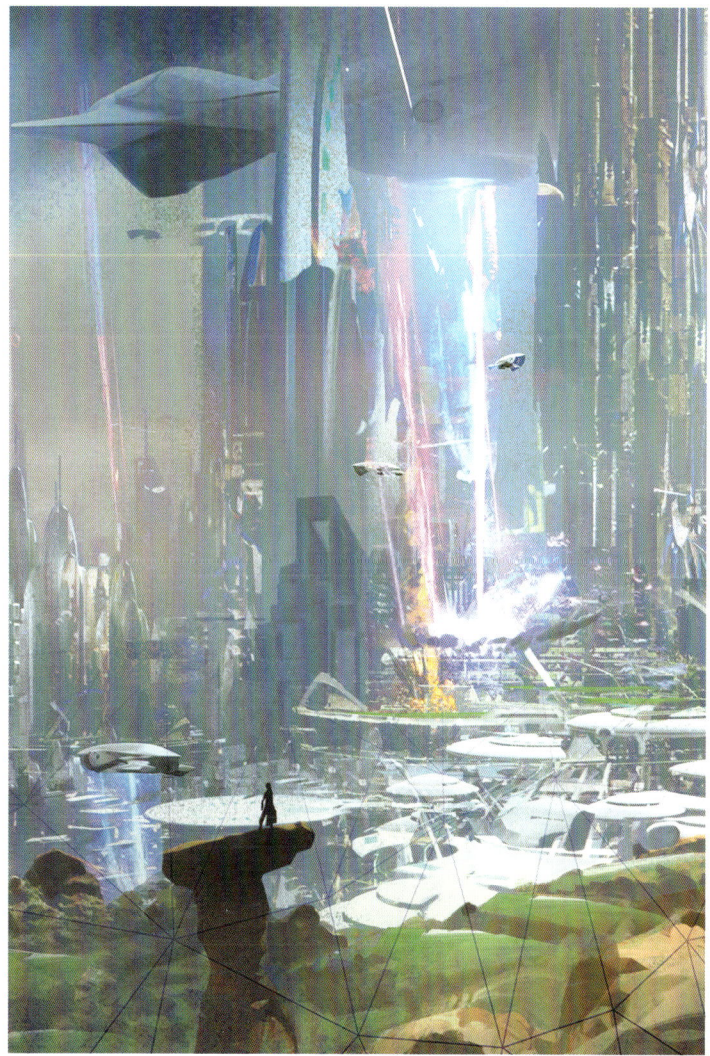

Smith's *Lords of Instrumentality*, a story of humanity and its animal and robotic counterparts set forty thousand years in the future. There, C'mell the cat-woman teaches Lord Jestocost what it means to be human and free. And cats battle alien nightmares so that human pilots can travel between the stars. Fritz Leiber's love of and affinity for cats permeates much of the great American fantasy writer's work. From the creation of one of his best-known heroes, the Gray Mouser, to the Tigerishika featured in his award-winning novel, *The Wanderer*, felines were a never-ending source of inspiration right up until his death in 1992. And Tigerishika is just one representative of the many feline races that populate fiction. In comics, films (such as *The Cat from Outer Space*, a Disney production for the whole family), and books (such as Luce Basseterre's various wildcats in *Le Chant des Γenjicks* and *La Débusqueuse de mondes*, or Ayerdhal's giant cats in *Mytale*), these creatures, whether quadruped or biped, fascinate us. Although foreign to us, they seem very close in their motivations. 🐾

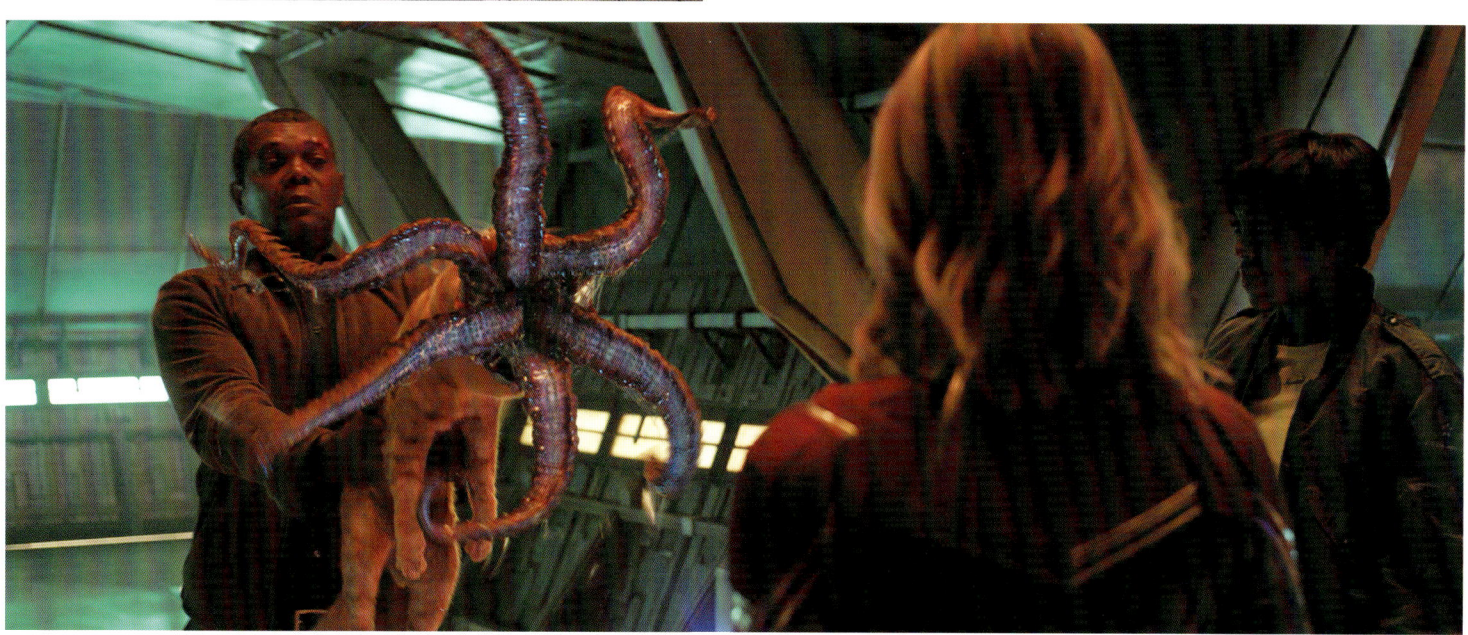

Goose is a Flerken who takes on the appearance of a cat in *Captain Marvel*.

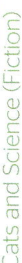

Viewpoint

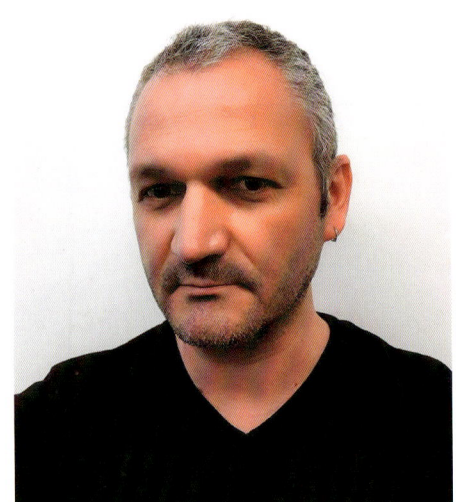

Renaud Guillemin, aka L'Épaule d'Orion

When he's not trying to blow up the planet in his molecular physics laboratory at the CNRS, he's unearthing new texts and polishing up old works of science fiction for the Ailleurs et Demain collection published by Robert Laffont. A slave to two cats, he explains the connections between science and science fiction and these animals.

Science's most famous cat— Schrödinger's cat—doesn't exist, since it's the subject of a thought experiment. What's a thought experiment?
A thought experiment is what we all do on Monday mornings, when we say to ourselves, "What would happen if I stayed under the covers instead of going to work?" You know you can't do it, but imagining it leads you to draw conclusions about the meaning of life, the universe, and everything else. In physics, a thought experiment is a form of abstraction that allows you to extrapolate a theory, model, or equation beyond the experimental means at your disposal, to test its limits when you push your logic to the limit, even to the point of the absurd. In the case of Schrödinger's cat, this means asking what the consequences are of the postulates of quantum mechanics, whose focus is the microscopic world, on the macroscopic world that is directly perceptible to us. The indeterminate state of a quantum system (radioactive decay) is associated with a macroscopic system (a cat), leading to the somewhat caricatured conclusion that the cat is now the living dead (poor Church!). On a more basic level, a thought experiment is simply an intellectual process that helps us devise experiments to test models in our daily work in the lab.

Why was Schrödinger's cat important to physics? Is the experiment still relevant today?
Looking back, I think Schrödinger's cat was more a source of misunderstanding about quantum mechanics than anything else, even among physicists. The formulation is basically linked to what is known as the "measurement problem." But what it really questions is the manifestation of quantum effects on a macroscopic scale. From a modern point of view, there is no paradox. Quantum effects don't resist the transition from the microscopic to the macroscopic. The main reason is that the universe exists even when we stop looking at it. What we define as a "measurement" doesn't require the presence of consciousness but may simply be the consequence of the interaction between two particles. In other words, once your system is no longer isolated from the rest of the world, it rapidly loses its quantum properties. The cat's fate is sealed long before you open the box; you just don't know what it is. Quantum mechanics says nothing about the nature of the universe. It only tells you what you can learn from it. Is the experiment still relevant? Yes, as long as there are people to ponder it.

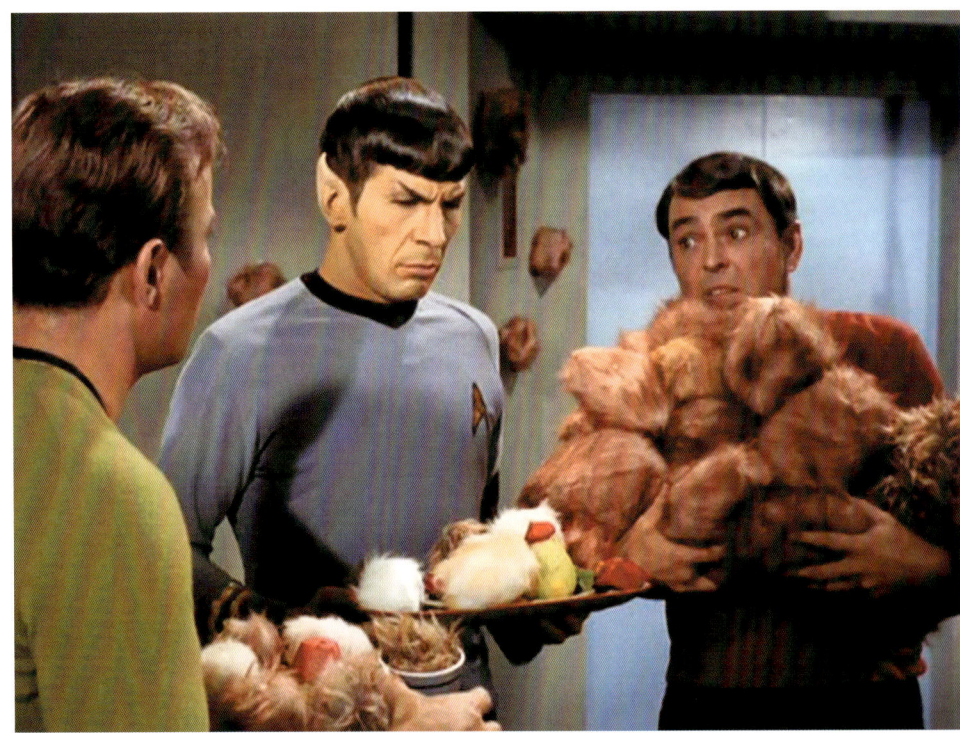

Dangerously invasive Tribbles in *Star Trek.*

As far as I'm concerned, I don't think so. Having said that, a few years ago, I published an article[1] that drew a parallel between Schrödinger's cat and the indistinguishability of two atoms from the point of view of a photon. Simply because it's fun, because everyone knows Schrödinger's cat, and it remains a communication icon.

Cats have also greatly inspired science-fiction writers (Heinlein, Pohl, Leiber, Werber, Cordwainer Smith, as well as *Star Trek*'s Tribbles, etc.), particularly with this paradox, but not exclusively. Why is it so fascinating?

In the armed race between prey and predator that has been going on for 3.5 billion years on planet Earth, cats are the pinnacle of evolution. Whether in terms of equipment, agility, strength, or perception, these beasts have reached a perfection that is focused on a single goal: killing. Cats are just miniature tigers, only more violent. In fact, unlike dogs, cats have evolved very little since they first domesticated man. Simply because they haven't needed to; they're perfect! Everything about cats—their claws, their teeth, their look—evokes an atavistic fear in humans. We instinctively recognize danger. The proximity of a cat exerts a fascination on us that's linked to this ancestral conditioning.

And if that weren't enough, cats have become shrouded in an aura of mystery. While it's easy to anthropomorphize the mimetic behavior of a dog, it's impossible to do it with a cat. Cats represent otherness. Nothing about cats' behavior is familiar. Even their perception of space is different from ours. Proof of this is their eternal quest for the door to summer. Finally, they're fluffy. 'Nuff said. They're pretty, ultimate weapons that are totally beyond our

comprehension. It's easy to see why cats inspire science-fiction writers. To the list of authors mentioned above, I'd add A. E. van Vogt's Coeurl in *The Voyage of the Space Beagle*, who is the ultimate predator. Then there are Ayerdhal's ksins in *Mytale*, which are two-hundred-kilo cats that embody both companionship and pure violence. And Aineko, an AI manipulating humanity for its own benefit in Charles Stross's *Accelerando*. I think these three examples illustrate my answer quite well.

In *Men in Black*, the pendant on the cat Orion's collar contains a whole universe. Is this poetic license on the part of the screenwriters or directors, or could it correspond to a particular scientific theory?

The idea of nested universes is nothing new; it can be traced back to the idea of an organized, geometric universe, as found among the mathematicians of ancient Greece. Today, it's concomitant with the multiverse theory. If we ignore the laws of physics, we can imagine anything. But the four fundamental interactions we know limit the amount of matter we can fit into a given volume. Electromagnetic interaction, for example, allows you to sit on a chair without passing through it. If we imagined a galaxy where chemistry was possible, meaning composed of atoms and molecules, it would have to be roughly the same size as the one we live in. We can imagine other states of matter. There are very high-density stars, composed essentially of neutrons. And if we go even further, there are black holes. But here again, size is finite.

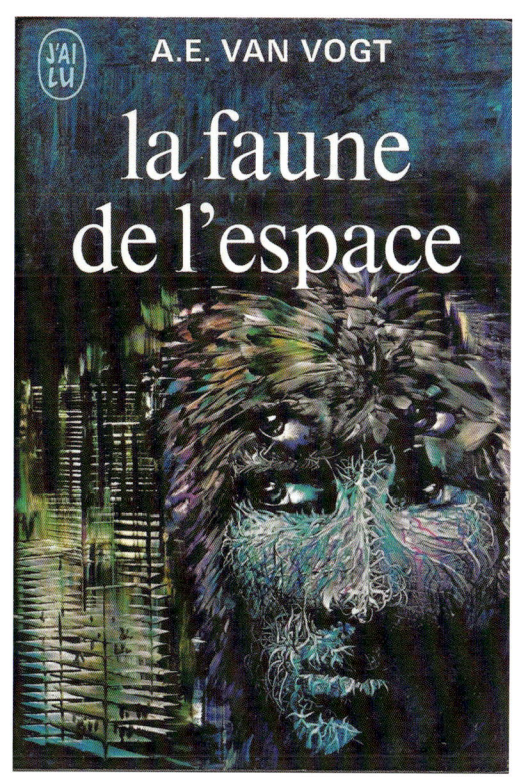

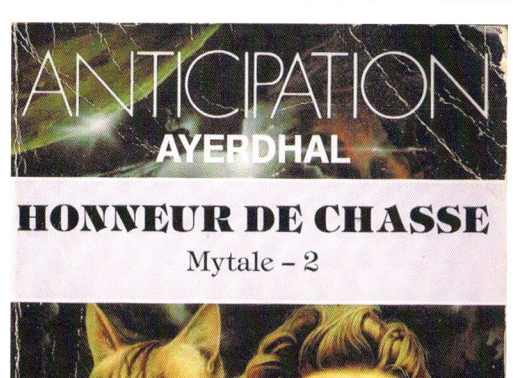

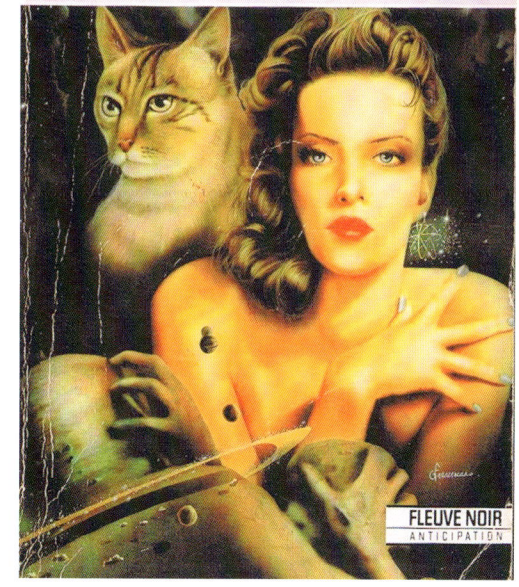

[1] R. Guillemin et al., *Nature Communications 6*, 6166 (2015). https://www.nature.com/articles/ncomms7166

A hole the mass of the sun would have a radius (known as the Schwarzschild radius) of three kilometers. So, no, you can't fit a galaxy into the volume of a marble unless you radically alter the laws of physics.

But more than just poetic license, Orion's pendant is a plot device, a magic trick designed to divert attention. I'm going to reveal something to you: The universe isn't contained in Orion's pendant, but in cats' eyes. Take a basin and fill it with water. Dip your feet into it. Grab a cat and look deeply into its eyes. You're about to travel. 🐾

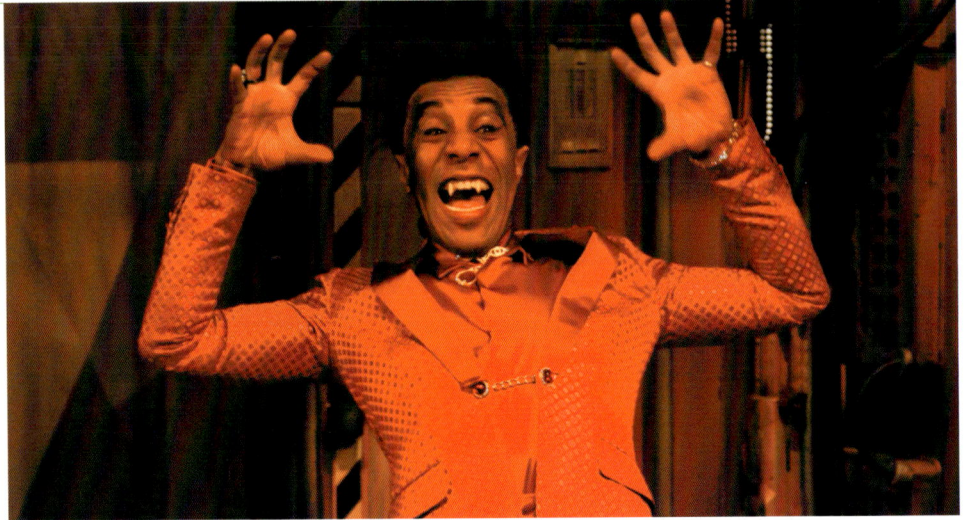

Cat in *Red Dwarf.*

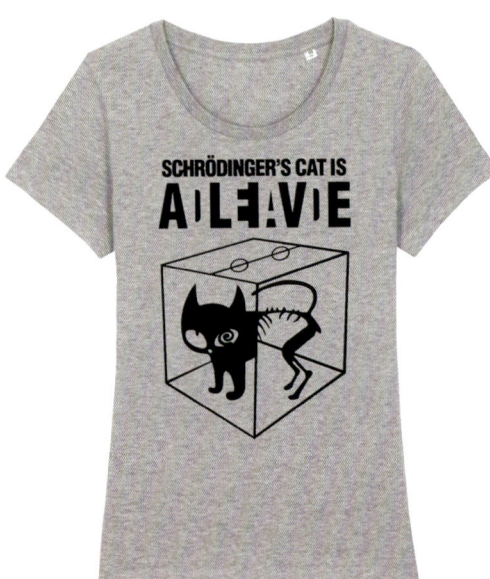

A Schrödinger's cat T-shirt.

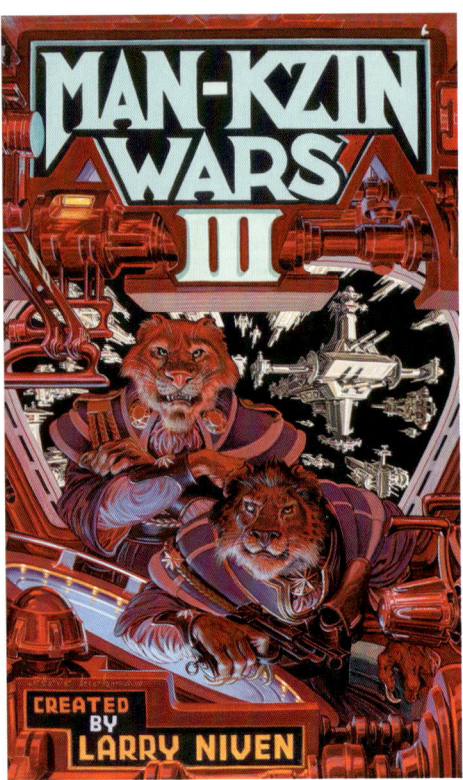

Science-fiction author Larry Niven's *Man–Kzin Wars III.*

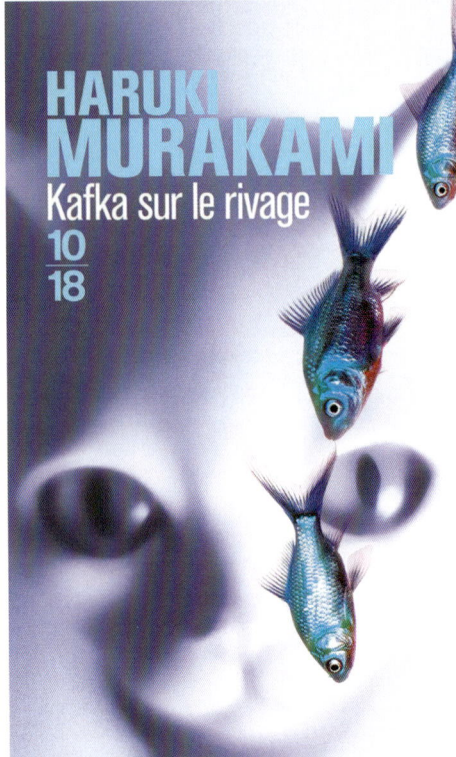

French cover design for the Japanese author Haruki Murakami's novel *Kafka on the Shore.*

Schrödinger's Cat

Both alive and dead, this poor locked-up cat is a geek's delight and the subject of many jokes. Originally, however, it was an attempt to understand how quantum mechanics works.

Austrian philosopher and physicist Erwin Schrödinger is best known for laying the foundations of quantum mechanics by developing an equation for the wave function, one of its fundamental concepts. And for those who are not particularly scientific, for his thought experiment to explain the paradox of quantum states in relation to the visible world. This is the famous Schrödinger's cat, which he first discussed in his correspondence with another famous physicist, Albert Einstein.

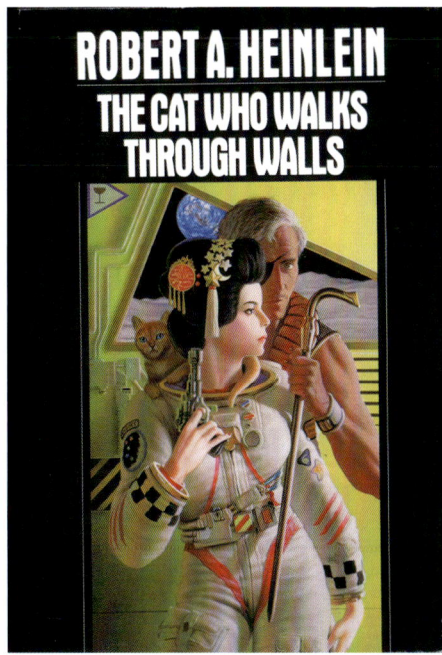

This experiment imagines a closed box containing a cat. A device kills the animal as soon as it detects the disintegration of an atom of a radioactive body. He uses the example of a radioactivity detector, connected to a switch that causes a hammer to fall and break a vial of deadly gas. How do we know whether the cat is dead or alive? As long as the outside observer hasn't opened the box, the cat's survival depends on that of the radioactive particle, and it is, therefore, like the particle, both alive and dead. And the very fact of trying to find out, by lifting the lid of the box, would automatically trigger the cat's death by shattering the vial.

While it may no longer be of great interest to twenty-first-century quantum physicists, this rhetorical question from 1935 continues to fascinate, and it's used and hijacked by popular culture. In *The Cat Who Walks Through Walls*, Robert Heinlein depicts a kitten that can sneak up on any human it wants to see, regardless of trivial obstacles such as walls or doors. The story emphasizes that the kitten is a Schrödinger's cat. In *Witches Abroad*, Terry Pratchett adds a third possible state to the experiment: "Alive, Dead, and Bloody Furious." In the manga *Hellsing*, Schrödinger is a feline android who defines himself as being both everywhere and nowhere, and existing only as long as he is self-aware. And more recently, the German science-fiction series *Dark* uses the metaphor to explain how one of its characters can be both alive and dead, and the entanglements between the various threads of the story. 🐾

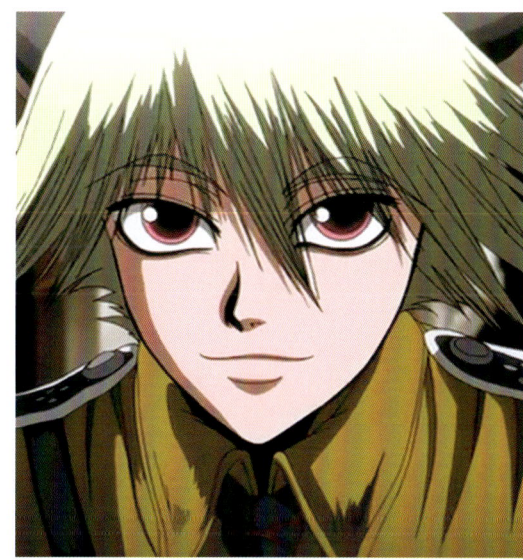

Schrödinger, *Hellsing*.

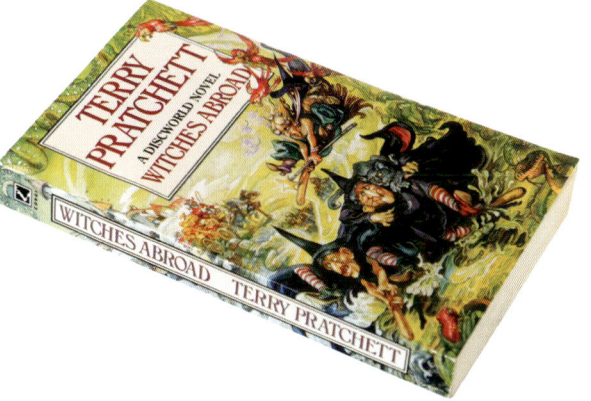

SPEC SHEET

CAT'S NAME: Anonymous.
ROLE: Guinea pig in a theoretical experiment.
CREATOR: Erwin Schrödinger.
DATE CREATED: 1935.
CAT'S CHARACTERISTICS: Both alive and dead.

Phosphorescent Cats for Medical Advances

If there's one power that cats don't naturally have, it's phosphorescence. Yet scientists have gone to great lengths to modify feline genes so that they can be seen better in the dark.

Some animals are naturally phosphorescent, i.e., capable of emitting light in the dark. This is the case for fireflies, certain squid, and deep-sea fish, for example. This isn't the case with cats, even though their eyes, which are better equipped than ours to see in the dark, can shine by reflecting the slightest flash of light. And yet, in 2011, researchers at the Mayo Clinic in Rochester, Minnesota, created a litter of phosphorescent kittens. Not for the sake of novelty, cosmetic interest, or to have a companion to help them read quietly in bed, but to advance medicine. Dr. Eric Poeschla and his team were looking to modify cats to increase their resistance to FIV (feline immunodeficiency virus, commonly known as "feline AIDS" because it's a cousin of the HIV virus responsible for

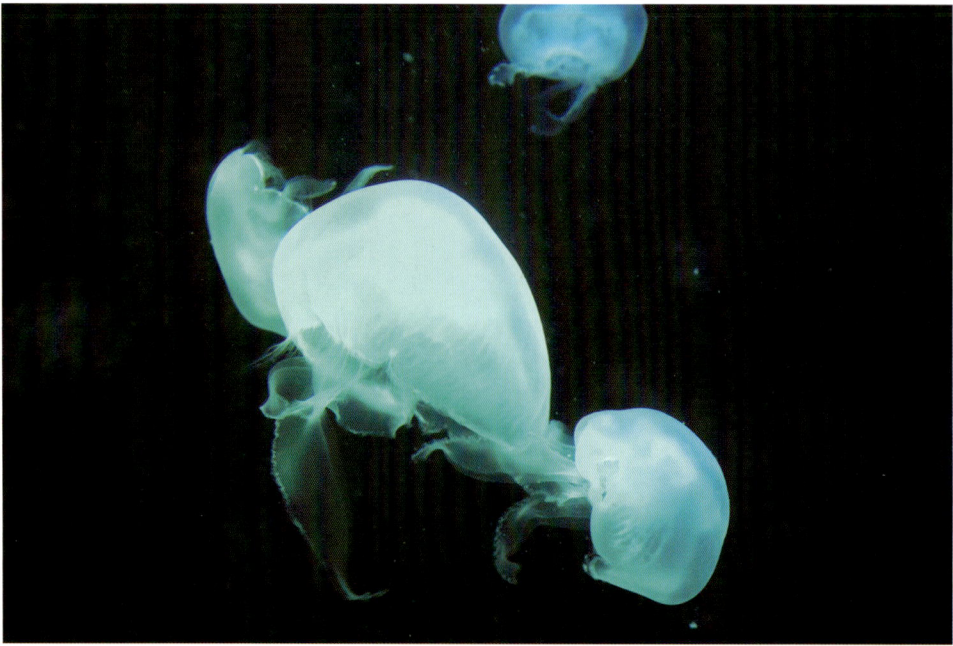

Jellyfish, Sydney Zoo, Australia. Photo by Ank Kumar.

human AIDS). They introduced a protective rhesus macaque gene into the cats' DNA and, to verify that the gene was activated, coupled it with the jellyfish gene responsible for its bioluminescence. If the cats glowed in the dark, it meant that the macaque gene had been properly implanted and activated.

The experiment was a success, and the cats developed a form of resistance to the disease. But as Eric Poeschla explained, "We haven't shown cats that are AIDS-proof. We still have to do infection studies involving whole cats. That the protection gene is expressed in the cat lymphoid organs, where AIDS virus spread and cell death mostly play out, is encouraging to us, however."[1] Ten years on, AIDS research has progressed, with numerous vaccines in trial and new therapies under development. Perhaps thanks in part to these kittens? 🐾

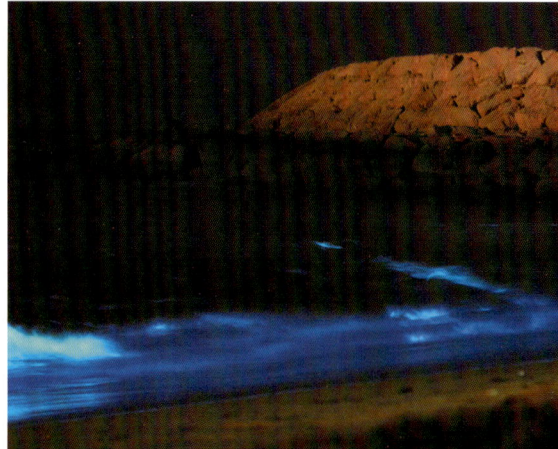

Plankton, Chabahar beaches, Iran. Photo by Safa Daneshvar.

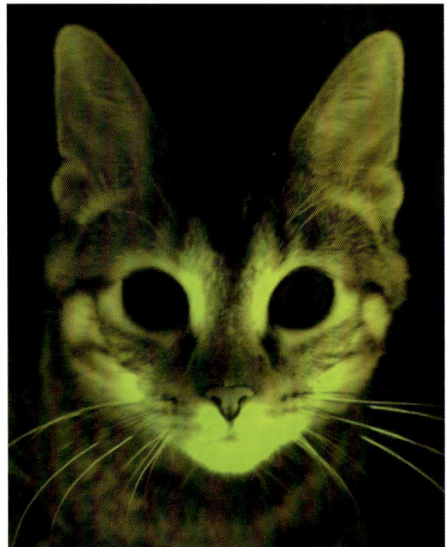

Phosphorescent kitten. Photo by the Mayo Clinic.

SPEC SHEET

CATS' NAMES: Anonymous.
ROLE: Guinea pigs from a medical experiment.
CREATORS: Dr. Eric Poeschla and his team at the Mayo Clinic.
DATE CREATED: 2011.
CATS' CHARACTERISTICS: Transgenic phosphorescent cats.

---

[1] https://www.livescience.com/15994-glow-dark-cats-aids-virus-research.html

Although cloning experiments on animals no longer make the headlines, one of the first experiments involved a cat whose clone, CC, lived a normal life, including having a litter of kittens.

Not all animals are easy to clone. And when scientists succeeded in cloning the first mammal, Dolly the sheep,[1] in 1996, some saw it as a dream opportunity to give our pets a semblance of immortality by cloning them. The first viable cloned cat was CC (or Carbon Copy), born on December 22, 2001. Despite her name, she didn't really resemble her mother, Rainbow. While Rainbow was a calico (a tricolored cat with large white spots covering between 25% and 75% of her body), CC was a perfectly ordinary tabby and white cat. This difference in pigmentation, which can also be found in natural identical twins, is explained by the way coat color is encoded in chromosomes. Tricolored coats (tortoiseshell or calico) are specific to females of the species, due to the fact that one of the two X^2

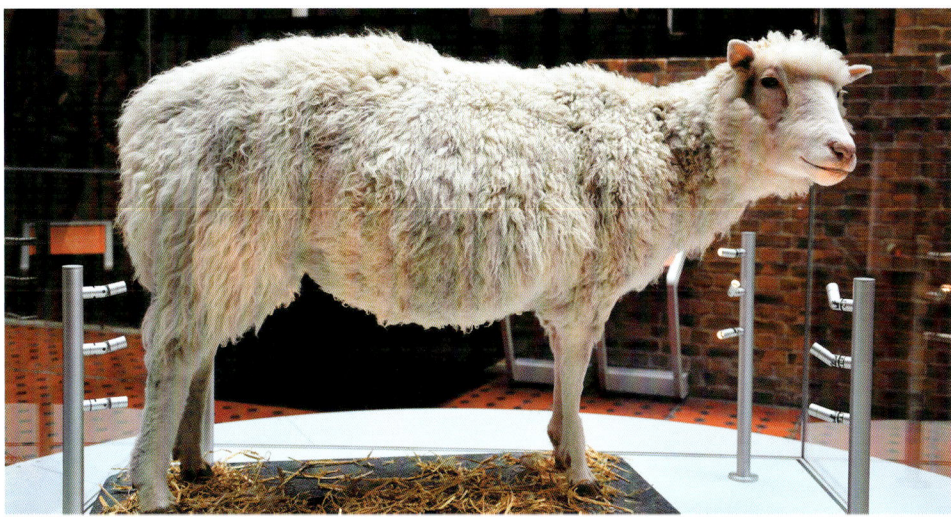
Dolly (stuffed), National Museum of Scotland, Edinburgh. Photo by Mike McBey.

chromosomes carries the orange gene and the other the black gene. To prevent both genes from being expressed at the same time, each cell randomly deactivates one of them. Therefore, the orange gene wasn't activated in the cell used to create the daughter CC.

Apart from this cosmetic difference, the cat was born healthy, had kittens that were also completely normal, and lived until 2020, reaching the respectable age of eighteen (which is good for a cat).

Following this successful publicity, Genetic Savings & Clone launched its pet cloning business in 2004 with the first commercial "product," Little Nicky, a Maine Coon born on October 17, 2004, from the cells of another male, who died at the age of seventeen. However, unlike his "father," Little Nicky suffered a lifetime of health problems, with no proof or denial that these were cloning-related. In any case, Genetic Savings & Clone closed its doors two years later, in part due to a campaign arguing that the $50,000 it cost to clone an animal could be more effectively invested in protecting pets in general. Since then, pet cloning has become a commercial

venture, with American, Korean, and Chinese companies promising to create a duplicate of one's pet cat for sums ranging from €30,000 to €50,000 per animal. 🐾

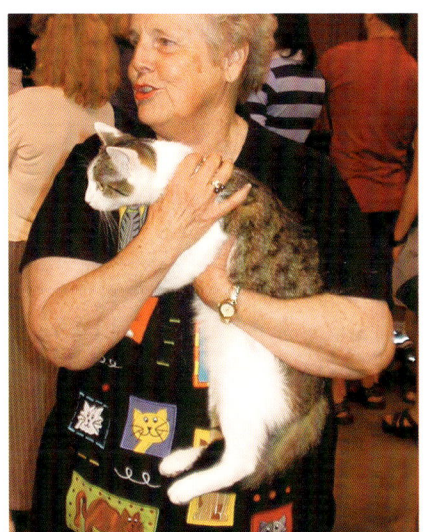
CC, the first cloned cat, age two, white and tabby. 2003, with owner, College Station, Texas. Photo by Pschemp.

SPEC SHEET

CAT'S NAME: CC.
ROLE: Clone.
CREATORS: Texas A&M University and Genetic Savings & Clone.
BIRTH DATE: December 22, 2001.
CAT'S CHARACTERISTICS: Shorthaired tabby and white cat.

---

[1] https://www.nms.ac.uk/dolly
[2] Rare tricolored male cats, known as "tortoiseshells" or "calicos", are sterile, as they carry a genetic anomaly giving them three sex chromosomes: two X and one Y.

Cats in Antarctica

Wherever humans go, cats go, too. Already valued as rat hunters on ships, cats and kittens have ventured as far as the South Pole during scientific expeditions.

Despite the species' general aversion to water, cats have often been welcomed on ships. One thing led to another, and some had the opportunity to set foot on the icy continent of Antarctica. From the first expeditions in the nineteenth century to today's stations, cats have always accompanied people, often sharing with them a tragic fate in the face of harsh climatic conditions.

One of the most famous was Mrs. Chippy, who, despite the name, was a tomcat who stowed away on the *Endurance*, the ship belonging to Ernest Shackleton (a distinguished British explorer), on an exploratory voyage to the south. He hid in the belongings of his master, the ship's carpenter, on

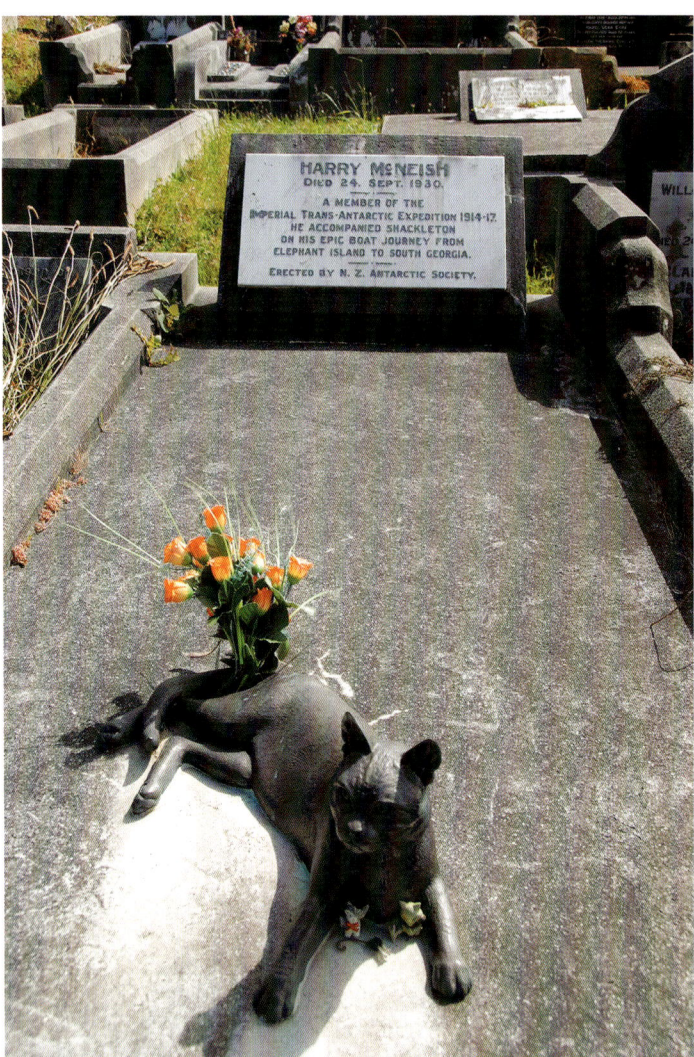

Mrs. Chippy, portrayed on the grave of his master, Harry McNish, Wellington, New Zealand.

August 1, 1914, and was only discovered once at sea. Loved and pampered by most of the crew, he met a tragic end on October 29, 1915. On that date, the *Endurance* was so icebound that the hull broke, and the men had to evacuate. Faced with the meager provisions available, they had to resort to slaughtering the animals that couldn't leave in the lifeboats with them. Mrs. Chippy was put to sleep beforehand with a tin of sardines covered in sleeping pills.

WHAT ABOUT THE ARCTIC?

At least one cat is famous for visiting the North Pole and the Arctic Ocean. That was Halifax, a calico cat owned by Diana White and her husband, Alvah Simon. The couple decided to spend an entire winter on an icebound vessel above the Arctic Circle, taking the cat with them as a traveling companion. When Diana White had to return to New Zealand to care for her ailing father, Alvah was left alone with Halifax in the polar night from October 1994 to March 1995. Diana returned, and the couple finally decided to leave in August 1995.[1] Halifax was luckier than her colleagues at the South Pole, dying of old age in June 2009.

She wasn't the only one to venture so far north. When Nigeraurak found herself in the western Arctic, the poor animal hadn't asked for any of it. It all began on June 17, 1913. A scientific expedition embarked on the *Karluk* to sail from British Columbia to the Banks Islands. One of the crew members smuggled aboard a small black kitten, the famous Nigeraurak ("little black thing" in Inuit). Despite initial reluctance, the animal was quickly adopted by the crew. But the *Karluk* was caught in the ice and drifted far from its destination. The crew had to abandon ship and set off for Siberia on foot and dog sled. Unlike poor Mrs. Chippy, no one had the heart to kill Nigeraurak, who was the companion of two young Inuit sisters (aged eight and three) who were also part of the expedition. The cat survived by eating the pemmican (a native dish) given to her by the other members of the expedition and by sticking close to them inside the igloos where they slept at night. Like the others, she was rescued in September 1914 and lived a full life with one of the shipwrecked sailors, having several litters of kittens.

[1] *North to the Night* by Alvah Simon.

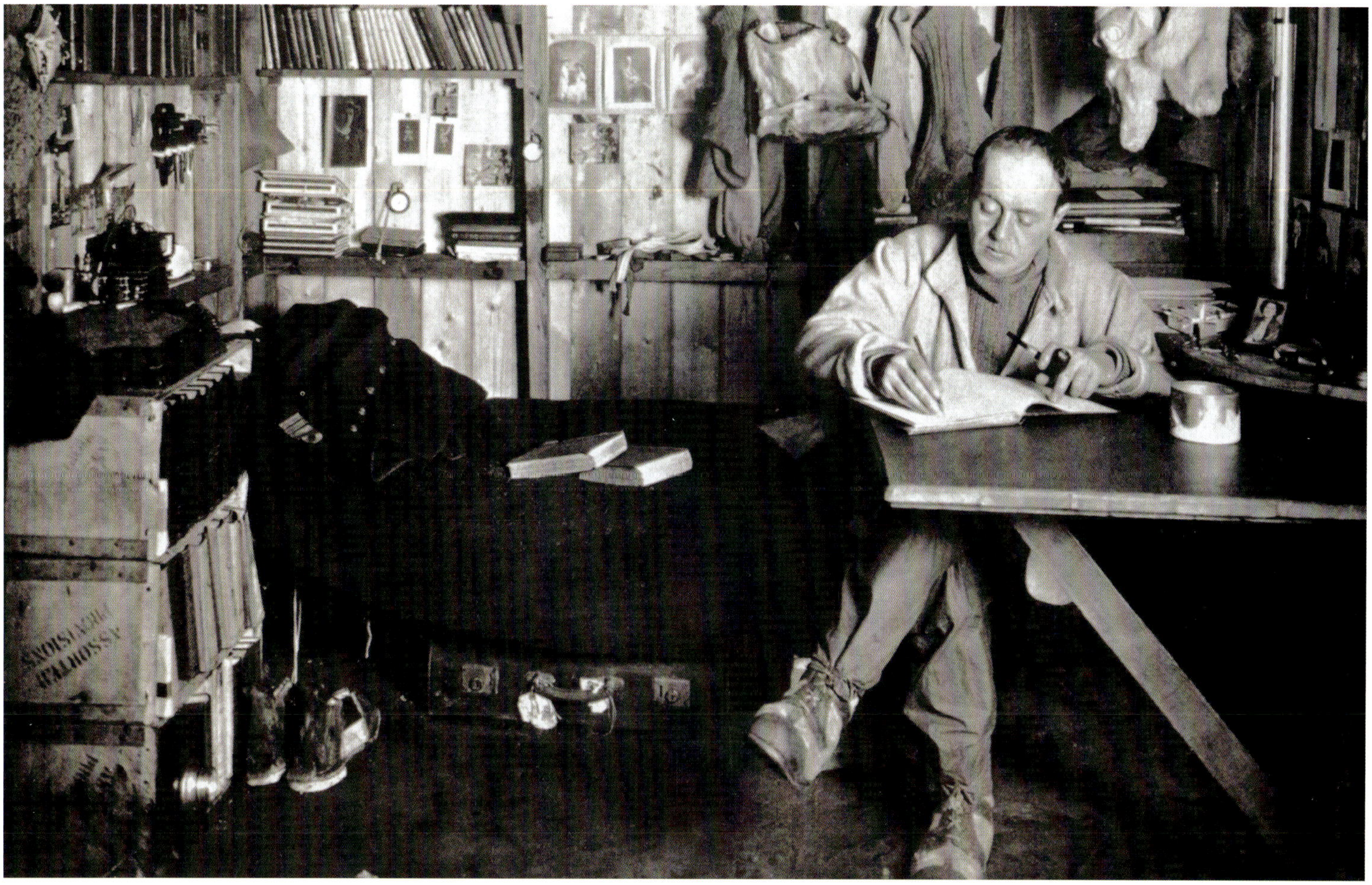

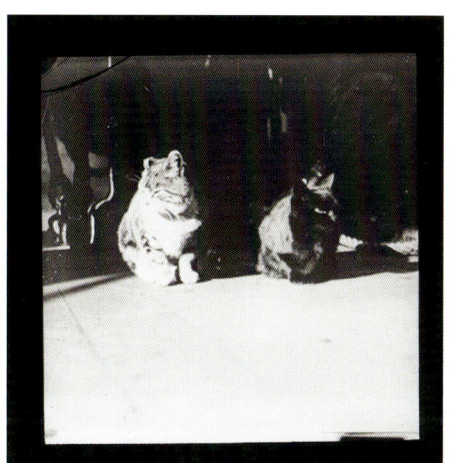

Robert Falcon Scott, 1911. Photo by Herbert Ponting.

Robert Falcon Scott also had cats on board during his two expeditions to the southernmost continent. The *Discovery* expedition (1901–1904) had two cats among the crew: the male Blackwall and the female Poplar. They reached the continent, but neither they nor the kittens that resulted from their union survived. The cat from the *Terra Nova* expedition (which also proved fatal for Robert Scott) didn't even make it to Antarctica: A gust of wind blew him overboard first.

Since World War II, the Antarctic has been occupied by permanent scientific bases, and many of them have taken in cats, always with a view to rodent control, but also for moral support. 🐾

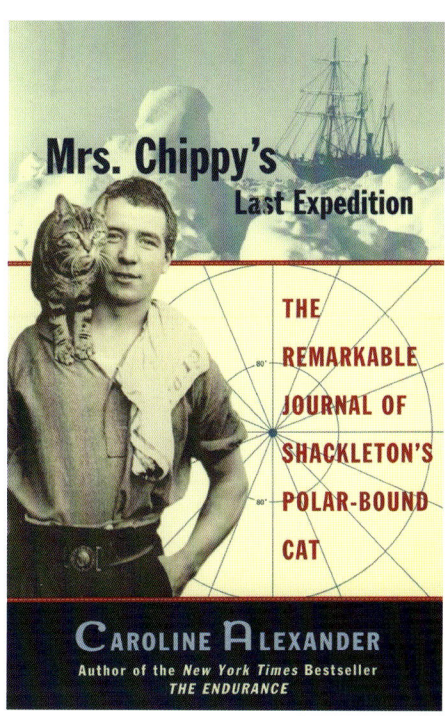

Poplar and Blackwall on ship's deck, Antarctica, 1901–1904. ANMM Collection.

Mrs. Chippy's Last Expedition

THE REMARKABLE JOURNAL OF SHACKLETON'S POLAR-BOUND CAT

CAROLINE ALEXANDER
Author of the *New York Times* Bestseller *THE ENDURANCE*

Félicette, a Cat in Space

While the first living creature sent to space was a Soviet dog named Laïka, at least one cat has also had the chance to leave the Earth's atmosphere: France's Félicette.

It was October 18, 1963, and a Véronique rocket soared eighty-one miles above the ground from the Algerian Sahara. On board was subject C341, a 5.5-pound black-and-white

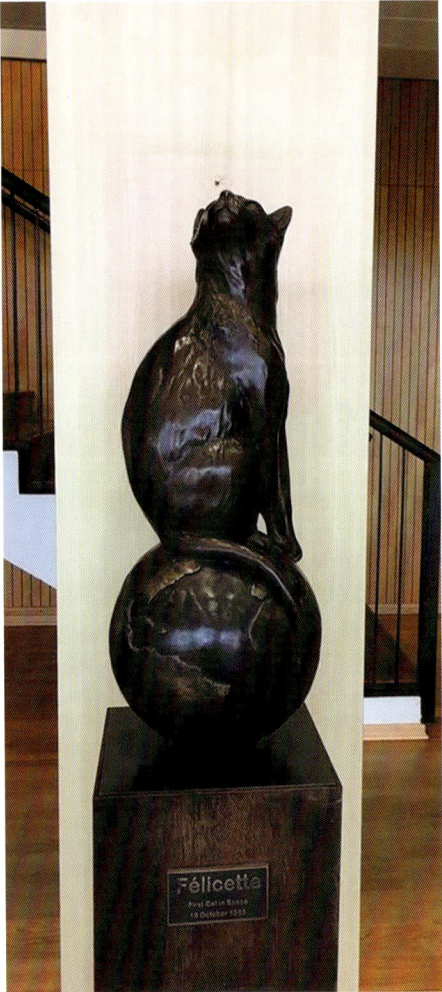

Statue of Félicette, International Space University, Strasbourg.

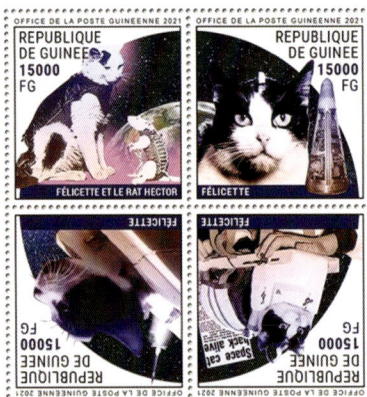

FÉLICETTE
La première chatte lancée dans l'espace

Stamps from the Republic of Guinea.

cat nicknamed Félicette. After thirteen minutes of turbulent flight and five minutes of weightlessness for its passenger, the rocket returned to Earth. Félicette was alive, and to this day, she remains the only cat ever to have gone into space and returned safely. A few days later, on October 24, the French launched a second cat into space, but a jammed bolt caused a chaotic launch and a difficult recovery, with a delay of more than twenty-four hours. By the time help arrived, the animal had not survived. The twelve other cats in the French space program were decommissioned, and the electrodes implanted in their heads to monitor their in-flight vitals were removed. Thereafter, before moving on to human flights, French scientists, like their American counterparts, used monkeys.

And what happened to Félicette? The poor thing didn't survive long. Two months later, she was euthanized and then autopsied to examine the state of her brain after experiencing an acceleration of 9.5 Gs during ascent and five minutes of microgravity. Unlike the other animals who gave their lives for the conquest of space, Félicette went a long time without honors in her home country, although some former French territories (such as the Comoros, Chad, and Niger) issued stamps bearing her likeness. In 2017, an international crowdfunding campaign was launched so that the little cat could finally have a statue in her honor. Created by British artist Gill Parker, the statue now sits alongside that of Yuri Gagarin at the ISU (International Space University) in Strasbourg. 🐾

SPEC SHEET

CAT'S NAME: C341, called Félicette.
ROLE: Astronaut.
ORIGINATOR: CERMA (Centre de recherche et de médecine aéronautique).
LAUNCH DATE: October 18, 1963.
CAT'S CHARACTERISTICS: Black-and-white alley cat.

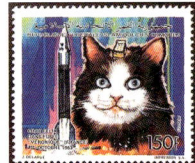

Stamp from the Comoros.

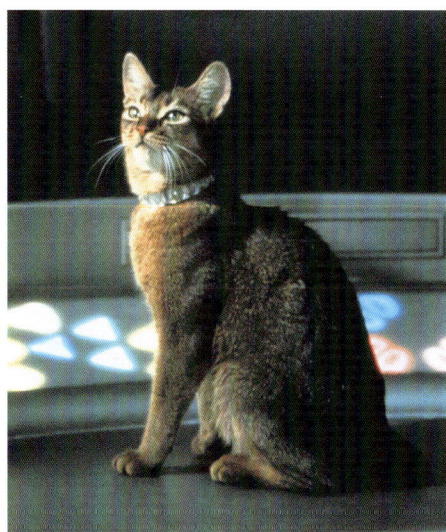

Long before the versions of The Lion King and The Jungle Book combining CGI and real images, Disney Studios had already tried its hand at putting real cats in front of the cameras, such as in this sci-fi comedy.

Released a year after *Close Encounters of the Third Kind*, *The Cat from Outer Space* is one of a long series of live-action films made by Walt Disney Productions that strayed a little from their core target audience of children. Although not as gritty as its forays into horror (such as 1983's *Something Wicked This Way Comes*), this 1978 comedy stands out from the rest of the Disney catalog of the time for its fairly critical take on the US military and its shortcomings in the midst of the Cold War, as well as its rather positive depiction of sports betting and gambling. The hero cat even uses his technology and powers to cheat and achieve his aims.

Based on a storyline from the old science-fiction films of the 1950s, *The Cat from Outer Space* portrays an alien whose saucer is stranded on Earth. While he waits for the main

ship to arrive, he has just forty-eight hours to find something to repair it. And to make matters worse, he looks like an ordinary cat, except for his collar, which gives him telepathic and telekinetic talents. To repair his ship, he teams up with an army scientist who is mocked for his outlandish ideas, but not everything goes according to plan. Released thirteen years after Walt Disney Productions' *That Darn Cat!*, a live-action film starring a Siamese cat that parodies spy films, *The Cat from Outer Space* is a spirited romp whose special effects have aged considerably. Nevertheless, it remains an enjoyable

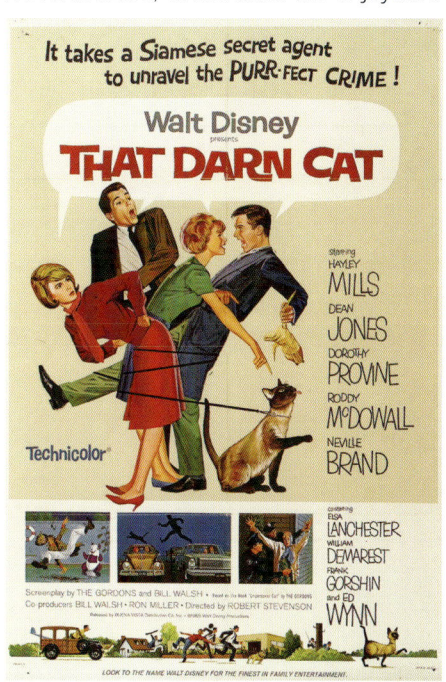

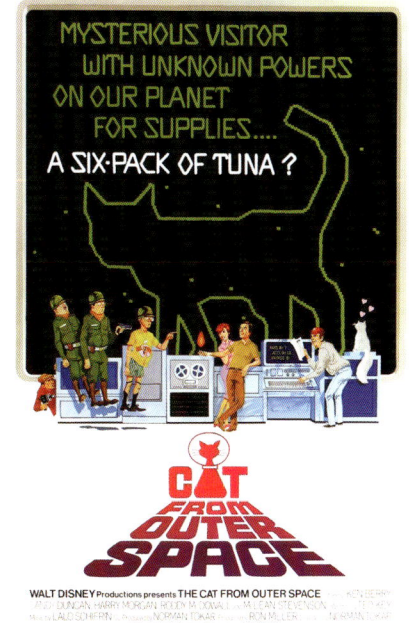

family comedy, and the film made enough of an impact at the time to have inspired other works. Rumor has it that Steven Spielberg came up with the idea for *E. T. the Extra-Terrestrial* after seeing it. But the opposite scenario can also be found in the series *ALF* (see p. 100), where a cat-eating alien is stranded on Earth. Or even in *Men in Black*, where Orion's physical appearance (see p. 156) and necklace are reminiscent of Jake in this film. 🐾

SPEC SHEET

WORK: *The Cat from Outer Space*.
CREATORS: Norman Tokar (director) and Ted Key (screenwriter).
DATE CREATED: June 9, 1978.
DISTRIBUTOR/AVAILABILITY: Walt Disney Productions, available on DVD and on Disney+.
NAME OF THE CAT AND ROLE IN THE WORK: Zunar-J-5/9 Doric-4-7, aka Jake, the story's protagonist alien cat that is stranded on Earth.

Orion

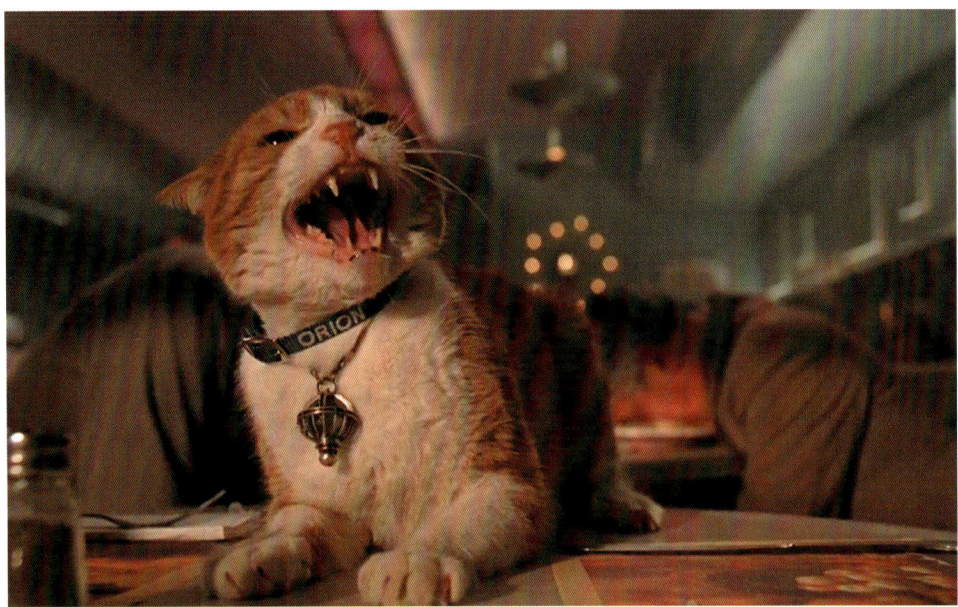

In 1997, two agents dressed in black save the world from destruction by aliens in a comedy produced by Steven Spielberg. The key to averting the galactic apocalypse lies with Orion, an orange cat with a white chest.

Adapted from a comic book and paving the way for three other films, an animated series, and a slew of spin-off products, *Men in Black* presents our planet as a zone of peace, a kind of Switzerland of the universe. The eccentric ETs sometimes wear funny human disguises, like Michael Jackson playing himself. From an animal point of view, audiences will especially remember the alien Frank, whose costume is that of a pug. He appears in all the other films.

Yet a cat is at the heart of the story. The feline's master is an extraterrestrial guardian of the "galaxy." This galaxy is in fact a small pendant attached to the animal's collar. It's the best source of subatomic energy in the universe.

With humor and absurdity predominating in the film, it's no coincidence that a simple house cat is used to transport the precious object. The cat's name, Orion, also leads to a number of twists and turns. The two protagonists think that what they're looking for is in the middle of Orion's band, which they then interpret as the constellation Orion's Belt. When the cat has the galaxy removed from its neck, this leads to the resolution of the film's final dramatic twist and the action scenes that accompany it.

The film is a satire of the real world and its bureaucracy in a near-future universe where aliens live among us. It alternates computer-generated images and ultra-modern sets with shots taken in the New York underworld. Director Barry Sonnenfeld, who had already

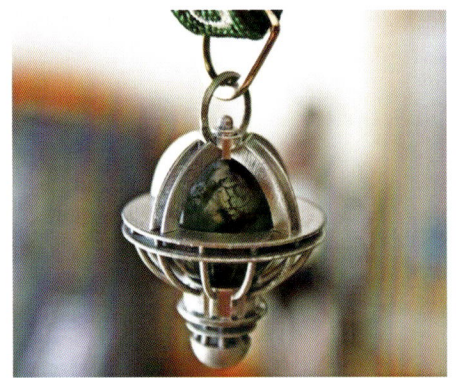

directed *The Addams Family*, succeeded in blending these two elements. These paradoxes are what made the film such a success. For an investment of $90 million, it grossed almost $590 million at the box office.

Absurdity and science form an explosive mix. The Orion galaxy, in which the viewer glimpses thousands of planets, represents an infinitely large universe in a tiny object. This pseudo-scientific theme recurs throughout the films. The first opus ends on Earth, which itself belongs to a galaxy that an alien is using to play marbles. 🐾

SPEC SHEET

CAT'S NAME: Orion.
WORK: *Men in Black*.
CREATORS: Barry Sonnenfeld (director) and Ed Solomon (screenwriter), based on the comics by Lowell Cunningham.
DATE CREATED: August 6, 1997.
DISTRIBUTOR/AVAILABILITY: Sony Pictures. Available on DVD, Blu-ray, and streaming services.
CAT'S CHARACTERISTICS: Orange cat with a white chest. Wears a galaxy on his collar.

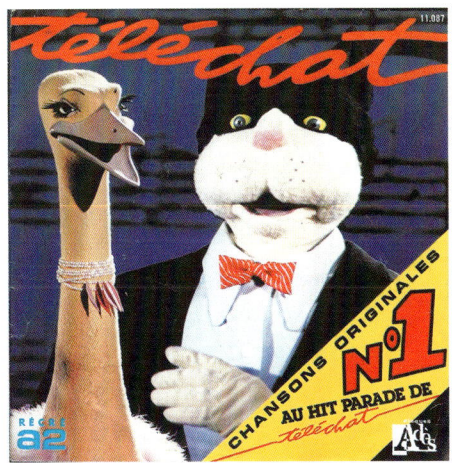

Touting itself as a news program for cats and presented by a cat, Telecat was a Franco-Belgian puppet program for young people that left its mark on the 1980s with its absurd logic and imagination.

A black-and-white cat with one paw in a cast, an ostrich sticking its head in a hole at the slightest annoyance, a green orangutan, a superhero full of chlorophyll . . . No need to wonder; this is *Telecat*, the children's program that left its mark in the 1980s. Co-created by Roland Topor and Henri Xhonneux, this TV news parody was divided into five-minute episodes. With its talking animals and objects (notably Durallo, the doll-faced telephone), it impacted a whole generation during its run from 1983 to 1986. Some young viewers were terrified, while others were fascinated.

Mixing absurd logic (which is the first step: the one at the top or the one at the bottom of the staircase?), a critique of TV programs and the ads they ran, puppets, and dated special effects that were quite well done for the time (like the flying boot with glasses that made predictions), *Telecat* was a surreal version of what young children otherwise saw on TV. And some of the craziest elements, such as the chattering gluons at the heart of matter,

were based on actual elementary particles discovered in 1979.

In this world, Groucha served as an entry point for young audiences, along with his ostrich colleague, Lola. A typical domestic cat, he embodied the slightly macho, grumpy TV anchor as seen on the evening news at the time. A mixture of good sense and bad faith, he has feline vanity that makes him reluctant to accept criticism and mockery (notably when he refuses to say why his paw is in a cast). But that doesn't stop him from making eyes at his avian co-anchor, on set or post-credits at the Milk Bar. And through his questions and reports, he helps viewers enter this lunar universe, albeit with his own logic. 🐾

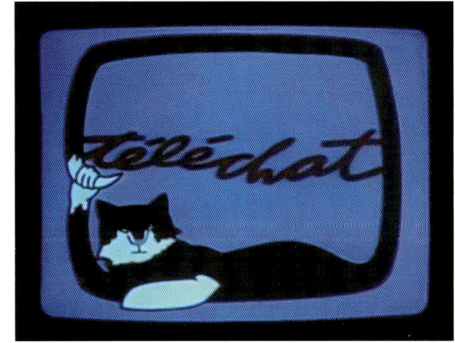

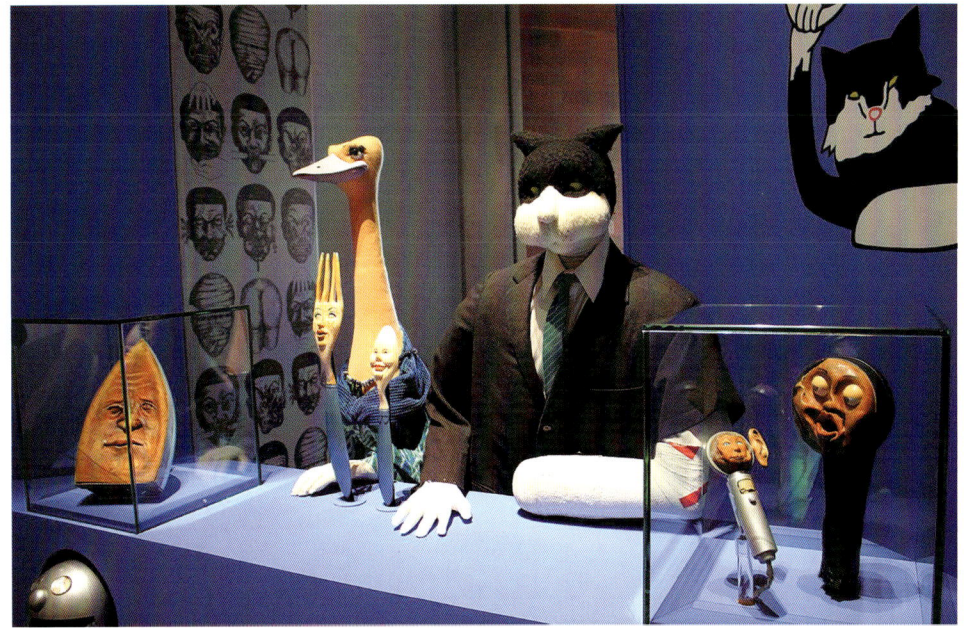

SPEC SHEET

WORK: *Telecat* (*Téléchat* in the original French).
CREATORS: Roland Topor and Henri Xhonneux.
ORIGINAL BROADCAST DATES: September 19, 1983 to September 10, 1986.
DISTRIBUTORS/AVAILABILITY: France 2 (then Antenne 2) and RTBF. Now available on DVD (in French).
CAT'S NAME AND ROLE IN THE WORK: Groucha, a black-and-white cat in a suit with one paw in a cast, the show's anchor.

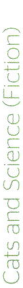

The Door into Summer

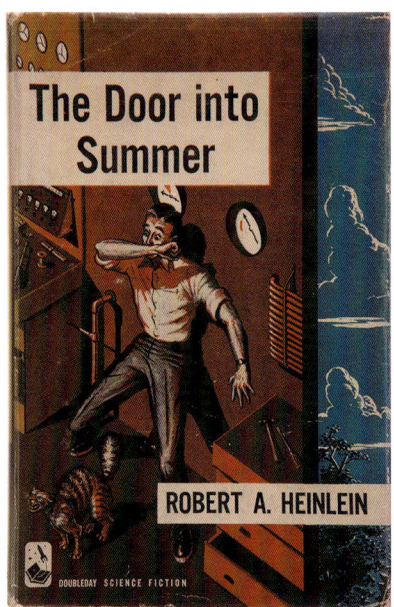

A prolific writer in the golden age of English-language science fiction, Robert Heinlein was also an aeronautical engineer and a great lover of cats. Of all the cats in his work, Petronius in The Door into Summer is the hero's true support and one of the driving forces behind the action.

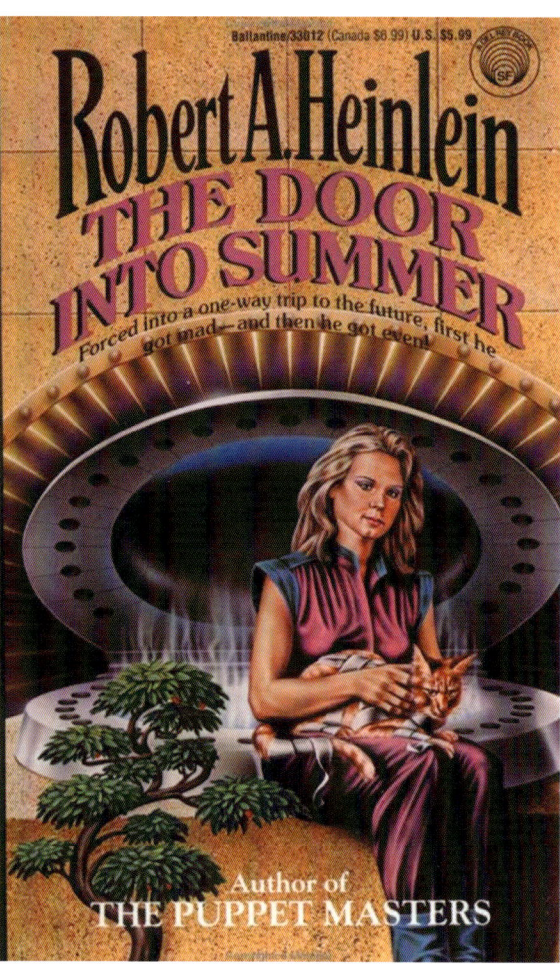

"Pete, being a proper cat, prefers to go outdoors, and he has never given up his conviction that if you just try *all* the doors one of them is bound to be the Door into Summer." Written in 1956, *The Door into Summer* has a special place in Robert Heinlein's work. It contains the best and the worst of Robert Heinlein, condensed into a short novel. The worst? Robert Heinlein is incurably macho and opinionated. His adult female characters are at best delightful idiots (including poor Ricky, who loses her intelligence as she grows up), and at worst, obnoxious, cat-hating manipulators. As his writing progressed, Robert Heinlein would flesh out his characters, but here, we're still a long way from Maureen Johnson in *To Sail Beyond the Sunset* and Hazel Stone

in *The Cat Who Walks Through Walls*. As for his general ideas, let's just say they were those of a staunch American libertarian of the time.

And the best part? *The Door into Summer* is an engaging tale of time travel and revenge. It's easy to follow, despite how it jumps back and forth between eras, and very well told, funny, and ingenious in its various methods of time travel. On the other hand, whatever the era, Robert Heinlein's cats, like those in everyday life, are always obstinate in their search for the "door into summer," and for their own personal happiness. In this case, it's to stay with their human of choice, whatever the cost. Like Petronius the Arbiter, other cats would leave their mark on Robert A. Heinlein's work,

such as Pixel, the famous cat who could walk through walls, and Random and Princess Ponderosa Peach Fuzz, who are part of the Johnson-Long family in his *Future History* series. In *Time Enough for Love*, the author, who's a fervent lover of cats and women (if not a feminist), has his favorite character, Lazarus Long, say, "Women and cats will do as they please, and men and dogs should relax and get used to the idea." 🐾

Although best known for his two great cycles, the Foundation series and the Robot series, Isaac Asimov was a prolific writer from a young age. Among his early works was this short story about cats and time travel.

One of Isaac Asimov's shortest texts is "Time Pussy," a commissioned text he wrote and delivered on December 7, 1941, the very morning that the attack on Pearl Harbor plunged his adopted country, the United States, into World War II.

This short story of fewer than one thousand words is the tale of a former space miner, Mac. When asked about his love of felines, he explains that these earthly pets remind him of the cats of Pallas, four-dimensional creatures stretching across space and time. "These pussies was about a foot long and six inches high and four inches wide and stretched somewheres into middle o' next week," he tells his neighbor.

Living with miners on the asteroid that gave the species its name, these cats played the role that canaries in coal mines do on Earth. Where the canary asphyxiates before humans, signaling pockets of gas before it affects humans, the Pallas cats, living partially in the future through their state of health, indicated to Mac and his colleagues the setbacks to come. Written to fill a new category in *Astounding Science Fiction* magazine, the story is light-hearted. On the other hand, Isaac Asimov, who was a scientist by training, played with timelines and cause-and-effect relationships for one of the first times in his career. He would later explore these ideas in detail throughout his Foundation cycle, in which psychohistory—a science invented to predict the future based on past history and psychology to explain human behavior—guides the destiny of the entire species. And, of course, there are twists and turns from one book to the next to keep the plot moving. And less dramatic endings than for those poor time pussies. 🐾

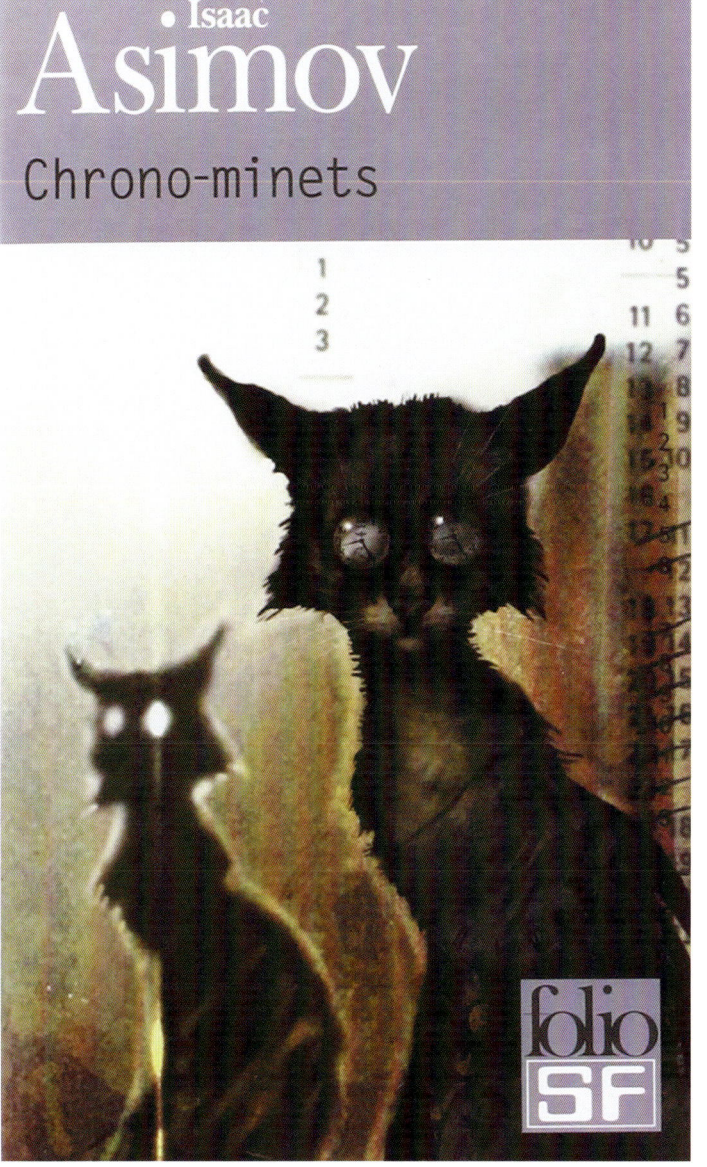

SPEC SHEET

WORK: "Time Pussy."
CREATOR: Isaac Asimov.
FIRST PUBLISHED: December 7, 1941.

PUBLISHER: Various publishers.
CATS' NAMES AND ROLE IN THE WORK: Unnamed time pussies, the four-dimensional extraterrestrial companions of space miners.

Fritz Leiber and Cats

Fritz Leiber is best known for his fantasy cycle that spawned the sword-and-sorcery genre, Fafhrd and the Gray Mouser, but he has tried his hand at every imaginative genre. And no matter how his works are classified, one animal always haunts his writing.

Many writers have cats, but some are cat writers. In the realm of the imaginary, Fritz Leiber (1910–1992) falls into the second category. A prolific author who wrote constantly from the mid-1930s until his death at the end of the 20th century, he drew heavily on his daily life and his surroundings to create his stories and characters. He and his first wife, Jonquil, had many cats, both male and female, pedigree and alley cats, until her death in 1969. And they inspired a lot of his characters, be they domestic cats, feline aliens, or human beings borrowing some of their characteristics from the animals. He himself inspired other authors to write certain characters or cat stories.

The Gray Mouser in the Fafhrd and the Gray Mouser Series

Fafhrd and the Gray Mouser is a collection of short stories published from 1939 onward in seven volumes (*Swords and Deviltry*, *Swords Against Death*, *Swords in the Mist*, *Swords Against Wizardry*, *The Swords of Lankhmar*, *Swords and Ice Magic*, and *The Knight and Knave of Swords*). Set entirely in the fantasy world of Nehwon (literally "no when" backwards), these stories feature two characters so diametrically opposed to each other that they have become archetypes of the genre and have since spread to role-playing and video games: Fafhrd,

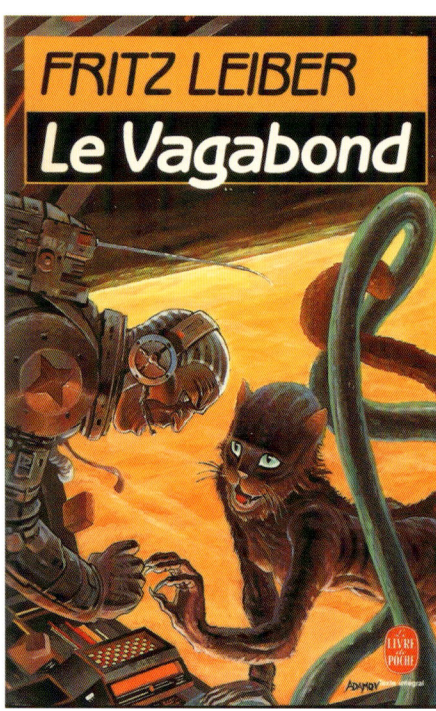

the great barbarian warrior, and the Gray Mouser, a cunning little thief skilled with sword and magic. The latter, who would be at the origin of game classes such as the thief, the mage, and sometimes the demonist or necromancer in some of the short stories, is the one most inspired by the cat. They even share the same predatory nickname: "mouser." The Gray Mouser is a pure product of the city (in this case Lankhmar) and its alleyways. His strengths? Discretion, agility, and an uncanny talent for thievery. Weaknesses? He's a lady's man and will fall for the first face that gives him the slightest hope, but he's also rather lazy, fond of gossip, and devious enough to trick the naivest of opponents with his fine words and manners. All attributes that popular wisdom attributes to house cats. It's worth noting that, in addition to animals, the Gray Mouser was inspired by another fantasy writer and friend of Fritz Leiber, Harry Otto Fischer, who

co-wrote the short story in the cycle entitled "The Lords of Quarmall."

Tigerishka in *The Wanderer*

Published in 1964 and winner of a Hugo Award the following year, *The Wanderer* is a novel set in the twenty-first century, with the Cold War between the USSR and the United States still raging. A roving star, the Wanderer, approaches the Earth and pushes the Moon out of its orbit, generating an immeasurable number of climatic catastrophes. Paul Hagbolt and his cat Miaow are rescued from the waves during a tidal wave by a humanoid feline, Tigerishka. Clearly of the feminine gender and appealing to the tastes of male *Homo sapiens*, Tigerishka comes from the Wanderer. The alien then tries, unsuccessfully, to communicate telepathically with the cat, mistaking it for the most evolved life-form, like on her planet, before she realizes her mistake and admits that the lecherous monkey accompanying her, Paul, is sentient. She then explains to him the origin of the Wanderer and the reason for its presence in the area: to replenish its energy before setting off again. Tigerishka is the archetypal sexy cat-woman, even though her seduction is unintentional and she's rather disgusted by the advances she receives.

Lucky in *The Green Millennium*

Like the adventures of the cat Gummitch and many other Fritz Leiber stories featuring felines, *The Green Millennium* is a psychedelic novel written in 1953, just after World War II and just as tensions between the two blocs were leading to the Korean War. Fritz Leiber, a staunch pacifist, projects himself into a twenty-first century that bears little resemblance to our own. In a world where robotization has forced many people out of work, and in a city built in successive layers, protagonist Phil Gish is daydreaming while contemplating his neighbors when a green cat, quickly named Lucky, enters his apartment. The man goes from depressed and shy to cheerful and self-confident whenever the cat is with him. He even confronts a gang of wrestlers and mobsters and, once the cat has disappeared, finds himself entangled with the mafia, the US government, a strange cult, and an odd psychoanalyst. And why does his neighbor look like a female version of a faun when she undresses? This story leads its reader, like its protagonist, through an endless succession of improbable situations, before concluding with a finale befitting a midnight movie. And the cat? Green he is, green he stays, but he's healthy and works miracles on all the characters in the story, improving the odds in their favor and inciting them to non-violence and benevolence.

Gummitch the Cat

Gummitch is a kitten, then an adult cat, who would be the subject of five different short stories ("Space-Time for Springers," "Kreativity for Kats," "Cat's

GRAND MASTER OF SCIENCE FICTION
FRITZ LEIBER
THE GREEN MILLENNIUM

Cradle," "The Cat Hotel," and "Thrice the Brinded Cat"). With an IQ of 160, he dreams of becoming human by drinking coffee. While some of these short stories have little to do with fantasy, apart from being told from the cat's point of view, others, such as "The Cat Hotel" and "Thrice the Brinded Cat," are full of it. They also deal with one of the author's favorite themes, female witchcraft, and associate cats with magical powers. In these two stories, cats are the "good" witch's pets, while the antagonists have other animals as pets (a toad, a rabbit,

and a hamster, all black). These are also some of Fritz Leiber's most personal short stories, in which he and his wife of the time are embodied as Old Horsemeat and Kitty-Come-Here, the human couple who take in Gummitch. Like Jonquil Leiber, Kitty-Come-Here is a Welsh woman exiled in the United States, and Old Horsemeat is a writer and former theater artist like Fritz himself. In writing these short stories from the perspective of a cat, Fritz Leiber takes a disillusioned yet affectionate look at a certain period in American history and tries his hand at a variety of literary genres.

Cats will be present, and not always in a favorable light, in Fritz Leiber's other texts, whether as protagonists as in "Ship of Shadows," "Cat Three," and "The Bump," or as accessories and secondary characters in his other stories, when they don't inspire certain vamps like the creature of "Gold, Black and Silver." 🐾

Cat the Psion

Cat, the protagonist in Joan D. Vinge's science-fiction series, has few outward feline characteristics. However, his behavior and relationships with the other characters are similar to those of an alley cat.

A young mixed-race orphan, Cat would look like any other puny human if he didn't have two straight pupils splitting his green eyes vertically, like those of a cat. That's how he got his nickname. He's half human and half Hydran, a humanoid extraterrestrial race endowed with the full range of classic psychic powers: telepathy, telekinesis, teleportation, prescience. These are the same powers that many legends attribute to domestic cats, thanks to their deep gaze and ability to flee danger before humans detect it, to walk lightly at will and, conversely, to knock over objects they dislike. A peaceful race thanks to the mental communion imposed by their talents, Hydrans were soon colonized and almost exterminated by humans. Rare mixed-race individuals like Cat and anyone else displaying psychic gifts are therefore exploited and suffer from racism.

An orphan surviving in a ghetto by raiding and fighting like a pure wildcat, he is "taken in" because of his telepathic talents and manipulated to serve various corporations over the course of the stories. Alas, he will emerge mentally "castrated," unable to open his mind to others, leading to his rejection by the two peoples he comes from, who see him as a traitor, each for opposite reasons. In the very structure of the novels, especially the first two, the comparison between Cat and a feral cat is obvious. He's successively abandoned and then taken in, only to be rejected again until he finds (or creates) a home of his own. 🐾

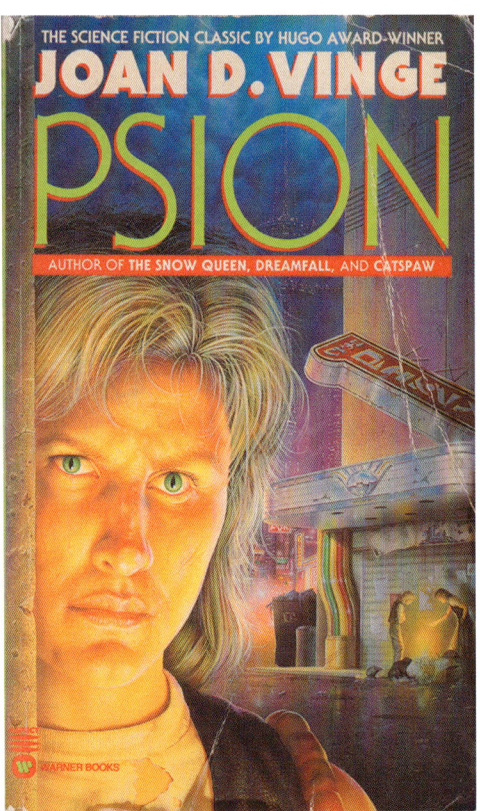

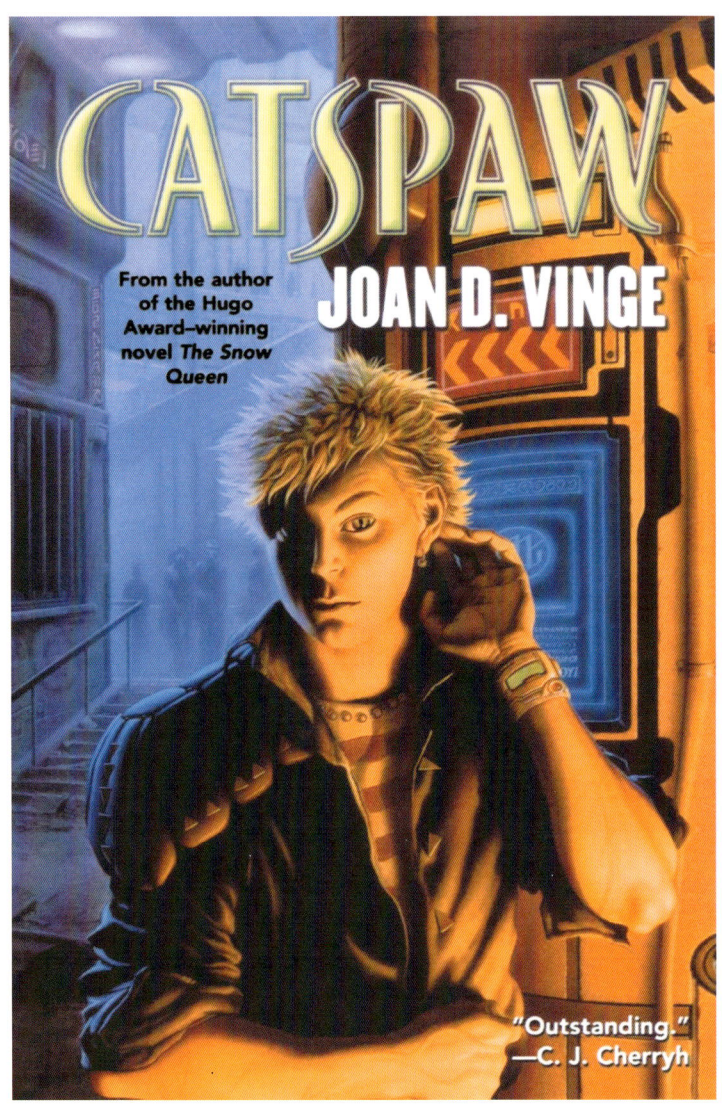

"Outstanding."
—C. J. Cherryh

Bernard Werber's Cat Trilogy

While he made his name with a trilogy about ants, the French writer aims to tell the story of civilization with one about cats. In a post-apocalyptic world, our feline companions are the only hope beyond immediate survival.

After a detour into the world of angels and gods, Bernard Werber is using the animal world again to talk about humanity. While he first made a name for himself with ants, the social insects that were the subject of his first trilogy, cats have been the focus of his attention since 2016. Through his trilogy—*Demain les chats* [*Tomorrow the Cats*], *Sa Majesté des chats* [*Her Majesty of the Cats*], and *La Planète des chats* [*The Planet of the Cats*]—he offers a rather dark vision of our future but uses felines and their various qualities as symbols of hope and renewal.

It all begins with *Demain les chats*, set in Paris. There, in Montmartre, live two cats: Bastet, the narrator who wishes to better communicate with and understand humans, and her balcony neighbor, Pythagore, a laboratory cat with a USB plug at the top of his skull that allows him to connect to the internet. When global warming and revolt bring down human civilization,

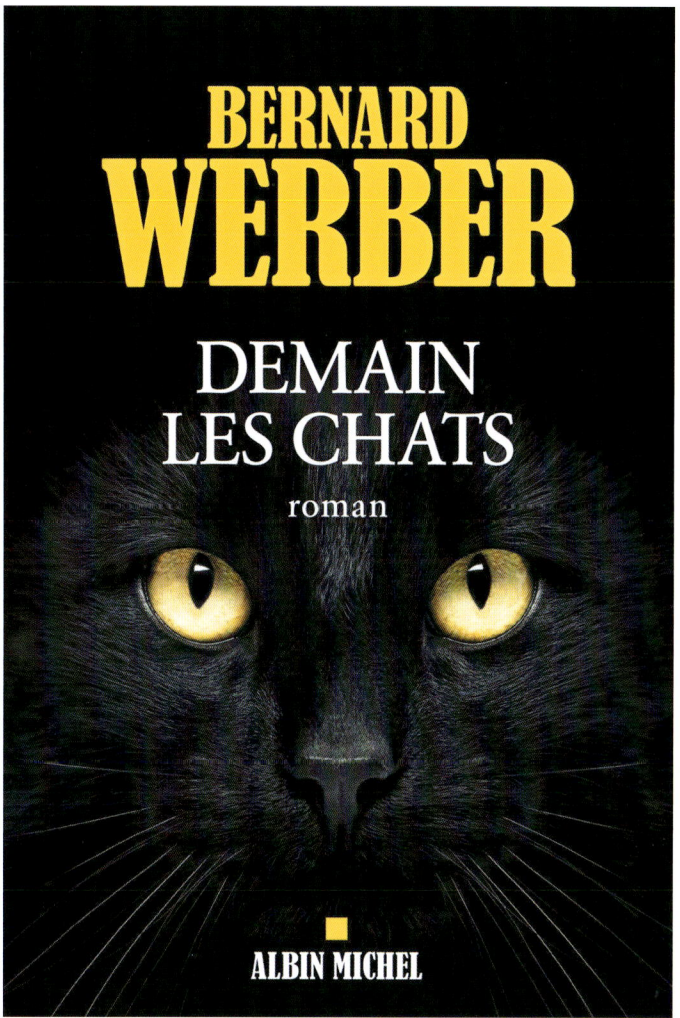

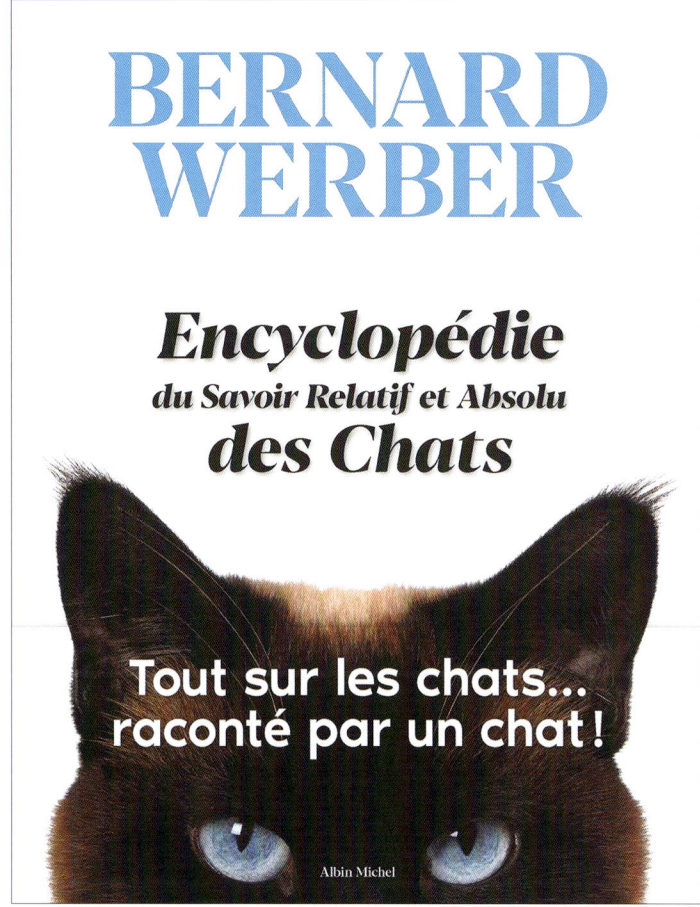

the plague returns, carried by rats who intend to impose themselves as the new dominant species. But resistance is growing, thanks to the collaboration between the cats and some of their surviving human "slaves."

The second volume, *Sa Majesté des chats*, sees Bastet attempt to lay the foundations of a new civilization in the image of the mixed human/cat community she, her human servant Nathalie, and Pythagore have created in the heart of Paris. To achieve this, she has to assimilate and recreate three purely human concepts: humor, love, and art. For an arrogant cat who dreams of being a queen, this is no easy task. Finally, the last leg of the journey, *La Planète des chats*, sees her cross the Atlantic at the head of her little group to put an end once and for all to the rats' supremacy.

As is often the case with Bernard Werber, who was once a science journalist, the story is interspersed with philosophical and historical considerations and provides an opportunity to slip in anecdotes that are a priori unrelated to the story (such as knowing that a surgeon operated on himself for appendicitis in 1921). These anecdotes are the stuff of popular science and will make even the most scientifically and historically literate readers roll their eyes at the liberties taken by the author. They can nevertheless serve as an entry point for those who want to know more about cats and civilization. Incidentally, the author has published a feline version of his *Encyclopédie du savoir relatif et absolu* [*Encyclopedia of Relative and Absolute Knowledge*] devoted to cats in 2019, using the other hero of his trilogy, Pythagore, as narrator.

Speaking of Pythagore, this Siamese cat is a former laboratory animal who has had a USB plug implanted in his head, which allows him to surf the internet and thus access human knowledge. This point is one of the countless moments in the story in which the reader should suspend disbelief—the same applies to the telepathic communication between Bastet and the various animals or the human shaman—but this

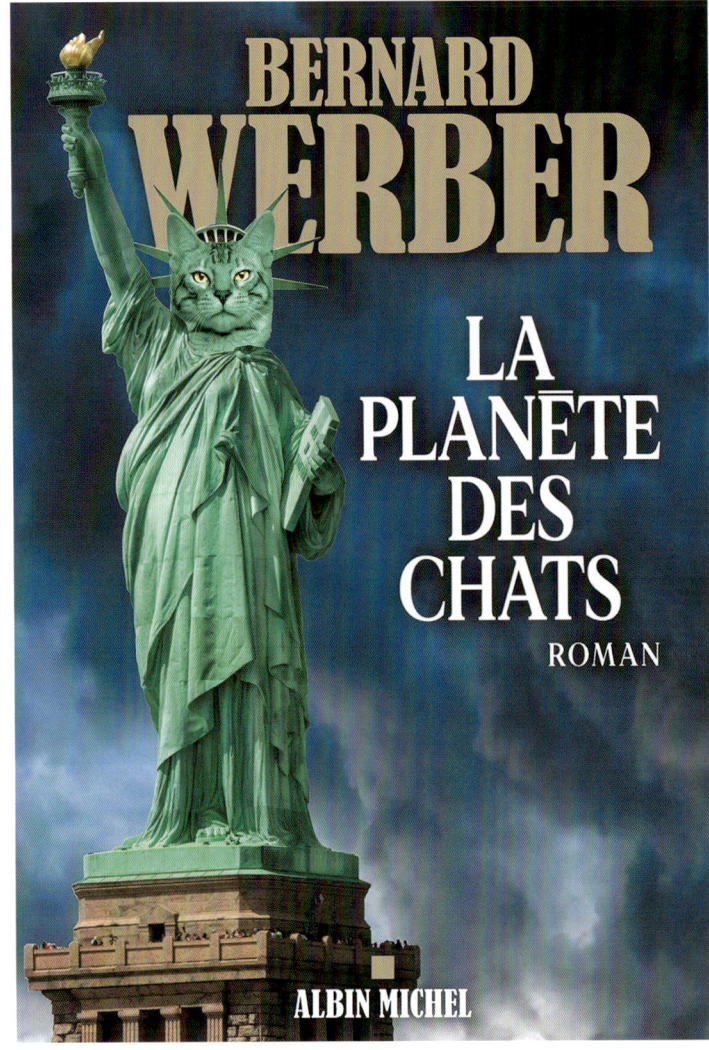

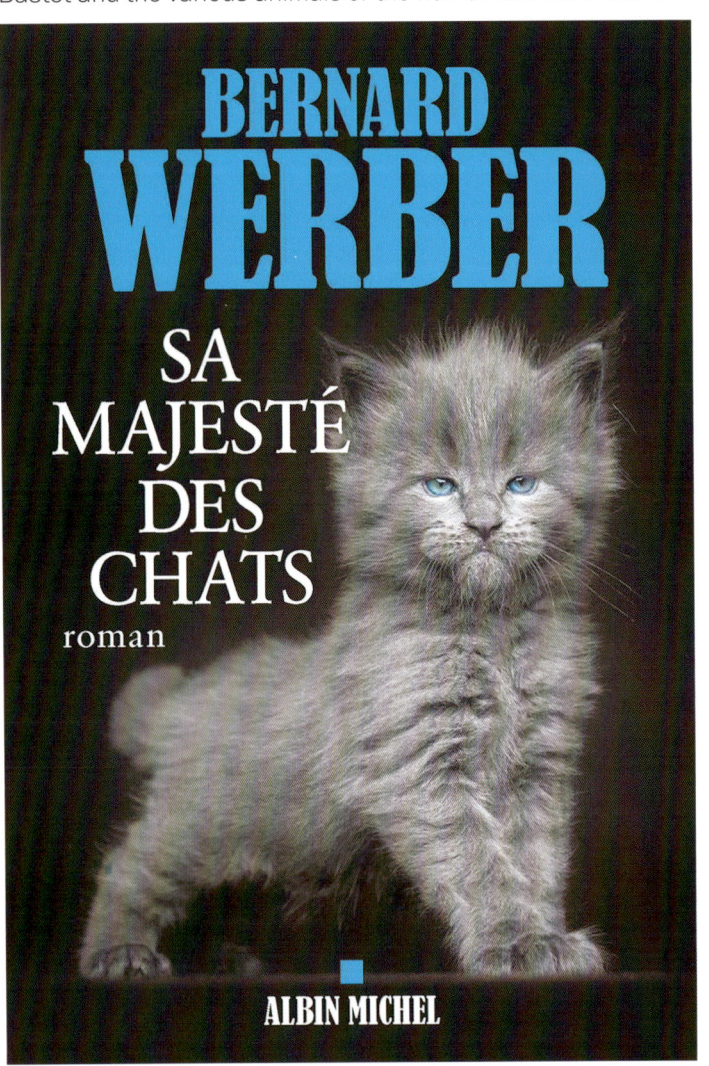

trick allows him to be used as a conduit for knowledge, and a shadowy adviser to move the story forward. It also allows us to present a darker side of the relationship between cats and humans: Even in the twenty-first century, when they seem to be cherished and pampered house pets, cats don't always have it easy with humans. Some are hunted for their meat and fur in Europe (the consumption of cat meat is legal in Switzerland, even if its sale is forbidden[1]), and others, like dogs, rabbits, and other pet species or monkeys, are used as guinea pigs in laboratories, for experiments of varying degrees of usefulness to human survival. Pythagore thus serves as a mirror to question the reader on the validity of certain practices, and to remind us that not everything is rosy in the relationship between cats and humans. In a story based on a utopian fusion between cat and human civilization, this is a necessary point before letting the reader's imagination run wild. For Bernard Werber, "Using animals to talk about people is probably the only valid method.

---

[1] https://www.fedlex.admin.ch/eli/cc/2005/801/fr

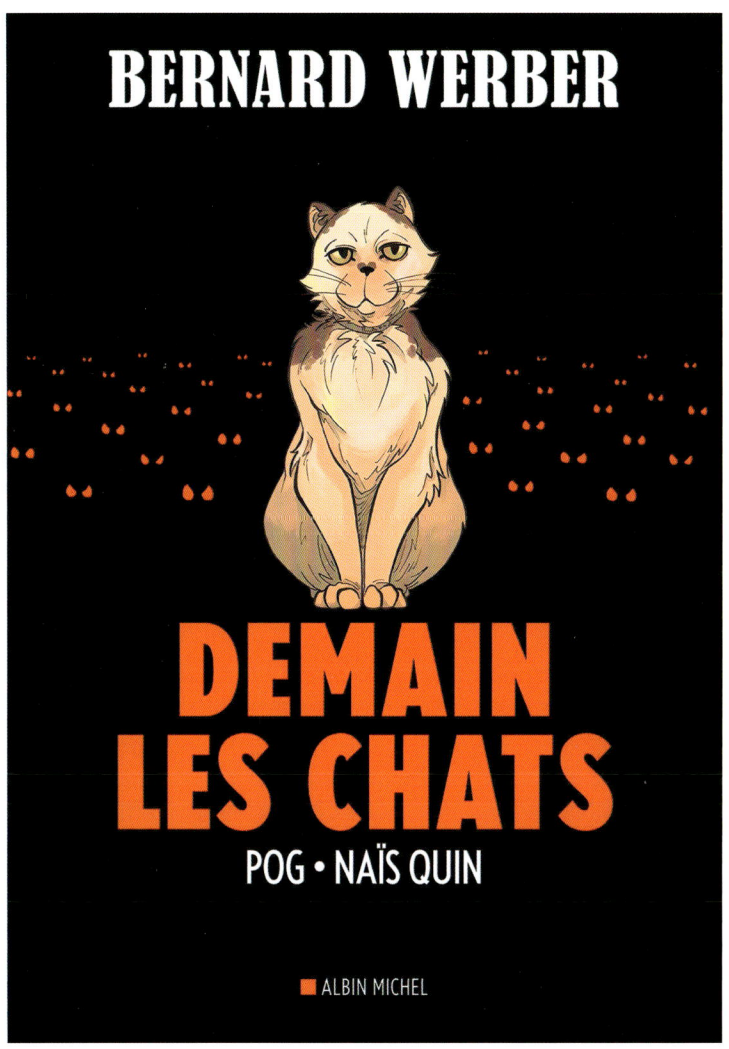

BERNARD WERBER

DEMAIN LES CHATS

POG • NAÏS QUIN

■ ALBIN MICHEL

[I'm] an absolute fan of La Fontaine, whose fables delivered political messages under the tyrannical reign of Louis XIV. If [I had to] sum up [my] work, [I'd say] it consists in thinking about the future, about the various possible scenarios." Pythagore, Bastet, and the others are his new messengers. 🐾

SPEC SHEET

WORKS: The Cats trilogy: *Demain les chats* [*Tomorrow the Cats*] (2016), *Sa Majesté des chats* [*Her Majesty of the Cats*] (2019), *La Planète des chats* [*The Planet of the Cats*] (2020). Comic book adaptation of *Demain les chats* by Pog and Naïs Ouin, released in 2021.
CREATOR: Bernard Werber.
DATE CREATED: First volume released on October 3, 2016.
PUBLISHER: Albin Michel (and Livre de Poche for the first two volumes). Available in print and digital. The novels are currently only available in French.
CATS' NAMES AND ROLE IN THE WORK: Bastet, a Persian cat and the heroine of the trilogy. Pythagore, a Siamese cat and former laboratory animal who acts as an interface between cats and human knowledge.

Nimitz

Of all the alien creatures based on cats, the treecats invented by David Weber are among the most striking. The best known of these is the cat that belongs to his heroine, Honor Harrington.

How do you make your hero endearing in a military sci-fi series? Give them a furry or feathered companion, a little smarter than the basic pet, but with whom conventional communication isn't intuitive. This principle gave rise to Chewbacca and the Ewoks in the *Star Wars* universe, and the genetically modified one-armed penguin Pen Pen in *Neon Genesis Evangelion*. And in genre literature, it gave us Nimitz, the treecat linked to Honor Harrington, the heroine of fourteen novels and a multitude of short stories. What's a treecat? In the Honorverse, it's a protected intelligent species native to the planet Sphinx. This species is the answer to the fantasies and nightmares of all humans living with cats: What if our favorite pets had hands and could communicate with us? Treecats look like ordinary

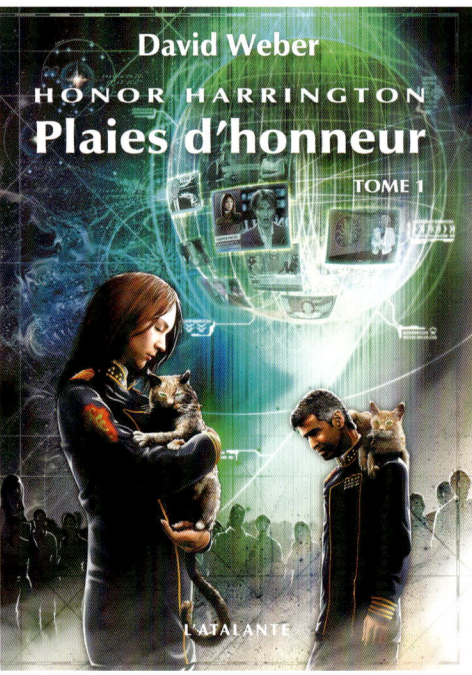

cats (large ones, like Maine Coons or Norwegian Forest Cats), but they have a third pair of limbs. The first two pairs serve as arms, with three-toed hands, including opposable thumbs. Individuals of this species communicate with each other by telepathy, the soul voice, and with humans by empathy and sending visual flashes. Nimitz is a treecat living on Honor's home world who has bonded with her (an interspecies relationship as strong as marriage, but without the carnal element) and accompanies her on her adventures. In addition to his role, like Pen Pen's, as comic relief (with his love of celery, his bad manners, and his reflections), he sometimes takes center stage and proves himself gifted at piloting and diplomacy. 🐾

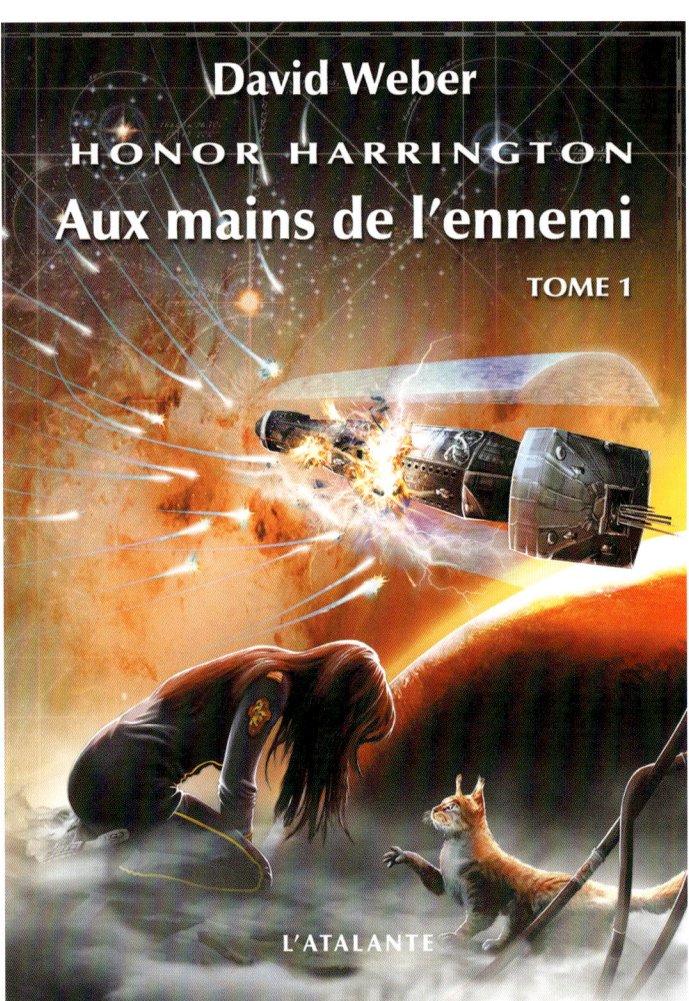

SPEC SHEET

CAT'S NAME: Nimitz to Honor Harrington, Laughs Brightly among his own kind.

WORKS: The Honor Harrington Saga, a military science-fiction series.

CREATOR: David Weber.

DATE CREATED: 1993 (he appears in the first novel, *On Basilisk Station*).

PUBLISHER: Baen.

CAT'S CHARACTERISTICS: Sixty-five-centimeter-long treecat with a cream-and-gray coat and bright green eyes. Companion to Honor Harrington, whom he adopted.

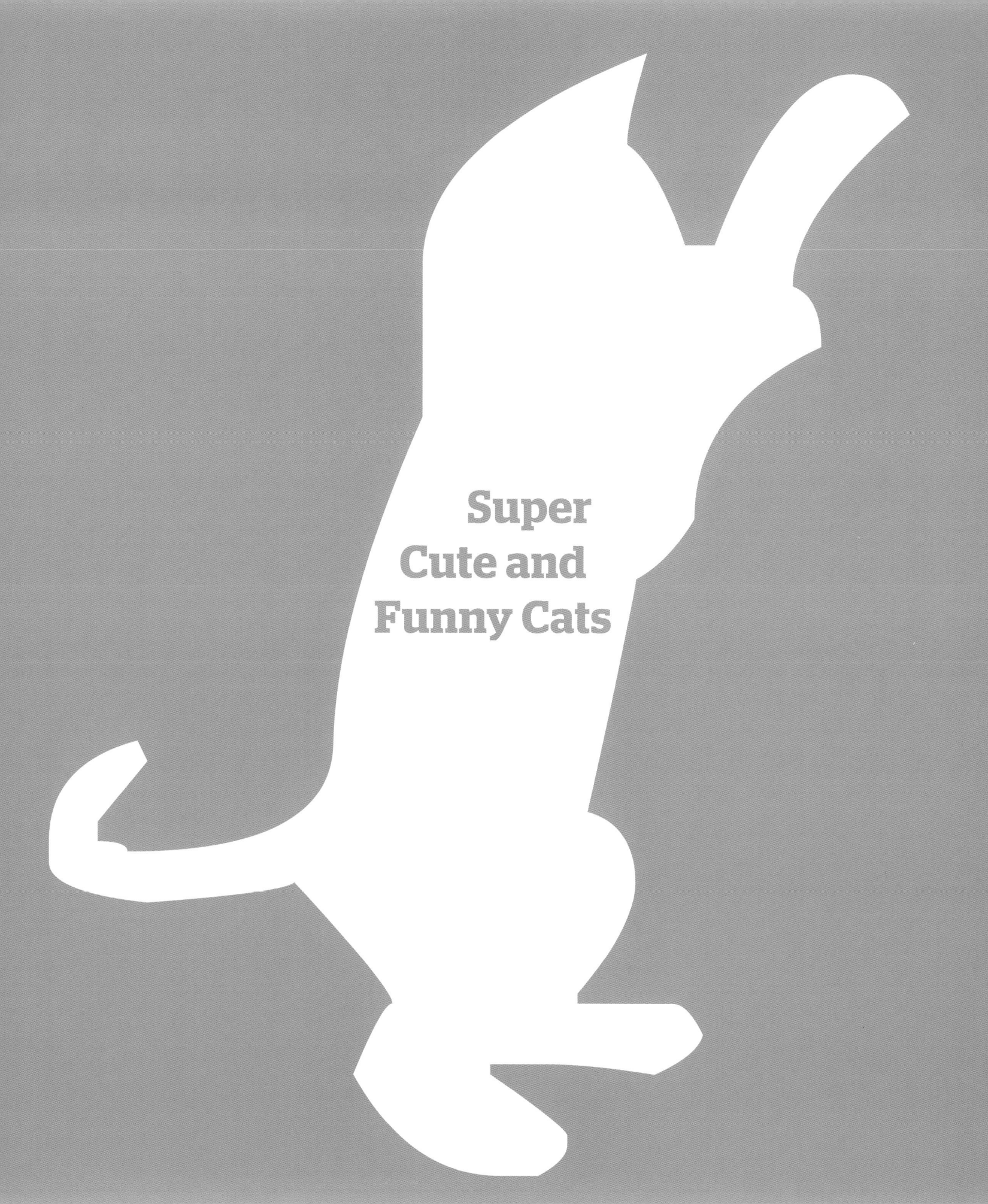

Super
Cute and
Funny Cats

Super Cute and Funny Cats

Cats are all over the internet in videos, memes, photos, and more. Why and how? Two major factors come into play: their kawaii *aspect and their great comic potential.*

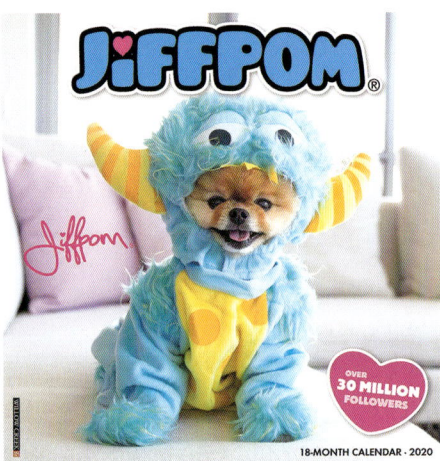

Felines are often the stars of memes and viral videos. They are regularly referred to as the kings of the internet. However, Google searches for the word "dog" far outnumber those for "cat." So, technically, the cat isn't in pole position according to this criterion. Internationally, the most popular animal is Jiffpom, a Pomeranian dog with more than ten million Instagram followers. Animals in general attract human attention on the internet, including rabbits, hedgehogs, and even raccoons. What's the reason for so much success? Undoubtedly the universal nature of animal language. The antics of our companions, whether carnivores or rodents, bring us together and reach every audience, whatever their language.

Are Cats the Kings of the Internet?

Animals, and therefore cats, provide videos with burlesque characteristics. Their comedy is often physical. The content is inexpensive in the digital age, as everyone has access to a high-quality camera in their phone. The matching algorithms used by modern technology also favor the consumption,[1] and therefore the production, of these types of photos and videos.

Whatever the photo or video content, anthropological projection can explain such enthusiasm, especially when it comes to memes. Cats are humanized by their worst faults: laziness, gluttony, and even malice.

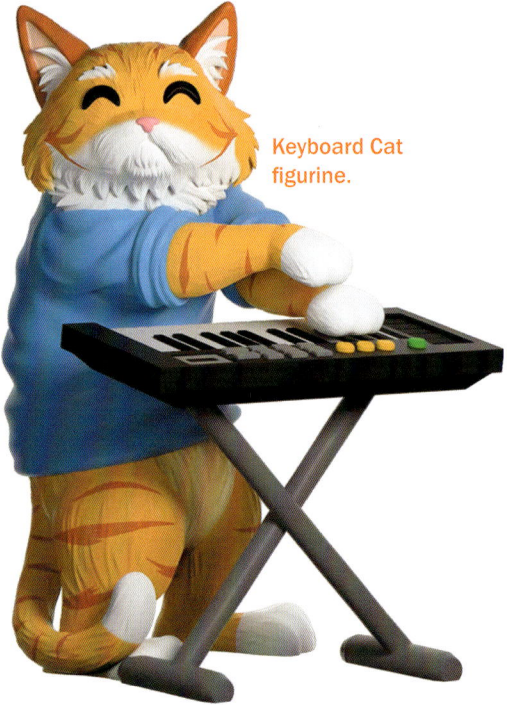

Keyboard Cat figurine.

The content can vary, from immortalizing an unusual action such as the heroism of a rescue, to the cowardice of a cat who is startled by a cucumber, or a cat who talks, to more commonplace events such as a spectacular fall.

The bizarre is also part of the equation, as in the case of Keyboard Cat, a cat playing the piano. The 1984 video went viral when it was posted online in 2004, with more than sixty-two million views.

Cats and Japan: *Kawaii* Culture

Japan has played a key role in the development of international pop culture, whether through technology, Japanimation, or *kawaii* culture in general. The term literally means "cute" and implies youth and innocence, often defining a sparkling, fluorescent aesthetic. Cats are extremely present in Japanese culture, both in legends (see p. 131) and in modern fiction. There are eleven cat islands where felines are so numerous that they are part of the local culture, demonstrating the Japanese attachment to the creatures. However, the development of *kawaii* culture in the 1970s popularized a certain vision of cats in Japan, with the creation of characters such as Hello Kitty.

While most Western countries experienced periods of youth protest around the same time, with May 68 in France and the anti-segregation movement in the United States, Japanese students also took part in

---

[1] https://www.lesechos.fr/idees-debats/cercle/opinion-les-chats-et-internet-itineraire-dune-conquete-140077

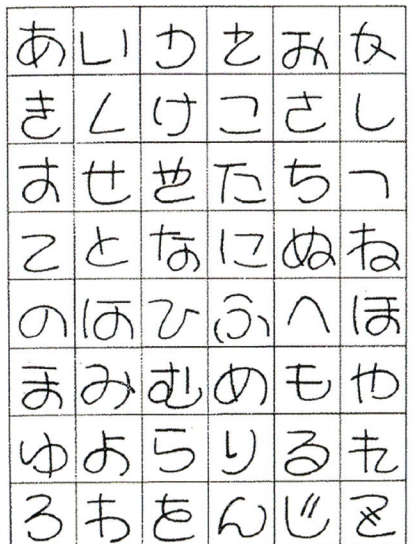

Kitten writing (hiragana).

libertarian demonstrations.[2] At the same time, the new generation rebelled with a more rounded script and the use of *koneko-ji*, or kitten writing.[3] Japanese youth also opposed their rigid society by promoting immature values and skipping school to read manga. This led to the emergence of *kawaii* culture.

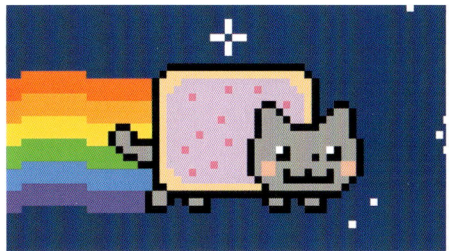

Nyan Cat

The word *kawaii* incorporates a notion of innocence that spread across the country between the 1970s and 1980s. As a result, the *kawaii* cat is almost never endowed with the classic flaws associated with cats in Western works, such as cunning or malice. The *kawaii* aesthetic can be found in Japanese music, fashion, and, of course, manga.[4] The common denominators of these trends are colorful, juvenile aspects and rounded designs.

The Land of the Rising Sun is no stranger to the conquest of the internet by cats, notably with Maru, the star of YouTube Japan with more than eight hundred thousand subscribers. However, the combination of the Japanese love of felines and this culture of cheeky cuteness has contributed to the cat's emergence in pop culture as we know it today, even through memes like Nyan Cat.

The Lolcat Phenomenon

What are lolcats? Quite simply, memes featuring cats. As the name suggests, they're meant to be funny ("lol" stands for "laugh out loud"). Cats are so cute, silky, and soft that they've often been immortalized in photos, and the combination of cat images and funny commentary is by no means a new thing. As early as the 1870s, the English photographer Harry Pointer was selling shots of cats accompanied by jokes, but it was the American Harry Whittier Frees who is considered the father of

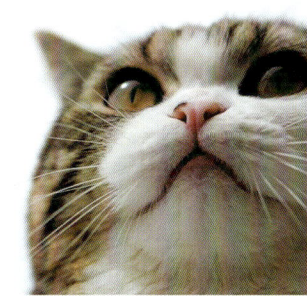

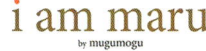

i am maru
by mugumogu

lolcats at the beginning of the twentieth century, with his animal photos. In one shot, a cat disguised as a baby in a highchair asks: "What's delaying my dinner?" The photo "Five O'Clock Tea" immortalized five cats in a box, helping themselves to tea. At the time, the staging around the cat took precedence over the commentary, whose humor was more a redundancy than a genuine addition to the scene. Modern lolcats may feature cats in staged situations, perhaps with costumes or props. However, cats are facetious and unpredictable animals that often get themselves into comic situations. This is the case with the "Ceiling Cat" memes, which show cats looking through a hole in the ceiling. They are often subtitled with a comment that includes "Ceiling Cat is watching you . . . " The cat may be making a face, looking like it's smiling, or sleeping in an unlikely position, but it's the commentary that prevails in most memes. The projection of human emotions onto the cat's face can also be a source of comedy. Anthropomorphism is at the root of success stories such as Grumpy Cat.

Lolcats have been around since the early 2000s on discussion forums, and more specifically on 4chan, and began to become an internet phenomenon[5] long before social media took off. As for the expression "lolcat," it wasn't used until 2006. There's a pattern in the way lolcats are presented. For example, the commentary is often in Arial or Impact font, in white with a black outline. It may contain spelling mistakes when the words are supposedly spoken by the cat. 🐾

[2] https://www.geo.fr/histoire/1968-au-japon-comme-un-tremblement-de-terre-185811
[3] https://kdochats.com/mode-kawaii-histoire/
[4] https://universdujapon.com/blogs/japon/que-veux-dire-kawaii
[5] https://www.lepoint.fr/insolite/journee-du-chat-les-felins-envahissent-la-toile-08-08-2016-2059738_48.php

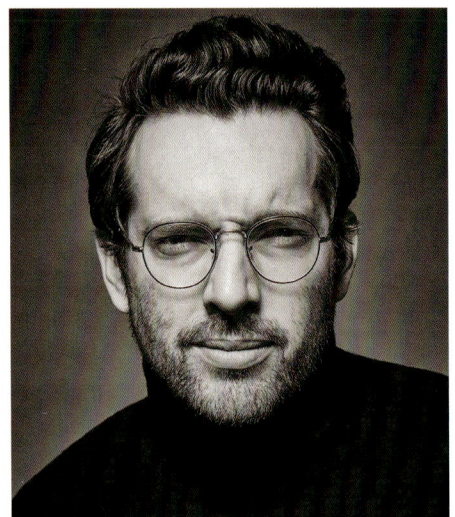

Fabien Loszach, Sociologist

"Geeks are the kings of the internet, and they love cats."

Fabien Loszach is an expert in digital strategy and web culture. When he's not teaching at the Université de Sherbrooke or the Université de Québec in Montreal, he writes about creativity and the internet, notably in WIKI, GIF & LSD: L'encyclopédie anecdotique du web. *And he tells us why cats seem to dominate the internet.*

Do you think cats are the kings of the internet?

Yes, because they've always been the geek's companions. Cats are solitary, independent, home-loving animals who don't go out and stay in their apartments, a bit like the geek's personality. It's the internet animal, unlike the dog, which is the faithful, almost social animal, whose "socializing" takes place in dog parks. The internet is the cat park. I don't really like going back in time, but cats have had many lives. In Egypt, they were deified. In the Middle Ages,

it was a little more complicated, but Romanticism rehabilitated them a little. There are poems about cats in Baudelaire's *Les Fleurs du Mal*. In the 1870s, with the advent of photography, Harry Pointer took photos of cats[1] that were, in a way, the ancestors of the lolcat. He dressed them up or put them on bicycles. In France, there was the postal worker's almanac. In the 1970s, 1980s, and 1990s, dogs received more public exposure because, unlike cats, they were easier to film. Of course, there were *The Aristocats*, but many films featured dogs, like *Lassie*, *Beethoven*, and *One Hundred and One Dalmatians*. It's easier to have dogs. Cats are getting their revenge on the internet.

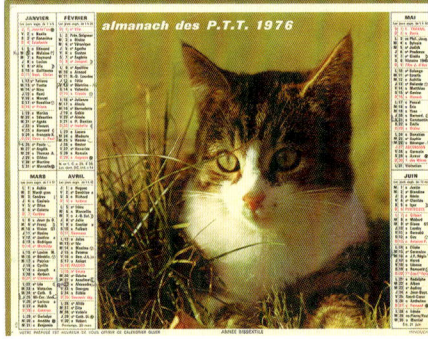

Post Office calendar, 1976.

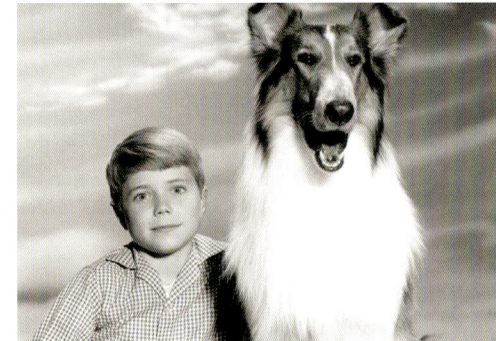

Lassie.

Did 4chan play a significant role in this?

In the 2000s, 4chan became an incubator for a mix of chat culture and internet meme culture. This kind of anonymous forum encouraged creativity. This was synthesized in an event called Caturday, a play on the words "cat" and "Saturday." On Caturday, people posted photos of their cats. Then, little by little, they started adding captions to them. The captions turned into jokes. Cats became part of meme culture and were given the name lolcat, a word made up of "lol" and "cat." From then on, a whole vernacular language would emerge from this culture, from this 4chan potpourri. Certain themes emerged: Surprised Kitty, Ceiling Cat, Limecat, the monorail

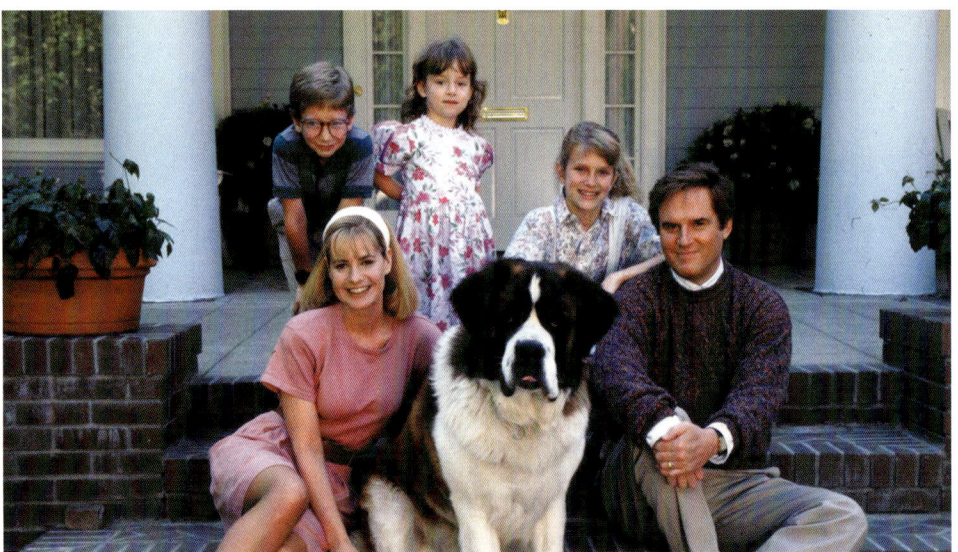

Beethoven.

---

[1] http://photohistory-sussex.co.uk/BTNPointerCats.htm

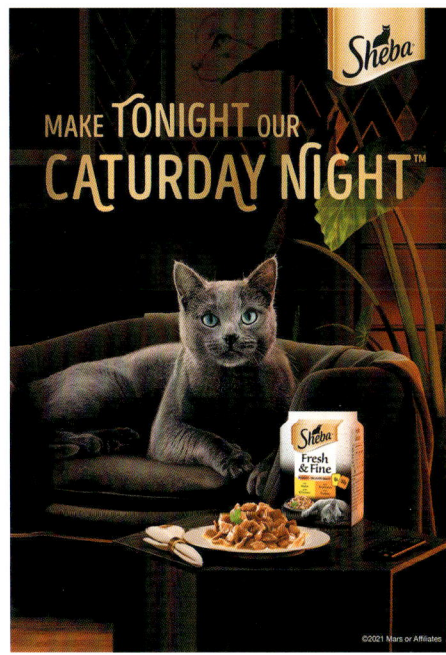

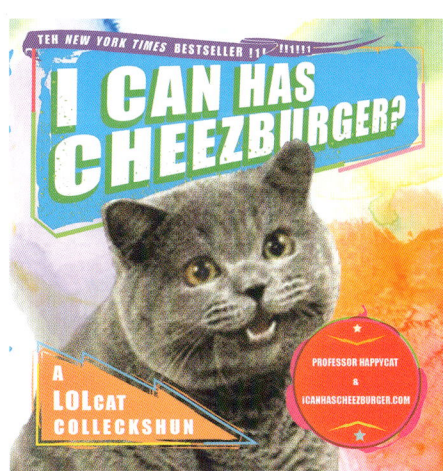

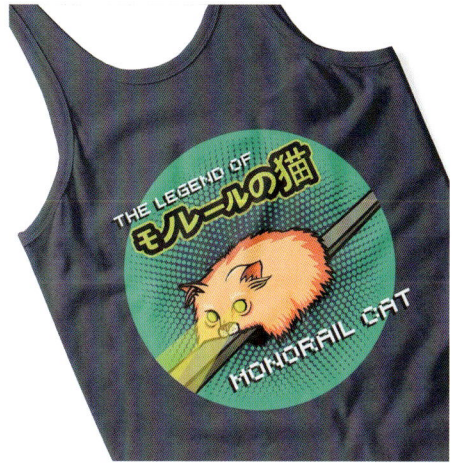

emerged, including the Impossible Frozen Ball Cat and the Impossible Sandwiches. It reached the point that in 2010, the Cat Video Festival was created in Minneapolis. The Cat Video Fest still exists, and it's a bit of a validation. It shows that the internet is creating a form of folklore. There is also a similar thing with dogs (Advice Dog, Cool Dog, Depression Dog), but cats really crystalized it.

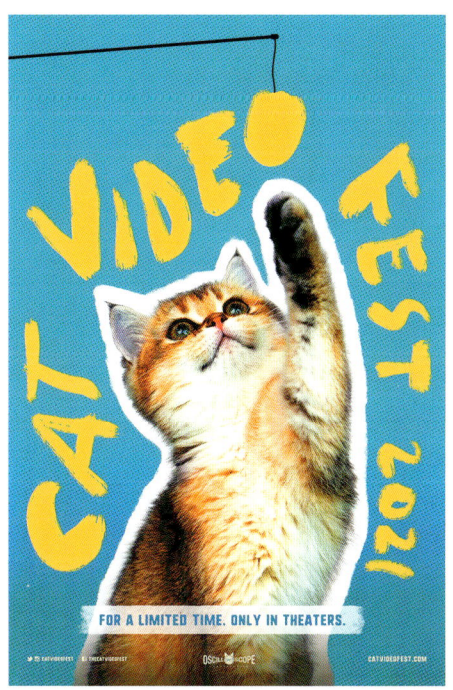

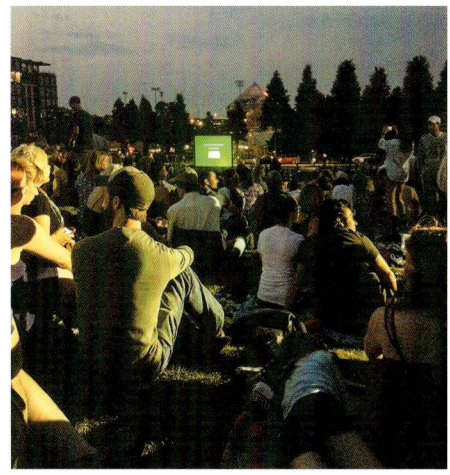

Internet Cat Video Festival, 2012. Photo by Tony Webster.

cat, and many others. At the same time, YouTube appeared, and people started sharing videos of their cats. It was really the first user-generated content platform that allowed everyone to share their own videos online. A video like *The Internet Is Made of Cats* got millions of views. Then came cat blogs like *That Cat Blog*[2] and *I Can Has Cheezburger?*[3] The latter grew so big that they even turned it into books sold in inner-city hipster stores. Between 2005 and 2010, a whole lolcat culture emerged. Always the same model: a photo of a cat, it was cute, it was funny, and then there was a caption. A whole range of forms

Why are they the kings of the internet?

I think there's really something about humor with cats. The emphasis is on the easy life they lead, unlike their masters. The Japanese cat, Maru, is a good example. He's a paunchy, lazy cat, and the only thing he knows how to do is run around and get into boxes. The other driving force is what Henri Bergson identified with humor: anthropomorphism. Bergson says that we'll laugh at an animal because we've caught in it a human attitude, a human expression. The lolcat is a hybrid between man and animal. We try to transpose our life into this companion, an animal that is not completely domesticated, that is always a little independent, that has its own life. I met the creators of the lolcat festival at a seminar. They explained that the cat festival was the product of a 4chan culture that, with hindsight, could be described as a little toxic, or at any rate very anonymous, but that in joke culture, cats are a form of humor that is devoid of any cynicism or irony. It's something that's perhaps out of step with a lot of other art forms or other things on the internet, especially today, when the internet has become an ideological battleground between the far right and the far left.

[2] https://www.thatcatblog.com/
[3] https://icanhas.cheezburger.com/

Why, with all the content on the internet, do we look at things that are as simple as cats?

I think it's because it's depoliticized. We also use cats because they've become a way of expressing our feelings and moods in something very simple, effective, fast, and that everyone understands. On the other hand, cats also embody the values advocated by our society: freedom, autonomy, individualism. They're at once autonomous, close, semi-domesticated, and can't be controlled. It's something that everyone in our society can embody and identify with. They're the geek's companion because they share the same characteristics. They're independent, asocial, and solitary. They sleep as much as geeks spend time online, in a way. They're low-maintenance, and we might jokingly say that geeks are a bit like that. They never need to get fresh air, much like geeks who stay at home. Cats may not be the kings of the internet, but geeks are. When I was a kid growing up in the countryside, the geek, the person who wore glasses and got good grades, would get slapped on the way out of school before getting on the bus. It was tough; nobody envied them. They were social misfits. In the space of one generation, our generation, they became rock stars. Today, Jeff Bezos, Mark Zuckerberg, and Steve Wozniak have become social role models. As Booba said on one of his last albums, "You can't rob anymore; you have to code. I'm not coding anything; I've got the BEP [vocational diploma]." Even he says that these guys have become stars. Have you ever heard of the cute cat theory?

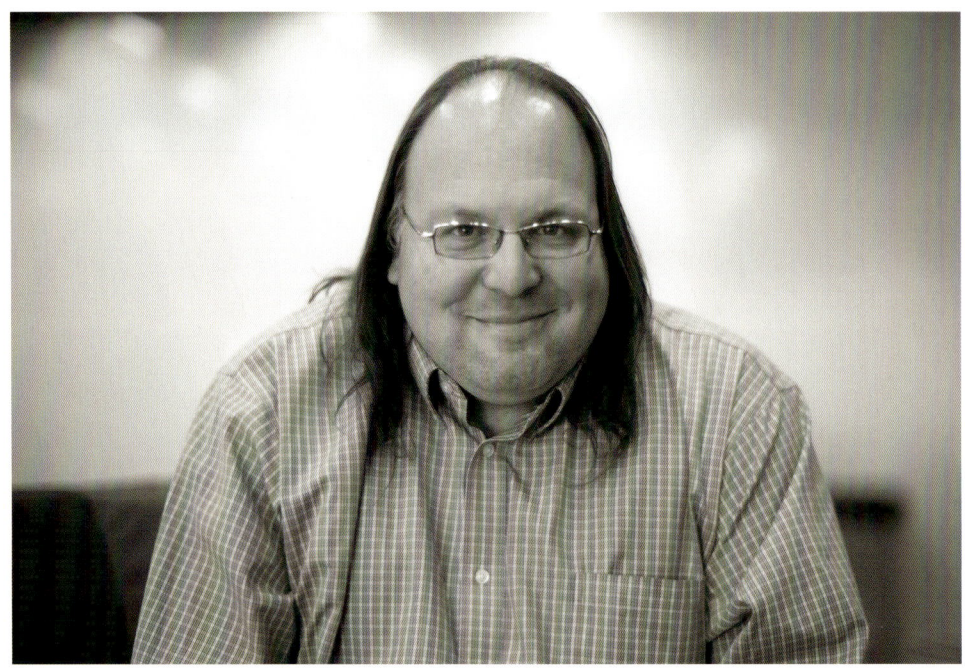

Ethan Zuckerman. Photo by Joi Ito.

No. What is it?

It's a theory developed by Ethan Zuckerman. He says that in the world of technology, there's a form of magical thinking that claims to solve all social and human rights issues through technology. This is what Evgeny Morozov calls "technological solutionism." Technology is going to solve all our problems, whether it's social cohesion or depression. It's going to liberate people and make them more cultured, more autonomous, and so on. It's a bit like the ideology of Silicon Valley. When the Arab Spring broke out in early 2010, *New York Times* columns talked about the Twitter revolution or the Facebook revolution. In his cute cat theory, Ethan Zuckerman says that even if we were to build the best social network that would enable us to organize ourselves in the best possible way to achieve democratic goals, most people would only use the simplest features of this tool and share photos of cute cats. So, the general

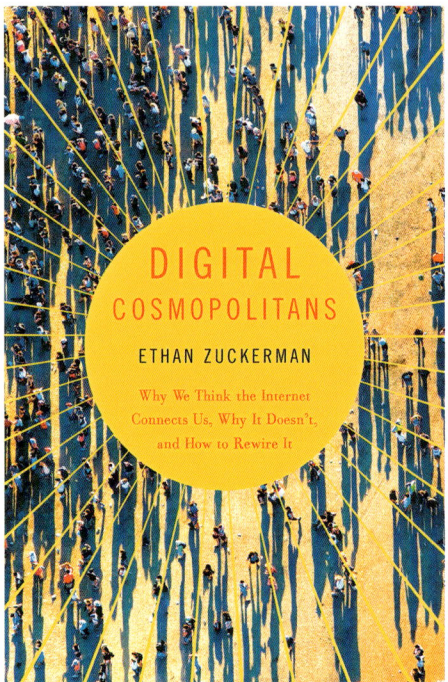

population isn't interested in militant activism. People aren't interested in these big issues. They prefer to use the web for everyday social activities like lolcat distribution. The theory behind lolcat is that you can give people the most beautiful communication tools, and they'll use them for trivial things. When I say "people," I'm obviously including myself.

And yet, dogs dominate Google searches. What's behind the perception that cats dominate the internet?

It's because geeks are the kings of the internet, and they love cats. There are also the effects of what's fashionable. In other words, there's been a lot of talk about lolcat in publications. There are effects of viewpoint, of perspective. As humans, we believe that things are happening.

On Instagram, in particular, certain cats have achieved influencer status. Why is this?

If you have a certain kind of cat, funny and a bit stupid, and you put it on the internet, it will quickly become a hit because, once again, it's easy humor, devoid of any politics, cynicism, or malice. It's a bit like a baby's smile; you just naturally like it. Not all cats can become internet stars. It's the cats that have particular qualities, that already have the basic things that lend themselves to a joke. 🐾

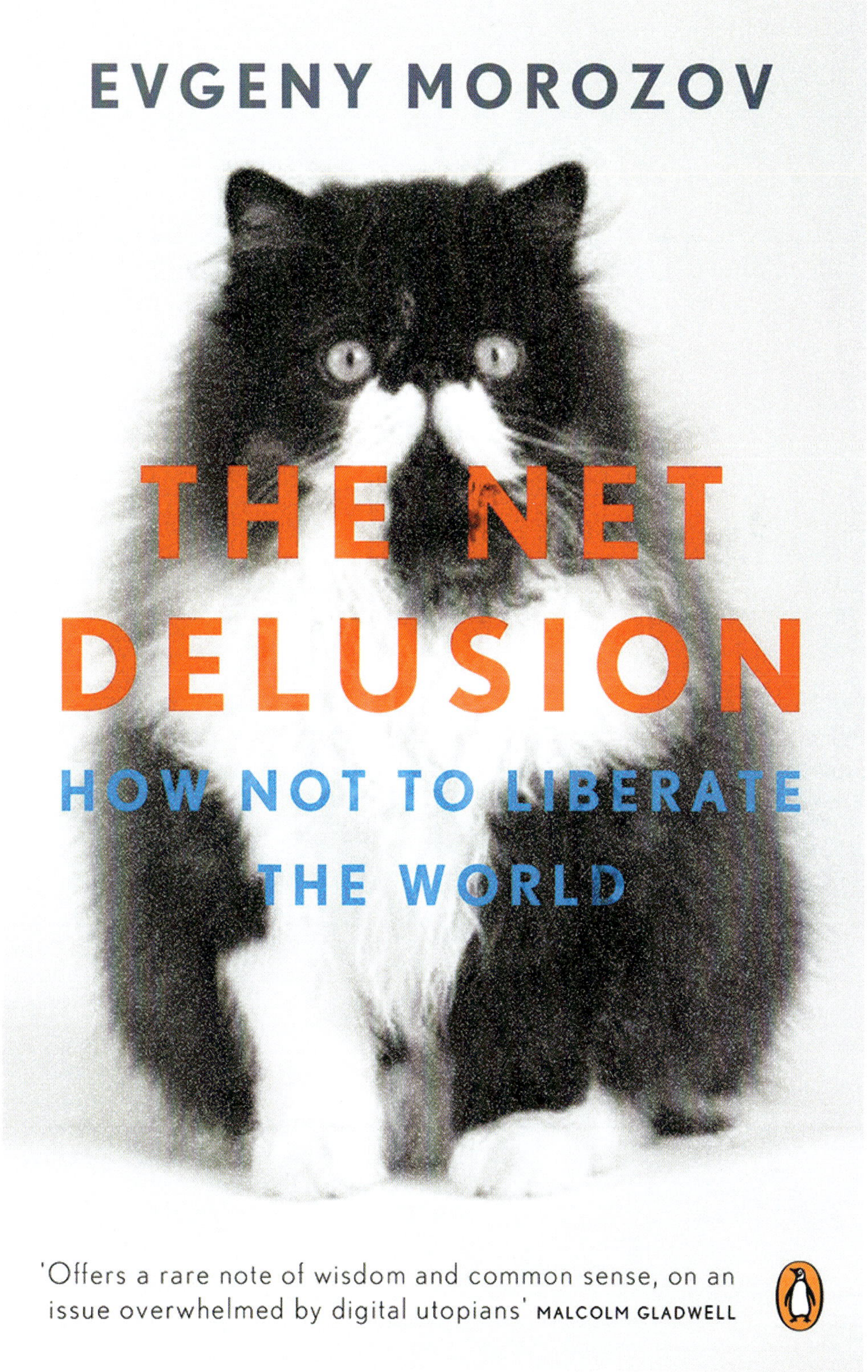

EVGENY MOROZOV

THE NET DELUSION

HOW NOT TO LIBERATE THE WORLD

'Offers a rare note of wisdom and common sense, on an issue overwhelmed by digital utopians' MALCOLM GLADWELL

Nyan Cat

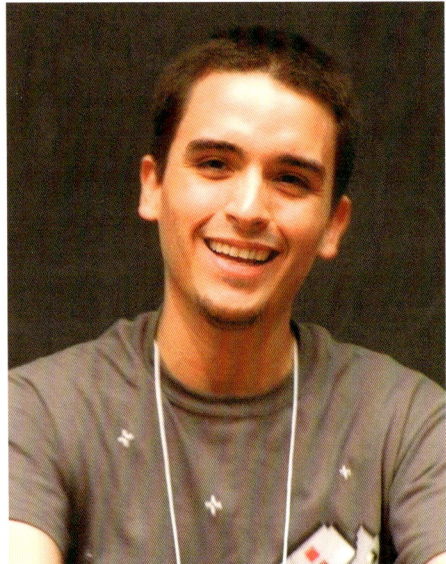

Chris Torres, 2012. Photo by Matt DiGirolamo.

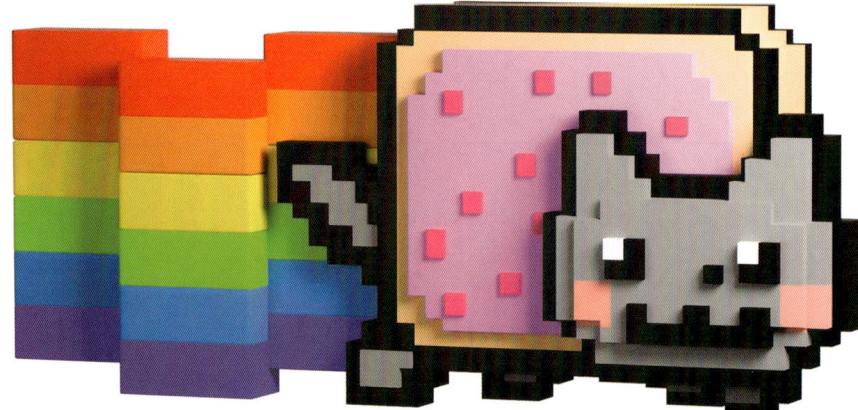

Nyan Cat figurine.

In April 2011, Chris Torres, age 25, was creating comic strips that he published online. He asked his readers to suggest keywords to give him drawing ideas. The words "cat" and "rainbow" came up several times, inspiring him to create the Nyan Cat GIF.[1]

Chris Torres quickly drew his first model of a cat with a Pop-Tart body, flying over a rainbow. He took his inspiration from his gray cat, Marty. He spent the night programming his drawing in 8-bit pixel animation. The deliberately kitsch retro style, flashy rainbow colors, and Pop-Tart were a direct hit, making the GIF go viral. However, it wasn't until Sara June released the GIF, accompanied by the Japanese electro-pop *Nyanyanyanyanyanya!* (literally meaning "meow") that the Nyan Cat caught on. Today, more than 180 million people have seen the video on YouTube.

While Chris Torres is the original author of "Pop-Tart Cat," the music by daniwellP and the association made by Sara June were what created a sensation. However, a legal battle began not between these three, but between Torres, Warner, and 5th Cell in 2013[2] for copyright infringement in the video game *Scribblenauts*. Raising the debate of copyright in a work distributed online and memes in general, lawyers on both sides finally managed to reach an agreement on financial compensation.[3]

In February 2021, an auction was held for the Nyan Cat meme. It was sold for almost $600,000 (300 Ether) on the crypto art platform Foundation.[4] Whereas a GIF is in essence totally reproducible, the sale of the Nyan Cat through the concept of a non-fungible token (NFT) gives a certificate of authenticity like that of an original[5] to its buyer. 🐾

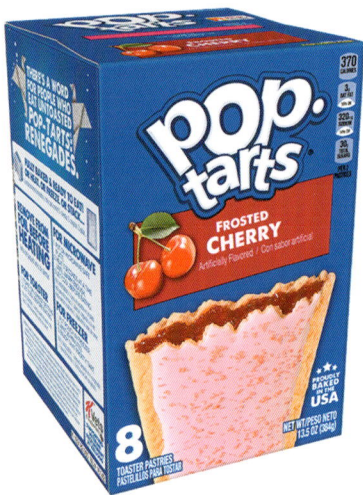

SPEC SHEET

CAT'S NAME: Nyan Cat.
WORK: *Original Nyan Cat*.
CREATORS: Chris Torres, video by Sara June, music by daniwellP.
DATE CREATED: April 2011.
AVAILABILITY: YouTube.
CAT'S CHARACTERISTICS: Gray and pixelated, with a Pop-Tart body. Flying on a rainbow.

[1] https://www.youtube.com/watch?v=AmnmjHqd52E&t=166s
[2] https://scinfolex.com/2013/05/09/le-nyan-cat-appartient-au-public-un-meme-nest-pas-une-marque/
[3] https://www.lemonde.fr/pixels/article/2014/07/09/le-meme-internet-doge-est-devenu-unemarque_4453433_4408996.html
[4] https://korii.slate.fr/biz/non-fongible-token-nft-nyan-cat-500000-dollars-blockchain-possession-memesmarche-art
[5] https://ici.radio-canada.ca/nouvelle/1776627/le-createur-du-nyan-cat-organise-des-encheres-pour-la-ventede-memes-celebres

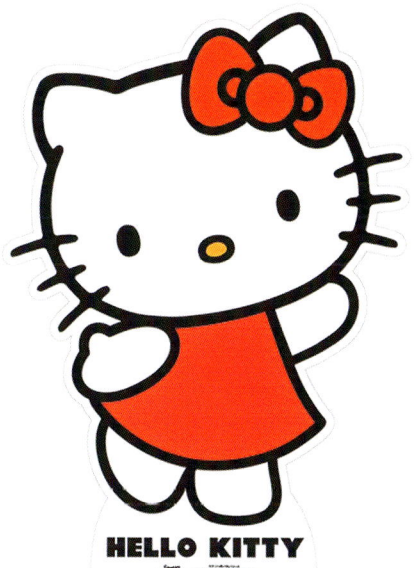

Promotional figure.

A worldwide phenomenon that symbolizes kawaii culture, Hello Kitty is a white cat with a clean, cartoonish design. Recognizable by her lack of mouth and her red bow, she stands upright and wears a variety of costumes to accentuate her cute, childlike side.

History and Urban Myths

Sanrio, a Japanese company specializing in all kinds of products (stationery, clothing, plush toys, etc.), was looking to create a product aimed at teenage girls. To that end, it asked an employee, stylist Yuko Shimizu, to create a design for a small purse. The cat was named "Hello Kitty," recalling the concept of *maneki-neko*, the cats that greet customers and invite them in. The character's creator explains that the name "Kitty" was chosen in reference to one of the cats in Lewis Carroll's novel *Through the Looking Glass*.[1]

A year after the mascot's creation, Yuko Shimizu left Sanrio, but the company continued to use the character's image, creating a story and background for her. Hello Kitty's real name is Kitty White. She lives in London with her parents, her twin sister Mimmy, and her pets, including a cat and a hamster. How can a cat be the owner of a cat? Sanrio answered in 2014 at an exhibition for the fortieth anniversary of its *kawaii* muse: Hello Kitty isn't a cat.[2] She may look like a feline, but she's actually a little girl. The character's lack of a mouth fuels the wildest urban myths. The most widespread is a story linking the mother of a child with cancer to a satanic pact.

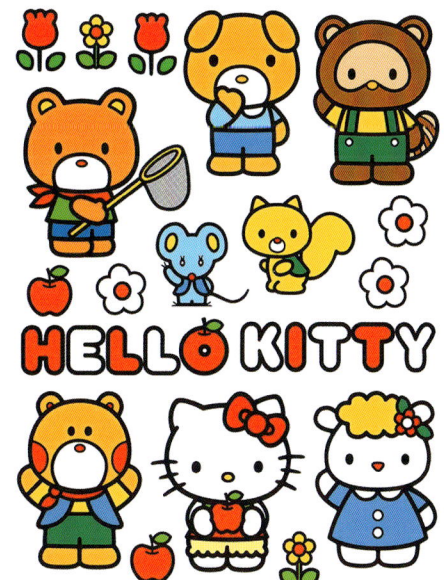

Character stickers.

These stories are obviously untrue, but they are a testament to the notoriety of Sanrio's mascot.

Spin-off Products and Brand

Originally created for a change purse, the design's success led Sanrio to exploit its character extensively on all kinds of objects. Today, the company is present in more than 130 countries and offers more than fifty thousand products featuring its star. The Hello Kitty franchise is now the second most lucrative in the world (behind Pokémon), with $80 billion generated since its creation.[3]

Hello Kitty is suitable for all kinds of merchandising, from textiles and accessories to food and hygiene; nothing escapes her. She's become a social phenomenon and has even found her way into pop culture, with singers such as Micky Green sporting a Hello Kitty guitar and Avril Lavigne dedicating a song to her.

In Japan, the mascot has also been adapted for video games. The first arrived in the 1990s, and since then more than seventy games have been released, with all platforms represented.

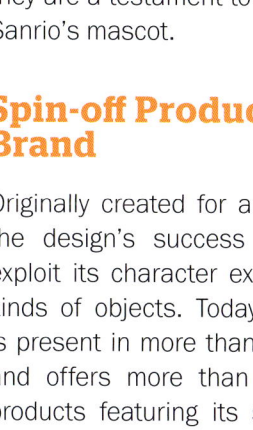

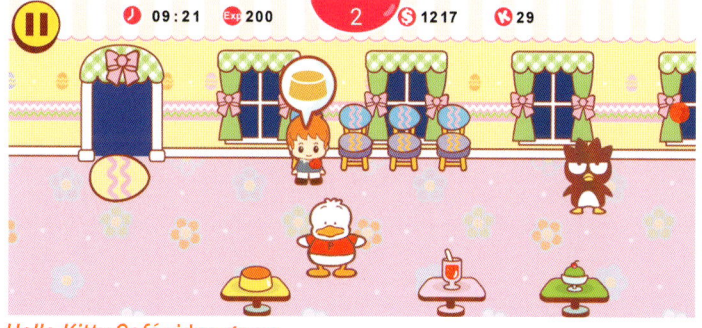

Hello Kitty Café video game.

[1] https://www.dailymotion.com/video/xdvy28
[2] https://www.lci.fr/culture/hello-kitty-na-jamais-ete-un-chat-selon-la-societe-qui-la-commercialise-1555404.html
[3] https://www.allocine.fr/article/fichearticle_gen_carticle=18679562.html

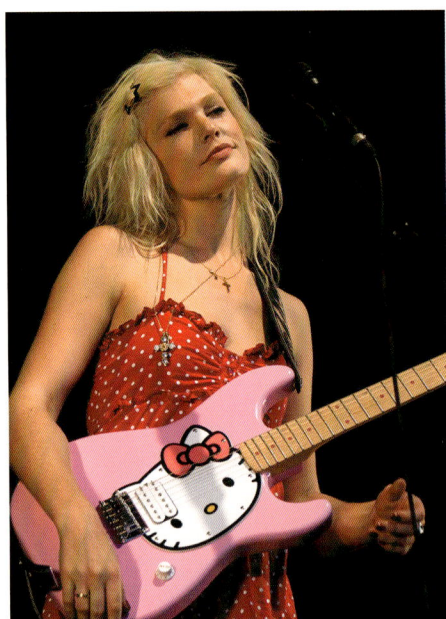

Micky Green, Festival aux Zarbs, Auxerre 2008. Photo by Benoît Derrier.

Animated Series

The first animated series, *Hello Kitty's Furry Tale Theater*, was produced in 1987. This thirteen-episode Japanese-American co-production blends the world of cute plushies with American film culture, with Kitty and her friends performing their version of great films like *King Kong* and *Star Wars*, and fairy tales like "Little Red Riding Hood."

Four more animated series followed. *Hello Kitty and Friends* in 1993, *Hello Kitty's Paradise* in 1999, and *Hello Kitty: Stump Village* in 2005 each only lasted one season. In 2006, the character went 3D with a fifty-two-episode series: *The Adventures of Hello Kitty and Friends*.

In 2009, Sanrio launched the prolific *Hello Kitty and Friends* YouTube channel, which includes the cartoon *Hello Kitty and Friends Supercute Adventures*, a sleekly designed series aimed at young viewers.

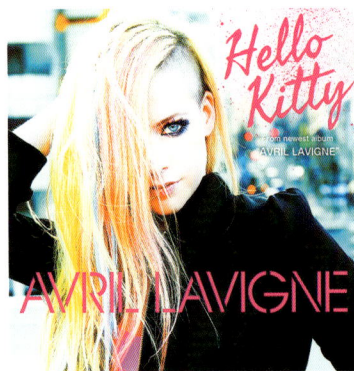

A Movie

Hollywood is always on the lookout for lucrative licenses, and it was only logical that it should seize on the little cat's success to want to produce a film. A project was announced in 2019, although little concrete information is circulating on the subject. The film is to be directed by Jennifer Coyle and Leo Matsuda. The film is expected to be a live-action/animated hybrid, produced by a Warner Bros. subsidiary in co-production with Flynn Picture Company, the production company behind some of The Rock's hit films.[4] However, no casting or release date has been given, so it remains to be seen if it will ever see the light of day.

Amusement Parks

Disney created the concept of making you pay to see its mascots, and therefore its live advertising, and to buy its products at its Disney Parks. Sanrio had a strong enough character and a wide enough range of merchandising to open a park based on the same principle. In 1990, the company opened Sanrio Puroland (nicknamed Hello Kitty Land) in the Tokyo suburb of Tama. Today, it's one of the most visited parks in Japan.

While the attractions lack the sensationalism of its American competitors, the company relies on the strength of its characters and their *kawaii* appeal. Hello Kitty shows take place several times a day to liven things up,[5] and you can visit the heroine's house and meet the various characters from the universe that Sanrio created around her. Admission to the Japanese park costs around $20 to $30. Another park opened in China near Shanghai in 2015. 🐾

---

[4] https://www.bbc.com/news/business-47466811
[5] https://www.kanpai.fr/tokyo/sanrio-puroland

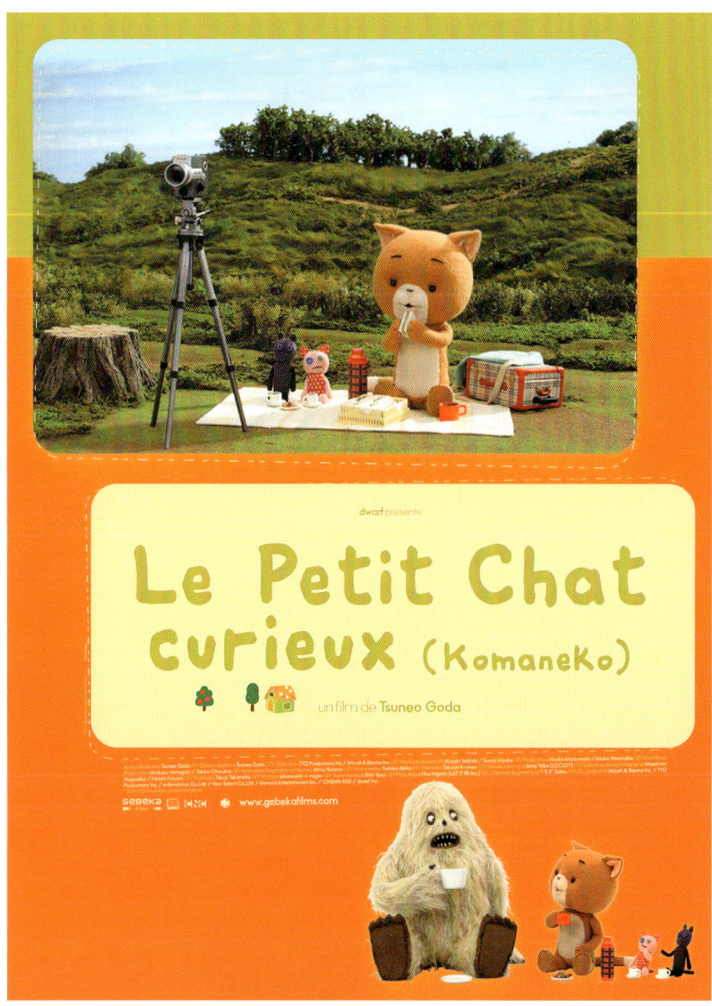

A stop-motion film conceived as five short episodes, Komaneko: The Curious Cat is one of the very first films offered to young audiences. Following along with Komaneko, viewers discover the magic of cinema.

Why do people make films? How is a film made? What does it mean to make a film? And for that matter, what is a film? Through five different stories, Tsuneo Goda's *Komaneko: The Curious Cat* (*Koma Tori Eiga Komaneko*) answers these questions for little ones. Recommended for children aged three and up, *Komaneko: The Curious Cat* is often used in kindergarten classes as an introduction to cinema, thanks to its length and the cute character of Komaneko, the little cat heroine of these stories.

What's it about? The summary is rather vague: "In Grandpa's charming house, life flows peacefully to the rhythm of the seasons. Komaneko, the little cat, has no shortage of ideas or friends to occupy her days. But sometimes, strange creatures come to disrupt the peaceful course of life." From story to story,

little Komaneko goes through the various stages of making a film: script and storyboard in "First Step"; filming what's around her, in this case a ghost, in "Camera in Hand"; meeting the public through her toys, which, from actors in her film, become a sort of currency with the yeti in "True Friends," and more.

While the summary specifies Komaneko's gender, there's nothing on-screen to indicate this, and the scenes with the young animal are perfectly unisex. The only clues are for film-loving parents, who might see similarities between the on-screen action and certain film classics: the yeti holding Komaneko's doll like King Kong holding the blond Ann Darrow (Fay Wray) in the 1933 black-and-white film of the same name, or the same yeti with a red umbrella in the forest reminiscent of Satsuki at the bus stop in *My Neighbor Totoro*. On the other hand, like a good little kitten, Koma is curious, likes to experiment with what she finds, and gives free rein to her imagination in the same way a young feline does with a piece of string or a ball of paper. 🐾

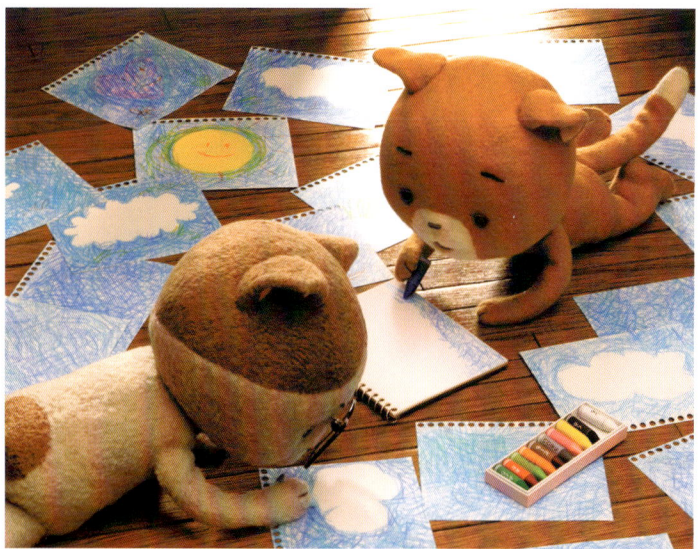

SPEC SHEET

WORK: *Komaneko: The Curious Cat*.
CREATOR: Tsuneo Goda (director and screenwriter).
DATE CREATED: March 25, 2006.
DISTRIBUTOR: Possibly available on DVD as a Japanese import (there's no talking in the film, so it would be watchable to an English audience).
CAT'S NAME AND ROLE IN THE WORK: Komaneko, a little anthropomorphic cat who wants to make her own animated film.

Cats Sell

Cats were advertising stars long before the rise of the internet or even television. Sometimes featured as a comical element for their cunning, they are more often used for their cleanliness, silkiness, or just plain cuteness.

There are far too many cats in advertising to mention them all, but it is possible to divide them into two groups: those intended to sell feline-related products (like food and litter) and those used to promote products that have nothing to do with cats.

Advertising for Cat Products

The first group includes mostly cat food brands. Their advertising emphasizes how soft cats are. The light brings out the silkiness of their fur and the beauty of their eyes. This is true of Sheba ads, which use cats in a seductive way. They are quick to rub their heads against their master's head, and the food is always highlighted as a high-quality delicacy. Friskies

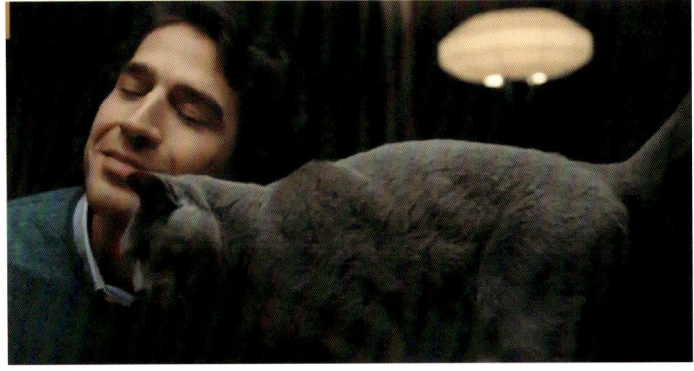

ads take another approach, playing up their cats' vitality. The cats are orange, like on the packaging, and often on the move. The animals' grace and effortless movement are emphasized by showing them jump, sometimes in slow motion. The Felix

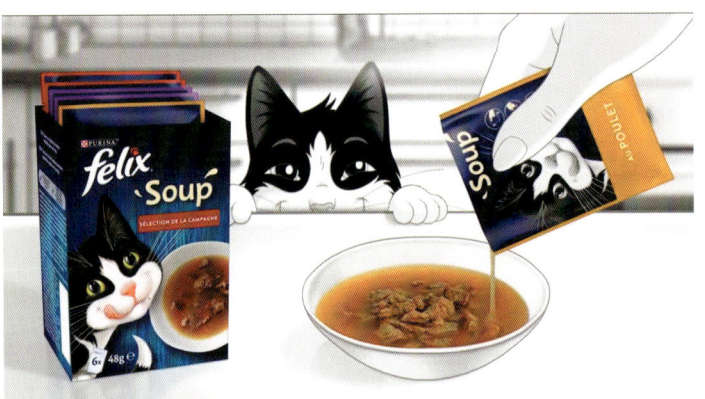

brand opted for animation, playing on how close its name is to one of the first silent film stars (see p. 106).

Advertising Featuring Cats

Before cats became a lucrative market, advertisers had already understood that the animals could help sell. The Philips brand, for example, regularly used cats on its posters in the 1960s. An illustration by Elvinger showed a cat looking at a fish through a television set to emphasize the realism of the image. In the field of soap and laundry detergent, cats quite naturally became ambassadors of choice. Since cats spend their days cleaning themselves, the general public perceives them as being clean.

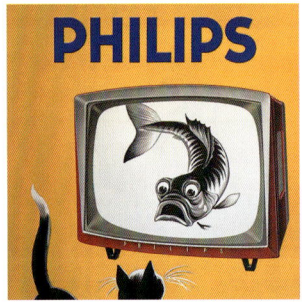

Very early on, cats appeared on posters for Marseille soap. The Marseille soap manufacturer C. Ferrier et Cie decided to make the feline its representative on posters in the early twentieth century, giving its brand the name "Le Chat." Paradoxically, apart from its name and logo, the brand hasn't used the animal in its communications for decades.

Today, cats are a fixture in advertising. They are used in many different ways, and some creative minds have managed to stand out for their use of felines.

In 2014, the jeweler Gemmyo launched ad campaigns featuring a pink kitten playing with a ring against a backdrop of classical music and pop art imagery. The slogan "adopt us" referred to both the feline and the jewelry collection. The cat was used for its adorable, playful side, with the message that playing is fun, just like the ring.

In 2005, Feu Vert, a company specializing in car maintenance and accessories, decided to use a cat as its mascot. Ramsès, who was white with green eyes, was supposed to be an animal

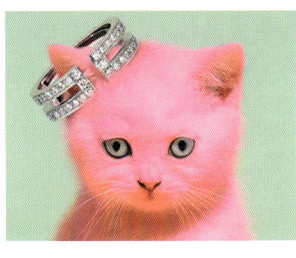

that inspired confidence. Dogs are innocent animals but are also often associated with innocence bordering on stupidity. Cats are seen as clever, even if they are also sometimes identified as devious, which is skillfully glossed over in advertising.

In 2007, the company decided to use computer-generated images for its cat, before returning to a real cat in 2017. In 2021, Feu Vert not only went back to CGI, but also announced the retirement of Ramsès. An ad campaign then began with

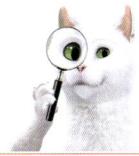

fake animal casting calls to replace the "expert" cat. These were most certainly inspired by the fake character bloopers shown at the end of Pixar Studios films. In this case, they intended to show that the cat—and, therefore, the company—was the only one who could be trusted. Feu Vert's advertising strategy is to assimilate its mascot with its company, since its slogan has become "La patte de l'expert" in French, which can be translated as either "The expert touch" or "The expert's paw."

Lolcats Invade Advertising

In 2011, the explosion of cats and lolcats on the web prompted Bouygues Télécom to create a viral ad. The cell phone and internet provider created a spot featuring a world full of kittens. Humans were replaced by small felines, who went to the office, clicked on rodent-shaped computer "mice," wore astronaut costumes, watched TV, spoke in little voices, made phone calls, and even took cabs, all with hilarious dialogue. The ad even went so far as to create a parody of the film *Machete* with a cat entitled *Catchete*. Comedian Alain Chabat's voice-over added to the comedy of the situation, as he had written fake ads for the television show *Les Nuls*. His detached tone and dialogue added flavor to the ad: "And it's because we at Bouygues Télécom know that you like internet movies with little kittens that we decided to make this internet movie with little kittens."

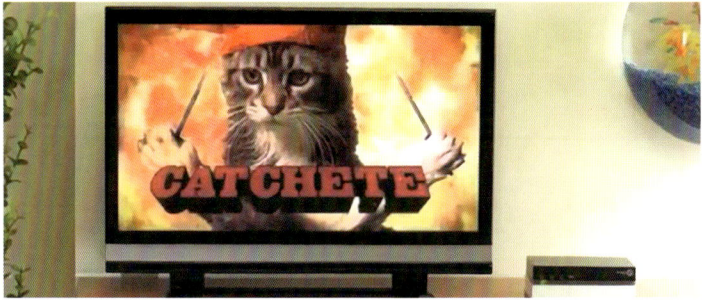

Humor is often used in ads that feature cats. One example was the 2012 Brazilian campaign for the energy drink Flying Horse, which used the cat's property of landing on its feet and that of a piece of toast of systematically landing on its buttered side to create an unlimited source of energy. 🐾

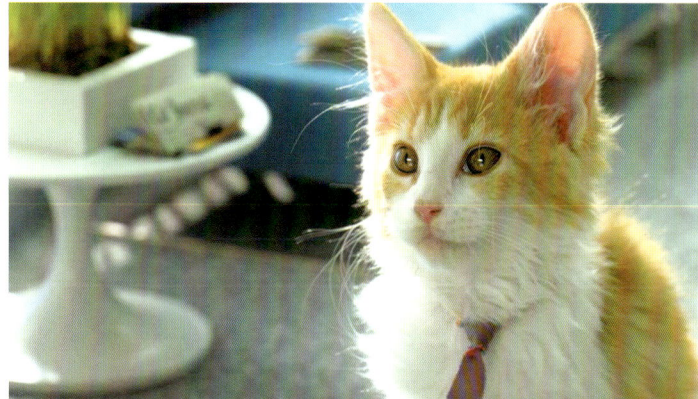

Bouygues Télécom ad.

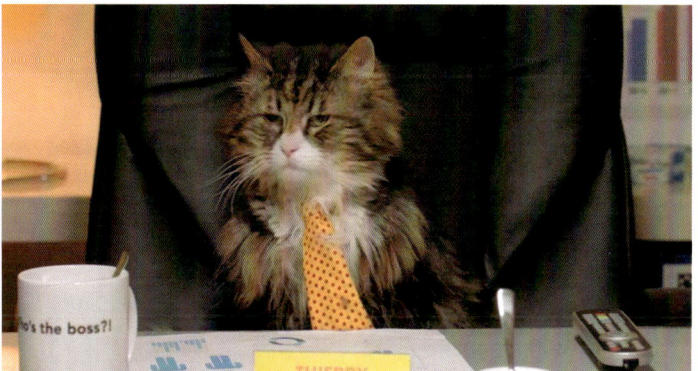

Netto ad.

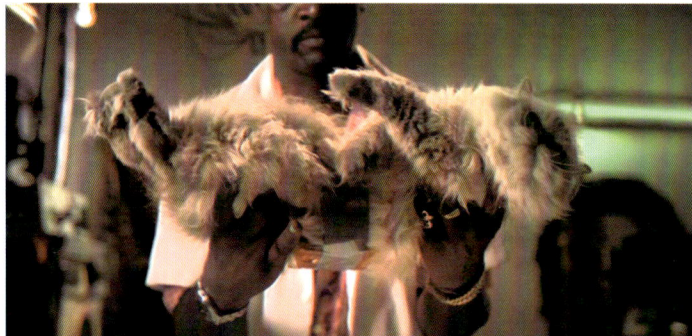

Flying Horse ad.

Nala

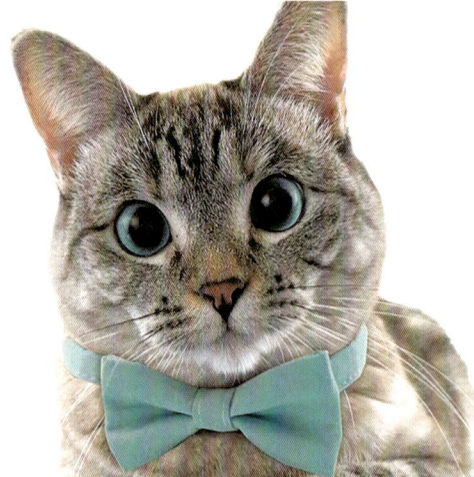

Photo by R.R.

If Instagram is the kingdom of cats, Nala is surely its queen! With 4.3 million followers, she has been awarded a Guinness World Record for the most followers of any cat.[1]

No doubt taking her name from the character in the film *The Lion King*, Nala was adopted at five months old by Varisiri Methachittiphan and her partner Shannon Ellis[2] from a Los Angeles shelter in 2012. At the time, the animal had a respiratory infection—a fairly common phenomenon in shelter living conditions—and her owners wanted to raise awareness of it. Seventy-five percent of animals are euthanized due to overcrowding in the country's shelters, so part of Nala's fortune is invested in Love, an animal protection organization.

Was Nala's success calculated? Not according to her owners. Varisiri Methachittiphan's sister, who was living in Thailand, suggested that they create an Instagram account for the little cat to share her photos more easily. The account quickly grew well beyond the family. Her blue eyes, gray tabby coat, and feline games (hiding in boxes or drawers, tearing toilet paper, etc.) won over the web. Photos taken by her mistresses with an amateur camera or cell phone soon turned into professional photo shoots. Today, at fourteen years old, the light in her shots mainly highlights the silky character of her coat, as well as the animal's mischievous expressions (when she squints or yawns, for example). Many of the photos also feature costumes (like a cosmonaut, Superman, or Princess Leia) for comic effect, especially in her annual calendar.

While it's difficult to pinpoint the reasons for Nala's success, the public loves her cute, playful temperament. This may be due in part to the size of her short legs, which could be the result of difficult living conditions in her first few months of life. Given her popularity, the little ball of fur is now the darling of advertisers, particularly in the field of pet products (food, accessories, cosmetics). She has her own website[3] and an online boutique. 🐾

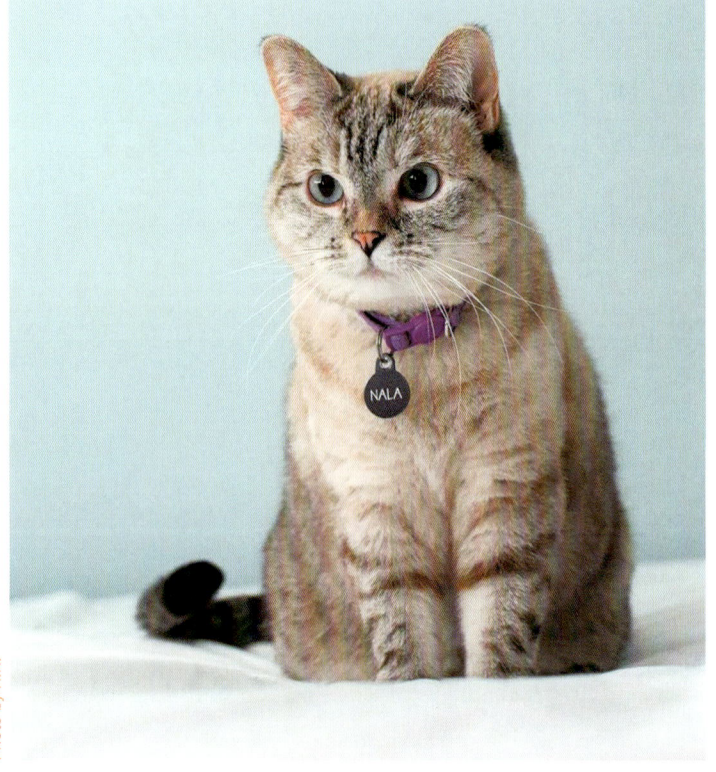

Photo by R.R.

SPEC SHEET

CAT'S NAME: Nala.
WORKS: Photos, advertising, merchandising.
HUMAN GUARDIANS/OWNERS: Varisiri Methachittiphan and Shannon Ellis.
DATE CREATED: First photo in March 2012.
DISTRIBUTOR: Instagram @nala_cat.
CAT'S CHARACTERISTICS: Cute, *kawaii*.

[1] https://www.youtube.com/watch?v=76Bm8W6W3Oo
[2] https://www.chakipet.com/lincroyable-histoire-de-nala-le-chat-le-plus-celebre-dinstagram-23-millions-dabonnes/
[3] https://nalacat.com/

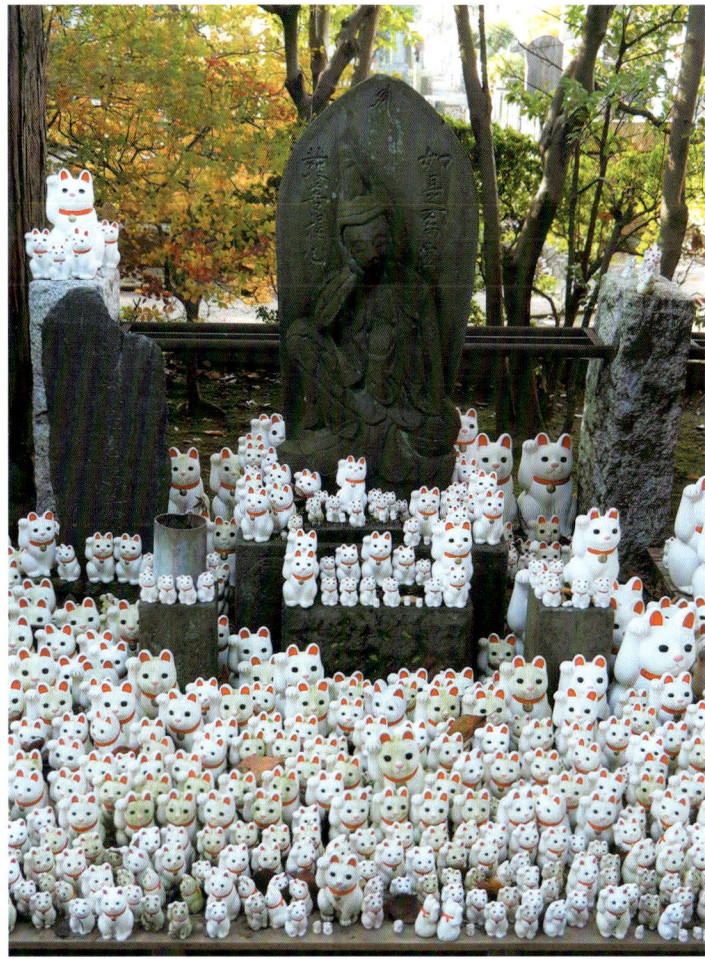

Gōtoku-ji Temple, Tokyo, Japan. Photo by Laika_ac.

Often standing at the entrance or near the checkout of Asian stores and restaurants, these cats with their paws raised will make you smile. And who knows? They might bring you good luck.

While most feline *yokai* get bad press in Japan, the *maneki-neko* (aka lucky cat or waving cat), is seen as a symbol of good luck and prosperity.

What are they? Small statuettes that were traditionally made of ceramic but are now also available in metal or plastic, depicting a cat—usually white or calico, but Chinese versions are often gilded—raising one of its front paws as if to greet passersby and invite them in. If he's raising his left paw, it's to draw customers into the store. If he's raising his right paw, it's to attract prosperity to the home where he's settled. Sometimes, other colors are used. As black cats in Asia have a good reputation and are believed to see the invisible world, a black *maneki-neko* would be placed in the business or home to ward off evil spirits. Red, the lucky color of brides in China

and the traditional skin color of oni, the Japanese ogres whose image is also used to ward off bad luck, is also used on *maneki-neko* to ensure the health of the occupants of the premises. Why? Because it was long believed that this color would ward off diseases such as smallpox or measles, by analogy with the color of the rash.

Where did *maneki-neko* come from? There are many legends about them, but the most common involve a monastery that

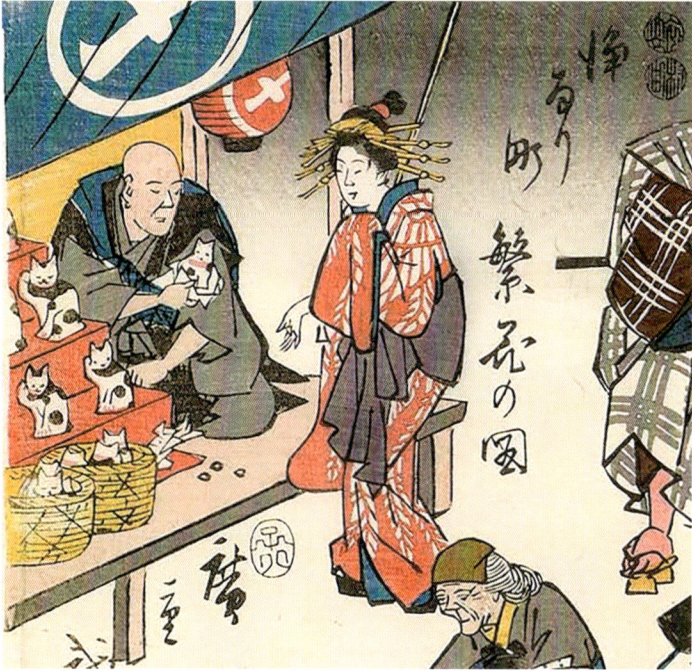

Maneki-neko, detail of *Flourishing Business in Balladtown*, Utagawa Hiroshige, 1852.

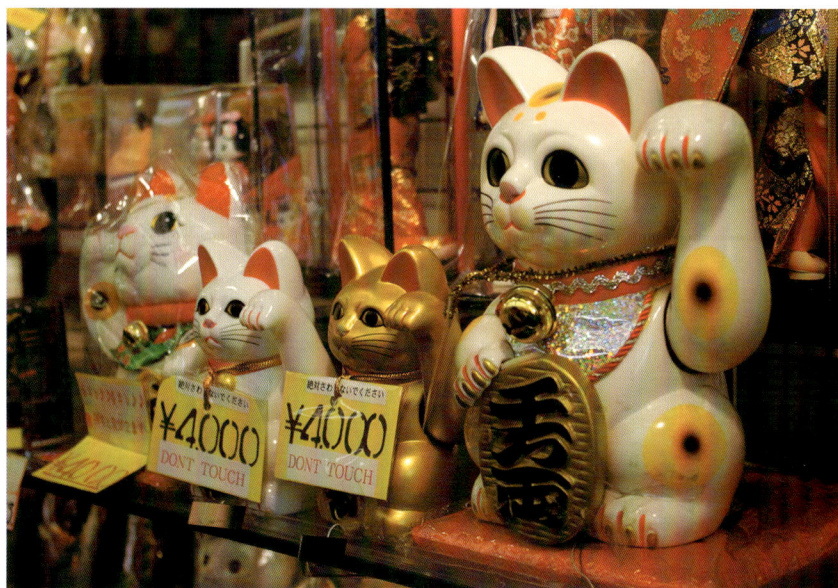

Maneki-neko, Tokyo, 2010. Photo by Jakub Halun.

became prosperous after housing a cat. It's said that around 1620, Gōtoku-ji Temple in the Setagaya district of Tokyo was on the verge of ruin. One day, a samurai returning home from a hunt empty-handed saw a cat in the temple, its paw raised in invitation. He entered the temple just as a terrible storm broke out. The samurai was happy to have escaped a major soaking and donated a large sum of money to the temple, which was able to carry out renovations and regain a certain prosperity. Since then, the place has become known as the *maneki-neko* temple, attracting tourists with its many cat statuettes. Another version of the story places it two centuries earlier, when the temple was just the hut of a single monk and his cat, who attracted the samurai and invited him to share his owner's tea and teaching. Enlightened in the way of Buddha, the samurai gave the monk rice paddies and fields to establish the present monastery, and the cat was deified on his death as Shobyo Kannon.

The *maneki-neko* gesture can also be seen as a cat washing its ear, recalling an even older Chinese proverb (from the ninth century CE) that says that if a cat lifts its paw over its ear and

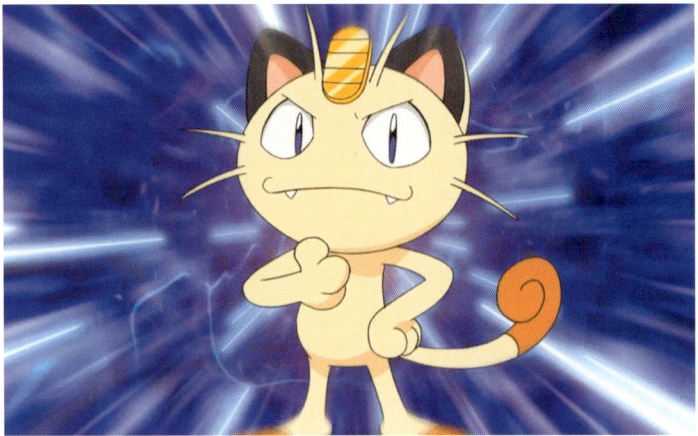

Meowth in *Pokémon*. Inspired by the *maneki-neko*, but not lucky for Team Rocket, the hero's antagonists in the franchise's cartoon.

washes its face, customers will come. Or it could recall the little tortoiseshell cat of a Tokyo courtesan that was unjustly decapitated by a client when she tried to warn her mistress of the presence of a venomous snake in the room. The client and brothel owner were abashed because they had believed the animal was attacking the woman for no reason, so they had a wooden statuette made of the cat. It was so beautiful and faithful that the courtesan regained her smile. And her employer got back a significant source of income.

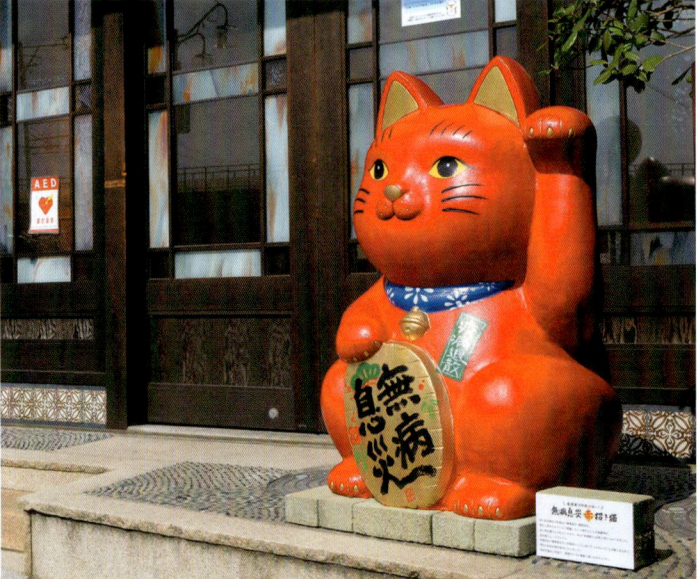

Maneki-neko, Cat Museum, Seto, Japan, 2020. Photo by Asturio Cantabrio.

In any case, this type of statuette became popular in Japan and soon after in China at the end of the Edo period (1603–1867), with the first one found dating back to 1852. Then, as migrations progressed, the lucky cat spread throughout Southeast Asia and to various Chinatowns around the world, before seducing people far beyond the Asian community. They're now available in new variations: pink to attract love; gold to attract money, whichever paw is raised; blue for success in studies and research; green to guarantee safety in the home or when traveling; and so on. They can be found as key rings, charms to hang from a wrist or telephone, teapots, plush toys, and piggy banks, and they inspired the appearance of Meowth, the chatty Pokémon that accompanies Team Rocket. 🐾

SPEC SHEET

CAT'S NAME: *Maneki-neko*.
ORIGIN: Various legends from Japan, all relating to the Tokyo area when the city was called Edo.
CREATOR: Anonymous.
DATE CREATED: Late Edo period, mid-nineteenth century.
CAT'S CHARACTERISTICS: Seated cat holding one paw up in invitation. The cat is usually white or calico, but other colors are possible.

With 2.5 million followers on Instagram, Grumpy Cat is, despite her death in 2019, currently the second most followed cat on Instagram. Her fame rests on a mix of the cuteness and attitude the social media site is so fond of, and the anger that can be read in her features, which are widely featured in memes.

Tardar Sauce was born in Arizona in 2012. Adopted by Tabatha Bundesen, she became famous after her owner's brother, Bryan, posted photos of her on Reddit that same year. One of the photos was quickly reposted and hijacked. It went viral thanks to the many memes playing on the animal's scowl. Because of this characteristic, she soon became known as Grumpy Cat.

Among the memes, the most famous will undoubtedly remain "I hate Mondays," "I had fun once, it was awful," and "I like the sound you make when you shut up."

The first video posted on YouTube, *The Original Grumpy Cat*, in 2012, was

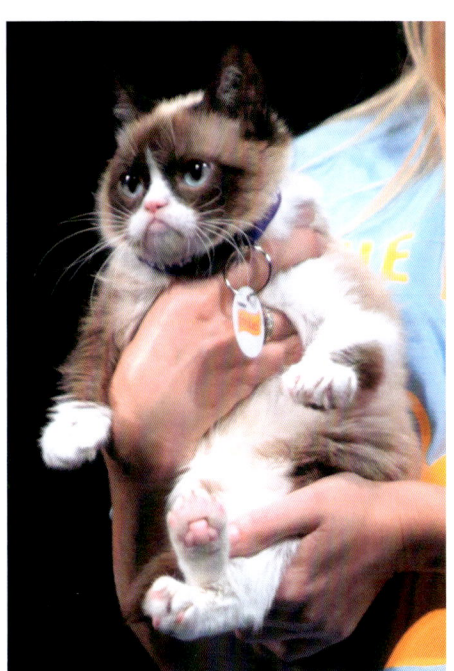

Grumpy Cat, VidCon 2014. Photo by Gage Skidmore.

viewed sixteen million times at the time. Taking advantage of the explosion in social media, the Grumpy Cat phenomenon was then spun off into a wide range of products, from plush toys and Pop! figurines to various textile products bearing her likeness.

Her fame enabled Tabatha Bundesen to quit her job as a waitress just a few days after Grumpy Cat's first online appearance. Suffering from dwarfism and a dental malocclusion that gave her a grumpy look, the animal passed away in 2019. She left her owner a fortune of $82 million.[1] She still has 8.1 million subscribers on her Facebook page.

Hollywood is always quick to jump on a bandwagon, so some producers decided to produce a Christmas TV movie: *Grumpy Cat's Worst Christmas Ever*. Released in 2014, this children's comedy in the vein of *Home Alone* revolves around the duo of Grumpy Cat and a twelve-year-old girl who hears the cat's thoughts.

Directed by Tim Hill, who had already created such children's films as *Garfield 2* (2006) and *Alvin and the Chipmunks* (2007), the film was, above all, an opportunity to dress the cat in a variety of cute costumes to accentuate her blasé air.

Unlike most feline stars, Grumpy Cat didn't necessarily fit the archetype of the cute cat on social media. Her temperamental, even angry expression contrasted with her soft, silky fur to give her great comic power.

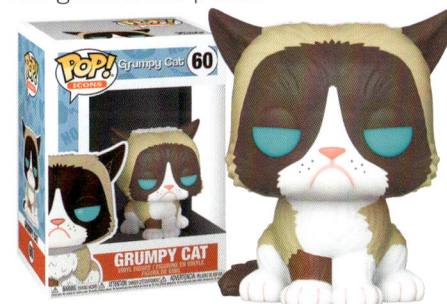

Grumpy Cat figurine.

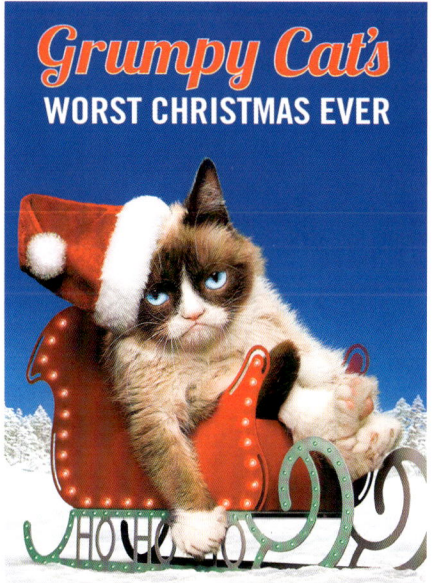

SPEC SHEET

CAT'S NAME: Tardar Sauce, aka Grumpy Cat.
WORKS: Photos, memes, online videos, TV movie *Grumpy Cat's Worst Christmas Ever* (2014).
HUMAN GUARDIAN/OWNER: Tabatha Bundesen.
DATE CREATED: First photos released in September 2012.
AVAILABILITY: Instagram @realgrumpycat.
CAT'S CHARACTERISTICS: Scowling face, always looking annoyed.

1   https://www.20minutes.fr/insolite/1496975-20141208-proprietaire-grumpy-cat-gagne-pres-82-millions-euros-grace-chat

"Le Chat"

In 1992, the song "Le Chat" [The Cat], a veritable musical UFO, spent seven weeks at the top of the French Top 50. The four-member group Pow woW sang "Moi vouloir être chat" [I want to be a cat], a metaphor between man and feline, a cappella. The life of a cat can make some men dream. Such is the case with the narrator of this song, in which he describes the animal's freedom to go out and play, and to "find [his] litter mates in the gutters." He also evokes his sexual relationship with the woman, as he remains "snuggled in [her] arms."

Throughout the verses, this ritornello draws a metaphor between the cat's behavior and that of a fickle man. The line "Lick my lips, when your girlfriends come over" emphasizes the cat's unfaithful nature. The animal's possessiveness is also reflected in his jealousy over his mistress, whom he warns about, "If one day you prefer the canines of a dog on a leash to my feline caresses." The song isn't really an ode to cats; it compares human relationships to a game of cat and mouse. The lyrics "And you'll be the mouse" are along the same lines. They cleverly mix the slang term "mouse" used to designate the woman as the game played by the cat or the man, when it comes to biting her, in a literal or seductive way.

Apart from presenting the group as crooners, the video from the time shows a woman disguised as a cat roaming the rooftops at dusk. While it may look dated today, the video was no doubt intended to reinforce the nonchalance of the feline in the lyrics.

Following the success of the song, Pow woW, whose members were Ahmed Mouici, Pascal Periz, Bertrand Pierre, and Alain Chennevière, won the 1993 Victoire de la Musique (a French music award) for best song with another feline track. The quartet sang "Le Lion est mort ce soir," which Henri Salvador had already covered in 1962. The original song was actually South African. Created in 1939 by Solomon Linda, it was later adapted in the United States as "The Lion Sleeps Tonight." Also used in the 1994 animated film *The Lion King*, the song was the subject of a court battle.

Pow woW's retro jazz a cappella style was well received, but the group struggled to establish itself over time. "Devenir Cheyenne" was their last hit, and they broke up in 1996. The group only partially reunited in 2005 for an album and in 2016 for a tour. 🐾

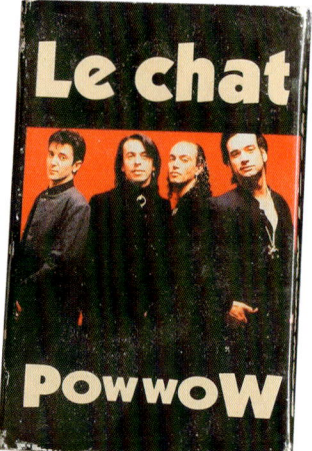 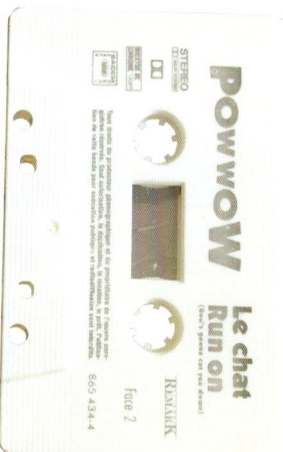

The cassette.

SPEC SHEET

WORK: "Le Chat" [The Cat].
CREATOR: Performed by the group Pow woW (Ahmed Mouici, Pascal Periz, Bertrand Pierre, and Alain Chennevière).
DATE CREATED: May 1992.
DISTRIBUTOR: Remark Records. Available on pre-owned CDs and streaming services.
CAT'S NAME AND ROLE IN THE WORK: An anonymous imaginary cat that serves as protagonist and parable.

The two-track 45.

Among the many musical artists who have drawn inspiration from cats for their music, the Stray Cats have taken the concept to the extreme. From the band's name to the lyrics of certain tracks and their musical style, everything evokes the alley cat.

Cats are often discreet, but they can also be noisy, whether wild or domesticated, especially during the mating season, when females in heat meow insistently to attract males, and the toms may compete noisily for the ladies' favor. So, it's hardly surprising that some rock bands have drawn inspiration for their music from these animals. Along with the French rock band Les Chats Sauvages with Dick Rivers in the 1960s, one of the most striking examples was formed in the late 1970s and is still intermittently active today: Stray Cats.

Right from the start, this American rockabilly trio made no secret of their passion for felines. But The Tomcats (the name of their first band) didn't work on their side of the Atlantic, so they renamed themselves "Stray Cats" and emigrated to London. There, at the height of the punk scene, their retro

rockabilly and energetic live shows (double bass included) attracted the attention of Dave Edmunds, a rock singer and producer, who released their first single, followed by an album in 1981. From "Stray Cat Strut" to "Cat Fight (Over a Dog Like Me)," cats often serve as metaphors for an idealized version of the band's members: boastful, seductive, sometimes brawling musicians wandering from city to city, groupie to groupie, unattached, like alley cats. The kind of musicians who, in twentieth-century jazz slang, were known as "cool cats."

Their career only lasted until 1984, when each member went off to try his luck as a solo artist. And yet, the band reunited regularly for concerts. Thanks to the *Guitar Hero* video game franchise, their two best-known songs, "Rock This Town" and "Stray Cat Strut," found a new audience. This generated enough interest to prompt the release of a final album in 2020, following the band's fortieth anniversary world tour. 🐾

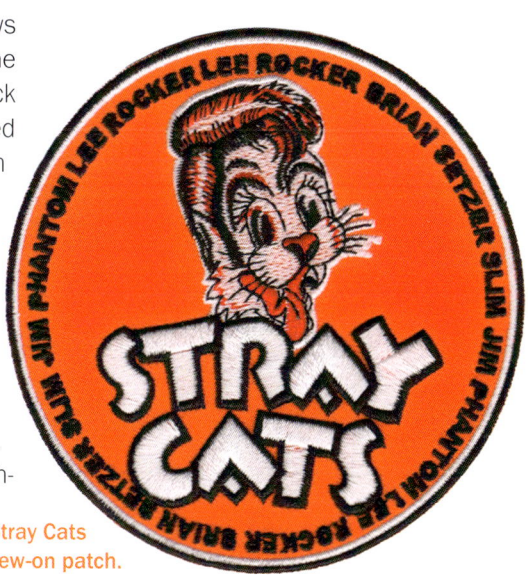

Stray Cats
sew-on patch.

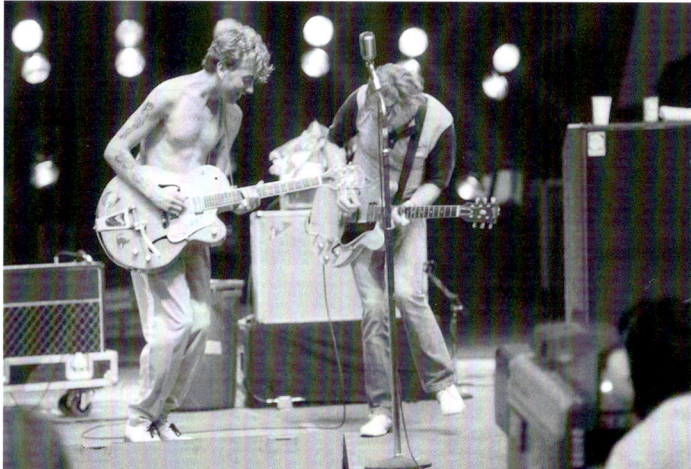

Stray Cats on the German TV show *Rockpalast*, 1983.

SPEC SHEET

GROUP'S NAME: Stray Cats.
MEMBERS: Brian Setzer, Lee Rocker, Slim Jim Phantom.
DATE FORMED: 1979–1984, then on and off. Their most recent live album, *Rocked This Town: From LA to London*, was released in 2020.
CHARACTERISTICS: Rockabilly trio with a double bass that reproduces the sound of marauding cat feet.

Choupette

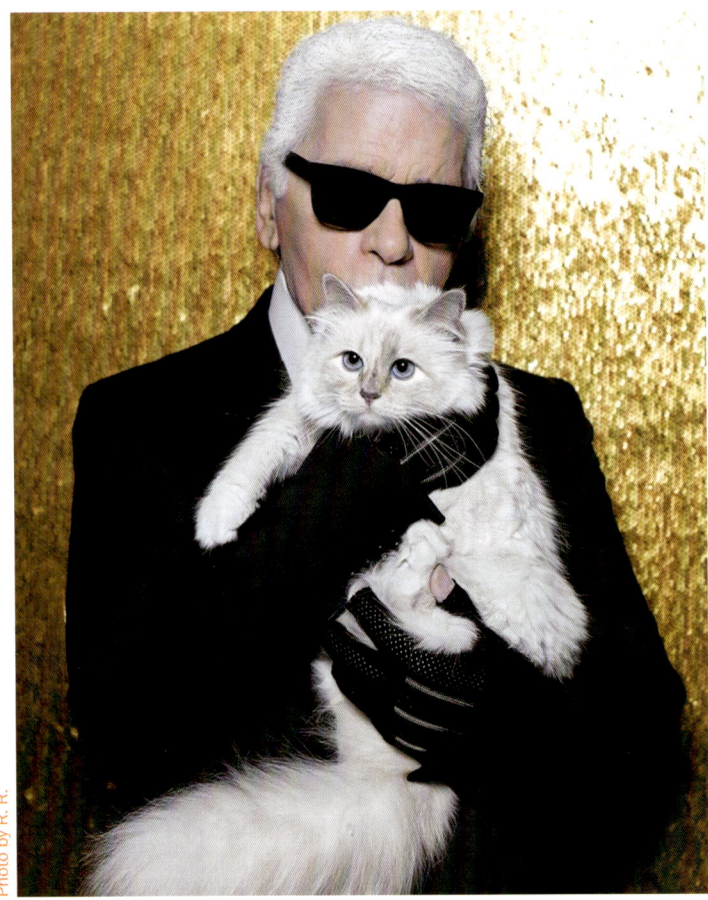

Photo by R. R.

Karl Lagerfeld and Choupette, promotional poster.

In 2015, Chanel's renowned artistic director, Karl Lagerfeld, announced on the Le Divan television show that his Birman cat was his heir and would be safe from want after his death.

In 2011, model Baptiste Giabiconi gave Choupette to his German mentor, who had fallen in love with his feline companion. By 2012, she had launched a career, appearing on Twitter and on the covers of fashion magazines such as *Grazia* and *German Vogue*. With photo shoots and an Instagram account with almost seventy thousand subscribers at the time (and topping eighty-five thousand since), the blue-eyed white cat alone generated $3 million in 2015.[1]

A Shupette makeup line was launched in her likeness, in a collaboration between Shu Uemura and her owner. He kept a close eye on her image: "I wouldn't allow her to advertise cat food; she's too sophisticated. There's something unique about her."[2] He refused to allow his cat to pose in costume, deeming the practice grotesque. In 2012, he dedicated a bag from the Chanel collection to her, naming it after her.

In 2014, the book *Choupette: La Vie enchantée d'un chat fashion* (which was released two years later in English as *Choupette: The Private Life of a High-Flying Cat*) presented a diary-like collection of anecdotes from the cat's daily life, veterinary advice, and artistic photos of the animal immortalized by her owner's talents.

Whether it was an old man's desire to show his affection for his feline companion or the fashion genius's ultimate touch of humor, when Lagerfeld passed away in 2019, Choupette was presented as both the major heiress and the richest cat

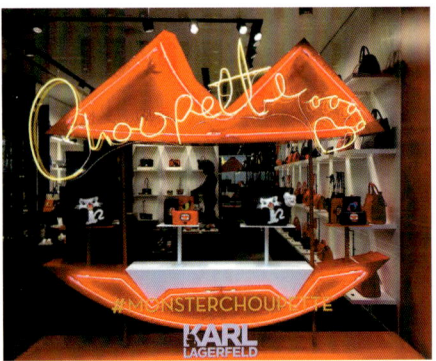

London boutique. Photo by R. R.

in the world. Obviously, from a legal point of view, this wasn't the case. In France, an animal can't inherit from its owner. So, while the designer's fortune was worth at least $200 million,[3] Choupette's money was entrusted to her caretaker and friend of the designer, Françoise Caçote. She was also one of the seven heirs to the designer's fortune, which is currently at the heart of a legal dispute. 🐾

SPEC SHEET

CAT'S NAME: Choupette Lagerfeld.
WORK: *Choupette: La Vie enchantée d'un chat fashion* (*Choupette: The Private Life of a High-Flying Cat*).
AUTHORS: Patrick Mauriès and Jean-Christophe Napias. Karl Lagerfeld photos.
DATE CREATED: 2014.
PUBLISHER: Flammarion.
CAT'S CHARACTERISTICS: A fashion ambassador, Choupette is a Birman cat with a fawn point coat (i.e., with a pinkish-beige mouth and tips that are relatively light compared to the rest of the white coat).

---

[1] https://www.courrierinternational.com/article/vu-des-etats-unis-quest-devenue-choupette-la-chatte-de-karl-lagerfeld
[2] https://madame.lefigaro.fr/style/choupette-lagerfeld-est-millionnaire-010415-95820
[3] https://www.lepoint.fr/people/le-testament-de-karl-lagerfeld-un-vrai-sac-de-noeuds-25-02-2020-2364270_2116.php

Cat Manga: More Than a Genre

Kawaii *and cats have long gone hand in hand. So, cats were a natural match for manga. From simple characters like Master Korin in Dragon Ball, they gradually developed into a genre in their own right, even though it meant borrowing the conventions of other manga genres.*

Cats have always seduced artists, particularly in Japan, where they have been present since the days of *emakimono* and prints. A kitten knocking down a folding screen launched the epic *The Tale of Genji* (eleventh century CE), giving Genji's nephew a glimpse of his mistress, the third princess. It's only natural, then, that in more modern times—when the country is dotted with cat bars, cat temples, and no fewer than fourteen cat islands—cats have also found their way into literature and the arts, especially manga (and later, anime). Right from the start of the comic book era, cats have featured among the characters, including Master Korin in *Dragon Ball*, Nekomamushi in *One Piece*, and Juliano in *Love Me, My Knight*.

The Ancestors: Doraemon and Michael

Doraemon, the earless blue robot cat from the future, starred in a manga from 1970 to 1995. The series of the same name, which was intended for children, features an anthropomorphic cat who uses a variety of wacky gadgets to help Nobita Nobi, his creator's grandfather, when he was a little boy. The robot's feline side is derided; having had his ears eaten off by a robot mouse, he's scared to death of mice. He does have

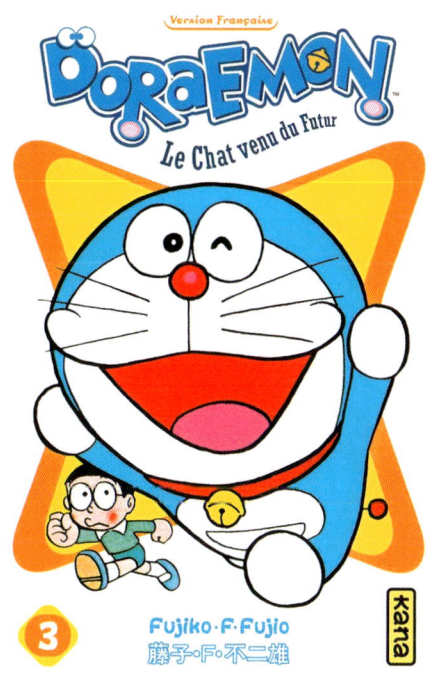

a slight tendency toward laziness and trickery, however, when he pretends to be too busy to make time for a walk with Mii-chan, the neighbor's little cat. The manga has been turned into anime (three different series in 1973, 1979, and 2005, as well as several films and TV movies), video games, a musical, and even a mascot.

But soon, another kind of cat would take center stage in the world of manga: the ordinary cat, whether a house cat or a cat roaming the streets. With no special powers or strange origins, these cats found their audience. One of the first manga of this type, *What's Michael?*, ran from 1984 to 1989, before generating OAVs and an animated series. Michael and his family are ordinary cats, most often on all fours and sometimes anthropomorphized (notably in an escape "dance"), to whom all sorts of funny adventures happen for the reader to enjoy. And with Michael's

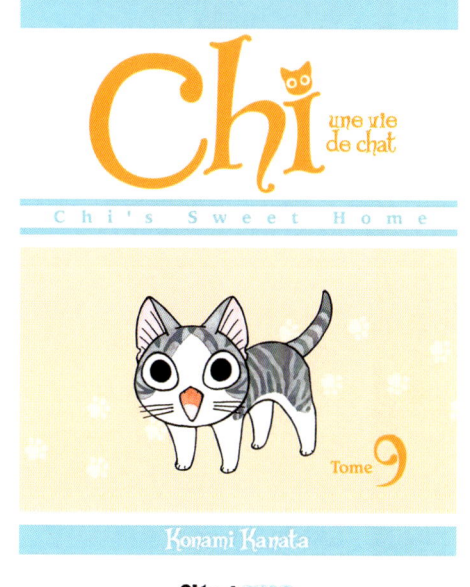

success, and even more so since the late 1990s, the dedicated "cat manga" genre was born.

What's Cat Manga?

What exactly is cat manga? Most often, it's a manga about ordinary life, without any adventure, supernatural elements, or science fiction involved, which features one or more cats. It may be intended for any audience, from young children to fans of *shōjo*, *shōnen*, or even *seinen* manga. Some mangakas have even specialized in this kind of manga, devoting their entire body of work to domestic felines. One example is Konami Kanata, who has drawn nothing but cat stories since the beginning. Her best-known title is *Chi's Sweet Home*. It tells the story of a small cat, Chi, who gets lost and is adopted by a little boy, Yohei, and his family. Initially aimed at children, this gentle series could be the archetype for cat manga: It begins with the meeting between the cat and its new family and then follows

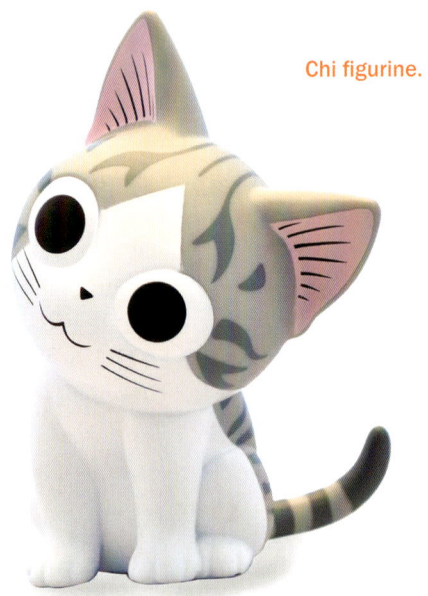

Chi figurine.

their everyday micro-adventures as the animal grows and ages (or even dies, as the lives of our feline companions are shorter than ours). Chi was later turned into an anime (produced by Madhouse studio). Konami Kanata's other titles (*Sue & Tai-chan* and *FukuFuku: Kitten Tales*) are variations on the same theme.

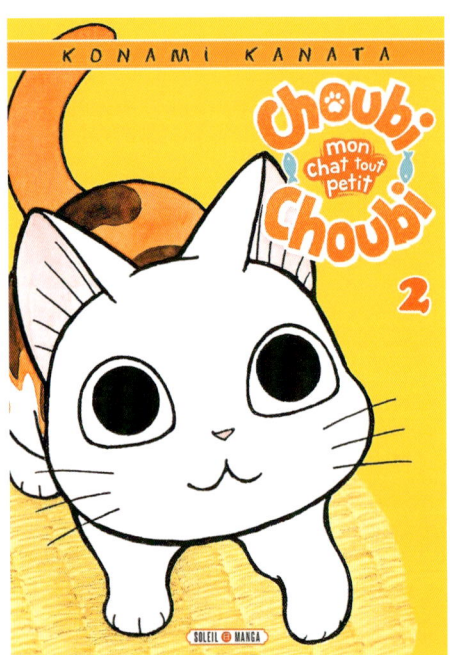

Other titles, such as *Plum Crazy! Tales of a Tiger-Striped Cat* by Hoshino Natsumi (which tells the stories from the point of view of one of the cats), follow the same principle. It's also parodied in *Oh My Cats!* by Kotsubu Sakaki, in which the mangaka may adore her

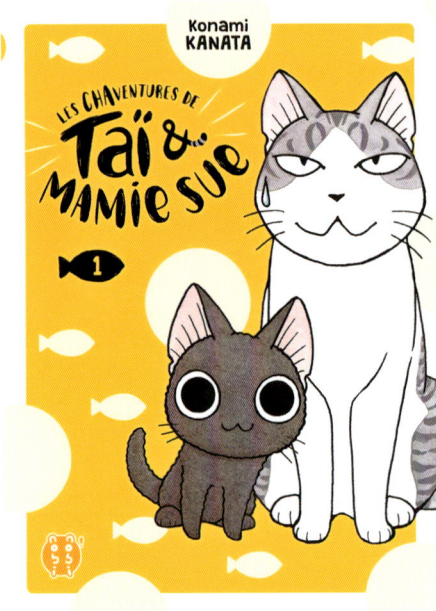

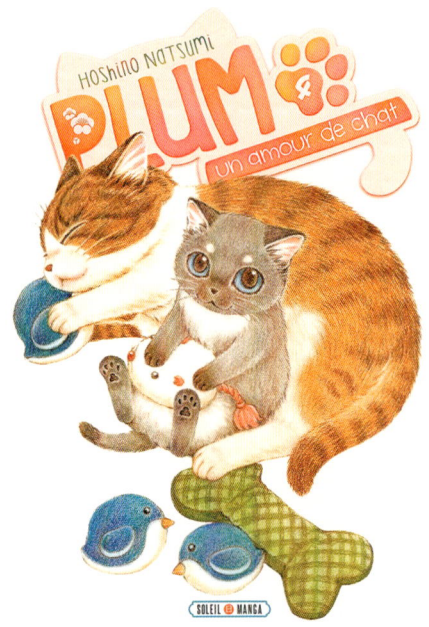

cats, but they (a mother and son) don't exactly reciprocate, preferring the other members of the household over her.

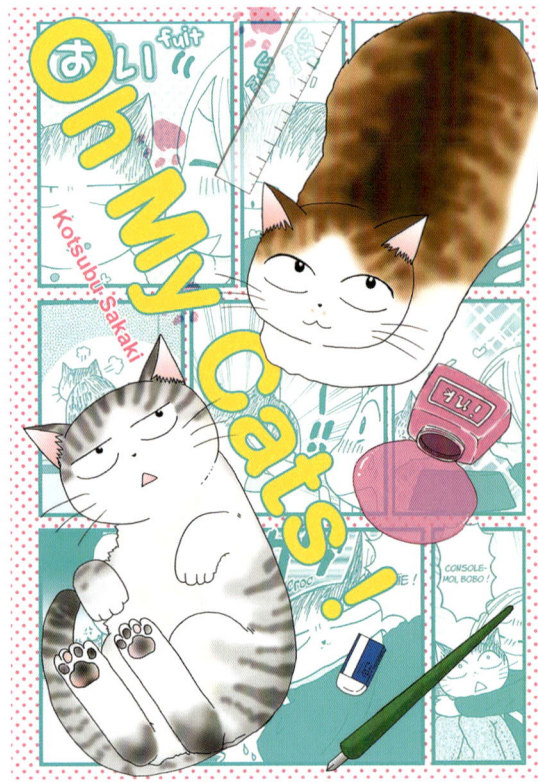

Even Junji Ito, who is better known for his horror manga, got in on the act with *Junji Ito's Cat Diary: Yon & Mu*, an autobiographical account of moving in with his wife and her cats, and the first days of life with these unfamiliar monsters. Watching a man who's a bit of an ailurophobe forced to cohabit with two felines and discover their habits, which are more or less invasive for his married life, before learning to love and appreciate them, is a treat. He turns everyday situations into comic/horror moments worthy of the slasher films of Wes Craven or John Carpenter.

Using Cats to Talk About Humans

Cat manga then evolved to focus on more specific issues and tackle more serious themes. In *A Story of Seven Lives*, Gin Shirakawa interweaves the daily lives of stray cats and lonely city dwellers in three volumes. This beautiful title is best reserved for

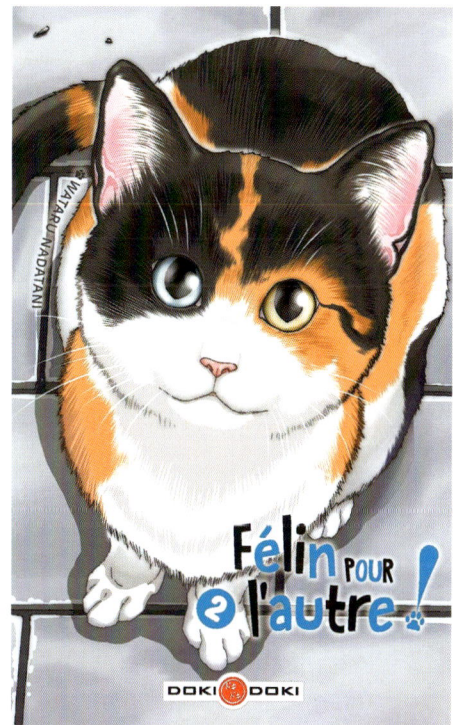

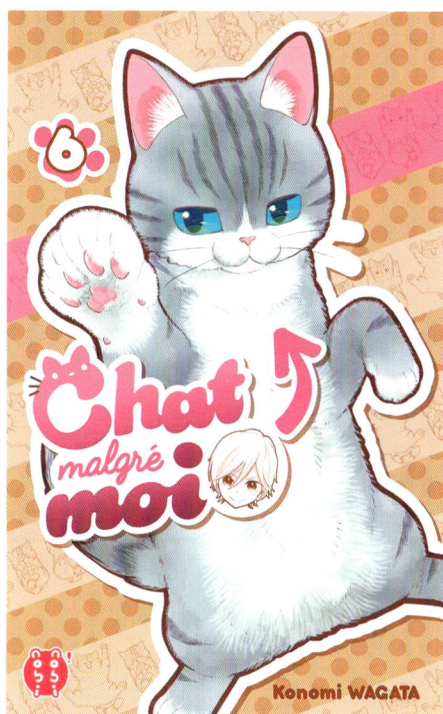

Gamer, shows the daily life of an independent woman who loves video games and how the kitten she adopts turns her life upside down. It's both an ode to cats and video game culture, and a touching portrait of a young woman who's unwilling to let herself be trapped in what traditional Japanese culture expects of her. In the same style, Tsubasa Yamaguchi has adapted Makoto Shinkai's first short film, *She and Her Cat*, into a manga, recounting the daily life of a lonely woman in the big city, as seen through the eyes of her cat, Chobi. Cat manga is becoming so diversified that it crosses over with other genres such as *isekai*, with titles such as *My New Life as a Cat* by Konomi Wagata, in which a boy is hit by a car and reincarnated as a cat. Adopted by a high school girl, he lives his life as a cat for eight volumes, while trying to regain his original body.

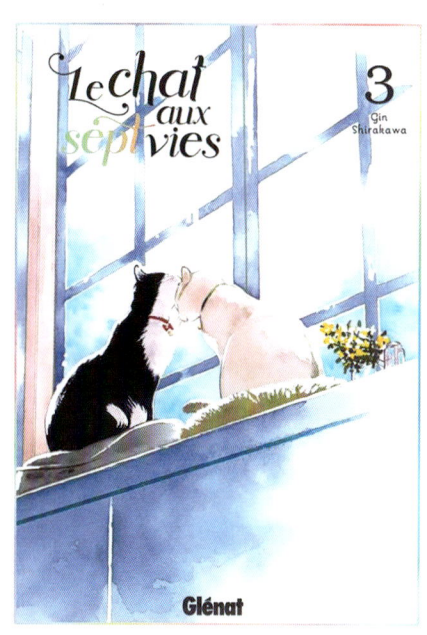

From Cat Manga to Cats in Manga

From cat manga, we move on to manga in which cats play the starring role, but

they slip into other very different genres, even if it means changing countries—with titles such as *Miss Kitty and Her Bodyguards* or *Cat Loaf*, which come from South Korea rather than Japan. The former is a combination of action and comedy in which anthropomorphic animals (mainly dogs) have to protect Anna, a Burmese cat who behaves like a perfect four-legged feline. The second

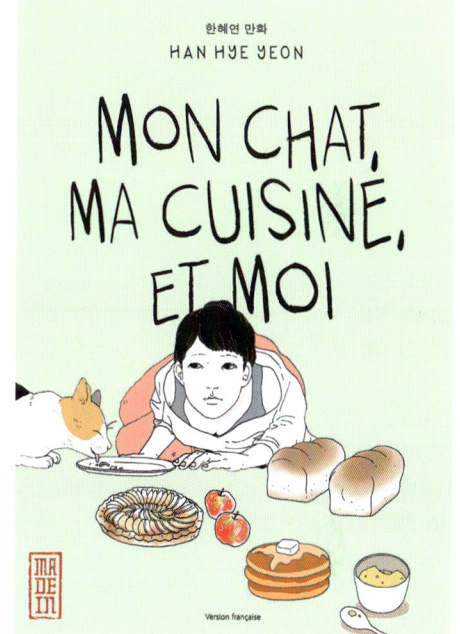

is a mix of *manwha* (Korean comic book) and cookbook, in which the author, Han Hye Yeon, combines the slice-of-life genre with her three cats and her love of baking. These variations also exist and thrive in Japan.

Bye, Bye, My Brother by Yoshihiro Yanagawa tells the sad story of two boxers haunted by death, except that all the characters in the manga are cats. And cats take over every realm, even the most unlikely. Tomo Kitaoka's *The Walking Cat* is a horror series in three volumes that follows an ordinary white cat, Yuki, in the midst of a zombie epidemic. He lives his life and crosses paths with a succession of humans looking for the island or corner of the world where they can live in peace

adults, as it tackles difficult themes such as grief and solitude. With *Cat + Crazy* and *Cat + Gamer*, Wataru Nadatani uses the cat manga form to tackle other subjects in a light, funny way. His most recent series, *Cat +*

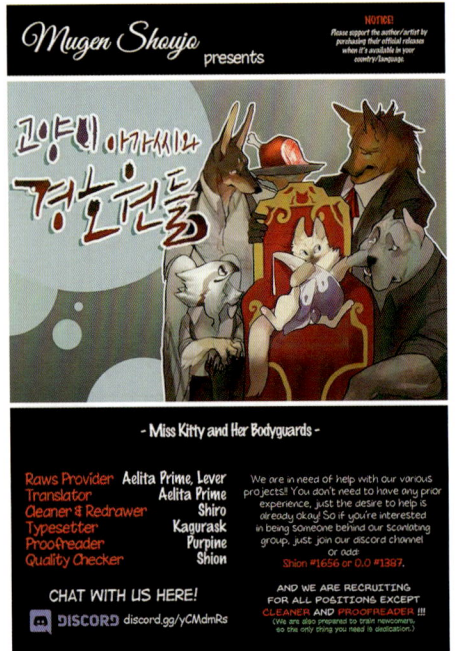

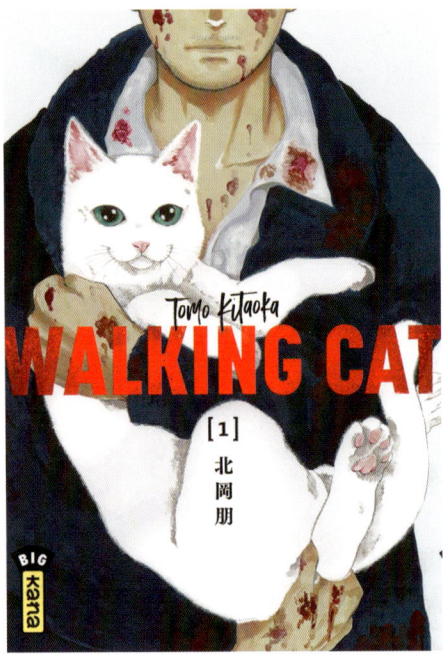

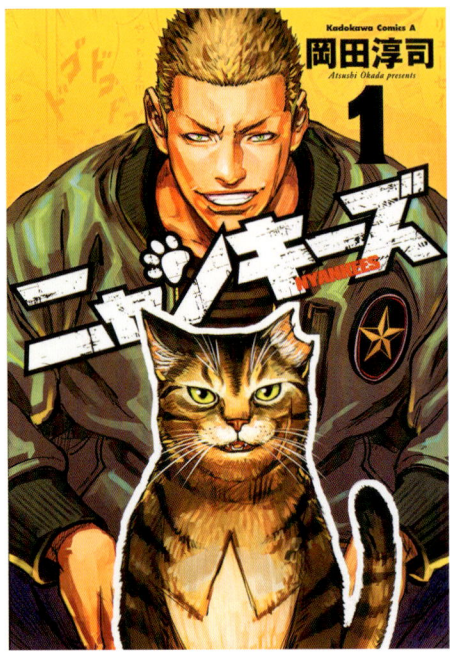

away from the infected. With no special talent, not even a gift of speech, Yuki motivates the humans to fight for their survival (and his protection), even when all seems lost.

Nekoten! by Yuji Iwahara imagines a world where female students fight monsters with the help of their cats. And Hiroyuki Takei's *Nekogahara: Stray Cat Samurai* is a classic samurai and ronin manga, embodied entirely by cats. It adds an extra layer of readability by playing on the opposition between street cats (the Stray Cat in the title) and those living with humans. Even *furyo* manga (which focus on gangs of thugs and petty crime in Japan) have been invaded by cats. One of these series, *Street Fighting Cat* by SP Nakatema, depicts a war

between various cat gangs in a city to take over the garbage cans of the best restaurants, and the rise to supreme leader of one of the most pathetic of cats, who is taken under the paw of a big, naive lump with a good right hook. Told entirely from the cat's point of view, this is a very funny book that explains the rules of feline Bushido: don't let a human see you on two legs, use your claws and teeth only as a last resort, and so on. Another series, *Nyankees* by Atsushi Okada, recounts the daily life of street cats, with a clever narrative trick. Where other mangakas choose to portray their characters as cats, Okada does the opposite, transforming his tomcats into young hooligans ready for a fight in the middle of the action. 🐾

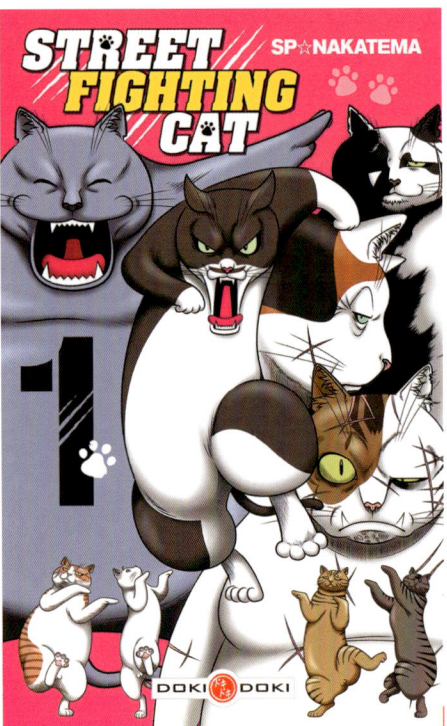

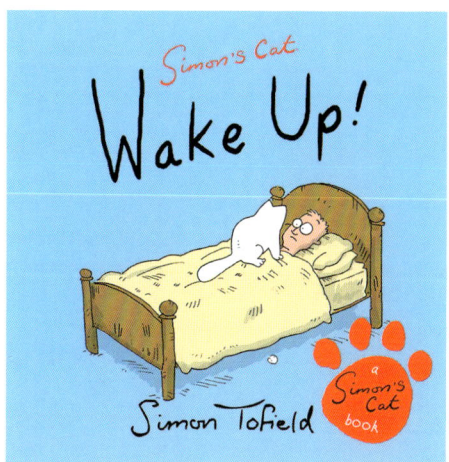

A snapshot of everyday life with a cat, the videos featuring Simon's Cat have made the rounds on the internet. They're deliberately uncluttered, allowing viewers to imagine themselves living out these sketches with their own cat. Simon's Cat has become our own.

An animator working mainly in advertising, Simon Tofield was dragged out of bed one morning by his cat, who was demanding his food. Over breakfast, he found the idea funny enough to turn it into a short, animated film. One of his customers at the time asked for permission to use it to test the video capabilities of their website. The film was such a success that it crashed the client's servers and ended up on YouTube. Not wanting to lose control of his creation, Simon created a second film, which he named *Simon's Cat*. A saga was born.

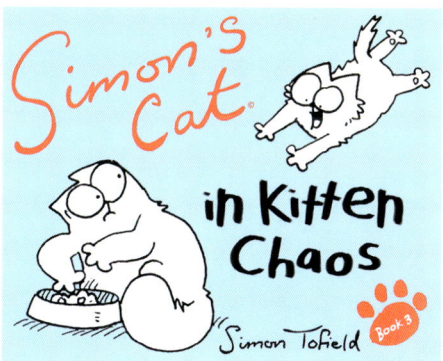

In his short films, Simon Tofield draws inspiration from life with his own cats, especially Hugh (a black shorthair, although Simon's cat is white) for the main feline character. The other cats that appear in the episodes are also inspired by the large feline family that has lived and lives with him, without being linked to any particular character.

In addition to the main cat, who is deliberately anonymous so that viewers can imagine their own cat in his place, *Simon's Cat* now features several cats: a kitten that Simon adopted in 2011, much to the main cat's displeasure (before making him his underling and accomplice),

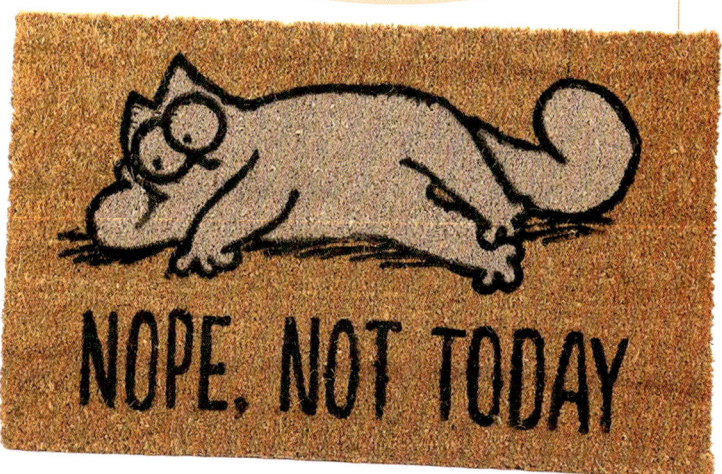

and the neighbors' cats, including two attractive females and a feisty male. Other animals are also present, playing on the humor of antagonism between species (dogs, birds, hedgehogs, mice). No more than four minutes long, these videos have created such a craze that there are now comics and mobile games developed around the *Simon's Cat* universe. As for Simon Tofield? He now has a full-time job thanks to his cats and even employs other animators. 🐾

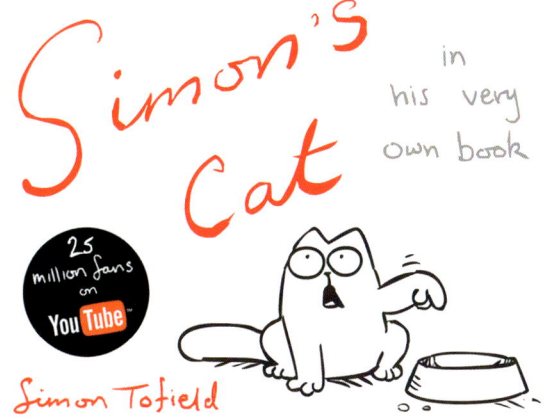

SPEC SHEET

CAT'S NAME: Anonymous.
WORK: *Simon's Cat*, a series of short, animated films on YouTube.
CREATOR: Simon Tofield.
DATE CREATED: March 4, 2008.
DISTRIBUTOR/AVAILABILITY: The videos have a dedicated channel, https://www.youtube.com/user/simonscat, and can be found on the animator's website, https://simonscat.com/.
CAT'S CHARACTERISTICS: A long-haired white cat who's very expressive and always hungry.

M. Chat

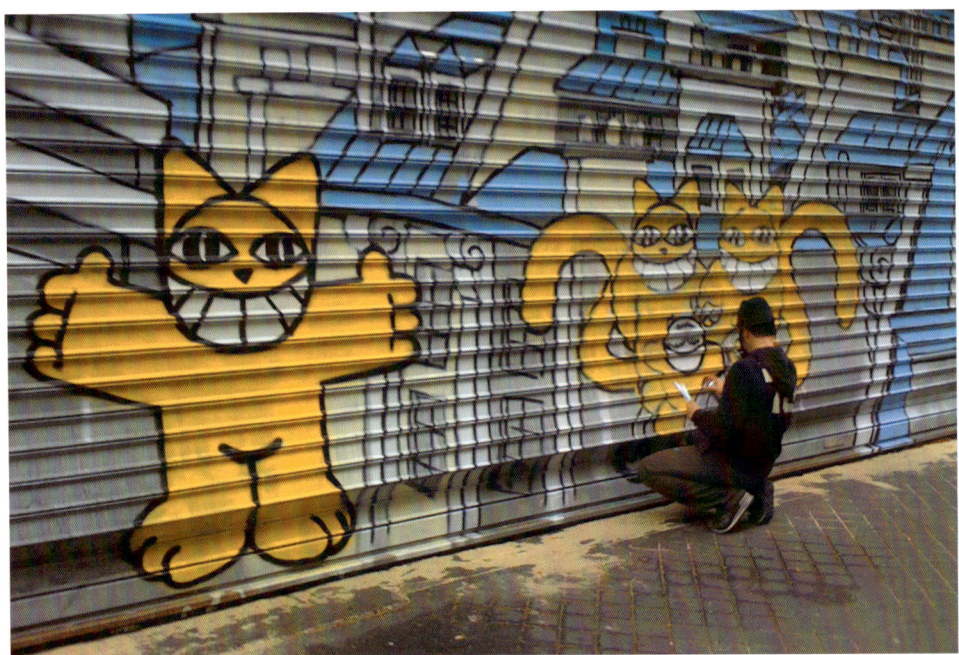

M. Chat, Paris, October 5, 2012. Photo by LoveBoat.

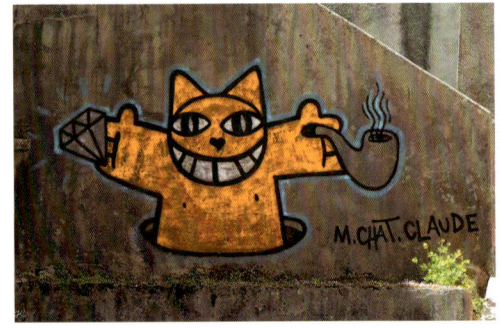

Cat, Saint-Claude, Jura. Photo by Céréaleskiller.

Since 1997, a big, orange, smiling cat—who often has wings—has graced the streets of European cities. He's named M. Chat (Mr. Cat) and is the creation of artist and painter Thoma Vuille.

Although they're often seen roaming the streets, scavenging for trash, or leaping nimbly over barricades, cats generally don't inspire graffiti artists and other street artists. But there is one notable exception, which first appeared on the walls of Orléans in 1997: an orange cat with a big toothy grin. It was M. Chat, Thoma Vuille's favorite character; he gave the feline a pair of white wings in 2003. He was inspired by "a drawing (equivalent to a bookplate) that [his] mother used to sign the letters she sent [him] as a child," he explained in an interview with Forbes. "It resurfaced when I was a student running an extracurricular drawing workshop at a school in Orléans. I had reworked the silhouette that a little girl had drawn on the city's walls."[1]

He drew him on the walls and rooftops of the cities he visited, gaining visibility when he took to the rooftops of Paris, and when his cat was taken up by demonstrators in the run-up to the 2002 French presidential election. Film director Chris Marker took an interest in him and decided to make this iconic character the focus of his documentary *The Case of the Grinning Cat*.[2] From that point on, M. Chat continued to adorn walls and rooftops, attracting a conviction for degradation and a €500 fine for his creator in 2016 for setting up on the walls of a Paris train station under construction. But he became respectable and found himself drawn by invitation all over the world, from Tokyo to Lima to Sète, when he's not being sold on canvas or in a variety of spin-off products, such as lighters or four-color BIC pens. 🐾

[1] https://www.forbes.fr/lifestyle/rencontre-avec-m-chat-de-paris-au-perou-un-artiste-au-sommet-du-street-art/
[2] https://www.youtube.com/watch?v=7fJb08wOc84

SPEC SHEET

CAT'S NAME: M. Chat.
WORKS: Various murals around the world, as well as spin-off products.
CREATOR: Thoma Vuille.
DATE CREATED: 1997.
AVAILABILITY: Look up at the city walls, especially in Paris.
CAT'S CHARACTERISTICS: Smiling orange cat who is always facing front, even when depicted in profile.

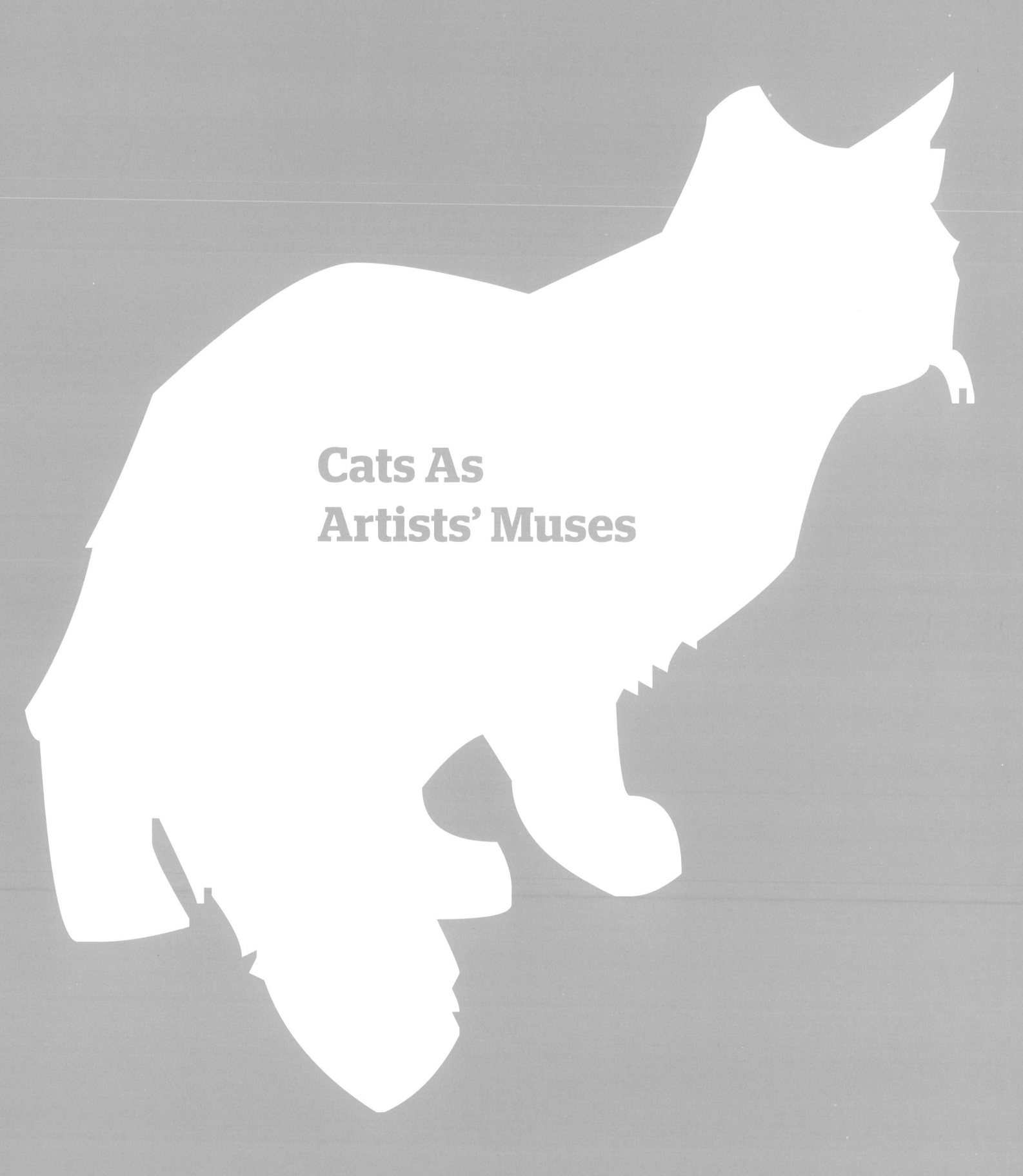

Cats As
Artists' Muses

When Cats Inspire

Alternately humans' companions or scapegoats, depending on beliefs and circumstances, cats have found their place in the hearts of poets, artists, and writers. And they never cease to inspire a story, a painting, a piece of music, or a poem.

It's simply impossible to list all the works that have been inspired by cats. As we have seen in the preceding pages, the relationship between humans and cats is so complex, so protean, that the very image of the cat in art in the broadest sense of the term could be the subject of another book on its own. Rather than repeating what we've already covered, here are a few examples of the genres in which cats play an integral role.

Colette's *The Cat* is one of the best-known novels to feature an ordinary cat as the main character. This device has been repeated several times, notably by Lilian Jackson Braun and her detective series *The Cat Who . . .* In this case, the cat, or rather the cats in question are two Siamese belonging to a grumpy journalist who left the big city to settle in a small town in the Northeastern United States. The male cat, Kao K'o-Kung (aka Koko), is the key helper in his owner's investigations, thanks to a sixth sense he seems to possess. The female cat, Yum Yum, is more affectionate and agile, and more the comic relief in the books, thanks to her antics. *The Cat Who . . .* series includes a total of twenty-nine novels written between 1966 and 2007.

Sometimes, cats are not only the main characters, but also the narrators of the story. This literary sub-genre can be found in children's books such as *The Diary of a Killer Cat* and its sequels by Anne Fine. But it has also found its way into "biographies," such

as *The Travelling Cat Chronicles* by Hiro Arikawa, *Les Mémoires d'un chat de gouttière* (*Memoirs of an Alley Cat*) by Miguel Haler, and many others. Through the eyes of the cat, the human writer reveals a slice of life in a specific time and place. The animal serves as a guide to the author's psyche or the society they wish to portray.

This is the same process used in painting and sculpture, in which cats are depicted slipping into the skin of humans as they go about their daily lives or are simply caught in the act of being cats. Whether they're the main subject of the work or just a detail in a

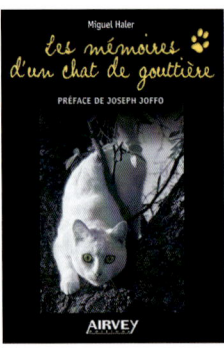 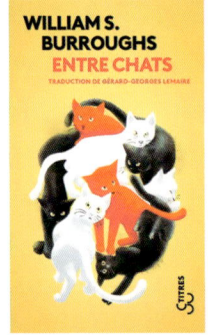

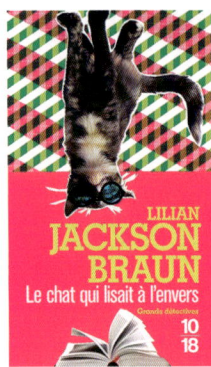 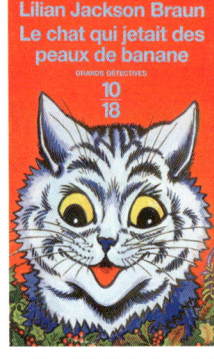

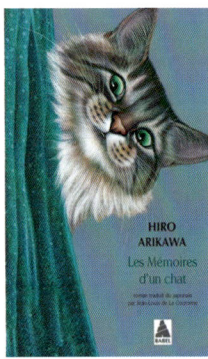 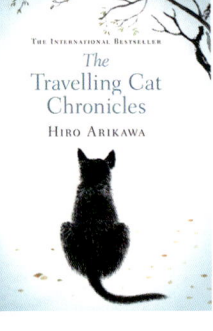

larger whole, they add a down-to-earth touch to the painting or sculpture, or else a touch of fantasy or humor.

The love of cats can also lead to wonderful essays and poems. While we've chosen to talk about Charles Baudelaire, he's far from alone. We might mention his friend and contemporary, Théophile Gautier, who devoted many pages to the felines sharing his life in *My Private Menagerie*, Stéphane Mallarmé, or, more recently, William Burroughs with *The Cat Inside*. Or, in a much funnier vein, Terry Pratchett's *The Unadulterated Cat*.

Lastly, the very image of the cat can become iconic. One example is the advertising lithograph produced for the cabaret Le Chat noir, which itself became an evocation of a certain French art of living. And while the poster itself was constantly being reproduced from one medium to another, slipping into works as improbable as video games, children's cartoons, and web series, the cabaret's name was also taken up by other establishments in real life. Restaurants, bars, and cabarets all over the world now bear the name, or variations of it, in homage to the establishment founded by Rodolphe Salis. It has also been reinvented in fiction, as in the case of the Golden Cat establishment in which much of the story of the video game *Dishonored* unfolds. 🐾

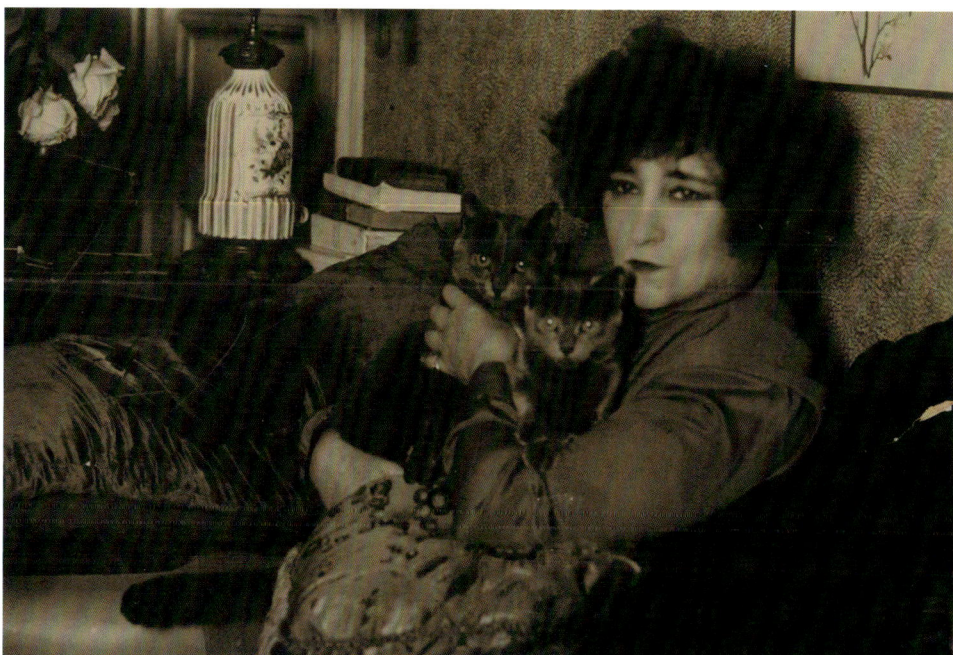

Colette and her cats, before 1947. Photo by Henri Manuel.

Cat-loving writer Colette was a scandalous figure all her life. In this short novel, in which a young wife sees a Chartreux cat as a rival in love, she shows the intensity of feelings that can unite human and cat.

A novelist who was well known, among other things, for her love of animals, and cats in particular, Sidonie-Gabrielle Colette, known as Colette, wrote *The Cat* in 1933. This very short novel can be seen as an ode to the beauty and fascination of cats, or, on the contrary, as a nightmare for anyone having to bring a new companion into their life and wondering whether the cat will accept and be accepted by this stranger.

The story is simple. Two young adults, who are pampered and idle in the terms used at the time, and rather spoiled and rotten in a more modern view, are getting married. Alain and Camille have known each other since childhood but have never lived together. Camille, who is used to being the center of attention, hasn't realized the fascination that Saha, the Chartreux cat, elicits from her master, Alain. Camille becomes insanely jealous, to the point of committing the irreparable act of throwing the animal out of their ninth-floor studio window. The human couple is shattered by this act; it ends with the woman's departure under the scornful gaze of both her ex-husband and his beloved Saha.

In this novel, even though the animal has no supernatural or fantastic characteristics and never speaks, Colette describes it as a character in its own right. And yet, she rarely mentions the animal's first name, instead referring to it as "the cat." This label establishes both distance and essence: Saha is the ultimate cat, the quintessential cat of all cats. She is also feminine, and as a female cat is the absolute mistress of Alain's heart, whether his young wife likes it or not. With journalistic precision and economy of words, Colette reinterprets the tragic love triangle in *The Cat*, describing a double obsession with animals that borders on madness. 🐾

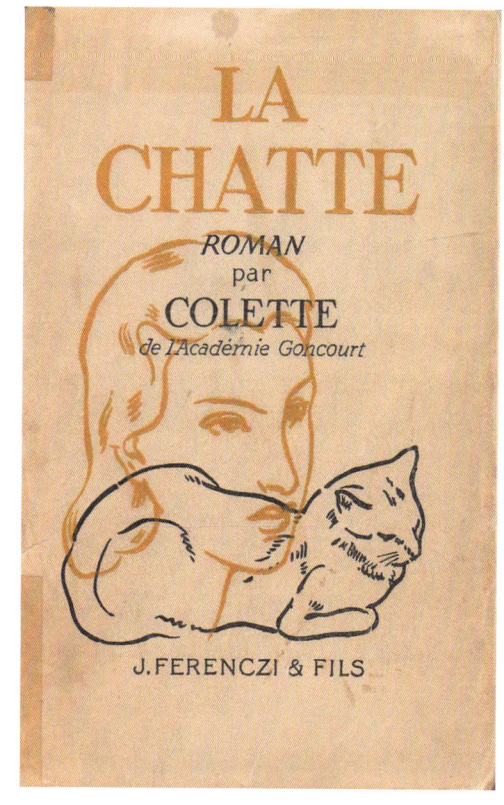

LA CHATTE

ROMAN
par
COLETTE
de l'Académie Goncourt

J. FERENCZI & FILS

SPEC SHEET

WORK: *The Cat*.
CREATOR: Colette.
DATE CREATED: From April 12 to June 7, 1933, in the newspaper *Marianne* and then as a novel on June 12, 1933.
PUBLISHER/AVAILABILITY: Available from various publishers.
CAT'S NAME AND ROLE IN THE WORK: Saha, Alain's Chartreux cat, triggers Camille's excessive jealousy.

A Cat's Life

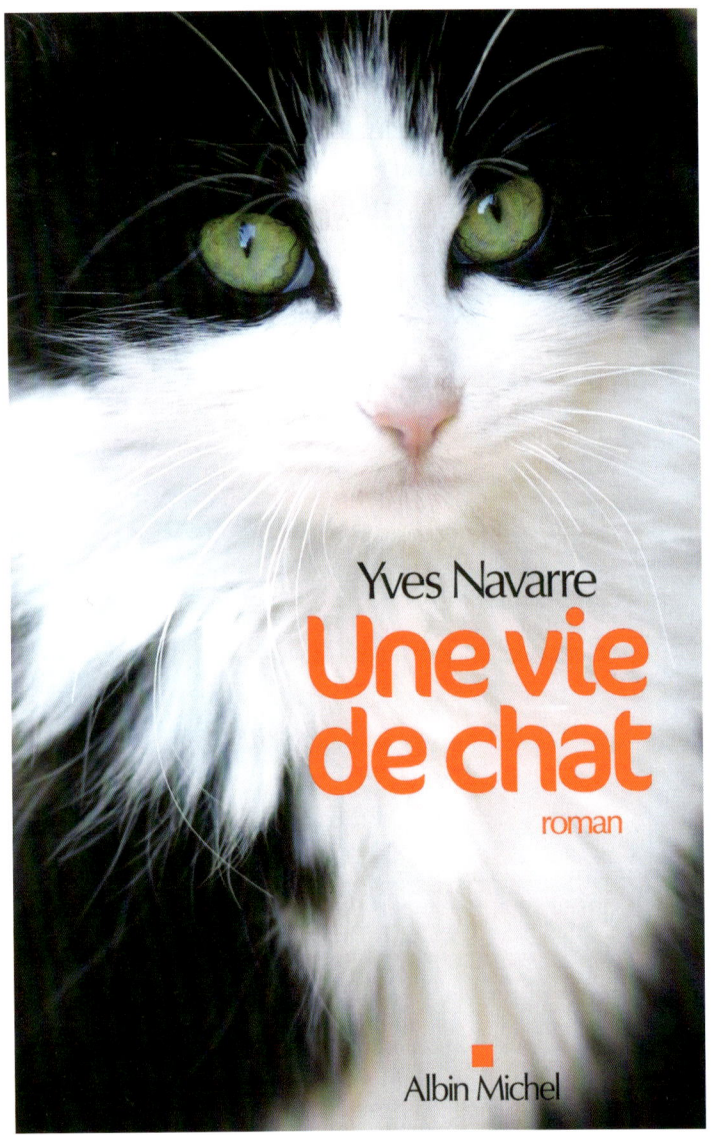

By taking the point of view of his cat, Tiffauges, and slightly romanticizing his life, in this novel, Yves Navarre invites us to discover his innermost being as a writer. It's as if he had to take on the role of his silent companion to better reveal himself.

"I'm the I. It's me. The cat. A cat. You have to take that as read. No alternative. You can still choose to cast this book aside. You are free to do so. This is my life. And my death. My name is Tiffauges. And I'm writing." Books supposedly written by cats abound in literature, whatever the language of origin. Whether they're aimed at young readers or tell the story of a more or less harsh life together, there's something for every taste and every audience. So why did we choose *A Cat's Life* by Yves Navarre? Quite simply because, in fewer than 250 pages, he succeeds in

drawing a touching, intimate, modest, faithful double portrait of the cat and his giant, the writer Abel (Yves Navarre's double). In the ten years, almost eleven, that they've lived together, these two have had time to tame each other, to get to know each other, to watch each other live, to understand each other better. The book talks about their life together between Paris and their home in the South of France. It's about their worries for the future (because, yes, cats worry about the future, too, and not just about their next bowl of wet food), and about the agonies of literary creation and the fact that it only seems to happen through suffering. But also, and above all, their respective love lives: Tiffauges with his two wives, Tiffany and Tityre, and Abel with his "catkins" who come and go without lingering, chased away by his inflexibility and uncompromising side.

By leaving the writing to his cat, Yves Navarre achieves two things. On the one hand, he mourns the loss of his beloved feline, who we gradually come to understand was brutally shot by a hunter trying to score a hit. On the other hand, he talks about his private life, his homosexuality, from an outsider's point of view (apart from being a cat, Tiffauges is resolutely a fan of female cats and, despite his castration, regularly services the two females who share his life), so as not to alarm the reader. Regardless of their sexual orientation, readers are taken into the daily life of a homosexual writer in the early 1980s, between embarrassment for those close to him, such as his parents, and open provocation for others. And for cat lovers, it's a wonderful insight into the life of a unique human/feline couple. 🐾

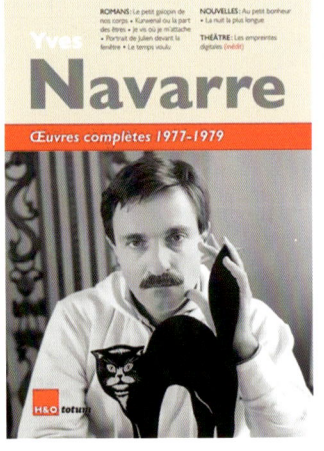

SPEC SHEET

WORK: *A Cat's Life*.
CREATOR: Yves Navarre.
DATE CREATED: 1986.
PUBLISHER/AVAILABILITY: Texas Bookman and Quartet Books. May be available used.
CAT'S NAME AND ROLE IN THE WORK: Tiffauges, a black-and-white cat with a pink nose, the novel's narrator.

Tournée du Chat noir

Originally a simple poster advertising a Montmartre cabaret, **Tournée du Chat noir** *is part of Paris's international iconographic heritage.*

When Swiss artist Théophile Alexandre Steinlen designed the poster to publicize the Chat Noir cabaret located on the hill of Montmartre, he had no idea that, more than a century after its publication, it would still have influence all over the world. It's true that the Chat Noir it promotes was a fashionable establishment in the nineteenth century, attracting customers such as Paul Verlaine, Alphonse Allais, Caran d'Ache, and Aristide Bruant, who wrote a song about it. But the poster itself was nothing spectacular. It shows a black cat with medium-length fur, yellow eyes, and very long whiskers, sitting facing forward, with the text *"Prochainement, Tournée du Chat noir de Rodolphe Salis"* [Coming soon: Rodolphe Salis's Black Cat Tour], with no date or place indicated.

And yet, it was soon reproduced, and still is, on a wide range of media: tea towels, postcards, cookie tins, trays, tiles, cups, and more. It came to be regarded as one of the symbols of the bohemian lifestyle and popular art of living in Paris.

Perhaps in part due to its presence in Blake Edwards's *Breakfast at Tiffany's*, it enjoyed a resurgence of interest in the late twentieth and twenty-first centuries. Representations of the poster have appeared in video games such as *Fallout* 1 and 2, *Overwatch*, *Resident Evil Survivor*, and *Dishonored*; in films such as *Gray Matters*, *The Secret Life of Pets*, and *The King of Staten Island*; and in TV series such as *Alvin and the Chipmunks*, *Bref*, and *Days of Our Lives*. Whenever someone wants to point out a French or Parisian element without resorting to the cliché beret/baguette/red wine, this poster is used. In post-apocalyptic environments (especially *Fallout*), it becomes a nostalgic reminder of the time before the catastrophe. And it's anyone's guess whether the tour in question was even a success! 🐾

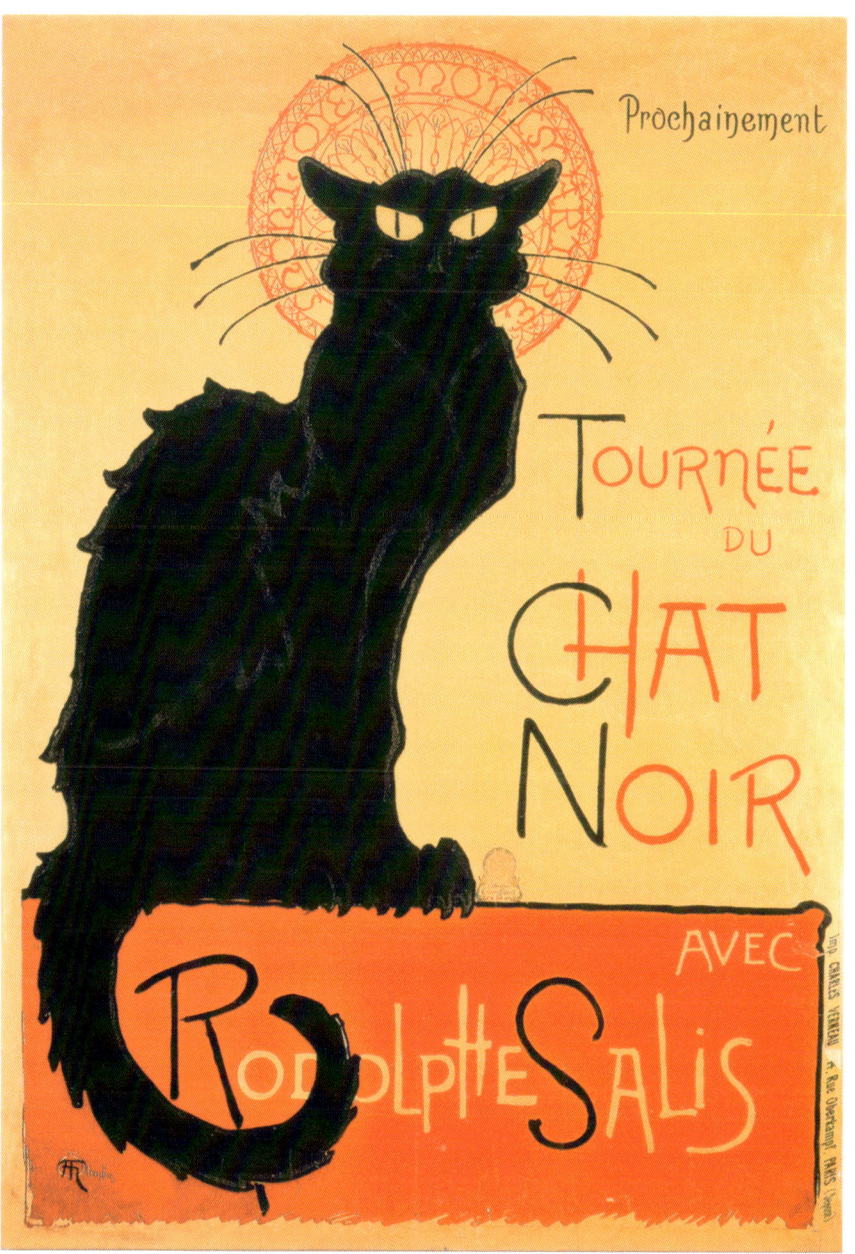

SPEC SHEET

WORK: *Tournée du Chat noir*.
CREATOR: Théophile Alexandre Steinlen.
DATE CREATED: 1896.
AVAILABILITY: The original lithograph can be seen at the Zimmerli Art Museum at Rutgers University in New Brunswick, NJ.
CAT'S NAME AND ROLE IN THE WORK: Anonymous black cat posing proudly. Its head is surrounded by a red halo.

Charles Baudelaire and Cats

The Romantic poet Charles Baudelaire was a sensual man. In his best-known collection, Les Fleurs du mal (The Flowers of Evil)**, he devotes no fewer than three poems to his favorite animals.**

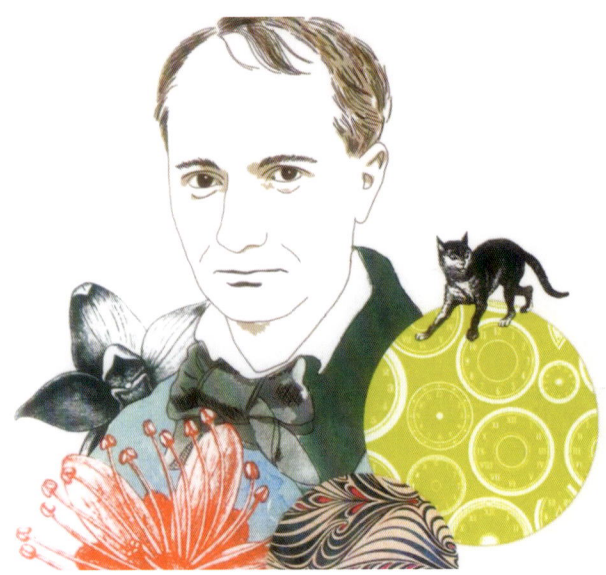

"In my brain walks,/As in his own apartment,/A beautiful cat that is strong, sweet, and charming./When he meows you can hardly hear him." "Come, my beautiful cat, to my loving heart/ Hold back your claws, and let me gaze into your beautiful eyes/ Mingled with metal and agate." "Passionate lovers and austere scholars/Both love in their ripe season/Gentle, powerful cats, the pride of the house/Who, like them, are easily chilled and sedentary." Anyone who has ever had to study Les Fleurs du mal in French class will remember the beginning of the three poems Charles Baudelaire dedicated to cats in the "Spleen" and "Ideal" sections.

Without going into lengthy commentary, these three works, which differ from one another in length and rhythm, show that the writer, who shared the life of a cat named Tibère, was fascinated by these animals. Sometimes he compares them to the woman who occupies his heart, like in the two poems both titled "The Cat"; sometimes he identifies with a cat dreaming of sticking close to his mistress's feet in "The Giantess." Or he may describe them in detail and imagine them as the muses of artists and scientists, taking up the mystical side of the cat: "Erebus would have made them his funeral steeds, if they could bend their pride to servitude" in "Cats." And beneath the poetic exterior, his comparisons have the accuracy of a keen observer of domestic felines. Charles Baudelaire's contemporaries and acquaintances had noticed this, noting that when he saw a cat, he "went to it, drew it in with cuddles, took it in his arms, and stroked it; even in the wrong direction." And his animals infuse all his work (sometimes using comparisons with their real qualities and defects, sometimes endowing them with supernatural gifts enabling them to see the spirit world) and can also be found in *Paris Spleen* and in his diaries (*Fusées*, published in 1851).

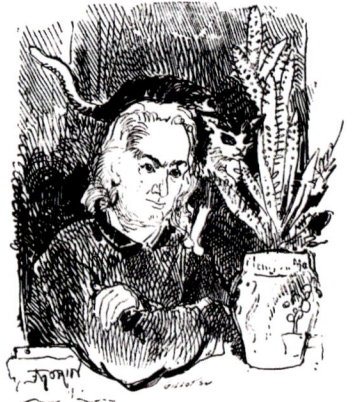

Charles Baudelaire, Edmond Morin, 1868.

SPEC SHEET

WORK: *Les Fleurs du mal* (*The Flowers of Evil*), in particular "The Cat" (no. XXXIV), "The Cat" (no. LXI), and "Cats" (no. LXVI).
CREATOR: Charles Baudelaire.
DATE CREATED: First published August 23, 1857.
PUBLISHER/AVAILABILITY: Available in several English editions.
CAT'S NAME AND ROLE IN THE WORK: The cats are never named in the poems.

"The Cat That Walked by Himself"

An English writer born in Bombay, India, Rudyard Kipling is best known for The Jungle Book, *in which the panther Bagheera and the tiger Shere Khan play key roles. He also wrote a short story about how the Cat and the Woman struck a deal.*

The question of whether human or cat tamed the other is a never-ending debate. In his 1902 collection, *Just So Stories for Little Children*, Rudyard Kipling offers a poetic prose explanation of how cats came into the home. This story, "The Cat That Walked by Himself," is dedicated to Best Beloved, Rudyard Kipling's daughter, to whom he told the tale (just as J. R. R. Tolkien's *The Hobbit* was initially a story for his children). Set at the dawn of time, it explains how the Woman convinces the Man to move into the Cave and then persuades the Dog, the Horse, and the Cow to join them, to the benefit of humans. All this under the watchful eye of the Cat: "He walked by himself and all places were alike to him."

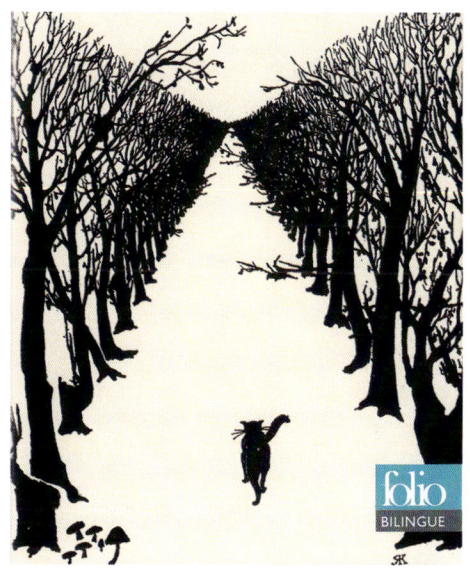

He then tricks the Woman into offering him three privileges: the right to enter the Cave, the right to warm himself by the fire, and the promise of good milk. The Man and the Dog are having none of it, and this little tale explains why three out of five men reject felines and why dogs chase them.

This poetically written text illustrates the duality of the Cat, which is both home-loving and independent. He's a protector and a friend to little ones, just as Bagheera takes Mowgli under his wing in *The Jungle Book*. And he refuses to make the concessions demanded by the Man and the Dog, even though he may suffer as a result. But his cunning, gentleness, and antics will win the heart of the Woman and her child, assuring him a permanent place among humans. 🐾

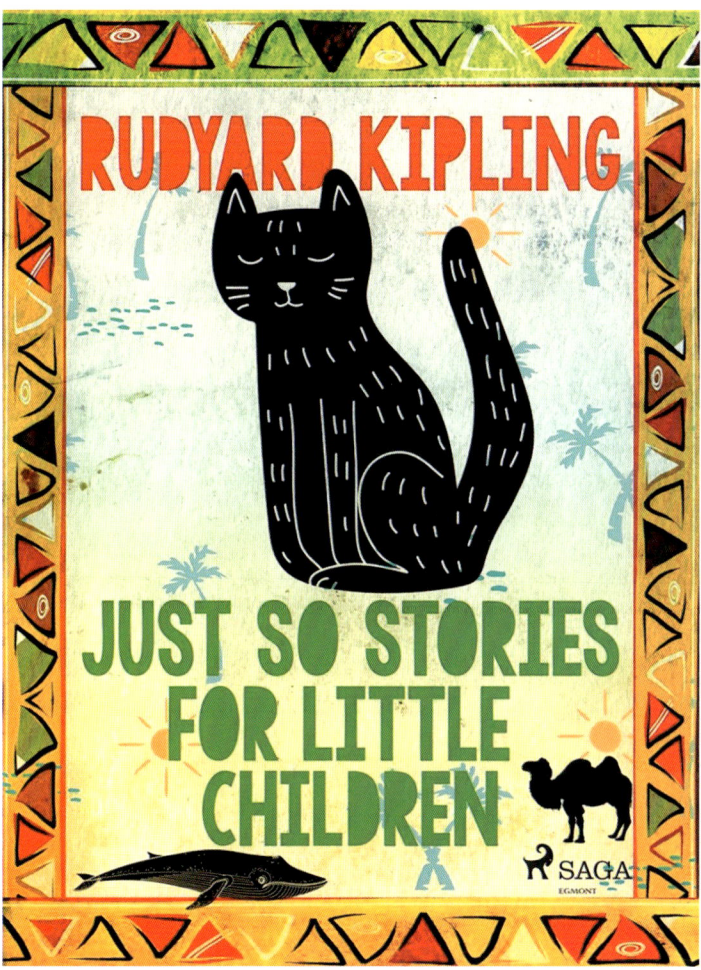

SPEC SHEET

WORK: "The Cat That Walked by Himself."
CREATOR: Rudyard Kipling.
DATE CREATED: 1902.
AVAILABILITY: Available in various editions, either alone or in *Just So Stories for Little Children*.
CAT'S NAME AND ROLE IN THE WORK: The Cat. The hero of the short story, he also observes the domestication of the Man and the other animals by the Woman.

Feline Muses for Artists

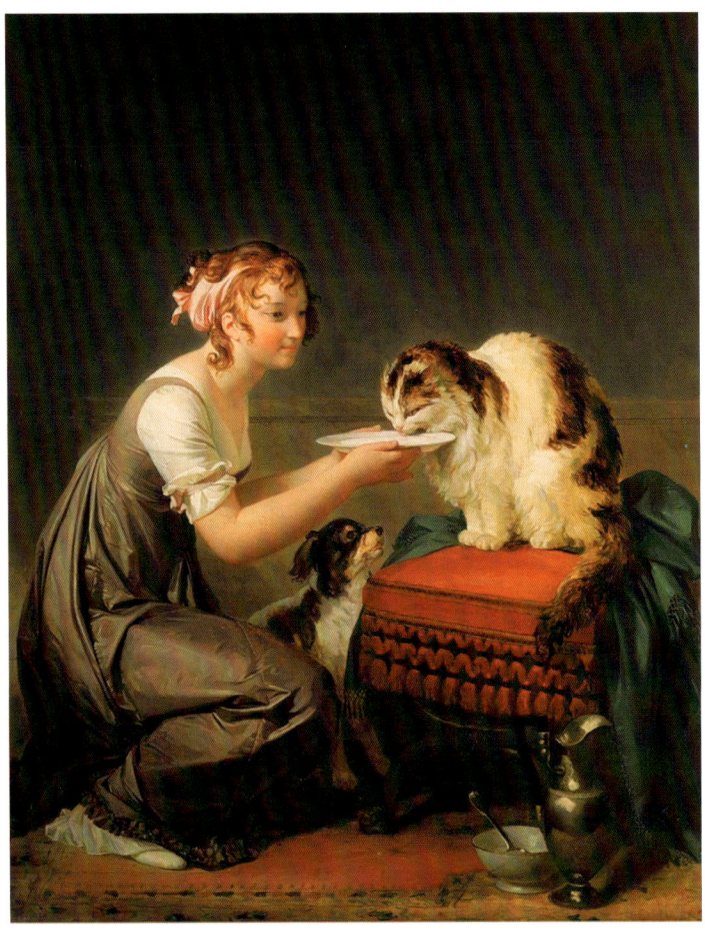

The Cat's Lunch, Marguerite Gérard, Musée Fragonard, Grasse, 1937.

With cats inspiring so many texts, films, characters, legends, myths, and memes, painters and sculptors couldn't be left out.

From the very beginnings of the special relationship between humankind and felines, cats have featured in works of art, whether in paintings, engravings, sculptures, or any other art form. In the beginning, these were often religious representations, such as the Sphinx or the various Egyptian depictions of Bastet, or the Babylonian Lion, emblem of the goddess Ishtar and symbol of royalty, or the guardians of Chinese and Japanese temples. Similarly, we find cats and lions in heraldry—in other words, on the coats of arms of cities and certain families. While lions have a royal symbolism, cats are more often used as "speaking weapons," a reminder of the name of the place or family whose coat of arms they adorn. Although, according to the *Dictionnaire archéologique et explicatif de la science du blason* [Archaeological and

Explanatory Dictionary of the Science of Heraldry], the cat "is the symbol of freedom. According to Marcus Vulson de la Colombière, the cat is vigilant, agile, light, flexible, and nervous; this is why it indicates warriors who defend the places where they command so well that it is impossible to attack them without incurring great danger. Since the cat is fonder of the home than its inhabitants, we can say that it personifies the citizens who have kept a town or city well-guarded."

Gradually, however, cats came to be regarded as figures of art for art's sake. In paintings adorning Egyptian tombs or Roman mosaics, cats were simply part of everyday life. And as the two species became closer, representations of cats in pictorial art developed. Cats have always been present in Asia, particularly in China and Japan. In the West, it wasn't until the Renaissance that painters and sculptors took up the subject, once the scorn cast on the animal associated with both plague epidemics and the devil began to wane. Since then, whether as a person's companion, like the black kitten next to Olympia in Édouard Manet's painting, or as the very subject of the work, as in Marguerite Gérard's *The Cat's Lunch*, the animal has played an increasingly important role in art. 🐾

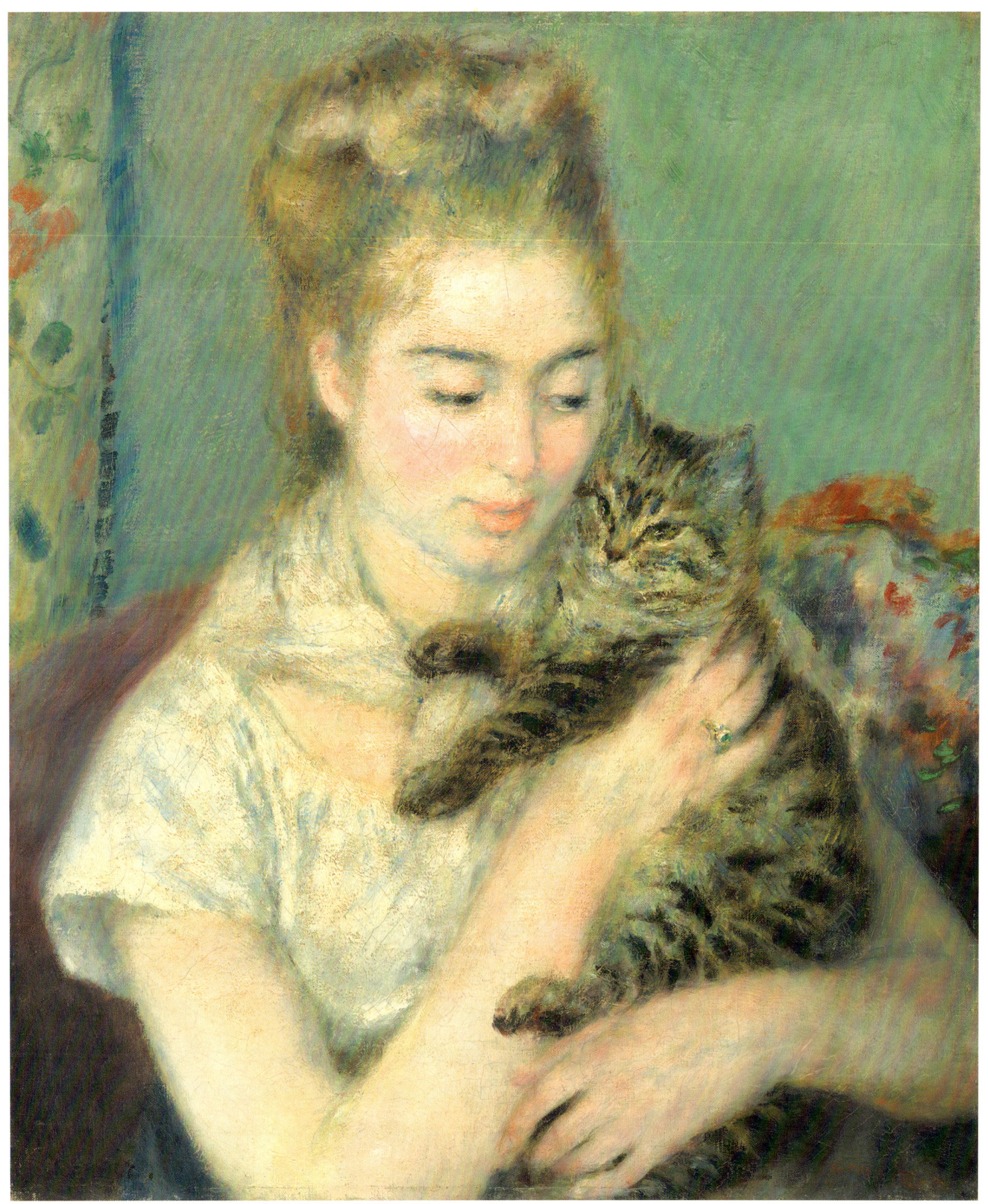

Woman with a Cat, Pierre-Auguste Renoir, 1875, National Gallery of Art, Washington, D.C., USA.

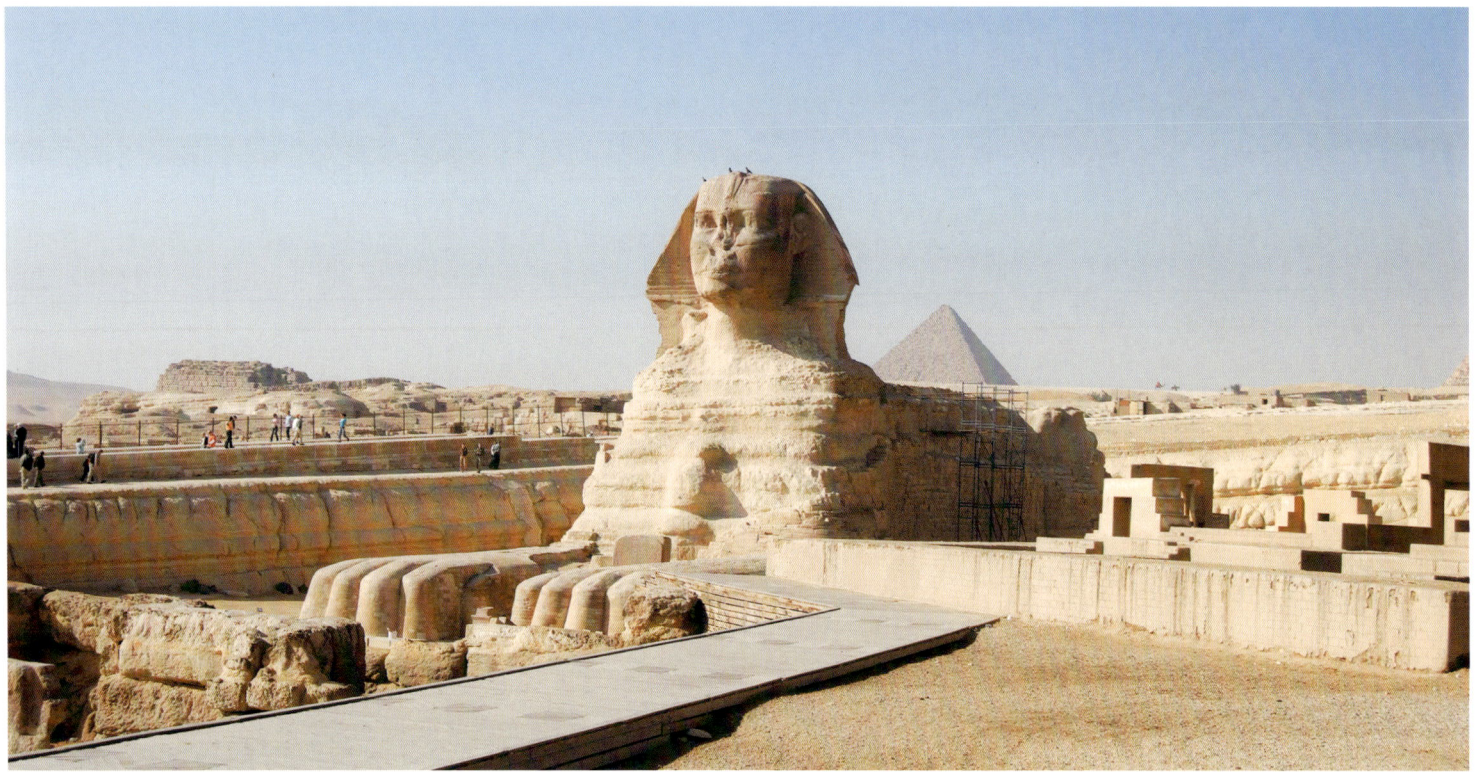

Great Sphinx of Giza, Egypt, 2500 BCE.

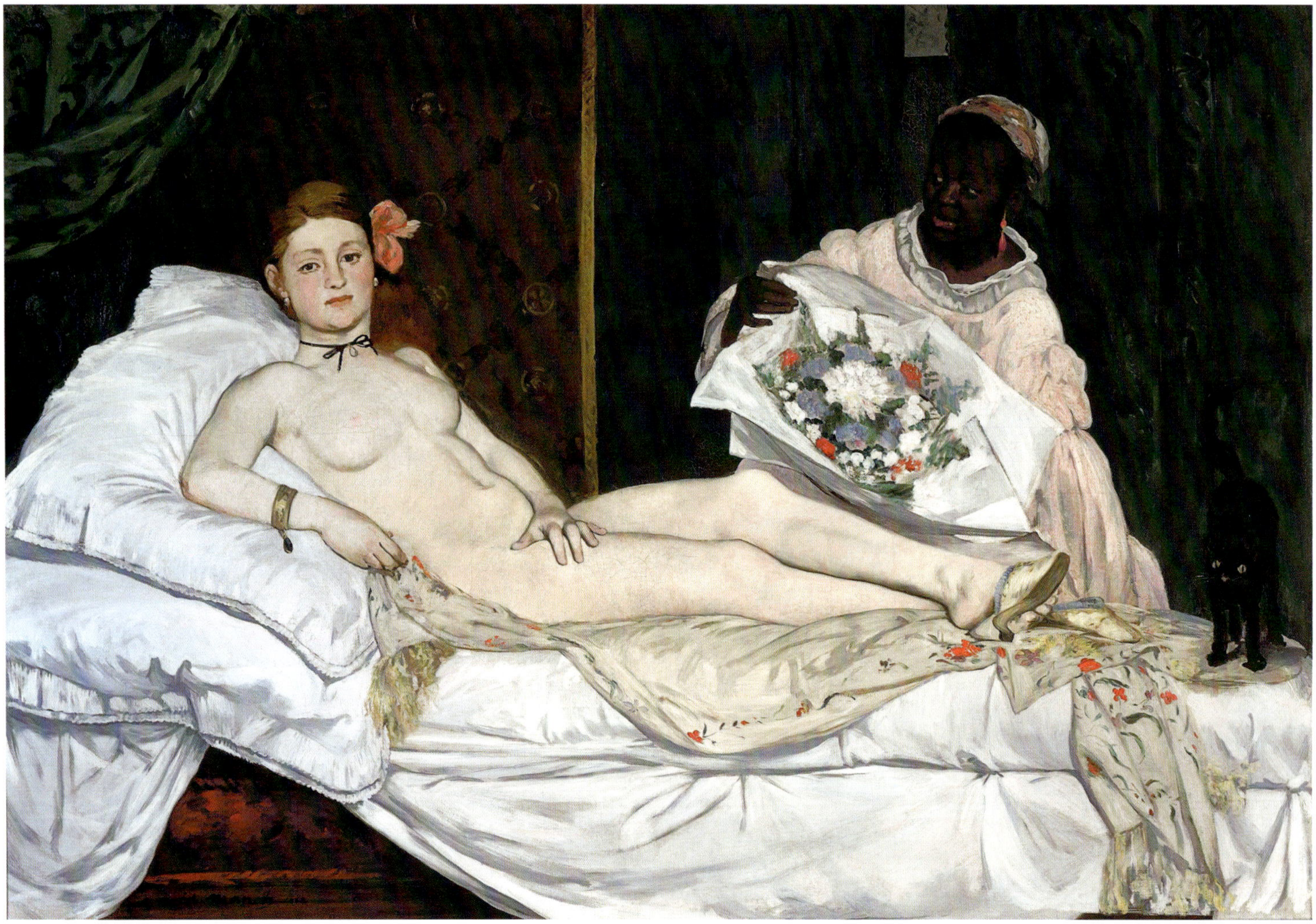

Olympia, Edouard Manet, Musée d'Orsay, 1863.

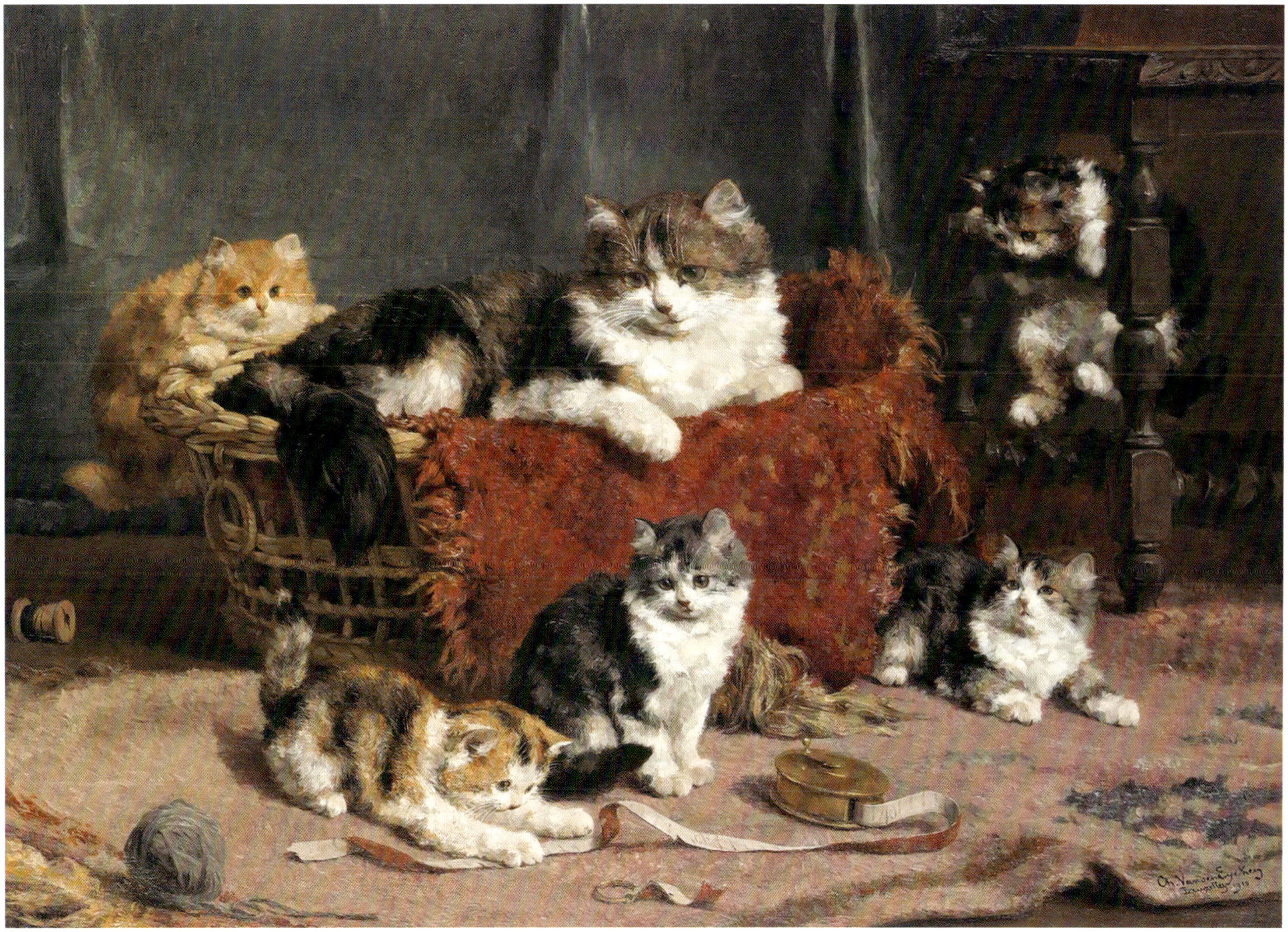

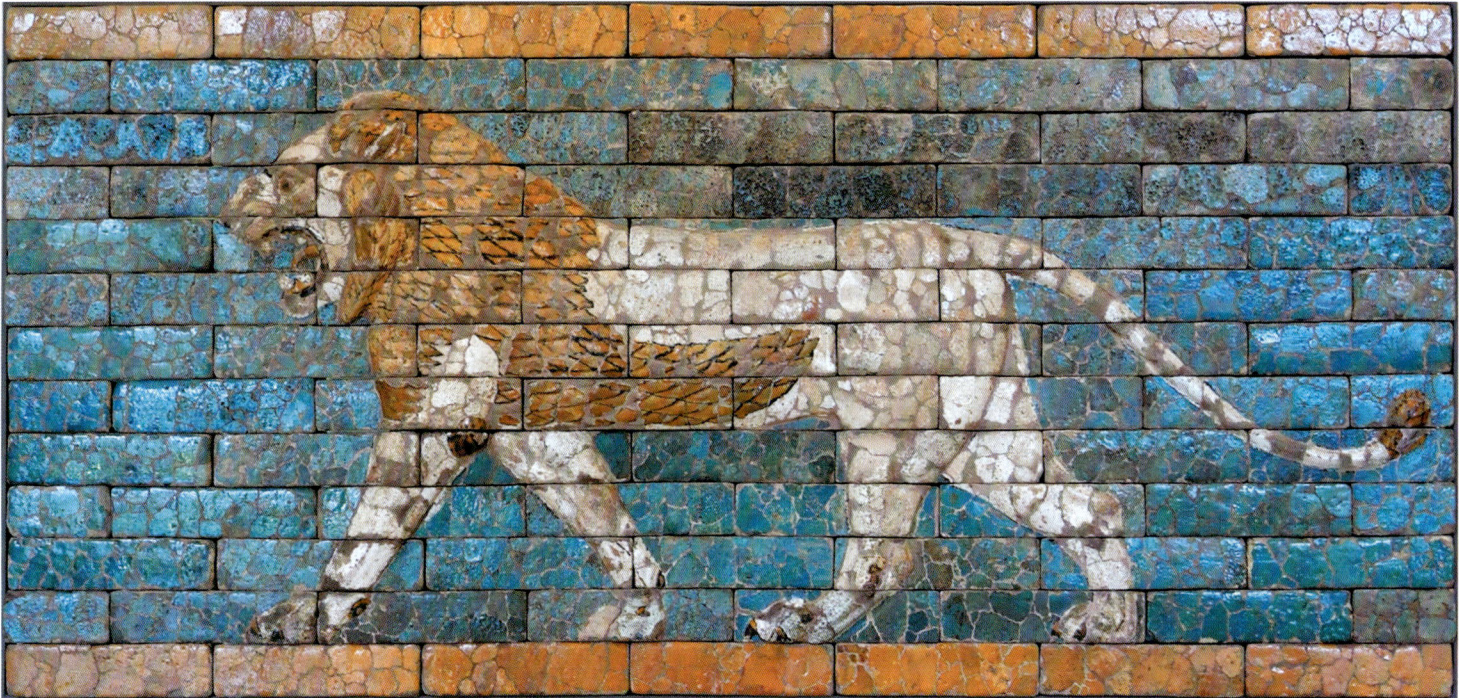

Playtime, Charles van den Eycken, 1910.

Lion of Babylon, Iraq, Louvre Museum, between 604 and 562 BCE.

Glossary

Anime: Pronounced "animay." A generic term used to designate cartoons in Japan (and by extension in the West, any short cartoon from Asia).

Calico: Cat coat color combining white and tortoiseshell. Almost all calico cats are females.

Coat: Appearance of an animal's fur, including color, density, and length.

Kodomo: From the Japanese word for "child." Outside of Japan, it indicates a manga, book, or anime intended for children age ten and younger.

Manga: A Japanese comic or, by extension, one that adopts the graphic and writing style of these comics.

Mangaka: Manga author, whether scriptwriter, illustrator, or both.

Mecha: Science-fiction theme that features characters using or embodying robotic armor, usually in humanoid form.

Neolithic: Prehistoric period corresponding to human groups adopting a subsistence model based on agriculture and animal husbandry, most often involving settling in one place.

Psychopomp: Divinity or being that guides the souls of the dead. By extension, any creature capable of predicting death.

Shōjo: Manga and anime for girls (ages ten to eighteen).

Shōnen: Manga and anime for boys (ages ten to eighteen).

Sphynx: Not to be confused with the mythical Egyptian and Greek animal (spelled Sphinx). This is a "hairless" cat breed, although they do have a fine, fuzzy coat.

Tortoiseshell: Cat coat color mixing red and black, as well as all derivative colors (cream, cinnamon, chocolate, blue). Almost all tortoiseshell cats are females.

Tuxedo: Black-and-white cat coloring that is reminiscent of a tuxedo.

Yokai: A type of supernatural creature in Japan. They range from mischievous but protective goblins to bloodthirsty ogres, ghostly apparitions, and tasteless jokes. Their appearance is extremely varied and is inspired by animals, objects, or human beings.

Selected Bibliography

In addition to all the works of fiction cited, read, reread, or reviewed for inclusion in this book, here's a list of other useful resources we used.

Banville (de), Théodore, *Le Chat*. Éditions Feedbooks. St-Hilaire, Paul, *Le Chat*. Éditions Philippe Lebaud.

Fouillet, Pierre and Lacotte, Daniel, *Les chats-mots*. First Editions.

Gaiman, Neil, *Norse Mythology*. W.W. Norton & Company

IMDb, internet database on cinema and audiovisual production. https://www.imdb.com

Loszach, Fabien, and Dugall Matthieu, *Wiki,GIF & LSD-L'encyclopédie anecdotique du web*. Éditions Cardinal.

Mizuki, Shigeru, *Dictionnaire des yokaï*. Pika.

nooSFere, French-language reference site for all fantasy literature, including science fiction, fantasy, and the fantastic. https://www.noosfere.org/

Patrick, Jean-Baptiste, *Dictionnaire universel: Dieux Déesses et Démons.* Éditions du Seuil.

Suares, J.-C., *Le Chat indispensable*. Éditions Herscher.

Walter, Virginie Valérie, *Contribution à l'étude de l'évolution historique du chat : ses relations avec l'homme de l'Antiquité à nos jours*. Thesis. Available here: https://oatao.univ-toulouse.fr/1817/1/cel- dran_1817.pdf

Acknowledgments

The two authors would like to thank those who shared their time and enthusiasm with them:

Cécile Callou, Emmanuelle Titieux, Pierre Dubois, Fabien Loszach, Renaud Guillemin, and Souillon for Maliki.

Thank you to my family and especially to Marie-Hélène Thévenon, who always helps me with her invaluable advice. And a special thank-you to my Brazilian jiu-jitsu team, the Panda Supa Crew.

To Bambou and all the cats who have shared my life, and to the one I put in the oven for the sake of a shoot.

Thank you to Minouche, Raven, Chani, Jethro, and the others who, with the tips of their whiskers and claws, were able to guide me through the twists and turns of feline mysteries.

Thank you, Nelly and Francis, for supporting me in this passion.

Printed in October 2021 by J.J Production (Turkey).

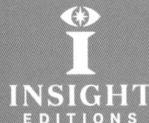

INSIGHT
EDITIONS

PO Box 3088
San Rafael, CA 94912
www.insighteditions.com

Find us on Facebook: www.facebook.com/InsightEditions
Follow us on Instagram: @insighteditions

Originally published in French as *Les Chats dans la Pop Culture* by
Ynnis Editions, France, in 2021. Legal deposit: November 2017

English translation by Beth Smith.
English translation © 2025 Insight Editions.

ISBN: 979-8-3374-0056-3

Publisher: Raoul Goff
SVP, Co-Publisher: Vanessa Lopez
VP, Creative: Chrissy Kwasnik
VP, Manufacturing: Alix Nicholaeff
Art Director: Matt Girard
Senior Editor: Stephen Fall
Editorial Assistant: Audrey Salo
Executive Managing Editor: Maria Spano
Senior Production Manager: Greg Steffen
Strategic Production Planner: Lina s Palma-Temena

YNNIS

© 2021 Ynnis Éditions. All rights reserved worldwide.

CEO: Cedric Littardi
Editorial and Artistic Director: Sébastien Rost
Correction: Mélissa Veludo
Graphic design: Stéphanie Lairet
Cover illustration: Eliot Trouttet
Images: Sébastien Rost, Jeanne Bucher
Production: Céline Antoine
Marketing & communication: Camille Nogueira

Ynnis Éditions
38 rue Notre-Dame-De-Nazareth
75003 Paris, France
www.ynnis-editions.fr
Instagram: @ynnis_editions
Facebook: Ynnis Éditions
X: @YnnisEditions

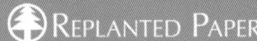
ROOTS of PEACE   REPLANTED PAPER

Insight Editions, in association with Roots of Peace, will plant two
trees for each tree used in the manufacturing of this book. Roots
of Peace is an internationally renowned humanitarian organization
dedicated to eradicating land mines worldwide and converting
war-torn lands into productive farms and wildlife habitats. Roots of
Peace will plant two million fruit and nut trees in Afghanistan and
provide farmers there with the skills and support necessary for
sustainable land use.

Manufactured in China by Insight Editions

10 9 8 7 6 5 4 3 2 1

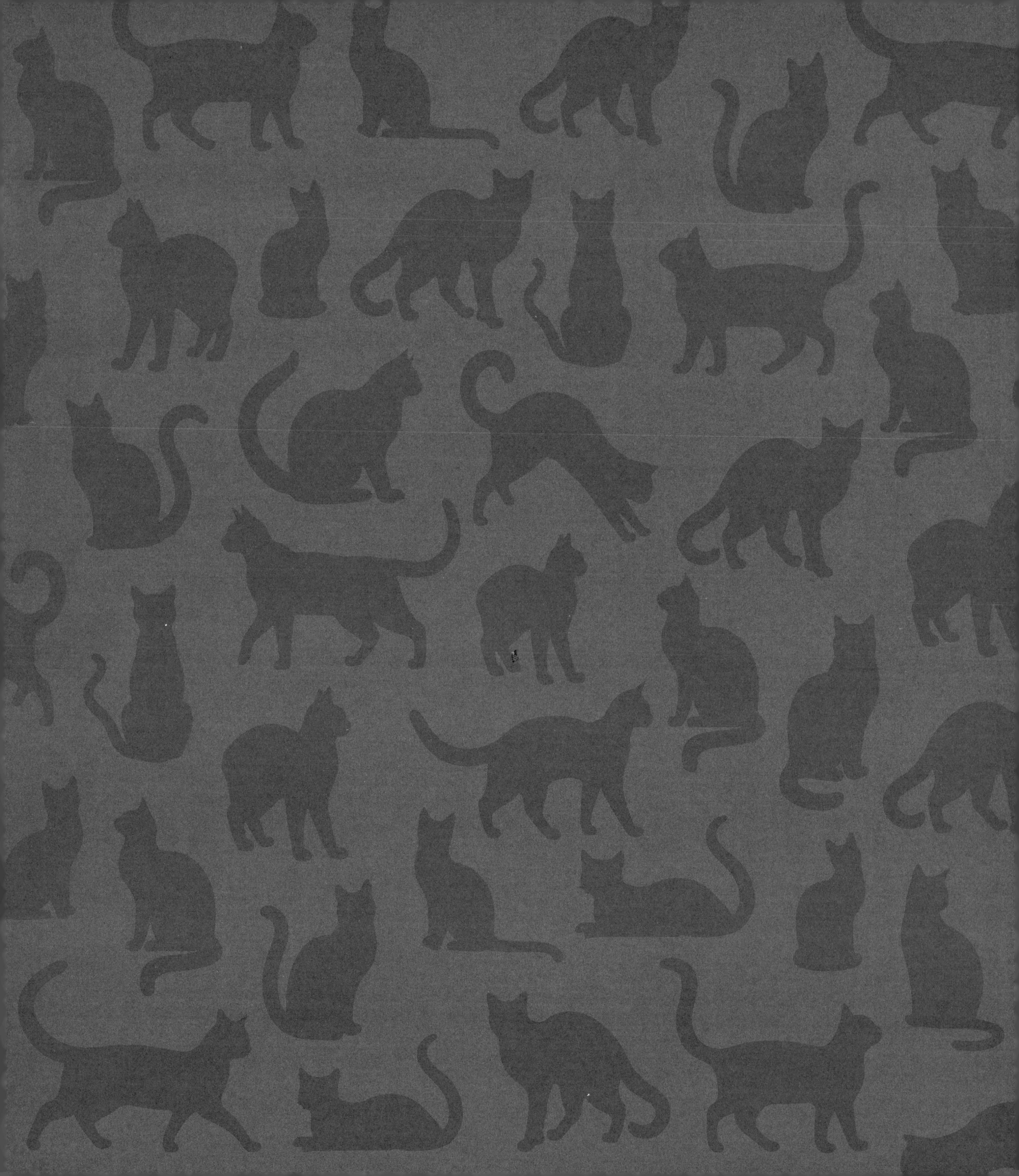